Prepublication praise for

Understanding and Using

dBASE III Plus

"I got carried away with some truly new approaches to the subject.
. . . This was really a great learning experience for me."

> Richard A. Bassler
> Professor Emeritus of Microcomputer
>   Applications
> Center for Technology and Administration
> The American University

"I like this book very much. It is a down-to-earth . . . introduction
to dBASE III+. The lessons flow easily, the examples are good. The
reader has every chance to become a good dBASE III Plus programmer with this book."

> Jay Siegel
> Quantitative Software Reports

"The chapters . . . on writing real-life application modules are quite
good, as are the sections using dBASE with other programs."

> Margaret Levine
> Author and Computer Consultant

Understanding and Using

dBASE III Plus

Rob Krumm

Brady

New York

BRADY

Simon & Schuster, Inc.
Gulf+Western Building
One Gulf+Western Plaza
New York, NY 10023

DISTRIBUTED BY PRENTICE HALL TRADE

Manufactured in the United States of America

5 6 7 8 9 10

Library of Congress Cataloging-in-Publication Data

Krumm, Rob, 1951-
    Understanding and using dBASE III Plus.

    "A Brady book."
    Includes index.
    I. dBASE III PLUS (Computer program) I. Title.
QA76.9.D3K794 1987   005.75'65   87-2574
ISBN 0-13-935859-5

To my sister Judy, with love
And to the memory of my Aunt Leslie,
who believed in me when there was no reason to.

Trademarks

dBASE II, dBASE III, dBASE III Plus, Framework, and *MultiMate* are trademarks of Ashton-Tate.

Lotus 1-2-3 and *Symphony* are trademarks of Lotus Development Corporation.

DBIII compiler and *Quicksilver* are trademarks of WordTech.

MS DOS, *Multiplan,* and *Word* are trademarks of Microsoft.

DisplayWrite 3, IBM PC, and PC DOS are trademarks of IBM Corporation.

WordStar Professional and *WordStar 2000* are trademarks of MicroPro Corporation.

WordPerfect is a trademark of SSI Software.

XyWrite is a trademark of XyQuest.

Sidekick is a trademark of Borland International.

Javelin is a trademark of Javelin.

V.P. Planner is a trademark of Paperback Software.

PFS Professional Plan is a trademark of PFS.

SuperCalc is a trademark of Computer Associates.

CONTENTS

INTRODUCTION

WHY BUY THIS BOOK?

If you are reading this introduction you are probably standing in a bookstore looking at a shelf full of books that includes *dBASE III* among its titles.

The obvious question is, which book should you buy? As the author, I would like to provide you with some information about *Understanding and Using dBASE III Plus* that should help you make the correct decision.

- This book is designed for both the new and experienced user. Unlike most books of this type it is not aimed at *just* beginners or *just* experienced users. The goal is to provide a full educational experience starting with the most basic level and moving on to advanced concepts, including advanced programming.

  The reason this book includes so wide a spectrum is that experience has shown that the topics included in this book are necessary for many practical applications. Many books make what I consider artificial distinctions between beginner, intermediate, and advanced uses of *dBASE III Plus*. In this book I have placed the *dBASE III* concepts into a continuum that will provide the tools necessary to attack almost any data base task.

- To make this approach workable, the majority of the book works with a single example. This means that the example discussed in the beginning chapters is also the example used in programming chapters. The single example unifies all the procedures and techniques shown in the book. It is my opinion that switching examples each time a new topic is introduced slows down the learning process. The use of a few simple examples throughout the book lets the techniques stand out more clearly.

- This book is the latest in a series of *dBASE* books begun in 1982. The original and all subsequent revisions have been used in my school in California to teach *dBASE* to hundreds of students before the manuscripts were published. This means two things to you, the potential buyer of this book.

First, the book has been fully tested with a variety of students. Second, the goal of the book is to educate you about *dBASE III Plus*, not just to provide a listing of sample programs.

- This book and its previous versions have been used successfully by managers, professionals, small business owners, programmers learning a new language, researchers, high school students, and others.

This book is specifically oriented to *dBASE III Plus*. While the majority of the concepts apply to *dBASE III* and to a lesser degree *dBASE II*, the commands and techniques include items that will execute properly only with *dBASE III Plus*.

Also note that the sequence of the book is based on the proper learning progression. Care has been taken to provide an index that will assist you in locating specific areas of interest so that the book can function as a reference guide as well as an educational book.

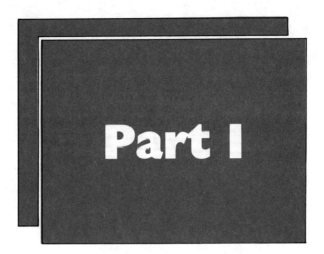

Part I

Data Management
with *dBASE III Plus*

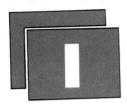

HOW TO USE

THIS BOOK

THE PURPOSE OF THIS BOOK is to teach the reader how to use the *dBASE III Plus* program from the beginning to advanced levels. The book can be used effectively by both users with almost no previous experience and experienced users.

If you are new to computers or data base management, you might want to repeat some of the chapters to make sure you have a firm understanding of each of the subjects covered.

The book is sequenced in the order that you need to work to learn about *dBASE III Plus*. A great deal of time was devoted to indexing this book to make referencing as simple as possible later on. However, keep in mind that the primary design consideration was the best possible learning sequence.

In order to make the book as consistent as possible, a few examples are used in almost every chapter in Part I. The major exception is Chapter 8, on labels, which uses a mail list example. The advantage of using the same example is that the names and data used throughout the book stay the same as the subjects change. This makes it easier to understand each new technique.

The primary concern is that you learn the *how* and *why* of *dBASE III Plus* operations so that you can apply them to your own practical uses. The book follows a hands-on approach to learning. As much as possible, the actual screen is displayed so you can check your results against the examples in the book.

This book is in three parts.

Part I

Part I, which consists of Chapters 1 through 11, covers all the major commands of *dBASE III Plus*. This section covers what are called the *ASSIST* and *DOT PROMPT* modes. In this section you learn how *dBASE III Plus* stores data, how files are retrieved and organized, how labels and reports are generated, and more.

You should have a good grasp of the subjects covered in Part I before you proceed to Part II.

Part II

Part II consists of programming *dBASE III Plus*. Chapters 12 through 14 cover basic programming concepts. The following chapters develop a series of business-oriented program systems.

Part III

Part III contains information about *dBASE III Plus* and other programs that can be used with it in a variety of ways. These include word processing programs, spreadsheets, and compilers.

Before discussing *dBASE III Plus*, it is necessary to explain the system of representations used for special keys found on the IBM PC keyboard.

SPECIAL KEYS

There are three "special" keys on the keyboard with which the user will need to become familiar: the RETURN key, the ESCAPE key, and the CONTROL key. The most frequently used of the three keys is the RETURN key.

The RETURN key is labeled "RETURN" on most keyboards. However, there are some exceptions. Some computers use "ENTER," while the IBM PC uses an arrow with a right angle. I will use < return > in this book to indicate when the RETURN key should be pressed.

Similarly, the ESCAPE key is usually labeled 'Esc' on the keyboard. In this book, < Esc > will be used to indicate when to press the ESCAPE key.

The CTRL key on the keyboard indicates the CONTROL key. The CONTROL key works like the SHIFT key in that it is used in combination with other keys. The CONTROL key is always pressed first and held down while a second key is pressed. Then both keys are released. *dBASE III Plus* makes use of various CONTROL key combinations (such as CONTROL q, CONTROL [End], etc) to issue special keystrokes recognized by the program. In this book, the symbol [**CTRL/**] will be used to indicate a CONTROL combination, for example, [**CTRL/q**].

This notation differs from that used by the *dBASE III Plus* manual, where ^Q is the symbol for CONTROL Q. It is hoped that the [**CTRL/q**] notation will be clearer for the new user.

The IBM PC, XT, and AT keyboards also contain some special keys that have specific names. For example, there are ten function keys labeled "F1" through "F10." In this book the symbols [**F1**], [**F2**], [**F3**], [**F4**], [**F5**], [**F6**], [**F7**], [**F8**], [**F9**], and [**F10**] are used to represent those keys.

Also present on the above keyboards are keys with special names. The following symbols are used for those keys:

<Tab>	= Tab Key
[Home]	= Home Key
[End]	= End Key
[Pg Up]	= Page Up Key
[Pg Dn]	= Page Down Key
[Ins]	= Insert Key
[Del]	= Delete Key
<right arrow>	= right arrow key
<left arrow>	= left arrow key
<up arrow>	= up arrow key
<down arrow>	= down arrow key

UPPER- AND LOWERCASE

Because this book contains complete hands-on instructions about the techniques needed to operate *dBASE III Plus*, the user will be asked to enter sequences of keystrokes while at the keyboard. To illustrate the differences between *dBASE III Plus* command words and user-defined terms (such as filenames), all *dBASE III Plus* commands will be typed in uppercase characters. The typical command,

SET INDEX TO clients<return>

asks you to type SET INDEX TO clients, and then requests that you press the <return> key. The words "SET INDEX TO" are *dBASE III Plus* command words, while "clients" is a user-defined term. The difference in case is used to make the command more understandable. *dBASE III Plus* will execute the command no matter what case is used. Examples:

> **Set Index To Clients**
> **SET index to clients**
> **set index to clients**
> **SET INDEX TO CLIENTS**

All of the commands above are considered equivalent by *dBASE III Plus*.

There is one exception. Letters, when surrounded by quotation marks, are used to compare text. *dBASE III Plus* recognizes the difference between uppercase text and lowercase text when it is surrounded by quotes. Example:

> **LIST FOR NAME="SAM"**
> **LIST FOR NAME="Sam"**
> **LIST FOR NAME="sam"**

Each of these commands would have a different effect because the quotation marks tell *dBASE III Plus* that you want a listing that matches the letters exactly as they were typed. Don't be concerned if this exception is not clear to you now. You will be reminded of the distinction later in the book.

WHAT IS A DATA BASE?

The invention and proliferation of inexpensive microcomputers has brought tools of spectacular ability into the hands of the average user. One of the most powerful tools available for microcomputers are the *dBASE* data management programs. The first product in this family was *dBASE II*. Its successor, *dBASE III,* has now been enhanced into the latest program, *dBASE III Plus*. The purpose of this book is to provide a detailed, educational experience that will teach the reader how to use *dBASE III Plus*.

What *dBASE III Plus* is can be determined by discussing what a data base program is and what it can do for you. Although much has been written about this complex subject, it is possible to boil it down to the two basic functions provided by any data base program. They are:

1.   Sequencing
2.   Selection

Sequencing refers to any action that alters the order in which information is stored or presented. When a list of names is placed in alphabetical order, sequencing is taking place. The same is true when you arrange your canceled checks in numerical order.

Although most people perform sequencing as part of their daily routine, sequencing remains a difficult and demanding task. Computerized data bases can perform complex sequencing tasks with great power and accuracy. Why sequencing is important, and why so much time and effort is spent in ordering information, will be discussed in detail when more is learned about how *dBASE* performs sequencing.

The other major function of a data base is *selection.* Selection refers to the process by which certain items are selected from a larger group. For example, suppose you had a list of recent college graduates. You might wish to select a list of only those students, if any, who reside in New York State. Selection can be done in a number of ways for a wide variety of reasons.

However, the process always consists of testing the elements of the collection to select a subgroup of some kind. Anytime you want to sequence information, select a subgroup, or some combination of the two actions, you are performing a data base management task. Any program that performs these tasks is said to be performing data base functions. Not every program that sequences or selects is a data base management program. For example, *Lotus 1-2-3* is primarily a program that creates mathematical models. However, it is advertised as a spreadsheet, as well as a data base manager and a graphics program.

While it is true that *1-2-3* can perform sequencing and selection functions, only a small part of the program's power is used to implement these functions. In baseball terms, *1-2-3* is like a pitcher who can hit. The fact that the pitcher can hit is a plus, but you wouldn't build your offense around him. Sequencing is one of the most difficult tasks for a computer to deal with. Therefore it is not enough to ask "Can a program sequence?" You must look deeper and ask how the sequencing is accomplished.

True data management programs offer very powerful sequencing and selection commands and functions.

The sequencing and selection functions imply that two other areas are required of a data base program. For instance, how do the data to be sequenced or selected get into the computer? The answer is that the program must provide a structure, or a means by which the data can be put into the system.

The opposite end of the process is the output. The ultimate goal of sequencing and selecting is to create something that a human being can understand and evaluate. Production of those data by screen display or printed information is called *output.*

Thus to be of practical value, a data base program must provide input, selection, sequencing, and output functions.

THE THREE BASIC OPERATIONS

There are three basic operations that a data management system must perform. Whereas the medium with *dBASE III Plus* is a computer, the functions that are described apply to other forms of data management as well. Any office that does not use computers must still find a way to perform these basic operations.

1. **Data Entry.** The system must provide a structure in which data can be stored. The system must also allow for inspection of the data and the making of changes and corrections in order to maintain the validity of the information. For instance, a job application form is an example of a data structure produced with paper and ink.

2. **Data Organization.** Once data have been entered, you will want to use the program's powerful functions to organize and change the data. This includes sequencing, selection, and mathematical calculations.

3. **Report Generation.** From time to time, the information in the data base must be organized and summarized. This is different from a query in two respects: first, a report usually involves the entire data base, not just one part. Second, the information is often transformed in some way. Reports not only reflect the contents of the data base, but show some analysis of it as well. Balancing a checkbook, or doing end-of-the-month accounting are similar to report generation.

DATA ENTRY

Most of the exciting and intriguing aspects of data management take place after you have some data to manage. To get to that point it is necessary to create a means by which data can be entered. How is computer-based data entry special? This is a simple but important question. In the typical paper-based data systems, questions of form and structure are much less important than they are in a computer-based system. The reason is that the understanding of a common language possessed by most humans allows them to recognize data in a wide variety of forms. It is certainly possible to make notes on a napkin while you are having lunch. It might be easier to have a notepad with you, but it is not necessary.

Computers, on the other hand, do not possess anything like an understanding of language. They have no way of telling a first name from a last name, or a company name from a street name. To the computer, names are simply random sequences of characters. In word processing, this limitation generally does not pose a problem because the computer is not required to understand the text, but only to print it.

However, in data base systems, the data stored are subject to some analysis. It is necessary to create some way by which the computer can identify or associate some simple meanings with the data. *dBASE III Plus* employs a master "structure" technique often used by computer data bases. The master structure technique divides the data input into distinct items. For example, when creating a checkbook ledger, you might specify that the first eight characters entered will be the date, while the next three characters (9 through 12) are the check number, and so on.

The structure serves to make the data more than just a random sequence of characters. In turn, the structure is used to help analyze and organize the data. Before you can do anything with *dBASE III Plus*, you must create a structure for the data you want to store.

CREATING THE STRUCTURE

The heart of any computer information system is the *file*. The file has two distinct parts, structure and data, and is where the information actually is stored.

How do computers deal with information? First, an explanation of how humans usually record information is necessary. Look below:

NAME: Carolyn Rigiero
AREA CODE: 212
PHONE: 245–0929

If you look carefully, you can see the elements of a computer data file. Note that there are fundamentally two types of information merged together. Some of the writing (boldface) is used to identify the other information. If they were separated, you would get something like this:

STRUCTURE	*INFORMATION*
NAME:	Carolyn Rigiero
AREA CODE:	212
PHONE:	245–0929

One basic difference between the structure and the information is that the structure will be the same each time, but the information will change with every entry.

You will need to know some terms when talking about information stored in computer files:

1. **FIELD.** Each piece of information is called a *field*. In the example above, 212 is a field. AREA CODE is the label that identifies the field.
2. **RECORD.** All the fields of information that are grouped together constitute a RECORD. In the example, the information below is a single record.

   Carolyn Rigiero
   212
   245–0929
3. **FILE.** A *file* is made up of all the records that have been stored.

A FILE COMPOSED OF RECORDS ORGANIZED BY FIELDS

NAME	AREA CODE	PHONE
Carolyn Rigiero	415	657–0505
Walter La Fish	215	567–0494
Robert Kurnick	103	645–9874
Louis Krumm	215	756–0595

FIELDS

RECORDS

A word about computer terms: the words *field, record,* and *file* have many meanings. In terms of data base management, however, they are used in the narrow context that has been described above.

FILE STRUCTURE

When a file is created there are certain key questions that the creator must answer:

1.   What fields do I want to have?
2.   What are the names of the fields?
3.   What kind of information will these fields contain?

For the sake of expediency and consistency, the information needed to create files is provided for you in this book. In real life, however, you must think about the tasks you want the computer to perform, and answer the three questions above based on your understanding of the problem.

Question number three is a bit unusual. Computers generally make a distinction between two types of information: characters and numbers. Basically, characters are used as text, while numbers are values used in calculations. There are times, however, when what you think of as numbers, 215 for instance, are treated as letters. As you go along, the distinction will become clear.

LIMITATIONS

In *dBASE III Plus*, the file structure is created with the CREATE command. Like all programs, *dBASE III Plus* has limits in the number of fields, the total number of characters, and the types of fields allowed in a given file:

Number of fields in a data base:	**128**
Total number of characters in all fields:	**4000**
Maximum number of characters in a field:	**254**
Total number of records in a file:	**1 billion**
Number of data files in use at one time:	**10**

dBASE III Plus accepts five types of fields, as listed below.

Character

This field accepts any characters and stores them as left-justified text, with a limit of 254 characters. No calculations can be performed on CHARACTER fields.

Numeric

NUMERIC fields contain only numbers and are right-justified. Calculations can be performed only on NUMERIC fields. NUMERIC fields are limited to 19 characters in length.

Logical

A LOGICAL field is limited to a single character. Entry into a LOGICAL field is limited to the characters T, t, Y, y for a logical TRUE, or F, f, N, n for a logical FALSE.

Date

DATE fields hold calendar dates. All DATE fields are automatically set at eight characters in length. Dates are entered as MM/DD/YY. DATE fields allow the use of special date functions built into *dBASE III Plus*. Addition and subtraction can be performed on DATE fields.

Memo

MEMO fields are special fields that allow you to attach a text memo of up to 4096 characters to each record. The memos are not stored with the other fields, but are stored in a separate memo file. MEMO fields have an automatic length of ten characters. They are different from CHARACTER fields in that they are not subject to sequencing or selection actions of the data base. You will learn more about MEMO fields later in this chapter.

In the section that follows and throughout, the book becomes "hands-on." It is assumed that you are using your computer and the *dBASE III Plus* software as you are working along.

If you have not already done so, please load your *dBASE III Plus* program.

The assumption is made that you are working with a hard disk system and that the hard disk is designated as drive C. If this is not the case on your system, it will not make much difference in how the program operates. Simply substitute the letter of your drive for C when necessary.

The same is true of users with floppy drive systems. For the most part, it will not make any difference if a floppy drive system is used. When differences occur, they will be noted. If you are using *dBASE* on a floppy drive system, you should enter the following command to change the data disk to drive B. Insert a formatted disk, preferably blank, into drive B. Then type

> **SET DEFAULT TO b:<return>**

You are now ready to begin.

THREE MODES OF OPERATION

dBASE III Plus can operate in one of three modes:

1. **DOT PROMPT.** The DOT PROMPT mode is the basic mode of operation for *dBASE III Plus*. In this mode, the program displays a . (dot) character as a prompt. You can then enter commands directly for *dBASE III Plus* to interpret. The DOT PROMPT mode requires you to know the proper commands and command syntax.

2. **ASSISTANT.** The ASSISTANT (or ASSIST) mode is designed to implement *dBASE III Plus* by selecting choices from a series of menus. The advantage of the ASSISTANT is that you do not have to know the exact commands or command syntax in order to execute a command.

3. **PROGRAM.** The PROGRAM mode is one of the most powerful tools available in *dBASE III Plus*. In this mode, commands are entered into a file. Rather than executing the commands as they are entered, the program stores them for later reference. When you ask the program to execute the commands, they are automatically read from the file and executed one after the other. *dBASE III Plus* operates automatically in the PROGRAM mode.

Which mode should you begin with? The ASSISTANT mode is well executed in *dBASE III Plus* as compared with its predecessor, *dBASE III*. The most obvious difference between *dBASE III* and *dBASE III Plus* is the design and use of the ASSISTANT. The difference is that in *dBASE III* the program begins in the DOT PROMPT mode, and *dBASE III Plus* begins in the ASSISTANT mode.

Because of the improvements made in the ASSISTANT mode for *dBASE III Plus*, all three modes will be covered.

The reason dBASE III Plus begins in the ASSISTANT mode and dBASE III does not is because of a difference in the CONFIG.DB file. If the CONFIG.DB file contains the command COMMAND=ASSIST, the program will automatically enter the ASSISTANT mode whenever it is loaded. This is true for both dBASE III and dBASE III Plus. The difference between the programs is a result of the fact that dBASE III Plus is supplied with a CONFIG.DB file that already contains this command. dBASE III is not supplied with that file.

Once you have loaded the program you are ready to learn how to create a file structure.

CREATE A FILE STRUCTURE

The initial *dBASE III Plus* display shows the SETUP menu as presented by the *dBASE III Plus* ASSISTANT. The ASSISTANT consists of a series of menus that help you operate *dBASE III Plus*. The screen will look like this:

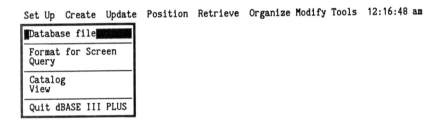

dBASE III PLUS ASSISTANT

The ASSISTANT screen display is divided into six areas:

1. **Menu Bar.** The menu bar consists of a series of items listed on the top line of the screen.
2. **Clock Display.** The section shows the current system time in the upper right hand corner of the screen.

   The time displayed is taken from the DOS system time. If you have a battery-powered clock installed in the computer, DOS will take its time from the clock. Note that many clocks require you to run a special software program supplied with the clock in order to transfer the time to the system (e.g., AST-Six-Pak uses a program called ASTCLOCK.COM). Otherwise, DOS begins keeping time starting from when you booted the system.

3. **Pull Down Menu.** The pull down menu appears as a box that contains a list of choices. Each item on the menu bar has its own pull down menu.

4. **Command Line.** This line shows you the *dBASE III Plus* command that is being created in response to your menu choices. Right now, the line is blank because no command has been chosen from the menu.

5. **Status Line.** The status line displays information about the current status of the program. The status line itself has six sections:

   1. **Mode.** This shows the current mode, either ASSIST, Command Line (DOT PROMPT), or Command (PROGRAMMING).

   2. **Drive.** This area shows the selected disk drive.

   3. **File.** This area shows the selected data file, if any.

   4. **Location.** This area shows the location of the highlight. For example, Opt: 1/6 means that the highlight is in a pull down menu positioned in the first of six possible choices.

   5. **Insert/Overtype.** This area indicates the status of typing, either insert or overtype.

   6. **Locks.** This area indicates whether or not the CAPS or NUMLOCK key has been activated. This is helpful because the IBM PC and XT keyboards do not have indicator lights to show the status of these keys.

6. **Message Area.** The message area is used to display information that helps you operate the program.

In order to create a structure you must change to the CREATE menu. Enter

< right arrow >

The highlight on the menu bar moves to the right, and the pull down menu for CREATE appears.

```
Set Up  Create  Update  Position  Retrieve  Organize Modify Tools  01:17:02 am
        ┌────────────────┐
        │ Database file  │
        │ Format         │
        │ View           │
        │ Query          │
        │ Report         │
        │ Label          │
        └────────────────┘
```

```
ASSIST            ‖<C:>‖                          ‖Opt:‖1/4‖           ‖     ‖
Move selection bar - ↑↓. Select - ↵. Leave menu - . Help - F1. Exit - Esc.
```

The highlight is positioned on Database file, the type of file you want to create. Select that option by entering

< return >

dBASE III Plus displays

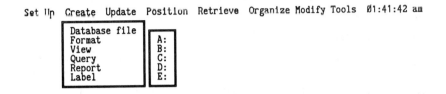

Note that two things happen when you enter < return >:

1. A new box appears on the screen listing the disk drives active in the system. You can now use the highlight to select the drive on which the data file will be created. The highlight is positioned on the current active drive.

    The number of drives that appear in the box will reflect the number of disk drives DOS believes are available. In most systems this would mean A and B for the floppy drives and C for the hard disk, if present. However, if you are using DOS 3.1, the box will contain D and E. DOS 3.1 creates the fictional drives D and E to allow the creation of ram disks, or substitution of a disk drive for a subdirectory using the SUBST command. The main point is not to be concerned if more drive letters are displayed than are physically present in your computer system.

2. The command line now shows the actual *dBASE III Plus* command that will carry out your menu selections. This means that selecting Database file from the CREATE menu is equivalent to entering the *dBASE III Plus* command, CREATE, at the dot prompt.

    The reason for the display is that the ASSISTANT mode has two functions. The first is to make *dBASE III Plus* simple for the new user. Many programs employ systems of menus for this purpose.

    Where *dBASE III Plus* differs from other programs is in the second purpose of the ASSISTANT display. If you intend to master *dBASE III Plus* commands and eventually create your own programs, it is necessary to learn the *dBASE III Plus* language. By watching the command line as you select options from the menus, you will learn the correct form of entry for the other two modes of *dBASE III Plus*. While the ASSISTANT makes *dBASE III Plus* easier to use, it also teaches you the more difficult but more powerful method of direct entry of commands. You will learn more about direct entry later in this book.

If you are using dBASE III Plus *on a floppy drive system, make sure that the highlight in the drive box is on B:. Also make sure that you have a formatted disk in drive B.*

Select the highlighted disk by entering

< return >

The next box asks you to enter the name of the file that you want to create.

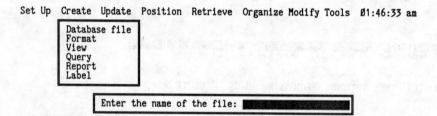

Filenames in *dBASE III Plus* can be from one to eight characters and cannot contain spaces.

Enter the name as follows:

expenses < return >

dBASE III Plus *automatically adds a .DBF extension to a data base file. Thus EXPENSES will appear as EXPENSES.DBF on the disk directory.*

The screen will look like this:

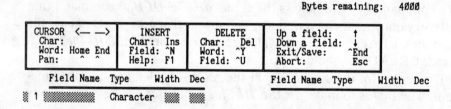

The top portion of the screen shows a menu of editing commands that can be used in this mode. You can make the screen display less cluttered by turning off the HELP menu. The **[F1]** key is the Help key in *dBASE III Plus*. Enter

> **[F1]**

You are now ready to enter the specifications for the individual fields.

SPECIFYING FIELDS

Note that the name of the file you are creating appears in the upper left-hand corner of the screen. In the upper right-hand corner, the program displays the number of characters left for you to use and the number of fields defined. The values change as you add fields. Enter the name of the first field:

> **date < return >**

Field names in dBASE III Plus must begin with a letter and can be up to ten characters in length. You are allowed to use letters or numbers following the first character, but you cannot use blank spaces in a field name. If you wish to create a name with a gap, you can use an underscore character. Examples:

> *birth   date   WRONG*
> *birth__date   CORRECT*

The cursor has moved to the next area where the type of field will be entered. *dBASE III Plus* has already entered Char/text. Enter

> **< space bar >**

The entry changes to NUMERIC. The note at the bottom of the screen explains the type of data you can enter into a NUMERIC field. Enter

> **< space bar >**

DATE appears in the area. Because this is the proper type for this field, enter

> **< return >**

dBASE III Plus automatically enters a length of eight for the DATE field. The cursor now moves to the second field. The display looks like this:

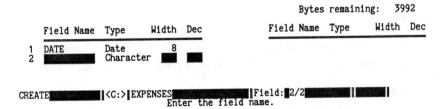

	Field Name	Type	Width	Dec		Field Name	Type	Width	Dec
1	DATE	Date	8						
2		Character							

Bytes remaining: 3992

CREATE ▮▮▮▮ |<C:>|EXPENSES▮▮▮▮▮|Field:▮2/2▮▮▮ ▮ ▮▮▮▮|
Enter the field name.

You are now ready to define another field. Enter

    payto < return >

Because this is a CHARACTER field, enter the following to accept the default.

    < return >

The cursor is now in the width column. Enter

    20 < return >

Once again, the cursor moves to the next field. Because the previous field was defined as CHARACTER, the program skipped the decimal column. Enter the next field as follows:

    item < return >
    < return >
    20 < return >

Next, enter the NUMERIC field, amount:

    amount < return >

To change the field type to NUMERIC, press the space bar until the desired field type appears. There is another method, however. You can directly select the field type you want by entering the first letter of the field type. You could enter one of the following:

N   for NUMERIC
L   for LOGICAL
D   for DATE
M   for MEMO
C   for CHARACTER

In this case, enter

    n

Note that no < return > was needed. Enter the number of characters

    6 < return >

Because this is a numeric entry, *dBASE III Plus* stops in the decimal column to allow you to define the number of decimal places for this field. Enter

    2 < return >

MEMO FIELDS

MEMO fields are more complicated than DATE fields. The purpose of the MEMO field is to allow entry of large blocks of text into records. For example, the EXPENSES file you are creating contains four fields, DATE, PAYTO, ITEM, and AMOUNT. Suppose you wanted a place for comments. Occasionally, an expense might need a paragraph or two to explain something about it (e.g., when to expect a refund of a deposit made to a utility company).

You might choose a CHARACTER field to create a COMMENT field. The largest number of characters allowed in any CHARACTER field is 254. Thus if you created a character-type field called "comments" for your memos, there would be two major disadvantages:

1. If you define the field as a CHARACTER-type field it will take up space for every record entered, whether you use the space or not. Considering the size of a field like COMMENTS, you will be wasting a great deal of disk space, which in turn slows down the processing speed of the computer.
2. *dBASE III Plus* provides no formatting to deal with input areas greater than 70 characters. When a field is wider than 70 characters, it merely wraps around the screen when it reaches the right edge of the video display. If you enter text into the field, *dBASE III Plus* has no facility to keep from breaking words in the middle when they are typed at the edge of the screen, as a word processor does.

The purpose of the MEMO field is to solve these problems. When text is entered into a MEMO field, it is not stored in the same file with the information from the other fields. Rather, a special file is created to store the memo file. It shares the same name with the data file but it uses a .DBT extension.

The .DBT file does not function like a *dBASE* data file. No space is reserved for data; space is used only as actual text is entered. Thus the .DBT file takes up only as much space as is actually needed. A MEMO field can contain up to 4096 characters of text. Note that spaces and carriage returns count as part of that 4096 total.

When a MEMO field is defined, it is automatically set to a length of ten characters. *dBASE III Plus* uses these characters to create a link between the records in the data file (.DBF) and the entries in the memo file (.DBT).

To create a MEMO field in this data file, enter

comments < return >

m

Note that no <return> was necessary after typing the m. The MEMO field is automatically defined as ten characters.

```
                                        Bytes remaining:   3936

     Field Name   Type    Width Dec    Field Name   Type     Width  Dec
  1  DATE         Date        8
  2  PAYTO        Character  20
  3  ITEM         Character  20
  4  AMOUNT       Numeric     6   2
  5  COMMENTS     Memo       10
  6  ███████      Character  ███  ███
```

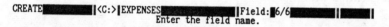
```
CREATE████████    ██<C:>│EXPENSES███████████████│Field:█6/6████████ ██████████
                        Enter the field name.
```

To terminate the entry of fields and save this file definition, enter the following:

> **<return>**

dBASE III Plus will display

```
Press ENTER to confirm.  Any other key to resume.
```

The purpose of this prompt is to make sure you really want to end the create command. If you enter <return>, then the file structure will be defined. Hitting any other key will return you to the create process. Enter

> **<return>**

dBASE III will display

```
Input data records now? (Y/N)
```

If you wanted to enter data, you would enter Y or y. In this instance, enter

> **n**

dBASE III Plus returns to the CREATE menu.

```
Set Up  Create  Update  Position  Retrieve  Organize Modify Tools  12:37:49 am
       ┌───────────────┐
       │█Database█file█│
       │ Format        │
       │ View          │
       │ Query         │
       │ Report        │
       │ Label         │
       └───────────────┘
```

```
ASSIST████████    ██<C:>│EXPENSES███████████████│Rec:█None████████ ██████████
```

LISTING THE STRUCTURE AND DATA ENTRY

After you have completed the creation of the file's structure, you are returned to the CREATE menu. The name of the active file, EXPENSES, appears in the center section of the status line. The section to the right shows Rec: None. This indicates that you have merely created the structure for the file and have not actually entered any data into it.

Right now the structure of the file is fresh in your mind. In addition, you can refer to this book should you forget. But this is not the way things really are when you begin to create your own files. Often, you need to refer to the file structure to see how it was set up.

dBASE III Plus anticipates that and provides a command that will display the structure of the active file. The command is located on the TOOLS menu. A quick way to access any of the menus on the menu bar is to type the first letter of the menu. For example, the TOOLS menu could be accessed by typing t. Enter

t

```
Set Up  Create  Update  Position  Retrieve  Organize Modify Tools  06:47:08 am
                                                     ┌─────────────┐
                                                     │█Set drive███│
                                                     │ Copy file   │
                                                     │ Directory   │
                                                     │ Rename      │
                                                     │ Erase       │
                                                     │ List structure│
                                                     │─────────────│
                                                     │ Import      │
                                                     │ Export      │
                                                     └─────────────┘


ASSIST████████│<C:>│████████████████│Opt:█1/7█████████│████│
```

The command you want to use is LIST STRUCTURE. Note that you cannot access choices on the menu by typing the first letter. You must use the cursor to move the highlight to the option that you desire. In this case, select LIST STRUCTURE by entering

<down arrow> (5 times)
<return>

dBASE III Plus gives you the option of sending the listing to the printer. In this instance, enter

n

dBASE III Plus displays

```
Structure for database : B:expenses.dbf
Number of data records :        0
Date of last update    : 01/01/80
Field  Field name  Type       Width  Dec
    1  DATE        Date           8
    2  PAYTO       Character     20
    3  ITEM        Character     20
    4  AMOUNT      Numeric        6    2
    5  COMMENTS    Memo          10
** Total **                     65
```

Your fields total 64 (8 + 20 + 20 + 6 + 10) characters, but the structure shows 65. Why?

As in its predecessor *dBASE III, dBASE III Plus* adds an overhead character to the file structure to keep track of a special characteristic of each record. The extra character is used to mark a record as deleted or undeleted. You will learn more about deletion later. To return to the ASSISTANT you can press any key. Enter

<return>

Next, you can produce a printed copy of the structure. Make sure your printer is on-line and properly connected before you enter any printing commands. Enter

<return>
y

Notice that *dBASE III Plus* stopped the printing in the middle of the page. To get the paper feed to the top of the next form, it is not necessary to manually adjust the printer. *dBASE III Plus* has a special command called EJECT that causes the printer to advance to the top of the next form. However, there is a problem. The EJECT command does not appear on any of the ASSISTANT menus. Remember that the ASSISTANT mode does not provide complete access to the entire set of *dBASE III Plus* commands.

EXITING AND ENTERING ASSIST

In order to gain access to *dBASE III Plus* commands that are not included in the ASSISTANT menus, you must exit the ASSIST mode. Only a single keystroke is required. Enter

<Esc>

The ASSIST menus disappear and the screen displays a single period positioned just above the status line. You are now in the COMMAND mode, usually referred to as the DOT PROMPT mode. In this mode, commands are entered by typing in the text of the commands, instead of selecting options from a menu. To feed the paper, enter

EJECT <return>

and the paper aligns at the top of the next page.

You can now continue to work and issue commands in the DOT PROMPT mode, or you can return to the ASSIST mode. To return, enter the ASSIST command:

ASSIST <return>

The ASSIST menus appear. Notice that the SETUP menu is always the first one displayed whenever the ASSIST mode is first entered. To practice exiting and entering the ASSIST mode, try the following (the correct commands are listed at the end of the chapter):

Exercise I   Exit the ASSIST mode, feed a page, and return to the ASSIST.

Once you have defined your file structure, your next task is to enter information into the file. The command used to enter new data into a data file is APPEND. APPEND is found on the UPDATE menu. Enter

u

```
Set Up  Create  Update  Position  Retrieve  Organize Modify Tools  06:49:04 am
                ┌─────────┐
                │ Append  │
                ├─────────┤
                │ Edit    │
                │ Display │
                ├─────────┤
                │ Browse  │
                │ Replace │
                ├─────────┤
                │ Delete  │
                │ Recall  │
                │ Pack    │
                └─────────┘
```

When the APPEND command is issued, the computer checks the data file to determine how many records have already been entered. *dBASE III Plus* allows one billion records, disk space permitting, of course. Since APPEND is already highlighted, you can begin adding records by entering

<return>

dBASE III Plus displays the following:

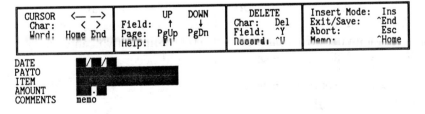

```
┌──────────────────────┬───────────────────┬──────────────────┬──────────────────────────┐
│ CURSOR   <── ──>     │         UP   DOWN │    DELETE        │ Insert Mode:  Ins        │
│ Char:     <  >       │ Field:   ↑     ↓  │ Char:    Del     │ Exit/Save:    ^End       │
│ Word:   Home End     │ Page:   PgUp PgDn │ Field:   ^Y      │ Abort:        Esc        │
│                      │ Help:    F1       │ Record:  ^U      │ Memo:         ^Home      │
└──────────────────────┴───────────────────┴──────────────────┴──────────────────────────┘
DATE        / /
PAYTO
ITEM
AMOUNT           .
COMMENTS    memo
```

APPEND |<C:>|EXPENSES |Rec: None

The cursor appears in the first field, DATE, and you are now ready to enter the actual information into the data file.

ENTERING INFORMATION

The next step is to enter the data. Enter

010283

Note that the slash marks are automatically inserted in the date.

What happened when you typed the final character, 3? The computer made a beep and the cursor jumped to the next field. This is an "automatic advance" feature built into the program that happens when all the spaces are filled. The feature can be disabled by entering a SET CONFIRM ON command before you APPEND. Further information concerning this command is forthcoming when environmental commands are discussed.

DATE FIELDS

The DATE field helps solve many of the problems that would be created by using the CHARACTER field to hold dates. DATE fields in *dBASE III Plus* have the following characteristics:

1. DATE fields are automatically defined as eight characters in length.
2. When entries are made in DATE fields, the slash marks are automatically entered. If you enter 010184 into a DATE field, the entry is stored as 01/01/84.
3. DATE fields default to a MM/DD/YY format. The PICTURE clause can be used to change the format to DD/MM/YY.
4. DATE fields will be correctly sorted even though they are entered in MM/DD/YY form. The program knows that YY is more important than MM even though the MM is entered first. For example, if you entered dates in a CHARACTER field, the sequencing would occur as follows:

Initial Order	Sorted Characters
10/25/82	10/01/81
10/01/81	10/14/79
10/14/79	10/25/82

If the sorting is performed on a DATE field in *dBASE III Plus*, the results are as follows:

Initial Order	Sorted by *dBASE III* or *Plus*
10/25/82	10/14/79
10/01/81	10/01/81
10/14/79	10/25/82

5. DATE entries are checked for validity when they are entered. For example, 13/01/84 or 02/31/83 would cause *dBASE III Plus* to display INVALID DATE (hit Space). The user should then press the <space bar>. When the cursor returns to the beginning of the DATE field, a correct date can be entered. The program will continue checking the date until a valid date is entered.

6. Because DATE fields are a distinct category apart from other types of fields, you can perform a special type of addition and subtraction. DATE field arithmetic can determine the number of days between two dates. *dBASE III Plus* offers a variety of new functions specifically designed to take advantage of the DATE field.

7. Because DATE fields are distinct from CHARACTER fields, logical expressions involving DATE fields must use the special date functions to avoid type mismatch errors. For example, a typical logical expression might be

date='01/01/84'

This expression tests the value of the field called DATE. It assumes that the field called DATE is really a CHARACTER field. However, if the field called DATE is a DATE-type field, the expression above is invalid. The correct expression would look like this:

DTOC(date)='01/01/84'

You will learn more about dates and special date functions as you progress.

You can now enter the rest of the information needed to complete the record. When entering data, the use of uppercase or lowercase characters is significant. Though the program does not care if data are entered in upper- or lowercase letters, when you attempt to select data, *dBASE III Plus* does make a distinction between upper- and lowercase:

Asked for	Found	Match?
CROW CANYON LUMBER	CROW CANYON LUMBER	YES
CROW CANYON LUMBER	crow canyon lumber	NO
crow canyon lumber	CROW CANYON LUMBER	NO
Crow Canyon Lumber	CROW CANYON LUMBER	NO
crow canyon lumber	crow canyon lumber	YES

dBASE III Plus will find a match only if the type is exactly the same as far as case is concerned. Therefore you need to be consistent in the way you enter and search for data.

Type the following into the PAYTO field:

CROW CANYON LUMBER < return >

In this case, you needed to press < return > at the end of the entry because the text did not fill all the 20 characters allocated for that field.

In case of a typing mistake, *dBASE III Plus* offers full screen editing in the APPEND mode. To see this menu, enter

[F1]

The program displays a menu of the editing commands available in the APPEND mode. Enter

[F1]

again, and the HELP menu is removed. Next, enter the ITEM field:

10 2 BY 4 < return >

Finally, enter the AMOUNT field:

65.39 < return >

dBASE III Plus displays the following:

```
Record No.         1
DATE              01/02/83
PAYTO             CROW CANYON LUMBER
ITEM              10 2 BY 4
AMOUNT            65.39
COMMENTS          memo
```

Since no memo is needed in this record, enter

< return >

When the last < return > is pressed, the screen clears the information and you are presented with record no. 2, waiting to be filled in.

While you are entering data, you can skip backward and look at some of the records previously entered. Enter

[Pg Up]

The display has moved back to record no.1. If you spot any mistakes, you are free to edit the record. To return to record no. 2, enter

[Pg Dn]

Enter the following information into record no. 2. Since there is no memo to be entered into the COMMENTS field, simply press < return > when you reach that field.

DATE	PAY TO	ITEM	AMOUNT	MEMO
01/15/83	GREEN ACRES FURN	DESKS	220.57	none

Now enter record no. 3. When you get to the MEMO field, do *not* press < return >. Leave the cursor there for entry of a memo. Enter the following data into record no. 3.

DATE	PAY TO	ITEM	AMOUNT	MEMO
01/21/83	P G & E	TURN ON ELEC	45.87	

MEMO FIELDS

Entering text into a MEMO field is different from entering text into CHARACTER, NUMERIC, LOGICAL, or DATE fields. When you enter the APPEND or EDIT commands to add or revise data, the contents of the MEMO field will appear as the word *memo*. If you want to enter or display the contents of that field, you must position the cursor at the MEMO field and enter [**CTRL/Home**].

When you enter this command, the display changes from the normal EDIT or APPEND format to a word processing format. In this mode, *dBASE III Plus* allows you to enter text in a word processing environment. As you type, your lines wrap around the screen and break between words, just as you would expect with a word processor.

After you have entered the text, [**CTRL/End**] will save the text and return you to the EDIT or APPEND mode. The cursor will be positioned in the MEMO field of the record you were working with, before you entered the word processing mode.

To enter a memo for this record, enter

    [CTRL/Home]

dBASE III Plus displays

```
Edit: COMMENTS
```

Both of these displays indicate that you have entered a word processing mode. This means that the text will automatically wrap around as you type. Enter the following text:

This amount is a deposit held by the electric company because of our current lack of credit. If all bills are paid on time for a period of one year, this deposit will be refunded.

dBASE III Plus *users can display a list of editing functions by pressing the Help key,* [**FI**].

To end the memo and save it as part of record no. 3, enter

[CTRL/End]

You return to the entry form display. Note that the memo itself is not visible. Only the word "memo" appears in the field. To see the memo again, enter

[CTRL/Home]

and the program displays the memo you have just entered. You are now free to add, delete, or change the text. You are limited to 4096 characters for each memo created.

This limit can be overcome by substituting for the dBASE III Plus word processor, another word processing program that can handle larger files (e.g., WordStar 3.3., WordStar 2000, WordPerfect, or Microsoft Word). The technique used to configure a word processing program to dBASE III Plus is covered in detail in Chapter 20.

Return to the entry form. Enter

[CTRL/End]

Move to the next record by entering

[Pg Dn]

Enter the following data:

DATE	PAY TO	ITEM	AMOUNT
01/25/83	PACIFIC BELL	INSTALL TELE	36.90

When you reach the MEMO field, enter the following:

[CTRL/Home]

At this time, use AT&T as the long-distance carrier. However, other possible long-distance services should be examined in light of their potential savings.

[CTRL/End]

Complete the record. Enter

<return>

Enter a fifth record using the following information:

DATE	PAY TO	ITEM	AMOUNT	MEMO
01/30/83	BRITZ PRINTING	BUSINESS CARDS	56.93	none

When you have entered the information, you should have a blank record, no. 6, on the screen. To end the APPEND function, enter

<Esc>

<Esc> is used generally in *dBASE III Plus* to quit a function or a mode. In this case, <Esc> terminates adding records and returns the user to the UPDATE menu.

CLOSING THE FILE

The final step in this chapter is to close the file you have created. This step is very important because the data you have entered have not yet been saved in a file on your disk drive.

Though the following explanation is technical, it is important to understand how *dBASE III Plus* works with the computer's memory. All computers use two types of memory: internal and external. The internal memory, called RAM (Random Access Memory), is where the data are stored when typed into the computer. The internal memory of your computer has two important characteristics:

1. Data can be stored and retrieved at a very high speed.
2. All data are lost when the computer is turned off.

Since internal memory cannot maintain data from session to session, the computer contains a second form of memory called *external*. The disks, both hard and floppy, are used to record data entered into the internal memory. External memory is characterized as follows:

1. Data can be stored for an indefinite period of time.
2. The rate of storage and retrieval is slower than internal memory.

What does all this have to do with *dBASE III Plus* files? The answer is that when you enter data into a *dBASE III Plus* file, your entry is initially stored in the internal memory. The data are therefore subject to loss if something should go wrong with the computer like a power failure or operator error.

To guard against the loss of data, make sure that *dBASE III Plus* has written the data onto the disk. The tricky part is that *dBASE III Plus* writes data to the disk under only two conditions:

1. You have entered more records than the internal memory can hold.
2. You force the program to close the file.

As you enter each record, *dBASE III Plus* does not bother to write the data to the disk because it would slow down the entry process. If the number of records you are entering is small, such as in the examples shown, the program will not write the records to the disk until a command is issued that forces it to close the file.

There are many commands that do this. The first and most direct command is the CLOSE command. When entered, this command tells *dBASE III Plus* to put away the data file that you have been working on. Once this has been done, you can reopen the file and continue working. Should the power go off, your work will be interrupted but no data will be lost.

CLOSE DATABASE

dBASE III Plus users should note that the CLOSE command does not appear on the ASSIST menu. To enter the command, leave the ASSIST mode by entering

<Esc>

dBASE III Plus now is in the DOT PROMPT mode. Enter

CLOSE DATABASE<return>

Notice that the disk drive upon which the data are being saved became active. You can tell by the sound it makes, and by the flashing red light on the drive. Don't be concerned if you missed the light flash; it happens very quickly on some computers.

If you look at the status line, you will see that the portion of the line that contained the name of the file is now blank. This indicates that no file is currently open.

THE DIRECTORY

The directory refers to the list of files stored on a disk. Once a file has been created, it will appear on the disk directory. To check to see if the file really is there, enter

DIR<return>

The DIR command displays a DIRectory of the data base files on the disk. You should see something like this:

```
Database Files   # Records   Last Update   Size
EXPENSES.DBF           5      01/01/80      519
     519 bytes in      1 files.
5062656 bytes remaining on drive.
```

The directory displays the name of the file, the number of records, the system's date of the last update, and the total number of characters in the file. The total number of characters includes both the structure and the five records you entered. Note that a .DBF file extension was automatically added to the EXPENSES file.

In addition, the directory displays the amount of free space remaining on the disk. This number is very important if you are working with a floppy disk system.

The figure used for the size of a file can be deceptive. The number indicates the exact number of characters stored in the file, but that is not the same as the amount of disk space used by the file.

MS DOS systems allocate space on disks in terms of "clusters." The cluster is the minimum allocation unit used for a file. For example, on a double-sided, double-density floppy disk, the cluster size is 1021 characters. Even though the EXPENSES.DBF file is only a little over 500 characters, DOS will allocate a full cluster for that file.

Interestingly enough, the size of the cluster changes as the total capacity of the disk changes. For example, a typical 20-megabyte hard disk has a cluster size of 4096 characters. Thus the same EXPENSES.DBF file would take up to four times the room on a 20-megabyte drive as it would on a floppy disk. Note that DOS 3.2 uses smaller clusters, 2048 bytes.

It is important to remember that the amount of space used up by a file will vary somewhat from the size as shown in the directory listing.

The QUIT command is used to exit the program. Enter

QUIT <return>

The system's prompt appears, indicating that you have left *dBASE III Plus*.

SUMMARY

1. The basis for all data management work is the data base file. Files are produced by creating a file structure. The CREATE command is used to initiate the creation of a file structure.
2. File structures are composed of fields. Each data base file can have up to 128 fields. The size of all fields cannot exceed 4000 characters. No one field can be more than 254 characters.
3. Fields can be either CHARACTER, NUMERIC, DATE, LOGICAL, or MEMO.
4. After the structure is created you can add data to the file by filling in the fields. Each set of fields is called a *record*. Files can have up to a billion records. The APPEND command places *dBASE III Plus* in a data entry mode.

Commands

CREATE (filename)
USE (filename)
APPEND
CLOSE DATABASE
LIST STRUCTURE (TO PRINT)

ANSWER KEY

Exercise 1

< Esc >
EJECT <return >
ASSIST <return >

2

RETRIEVING DATA

THE ENTRY OF DATA IS the slowest of the data base management processes. Once the data have been entered, you can begin to take advantage of the power of the computer and *dBASE III Plus* to retrieve the data from the file. Data retrieval introduces one of the most important concepts in data base management, known as *multiple form output*. This concept separates *dBASE III Plus* (and other full data base programs) from typical word processing or spreadsheet applications.

In Chapter 1 you learned how to create a structure and input data. *dBASE III Plus* automatically created a form in which you entered the data. However, that form is not the form in which the data will finally appear. The whole point of programs like *dBASE III Plus* is that the data entered into the entry form can be retrieved in an almost limitless variety of forms. Some of the forms, such as mailing labels and column reports, are already built into *dBASE III Plus*. Also, personalized output forms can be created to fit almost any need by using some of *dBASE III Plus*'s advanced features.

The point to remember is that the way the data are input does not determine the way in which the data will finally be output. The term *multiple form outputs* refers to that quality which is so important in data management.

In this chapter you will learn some simple but powerful ways to retrieve information from your data base file.

TYPES OF RETRIEVAL

When retrieving records that have already been entered into a data file, there are two questions to be considered:

1.   Do you want to display one record at a time or more than one?
2.   Do you want to allow changes to be made in the data or not?

The four possible commands based on these two questions are EDIT, DISPLAY, LIST, and BROWSE. Why such a variety?

dBASE III Plus seeks to provide as flexible as possible a means of displaying and updating data. For example, commands that do not allow updating prevent you from accidentally changing the information. Each command has its own advantages, and provides a different way of looking at the same information.

In order to continue with the "hands-on" section of this chapter, you should load the *dBASE III Plus* program in the usual manner.

OPENING A FILE

The first step in working with data stored in a file is to "open" the file. "Open" simply refers to a command that tells *dBASE III Plus* that you want to work with the data in a particular file. To open a data base file, you need to select the SETUP menu. If you have just loaded the program, *dBASE III Plus* automatically displays the SETUP menu, with the highlight on the data base file option. This is the option that is used to open a file. Enter

< return >

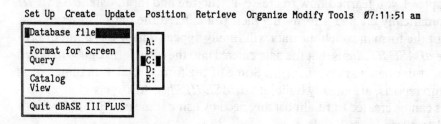

```
Set Up  Create  Update  Position  Retrieve  Organize Modify Tools  07:11:51 am
 Database file                    A:
                                  B:
 Format for Screen                C:
 Query                            D:
                                  E:
 Catalog
 View

 Quit dBASE III PLUS
```

```
Command: USE
ASSIST          |<C:>|                        |Opt: 3/5
```

Two things have happened. In the menu area of the screen, *dBASE III Plus* displays the drive box. In addition, the USE command is displayed on the command line.

It is this command that tells *dBASE III Plus* to open a specific file. To complete the command, you must specify the name of the file. However, you must first select the drive on which the file is stored. Hard disk users can select drive C by entering

<return>

Floppy disk users should position the highlight to B: and then enter

<return>

dBASE III Plus now displays a box that lists all the data base files on a particular disk directory.

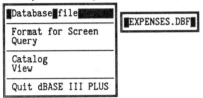

```
Set Up  Create  Update  Position  Retrieve  Organize Modify Tools  07:15:33 am
┌─────────────────┐
│ Database file   │   ┌───────────────┐
├─────────────────┤   │ EXPENSES.DBF  │
│ Format for Screen│  └───────────────┘
│ Query           │
├─────────────────┤
│ Catalog         │
│ View            │
├─────────────────┤
│ Quit dBASE III PLUS │
└─────────────────┘
```

You can use the up and down arrow keys to highlight the file that you want to use. In this example, there is only one file, EXPENSES. If you have been working with *dBASE III Plus* you may have more than one filename appearing in the box. If so, use the arrow keys to highlight EXPENSES.

You can select files only by moving the highlight and pressing <return>. You cannot select the file by typing in the first letter.

Enter

<return>

The next box displayed asks if the file is indexed.

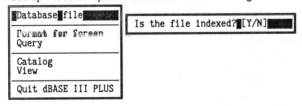

```
Set Up  Create  Update  Position  Retrieve  Organize Modify Tools  07:16:08 am
┌─────────────────┐
│ Database file   │   ┌──────────────────────────┐
├─────────────────┤   │ Is the file indexed? [Y/N]│
│ Format for Screen│  └──────────────────────────┘
│ Query           │
├─────────────────┤
│ Catalog         │
│ View            │
├─────────────────┤
│ Quit dBASE III PLUS │
└─────────────────┘
```

```
Command: USE C:EXPENSES
ASSIST            <C:>                          Opt: 1/1
```

An index file is used to maintain a file in a specific sequence. You will learn how to create and use index files in Chapter 4. For now, enter

n

The display returns to the SETUP menu; however, there has been one change. The STATUS line shows the name of the file that is open, EXPENSES. The STATUS line also contains the information Rec: 1/5.

Rec: 1/5 tells you about the number of records in the file. The 1 indicates the position of the pointer. The pointer is always positioned at the first record in the file when it is opened. You will learn more about the significance of the pointer later in this chapter. The 5 indicates the total number of records in the file.

LISTING DATA

Now that the file is open you can retrieve the data that are stored in it. Select the RETRIEVE menu by entering

r

Set Up Create Update Position Retrieve Organize Modify Tools 07:17:03 am

The first command on the menu, LIST, is automatically highlighted. Enter

< return >

When you have selected the command, *dBASE III Plus* displays the command options box.

Set Up Create Update Position Retrieve Organize Modify Tools 07:17:42 am

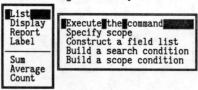

The box has five options:

1. **Execute the command.** Perform command as currently specified.
2. **Specify scope.** Specify a certain area of the data base to work with.

3. **Construct a field list.** Select fields to work with.

4. **Build a search condition.** Select records to work with.

5. **Build a scope condition.** Select a limit for command.

Options 2 through 5 are used to modify the effect of the command. If these options are not used, *dBASE III Plus* executes the command you have selected with its default settings. What is meant by "default" settings?

Each command in *dBASE III Plus* is designed to operate with a specific set of assumptions. For example, the LIST command is designed to retrieve all the fields from all the records in the data base file. However, there are times when you might want to limit the effect of the LIST command. In order to do that you would use options 2 through 5 on the COMMAND menu to modify the default assumptions.

The term *default* also implies that every time you issue a command, *dBASE III Plus* assumes you want to use the default assumptions. If you want to limit the command, you must specify the limits each time the command is used.

The command options menu box is used with many *dBASE III Plus* commands. It is not specific to the LIST command.

To see how LIST works with the default values, enter

     < return >

dBASE III Plus offers you the option of sending the output to the printer.

```
Set Up  Create  Update  Position  Retrieve  Organize Modify Tools  07:31:45 am
                                  ┌────────┐
                                  │■List■■■│
                                  │Display │
                                  │Report  │
                                  │Label   │
                                  ├────────┤
                                  │Sum     │
                                  │Average │
                                  │Count   │
                                  └────────┘
           ┌──────────────────────────────────────────────┐
           │ Direct the output to the printer? [Y/N] ■■    │
           └──────────────────────────────────────────────┘
```

Enter

       n

The records are displayed. Note that the MEMO fields, COMMENTS, lists the word *memo* for each record. The memos you entered are not displayed. In fact, from this display there is no way that you can tell which records have memos and which don't. You will be reminded of how to display the memo later in this chapter.

Notice that *dBASE III Plus* automatically numbers the records as they are listed. To continue, enter

     < return >

The display is cleared from the screen and the RETRIEVE menu appears.

FIELD LISTS

The default value for the LIST command is to list all the fields in the data base file. However, you can change which fields are listed, and the order in which they are listed, by using the FIELD LIST option on the COMMAND OPTIONS menu. Select the LIST command again by entering

> **< return >**

Select the field list option by entering

> **< down arrow >**
> **< down arrow >**
> **< return >**

dBASE III Plus displays two more boxes.

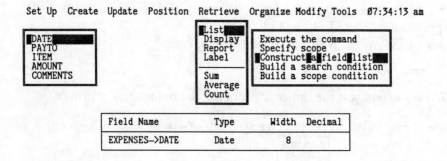

The box in the upper left-hand corner of the screen lists the names of the fields in the data base. These names are the names of the fields as entered during the CREATE command.

The box in the center of the screen displays details about the field currently highlighted.

The field name as shown in the center box is EXPENSES– >DATE. This form of the field name includes an "alias," and the field name. The alias is the name of the file, EXPENSES. It is used to indicate which file the field name comes from. dBASE III Plus has advanced features that allow data from several files to be used at the same time. Alias names help distinguish fields from different files even if they have the same name. For now, you are working with only one file at a time. You will learn more about the use of field aliases later on.

You can now select fields by moving the highlight with the up and down arrow keys. For example, to select the PAYTO field, enter

> **<down arrow>**
> **<return>**

Notice that PAYTO now appears in duller video, indicating that it has been selected. Select AMOUNT by entering

> **<down arrow>**
> **<return>**

When you have selected the fields you want to list, exit the FIELDS menu by entering

> **<right arrow>**

Look at the command line. It shows the command you have created with your choices: LIST PAYTO, AMOUNT. The command line shows the *dBASE III Plus* command language equivalent to the menu selections you have made. To execute the command, enter

> **[Pg Up]**
> **<return>**
> **n**

When you are finished viewing the display, enter

> **<return>**

Enter another LIST command.

> **<return>**
> **<down arrow> (2 times)**
> **<return>**

Select the ITEM field by entering

> **<down arrow>**
> **<down arrow>**
> **<return>**

Execute the command by entering

> **<right arrow>**
> **[Pg up]**
> **<return>**
> **n**

When you have finished viewing the display, enter

> **<return>**

The field selection option allows you to display one or more fields in a listing. In addition, you can arrange the list in any order you desire.

LISTING MEMOS

When a LIST command is used to list all the fields in the data base file, *dBASE III Plus* does not display the contents of the MEMO fields. To display the contents of a MEMO field, you must select the MEMO field as part of your field list. For example, if you wanted to list the dates and memos in your file, you would begin by selecting fields. Enter

> **<return>**
> **<down arrow>**
> **<down arrow>**
> **<return>**

Select the DATE field by entering

> **<return>**

Now select the COMMENTS field. Enter

> **<down arrow> (3 times)**
> **<return>**

Execute the command by entering

> **<right arrow>**
> **[Pg Up]**
> **<return>**
> **n**

To continue, enter

> **<return>**

The contents of the MEMO field are listed in lines no wider than 50 characters. You may remember that when you entered the memos, dBASE III Plus allowed you to type in a line 65 characters wide. The memo lines are listed in a slightly different form than the one in which you entered them.

MEMO fields can create a problem when they are listed with a number of other fields because they are so wide. For example, you might use the field selection option to select all the fields that include the COMMENTS field. Enter

> **<return>**
> **<down arrow>**
> **<down arrow>**

> < return >
> < return > (5 times)
> [Pg Up]
> < return ⋗n

The records that contained memos were too wide to be displayed on the screen. The screen can display lines that are only 80 characters or fewer. When the lines exceed the 80-column limit, the remainder of the line is displayed on the next line. This problem can occur even without a MEMO field if the file contains fields that add up to more than 71 characters (9 characters are used for the record number).

If your printer can print more than 80 characters, the data will appear correctly on the printer even though it looks scrambled on the screen.

This type of display can be very hard to read. However, *dBASE III Plus* allows you to change the width of the lines used to display the contents of a MEMO field. Since the command is not on the ASSIST menu, you must leave the ASSIST mode and access the DOT PROMPT mode. Enter

> < Esc > (2 times)

Enter

> SET MEMOWIDTH TO 30 < return >

Now enter the ASSIST mode again by entering

> ASSIST < return >

Now list the COMMENTS field. Enter

> r
> < return >
> < down arrow >
> < down arrow >
> < return >
> < down arrow > (4 times)
> < return >

The COMMENTS field has been selected for listing. Enter

> < right arrow >
> [Pg Up]
> < return >
> n

The memo's line width has been altered. Enter

> < return >

Try the exercise below.

Exercise 1   Change the memo line width back to 50 characters. Then return to the ASSIST mode. The correct commands can be found at the end of the chapter.

The next section shows how the LIST command can be used in the DOT PROMPT mode. Exit the ASSIST mode, by entering

< Esc >

Reset the memo width to 50 characters. Enter

SET MEMOWIDTH TO 50 < return >

Open the EXPENSES file with the USE command:

USE expenses < return >

Though the EXPENSES file is already open, entering the above command is perfectly acceptable.

Note that nothing much seems to happen when you open a file, except that another DOT PROMPT appears. Because nothing visual happens when you enter a USE command, many new users think that the command didn't work. That is not the case. Remember, not every command has a visual effect. Many *dBASE III Plus* commands have a "behind the scenes" effect.

Suppose you wanted to confirm that the file was really open. You could ask the program to list the structure. Enter

LIST STRUCTURE < return >

The structure of the file is listed. Notice that the structure contains the name of the file, EXPENSES.

LISTING FROM THE DOT PROMPT

The LIST command allows you to list all the data you have entered into a data base file (all fields, all records). Enter

LIST < return >

All the information that was entered into the file EXPENSES is displayed.

```
Record#  DATE      PAYTO               ITEM            AMOUNT  COMMENTS
      1  01/02/83  CROW CANYON LUMBER  10 2 BY 4        65.39  Memo
      2  01/15/83  GREEN ACRES FURN    DESKS          220.57  Memo
      3  01/21/83  P G & E             TURN ON ELEC    45.87  Memo
      4  01/25/83  PACIFIC BELL        INSTALL TELE    36.90  Memo
      5  01/30/83  BRITZ PRINTING      BUSINESS CARDS  56.93  Memo
```

In large data base files, you might wish to terminate the listing before the end of the file is reached. Entering < Esc > stops the listing.

When used as above, the LIST command lists all fields of all records; however, you can also list the contents of specified fields. For example, all the entries in the PAYTO field can be listed by entering

LIST payto < **return** >

```
Record#  payto
      1  CROW CANYON LUMBER
      2  GREEN ACRES FURN
      3  P G & E
      4  PACIFIC BELL
      5  BRITZ PRINTING
```

Thus by adding the name of the field to the LIST command, you are able to produce a list of just the entries made into the PAYTO field. Enter the following commands:

LIST amount < **return** >
LIST date < **return** >
LIST item < **return** >

It is possible to select more than one field for listing. Enter the following:

LIST payto,amount < **return** >
LIST date,item < **return** >
LIST amount,date,payto < **return** >

Exercise 2   Enter a command that will list the date and the amount only. The correct command can be found at the end of the chapter.

When a LIST command is used to list the fields in the data base file, *dBASE III Plus* does not display the contents of the MEMO fields. In order to display the contents of a MEMO field, you must select the MEMO field as part of your field list. For example, if you wanted to list the dates and memos in your file, you would begin by selecting fields. Enter

LIST date,comments < **return** >

The program displays

```
Record#  date      comments
      1  01/02/83
      2  01/15/83
      3  01/21/83  This amount is a deposit held by the electric
                   company because of our current lack of credit. If
                   all bills are paid on time for a period of one
                   year, this deposit will be refunded.
      4  01/25/83  At this time we will use AT&T as our long-distance
                   carrier. However, other possible long-distance
                   services should be examined in light of their
                   potential savings.
      5  01/30/83
```

The memos are listed with a line width of no more than 50 characters. dBASE III *Plus can alter the width of the line used to display a MEMO field, if you choose.*

Enter the following command:

LIST payto,comments < return >

The program displays

```
Record#  PAYTO                 COMMENTS
      1  CROW CANYON LUMBER
      2  GREEN ACRES FURN
      3  P G & E               This amount is a deposit held by the electric
                               company because of our current lack of credit.  If
                               all bills are paid on time for a period of one
                               year, this deposit will be refunded.

                               On or about January 21, 1984, contact Walter LaFish
                               of the small business accounts department
                               415-897-2626.

      4  PACIFIC BELL          Now that break up of AT&T has become effective—return
                               phones which are rented from AT&T and replace them
                               with company—owned equipment

      5  BRITZ PRINTING
```

The OFF clause is a special clause that can be added to a LIST command at the DOT PROMPT. Its purpose is to tell *dBASE III Plus* not to include the record numbers with the listing. Enter

LIST OFF < return >

OUTPUT TO THE PRINTER

If you want a printed copy of the data, you can add the TO PRINT clause to the LIST command. Before you enter this command, make sure your printer is turned on and cabled correctly to your computer. Enter

LIST TO PRINT <return >

Note that the printing stops as soon as the data have been exhausted. You can command the program to skip to the top of the next form (assuming you are using continuous-form paper) by entering

EJECT <return >

The EJECT command issues a form feed code that is recognized by most printers.

LISTING ARITHMETIC EXPRESSIONS

dBASE III Plus can perform arithmetic functions (i.e., addition($+$), subtraction($-$), multiplication($*$), and division($/$)) while listing. This is accomplished by specifying not just a field but an arithmetic expression.

The computer symbol for multiplication is an *. *Thus 2*5 equals 10.*

For example, you might want to increase the amounts by 6.5 percent, and list them. Enter

LIST amount*1.065 < return >

The amounts listed are 6.5 percent higher than you entered. You can list several arithmetic expressions with the same command. Each one can be based on the same field. Enter

LIST amount,amount*.065,amount*1.065 < return >

The screen will show

```
Record#   amount  amount*.065  amount*1.065
   1       65.39      4.25035       69.64035
   2      220.57     14.33705      234.90705
   3       45.87      2.98155       48.85155
   4       36.90      2.39850       39.29850
   5       56.93      3.70045       60.63045
```

Exercise 3   Enter a command that will list 50 percent of the value of the amount entries. The correct command can be found at the end of the chapter.

SPECIAL DATE FUNCTIONS

One of the reasons that a DATE-type field is advantageous is that *dBASE III Plus* has a number of special functions that operate on the contents of DATE fields in special ways. Enter

LIST YEAR(date) < return >

The program will display

```
Record#   YEAR(date)
   1         1983
   2         1983
   3         1983
   4         1983
   5         1983
```

The program can produce the character name of a month entered as a number. Enter

LIST CMONTH(date) < return >

The program will display

```
Record#   CMONTH(date)
   1       January
   2       January
   3       January
   4       January
   5       January
```

The program can list the day of the week (DOW) of the dates in the data file. Enter

LIST DOW(date) < return >

The program will display

```
Record#   DOW(date)
    1         1
    2         7
    3         6
    4         3
    5         1
```

The number 1 corresponds to Sunday, 2 to Monday, and so on. However, *dBASE III Plus* can directly list the character name for the day of the week. Enter

LIST CDOW(date) < return >

The program will display

```
Record#   CDOW(date)
    1      Sunday
    2      Saturday
    3      Friday
    4      Tuesday
    5      Sunday
```

You can combine several date functions to get almost any type of desired date display. Enter this example:

LIST CDOW(date),CMONTH(date),DAY(date),YEAR(date) < return >

The program will display

```
Record#   CDOW(date) CMONTH(date) DAY(date) YEAR(date)
    1      Sunday     January           2      1983
    2      Saturday   January          15      1983
    3      Friday     January          21      1983
    4      Tuesday    January          25      1983
    5      Sunday     January          30      1983
```

Dates are also subject to a special type of arithmetic. For example, you might want to know the date 45 days from a particular date. Enter

LIST date+45 < return >

The program lists

```
Record#   date+45
    1      02/16/83
    2      03/01/83
    3      03/07/83
    4      03/11/83
    5      03/16/83
```

dBASE III Plus *assumes that all values added to dates are in terms of days. To add a year, you would add 365.25 to a date.*

You can combine the special functions along with the date arithmetic to find out what day of the week 45 days from the date falls on. Enter

LIST CDOW(date+45)<return>

The program lists

```
Record#  cdow(date+45)
      1  Wednesday
      2  Tuesday
      3  Monday
      4  Friday
      5  Wednesday
```

Dates can also be subtracted. Enter

LIST date−15<return>

The program lists

```
Record#  date−15
      1  12/18/82
      2  12/31/82
      3  01/06/83
      4  01/10/83
      5  01/15/83
```

THE DISPLAY COMMAND

The DISPLAY command differs from the LIST command in the respect that the default is to display all the fields in one record. To see how the DISPLAY command operates, enter

DISPLAY <return>

What happens? The headings are displayed but no data appear. Is there something wrong with the program or the file?

The answer may become clear if you consider the function of the DISPLAY command. Remember, the DISPLAY command shows the contents of only one record at a time. But what record will that be? Will it be the first record in the file, the last, or some other record?

The answer lies in the concept of the pointer. The pointer is really a value *dBASE III Plus* stores in the memory of the computer that can be either a number representing a record number, or a special function called EOF, End Of File.

When you use the LIST command, *dBASE III Plus* automatically sets the pointer back to record no. 1. The program then lists the data from that record on until it reaches the end of the file. When the end of the file is encountered, the pointer is no longer pointing to a valid record.

That is exactly the case in this example. After each LIST command the pointer is positioned at the end of the file. Entering a DISPLAY command at this point will display no data. To visually enforce that, *dBASE III Plus* displays on the status line Rec: EOF/5, to indicate that the pointer is at the End Of the File.

There are several concepts to keep in mind when the pointer is discussed:

1. The pointer refers to a position within the data base file. If you do not have a data base file open, there is no pointer.

2. Whenever a data base file is open, the pointer is positioned at the top of the file. *dBASE III Plus* possesses the ability to open up to ten data base files at once. Each file has its own pointer independent of any other.

3. The terms *current record* and *active record* refer to the record that the pointer is indicating at that moment.

4. There can be only one active record in each data base. The pointer cannot point at two records in the same data base file at the same time.

5. Many *dBASE III Plus* commands affect the position of the pointer. When issuing a series of commands, you should consider the effect that each command will have on the position of the pointer.

ADJUSTING THE POINTER

dBASE III Plus has a simple command for positioning the pointer, called the GOTO command. Enter

        GOTO 3 < return >

The pointer has moved to record no. 3. The positioning of the pointer is visually enforced on the status line. It reads Rec: 3/5. Enter

        DISPLAY < return >

The program displays record no. 3.

```
Record#  DATE    PAYTO          ITEM          AMOUNT COMMENTS
     3  01/21/83 P G & E        TURN ON ELEC   45.87 Memo
```

dBASE III Plus will recognize an abbreviated form of the GOTO command. Simply enter the number of the record. Enter

        4 < return >
        DISPLAY < return >

Enter

        7 < return >

What happens? The screen displays

```
Record is out of range.
  ?
7
```

The record out of range message tells you that you have requested that *dBASE III Plus* position the pointer beyond the end of the file. The program cannot execute this command and an error is caused.

The program also displays a message asking if you want some help. Enter

> **y**

The screen display is changed to the *dBASE III Plus* help screen. A brief explanation of the command is given to remind you of what you did wrong. To return to the DOT PROMPT mode, enter

> **<Esc>**

Help in *dBASE III Plus* is context sensitive. This means that you will see a help screen related to the action you were performing when the error occurred.

MORE ABOUT GOTO

The GOTO command will respond to any valid numeric expression. Enter

> **GOTO 7−5 <return>**
> **DISPLAY <return>**

Why is record no. 2 displayed? The entry 7−5 is interpreted by *dBASE III Plus* as an arithmetic expression (seven minus five) whose result is the value two. The program then executes the GOTO command for the result of the calculation and positions the pointer at record no. 2. This ability will be more meaningful when you begin to write programs than it is right now.

TOP AND BOTTOM

Besides numbers or arithmetic expressions, the GOTO command recognizes two special words: TOP and BOTTOM. TOP tells the program to position the pointer at the first record in the file, and BOTTOM positions the pointer at the last record in the file. Enter

> **GOTO TOP <return>**
> **DISPLAY <return>**

The commands GOTO TOP and GOTO 1 will perform the function in a nonindexed data base. When an index file is open, the GOTO TOP positions the pointer at the logical top of the file. This record may or may not be record no. 1, depending on the order by which the file has been indexed. GOTO 1 always positions the pointer at record no. 1 regardless of where it appears in an index file. Indexing will be covered in Chapter 5.

Move the cursor to the bottom of the file by entering

> **GOTO BOTTOM** < **return** >
> **DISPLAY** < **return** >

You cannot take the same shortcut using the TOP and BOTTOM specifications as you can with a numeric value (e.g., BOTTOM in place of GOTO BOTTOM). The GOTO command must precede the TOP and BOTTOM specifications.

The bottom of the file is not the same thing as the end of the file. Bottom refers to the position at the beginning of the last record. End of file refers to the position following the last record in the file. When a LIST command is completed, the pointer is at the end of the file. Enter

> **LIST** < **return** >
> **DISPLAY** < **return** >

Notice that the DISPLAY command does not display any data because the pointer position is beyond the last record. Enter

> **GOTO BOTTOM** < **return** >
> **DISPLAY** < **return** >

This time record no. 5, the last record in the file, is displayed because the pointer was positioned at the first character in the last record. Keep this distinction in mind when you are performing searches in your data base.

Almost all *dBASE III Plus* commands have a default scope. The scope refers to the portion of the data base that is affected by a command. *dBASE III Plus* allows you to modify the scope of a command by specifying an alternate scope. For example, the DISPLAY command will display the contents of a single record. However, that can be changed by adding a scope to the command. Enter

> **DISPLAY ALL** < **return** >

This time, DISPLAY listed all the records. DISPLAY ALL performs the same function as LIST.

The statement above is true with the exception that when a data file has more records than can be displayed on the screen, DISPLAY ALL will pause automatically to give you a chance to read the display. LIST will display the entire file without pausing.
In dBASE III Plus, the pause occurs every 19 records.

dBASE III Plus uses the following SCOPES:

1. **ALL.** This scope will process all the records in the file beginning at the top and working sequentially to the end of the file.
2. **RECORD #.** This scope will process only the one specified record.
3. **NEXT #.** This scope will begin at the current pointer location and process the number of records specified. If the end of the file is encountered first, the processing will stop. No error message will be displayed if the number specified next is beyond the end of the file.
4. **REST.** This scope tells *dBASE* to process all records beginning with the current record until the end of the file is reached.

For example, you could LIST a single record by entering the following:

> LIST RECORD 3 < return >

The contents of record no. 3 are displayed. The display command works exactly the same way with the RECORD scope. Enter

> DISPLAY RECORD 3 < return >

There is no difference between LIST RECORD # and DISPLAY RECORD # because the RECORD scope displays only one record at a time. The automatic pause used by DISPLAY is irrelevant when the scope is limited to a single record.

DISPLAY can be used in combination with GOTO to display a series of nonadjacent records. Enter

> 2 < return >
> DISPLAY < return >
> 4 < return >
> DISPLAY < return >

Note that when DISPLAY is used without a scope, the record displayed depends on the pointer position. This may seem like a small point at this moment. However, when you begin to program, the significance of this type of command will become clearer.

RELATIVE MOVEMENT

The ALL and RECORD scopes are not affected by the position of the pointer at the moment when the command is issued. The ALL scope always repositions the pointer at the beginning of the file before the processing begins. You could say that commands with an ALL scope contain a GOTO TOP command within them. ALL and RECORD are considered absolute scopes because they always operate the same way.

NEXT and REST are relative scopes because they do depend on the current position of the pointer.
Enter

GOTO 2 < return >

Next, enter a DISPLAY command with a next scope. Enter

DISPLAY NEXT 3 < return >

The program displays

```
Record#  DATE      PAYTO                ITEM          AMOUNT  COMMENTS
     2   01/15/83  GREEN ACRES FURN     DESKS         220.57  Memo
     3   01/21/83  P G & E              TURN ON ELEC   45.87  Memo
     4   01/25/83  PACIFIC BELL         INSTALL TELE   36.90  Memo
```

The scope, NEXT 3, does display three records. However, they may not be the records you expected. It is quite logical to assume that since you are starting at record no. 2, the next three records would be 3, 4, and 5. *dBASE III Plus* begins the display with the current pointer position, record no. 2, and proceeds to the next two records, 3 and 4.

Why does the NEXT scope operate in this manner? The reason for counting the current record as the first one to be displayed is that the GOTO command does not display the information; it only positions the pointer. Suppose that you had a large data base file with hundreds of records. If you wanted to see the ten records beginning at record 550, you would enter GOTO 550, then you would enter DISPLAY NEXT 10.

What would happen if you entered the command DISPLAY NEXT 1 in the EXPENSES file? Which record would be displayed? Enter

DISPLAY NEXT 1 < return >

Record no. 4 is listed. Using a scope of NEXT 1 processes only the current record.

One of the major advantages of the NEXT scope is that it begins processing records at the current cursor position, and not at the beginning of the file. In a small data base like the one in which you are working, the position of the pointer before a command is not very significant. However, as the data base file gets larger, the distinction becomes important.

Suppose you have a file of over a thousand records. You are currently positioned at record 400. Entering a LIST command would begin listing records starting at the beginning of the file. LIST NEXT 100 would begin the listing at the current record and continue to record 499 (assuming that many records are in the file).

The NEXT scope has an awkward limitation. If you want to tell the program to process all the records from the current record to the end of the file, you would have to make an estimate of the number of records remaining in the file. Since there is no harm in entering too large a number, you could enter some large number that you are sure exceeds the number of records in the file, for example, LIST NEXT 10000. To overcome this awkwardness *dBASE III Plus* adds an additional scope.

THE REST SCOPE

The REST scope appearing in *dBASE III Plus* solves the problem posed by the NEXT scope. Using REST processes all the records from the current record until the end of the file. Enter

```
3 < return >
DISPLAY REST <return >
```

dBASE III Plus displays the current record and all the remaining records until the end of the file is encountered.

MORE ABOUT RELATIVE MOVEMENT

The GOTO command is used to position the pointer to a specific record in the data base file. Another method by which the position of the pointer can be changed is the SKIP command. The SKIP command moves the pointer relative to its current position. Begin by entering

```
GOTO 3 < return >
```

The SKIP command below will move the pointer a specified number of records from the active record. If used with any numeric values, the SKIP command moves the pointer one record toward the end of the file. Enter

```
SKIP < return >
```

Note that the SKIP command displays a message that indicates the current record. The current record is now no. 4. To move backwards in the file (i.e., toward the beginning of the file) you should enter a negative value. Enter

```
SKIP −1 <return >
```

The current record is now record no. 3. You can change the pointer's position by more than one record by entering a larger numeric value. Enter

```
SKIP 3 < return >
```

The program tells you that you are positioned at record no. 6. This may be confusing since there are only five records in the file. Enter

```
DISPLAY <return >
```

Nothing is displayed because record no. 6 is really the end of the file. The SKIP command does not explicitly show that you have reached the end of the file. Enter

SKIP 10 < return >

What happened? The screen displays

```
. SKIP 10
End of file encountered.
         ?
SKIP 10
```

dBASE III Plus is telling you that it cannot carry out the command. This makes sense because you don't have enough records to move 10 beyond where you are already positioned, at the end of the file.

Because you were positioned at record no. 6, entering a SKIP 10 command implies movement beyond the end of the file.

When you enter a command that *dBASE III Plus* does not understand, a message appears at the bottom of the screen asking you if you want help. Enter

y

dBASE III Plus will display

SKIP

<u>SKIP</u>

```
Syntax      :  SKIP [<expN>]

Description :  Moves the record pointer in the active data base file
               forward or backward.  You specify the number of records
               to be skipped using the numeric expression.  The default
               is forward one record.

See also    :  GO, RECNO()
```

The purpose of this screen is to give you a short description of how the SKIP command works. To return to the DOT PROMPT mode, enter

< Esc >

Note that the error you just encountered happens when you are positioned at the end of the file and you try to SKIP in a forward direction. If you are not already at the end of the file, you can attempt to skip beyond the end without creating an error. For example, if you are at record no. 5 and enter SKIP 10, dBASE III Plus moves the pointer to the end of the file and stops without an error message.

As with GOTO, the numeric value used with SKIP can be any valid *dBASE III Plus* numeric expression. Look at the command below. To what record will that command position the pointer? Enter the command to find out if your estimate was correct.

SKIP 2*2/4* –1 <return>

The advantage of the SKIP command is that the pointer is moved relative to its current position. The SKIP command is used more in the programming mode than in the manual entry modes.

THE ? COMMAND

So far, you have learned two commands that retrieve data from the data base file: LIST and DISPLAY. Both commands are oriented toward producing lists of fields and records. *dBASE III Plus* also contains a command designed to display a very limited amount of information. That command is the ? command.

The ? command is often called the *print* command. The reason for this name is related to the BASIC programming language in which the ? is used as an abbreviation for the PRINT command. The ? functions in a similar manner to the BASIC command, PRINT.

The ? command has a default scope of NEXT 1, the same as the DISPLAY command. However, unlike DISPLAY, ? does not automatically display any fields. You must specify the fields or expressions that you want retrieved with the ? command. The data are drawn from the current record.

For example, suppose you wanted to display the amount entered into record no. 3. Enter the following command:

DISPLAY amount RECORD 3 <return>

dBASE III Plus displays

```
Record#   AMOUNT
     3    45.87
```

Now try another method. First use the short form of the GOTO command to position the pointer. Enter

3 <return>

Now use the ? command to print the field. Enter

? amount <return>

dBASE III Plus displays

```
45.87
```

What are the differences in the two methods? First, the method that employs the ? command requires you to enter fewer keystrokes. In addition, the DISPLAY command creates two lines: one for the heading and one for the data. The ? command displays only the value of the AMOUNT field, with no heading. Furthermore, the DISPLAY command prints the record number and the ? command does not.

Which is the better? The answer depends on what type of information you want. The advantage of the ? command is that it displays a very limited amount of data. It allows you to isolate the contents of a field without headings or record numbers.

You can display several fields at once by entering a list of fields separated by commas. Enter

? CMONTH(date),amount,payto < return >

dBASE III Plus displays

```
January  45.87 P G & E
```

Notice that like LIST and DISPLAY, you can include special functions like CMONTH(), character month, in the list of fields to print.

COMMAND HISTORY

One advantage of working in the DOT PROMPT command mode is that *dBASE III Plus* records the commands you enter and allows you to access the previous commands. The up arrow key can be used to move backward through the commands you have previously entered.

To see how this works, enter

< up arrow >

dBASE III Plus displays the last command you entered

```
? CMONTH(date),amount,payto
```

Move to the command before that one by entering

< up arrow >

dBASE III Plus displays

```
? amount
```

You can execute the command by entering

< return >

The command prints the value in the AMOUNT field.

In addition to repeating a command, you can edit the command. Enter

> **<up arrow>**

The cursor is now at the beginning of the line. The right and left arrow keys allow you to position the cursor on the line. The [**End**] key moves the cursor one word to the right, the [**Home**] key one word to the left. Enter

> **[End]**
> **[End]**

The cursor moves to the end of the command. Enter

> **,date**

You have now added something to the command. Enter

> **<return>**

dBASE III Plus executes the modified command.

   The history editing is very handy for correcting mistakes. Enter the following command.

> **LIST date,payee,amount<return>**

dBASE III Plus cannot carry out the command because you have entered PAYEE instead of the correct field name, PAYTO. To correct this mistake it is not necessary to reenter the entire command. First tell *dBASE III Plus* that you do not want the help screen displayed by entering

> **n**

Next, display the incorrect command by entering

> **<up arrow>**

The command is displayed for editing. Use the right arrow key to position the cursor under the first *e* in payee. Enter

> **to**

   The command now reads correctly. You do not have to move the cursor to the end of the line in order to execute the command. Enter

> **<return>**

The corrected command is displayed.

> *The [**Ins**] key can be used to place dBASE III Plus in or out of the insert mode. The default is a typeover mode. Pressing [**Ins**] will allow inserting while editing. The [**Ins**] key is a toggle. Pressing it a second time will return dBASE III Plus to the overtype mode.*

The ability to access commands previously entered makes command entry from the DOT PROMPT a much simpler matter. Many times it is easier to cursor up and find a similar command to the one you want to enter and make changes than to type the entire command again. In this book you will find that some command sequences use the same or similar commands in a series. If you want to avoid typing, feel free to cursor up and use the history commands available to you.

LISTING HISTORY

dBASE III Plus allows you to list the sequence of commands stored in the history area of the memory. Enter

LIST HISTORY <return>

dBASE III Plus will display

```
GOTO 2
DISPLAY NEXT 3
DISPLAY NEXT 1
3
DISPLAY REST
GOTO 3
SKIP
SKIP -1
SKIP 3
DISPLAY
SKIP 10
SKIP 2*2/4-1
DISPLAY amount RECORD 3
3
? amount
? CMONTH(date),amount,payto
? amount,date
LIST date,payee,amount
LIST date,payto,amount
LIST HISTORY
```

dBASE III Plus keeps the last 20 commands in a special area of its memory called the *history buffer*. Every time you enter a new command, the 21st command in the buffer is erased and the new command is placed at the bottom of the stack. You can print the list by entering

LIST HISTORY TO PRINT <return>

Listing the history enables you to see the sequence of commands that you used to accomplish a particular task. This can be of great value when you are entering a complex sequence.

> dBASE III Plus *normally keeps 20 commands in the history buffer. However, you can change the number of commands stored by using the* SET HISTORY TO *command. For example, entering* SET HISTORY TO 100 *tells* dBASE III Plus *to store the last 100 commands in the history buffer. If you are entering a lot of commands, this may*

be helpful in recording a longer sequence of actions. The number of commands that can be stored in the history buffer is limited chiefly by the amount of internal memory (RAM) installed in your computer.

SCOPES IN THE ASSIST MODE

The *dBASE III Plus* ASSIST mode allows you to specify scopes. Return to the ASSIST mode by entering

      ASSIST <return>

      p

```
Set Up  Create  Update  Position  Retrieve  Organize Modify Tools  07:48:07 am
```

The POSITION menu contains commands that affect the location of the pointer but do not actually display data. Move the highlight to the GOTO command by entering

      <down arrow> **(2 times)**

Select the GOTO command by entering

      <return>

Another menu box opens to display the three choices.

```
Set Up  Create  Update  Position  Retrieve  Organize Modify Tools  08:09:32 am
```

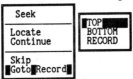

In this example you want to move the pointer to record no. 2. Enter

      <down arrow> **(2 times)**
      <return>

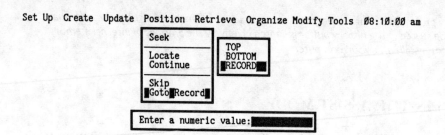

Look at the command line at the bottom of the screen. It displays the command GOTO RECORD. This indicates that the menu selections you have entered are the equivalent of typing in a GOTO RECORD command at the DOT PROMPT. Continue by entering the number of the record that you want to go to. Enter

2 < return >

The record indicator changes to Rec: 2/5 representing the pointer's position at record no. 2.

Display the RETRIEVE menu by entering

r

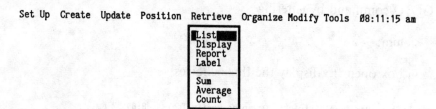

To select the LIST command, enter

< return >

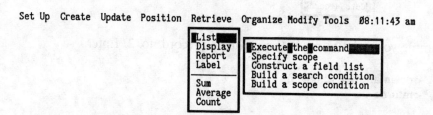

The second item in the command box is Specify scope. Select this option by entering

> **< down arrow >**
> **< return >**

```
Set Up  Create  Update  Position  Retrieve  Organize Modify Tools   08:13:20 am
                                 ▐List▌
                                 Display        Execute the command
                                 Report         ▌Specify▌scope▌
                                 Label          Construct a field list
                                 ─────────      Build a search condition
                                 Sum            Build a scope condition
                                 Average
                                 Count          ─────────────────────
                                                ▌Default▌scope▌
                                                ALL
                                                NEXT
                                                RECORD
                                                REST

Command: LIST
ASSIST▐▐▐▐▐▐▐▐▐▐▐▐▐|<C:>|EXPENSES▐▐▐▐▐▐▐▐▐▐▐▐▐|Rec:▐2/5▐▐▐▐▐▐▐▐▐▐|▐▐▐▐|
```

The scope box appears. The first choice, Default scope, refers to the default scope that *dBASE III Plus* associates with a specific command (e.g., LIST, default scope equals ALL; DISPLAY, default scope equals NEXT 1). Enter

> **< down arrow >**

The highlight skipped ALL and went directly to RECORD. *dBASE III Plus* skipped the ALL scope because the default scope for LIST is ALL. There is no need to select ALL when using LIST.

> *The ALL on the SCOPE menu appears in a different color or shade than the rest of the text. This is to indicate that ALL would not be a valid choice. dBASE III Plus uses the video display to indicate which of the menu choices are active at any given moment. The purpose is to avoid entry of commands that cannot be logically carried out. This protection is one of the advantages of the ASSIST mode. When you enter commands at the DOT PROMPT, dBASE III Plus does not offer such protection. Entry of an invalid command will result in an error message.*

Select the NEXT scope by entering

> **< return >**

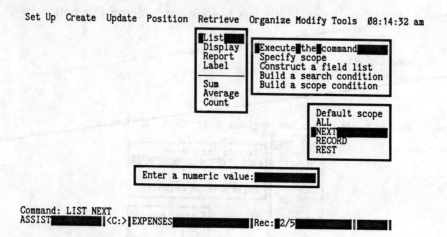

Set Up Create Update Position Retrieve Organize Modify Tools 08:14:32 am
```
                                    List
                                    Display      Execute the command
                                    Report       Specify scope
                                    Label        Construct a field list
                                                 Build a search condition
                                    Sum          Build a scope condition
                                    Average
                                    Count
                                                        Default scope
                                                        ALL
                                                        NEXT
                                                        RECORD
                                                        REST

                    Enter a numeric value:

Command: LIST NEXT
ASSIST           <C:> EXPENSES              Rec: 2/5
```

Next, enter a numeric value for the number of records to list. Enter

> **2 <return>**

Look at the command line. It shows LIST NEXT 2, the DOT PROMPT command that is equivalent to the one you are creating by menu selection. To execute this command, enter

> **[Pg Up]**
> **<return>**

dBASE III Plus asks if you want to send the output to the printer.

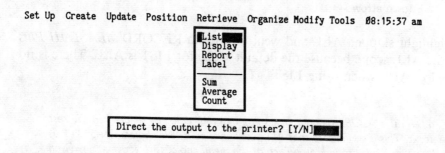

Set Up Create Update Position Retrieve Organize Modify Tools 08:15:37 am
```
                                    List
                                    Display
                                    Report
                                    Label

                                    Sum
                                    Average
                                    Count

                    Direct the output to the printer? [Y/N]

Command: LIST NEXT 2
ASSIST           <C:> EXPENSES              Rec: 2/5
```

Enter

> **n**

```
Records  DATE     PAYTO              ITEM                    AMOUNT COMMENTS
      2  Ø1/1Ø/85 SEARS              TRASH CAN                17.95 Memo
      3  Ø1/15/85 GREEN ACRES FURN   DESKS                   264.68 Memo
ASSIST             <C:> EXPENSES                 Rec: 2/5
```

Records no. 2 and 3 are listed. To exit the ASSIST mode, enter

> **<return>**
> **<Esc>**

SUMMARY

The major concepts in this chapter are listed as follows:

1. **Opening a File.** Before you can perform data management tasks, such as listing records, you must place the data base file you want to work with in use. The USE command opens a file.

2. **The Pointer.** When a data base file is opened, the program selects one record in the data base as the active or current record. When a data base is first opened, the active record is always the first record in the file. Commands such as LIST, DISPLAY, and GOTO, change the position of the pointer within the data base. The pointer is important because certain commands (e.g., DISPLAY) begin processing with the current record. By changing the position of the pointer, you can control the effect of these commands.

3. **Scopes.** When issuing commands, you must consider what part of the data base file will be processed by that command. The portion of the data base file affected by a command is called the *scope*. *dBASE III Plus* recognizes three scopes: ALL, RECORD n, and NEXT. *dBASE III Plus* recognizes an additional scope, REST. Every command has a default scope that is used unless you specify an alternative scope.

4. **End of File.** *dBASE III Plus* keeps track of the pointer position as long as a data base file is open. One special position is the End of File (EOF). If a command is entered that processes the last record in a data base file, the pointer position is considered to be EOF. When the pointer is at the end of the file, there is no active record.

5. To send the output to the line printer, use the TO PRINT clause with the LIST or DISPLAY command. EJECT issues a form feed command to align the printer at the top of the next form.

Commands

LIST (OFF) (TO PRINT)
DISPLAY (OFF) (TO PRINT)
GOTO (TOP, BOTTOM)
SKIP (+/−n)

Scopes

ALL
NEXT #
RECORD #
REST

ANSWER KEY

Exercise 1

<Esc>
SET MEMO TO 30 < return >
ASSIST <return>

Exercise 2

LIST date,amount < return >

Exercise 3

LIST amount/2 < return > *or* LIST amount*.5 < return >

CHANGING DATA

ONE OF THE MOST VERSATILE aspects of a data base program like *dBASE III Plus* lies in its ability to update and change data that have already been entered into a file. The topic of this chapter concerns those commands that can be used to take advantage of this ability. The reader will also learn how to add new records to a data base file by using commands other than the APPEND command, which was covered in Chapter 1.

This chapter begins where the last chapter left off.

THE EDIT COMMAND

The EDIT command displays the contents of a single record, and allows you to change the data in any of the fields. The record displayed when you enter the edit mode is the current record, unless otherwise specified. For example, to begin editing the file at the first record, enter

        GOTO TOP < return >
        EDIT < return >

dBASE III Plus displays record no. 1:

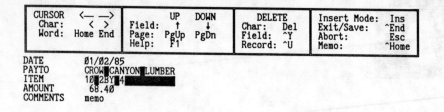

```
CURSOR   <— —>          UP   DOWN    DELETE           Insert Mode:   Ins
 Char:    <  >    Field:  ↑     ↓    Char:    Del     Exit/Save:    ^End
 Word:  Home End  Page:  PgUp  PgDn  Field:    ^Y     Abort:         Esc
                  Help:   F1          Record:   ^U     Memo:        ^Home
```

```
DATE       01/02/85
PAYTO      CROW CANYON LUMBER
ITEM       10 2BY 4
AMOUNT        68.40
COMMENTS   memo
```

```
EDIT            <C:>│EXPENSES              │Rec: 1/5
```

The top portion of the screen displays the editing commands that can be used in this mode. If the top of your screen does not show the editing commands, you can display them by pressing the Help key, **[F1]**. Note that the display of these commands is purely informational. It has no effect on the functions of the program. The screen display is a little less cluttered when the HELP menu is not shown, so you might prefer to turn the display off. You can do this by using the **[F1]** key again. The **[F1]** key is a toggle key, and turns the help display on or off.

*The IBM PC and compatible computers have ten function keys. In dBASE III Plus, [**F1**] is reserved as the Help key. The other nine function keys are assigned the following commands:*

F2	assist
F3	list
F4	dir
F5	display structure
F6	display status
F7	display memory
F8	display
F9	append
F10	edit

These keys can be reprogrammed to issue commands of your own design using the SET FUNCTION command. Example: The following command sets F10 equal to a CLOSE DATABASE command:

SET FUNCTION 10 TO "CLOSE DATABASE;" <return>

The **[Pg Dn]** and **[Pg Up]** keys move you forward and backward in the file, respectively. Enter

[Pg Dn]

Record no. 2 is displayed. Enter

[Pg Dn]

In dBASE III Plus, the record number is displayed at the right side of the status line. Currently, the display reads Rec: 2/5, meaning that the pointer is positioned at record no. 2, in a data base of five records.

Record no. 3 is displayed. To move between fields, enter

<return>

The cursor moves down to the PAYTO field. Enter

<return>
<return>

The cursor is now in the AMOUNT field. Enter a change in the amount.

50.50

Move to the next record by entering

[Pg Dn]

Return to record no. 3 by entering

[Pg Up]

You can see the revised value of 50.50 for the amount. Enter

[Pg Dn] (3 times)

What happened? You have automatically exited the EDIT mode because you reached the end of the file. By pressing **[Pg Dn]** while the last record in the file was active, the program automatically exits the EDIT mode. The same is true when you reach the top of the file using the **[Pg Up]** key.

Since the EDIT command begins with the active record, you can reenter the EDIT mode by entering

EDIT <return>

The program displays record no. 5, because that was the current record when you entered the EDIT command. Note that when you move from record to record while in the EDIT mode, the pointer moves along with the edit display. In the previous example, you entered the EDIT mode when record no. 1 was the active record, and exited at the end of the file. At that point, record no. 5 was the active record.

Leave the EDIT mode by entering

<Esc>

You can specify a particular record to begin with when you enter the EDIT command. Enter

      EDIT 3 < return >

The program displays record no. 3. Enter

      < Esc >

If you want to begin the editing process at the first record, enter

      EDIT 1 < return >

      EDIT 1 is the equivalent of GOTO TOP, then EDIT.

MAKING AND SAVING CHANGES

Entering the EDIT command places you in a mode in which the data in your file can be changed. Data retrieval, as explained in Chapter 2, allows data to be displayed, but not changed. In computer terminology, data retrieval is termed the *read-only* mode, while editing is known as the *read-write* mode.

It is important to understand at which point changes entered into a record actually become a permanent part of the data base file. At this moment record no. 1 is displayed on the screen. Change the date of the transaction by entering

      01/04/87

Suppose you had intended to change the date of record no. 3, not record no. 1. You can recover the original data because *dBASE III Plus* does not immediately store the changes made in a record. When you make changes, the program displays them on the screen, but records them only when you do one of the following:

1. Move to another record. This can be done by pressing < return >, or [**Pg Up**] or [**Pg Dn**]. If you move to another record, any changes made in the record previously displayed become part of the data file.
2. Exit the EDIT mode by entering either [**CTRL/End**] or [**CTRL/w**].

On the other hand, you can tell the program to ignore any changes made in the record displayed on the screen by exiting the EDIT mode with < Esc > or [**CTRL/q**].

    *The use of the [**CTRL/w**] and [**CTRL/q**] key combinations is a remnant of dBASE II in dBASE III Plus. Since dBASE II was designed for a variety of computer terminals and keyboards, the editing features did not employ special keys such as [**End**], [**Pg Up**], and so on, found on the IBM PC keyboard.*

*If you are a former dBASE II user you will find that most of the [**CTRL**] key commands used in dBASE II are still available in dBASE III Plus. For example, [**CTRL/R**] operates the same as the [**Pg Up**] key does.*

To negate the new date entry, press

> < Esc >

Enter

> DISPLAY <return>

The date in record no. 1 is still 01/02/83. The new date that was entered in the EDIT mode was not saved because the < Esc > key was used.

*Remember that the retention of changes applies only to the record that is displayed on the screen at the moment you enter the command to exit, <Esc> or [**CTRL/q**].*

For example, suppose that you edited records no. 1 and no. 2. Record no. 3 is now displayed on the screen. If you enter <Esc>, it will have no effect on records no. 1 and no. 2 because they were already automatically saved when you moved to record no. 3. Only the changes made in the active record, the one on the screen, are affected by the use of the <Esc> key.

*If you want to preserve the changes made on the active record, use [**CTRL/End**] or [**CTRL/w**] to exit the EDIT mode.*

EDIT WITH SCOPES

dBASE III Plus contains a number of additional ways in which the EDIT command can be used. These uses do not affect the basic purpose (changing data) and operation of the EDIT command. They do, however, allow you more control over which records and which fields are edited. For example, the EDIT command can be used with a list of field names, and can recognize scopes.

As with the DISPLAY and LIST commands, scopes are used to select areas of the data base file to be processed by the EDIT command. For example, if you used the ALL scope, it would have the same affect on EDIT as it does on DISPLAY; the pointer would be positioned at the top of the file and all the records in the data file would be accessible for editing by using the [**Pg Up**] and [**Pg Dn**] commands. (EDIT ALL would have the same effect as EDIT 1.)

Using a NEXT scope would limit the number of records that could be edited. Enter

> EDIT 1 NEXT 3 <return>

The first record appears in the EDIT mode.

To understand the previous command, it might be helpful to break down its parts:

1. **EDIT** specifies the EDIT command.

2. **1** indicates the pointer position for the first record to be edited.
3. **NEXT 3** limits the number of records available for editing to the next 3 including the starting record.

Enter

[Pg Dn] (3 times)

What happened? Because the NEXT 3 scope was specified, the EDIT mode automatically terminated when you advanced the pointer beyond the scope of the command. Enter the following command:

EDIT 3 NEXT 2<return>

The first record displayed is record no. 3. Enter

[Pg Up]
[Pg Dn]

What happened? The program automatically exited. Why? The pointer is still positioned to record no. 3 (Rec: 3/5). Usually the NEXT 2 scope beginning at record no. 3 would end at record no. 4. It is interesting to note that the NEXT scope takes on a slightly different meaning with the EDIT command than it does with the LIST and DISPLAY commands.

The LIST and DISPLAY commands always process records in the same direction, from their starting point toward the end of the file. EDIT processes records from the beginning or the end of the file. When a NEXT scope is used, *dBASE III Plus* uses the value to count the number of records to be edited no matter what direction the pointer is moved. If you move the pointer forward and backward, a record is counted as part of the scope each time it is displayed. Enter

EDIT 3 NEXT 6<return>

Now enter

[Pg Up][Pg Dn] (3 times)

Notice that the commands simply flip back and forth between the same pair of records. When the total number of records displayed (including the first record displayed) reaches the scope value (6), the EDIT mode is automatically terminated.

The REST scope functions in the same manner as the ALL scope, with one exception. The ALL scope repositions the pointer to the top of the file before editing. The REST scope begins editing at the current pointer position. You can use as many **[Pg Up]** or **[Pg Dn]** commands as you desire.

You can also limit the fields that are displayed for editing. As with the LIST and

DISPLAY commands, you can specify fields by listing their names separated by commas. Unlike those commands, EDIT requires the phrase FIELDS to be inserted before the field list. Enter

EDIT ALL FIELDS payto,amount < return >

Enter

[Pg Dn]
[Pg Dn]

You can flip through the records as in the usual EDIT mode, but only the selected fields appear. Enter

< Esc >

You can use FIELDS to rearrange the order of the fields in the display. You can place the fields that require the most changes at the top of the display and avoid having to move the cursor down to the bottom of the display each time you want to edit that field. For example, the AMOUNT field is located toward the bottom of the display. If you wanted easy access to the AMOUNT field, you would enter

EDIT ALL FIELDS amount,date,payto,item < return >

Enter

[Pg Dn]

Notice that the cursor moves to the first field in the display, which is AMOUNT. Enter

< Esc >

Position the pointer at the top of the file for the next section by entering

GOTO TOP < return >

BROWSE

Another command that allows you access to your records is the BROWSE command. The primary advantage of BROWSE is that it displays more than one record at a time. Enter

BROWSE < return >

The differences between dBASE III Plus displays have to do with the positions of the record number display and the default display of the help screen.

You can suppress the *dBASE III Plus* HELP display by entering

[F1]

The BROWSE display is a row-and-column display in which each row is a record in the data base file and each column is a field. The data base in this example is so small that all the records and fields can be displayed at the same time. However, larger data files will not be visible in a single screen display. To accommodate these files, BROWSE will scroll horizontally to display additional fields. **[CTRL/right arrow]** moves the screen display one field to the right. **[CTRL/left arrow]** scrolls the display one field to the left.

Enter

<down arrow>

The highlight moves to record no. 2. Enter

<return>

The cursor moves to the PAYTO field in record no. 2. When you are in the BROWSE mode you can change any part of the data base that you desire. All fields in all records are open for editing. By positioning the cursor at the record and field you want to change, you can alter the data base file in any way you wish. Enter

<down arrow>

Notice that the highlight has moved to record no. 3, but that the cursor is still positioned in the PAYTO field. This is in contrast to the EDIT mode, where when moving to the next record, the cursor is automatically positioned in the first field of the data base structure. In BROWSE, the cursor position remains in the same field as you move from record to record.

The BROWSE command will display up to 17 records on the screen at one time. (The number of records displayed is reduced to 11 if the HELP menu is displayed.) The **[Pg Up]** and **[Pg Dn]** keys will scroll an entire screen of records.

ADDING RECORDS IN BROWSE

Another difference between EDIT and BROWSE is that BROWSE allows you to add new records to the data base. Enter

[Pg Dn]

This positions the highlight to the last record in the file. Enter

<down arrow>

Attempting to move past the last record automatically terminates the EDIT mode. In BROWSE, attempting to move the cursor past the last record causes the program to display the prompt = = = > Add New Records? (Y/N). Entering n will return the cursor to the last record in the file. Entering y will allow you to enter a new record. Enter

y

A new blank line appears below the last record and you can enter a new record:

02/02/83
GIFT STORE < return >
GROUND HOG DAY CARDS
4.95 < return >

The cursor is now in the MEMO field, COMMENTS. Data cannot be entered into MEMO fields while in the BROWSE mode; MEMO fields can be edited only while in the APPEND or EDIT modes. To exit BROWSE and save the new record as part of the data base file, enter

[CTRL/End]

The DOT PROMPT returns. As in the EDIT mode, the last active record in the BROWSE mode determines the pointer position when you exit the mode. Enter

DISPLAY <return>

The new record, no. 6, is the active record.

SELECTING FIELDS

The BROWSE command in *dBASE III Plus* can be used with a specified list of fields. This allows you to browse only those fields with which you want to work. The field columns will be displayed in the order in which the field names appear in the BROWSE command; thus the fields can be ordered differently from the field order in the file structure. Enter

GOTO TOP < return >
BROWSE FIELDS amount,payto,date < return >

Exit the BROWSE by entering

< Esc >

```
AMOUNT PAYTO──────────── DATE────
█68.40 CROW CANYON LUMBER█ 01/02/85
 17.95 SEARS               01/10/85
264.68 GREEN ACRES FURN    01/15/85
 59.50 INSTANT PRINTING    01/17/85
 60.60 PG&E                01/21/85
```

```
BROWSE█████████║<C:>║EXPENSES███████████║Rec:█1/5█████║█████║
```

> *It is possible, though not usual, to specify the same field more than once in a field list. For example, you might enter BROWSE FIELDS amount,payto,date,amount. dBASE III Plus will display four field columns and place the identical information in the first and the fourth columns. You can edit either field, but the program will store the last entry in the right-most amount column as the value for the record.*

THE BROWSE MENU

The BROWSE mode has its own special menu bar that appears only when you are working in BROWSE. The menu bar does not appear when you enter BROWSE but can be displayed when you enter [**CTRL/Home**]. In *dBASE III Plus* the [**F10**] key can be used in place of [**CTRL/Home**]. Enter

BROWSE < return >

To display the BROWSE menu enter

[CTRL/Home]

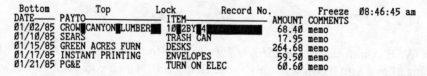

```
   Bottom        Top        Lock      Record No.        Freeze  08:46:45 am
DATE──── PAYTO────────────── ITEM────────────── AMOUNT COMMENTS
01/02/85 CROW█CANYON█LUMBER█ 10█2BY█4██████████  68.40 memo
01/10/85 SEARS               TRASH CAN           17.95 memo
01/15/85 GREEN ACRES FURN    DESKS              264.68 memo
01/17/85 INSTANT PRINTING    ENVELOPES           59.50 memo
01/21/85 PG&E                TURN ON ELEC        60.60 memo
```

The menu displays five commands. The BOTTOM, TOP, and RECORD NO. commands allow you to duplicate the GOTO BOTTOM, GOTO TOP, and GOTO

RECORD # commands that operate from the DOT PROMPT or ASSIST modes. The highlight is initially positioned on the BOTTOM command. Enter

> < return >

The cursor moves to record no. 6. Note that the BROWSE menu disappears after each BROWSE menu command is issued. Enter

> [CTRL/Home]
> t

The highlight moves to the top of the file. Enter

> [CTRL/Home]
> r

Enter the number of the record where you want the highlight to be positioned.

> 3 < return >

The highlight moves to record no. 3. Notice that record no. 3 becomes the first record displayed on the screen.

The FREEZE option allows you to limit the highlight to a particular field. Enter

> [CTRL/Home]
> f

Enter the name of the field you want to freeze. In this example, enter

> amount < return >

The highlight is now only as wide as the AMOUNT field. Enter

> < return >
> < return >

The highlight moves down one record but stays in the AMOUNT field. While the freeze is active, editing can take place only in the frozen field. All other fields are protected from editing. To unfreeze the highlight use the FREEZE command again, but do not enter a specific field name. Enter

> [CTRL/Home]
> f
> < return >

The highlight widens to include all the fields in the file's structure.

The final command on the menu is the LOCK command. LOCK is used when the data base file contains more fields than can be displayed at one time. The LOCK command allows you to specify a field column or columns on the left side of the screen that will remain displayed as you use the [CTRL/right arrow] command to scroll the columns. (The command is similar to the TITLES command found in *Lotus 1-2-3* and other spreadsheet programs.)

Exit the BROWSE mode by entering

<Esc>

THE CHANGE COMMAND

Because of the modifications made to the EDIT command when *dBASE III* was upgraded to *dBASE III Plus*, the CHANGE command is of little consequence. The primary purpose of the CHANGE command is to allow you to make editing changes in selected fields of a data base file. Thus in *dBASE III Plus*, CHANGE and EDIT are identical commands and are functionally interchangeable.

For example, if you wanted to edit the AMOUNT and PAYTO fields only, enter the following command:

CHANGE ALL FIELDS amount,payto<return>

The CHANGE display shows only the selected fields. Note that the order in which the fields are displayed is not that of the file's structure but the order in which they were listed in the command. Enter

[Pg Dn]

The next record's AMOUNT and PAYTO data appear. To exit the CHANGE mode, enter

<Esc>

In *dBASE III Plus* the commands CHANGE FIELDS payto and EDIT FIELDS payto perform exactly the same function.

MASS CHANGES

The three commands discussed in this chapter have one thing in common: they all require manual entry of the changes you want to make in the data base file. One of the most powerful features of *dBASE III Plus* is its ability to make mass changes in the data base with a single command.

Mass changes can affect one record or the entire data base file. The REPLACE command implements mass changes; it has a default scope of NEXT 1. The ALL scope can be used with the REPLACE command to change all the records in a data base file.

The REPLACE command takes the following general form. Do not enter this command at this time; it is only a model of an actual command.

REPLACE [scope] [field] WITH [expression]

For example, you might have noticed that the dates used in the example file, EX-PENSES, are for 1983. It would be more timely to add a few years to those dates. This could be done manually by using the BROWSE, EDIT, or CHANGE modes to type in 85 in place of 83. However, *dBASE III Plus* offers an alternative method. The REPLACE command can be used to add two years to all the DATE fields at once.

All date arithmetic is calculated in terms of days. In order to increment a date by a year you must add the number of days in a year, approximately 365. This method does not account for leap years. If a leap year is involved you must use 366 for the length of a year.

First, list the dates as they now exist. Enter

LIST date < return >

The programs displays

```
Record#  DATE
      1  01/02/83
      2  01/15/83
      3  01/21/83
      4  01/25/83
      5  01/30/83
      6  02/02/83
```

Enter the following command:

REPLACE ALL date WITH date+365+366 < return >

dBASE III Plus displays the message, 6 records replaced. This message means that the specified replacement has taken place in 6 records. Enter

LIST date < return >

The program displays

```
Record#  DATE
      1  01/02/85
      2  01/15/85
      3  01/21/85
      4  01/25/85
      5  01/30/85
      6  02/02/85
```

With a single command, you have updated all the records in the data base file. The REPLACE command offers a good example of why *dBASE III Plus* is so powerful. While manual entry is the basic technique by which data are initially entered, commands like REPLACE can perform alterations on a large number of records without any manual entry at all.

One of the primary advantages of REPLACE is that it can replace the contents of a field with the results of any valid *dBASE III Plus* expression. To illustrate the use of expressions with the REPLACE command, suppose that while entering the data into the EXPENSES file, you were not consistent in using uppercase characters. In this book, the assumption is made that you have entered all the data as uppercase characters. If that is not true, you might have to manually retype all the entries to be consistent with the assumption. However, *dBASE III Plus* has special functions that can convert the case of characters; they are UPPER() and LOWER(). Combining the functions with the REPLACE command can create a case-consistent file without any additional entry.

For those of you who followed the case convention correctly, you can create the problem by converting all your data to lowercase. Enter

REPLACE ALL payto WITH LOWER(payto),item WITH LOWER(item) < return >

Enter

LIST < return >

All the characters in the PAYTO and ITEM fields are now lowercase:

```
Record#  DATE     PAYTO               ITEM                   AMOUNT COMMENTS
      1  01/02/85 crow canyon lumber  10 2 by 4               57.00 Memo
      2  01/15/85 green acres furn    desks                  220.57 Memo
      3  01/21/85 p g & e             turn on elec            50.50 Memo
      4  01/25/85 pacific bell        install tele            36.90 Memo
      5  01/30/85 britz printing      business cards          56.93 Memo
      6  02/02/85 gift store          ground hog day cards     4.95 Memo
```

Notice that you can perform replacement on more than one field at a time by creating a list of replacement statements separated by commas. You can perform as many replacements as you like as long as the text of the entire command does not exceed 254 characters.

Now reverse the process and convert all the characters to uppercase. Enter

REPLACE ALL payto WITH UPPER(payto),item WITH UPPER(item) < return >

Display the data by entering

LIST < return >

```
Record#  DATE     PAYTO               ITEM                   AMOUNT COMMENTS
      1  01/02/85 CROW CANYON LUMBER  10 2 BY 4               57.00 Memo
      2  01/15/85 GREEN ACRES FURN    DESKS                  220.57 Memo
      3  01/21/85 P G & E             TURN ON ELEC            50.50 Memo
      4  01/25/85 PACIFIC BELL        INSTALL TELE            36.90 Memo
      5  01/30/85 BRITZ PRINTING      BUSINESS CARDS          56.93 Memo
      6  02/02/85 GIFT STORE          GROUND HOG DAY CARDS     4.95 Memo
```

The data have been converted to uppercase characters. This simple conversion can insure consistency in the data base and avoid retyping, which often creates more problems than it solves. Whenever possible it is better to have the computer make the changes than to have a person reenter data.

> dBASE III Plus does not contain a function that will convert a text item into a string that has the first letter of each word in uppercase and the remainder in lowercase (e.g., "JOHN SMITH" converted to "John Smith"). In the programming portion of this book, an example of a program that will accomplish this conversion is given.

The REPLACE command can be used to perform numeric operations. For example, you could increase all the amounts by 20 percent with a single REPLACE command. Enter

```
REPLACE ALL amount WITH amount*1.2 < return >
LIST <return >
```

```
Record#  DATE     PAYTO            ITEM                 AMOUNT COMMENTS
      1  01/02/85 CROW CANYON LUMBER 10 2 BY 4           68.40 Memo
      2  01/15/85 GREEN ACRES FURN  DESKS               264.68 Memo
      3  01/21/85 P G & E           TURN ON ELEC         60.60 Memo
      4  01/25/85 PACIFIC BELL      INSTALL TELE         44.28 Memo
      5  01/30/85 BRITZ PRINTING    BUSINESS CARDS       68.32 Memo
      6  02/02/85 GIFT STORE        GROUND HOG DAY CARDS  5.94 Memo
```

The amounts have automatically been increased and the results stored in the AMOUNT field. In performing calculations with the REPLACE command you must be careful not to create a numeric overflow. A numeric overflow occurs when the field is not large enough to hold the number that is to be placed in that field. For example, the AMOUNT field in expenses was not designed to hold values greater than 999.99 (six characters including two decimal places). If you have entered a command like REPLACE ALL amount WITH amount*100000, *dBASE III Plus* would display Numeric overflow (data was lost).

Take care when performing this type of replacement, since the lost data cannot be recovered.

CHANGING THE FILE STRUCTURE

While it is important to plan the structure of your data base file carefully, there will be times when you need to alter its structure to add new fields, change the size of existing fields, or delete fields that are no longer needed. The command that allows you to make alterations in the file's structure is MODIFY STRUCTURE.

In order to modify the structure of a file, the file must be in use. If no file is in use when you enter the command, you will be prompted by the program to enter the name of a data base file.

In the example you are working with, the EXPENSES file is currently open. Suppose you wanted to add some additional fields to the structure of the file. One field might be used to store an account number for the expense, while another might be used to hold the name of the month in which the expense was made. A third might be used to hold a logical value that indicates whether or not the item is tax deductible. Enter

MODIFY STRUCTURE < return >

The screen display is exactly the same as the one that is used by the CREATE command.

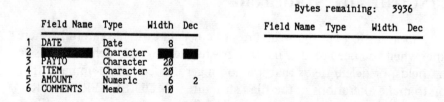

```
                                                        Bytes remaining:  3936
       Field Name   Type      Width  Dec    Field Name  Type    Width  Dec
   1   DATE         Date          8
   2   PAYTO        Character    20
   3   ITEM         Character    20
   4   AMOUNT       Numeric       6   2
   5   COMMENTS     Memo         10


MODIFY STRUCTURE |<C:>| EXPENSES                | Field: 1/5              |
```

You can add new fields at any place in the structure. For instance, suppose you want the CATEGORY field to follow the date. Move the cursor to field no. 2 by entering

< down arrow >

To make room for a new field, enter

[CTRL/n]

```
                                                        Bytes remaining:  3936
       Field Name   Type      Width  Dec    Field Name  Type    Width  Dec
   1   DATE         Date          8
   2                Character
   3   PAYTO        Character    20
   4   ITEM         Character    20
   5   AMOUNT       Numeric       6   2
   6   COMMENTS     Memo         10


MODIFY STRUCTURE |<C:>| EXPENSES                | Field: 2/6              |
```

The [**CTRL/n**] command inserts a blank field into the structure at the position of the highlight. Now enter the information for the new field.

> **cat** < return >
> **n**
> **5**
> < return >
> < return >

Add the next two fields at the end of the structure. Enter

> **[Pg Dn]**

The highlight moves to the end of the structure to a new field, no. 7. Enter

> **month** < return >
> < return >
> **15**
> < return >

The last field will be a LOGICAL field. Enter

> **deduct** < return >
> I

Because a LOGICAL field is always a single character, there is no need to enter the field length. *dBASE III Plus* automatically enters the length of 1.

The screen shows the seven fields that make up the new structure of the file. *dBASE III Plus* will display

Bytes remaining: 3915

	Field Name	Type	Width	Dec
1	DATE	Date	8	
2	CAT	Numeric	5	0
3	PAYTO	Character	20	
4	ITEM	Character	20	
5	AMOUNT	Numeric	6	2
6	COMMENTO	Memo	10	
7	MONTH	Character	15	
8	DEDUCT	Logical	1	
9	▓▓▓	Character	▓	▓

Field Name   Type   Width   Dec

MODIFY▓STRUCTURE|<C:>|EXPENSES▓▓▓▓▓▓▓▓▓|Field:▓9/9▓▓▓▓▓▓ ▓ ▓▓▓▓▓▓|

To save the changes, enter

> **[CTRL/End]**

Because this command effects a major alteration of the data base file, *dBASE III Plus* asks you to confirm the decision by entering

<return>

There is a slight delay as the program modifies the file. When the DOT PROMPT returns you can confirm the changes by listing the structure. Enter

LIST STRUCTURE<return>

The new file now contains an 86-character structure. List the contents of the file by entering

LIST<return>

Because the file contains records that have 86 characters, the data from each record cannot be listed on a single line of the screen display.

> *The LOGICAL field, DEDUCT, is automatically listed as containing .F., false values. When you create a LOGICAL field, the program automatically assumes a false value for the field. To make the value true you must input either a Y or T into that field.*

You can now add data to the new fields. Before you continue with the data entry, there are some aspects to the MODIFY STRUCTURE command that you need to consider.

When you modify the structure of a file, *dBASE III Plus* makes a backup copy of the original data base file. The program then compares the new structure with the old data file, and attempts to copy data from the old file into the new file, where the fields correspond. Naturally, the new fields added to the structure will appear blank in the new file.

If you make changes in the names or lengths of existing fields during MODIFY STRUCTURE, you should be aware that problems can occur that prevent *dBASE III Plus* from correctly copying data into the new structure. The basic rule to remember is that you can change field names or field lengths, but not both. If you change field names, *dBASE III Plus* uses the field lengths to match corresponding data. If you change field lengths the program uses the names to ascertain corresponding data. However, when you change both names and lengths, you will produce a new file with blank data fields.

The solution is to make the changes in two consecutive modifications. For example, use MODIFY STRUCTURE to enter all the field name changes. Complete the modifications and enter another MODIFY STRUCTURE command. This time, enter all the field length changes. The final result will have both types of alterations and your data will be preserved.

Note that if you make changes that cause you to lose data, there is no way to recover those data.

FILLING IN NEW FIELDS

Now that you have added new fields to the data base, you will want to fill the fields with data. To do so, you can use some of the data revision commands discussed in this chapter.

The MONTH field can be filled by using the REPLACE command. Enter

REPLACE ALL month WITH CMONTH(date)< return >

Enter

LIST date,month < return >

The program displays

```
Record#  date      month
      1  01/02/85  January
      2  01/15/85  January
      3  01/21/85  January
      4  01/25/85  January
      5  01/30/85  January
      6  02/02/85  February
```

Now you have stored the text name of the month along with the numeric date. The text name will come in handy later when you design reports.

The next step is to fill in the remaining two fields. Those fields will have to be manually entered. Enter the BROWSE mode:

BROWSE < return >

Move to the top of the file by entering

[CTRL/Home]
t

You now want to enter the category numbers for the various expenses. The best way to enter new data into a single field is to use the FREEZE option. Enter

[CTRL /Home]
f
cat
< return >

The highlight is limited to the CAT field. Enter

110 < return >
120 < return >
130 < return >
130 < return >
140 < return >
140 < return >

The program asks if you wish to enter a new record. Enter

    n

Now you will need to enter data into the DEDUCT field. The DEDUCT field is not displayed on the screen because the records are wider than the screen display. You can scroll to the right by entering

    [CTRL/right arrow]

The screen scrolls one column to the right. Enter

    [CTRL/right arrow]
    [CTRL/right arrow]

The DEDUCT column appears.

```
ITEM                AMOUNT COMMENTS MONTH           DEDUCT
10 2 BY 4            68.40 memo     January         ?
DESKS              264.68 memo     January         ?
TURN ON ELEC        60.60 memo     January         ?
INSTALL TELE        44.28 memo     January         ?
BUSINESS CARDS      68.32 memo     January         ?
GROUND HOG DAY CARDS 5.94 memo     February        ?
```

There is one problem. In displaying the DEDUCT column, you have scrolled the PAYTO and CAT columns off the screen. Since it may be necessary to see the contents of those columns in order to determine what should be entered into the DEDUCT column, PAYTO and CAT can be locked in place. First display the desired columns by entering

    [CTRL/left arrow]
    [CTRL/left arrow]

Now enter the LOCK command.

    [CTRL/Home]
    L

Since you want to lock the first two columns, enter

    2 < return >

Now scroll again by entering

    [CTRL/right arrow] (3 times)

The screen now displays all the columns that need to be visible at one time.

```
CAT  PAYTO              AMOUNT COMMENTS MONTH           DEDUCT
110 CROW CANYON LUMBER  68.40 memo     January         ?
120 GREEN ACRES FURN   264.68 memo     January         ?
130 P G & E             60.60 memo     January         ?
130 PACIFIC BELL        44.28 memo     January         ?
140 BRITZ PRINTING      68.32 memo     January         ?
140 GIFT STORE           5.94 memo     February        ?
```

Now freeze the cursor in the DEDUCT field. Enter

>**[CTRL/Home]**
>**f**
>**deduct < return >**

Move the cursor to the first record by entering

>**[CTRL/Home]**
>**t**

When you enter data into a LOGICAL field, you are restricted to typing one of only eight characters: f, F, n, N (meaning false) or t, T, y, Y (meaning true). *dBASE III Plus* will regard Y and T as the same value (i.e., a logical TRUE). The same applies to N and F. In this example, you will use Y and N as the logical entries. Enter

>**y**
>**y**
>**n**
>**n**
>**n**
>**n**

The program asks if you want to add a new record. Enter

>**n**

To exit the BROWSE mode, enter

>**< Esc > (2 times)**

Save the new data by entering

>**CLOSE DATABASE < return >**

DATA ENTRY COMMAND: THE ASSIST MODE

The DATA REVISION command can be implemented by using the ASSIST mode. Enter

>**ASSIST < return >**

First open the data file by entering

>**< return >**

Highlight the drive on which you have stored the EXPENSES file. Enter

>**< return >**

Highlight the EXPENSES file. Enter

> **<return>**

Since you have not learned how to index yet, enter

> **n**

The EDIT, BROWSE, and REPLACE commands are found on the UPDATE menu. Enter

> **u**

The EDIT, DISPLAY, and BROWSE commands viewed on the menu function exactly as they do at the DOT PROMPT. However, when they are selected from the menu, you cannot specify scopes or field lists as you can at the DOT PROMPT.

> *The DISPLAY command appears on two ASSIST menus, UPDATE and RETRIEVE. The DISPLAY command on the UPDATE menu is the default DISPLAY command with no options. The DISPLAY command on the RETRIEVE menu allows you to enter scopes and field lists.*

The REPLACE command acts differently in the ASSIST mode. Enter

> **<down arrow> (4 times)**
> **<return>**

The ASSISTANT displays two boxes, one listing the fields in the file's structure, the other showing the detail of the highlighted field. Note that the COMMENTS field (a MEMO-type field) is shown in dull video, indicating that it is not available for use with the REPLACE command. Enter

> **<return>**

By pressing <return>, you have selected the DATE field for replacement. You are now prompted to enter a date value. If you look at the command line, you will find that it shows

```
Command: REPLACE DATE WITH CTOD('.
```

This means the ASSIST mode limits the actions you can take on a DATE field to entering a replacement date in the MM/DD/YY format. The CTOD is a special *dBASE III Plus* function that converts character entries into DATE-type entries. The point to remember is that the ASSIST mode often makes assumptions that limit your options when using *dBASE III Plus* commands. The assumptions are made to facilitate learning the *dBASE III Plus* program. Cancel this command by entering

> **<Esc>**

Enter another REPLACE command.

> **<return>**

Move the highlight to the AMOUNT field by entering

> **<down arrow> (4 times)**

Enter

> **<return>**

You are now prompted to enter a numeric expression. Look at the command line. It shows that *dBASE III Plus* has entered the text of the REPLACE command just as you would if you were entering it at the DOT PROMPT. Enter

> **amount+10 <return>**

The field choice boxes are redisplayed. If you wanted, you could choose another replacement to make. To execute the command, enter

> **<right arrow>**

The command option box appears. You can now select a scope for the REPLACE command. Enter

> **<down arrow>**
> **<return>**

The scope box appears. Enter

> **<down arrow>**
> **<return>**

Execute the command by entering

> **[Pg Up]**
> **<return>**

dBASE III Plus displays the message that indicates six replacements have been made. To return to the ASSIST menu, enter

> **<return>**

To see the results of the command that you have just entered, use the BROWSE command. Enter

> **<up arrow>**
> **<return>**

Move the cursor to the top of the file by entering

> **[CTRL/Home]**
> **t**

You can see that each of the amounts has been increased by ten. To put the file back the way it was, use the REPLACE command to subtract ten from all the amounts. Enter

>**<Esc>**

Select the REPLACE command.

>**<down arrow>**
>**<return>**

Select the AMOUNT field by entering

>**<down arrow> (4 times)**
>**<return>**

Enter

>**amount−10<return>**

Display the command option by entering

>**<right arrow>**

Set the scope to ALL by entering

>**<down arrow>**
>**<return>**
>**<down arrow>**
>**<return>**

Execute the command by entering

>**[Pg Up]**
>**<return>**

Exit the ASSIST mode by entering

>**<Esc>**

Close the data base by entering

>**CLOSE DATABASE<return>**

SUMMARY

This chapter discussed the techniques used to alter an existing data base file.

1. **Manual Data Revision.** There are three commands that allow you to access the data in a data base file for revision: EDIT, BROWSE, and CHANGE.

EDIT and CHANGE display one record at a time; you can flip forward or backward. BROWSE displays up to 17 records at a time, and the fields are arranged in column form. BROWSE also contains its own menu bar that allows you to move the pointer to the top, bottom, or selected record number without leaving the BROWSE mode. In addition, BROWSE allows you to add new records to the data base. EDIT and CHANGE do not permit additional records.

> *If you enter APPEND and then use [**Pg Up**] to flip back to the previous record, you can perform editing actions in exactly the same way as you can in EDIT. You can also flip to the end of the file and add new records.*

2. **Mass Changes.** The REPLACE command is used to perform indirect data revision or entry and can affect one or more records. It can also perform replacements on more than one field at a time. You can use the command to replace the data in a field with the result of any valid *dBASE III Plus* expression. Keep in mind that the expression must evaluate to the same data type as the field into which the replacement is made (i.e., only DATE-type values can be placed in a DATE field, numeric values into a NUMERIC field, and so on).

   When replacing a NUMERIC field, take care that the value placed in the field does not exceed the field width. Attempting such a replacement can cause an unrecoverable loss of the data in that field. *dBASE III Plus* calls this a *numeric overflow.*

3. **File Structure.** The structure of a file can be changed by using the MODIFY STRUCTURE command. Fields can be added, deleted, or modified. *dBASE III Plus* will attempt to copy all data from the old file into the new structure. If you change field lengths and field names at the same time, a loss of data is possible. This loss can be avoided by making the modifications in two separate stages: first, modify the field names; then modify the new structure again to change field lengths.

SELECTION

In Chapter 3 you learned how scopes are added to a command to specify what area of the data base file should be processed by that command. Scopes select records by their physical location in a file. To achieve a logical selection of records, the user must find a way to select records based on the information contained within them.

THE FOR CLAUSE

Selection is one of the two major functions of data base management software. It refers to a program's ability to pick out a group of records that are related by some logical criterion. The addition of a FOR clause to a command allows the user to specify a condition that a record must have in order to be processed.

Since this chapter begins where Chapter 3 left off, the ASSIST mode may be active. It should be exited by pressing < Esc >. Now place the data base file in use by entering

    USE expenses < return >

The key to understanding the selection process is to understand what a "logical expression" is. Consider the text below:

amount = 60.6

There are three parts to the expression:

Field name:	**amount**
Logical operator:	= (equals)
Numeric object:	**60.6**

The expression asks a question: Is the value in the AMOUNT field equal to 60.6? The answer is either true or false, depending on what has been entered into the data base file. An expression like the one above can be added to a command by using the FOR clause. It tells the program to work with only those records for which the expression evaluates as true. Enter the following command:

LIST FOR amount=60.6 < return >

The program displays

```
Record# DATE         CAT PAYTO            ITEM            AMOUNT COMMENT
S MONTH              DEDUCT
      3  01/21/85     130 P G & E         TURN ON ELEC    60.60 Memo
   January            .F.
```

The FOR clause selected just the record or records that contained the value 60.6 in the AMOUNT field (the trailing zero in 60.60 has no numeric value and is considered an exact match for 60.6).

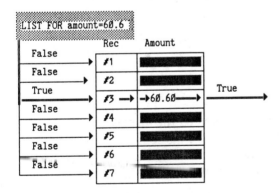

dBASE III Plus recognizes other logical operators. For example, the > represents a "greater than" relationship. Enter

LIST FOR amount > 60.6 < return >

Records no. 1, 2, and 5 appear, but why not record no. 3? Remember that the amount in record no. 3 was exactly 60.60. The criterion used with the command specified a value greater than 60.6. Record no. 3 didn't qualify.

To include record no. 3 in the selection, you could use the "greater than or equal to" symbol, > =. Enter

LIST FOR amount > =60.6 < return >

This time records no. 1, 2, 3, and 5 are listed. *dBASE III Plus* recognizes the following relational operators:

<	Less than
>	Greater than
=	Equal
< > or #	Not equal
< =	Less than or equal
> =	Greater than or equal

Enter

LIST FOR amount#60.6 < return >

The # stands for "not equal to." The program listed all the records except record no. 3. You can use the FOR clause with a number of *dBASE III Plus* commands. Enter

DISPLAY date,payto FOR amount > 50 < return >

The program displays

```
Record#  date     payto
     1   01/02/85 CROW CANYON LUMBER
     2   01/15/85 GREEN ACRES FURN
     3   01/21/85 P G & E
     5   01/30/85 BRITZ PRINTING
```

To understand why the previous command created the display that it did, you need to understand the grammar used in *dBASE III Plus* commands. The previous command breaks down into the following parts:

1. Command: **DISPLAY**
2. Field list: **date,payto**
3. Clause: **FOR**
4. Test field: **amount**
5. Operator: **=**
6. Criterion: **50**

The last three items (test field, operator, and criterion) are called a *logical expression*. A logical expression, which is one that evaluates as either true or false, is in contrast to a *numerical expression* (e.g., amount*.065), which evaluates to some numeric value.

The purpose of a logical expression is to create a test that when used with the FOR clause selects records for processing. You may have noticed that adding the FOR clause to the DISPLAY command affected the scope of the DISPLAY command. Normally, the command DISPLAY date,payto has a default scope of NEXT 1. The program then displays the DATE and PAYTO fields of the active record only.

However, *dBASE III Plus* assumes that when you add a FOR clause to a command, you want to test all the records in the data base file for possible selection. The command below has exactly the same meaning as the previous command. Enter

DISPLAY ALL date,payto FOR amount > 50 < return >

Notice that the result of this command is exactly the same as the previous DISPLAY command entered without the ALL scope. Using a FOR clause implies that the program should rewind the pointer to the top of the file and begin testing all the records sequentially, until the end of the file is encountered.

You can limit the scope of a FOR clause by using a restrictive scope, such as NEXT, RECORD #, or REST. Enter the following commands as an example:

GOTO TOP < return >
DISPLAY NEXT 3 date,payto FOR amount > 50 < return >

This time, only records no. 1 and 2 appear. This is because the NEXT 3 scope terminated the command after it searched the first three records.

SELECTING FOR CHARACTER FIELDS

FOR clauses can also be used to select records based on CHARACTER fields. However, there is a difference in the way that character criterion is specified. *dBASE III Plus*, for instance, requires that character criterion be delimited. The term *delimited* refers to special characters, such as quotation marks, that are used to mark the beginning and the end of a group of characters. Enter

LIST FOR payto = "P" < return >

The effect of the expression payto = "P" is that it selects records for which the first letter in the PAYTO field is P. Keep in mind that when you test for a character, the case of that character is significant. Enter

LIST FOR payto = "p" < return >

Notice that this command failed to list any records because the character specified in the expression is entered in lowercase, while the data in the fields are entered in uppercase.

Groups of characters surrounded by quotation marks are called text literals. For example, in the expression payto="P", payto is not a literal value, but a symbol for whatever data might be entered into the PAYTO field. On the other hand, "P" is a literal because it represents the letter P. If you enclose any group of characters in quotation marks, the program treats the item as a text literal, not a symbol. If you enter LIST FOR payto=P, the program would attempt to compare the contents of the PAYTO field to a field named P. If no such field existed, the program would display the error message Variable not found.

Furthermore, if you forget to include the quotation marks, the program will attempt to find a meaning for what appears to be a symbol or command word.

If you were not sure of the case in which the data were entered, you could use one of the *dBASE III Plus*'s special functions to eliminate the case sensitivity of a command. In the following command, the UPPER() function is added to prevent the program from skipping over records that begin with p. Enter

LIST FOR UPPER(payto)="P" <return>

The command works because it tells *dBASE III Plus* to convert the contents of the PAYTO field to uppercase and then compare the first letter of the field with P. Note that the converted value of the PAYTO field is not stored but used only momentarily to perform the selection test. (See Chapter 3 for an explanation of how to permanently convert the case of data stored on CHARACTER fields.)

dBASE III Plus recognizes three different pairs of delimiters for text literals: " ", ', and []. The ' is the single quotation, or apostrophe character, not the ' (accent) key, which also appears on the IBM PC-style keyboard. For example, all the following commands are acceptable to *dBASE III Plus*:

LIST FOR payto="P"
LIST FOR payto='P'
LIST FOR payto=[P]

However, take care that the literal is ended with the same delimiter with which it began. The following commands would cause an error:

LIST FOR payto="P'
LIST FOR payto="P]

The advantage of having several valid delimiters is that you can include the ', the ", or the square brackets in a text literal if necessary. The example below shows how an apostrophe is included in a text literal.

LIST FOR payto="JOE'S BAR AND GRILL"

If you required a more selective search, you could test the first two letters of a field. Enter

LIST FOR payto="PA" <return>

The only record that qualifies this time is the one that contains exactly PA in the PAYTO field. You can be very specific when entering a criterion. Enter

LIST FOR payto="PACIFIC BELL"<return>

Notice that the result is the same. Which is the better method? As a rule you should enter only as many characters as needed to make your match. The more characters you enter, the more likely you are to make a typing mistake. Also keep in mind that spaces are as significant as letters. Look at the following entries:

1. **P G & E**
2. **PG&E**
3. **PG & E**
4. **PAC. GAS & ELEC**
5. **PAC G&E**

All of them are meant to signify the same utility company. Most people would instantly recognize that fact and treat all the entries as equal. But computers lack the kind of intuition that humans bring to data recognition. For example, the command LIST FOR payto="PG&E" would display only one record, number 2. The others would appear to be missing from the data base file. Entering LIST FOR payto="P" would display all five records (along with any other payee that begins with P).

When you suspect that missing records are the result of inconsistent data entry, enter the broadest possible criterion first. Should too many undesired records appear, you can make the criterion more restrictive. Thus the general rule is to work from broad to restrictive criteria when retrieving data.

USING OTHER OPERATORS WITH TEXT

Earlier in this chapter, you learned that *dBASE III Plus* can test numeric values for such qualities as greater than or less than a specified amount. These same operators can be applied to character fields as well. Enter

LIST FOR payto>"G"<return>

What has happened? The program understands the expression payto>"G" as asking "Does the first letter in the payto field fall after the letter G in the alphabet?" If so the record is listed; if not the record is skipped. Enter the following command, which tests the contents of the ITEM field:

LIST FOR item<"M"<return>

This should select records for which the first letter in the ITEM field precedes the letter M in the alphabet. But what about record no. 1? The ITEM field begins with a number, not a letter. Why was it included in the selected records?

The answer lies in the method that many programs use to arrange text information. The most common method, and the one used by *dBASE III Plus*, utilizes the ASCII (American Standard Code for Information Interchange) coding system. The ASCII system assigns numeric values to the keyboard characters. (The system was designed for use with teletype systems. In fact, the term *teletype-like device* refers to an ASCII-compatible device such as a typical printer.) The ASCII rankings are listed as follows:

32	blank space
33–47	special characters !"#$%&|()*+ −./
48–57	numbers 0123456789
58–64	special signs :;< >=?@
65–90	capital letters A-Z
91–96	special symbols []^'
97–122	lowercase letters a-z
123–126	special characters {|}~

The entry ASCII code consists of 128 codes, 0 through 127. Some of the codes are used to represent special keys or key combinations. For example, ASCII code 1 represents the **[CTRL/A]** key combination.

> dBASE III Plus *conforms to the ASCII coding sequence; character entries that begin with numerals are ranked ahead of character entries that begin with letters. Also note that blank spaces are ranked ahead of visible characters. This means that fields that begin with blanks (e.g., empty CHARACTER fields) are always ranked ahead of fields that contain visible character data.*

Also keep in mind that uppercase letters precede lowercase letters in rank. If your data are entered inconsistently in terms of case, you may find your records appearing in improper order when you sort them.

All the operators that can be used with numeric values can be used with character data. This makes sense because the computer is really using the ASCII numeric values to rank the character data. Enter

LIST FOR payto#"P"<return>

The LIST command selects all the records except the one that begins with P.

Exercise 1   Enter a command that will list all the records in category 130. The correct command can be found at the end of this chapter.

SUBSTRING SEARCH

Up to this point, the criterion employed to select records on the basis of character fields has been position specific. This means that the expression payto="P" tests the first character in the field, while payto = "PA" tests the first two characters in the field, and so on.

There may be times when you want to test if a character, or group of characters, is entered into a field, even if they are not included in the first few characters. This type of search is called a *substring search*.

The term *string* is commonly used in computer languages to refer to character or text information. The idea is that text, to the computer, is simply a string of unrelated characters. This is in contrast to a numeric value in which the order of the numbers has a mathematical significance.

In recent years, as computer software has reached users that are technically less sophisticated, manufacturers have begun to use the words *character,* or *text,* in place of the more obscure technical word, *string.* In computer terminology, string, text, and character are used interchangeably. This inconsistency in terms is unfortunately embedded in *dBASE III Plus*'s command structure and cannot be avoided.

A substring is a section of a text entry. For example, PA is a substring of PACIFIC BELL; so is BELL, or PACIFIC. A substring can be any size, as long as it is smaller than the whole text item to which it refers.

dBASE III Plus recognizes a special operator symbol that works only with character (string) data. The $, used to test if a specified string is contained within a larger string, takes the following general form:

A$B

A stands for the substring, while B stands for the larger string. The expression asks the question, "is A some part of B?" As with the other operators, the answer is always either true or false. Enter

LIST FOR item="CARDS" <return>

No records are listed. Now enter

LIST FOR "CARDS"$item <return>

Record no. 5, which has an ITEM entry of BUSINESS CARDS, is displayed. Using the = operator failed to retrieve the record because CARDS was not the first part of the text.

SEARCHING SPECIAL FIELDS

Up to now, you have seen how selection can be performed on NUMERIC and CHARACTER fields. Two other special fields can also be searched: DATE and LOGICAL.

DATE fields pose a complicated problem because dates are stored in a different format than they appear on the screen. To perform selection on DATE fields, you have to use the *dBASE III Plus* date functions to convert dates into character or numeric data.

When selecting by a DATE field, the first criterion to consider is what date function will be used with the date. Some date functions return numeric values, while others return character values.

The following functions evaluate as characters:

1. **DTOC()** This function converts a date into a character string.
2. **CMONTH()** This function produces the text name of the month.
3. **CDOW()** This function produces the text day of the week.
4. **DAY()** This function produces the number indicating the day of the month.
5. **DOW()** This function produces the number of the day of the week.
6. **MONTH()** This function produces the number of the month.
7. **YEAR()** This function produces the number of the year.
8. **CTOD()** This function produces a date from a character string.

For example, suppose you wanted to locate records with the date 01/25/85. Enter

LIST FOR date="01/25/85" <return>

The program displays the message Data type mismatch. The program is reporting that DATE is a DATE-type field and cannot be compared with a character entry, "01/25/85". To overcome this problem the DTOC (Date to Character) function can be used to convert the date into a character string so that it can then be correctly compared with that string. Enter

LIST FOR DTOC(date)="01/25/85" <return>

The program can now make the selection correctly. The string used to match the date must follow the MM/DD/YY format and must be exactly eight characters in length. For example, LIST FOR DTOC(date)="1/25/85" would not be correct because the leading zero was not included in the match string.

If you want to select records by month, you can match for character or number. Enter

LIST FOR MONTH(date)=1 <return>

The same results can be achieved by entering

LIST FOR CMONTH(date)="Jan" <return>

Note that the text literal, Jan, was used instead of JAN because *dBASE III Plus* automatically converts a month into a text string, with the first letter uppercase and the remainder lowercase. If you want to use all uppercase letters in your text literal, you could enter

LIST FOR UPPER(CMONTH(date))="JAN" <return>

Notice that you get the same results with any of the commands.

In the previous command, two functions were used on the same field at the same time, UPPER(CMONTH(date)). This method, called *nesting,* allows you to make a series of computations in a single formula. In the example above, the CMONTH() function creates a text string for the month, and the UPPER() function converts the text string into all uppercase characters.

You must take care to properly enclose each function with the correct parentheses. Since the CMONTH() function operates on the DATE field, DATE, the name of the field should appear in the parentheses for that function. The UPPER() operates on the results of the CMONTH() function. Therefore the entire CMONTH(date) expression should be enclosed in the UPPER() function.

When the functions are correctly written, they are properly "nested."

DATE fields also offer another way to use the substring operator. Suppose you want to list all the records that have dates that fall on a Wednesday or a Friday. Look at the expression below (do not enter):

CDOW(date)$"Wednesday Friday"

Remember that the $ operator tests to see if the left string is any part of the right string. Usually the left string is a literal and the right a field. However, in this example the left string is the result of a date function that could evaluate to one of the seven days of the week. The test compares the day of week of the date with a string that contains the names of two days, Wednesday and Friday. Enter

LIST FOR CDOW(date)$"Wednesday Friday" <return>

The program selects records no. 1, 4, and 5.

How can you be sure that the records listed really do fall on one of the two days for which you want to select? Enter the following command:

LIST date,CDOW(date) FOR CDOW(date)$"Wednesday Friday" <return>

The program displays

```
Record#  date     cdow(date)
      1  01/02/85 Wednesday
      4  01/25/85 Friday
      5  01/30/85 Wednesday
```

By specifying CDOW() as part of the field list, you were able to confirm the accuracy of the selection.

Using the $ operator to select data in the manner just illustrated can be applied to CHARACTER fields as well as DATE fields. However, there is a complication that might be confusing. Suppose you wanted to select all the records that contained either P G & E, or PACIFIC BELL, as payees. You may try the following command: LIST FOR payto$"P G & E PACIFIC BELL", but you would fail to locate any records because of the length of the PAYTO field.

In *dBASE III Plus*, when a character field is evaluated, all the characters in that field are considered, even the blank spaces. Since the PAYTO field is 20 characters long, the program expects a matching character string to have the same number of blank spaces as the field contains. In the example above, this is not the case: "PACIFIC BELL" is not part of "P G & E PACIFIC BELL".

In order for the function to work properly you would have to enter

LIST FOR payto$"P G & E   PACIFIC BELL   "

Note that this time the trailing spaces have been included in the text literal. The main disadvantage to this is that it is very easy to type in the wrong number of spaces. However, there are two methods by which the same result can be obtained without having to pad the text literal with spaces. One, the use of logical connectives, is described later in this chapter. The other, the TRIM() function, is described in Chapter 4.

SEARCHING LOGICAL FIELDS

LOGICAL fields share a specialness with DATE fields for the same reason (i.e., they contain data in a different form than what is displayed in the APPEND, BROWSE, EDIT, or CHANGE modes). When you enter data into a LOGICAL field, you have the option of entering Y and N, or T and F. However, when you list the contents of a LOGICAL field, you see something different. Enter

LIST deduct< return >

dBASE III Plus displays the following:

```
Record#  deduct
    1    .T.
    2    .T.
    3    .F.
    4    .F.
    5    .F.
    6    .F.
```

Notice that the contents of the LOGICAL field are displayed as .T. (true) or .F. (false) symbols. In contrast, when entering or editing data, the contents of the field appear differently. Enter

EDIT RECORD 1 <return >

The program displays

```
DATE        01/02/85
CAT           110
PAYTO       CROW CANYON LUMBER
ITEM        10 2 BY 4
AMOUNT        68.40
COMMENTS    memo
MONTH       January
DEDUCT      Y
```

In the EDIT mode, the original entry, the letter Y, appears. Enter

<Esc>

Since the data in the LOGICAL field appears in different forms in different modes, how should you structure a logical expression to select records? Perhaps you should test the field for .T. or .F. Enter

LIST FOR deduct=.T.<return>

The program displays invalid operator. Respond to the help prompt by entering

n

When you create an expression to select records based on the contents of a LOGICAL field, *dBASE III Plus* allows you to use an abbreviated form of a logical expression. Enter

LIST FOR deduct<return>

The program lists records no. 1 and 2. Because DEDUCT is a LOGICAL field, simply using the field name tests if the contents of the field are true (either Y or T). Remember, this short form of the expression can be used only for logical values. Enter

LIST FOR date<return>

dBASE III Plus displays the error message, Not a logical expression. Respond to the help prompt by entering

n

SELECTING FALSE RECORDS

Because selecting true records utilizes a special expression form, there must also be a special form for selecting false records. The form involves the use of the logical connective .NOT., which reverses the veracity of any expression. Enter

LIST FOR .NOT.deduct<return>

Records no. 3, 4, 5, and 6 are listed because they contain a false value in the LOGICAL field.

> When new records are added to the data base file, LOGICAL fields are given a default value of false.

The .NOT. connective is not restricted to use with LOGICAL fields, but can be used to give the opposite meaning to any expression. For example, the following command will select any expenses dated for a Saturday or Sunday. Enter

LIST date,CDOW(date) FOR CDOW(date)$"Saturday Sunday" <return>

If you wanted to display all the weekday expenses, the .NOT. connective can save you some typing. Instead of entering a text string that contains all the weekday names, you can enter the same command but use a .NOT. to reverse its meaning. Enter

LIST date,CDOW(date) FOR .NOT.CDOW(date)$"Saturday Sunday" <return>

OTHER CONNECTIVES

So far, you have used only simple expressions that perform true and false tests for a single condition. More complex expressions can be created by using logical connectives, three of which *dBASE III Plus* recognizes: .AND., .OR., and .NOT. The periods are part of the logical connectives and must be entered in order to be considered valid.

The .AND. and .OR. connectives are used to combine separate expressions into a single complex expression. For example, below are two propositions that can be evaluated as either true or false.

1. The man is **greater than** 6 feet tall.
2. The man is **less than** 40 years old.

These two ideas can be expressed in *dBASE III Plus* notations (assuming fields called HEIGHT and AGE) as follows:

1. height > 6
2. age < 40

You can use logical connectives to combine these two expressions into a single expression.

height > 6**.AND.**age < 40

What is the meaning of a combined expression like the one above? The .AND. indicates that both parts of the expression must be true in order for the whole expression to be considered true. If either element is false then the whole expression is false.

Below is a chart that shows how the combined expression would be evaluated.

Name	Height	Age	height > 6 .AND. age < 40
Smith	6'2"	45	FALSE
Jones	5'8"	29	FALSE
Erving	6'8"	36	TRUE
Johnson	5'7"	50	FALSE

Only Erving qualifies because he satisfies both conditions in the expression, over 6 feet and younger than 40.

The logical connective .OR. evaluates the entire expression as true if either of the conditions is true. Here is the expression with an .OR. connective:

height > 6**.OR.**age < 40

The chart would appear as follows with an .OR. connective:

Name	Height	Age	height > 6 .OR. age < 40
Smith	6'2"	45	TRUE
Jones	5'8"	29	TRUE
Erving	6'8"	36	TRUE
Johnson	5'7"	50	FALSE

Now only Johnson fails the test. When using an .OR. connective, the entire expression is considered false only if both conditions are false. In general, .AND. connectives tend to make the selection more restrictive, while .OR. connectives tend to be less restrictive.

In terms of the EXPENSES file, you might want to list all the records that contain amounts between 50 and 100 dollars. Enter

LIST FOR amount > = 50 AND.amount < =100 < return >

Records no. 1, 3, and 5 are selected. The other records are either too high or two low to satisfy the conditions specified in the expression. Notice that in creating a complex expression, each element is a complete expression capable of being used separately.

amount > = 50   (complete expression)
.AND.   (logical connective)
amount < = 100   (complete expression)

You cannot take a shortcut by entering the field name only once. Enter the following command:

LIST FOR amount > =50.AND. < =100 < return >

dBASE III Plus displays the error message Syntax error, because the command did not have a complete expression following the connective:

amount > =50	(complete expression)
.AND.	(logical connective)
< =100	(field name missing—expression incomplete)

Logical connectives can also be used to test data in two different fields. Enter

DISPLAY FOR DTOC(date) > "01/15/85".AND.amount > 35 < return >

Records no. 3, 4, and 5 qualify this time.

It is possible to use more than one connective in an expression. Enter the following command:

DISPLAY FOR DTOC(date) > "01/15/85".AND.amount > 35.AND.payto < "M"
< return >

When using the logical connectives, you can add as many expressions as you like to a FOR clause. Your only limitation is that the total number of characters in the command should not exceed 254.

The .OR. connective works in the same manner as the .AND. Enter

LIST FOR amount < 50.OR.deduct < return >

Four records are listed. The first two qualify by having a true value in the DEDUCT field. The second two qualify because their amount value is less than 50. In an OR relationship, evaluating true to either expression selects the record.

You can get even more complex by making expressions that use several connectives of different kinds. Look at the command below. Take a guess at what records it will display, and then enter the command.

LIST FOR payto="P".OR.amount < 50.AND..NOT.deduct < return >

dBASE III Plus displays

```
Record#  DATE      CAT PAYTO                ITEM                 AMOUNT COMMENT
S MONTH            DEDUCT
      3  01/21/85  130 P G & E              TURN ON ELEC          60.60 Memo
  January          .F.
      4  01/25/85  130 PACIFIC BELL         INSTALL TELE          44.28 Memo
  January          .F.
      6  02/02/85  140 GIFT STORE           GROUND HOG DAY CARDS   5.94 Memo
  February         .F.
```

How does *dBASE III Plus* decode the expression used in the previous command? If you look at the expression, you will notice that its meaning changes, depending on which connective you evaluate first. To create a consistent environment for commands, *dBASE III Plus* establishes an order of precedence for connectives. The order is as follows (note that *dBASE III Plus* recognizes parentheses as a means of altering the precedence of evaluation):

First Evaluated	.NOT.
Second Evaluated	.AND.
Third Evaluated	.OR.

In the previous command, *dBASE III Plus* began by evaluating the .NOT. Then it tested the record to see if it was both false for deduct and contained an amount less than 50. If both were true, the record was displayed. However, if either one was false, the program tested the PAYTO field for the first letter of P. If that was true, the record was displayed. In the event that the final condition was false, the record was skipped.

This may seem very complicated, and it is! It takes some practice to get the expressions that make the exact selections you want. When you have worked with the program for a while, this type of notation will make much more sense.

MEMO FIELDS

Operations, like selection, cannot be performed on MEMO fields. If you find that you want to perform selections based on MEMO fields, you will have to alter the structure of your file and create a CHARACTER field (maximum size 254 characters) to hold the data. If the limitation on the size of the CHARACTER field does not leave you enough room for the memo, you might consider using the CHARACTER field to store key words from the memo. Then you could use a substring operator to locate a record that has a certain key word; for example, LIST FOR "ELECTRIC"$UPPER(keywords).

Exercise 2   Enter a command that will list the records in category 130 with amounts greater than $50. The correct command can be found at the end of this chapter.

SELECTIVE REPLACEMENT

The use of the FOR clause to select records for processing is not limited to the LIST command. Many *dBASE III Plus* commands also operate selectively. For example, the REPLACE command used in Chapter 3 will operate using a FOR clause.

Suppose you realize that you entered a payee inconsistently (e.g., P G & E, PG&E). You would want to change one of the entry styles to be consistent with the other. This is where the REPLACE command comes in. It can be used to selectively change the data from one style to another. Enter

REPLACE payto WITH "PG&E" FOR payto="P G & E" <return>

The command selected the record (or records) that contained P G & E and replaced the PAYTO field with PG&E. In the example, only one record was replaced. Had there been more, *dBASE III Plus* would have searched the entire data base file and performed the replacement as many times as required.

FILTERS

Up to now, you have learned how a FOR clause can modify a command so that it selectively processes the records in the data base file. In each case, the effect of the FOR clause was limited to the command to which it was attached. *dBASE III Plus* allows you to create a data filter that consists of an expression just like the one used with a FOR clause. However, instead of being attached to a specific command, the filter controls all the commands you issue. It is as if the program were automatically adding a FOR clause to each command that entered.

The advantage of a filter is that you do not have to bother entering the same FOR clause over and over again. For example, suppose you wanted to work with only the records that were deductible. Enter

SET FILTER TO deduct <return>

Enter

LIST <return>

The data base file behaves as if the only records in the file were the ones that contained a true value for the DEDUCT field. The filter controls the records displayed for any command that you issue. Enter

BROWSE <return>
[CTRL/Home]
t

Notice that only two records are displayed in the BROWSE mode. Enter

<Esc>

To turn off the filter and allow display of the full data base file, enter

> **SET FILTER TO**< return >
> **LIST**<return >

The records are displayed once again. You can have only one active filter at a time. Entering another filter command cancels the first filter. Enter

> **SET FILTER TO amount > 60** < return >
> **LIST**<return >
> **SET FILTER TO DTOC(date) > "01/15/85"** <return >
> **LIST**<return >
> **SET FILTER TO**< return >
> **LIST**<return >

Exercise 3   Create a filter that displays only records with budget categories between 120 and 130. List the data base file, then remove the filter.

> *A filter is automatically removed from the memory of the computer whenever the active data base file is closed or a new one is opened. Filters are not maintained from session to session, either. Quitting* dBASE III Plus *eliminates any filter that might be active.*

dBASE III Plus contains QUERY files that can be used to store and recall filter specification.

SELECTION IN THE ASSIST MODE

The ASSIST mode of *dBASE III Plus* presents users with a menu-driven method of adding FOR clauses to their commands. To see how this is done, enter the ASSIST mode by entering

> **ASSIST**<return >

Select the RETRIEVE menu by entering

> **r**

Select the LIST command by entering

> < return >

The command options box appears. To create a search clause, enter

> **<down arrow>** (3 times)
> < return >

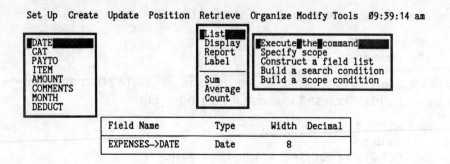

dBASE III Plus displays a list of fields and a box, which shows the detail of the highlighted field.

Note that COMMENTS appears in a duller video, indicating that COMMENTS (a MEMO field) cannot be used in a selection criterion. Select the PAYTO field by entering

> **< down arrow > (2 times)**
> **< return >**

dBASE III Plus now displays a box that lists the logical operators that can be used in the expression.

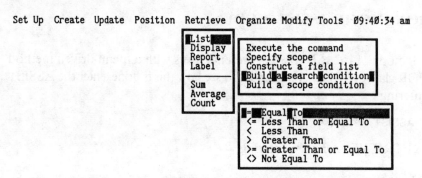

The $ (substring) operator is not available in the ASSIST mode.

Select the equal to operator by entering

> **< return >**

Now the displayed box asks you to enter the characters that you want to use as the criterion.

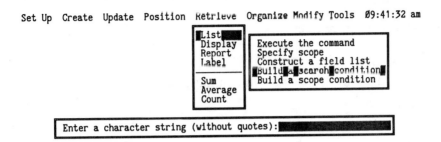

On the command line you see that LIST FOR PAYTO = ' has been entered. *dBASE III Plus* uses the single quotation mark (apostrophe) as the delimiter. Enter

P <return>

Yet another box is displayed that contains the logical connectives that can be used to create a more complex expression.

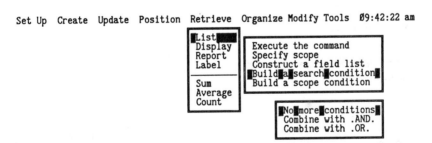

The command line shows LIST FOR PAYTO = 'P'. Notice that this is exactly the command you would type if you were working from the DOT PROMPT. To make a simple expression, enter

<return>

To execute the command, enter

[Pg Up]
< return >

When asked about printing, enter

n

The program lists the selected records. To continue, enter

< return >

QUERIES

The ASSIST mode does not allow direct entry of the SET FILTER command as seen at the DOT PROMPT. However, *dBASE III Plus* has another way of dealing with filter commands, called "queries." Each QUERY file holds a single filter specification. A QUERY differs from a filter in that a QUERY is stored in a file and can be recalled at some later time. SET FILTER, on the other hand, creates a filter condition that is terminated when you set another filter, close the data base file, open another data base file, or quit the *dBASE III Plus* program.

To create a QUERY file, display the CREATE menu by entering

c

Select QUERY by entering

< down arrow > (3 times)
< return >

Select the default drive by entering

< return >

Enter the name of the QUERY file. The filename can be only eight characters long and cannot contain spaces. *dBASE III Plus* allows you to enter more than eight characters in the box, but only the first eight will be used as the name of the QUERY file. Since the filter you will create is for deductible expenses in January, enter

janded< return >

The screen displays the QUERY file input screen.

```
██Set██Filter██        Nest          Display          Exit  09:44:06 am
┌──────────────────────────────────────────────────────┐
│ ██Field██Name██████████████████████                   │
│ Operator                                               │
│ Constant/Expression                                    │
│ Connect                                                │
│ ──────────────────────────────────────                │
│ Line Number        1                                   │
└──────────────────────────────────────────────────────┘
```

Line	Field	Operator	Constant/Expression	Connect
1				
2				
3				
4				
5				
6				
7				

```
CREATE█QUERY████ |<C:>|C:JANDED.QRY████████████|Opt:█1/2███████ ||█████|
```

It is here that you begin to create a QUERY file that specifies a filter that selects only those records for January that are deductible.

The QUERY display has three main sections. At the top is a menu bar with four options: SET FILTER, NEST, DISPLAY, and EXIT. Below the bar is the area for the pull down menus. The SET FILTER menu is automatically displayed. At the bottom of the screen, a table is displayed that shows the filter specifications as you enter them. The table is currently blank, but it can contain up to seven levels of nested expressions.

The first specification is to set the filter for the month of January. Enter

<return>

This activates the Field name area. *dBASE III Plus* displays the name of the field in a box on the right side of the display.

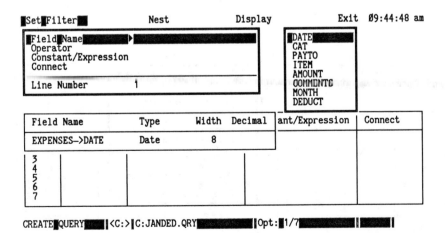

```
██Set██Filter██        Nest          Display          Exit  09:44:48 am
┌────────────────────────────────────────────┐  ┌──────────┐
│ ██Field██Name██████████████ ▶ ███████████   │  │ ██DATE██  │
│ Operator                                     │  │ CAT      │
│ Constant/Expression                          │  │ PAYTO    │
│ Connect                                      │  │ ITEM     │
│ ─────────────────────────────────────       │  │ AMOUNT   │
│ Line Number        1                         │  │ COMMENTS │
│                                              │  │ MONTH    │
│                                              │  │ DEDUCT   │
└────────────────────────────────────────────┘  └──────────┘
```

Field Name	Type	Width	Decimal	ant/Expression	Connect
EXPENSES→DATE	Date	8			
3					
4					
5					
6					
7					

```
CREATE█QUERY████ |<C:>|C:JANDED.QRY████████████|Opt:█1/7███████ ||█████|
```

Note that COMMENTS is not available for use in a QUERY file. In order to select by month, you must select the MONTH field.

In the DOT PROMPT mode, it is possible to enter a function (e.g., MONTH(date)) in the field name portion of the specification. However, the menu-driven ASSIST mode allows only the entry of a field name. If you want to select by month, it would not be possible using the DATE field.

However, in Chapter 3, you modified the structure of the file and created a new field that held just the name of the month. The addition of this field allows you now to specify the month by using the MONTH field.

Enter

> **<down arrow>** **(5 times)**
> **<return>**

The highlight is automatically positioned to the next item in the box, Operator.

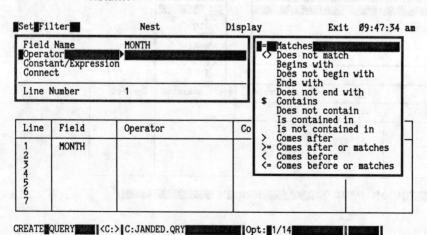

Enter

> **<return>**

dBASE III Plus displays a box that lists the logical operators; the box also contains a description of each. In this case, matches is the correct choice since it is the same as equal to. Enter

<return>

The highlight is now positioned at Constant/Expression. It is in this area that you can enter the criterion for the DATE field. The case of the text you enter is significant. The January text must be entered as an uppercase first letter and the remainder as lowercase. Enter

<return>
"January" <return>

Note that you *must* enter the delimiters with the text. The cursor is automatically moved down into the next item in the display, Connect.

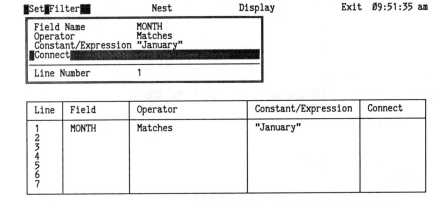

The connect area allows you to specify a logical connective to use if the filter is to have a second expression. Enter

<return>

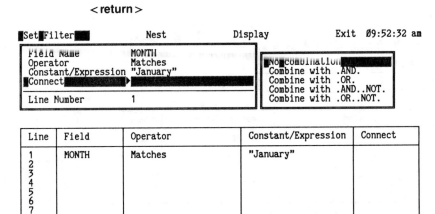

You can now use the highlight to select the proper connective. Enter

> **<down arrow>**
> **<return>**

The .AND. connective has been selected. *dBASE III Plus* then clears the filter box and inserts the number 2 in the line number section.

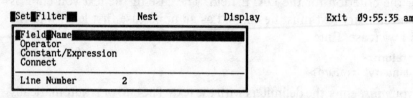

You can now enter the second criterion. Select the DEDUCT field by entering

> **<return>**
> **<down arrow> (6 times)**
> **<return>**

Select the operator by entering

> **<return>**

Because DEDUCT is a LOGICAL field, *dBASE III Plus* displays only two choices.

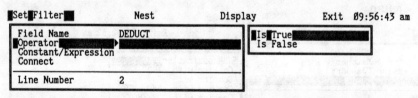

Enter

<return>

Note that *dBASE III Plus* automatically fills in True for the Constant/Expression area.

```
Set Filter            Nest           Display            Exit  09:58:01 am
  ┌─────────────────────────────────────────────┐
  │ Field Name          DEDUCT                    │
  │ Operator            Is                         │
  │ Constant/Expression True                       │
  │ Connect                                        │
  │                                                │
  │ Line Number         2                          │
  └─────────────────────────────────────────────┘
```

Line	Field	Operator	Constant/Expression	Connect
1	MONTH	Matches	"January"	.AND.
2	DEDUCT	Is	True	
3				
4				
5				
6				
7				

CREATE QUERY ▮ |<C:>| C:JANDED.QRY ▮ |Opt: 3/5 ▮ ▮

You have now entered the filter requirements. One of the advantages of the QUERY mode is that you can test the filter by entering the DISPLAY command. Enter

d<return>

The first record that fits the QUERY criterion appears. Enter

[Pg Dn]

The next record is displayed. Enter

[Pg Dn]

Nothing changes because there are no more records that meet the criterion. If you are satisfied with the results of the filters, you are ready to save the filters in a QUERY file. Enter

e

The EXIT menu displays two choices: SAVE or ABANDON. ABANDON tells *dBASE III Plus* to exit the QUERY mode and not to save the filter specification. SAVE exits the QUERY mode and stores the filters in a file.

All files created in the QUERY mode are given a QRY file extension. In this example, the file will be stored as JANDED.QRY.

Enter

<return>

The file is saved and you return to the CREATE menu. The filter that you just created is still in effect. Enter

>   **r**
>   **<return>**
>   **<return>**
>   **n**

dBASE III Plus lists the two records that meet the conditions specified by the QUERY file. Enter

>   **<return>**

To turn off the QUERY file you must go to the SETUP menu and open the EXPENSES file once again. Enter

>   **s<return>**

Move the highlight to EXPENSES. Enter

>   **<return>**
>   **n**

Test to see if the filter is really gone by entering

>   **r**
>   **<return>**
>   **<return>**
>   **<return>**

All six records are displayed. Enter

>   **<return>**

Opening a data base file actually serves two purposes. While the primary aim of the command is to allow access to a data base file, in order to do so, the command must first close any data base file that is already open. In addition, when the current file is closed, any auxiliary files, like QUERY files, are also closed. This is true even if the new file being opened is the one that is currently open. *dBASE III Plus* does not attempt to take a shortcut (i.e., simply leave the current file open). Instead it first closes the active data base file and then reopens it. When the file is reopened two things have changed: the pointer is reset to the top of the file, and no auxiliary files (e.g., QUERY files) are open.

USING QUERY FILES: DOT PROMPT MODE

QUERY files can be used in the DOT PROMPT mode to access filters that have been created previously. Exit the ASSIST mode by entering

>   **<Esc>**

First open the data base file. Enter

> **USE EXPENSES < return >**

Enter

> **LIST <return >**

Now that you have created a QUERY file, you can enter a modified form of the SET FILTER command. The SET FILTER command recognizes a TO FILE clause, which uses the data stored in the QUERY file to establish the filter criterion. Enter

> **SET FILTER TO FILE janded < return >**

The filter is now active. Enter

> **LIST <return >**

Now only two records, the ones that fit the filter criterion, are displayed. You can release the file from the filter by using the SET FILTER TO command. Enter

> **SET FILTER TO < return >**
> **LIST <return >**

All the records appear, indicating that the filter is no longer active.

ADVANTAGES OF QUERY FILES

QUERY files are designed to make the creation and use of filters simpler and faster. The QUERY mode does not add any capacity to the FILTER command but provides a menu-driven method of writing and testing filters.

The NEST command allows you to rearrange the filter specifications and the connectives, so that you get the proper logical nesting. Entering the filters at the DOT PROMPT requires the entire command to be reentered in order to correct a mistake in nesting.

The other advantage of the QUERY is that it offers a method by which you can store complicated filter specifications, and recall them when they are needed.

SUMMARY

The subject of this chapter is selection, a technique that allows the user to create groups of records that meet certain specific criteria.

The basic tool for selection is the FOR clause. When a FOR clause is added to a *dBASE III Plus* command, the command will process only selected records. The FOR clause must contain a logical expression. Logical expressions are those that can be evaluated as either true or false. When a FOR clause is used, the records in the data base file are tested, one by one, to see if the specified expression is true or false. Only records for which the expression evaluates as true are processed, while the other records are ignored.

Expressions can contain character, numeric, date, or logical values. You cannot test the contents of MEMO fields.

dBASE III Plus recognizes the following logical operations:

<	Less than
>	Greater than
=	Equal
< > or #	Not equal
< =	Less than or equal
> =	Greater than or equal

The ASCII coding sequence is used to evaluate greater or less than relationships between CHARACTER fields.

CHARACTER fields can also be evaluated for substring matches using the $ operator. Example: LIST FOR CDOW(date)$"Saturday Sunday". This command lists all records that occur on a Saturday or Sunday.

Logical connectives are used to link several logical expressions into a complex expression. *dBASE III Plus* recognizes

.AND.	true when both expressions are true
.OR.	true if either expression is true
.NOT.	true if the original expression is false

Filters create a global selection expression. When a filter is set, all commands are automatically treated as if a FOR clause were added to them. The filter remains in effect until

1. a SET FILTER TO command is entered
2. a new filter is set
3. the current data base file is closed.

Only one filter can be active at any one moment for a single data base file.

dBASE III Plus has the ability to create a view file. A view file stores a filter specification so that it can be recalled at a later date.

ANSWER KEY

Exercise 1

LIST FOR cat=130 < return >

Exercise 2

LIST FOR cat=130.AND.amount > 50 < return >

Exercise 3

SET FILTER TO cat > =120.AND.cat < =130 < return >
LIST < return >
SET FILTER TO < return >

5

SEQUENCING

In the last chapter you learned how to execute commands selectively by adding a FOR clause to a command. In this chapter you will explore the second basic technique of data base management, sequencing. Sequencing refers to methods by which *dBASE III Plus* can change the order in which records are stored or retrieved.

Sequencing is important for two reasons. First, ordering records is often required to create reports and lists. Second, ordering data base files is often an intermediate step to accomplishing some complex data base tasks like consolidations, summaries, or relations among several data base files.

It is important to learn how sequences are established, maintained, and, in turn, utilized by other commands; this is the goal of Chapter 5. To begin working through this chapter, *dBASE III Plus* should be loaded into the computer and the ASSIST mode should be exited by entering < Esc >.

MANUAL INSERTION OF RECORDS

So far you have encountered two commands that allow you to add new records to the data base file: APPEND and BROWSE. Both commands add the new records at the end of the file. However, there may come a time when you want a new record placed somewhere other than at the end of the file.

In the EXPENSES file you have been entering the records in date order. Suppose you want to add an expense for 01/10/85. Since the last record in the file is

120

dated 02/02/85, adding the record with APPEND or BROWSE would disrupt the date order of the file.

dBASE III Plus has a third command that adds records to the data base file called INSERT. INSERT allows you to add a new record anywhere in the data base file. To see how INSERT operates, open the EXPENSES file by entering

USE expenses< return >

To determine where to insert the new record, use the LIST command to display the dates already entered into the file. Enter

LIST date< return >

The program displays

```
Record#  date
    1    01/02/85
    2    01/15/85
    3    01/21/85
    4    01/25/85
    5    01/30/85
    6    02/02/85
```

The INSERT command adds a record immediately following the pointer position. For example, if the pointer is positioned at record no. 1, the INSERT command will create a new record numbered 2. When a record is inserted, all the records following the insert record will have their record numbers changed.

In this example, an expense made on 01/10/85 should be added following record no. 1. The first step is to position the pointer to that record. Enter

1< return >

Now enter the INSERT command.

INSERT < return >

The program displays the same entry screen format used by the APPEND command. Notice that the record number is 2/6. You can now enter the data for this record. Enter

01/10/85
140< return >
SEARS< return >
TRASH CAN< return >
17.95< return >
< return >
N

The record looks like this:

```
DATE        01/10/85
CAT            140
PAYTO       SEARS
ITEM        TRASH CAN
AMOUNT        17.95
COMMENTS    memo
MONTH
DEDUCT      N
```

When the record has been entered, *dBASE III Plus* automatically terminates the ENTRY mode and returns you to the DOT PROMPT. This automatic termination is in contrast to the APPEND or BROWSE modes, in which records continue to be added until you specifically exit that mode.

Entering <Esc> or [CTRL/q] while inserting a record cancels the insertion. The data base file remains as it was.

To fill in the MONTH field, use a REPLACE command. Enter

REPLACE month WITH CMONTH(date)<return>

Note that since no scope was specified, only one record, the active record, was replaced. To check the effect of the INSERT command, enter

LIST<return>

The program now displays seven records; the new record appears as record no. 2.

INSERT BEFORE

A variation on the INSERT command is INSERT BEFORE. This command inserts the record in front of the active record rather than after it. For example, suppose you wanted to add an expense dated 01/17/85. Enter

LIST date<return>

You can see that this new record falls between the current records no. 3 and 4 . To use the INSERT BEFORE command, enter

4<return>
INSERT BEFORE<return>

The entry display appears. This new record is record no. 4. Enter

0117/85
140<return>
INSTANT PRINTING<return>
ENVELOPES<return>
59.50
<return>
<return>
Y

MEMO fields can be accessed during the INSERT command by entering the [CTRL/Home] command when the cursor is positioned in a MEMO field. This makes four commands that allow entry into MEMO fields: APPEND, EDIT, CHANGE, and INSERT. BROWSE does not allow entry.

To fill in the MONTH field, use a REPLACE command. Enter

REPLACE month WITH CMONTH(date)< return >

AUTOMATIC SEQUENCING

The INSERT command allows you to maintain a data base file in sequence manually. The command is of limited use because it places the burden of organizing the data base file on you, not the computer. In the long run, INSERT should be used on occasion to enter a record or two. *dBASE III Plus* offers two power commands that will perform the sequencing of records automatically; the commands are SORT and INDEX.

While both commands are designed to sequence the data base file, they go about their tasks in two very different ways. Because these commands alter the data base file, it is important to have a clear and thorough understanding of the strengths and weaknesses of each method.

THE SORT COMMAND

The SORT command is used to organize a data base file by sequencing the records in a logical order. The records in the new file are arranged in either alphabetical (CHARACTER fields), chronological (DATE fields), or numerical (NUMERIC fields) order. The order is determined by the field or fields selected as keys for the sort.

The SORT command does not operate on LOGICAL or MEMO fields.

When a file is sorted, the original data base file is unaffected by the command. *dBASE III Plus* creates a new file with the same structure and records as the original file but with the records in a different order. The original file is always the file in use at the time the SORT command is issued. The name of the new file is specified as part of the SORT command.

```
Original File                 Sorted Copy of File

Record # 1   C           Record # 1   A
Record # 2   X           Record # 2   C
Record # 3   A           Record # 3   M
Record # 4   Z           Record # 4   X
Record # 5   M           Record # 5   Z
```

Note that because the SORT command creates a new data base file, it can be considered a special form of the COPY command. SORT not only copies the data but rearranges the records in specific logical order.

In its simplest form the SORT command uses a single field in the existing data base file as the key by which the new file is ordered. For example, suppose you want to create a file ordered alphabetically according to the name of the payee. Enter

SORT ON payto TO payorder < return >

The program now creates a new file. When the sorting is complete *dBASE III Plus* displays a message:

```
100% Sorted        8 Records sorted ... Copying text file.
```

The message tells you that the sorting is complete and that eight records have been copied to the new file. Looking at the screen display, one does not see much evidence to confirm the action taken by the SORT. The steps below show what has happened, and what has not happened.

1. A new file, PAYORDER, has been created.
2. The new file is not active. The EXPENSES file is still active. Any command given at this point (e.g., LIST, REPLACE) will affect EXPENSE, not PAYORDER.
3. The pointer in the active file has moved to the End of File.

Enter

LIST payto < return >

The program displays

```
Record#  payto
     1   CROW CANYON LUMBER
     2   SEARS
     3   GREEN ACRES FURN
     4   INSTANT PRINTING
     5   PG&E
     6   PACIFIC BELL
     7   BRITZ PRINTING
     8   GIFT STORE
```

The payees don't seem to be alphabetized. The reason is that you are not looking at the contents of the sorted file, PAYORDER, but you are still viewing the contents of the active file, EXPENSES. Enter

DIR < return >

The program displays a list of the data base files that should include these two files.

```
Database Files    # Records   Last Update   Size
EXPENSES.DBF            8      01/01/80      892
PAYORDER.DBF            8      01/01/80      978
     1870 bytes in     2 files.
```

The difference in the size of the two files is because *dBASE III Plus* has not written all the data in the records that were just inserted into the disk file EXPENSES. If you were to force the program to close the file (e.g., enter USE EXPENSES), the sizes would display the same.

PAYORDER exists but you cannot see the results of the SORT unless you make PAYORDER the active file. Enter

USE payorder< return >
LIST payto< return >

The program lists

```
Record#   payto
   1      BRITZ PRINTING
   2      CROW CANYON LUMBER
   3      GIFT STORE
   4      GREEN ACRES FURN
   5      INSTANT PRINTING
   6      PG&E
   7      PACIFIC BELL
   8      SEARS
```

You can now see the results of the SORT command. Notice that the records have different numbers than they do in EXPENSES. All the other data from EXPENSES have also been copied. Enter

LIST <return >

The records are displayed with all the fields. When a file is created by the SORT command, it is completely independent of the original data base file. The new file will function as if you had created it from scratch.

CAPITALIZATION

When sorting on a CHARACTER field it is important to remember that *dBASE III Plus* uses the ASCII coding system to determine the ranking of characters, as explained in Chapter 4. If records have been entered inconsistently from the point of view of capitalization, you may be surprised at the results of a sort. For example, suppose one of the records you inserted at the beginning of this chapter was entered in lowercase. Enter

REPLACE payto WITH LOWER(payto) RECORD 5< return >
LIST payto< return >

Record no. 5 is now in lowercase. Now sort on the PAYTO field by entering

SORT ON payto TO PAY1 <return>
USE pay1 <return>
LIST payto <return>

The program displays

```
Record#  payto
      1  BRITZ PRINTING
      2  CROW CANYON LUMBER
      3  GIFT STORE
      4  GREEN ACRES FURN
      5  PG&E
      6  PACIFIC BELL
      7  SEARS
      8  instant printing
```

The payee entered in lowercase is ranked at the bottom of the listing because the ASCII coding system ranks the lowercase letters after the uppercase letters.

You can use the REPLACE command to convert the key field to uppercase before you sort to avoid this type of problem. You may wish to go back to Chapter 4 to review the REPLACE command.

THE /C OPTION

In order to eliminate problems caused by the case of data entered into character fields, *dBASE III Plus* has incorporated a special option into the SORT command. Enter the following:

SORT ON payto/C TO pay2 <return>
USE pay2 <return>
LIST payto <return>

The program lists

```
Record#  payto
      1  BRITZ PRINTING
      2  CROW CANYON LUMBER
      3  GIFT STORE
      4  GREEN ACRES FURN
      5  instant printing
      6  PG&E
      7  PACIFIC BELL
      8  SEARS
```

The records are in the correct alphabetical sequence regardless of the case used. The case of the PAYTO fields was not altered when sorted. The /C option merely ignores the difference while sorting.

SEQUENCE ORDER

dBASE III Plus allows the user to specify either ascending (low to high) or descending (high to low) order for the sorting. In CHARACTER fields the ASCII coding will be used to determine a character's rank. This means that ascending will begin with numbers and special characters and then go from A–Z followed by a–z.

Return to the EXPENSES data base file by entering

USE expenses < return >

The order of the sort is specified by entering /A for ascending or /D for descending after the field name.

The SORT command assumes a default value of ascending when none is specified. It is not necessary to enter /A for an ascending sort. Its only purpose is to make the command more understandable to the person reading it.

To sort the file in descending order by amount, enter

SORT ON amount/D TO amtorder < return >
USE amtorder < return >
LIST < return >

The program lists the records starting with the highest amount. Return to the EXPENSES data base file by entering

USE expenses < return >

MULTILEVEL SORTS

Multilevel sorts are useful when the primary key is not unique. For example, a number of records have the same budget categories. When you sort the budget category, you may want to specify a second field by which the items with the same category number should be ordered (e.g., DATE). The SORT command accepts a list of fields that indicates a sorting sequence. For example, entering CAT,DATE would order the records by category and within each category order, by date. Enter

SORT ON cat,date TO catorder < return >
USE catorder < return >
LIST cat,date,payto,amount < return >

The program displays

```
Record#   cat date    payto              amount
   1      110 01/02/85 CROW CANYON LUMBER  68.40
   2      120 01/15/85 GREEN ACRES FURN   264.68
   3      130 01/21/85 PG&E                60.60
   4      130 01/25/85 PACIFIC BELL        44.28
   5      140 01/10/85 SEARS               17.95
   6      140 01/17/85 INSTANT PRINTING    59.50
   7      140 01/30/85 BRITZ PRINTING      68.32
   8      140 02/02/85 GIFT STORE           5.94
```

The records have been sorted on the primary level by category and on the secondary level by date.

When you are using more than one field as the sort key, you can specify an order for each field. If you do not enter an order, ascending is assumed. Enter

```
SORT ON cat,amount/D TO cat1 <return>
USE cat1 <return>
LIST cat,date,payto,amount <return>
```

The program lists

```
Record#    cat date       payto                  amount
      1    110 01/02/85 CROW CANYON LUMBER        68.40
      2    120 01/15/85 GREEN ACRES FURN         264.68
      3    130 01/21/85 PG&E                      60.60
      4    130 01/25/85 PACIFIC BELL              44.28
      5    140 01/30/85 BRITZ PRINTING            68.32
      6    140 01/17/85 INSTANT PRINTING          59.50
      7    140 01/10/85 SEARS                     17.95
      8    140 02/02/85 GIFT STORE                 5.94
```

The amounts are ranked by descending order within a category. Return to the EXPENSES data base file by entering

```
USE expenses <return>
```

You can specify up to ten fields in a single SORT command.

SELECTIVE SORTING

Up to this point, the sorting has included all the records in the original data base file. The SORT command can operate selectively using a FOR clause.

Suppose you wanted to sort a file by payee but select only those expenses that were deductible. Enter the following

```
SORT ON payto TO notax FOR deduct <return>
```

This time the message reports only three records have been sorted. Display the contents of the sorted file by entering

```
USE notax <return>
LIST <return>
```

The selected records appear ordered by payee. Return to the EXPENSES file by entering

```
USE expenses <return>
```

INDEXING

The second method by which *dBASE III Plus* organizes data is called *indexing*. Like sorting, indexing is designed to arrange a data base file in logical order. Indexing differs from sorting in that indexing does not copy all the data from the original file, but only a limited amount.

To understand the concept of indexing, look at the way a book like this one is indexed and how that index is used. When an index is prepared, it is not necessary to copy the entire paragraph into the index of the book. Rather a key word or phrase is selected. The index consists of an ordered listing of key words and the page number where the key word can be found.

When you want to find a particular topic, you search the index for the key word. The index then directs you to the correct page in the book.

The same idea can be applied to data base files. Instead of copying the entire record, only the sort key and record number are copied into the index file. This means that the index for a file can be much smaller than the original file. When you want to list the file, the program simply refers to the order of the record numbers as stored in the index file.

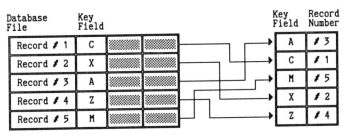

The illustration shows that when an index is prepared, only the key information and the record number of each record is copied to the new file. An index file operates much like an index in a book. It tells you on what page certain topics are discussed. An index file in *dBASE III Plus* tells you what record contains what key information.

Like the index of a book, an index file cannot be used without the data base file it is related to. This is very different from a sorted file, which is an exact duplicate of the original data base file and can be used independently of the original file.

In *dBASE III Plus* a sorted file has a .DBF extension indicating that it can be accessed with the USE command like any other .DBF file. Index files are given an .NDX extension. This tells you that you must use the .NDX file in conjunction with a .DBF file, not by itself.

Index files raise the idea that dBASE III Plus can produce several different types of files. The basic data file that you have been working with up to now carries a .DBF extension. As you proceed with dBASE III Plus you will see that there are a number of other specialized file types created by dBASE III Plus.

Indexing has a number of advantages over sorting; however, the differences, advantages, and weaknesses of sorting and indexing are discussed in detail later in this chapter. For now, you need to learn how index files are created and used.

CREATING AN INDEX FILE

Index files are created with the INDEX command. Like SORT, INDEX requires two pieces of information: the indexing key and the name of the index file to be created.

As with SORT, LOGICAL and MEMO fields cannot be used as an index key expression.

The first example entered in the SORT section was a sorting by payee. You can duplicate the task by entering the following INDEX command. Enter

INDEX ON payto TO payorder<return>

The program displays

```
100% indexed        8 Records indexed
```

Enter

LIST payto<return>

The program displays

```
7   BRITZ PRINTING
1   CROW CANYON LUMBER
8   GIFT STORE
3   GREEN ACRES FURN
4   INSTANT PRINTING
5   PG&E
6   PACIFIC BELL
2   SEARS
```

There are several significant points of difference between the results of an INDEX and a SORT. Look at the record numbers. Notice that the records maintain the same numbers that they had before the index, but they are now arranged so that the payees are in alphabetical order. Furthermore, note that it was not necessary to change files in order to view the results of the index. The INDEX command had a direct, immediate effect on the EXPENSES file.

When an INDEX command is issued, the file that is created is not considered a data base file. Enter

DIR *.ndx<return>

The program lists the file PAYORDER.NDX. *dBASE III Plus* attaches an .NDX extension to the filename to distinguish it from data base files (with .DBF extensions). The index file does not work alone but in conjunction with a data base file.

Because index files are assigned a different file extension (.NDX) than data base files (.DBF), it is possible to create an index file with the same name as a data base file. For example, if the file you were indexing is called EXPENSES, you could create an index file called EXPENSES with the following command: INDEX ON date TO expenses.

USING AN INDEX FILE

Once you have created an index file with the INDEX ON command the file can be opened and closed. When the index file is open, the data base acts as if it had been sorted. When the index file is closed, the data base returns to its original order. For example, to close the PAYORDER index file, enter

CLOSE INDEX< return >

Now list the payees by entering

LIST payto< return >

The program displays

```
Record#  payto
      1  CROW CANYON LUMBER
      2  SEARS
      3  GREEN ACRES FURN
      4  INSTANT PRINTING
      5  PG&E
      6  PACIFIC BELL
      7  BRITZ PRINTING
      8  GIFT STORE
```

The file reverts to the original order in which the records were entered. To open the index file, enter

SET INDEX TO payorder< return >

Now list the payees by entering

LIST payto< return >

The records now appear in the indexed order. Index files can be confusing at first. *dBASE III Plus* provides a command that helps the user to keep track of what files (data base and index) are open at any given moment. Enter

DISPLAY STATUS< return >

dBASE III Plus displays the following:

```
Currently Selected Database:
Select area:  1, Database in Use: C:expenses.dbf   Alias: EXPENSES
    Master index file:  C:payorder.ndx  Key: payto
         Memo file:   C:expenses.dbt
File search path:
Default disk drive: C:
Print destination:  PRN:
Margin =    Ø
Current work area =    1
Press any key to continue...

While dBASE III displays
Currently selected database:
Select area -  1, Database in use: B:expenses.dbf   Alias - EXPENSES
    Index file: B:payorder.ndx  key - payto
```

This screen shows that the EXPENSES file is open and that the PAYORDER index file is also open. In addition, it shows that the PAYORDER file uses the PAYTO field as the index key. When you have finished viewing the display, enter

<Esc>

dBASE III Plus displays the message, ***INTERRUPTED*** when you enter <Esc> and cancels the message.

Below is a review of the commands involved in indexing a file:

1. **INDEX ON (key expression) TO (index file name).** This command creates an index file for a data base file based on a key expression. The command creates a file with an .NDX extension. When the file is created, it immediately is put in use.

2. **CLOSE INDEX.** This command closes an index file but does not affect the status of the data base file. When the index is closed, *dBASE III Plus* will display the records in numeric order by record number.

3. **SET INDEX TO (index file name).** This command activates an index file. Remember that the data base file must already be open when you enter this command. SET INDEX TO has no meaning unless a data base is already in use.

Exercise 1   Suppose you wanted to index the file on budget category. What command would you enter? Use CATORDER as the name of the index file. The correct command can be found at the end of the chapter. Confirm that you have correctly indexed the file by entering

LIST cat<return>

The records list in category order.

Exercise 2   Create two more index files: AMTORDER indexed on amount and DATEORD indexed on date. You can find the correct commands at the end of the chapter.

CHANGING INDEX FILES

Now that you have created more than one index file, you can switch back and forth by using the SET INDEX TO command. Enter

> **SET INDEX TO payorder**< return >
> **LIST**<rcturn >

The file lists in payee order. Change the order to amount by entering

> **SET INDEX TO amtorder**< return >
> **LIST** <return >

The file is now ordered by the AMOUNT field.

TOP AND BOTTOM IN INDEXED FIELDS

The meaning of TOP and BOTTOM changes when a file is indexed. For example, in a nonindex file the TOP is the same as record no. 1. When an index is active the top of the file is the first record in the index order. The BOTTOM of the file is the last record in the index order, not necessarily the last record entered into the file. Enter

> **BROWSE**< return >
> **[CTRL/Home]**
> **t**

The screen displays the records in the index order. This means that the first record in the file is record no. 8 because its AMOUNT field contains the smallest value. Enter

> **[CTRL/Home]**
> **b**

The cursor moves to record no. 3, which contains the largest value in the AMOUNT field. Exit the BROWSE mode by entering

> **< Esc >**

THE ADVANTAGES OF INDEXING: UPDATING

At first glance the INDEX and SORT commands appear to be about the same. However, there are some crucial differences between them. To understand when to use one or the other, you will need to explore some of the advantages offered by indexing.

When a file is sorted, *dBASE III Plus* creates a copy of the file that is physically ordered according to the key field or fields. But what happens when you add new records to that file? Or when you change the data in some of the existing records?

The answer is that the sorted file has no way of updating the order of the file when additions or changes are made. The only way to get a correctly ordered file is to perform another SORT. This means that you create another new file each time a new record is entered, or an old record is revised (assuming the revision affects the index order).

The main disadvantage of SORT in this case is that it places two burdens on the user. First, you must remember to create the new sorted file; second, you must keep track of which file contains the latest version of the data base. While these burdens are not insuperable, the index system has a very different way of handling updates.

At this moment, the EXPENSES file is indexed on the AMOUNT field. Enter a new record:

> **APPEND** < return >
> **020585**
> **120** < return >
> **GREEN ACRES FURN** < return >
> **CHAIRS** < return >
> **175** < return >
> < return >
> < return >
> **Y**
> < Esc >

The record you entered was record no. 9. Enter

> **LIST date,payto,amount** < return >

The program displays

```
Record#   DATE      PAYTO                AMOUNT
     8   02/02/85  GIFT STORE              5.94
     2   01/10/85  SEARS                  17.95
     6   01/25/85  PACIFIC BELL           44.28
     4   01/17/85  INSTANT PRINTING       59.50
     5   01/21/85  PG&E                   60.60
     7   01/30/85  BRITZ PRINTING         68.32
     1   01/02/85  CROW CANYON LUMBER     68.40
     9   02/05/85  GREEN ACRES FURN      175.00
     3   01/15/85  GREEN ACRES FURN      264.68
```

Notice that without having to enter any additional command, *dBASE III Plus* placed the new record in its proper position in the file index.

Suppose a record is changed that was already part of the data base file. Enter

> **EDIT 7** < return >

Change the amount by entering

```
<down arrow> (4 times)
47.95<return>
[CTRL/End]
```

List the records again to see how the order affected the change in data:

```
LIST date,payto,amount<return>
```

The program displays

```
Record#  DATE      PAYTO               AMOUNT
     8   02/02/85  GIFT STORE            5.94
     2   01/10/85  SEARS                17.95
     6   01/25/85  PACIFIC BELL         44.28
     7   01/30/85  BRITZ PRINTING       47.95
     4   01/17/85  INSTANT PRINTING     59.50
     5   01/21/85  PG&E                 60.60
     1   01/02/85  CROW CANYON LUMBER   68.40
     9   02/05/85  GREEN ACRES FURN    175.00
     3   01/15/85  GREEN ACRES FURN    264.68
```

The position of record no. 7 has now changed in the file listing so that the new amount falls into step correctly.

One of the major advantages of indexing is that changes made when an index file is open immediately update the index file. Not only is this simpler than having to resort the file, it is considerably faster. *dBASE III Plus* can update an index file in a tiny fraction of the time it takes to sort or index an entire file.

The key to updating is to make sure that the index file you want to update is active whenever you use the APPEND, EDIT, CHANGE, or BROWSE commands to add new records or update existing records.

UPDATING MULTIPLE INDEX FILES

In the previous example, you saw that the active index file was immediately updated as records were added or changed in the data base file. The benefit is twofold:

1. Updating takes place immediately and automatically.
2. The amount of time required to maintain an accurate order is almost nil compared with the time it takes to reindex a file.

Indexing offers a much more accurate way of maintaining ordered files than is available in programs that perform physical sorts only.

However, you might have wondered about the effect the changes may have on the other index files you created: CATORDER, PAYORDER, and DATEORD. To see if these files are still accurate, you need to activate the index files. Enter

SET INDEX TO payorder < return >
LIST payto < return >

The program lists

```
7  BRITZ PRINTING
1  CROW CANYON LUMBER
8  GIFT STORE
3  GREEN ACRES FURN
4  INSTANT PRINTING
5  PG&E
6  PACIFIC BELL
2  SEARS
```

Where is record no. 9 placed? The fact is that record no. 9 does not even appear in the listing.

The problem encountered is a result of the fact that when PAYORDER was created, there were only eight records in the data base file. Record no. 9 was added when the PAYORDER index file was not active; thus PAYORDER displays only those records that were in the data base file at the time the index file was created.

dBASE III Plus offers a solution to this problem. The program allows you to activate more than one index file at a time so that updates and additions will be reflected in several index files. The limit on open index files is 7 for any one data base file.

The technique involved is a modification of the SET INDEX TO command. Enter

SET INDEX TO catorder,payorder,amtorder,dateord < return >

With so many index files open, what order are the records going to be listed in? *dBASE III Plus* considers the first index file in the list as the *master* index; it controls the sequence in which the records will be listed.

The other index files are open strictly for the purpose of receiving updated information for new or altered records. Now that all the files have been opened, you can make sure that they all take into account the latest changes by entering

REINDEX < return >

The screen displays

```
Rebuilding index - C:CATORDER.ndx
    100% indexed              9 Records indexed
Rebuilding index - C:PAYORDER.ndx
    100% indexed              9 Records indexed
Rebuilding index - C:AMTORDER.ndx
    100% indexed              9 Records indexed
Rebuilding index - C:DATEORD.ndx
    100% indexed              9 Records indexed
```

The display shows that now all the index files contain the same number of records. Now check the order of the files. Enter

> **LIST cat < return >**

The nine records list in correct order for category. To check the data order, first activate DATEORD as the master index file. Enter

> **SET INDEX TO dateord < return >**
> **LIST date < return >**

This display is also accurate.

Exercise 3   Enter the commands necessary to check the accuracy of the PAYORDER index file. The correct commands are at the end of the chapter.

USING DATA AND INDEX FILES

To facilitate the use of index files with data base files, *dBASE III Plus* allows you to open the index files and the data base file to which they are related in a single command. The command is a modification of the USE command. Enter

> **USE expenses INDEX payorder,catorder,amtorder,dateord < return >**

What effect has this command had?

The USE portion of the command placed the data base file EXPENSES in use. In addition, the record pointer was positioned to the first record in the file.

The INDEX portion of the file opened four index files to receive updates when any changes or additions are made to the data base file. The first file in the index file list, PAYORDER, is designated the master index file, meaning that records in the file will be sequenced according to the contents of the PAYTO field.

Is there any difference between the USE/INDEX command and the SET INDEX TO command? The commands are quite close in operation; however, one small but potentially significant difference does exist. Look at the two command sequences below:

Method 1

USE expenses INDEX payorder

Method 2

USE expenses
SET INDEX TO payorder

The two methods have the exact same effect on the program. Method 1 is probably the better method since it requires less typing. Close all the index files by entering

CLOSE INDEX< return >

DESCENDING INDEXES

One of the limitations of the INDEX command is that it sequences data in ascending order, while the SORT command is limited to using field names as keys. The INDEX command accepts any valid *dBASE III Plus* expression including numeric, chronological, and character expressions. For example, even though the INDEX command does not sequence in a descending order, you can create a key expression that will approximate the effect of a descending sort. Enter

LIST amount*–1 < return >

The listing looks like this:

```
Record#  AMOUNT*-1
    1      -68.40
    2      -17.95
    3     -264.68
    4      -59.50
    5      -60.60
    6      -44.28
    7      -47.95
    8       -5.94
    9     -175.00
```

In the list above the largest number is the one closest to zero, – 5.94, while the smallest number is – 264.68. Since INDEX always sequences in ascending order, from smallest to largest, an index of these amounts would give the same sequence as a descending sort of the actual values.

Amount*–1 is a numeric expression that qualifies to be used with the INDEX command. Enter

INDEX ON amount*–1 TO descend< return >
LIST amount< return >

The program displays

```
Record#  AMOUNT
    3     264.68
    9     175.00
    1      68.40
    5      60.60
    4      59.50
    7      47.95
    6      44.28
    2      17.95
    8       5.94
```

The effect is that the records appear in descending order.

A similar trick can be applied to a CHARACTER field in order to approximate a descending order. Suppose you want to list the payees in descending alphabetical order. Since *dBASE III Plus* will not allow you to multiply a character entry by negative 1, there is a way to treat characters as numbers using the ASCII code. (In Chapter 4 you learned about the ASCII code, which assigns numeric values to text characters.) *dBASE III Plus* has a special function, ASC(), that returns the ASCII numeric value for the first letter of a character string. Enter

> LIST ASC(payto) < return >

dBASE III Plus lists the numeric ASCII values of the first letter in the PAYTO field. Since these are numeric values, they can be multiplied by negative 1. Enter

> INDEX ON ASC(payto)*–1 TO descend1 < return >
> LIST payto < return >

The payees list in descending alphabetical order. Note that this technique only approximates a descending sort since only the first letter of each entry was used.

DATE fields pose another problem for descending indexing. Once again, a tricky conversion to numeric values can approximate the descending sort. In Chapter 4, you learned that *dBASE III Plus* provides special functions that convert DATE fields into numeric values for the year, month, and day. If you make the assumption that each year contains 365.25 days and each month contains 30.5 days, you could work out a numeric expression that evaluates each date as a single numeric value. Then you could multiply that value by negative 1 and achieve a descending order by dates. Enter

> INDEX ON (YEAR(date)*365.25+MONTH(date)*30.5+DAY(date))*–1 TO
>   descdate < return >
> LIST date < return >

The dates are listed in descending order. This expression may seem to be troublesome to design and implement. However, the advantages of indexing and the subsequent automatic updating of the index file as records are added and updated may in some circumstances far outweigh the complexity of the formula.

MULTIPLE FIELD INDEX FILES

As with the SORT command, the potential to create multilevel index files exists. However, because the INDEX command works with a single expression (as opposed to SORT, which uses a field list), it is necessary to learn the special techniques required to create multilevel index files.

The technique is quite simple if all the values to be included in the index key are character data. In this case the + is used to join the character items into a single expression. The + performs an operation called *concatenation,* the joining of character items to form a single string. The + has a different meaning when used with character items than it does with numeric items, where it indicates the arithmetic operation of addition.

As an illustration of concatenation, enter the following command (this command will index the file by payee and within payee, item):

```
INDEX ON payto+item TO string<return>
LIST payto,item<return>
```

The file is listed by payee. In the case of GREEN ACRES FURN, the two records for that payee are listed in order of the item field.

COMBINING FIELD TYPE

Using fields of different types makes indexing more complex. To create a single-key expression from fields of various types you need to convert the fields to a common data type. That usually means converting all the data to character-type data.

Suppose you wanted to index the data base file according to budget category and within that category, index by date. You must use special functions to convert both the category (NUMERIC field) and the date (DATE field) to characters. *dBASE III Plus* provides the STR() function that converts numeric values into character strings. The STR() function requires three items—STR(numeric value, length, and decimals):

1. **Numeric Value.** The numeric value can be the name of a field or any valid *dBASE III Plus* numeric expression.
2. **Length.** This is a number that specifies the length of the character string that will be created when the numeric value is converted.
3. **Decimals.** This is a number that specifies the number of decimal places (if any) to be included in the character string. If no number is entered, zero decimal places will be used.

The date can be converted to characters by using the DTOC() function. Enter the following:

```
INDEX ON STR(cat,3)+DTOC(date) TO string1<return>
LIST cat,date<return>
```

The command illustrated above works correctly for dates that occur in the same year. If the data base file contains dates from several years, the DTOC() function will not correctly index those dates. (See the section on DATE fields in Chapter 1.)

To make sure that dates from several years are correctly ordered, you must rearrange the parts of the date so that they are concatenated in year, month, and day order. The command below is an example of an INDEX command that correctly sequences the dates from different years.

Note that the command shown below is too large to be printed on a single line in this text. You can, however, enter this long command on a single line in dBASE III Plus. Make sure that you press < return > only at the end of the entire command.

> **INDEX ON**
> **STR(cat,3)+STR(YEAR(date),4)+STR(MONTH(date),2)+STR(DAY(date),2)**
> **TO catdate < return >**

INDEXING NUMERIC FIELDS

The ability of the INDEX command to operate based on the value of *dBASE III Plus* expressions also affects indexing done on NUMERIC fields. When you index on a single NUMERIC field, you can simply enter the field name. However, when you want to index on several NUMERIC fields, it is easy to make a mistake. Suppose you wanted to index on CATEGORY and subindex on AMOUNT. Enter

> **INDEX ON cat+amount TO numbers < return >**
> **LIST cat,amount < return >**

The screen displays

```
Record#    cat amount
     8     140     5.94
     2     140    17.95
     6     130    44.28
     1     110    68.40
     7     140    47.95
     5     130    60.60
     4     140    59.50
     9     120   175.00
     3     120   264.68
```

The program seems to have completely misunderstood the indexing order it was supposed to use. Remember that the expression you entered as the key was CAT+AMOUNT. Enter

> **LIST cat+amount,cat,amount < return >**

The program displays

```
Record#  cat+amount    cat amount
     8      145.94      140     5.94
     2      157.95      140    17.95
     6      174.28      130    44.28
     1      178.40      110    68.40
     7      187.95      140    47.95
     5      190.60      130    60.60
     4      199.50      140    59.50
     9      295.00      120   175.00
     3      384.68      120   264.68
```

You can see that the order of the records was determined by numeric value of the CAT field added to the AMOUNT field. The + indicates concatenation only when it is used with character data. When + is used with numeric data, addition is performed. In order to get the correct sequencing, enter

INDEX ON STR(cat,3)+STR(amount,6,2) TO numbers1 < return >
LIST cat,amount < return >

This time the records appear in the correct logical sequence.

CAPITALIZATION

The *dBASE III Plus* function UPPER() provides a simple means of overcoming indexing problems caused by inconsistent case entry of data. Enter

INDEX ON UPPER(payto) TO CAPS < return >

LIMITS ON INDEX KEYS

dBASE III Plus limits the INDEX command to key expressions that do not exceed 100 characters. The size of the INDEX expression is determined by the total of all the fields and functions used in the expression. For example, INDEX ON payto+item TO pays creates a key expression that is 40 characters (payto=20+item=20) in length.

The next chapter deals with how sorting and indexing are implemented in the *dBASE III Plus* ASSIST mode. To close all open index and data files, a CLOSE DATABASE command can be issued. When this command is entered, all open index files are automatically closed as well. Enter

CLOSE DATABASE < return >

SUMMARY

This chapter discussed methods by which *dBASE III Plus* could change the sequence of records in a data base file.

Differences between SORT and Index

The primary difference between the SORT and INDEX commands concerns the type of files generated by each command. SORT produces data base (.DBF) files, while INDEX produces index (.NDX) files. The data base file produced by the SORT command is capable of functioning as a full data base file on its own with no reference to the original file from which it was created. An index file is dependent on the original data base file and cannot be used unless the data base file is open.

The advantages of the SORT command are that it can perform mutlilevel sorts on combinations of DATE fields, NUMERIC fields, and characters, in ascending or descending order. SORT selects records while sorting, if a FOR clause is added.

The disadvantages of SORT are that because each SORT creates an independent data base file, there is no facility by which new or updated records can be automatically sequenced. SORT is slower than INDEX because it copies all the data in the original data base file.

The advantages of INDEX are that it is faster than SORT because it copies only the key information instead of the entire data base. Index files also take up less disk space. In addition, multiple index files can relate to a single data base file, and index files can operate on expressions composed of field names, functions, and operators. This last provides a greater variety in the way that index keys are created.

Index files can be automatically updated for new or altered records without having to reindex the entire file. Up to seven index files for a given data base file can be updated at one time.

The disadvantages of INDEX are that it does not offer a direct method of performing descending sequencing. It cannot select records and the entire data base file is indexed.

INDEX Commands

REINDEX is used to update index files.

SET INDEX TO opens index files.

CLOSE INDEX closes all open index files.

USE (file) INDEX (file list) opens a data base file and up to seven index files.

Other Topics

The INSERT command allows the user to enter records manually into specific positions within the data base file. INSERT adds one record at a time to the data file.

Functions

This chapter introduced a number of new functions:

ASC()—returns a numeric value equal to the ASCII code value for the first character in a text string.

STR()—returns a character string from a numeric value.

+—concatenates strings.

ANSWER KEY

Exercise 1

INDEX ON cat TO catorder < return >

Exercise 2

INDEX ON amount TO amtorder < return >
INDEX ON date TO dateord < return >

Exercise 3

SET INDEX TO payorder < return >
LIST payto < return >

6

HOUSEKEEPING: SEARCHING

FOR INDIVIDUAL RECORDS

THIS CHAPTER EXPLAINS THE TECHNIQUES and commands used in *dBASE III Plus* to maintain your data bases. The tasks include searching for individual records, deleting unneeded records, erasing files, and copying files, as well as ancillary tasks required to maintain control over the data base system.

The chapter also covers commands found in *dBASE III Plus* that help the user keep track of files that are logically related.

In Chapter 4 you learned how to select groups of records from a data base file using some logical criterion. In the first section below you will learn how to locate individual records stored in a file, and what the techniques are that *dBASE III Plus* uses to search those files. The following sections point out the strengths and weaknesses of each technique used.

To begin, *dBASE III Plus* should be loaded into the computer. Make sure that you have exited the ASSIST mode by entering <Esc>.

LOCATE

The LOCATE command positions the pointer to a specific record in the data base file, through use of a logical criterion. The LOCATE command operates with a

FOR clause. Unlike the other commands that use the FOR clause (the FOR clause is usually an option), LOCATE requires a FOR clause each time it is used.

To see how this command works, place the EXPENSES file in use by entering

USE expenses< return >

Suppose you wanted to find the record or records dated 01/30/85. You could use the LOCATE command to search the data base file for as many records as fit that criterion. Remember that you need to use a special date function to avoid a type mismatch error. Enter

LOCATE FOR DTOC(date)="01/30/85"< return >

The *dBASE III Plus* function CTOD(), character to date, can also be used to create an expression with the same meaning as DTOC(date)="01/30/85". For example, LOCATE FOR date=CTOD("01/30/85") has the exact same effect as the previous LOCATE command. For most purposes, the forms are interchangeable.

dBASE III Plus returns the number of the first record in the data base file for which the expression DTOC(date)="01/30/85" is true. When the record is found, the LOCATE command automatically terminates. In this example, the program displays Record=7.

The following has been accomplished:

1. The number of the first record that contains 01/30/85 is displayed. The default scope for the LOCATE command is ALL. The LOCATE command always begins searching at the top of the file regardless of any previous commands that might have affected the position of the pointer.
2. The LOCATE command always affects the position of the pointer; thus the pointer has been positioned to the record that contains the correct date.

Now that the pointer has been positioned to the correct record you can proceed to issue any position-specific commands such as EDIT or DISPLAY. Enter

DISPLAY <return>

The contents of record no. 7 are displayed. Enter

EDIT <return>

Record no. 7 is placed in the EDIT mode. To return to the DOT PROMPT, enter

<Esc>

The LOCATE command can operate on any valid *dBASE III Plus* expression. For example, you can locate based on other operators besides equal to. Enter

LOCATE FOR amount > 200 < return >

The command finds record no. 3.

The LOCATE command allows you to enter compound expressions that contain logical connectives. For example, you might want to search the data base file for phone bills that are over one hundred dollars. Enter

LOCATE FOR payto="PACIFIC BELL".and.amount>100<return>

The program displays the message End of LOCATE scope. This means that the program has searched all the records within the scope of the LOCATE command and failed to find any records that fit the criterion. Since the default scope of the LOCATE command is ALL, you can infer from the message that no such record has been entered into the data base file.

When using the LOCATE command with the default scope (ALL), the End of LOCATE scope message is synonymous with the end of the file.

THE CONTINUE COMMAND

What happens if more than one record in the file qualifies under the search criterion? The CONTINUE command is provided to continue the search initiated with the LOCATE command. To use CONTINUE, the user must first enter a LOCATE command. Enter

LOCATE FOR cat=120<return>

The first record found is record no. 3. To continue the search from that point, enter

CONTINUE<return>

The program stops at record no. 9. Enter

CONTINUE<return>

This time the End of LOCATE scope message appears, indicating that the end of the file has been reached.

The CONTINUE command always continues the search begun by the last previous LOCATE command. For example, you could change the position of the pointer by entering a GOTO command.

Enter

5<return>

When entering a number, in this case 5, GOTO is implicit.

Now enter

CONTINUE<return>

The pointer is positioned to record no. 9 again.

The search criterion established with the LOCATE command will remain active until

1. Another LOCATE command is entered.
2. The data base file is closed.

Enter

USE expenses < return >
CONTINUE < return >

Why does the program display the message CONTINUE without LOCATE? Remember that the USE command performs two actions. First, it closes any data base file that is open. Second, it opens the specified file. This is true even if the file specified for opening is the same file that is open at the time the command is entered. By entering the USE command, you told *dBASE III Plus* to close the EXPENSES file and, in the process, erase the search criterion established by the LOCATE command.

To return to the DOT PROMPT, enter

< Esc >

Exercise 1   Use the LOCATE command to find the records, if any, that are dated 02/02/85.

Exercise 2   Use the LOCATE command to find the record or records that contain the word "CAN" in the ITEM field. Note that the word does not have to be the first word in the field. The answers can be found at the end of the chapter.

THE FIND COMMAND

dBASE III Plus has a second command called FIND that can be used to find individual records. FIND differs from LOCATE in the following ways:

1. FIND will operate only when an index file is active. If you attempt to use FIND when no index file is open, the program will display an error message: Database is not indexed.
2. FIND will search only for records based on the key expression used to create the index file.
3. FIND will search for "equal to" relationships only. You cannot use FIND to locate records based on other relational operators such as greater than or less than.

To see how FIND works, enter

FIND SEARS < return >

Surprised at the results? Remember that FIND will not operate unless a data base file is active. To continue, enter

< Esc >

If you wanted to search for SEARS, you would have to use an index whose key expression was PAYTO. The PAYORDER.NDX file qualifies. Enter

SET INDEX TO payorder < return >

If you are not sure what key expression was used to create an index file, use the DISPLAY STATUS command to list the index file.

Now you can proceed to search for the record that contains SEARS. Enter

FIND SEARS < return >

The DOT PROMPT appears once again. What has happened? Enter

DISPLAY < return >

Record no. 2 is displayed. You can see that it contains SEARS as the payee.

The FIND command differs from LOCATE in several respects. The two most important ones are listed below:

1. The FIND command does not accept an expression as a criterion. You simply enter the characters that you want to search for. Thus you do not have to specify the field name to search. Also, the FIND command violates the rule that text literals must be delimited; no quotation marks are used with the FIND command.

2. When the FIND command locates a match, it does not display the record number or anything else for that matter (although the status line shows the new pointer position).

Enter the following to see what happens if the FIND command cannot find the records that match the criterion:

FIND PENNYS

dBASE III Plus displays the message No FIND. Remember that when you use the FIND command, you see a message only when the search has not been successful. When the match is found, no message is displayed.

You can search for a more general criterion by entering a few characters. Enter

FIND P < return >
DISPLAY < return >

Record no. 5 appears. This is not the only record in the file that begins with P, just the first record found. To continue the search, enter

> **CONTINUE** < return >
> **DISPLAY**

The program displays record no. 2 because the last LOCATE command entered was the one in Exercise 2. If you did not do Exercise 2, your results may differ. The CONTINUE command is not related to the FIND command in any way.

How can you get the next match when you use the FIND command if CONTINUE does not work? The answer is that there is no command that actually continues a FIND. FIND always stops at the first record that qualifies. But this is not as much a disadvantage as it appears to be.

Remember that FIND works only with indexed data base files. The searches made with the FIND command are limited to the data used as the index key. What this implies is that when you find the first record that qualifies, any other records that match will immediately follow the qualifying record.

Enter the FIND command again to search for records whose payees begin with P. Enter

> **FIND P** < return >
> **DISPLAY payto** < return >

Now move to the next record in the index order by entering

> **SKIP** < return >
> **DISPLAY payto** < return >

The payee in this record also begins with P. When you search an indexed file, the techniques for finding the next match are very different from when you search a file that has not been indexed.

THE WHILE CLAUSE

dBASE III Plus provides a clause designed to take advantage of the fact that index files group related records together. This is the WHILE clause. Like FOR, WHILE is attached to a command like LIST or DISPLAY and modifies the way it operates. Look at the following command:

LIST WHILE payto="P"

The WHILE clause is followed by a *dBASE III Plus* expression similar to the expression used with a FOR clause (i.e., one that will evaluate either true or false). The difference is that a WHILE clause tells the program to process records until the expression is false. When the expression is false, the command is automatically terminated. The WHILE clause is used to test a group of records, beginning with the active record, to see if they contain the same data.

The WHILE clause can be used with any data base file. However, it is more logical to use this clause with files that are indexed or sorted. In indexed or sorted files, records that have the same or similar data have already been grouped together.

The WHILE clause is logically related to the use of the FIND command. For example, to find all the records that have a payee that begins with the letter P, you would perform two actions:

1. Use the FIND command to position the pointer to the first record that qualifies.
2. Use a LIST command with a WHILE clause to list the adjacent records for which the expression is still true.

First, enter the FIND command:

FIND P<return>

Now enter the LIST command with a WHILE clause:

LIST payto WHILE payto="P"<return>

The program lists

```
Record#  payto
      5  PG&E
      6  PACIFIC BELL
```

The combination of the two commands locates and displays the correct records.

THE ADVANTAGES OF FIND

In the previous section, you may have questioned what advantage the FIND command offers, because the list obtained above could also have been generated using a LIST FOR command. Enter

LIST payto FOR payto="P"<return>

The results are exactly the same as the previous method, and you needed only one command to accomplish the task. Why bother to use FIND? What possible advantage could it have? The answer depends on the size of the data base file with which you are working. To understand why the size of the file is significant, you need to examine how the commands actually work.

When you enter a command such as LIST FOR or LOCATE FOR, the program automatically returns the pointer to the first record in the file. The program then evaluates the record according to the expression entered in the command. If the record is evaluated as true, it is processed. If it is false, the program skips to the next record and repeats the test. This process continues until the end of the file is encountered (i.e., there are no more records to test).

The number of tests performed is proportional to the size of the file. If the file contains 1000 records, then 1000 records must be tested. This is true even if none of the records in the file qualifies. In order to determine if the records qualify, *dBASE III Plus* must still examine each record.

This type of operation is called a *sequential search*. The term *sequential* refers to the fact that each record, beginning with the top of the file, must be tested in order to determine its qualifications. The amount of time needed to perform a sequential search increases in proportion to the number of records in the file. Therefore the more records you put into the file, the longer the processing time will be.

The FIND command works only when an index file is open; thus a search is not considered sequential. When a FIND command is entered, the program searches the index file to find a match rather than the data base file.

The new user may question what advantage is to be gained by searching the index file instead of the data base file. Obviously the index file must contain one entry for each record in the data base. One would assume, then, that the FIND command still has to perform just as many tests as the LIST FOR command, taking just as much time. The difference is, however, that FIND performs a binary search, not a sequential search. A binary search has several advantages to offer.

To illustrate a binary search, imagine that you are playing a number-guessing game. For example, you might pick a number from 1 to 100 and ask someone to try to guess the number you picked. How many guesses should it take the player to find the correct number?

Searching sequentially, the person would begin with 1, and proceed through the numbers until the match was made. By this method, the number of guesses would vary between 1 and 100. However, there is a more clever way to play this game. If the player were to begin with a guess of 50, and then know if the guess was either too high or too low, she could immediately eliminate half the numbers with a single guess. Then the next guess would halve the remaining 50 numbers. Because this method works by dividing the number by two each time, it is called a *binary* search.

Look at the list below. On the left are numbers, and on the right are the respective powers of two. The number 100 would fall between the sixth and seventh powers of two. Mathematics tells us that this means that a player can always guess the right number in seven tries.

1	2
2	4
3	8
4	16

5	32
6	64
7	128
8	256
9	512
10	1024
11	2048
12	4096

The list also shows that if the game is increased from 1 to 1000, a player will still find the correct number in 10 guesses.

This method greatly reduces the amount of time it takes to find the answer. There is one catch to a binary search. You must assume that the information that you are searching is already ordered. Thus to perform high speed searches, you must have the records in a data file in the proper order. When a file is indexed, the index file is created in such a manner that a binary-type search of the index file is possible.

The FIND command searches the index file for the number of the matching record. Then it performs a GOTO record number operation in the data base file. The result is that the FIND command can locate a specific record in a large data base file in a short period of time. The amount of time it takes to search records does not increase significantly as the data base file grows in size.

Look at the two sets of commands below:

Sequential	**Rapid Binary Search**
USE expenses	USE expenses INDEX payorder
LIST FOR payto="P"	FIND P
	LIST WHILE payto="P"

Both sets of commands list the same records. The difference is that the set of commands on the right executes at a high rate of speed, regardless of the size of the data base file. The method on the left slows down as the data base file increases in size. Thus another important advantage of index files is that they make rapid access to data possible where such access would have been impossible with a file that was merely sorted. Remember that the FIND command cannot act on sorted data base files, only on an index (.NDX) file.

In small data base files like the one used in these examples, it is hard to see the difference between SORT and INDEX. However, as the data base files increase in size, the ability to perform binary searches is crucial to making programs perform with the speed necessary for business applications. In the programming section of this book you will learn how to take advantage of index files to improve the speed of your applications.

FINDING RECORDS IN BROWSE

One *dBASE III Plus* command that takes direct advantage of the index file is the BROWSE command. In Chapter 3 you learned about the BROWSE command and its special menu of BROWSE subcommands. When BROWSE is used with a file that is indexed, *dBASE III Plus* adds an additional subcommand to the BROWSE menu called FIND. The subcommand is used to position the pointer to selected records within the BROWSE mode.

The addition of this command provides a way to locate and edit records in a single mode. The combination of BROWSE with an index file is ideal for making updates to existing records that may be scattered within a large data base file. Because the FIND subcommand operates on index files, it takes advantage of the high-speed search ability of *dBASE III Plus*.

THE FIND SUBCOMMAND

To use the FIND subcommand within BROWSE, you must open a data base file with an index file. Enter

USE expenses INDEX amtorder< return >

Enter the BROWSE mode by entering

BROWSE < return >

Access the BROWSE menu bar by entering

[F10]

As illustrated below, the sixth command on the menu bar is FIND:

```
     Bottom      Top      Lock      Record No.      Freeze      Find 12:14:41 am
     DATE─── CAT─ PAYTO─────────────── ITEM──────────── AMOUNT COMMENTS
     02/02/85    140 GIFT STORE         GROUND HOG DAY CARDS   5.94 memo
     01/10/85    140 SEARS              TRASH CAN             17.95 memo
     01/25/85    130 PACIFIC BELL       INSTALL TELE          44.28 memo
     01/30/85    140 BRITZ PRINTING     BUSINESS CARDS        47.95 memo
     01/17/85    140 INSTANT PRINTING   ENVELOPES             59.50 memo
     01/21/85    130 PG&E               TURN ON ELEC          60.60 memo
     01/02/85    110 CROW CANYON LUMBER 10 2 BY 4             68.40 memo
     02/05/85    120 GREEN ACRES FURN   CHAIRS               175.00 memo
     01/15/85    120 GREEN ACRES FURN   DESKS                264.68 memo
```

To select the FIND option, the arrow key is used to position the highlight to FIND. Note that, unlike the other commands on this menu, the function cannot be accessed by entering the first letter of the command. The reason is that entering the letter f would select FREEZE, not FIND. To select the FIND command, enter

< right arrow > (5 times)
< return >

dBASE III Plus now allows you to enter the characters you want to search for. Enter

44<return>

The entry has no effect because there is no amount that is equal to exactly $44.00. Remember that the current index file, AMTORDER, is based on the contents of the AMOUNT field. When a record cannot be found, *dBASE III Plus* clears the entry area and waits for you to reenter the criterion. This time, enter the exact amount that you are looking for.

44.28<return>

The highlight moves to record no. 6. To review, the FIND subcommand has the following limitations:

1. You can search only for data that is included in the index key of the active master index file.

2. You can search only for an "equal to" relationship. If the field indexed is numeric, the value must match the exact numeric value of the number for which you are searching. It is not necessary to enter trailing zeros because they have no numeric significance. For example, record no. 9 contains the amount 175.00. You can find that record by searching for 175 because the .00 has no mathematical significance. Record no. 5 contains 60.60. That record could be located by entering 60.6.

When you are using BROWSE with an index file, another important issue arises. BROWSE allows you to make alterations to any of the fields in the file. What would happen if you altered the contents of the field upon which the index order was based? To find out, return to the top of the file by entering

[F10]
t

Move to the AMOUNT field by entering

<return> (4 times)

Enter a new value in the AMOUNT field that is $100 more than the current value. Enter

105.94<return>

Because of the change you have just made, the screen display is not correctly arranged according to amount. Enter

<down arrow>

When you instruct *dBASE III Plus* to move to the next record, it automatically places the altered record in the correct position in the data base file, using the INDEX expression. The highlight moves not to record no. 2, which is the text record, but to record no. 9, which is the next record in logical order.

While this ability to automatically adjust the index file is useful, it might prove to be distracting when you are making a series of changes. If you wanted to change the values of the first three records, you would have to reposition the highlight after each change. *dBASE III Plus* provides an optional clause, NOFOLLOW, that can be used with BROWSE to stop the repositioning of the cursor after a change in the key field.

First, change the value in record no. 8 back to its previous value. Enter

> < up arrow >
> [Home]
> 5.94 < return >
> [CTRL/End]

Now enter the BROWSE command with NOFOLLOW.

> **BROWSE NOFOLLOW < return >**

Change the value of the record again by entering

> < return > (4 times)
> 105.94 < return >
> < down arrow >

Notice that this time the record is repositioned, but the highlight moves to record no. 2 not record no. 9. The NOFOLLOW option makes it simpler to make changes on the key field of an indexed data base file. Exit the BROWSE mode by entering

> [CTRL/End]

Exercise 3   Use a REPLACE command to change the value in record no. 8 back to 5.94. The correct command can be found at the end of the chapter.

COPYING

The COPY command is used to produce copies of the information stored in data base files. It can make an exact duplicate of an existing file, or it can copy portions of the existing file. The COPY command is one of the most useful commands in *dBASE III Plus*.

When you want to make a copy of a file, the file to be copied is always assumed to be the active file. That means if you want to make a copy of the EXPENSES file, you must first place that file in use. Once the file is in use, any COPY command that is issued will automatically draw data from the active file.

This is different from the operation of the DOS COPY command, which requires the entry of the name of a source file and a destination file, for example: COPY EXPENSES.DBF CASHOUT.DBF. The previous command will create a duplicate of the EXPENSES.DBF file called CASHOUT.DBF. Note that you must specify the file extensions when working in DOS.

To create a copy of the active file called CASHOUT, enter

> **USE expenses< return >**
> **COPY TO cashout< return >**

dBASE III Plus displays the message 9 records copied. List the disk directory of data base files by entering

> **DIR< return >**

The program displays a listing of the data base files that will look like this:

Database Files	# Records	Last Update	Size
CASHOUT.DBF	9	01/01/80	1064
EXPENSES.DBF	9	01/01/80	1536
PAYORDER.DBF	8	01/01/80	978
PAY1.DBF	8	01/01/80	978
PAY2.DBF	8	01/01/80	978
AMTORDER.DBF	8	01/01/80	978
CATORDER.DBF	8	01/01/80	978
CAT1.DBF	8	01/01/80	978
NOTAX.DBF	3	01/01/80	548

dBASE III Plus has automatically added the .DBF extension to the file. Enter

> **DIR *.dbt< return >**

The program displays a listing of the data base memo files that will look like this:

PATORDER.DBT	LL.DBT	EXPENSES.DBT	CASHOUT.DBT
PAY1.DBT	XX.DBT	DATE.DBT	PAYORDER.DBT
PAY2.DBT	AMTORDER.DBT	CATORDER.DBT	CAT1.DBT
NOTAX.DBT			

What significance does this display have? The .DBT files contain the memos for the records in the .DBF files. As mentioned in an earlier chapter, every time a new data base file is created that contains MEMO fields in its structure, it is necessary to create a .DBT file also. When you use the SORT or COPY commands, *dBASE III Plus* automatically creates the .DBT file.

When you use the DOS COPY command to copy a .DBF file, DOS will not know to create a corresponding .DBT file. You must remember to account for the .DBT file should the structure of the file you are copying contain a MEMO field. You can use the DOS wild card characters to make a copy of all files with the same filename but different extensions. For example, the DOS command COPY expenses.*newfile.* would copy EXPENSES.DBF and EXPENSES.DBT to NEWFILE.DBF and NEWFILE.DBT.

To test to see if CASHOUT is really a copy of the EXPENSES file, enter

USE cashout< return >
LIST<return >

The records are identical to the contents of EXPENSES. To check the memos, enter

LIST comments< return >

The memos are listed just as they would be in EXPENSES.

The COPY command has a default scope, ALL (records and fields). When you enter a COPY command, it does not matter where the pointer is positioned because *dBASE III Plus* automatically rewinds the data base to the top of the file before it begins to copy records.

LIMITED COPIES

There are occasions when you may want to copy only part of the information in the original data base file. For example, you may want to keep expense records from different years in separate files. To begin a new year, you would want to copy the file's structure, but not the records. *dBASE III Plus* employs a special form of the COPY command that copies only the structure of a file, not the records. Enter

COPY STRUCTURE TO exp1986< return >

To check the results of this command, enter

USE exp1986< return >
LIST<return >

No records are listed. Examine the structure by entering

LIST STRUCTURE< return >

The fields listed are identical to EXPENSES and CASHOUT. You could now proceed to use the EXP1986 file for the new year's expenses. Return to EXPENSES data base file by entering

USE expenses< return >

You can also use a scope to select records by their physical location. Enter

GOTO 2< return >
COPY TO scope NEXT 4< return >

This time, the four records beginning at record no. 2 are copied. Remember that scopes can also be used with the FOR clause to select records from a particular area of the data base file. Return to EXPENSES data base file by entering

USE expenses< return >

SELECTING FIELDS

Another type of selection you may want to perform when copying a file is to select certain fields to be copied. Selecting fields saves time and disk space because you do not have to copy fields you do not intend to use. In addition, you can specify the order in which the fields will appear in the new data base file. Changing the order of the fields is accomplished more easily through the COPY command than through the MODIFY STRUCTURE command. The following command creates a new data base file with selected fields. Enter

COPY TO cashout FIELDS payto,date,amount < return >

Notice that before the program carries out the command, it checks to see if the file CASHOUT.DBF already exists. Since it does, the program displays the prompt: cashout.dbf already exists, overwrite it? (Y/N).

dBASE III Plus inquires whether or not the new version of the file you have asked it to create should overwrite the existing file. If you enter Y for YES, any data in the existing CASHOUT.DBF (and CASHOUT.DBT) will be destroyed. DOS does not allow two files with the same name in the same directory. Keep in mind that copying can be destructive. Do not overwrite a file unless you are sure that you do not need its contents.

dBASE III Plus contains a method that allows you to determine how the program should react to name conflicts. The default mode is called SAFETY ON because a prompt, like the one above, is displayed whenever a file is about to be overwritten. Using the command SET SAFETY OFF eliminates the prompt. With the SAFETY OFF, files are overwritten without any warning about name conflict.

In this instance, you can enter

y

Examine the effect of the COPY command by entering

USE cashout < return >
LIST <return >

The program displays

```
1   CROW CANYON LUMBER   01/02/85   68.40
2   SEARS                01/10/85   17.95
3   GREEN ACRES FURN     01/15/85  264.68
4   INSTANT PRINTING     01/17/85   59.50
5   PG&E                 01/21/85   60.60
6   PACIFIC BELL         01/25/85   44.28
7   BRITZ PRINTING       01/30/85   47.95
8   GIFT STORE           02/02/85    5.94
9   GREEN ACRES FURN     02/05/85  175.00
```

The field list option can also be used with the COPY STRUCTURE command to create a blank file with an altered structure. Return to the EXPENSES file by entering

USE expenses < return >

SELECTING RECORDS

You can select records to be copied by adding a FOR clause to the COPY command. For example, you may want to copy the expenses for each month in its own file. To create a file that includes just January expenses, enter

COPY TO jan85 FOR MONTH(date)=1 <return>

This time the message tells you that only seven of the nine records were copied into the new file. Enter

USE jan85<return>
LIST date<return>

The screen shows

```
Record#  date
    1    01/02/85
    2    01/10/85
    3    01/15/85
    4    01/17/85
    5    01/21/85
    6    01/25/85
    7    01/30/85
```

All the dates in this file are for January. Return to EXPENSES by entering

USE expenses<return>

You can select fields and records in the same command. Enter

COPY TO feb85 FIELDS payto,amount,deduct FOR MONTH(date)=2 <return>

Check the results by entering

USE feb85<return>
LIST<return>

The screen displays the new file with a new structure.

```
Record#  PAYTO            AMOUNT DEDUCT
    1    GIFT STORE         5.94 .F.
    2    GREEN ACRES FURN  175.00 .T.
```

Return to the EXPENSES file by entering

USE expenses<return>

COPYING INDEXED FILES

If a file is indexed when copied, the records will be copied in the order indicated by the index file. The result of copying an index file is the same as a SORT; a new file is produced with the same data as the original, but in a different order. To see how this works, open an index file for the EXPENSES data base. Enter

SET INDEX TO payorder< return >

and the file is indexed on the PAYTO field. Now you can enter a command that will copy the file. In this case, you will also select fields to be copied. Enter

COPY TO cashout FIELDS amount,date,payto< return >
y

Check the results by entering

USE cashout< return >
LIST <return >

The screen displays

```
Record#  AMOUNT DATE     PAYTO
     1    47.95 01/30/85 BRITZ PRINTING
     2    68.40 01/02/85 CROW CANYON LUMBER
     3     5.94 02/02/85 GIFT STORE
     4   264.68 01/15/85 GREEN ACRES FURN
     5   175.00 02/05/85 GREEN ACRES FURN
     6    59.50 01/17/85 INSTANT PRINTING
     7    60.60 01/21/85 PG&E
     8    44.28 01/25/85 PACIFIC BELL
     9    17.95 01/10/85 SEARS
```

The resulting file is ordered as if it had been sorted. The new file is not indexed, nor is an index file created for it. If you want to use commands like FIND with the new file, you will have to create an index for that file.

There are two advantages to copying an indexed file:

1. The SORT command is limited to data base files of about 32,000 records. Copying an index file is not subject to that limitation.
2. The SORT does not recognize a FIELDS clause. If you want to select fields while making the new, sorted file, use COPY with an indexed file.

The COPY command will operate with a WHILE clause as well as a FOR clause. If you want to select a group of records to copy, you can increase the speed of the operation if the file is indexed. First, use the FIND command to position the pointer to the first record to be copied. Then use the COPY command with a WHILE clause to copy all the adjacent records that qualify. Below are the sequential and the binary methods of copying all the records for account 130. The binary method assumes you have already indexed the file by category in a file called CATORDER.NDX.

Sequential	Binary
USE expenses	USE expenses INDEX catorder
COPY TO newfile FOR cat=130	FIND 130
	COPY TO newfile WHILE cat=130

Although both commands accomplish the same task, the binary method performs many times faster on large data base files. Of course, the advantage depends on the existence of an up-to-date index file. As explained in Chapter 5, index files can be automatically updated when records are added or changed. You can see that planning ahead and keeping important index files updated can save you a considerable amount of time when performing *dBASE III Plus* operations.

ERASING FILES

When you no longer wish to use a file you have created, the ERASE command can be used to remove the file from the disk. The primary reason for erasing a file is to free up the disk space used by that file, or to avoid confusing yourself about which data base contains which data.

To use the ERASE command, you must enter the full name of the file including the extension. For example, try the command below to erase the JAN85 file:

ERASE jan85 < return >

dBASE III Plus responds with a message that says: File does not exist. The program is quite correct from its point of view. In order for *dBASE III Plus* to erase the file, you need to enter the extension as well as the name. Now enter

ERASE jan85.dbf < return >

The message File has been deleted appears on the screen, indicating that the file has been removed.

When you erase a .DBF file, *dBASE III Plus* does not erase the corresponding .DBT (memo) file. If the file you erased contained a MEMO field, you must remember to enter a separate command to erase that file. In the same vein, to remove an index file you must remember to add the .NDX extension. Enter

ERASE string1.ndx < return >

The file is erased. The *dBASE III Plus* command will not recognize the DOS wild card characters ? or *. The command ERASE *.NDX would not apply to the *dBASE III Plus* ERASE command. However, if you entered that command at the DOS level, it would erase all index files from a given directory.

The ERASE command performs the same function as the DOS commands DEL or ERASE. When a file is erased, the data in that file are lost and cannot be recovered by conventional means. For information about recovering erased files, see *Getting the Most Out of Utilities for Your IBM PC* (New York: Brady Company, 1987), by Rob Krumm.

ALTERNATIVE FILE CREATION

In looking at the operations performed by the COPY command, you can see that you can save time in creating a new file if the structure of the file is similar to an existing file. The COPY STRUCTURE command allows you to create a new file from an existing file. You can then use the MODIFY STRUCTURE command to change, add, or delete fields.

dBASE III Plus has a special form of the COPY and CREATE commands that allows you to take this logic one step further: you can create a file based on a list of specifications stored as data in a data base file.

To use the special form of the CREATE command, you must first have a data base that contains the information from which a file can be constructed. The data base file must have the following structure:

```
Field  Field Name  Type       Width  Dec
   1    FIELD_NAME  Character     10
   2    FIELD_TYPE  Character      1
   3    FIELD_LEN   Numeric        3
   4    FIELD_DEC   Numeric        3
** Total **                      18
```

Remember that the structure must contain exactly the field names shown here. You can create this special file manually, or take a shortcut by using a special form of the COPY command. Enter

```
USE expenses<return>
COPY TO fields STRUCTURE EXTENDED<return>
```

The COPY TO (new file) STRUCTURE EXTENDED command creates a file, FIELDS.DBF, with the special structure displayed above. Enter

```
USE fields<return>
LIST<return>
```

The screen displays

```
Record#  FIELD_NAME  FIELD_TYPE  FIELD_LEN  FIELD_DEC
   1     DATE         D              8          0
   2     CAT          N              5          0
   3     PAYTO        C             20          0
   4     ITEM         C             20          0
   5     AMOUNT       N              6          2
   6     COMMENTS     M             10          0
   7     MONTH        C             15          0
   8     DEDUCT       L              1          0
```

This special method of copying has translated the file structure of EXPENSES into a series of records in the file FIELDS. The file can now be edited using any of the *dBASE III Plus* editing commands, such as EDIT, CHANGE, REPLACE, or BROWSE. You can change the field names, types, or lengths. Enter

> **BROWSE < return >**
> **[CTRL/Home]**
> **t**

Change the name of the CAT and PAYTO fields by entering

> **< down arrow >**
> **CATEGORY**
> **< down arrow >**
> **PAYEE < return >**

Exit the BROWSE by entering

> **[CTRL/End]**

Close the FIELDS file. Enter

> **CLOSE DATABASE < return >**

Now that you have stored the FIELDS file, you can use the records in that file to create a new file structure. This requires the use of a special form of the CREATE command. Enter

> **CREATE exp FROM fields < return >**

The command creates a data base file, EXP, with the structure based on the records in FIELD. Enter

> **USE exp < return >**
> **LIST STRUCTURE < return >**

The screen displays the structure of the EXP data base file:

```
Structure for database: C:EXP.dbf
Number of data records:      Ø
Date of last update   : Ø1/Ø1/8Ø
Field  Field Name  Type       Width   Dec
    1  DATE        Date           8
    2  CATEGORY    Numeric        5
    3  PAYTO       Character      2Ø
    4  ITEM        Character      2Ø
    5  AMOUNT      Numeric        6       2
    6  COMMENTS    Memo          1Ø
    7  MONTH       Character     15
    8  DEDUCT      Logical        1
** Total **                     86
```

This technique is advantageous because sometimes it is simpler to edit records in a data base file than it is to use MODIFY STRUCTURE. For example, you could perform a SORT on the FIELDS data base file and get the field names alphabetized or grouped by field type, then use the sorted file to create a file structure.

The CREATE/FROM command and its companion COPY STRUCTURE EX-TENDED allow you to create applications in which users can modify and create files without having to learn how to use the *dBASE III Plus* CREATE command.

DELETING RECORDS

The next task, deleting obsolete or unneeded records from a data base, is a two-step process.

1. The records are marked for deletion, using one of five different commands: DELETE, EDIT, APPEND, CHANGE, and BROWSE. The DELETE command has no purpose other than to mark records as deleted. The others are editing commands that in addition to their other functions allow deleting.

   Deleted records are not immediatley removed from the data base file; they will remain in the file indefinitely until a PACK command is issued. Prior to that command, records can have their deletion marks removed by the RECALL, EDIT, APPEND, CHANGE, or BROWSE commands. The RECALL command has only one purpose, to unmark deleted records.

2. To remove records from the data base file, a PACK command is entered. The PACK command actually creates a new copy of the data base file but copies only the records that have not been marked as deleted. Following a PACK command, deleted records cannot be recovered.

   The reason for this two-part system is that packing a file consumes time. The larger the number of records in the file, the longer a PACK takes. Since records are marked for deletion one by one, *dBASE III Plus* delays packing until specifically told to do so. This way, you can make sure that all the records you want to delete are marked before you begin a PACK.

An additional benefit of this system is that you have an opportunity to change your mind about a record's deleted status before it is actually removed. To see how this system works, use the CASHOUT file. Since this is only a copy of the EX-PENSES file, it won't do any harm to remove records from it. Enter

   USE cashout < return >

During the full-screen editing allowed by APPEND, CHANGE, EDIT, and BROWSE, there are two ways to mark a record for deletion: (1) use the DELETE command, or (2) use the **[CTRL/u]** command. The DELETE command is handy for deleting a group of records selected by a scope or logical criterion. When you need to inspect the records to determine which ones should be deleted, using the full-screen mode is helpful.

Begin with an example of full-screen editing. Enter

BROWSE < return >

When in BROWSE, as well as EDIT, CHANGE, and APPEND, a record can be marked for deletion by entering **[CTRL/u]**. The record that is deleted is the current record, or in BROWSE, the highlighted record. (With EDIT, CHANGE, and APPEND, the record that is displayed on the screen is the current record.)
Enter

[CTRL/u]

dBASE III Plus indicates that the record has been marked as deleted by displaying the letters Del on the right side of the status line. See below.

```
BROWSE          :<C:>:CASHOUT              :Rec: 1/9        :   Del:   Caps
```

The **[CTRL/u]** command is a toggle command. If you enter the command and the record is already deleted, the record is changed to undeleted. Enter

[CTRL/u]

Note that the deleted symbol disappears from the screen. Move to the next record by entering

< down arrow >

Mark the record as deleted by entering

[CTRL/u]

Exit the BROWSE mode by entering

[CTRL/End]

List the records by entering

LIST <return >

The screen displays

```
Record#  AMOUNT DATE      PAYTO
     1    47.95 01/30/85 BRITZ PRINTING
     2 *  68.40 01/02/85 CROW CANYON LUMBER
     3     5.94 02/02/85 GIFT STORE
     4   264.68 01/15/85 GREEN ACRES FURN
     5   175.00 02/05/85 GREEN ACRES FURN
     6    59.50 01/17/85 INSTANT PRINTING
     7    60.60 01/21/85 PG&E
     8    44.28 01/25/85 PACIFIC BELL
     9    17.95 01/10/85 SEARS
```

Notice that record no. 2 is marked with an asterisk (*). The * indicates that the

record is marked for deletion and will not be copied if the file is packed. The *
is inserted into a special field in the record that does not appear in the file structure. This is a direct example of the explanation of the CREATE command in Chapter
1, where it was found that the total number of characters in the record structure
was one more than required by the specified field length. The extra character is reserved for the deletion mark.

The DELETE command is used to mark records for deletion when you are not
in a full-screen EDIT mode. DELETE is not a toggle and marks for deletion only.
If a record is already deleted, DELETE has no effect. The DELETE command has
a default scope of NEXT 1, meaning that it normally deletes only the active record.
For example, to delete record no. 7, enter

```
GOTO 7<return>
DELETE<return>
LIST<return>
```

The display now shows two records marked for deletion.

```
Record#  AMOUNT DATE      PAYTO
     1    47.95 01/30/85 BRITZ PRINTING
     2 *  68.40 01/02/85 CROW CANYON LUMBER
     3     5.94 02/02/85 GIFT STORE
     4   264.68 01/15/85 GREEN ACRES FURN
     5   175.00 02/05/85 GREEN ACRES FURN
     6    59.50 01/17/85 INSTANT PRINTING
     7 *  60.60 01/21/85 PG&E
     8    44.28 01/25/85 PACIFIC BELL
     9    17.95 01/10/85 SEARS
```

Now that the records have been marked, they can be removed in a single step
by packing the file. Enter

```
PACK<return>
```

dBASE III Plus displays a message indicating that seven records have been copied.
The message relates the number of records retained in the file, not the number removed. List the contents of the file by entering

```
LIST <return>
```

The screen displays

```
Record#  AMOUNT DATE      PAYTO
     1    47.95 01/30/85 BRITZ PRINTING
     2     5.94 02/02/85 GIFT STORE
     3   264.68 01/15/85 GREEN ACRES FURN
     4   175.00 02/05/85 GREEN ACRES FURN
     5    59.50 01/17/85 INSTANT PRINTING
     6    44.28 01/25/85 PACIFIC BELL
     7    17.95 01/10/85 SEARS
```

Since packing a file rewrites it, record numbers may be changed because of the
removal of some records.

With the use of a scope, the DELETE command can delete a group of adjacent records at once. Enter

> **GO TOP** < return >
> **DELETE NEXT 3** < return >
> **LIST** < return >

The first three records in the file are marked. The DELETE command will also function with FOR or WHILE clauses. For example, you might want to delete all the records for the month of January. Enter

> **DELETE FOR MONTH(date)=1** < return >
> **LIST** < return >

Only record no. 4 remains undeleted. Notice that record no. 2 has a February date but is marked as deleted because of a previous delete command. To rectify this situation, enter

> **RECALL FOR MONTH(date)=2** < return >
> **LIST** < return >

One record is recalled. The screen now shows

```
Record#  AMOUNT DATE      PAYTO
     1 *  47.95 01/30/85  BRITZ PRINTING
     2     5.94 02/02/85  GIFT STORE
     3 *264.68 01/15/85   GREEN ACRES FURN
     4   175.00 02/05/85  GREEN ACRES FURN
     5 *  59.50 01/17/85  INSTANT PRINTING
     6 *  44.28 01/25/85  PACIFIC BELL
     7 *  17.95 01/10/85  SEARS
```

Enter

> **PACK** < return >

Now there are only two records in the file. Enter

> **LIST** < return >

The screen displays

```
Record#  AMOUNT DATE      PAYTO
     1     5.94 02/02/85  GIFT STORE
     2   175.00 02/05/85  GREEN ACRES FURN
```

Return to the EXPENSES file by entering

> **USE expenses** < return >

PACKING INDEXED FILES

Because index files and data base files work together, packing a data base file affects the index files related to it. As explained above, packing a file causes some records to be removed; therefore some of the remaining records will have their record numbers changed. This means that the order of records stored in the index file for a given data base will no longer be accurate. When you use index files, there are some additional steps that must taken to update them.

Begin by making a copy of the EXPENSES file. Enter

> **COPY TO cashout < return >**
>
> **y**
>
> **USE cashout < return >**

Now you need to create some index files.

Exercise 4   Enter the commands needed to create two index files: (1) PAYTO.NDX index on PAYTO, and (2) AMOUNT.NDX index on AMOUNT. The correct commands can be found at the end of the chapter.

When the index files have been created, close the index file by entering

> **CLOSE INDEX < return >**

Now mark some records for deletion. Enter

> **DELETE FOR amount > 65 < return >**

Three records are marked. Pack the file by entering

> **PACK < return >**

Now that the pack is complete, open the index file by entering

> **SET INDEX TO payto < return >**
>
> **LIST <return >**

Nothing is listed. Why? The answer lies in the fact that the index file is attempting to display the file as it was before the PACK command was given. The first record in PAYTO order is record no. 7, BRITZ PRINTING. However, since the pack was performed, the data base file contains only six records. When the index file was opened, it attempted to list record no. 7, a record that is no longer in the data base file. (BRITZ PRINTING may still be in the file, but its record number has been changed.)

To resolve this contradiction you can use the REINDEX command to rebuild the index file to match the existing data in the data base file. Before you enter the REINDEX command, you should also consider that a second index file, AMOUNT.NDX, needs to be updated. You can update up to seven index files at once by opening them and then reindexing. Enter

> **SET INDEX TO payto,amount < return >**
>
> **REINDEX < return >**

To indicate that the reindexing is taking place, *dBASE III Plus* displays the following:

```
Rebuilding index — C:PAYTO.ndx
   100% indexed              6 Records indexed
Rebuilding index — C:AMOUNT.ndx
   100% indexed              6 Records indexed
```

You can now list the file correctly. Enter

LIST payto< return >

To avoid the extra step of reindexing, packing can be performed while the index files are open. For example, to delete some additional records, enter

DELETE FOR deduct< return >

One record is marked. Now pack the file by entering

PACK < return >

When the pack is complete the program automatically reindexes the open index files.

One common error message encountered with index files is RECORD OUT OF RANGE. Most often, the cause of this error is an index file that does not match the data base file. For example, suppose a pack reduces a 1000-record file to 700 records, and you have not updated the index file. When you enter the command USE (file) INDEX (file), the RECORD OUT OF RANGE message appears because the record at the top of the index file is 900 or 1000. The program tries to go to that record but finds that no such record exists, hence the error message. As in the previous example, reindexing the file will correct the problem.

Return to the EXPENSES file by entering

USE expenses< return >

IGNORING DELETED RECORDS

Packing a data base file has two disadvantages:

1. If the percentage of deleted records in a large data base file is small, you will be forced to wait while a pack is performed to eliminate these few records.
2. Once a file has been packed, the records cannot be recovered. There may be occasions when you might wish to delete certain records temporarily but restore them at a later time.

dBASE III Plus provides a method by which deleted records can be ignored without having to perform a pack. This saves time when the number of records marked for deletion is small; it also allows you to recover the records by simply recalling them.

The SET DELETED ON command tells *dBASE III Plus* to ignore all records that are marked for deletion even though no pack has been performed. The SET DELETED command is a special form of the SET FILTER TO command. The SET DELETED command filters only on the basis of the delete marker.

You can specify both SET FILTER TO and SET DELETED at the same time. To illustrate how this works, mark some records for deletion by entering

>**DELETE FOR cat > 120 < return >**
>**LIST cat < return >**

dBASE III Plus displays

```
Record#    CAT
     1     110
     2  *  140
     3     120
     4  *  140
     5  *  130
     6  *  130
     7  *  140
     8  *  140
     9     120
```

Now enter

>**SET DELETED ON < return >**
>**LIST cat < return >**

The program displays

```
Record#    CAT
     1     110
     3     120
     9     120
```

The file appears as if it has been packed. Enter

>**COPY TO NEWFILE < return >**

Only three records are copied. The SET DELETED ON command allows the file to function as if it had been packed.

The INDEX command does not recognize the SET DELETED ON command. If you create an index file while the DELETED is on, all the records in the data base file will be indexed.

To recover the records, simply turn the DELETED OFF. Enter

>**SET DELETED OFF < return >**
>**LIST cat < return >**

All the records are visible again.

THE DELETED FUNCTION

The DELETE command affects the contents of that special field reserved for the deletion mark. The field is not given a name in the file structure, but *dBASE III Plus* assigns the field a special name. The DELETED() function is used to refer to the value in the DELETE field. The function DELETED() is true if the record is marked for deletion, and false if the record is not marked.

For example, you could list all the deleted payees by entering

LIST payto FOR DELETED()< return >

The program displays

```
Record#  PAYTO
     2  *SEARS
     4  *INSTANT PRINTING
     5  *PG&E
     6  *PACIFIC BELL
     7  *BRITZ PRINTING
     8  *GIFT STORE
```

The () symbol is called a *null argument.* All *dBASE III Plus* functions require parentheses, and some functions like UPPER() require a field or expression to be placed within the parentheses. However, functions like DELETED() do not require anything to be placed inside the parentheses. *dBASE III Plus* requires you to include parentheses with every function for the sake of consistency in the command language.

You can list all the undeleted records by using the .NOT. connective with the DELETED() function. Enter

LIST payto FOR .NOT.DELETED()< return >

The command selects only the undeleted records. You can use the RECALL command to undelete all the deleted records. Enter

RECALL ALL< return >

If SET DELETED is ON, the RECALL command has no meaning. RECALL makes sense only when *dBASE III Plus* allows you to display deleted records. RECALL with SET DELETED ON will never find any records to recall because no deleted records will be processed.

Check the file by requesting that *dBASE III Plus* list all the deleted records. Enter

LIST FOR DELETED()< return >

No records are listed, indicating that all the records in EXPENSES are now marked as undeleted.

ZAPPING A FILE

If you wanted to remove all the records from a file, you could delete them and perform a pack. However, this method would waste a lot of time since *dBASE III Plus* must still check every record for a deletion mark when packing the file.

   dBASE III Plus provides a special command that will eliminate all the records in a file without sequentially searching it. The command is ZAP. Open the CASHOUT file by entering

> **USE cashout < return >**

Enter

> **ZAP < return >**

The program displays the prompt Zap C:cashout.dbf? (Y/N). Enter

> **y**

The prompt appears when the Safety is set on. When Safety is off, no prompt appears and the file is zapped as soon as the command is entered. Enter

> **LIST <return >**

   All the records in CASHOUT have been removed. The ZAP command does not inspect the data base file to determine which records should be eliminated as a DELETE ALL and PACK would do. ZAP simply places the end of file marker at what used to be the beginning of the file. When ZAP is used, the size of the file does not affect the amount of time required to remove the records.

   Remember that a file that has been zapped cannot be recovered. Return to the EXPENSES file by entering

> **USE expenses < return >**

USING DRIVES AND DIRECTORIES

Although this section is primarily of interest to users with hard disk drives in their systems, floppy disk users will also find the information useful.

   Now that you have learned how to copy data base files, you might wonder how you can copy the files to other drives or directories on your hard disk. Understanding how this is done requires some knowledge of MS DOS (Microsoft Disk Operating System), which controls the storage of data on the disks in your system. Although a full discussion of DOS is beyond the scope of this book, the following information explains how files can be copied to different devices in your system.

DOS recognizes three units of data storage:

1. **The File.** This is the smallest unit of storage. Files have 1 to 8 character names and 1 to 3 character extensions.

2. **The Directory.** Files can be grouped together in units called *directories;* directories contain one or more files. The idea of the directory is to create a file folder in which related files can be stored together. Directories are usually found only on systems with hard disk drives. Although it is entirely possible to create directories on floppy disks, the practice is not common because of the relatively limited number of files that can be stored on them. Hard disks typically hold several hundred files that can be divided into distinct groups, making the disk easier to manage.

    Directories are characterized by the \ character. For example, \DB3 stands for a directory called DB3.

3. **The Volume.** The volume is the name DOS gives to an entire disk. Volumes are always single letters followed by a colon. For example, A: represents the volume in drive A.

    Putting the three together creates what is called the *full pathname* of a file. The full pathname includes the filename, the directory (if any), and the volume. For example, C:\DB3\EXPENSES.DBF stands for a file (EXPENSES.DBF) in the DB3 directory (\DB3) of C drive (C:). If you leave out any part, DOS assumes that you want to use the last drive or directory selected. This assumption is called the *default*.

You can apply DOS grammar to the filenames used in *dBASE III Plus* commands, as follows:

COPY TO a:expenses<return>

Entering the command above will copy the EXPENSES file to the disk in drive A. Enter the command, then check the results by using DIR with a volume name:

DIR a:<return>

dBASE III Plus displays the data base files on drive A.

The file is copied to the disk in drive A. You can change the default by entering the SET DEFAULT TO command. For example, if you are working on a hard drive system, the default drive is C. If you have a disk in A, you can make that the default drive by entering

SET DEFAULT TO a:<return>

Enter

DIR<return>

Because drive A is now the default, the files from that drive are listed. Change the default back to C by entering

SET DEFAULT TO c:< return >

COPYING TO ANOTHER DIRECTORY

dBASE III Plus accepts path specifications in commands that require filenames. Suppose you are working on a hard disk in which a directory called DOS has been created. You can place a copy of the active file in that directory by entering

COPY TO \dos\cashout < return >

This command creates a file CASHOUT.DBF in the DOS directory of default drive C. Now that you have a data base file in another directory, you can place that file in use by entering

USE \dos\cashout < return >

Return to the EXPENSES file by entering

USE expenses < return >

You can list the data base files in another directory by adding the directory name to the command. Enter·

DIR \dos < return >

COPYING NON-DATA BASE FILES

The COPY command has a major limitation; it copies only the contents of data base files. If you want to make a duplicate of another type of file (e.g., index files), you have two options:

1. Use the COPY FILE command.
2. Use the RUN command to access the DOS COPY command.

The COPY FILE command does not require additional memory and can be used to copy any type of file. For example, suppose that you wanted to copy the index file PAYORDER.NDX to the DOS directory. Enter

COPY FILE payorder.ndx TO \dos\payorder.ndx < return >

dBASE III Plus displays a prompt that indicates the number of bytes copied.

The RUN command requires enough internal memory to operate both *dBASE III Plus* and the DOS command interpreter. Usually 384K of internal memory is sufficient. Running memory-resident programs such as ramdisks, spoolers, Sidekick, or Superkey reduces the amount of free memory for *dBASE III Plus*.

The DOS command has a slightly different syntax than do the *dBASE III Plus* commands, and will operate a good deal faster than the COPY FILE command when copying large files.

The RUN command allows you to enter valid operating system commands. Enter

RUN copy payorder.ndx \dos < return >

Note that DOS does not require the word "to" or the name of the new file.

RENAMING A FILE

dBASE III Plus also allows you to change the name of a file. The RENAME command performs the same function as the DOS command, REN, but uses a slightly different syntax. Suppose you wanted to change the name of the FIELDS.DBF file to EXPFLDS.DBF. You could perform either of the following commands:

1. Using the *dBASE III Plus* RENAME command, you would enter

    RENAME fields.dbf TO expflds.dbf < return >

    You must use the full filename, including extension. You cannot rename a file while it is in use. If you want to rename a current file, first close the file (CLOSE DATABASE) and then enter the RENAME command.

2. Using the RUN command to access the DOS REN command, you would enter

    RUN REN fields.dbf expflds.dbf < return >

    The RUN command requires the use of additional memory and therefore may not operate correctly on all systems.

HOUSEKEEPING IN THE ASSIST MODE

Most of the commands in this chapter can be carried out from the *dBASE III Plus* ASSIST mode. To illustrate how this can be done, access ASSIST:

ASSIST < return >

OPENING AN INDEX FILE

You can open an index file in the ASSIST mode by using the DATABASE file option on the SETUP menu. Enter

> < return >
> < return >

The program displays a list of data base files from which you can choose. Move the highlight to EXPENSES.DBF. Then enter

> < return >

Since the file will be indexed, enter

> y

The program displays a list of all the index files.
    Move the highlight to PAYORDER. Enter

> < return >

The file is selected as the master index file. If you want to open additional index files, you can do so by highlighting the names and pressing < return >. There is a limit of seven index files for each data base file open.
    To open the file and its index files, enter

> < left arrow >

POSITIONING

The ASSIST mode offers two search commands, SEEK and LOCATE. These commands are located on the POSITION menu. Enter

> p

The LOCATE command is the same as the LOCATE command used at the DOT PROMPT. Suppose that you wanted to locate all the records for category 140. Enter

> <down arrow>
> < return >

The program displays the command option box.
    Enter a selection criterion by entering

> <down arrow> (2 times)
> < return >

Enter

>   **< down arrow >**
>   **< return >**

Select equal to by entering

>   **< return >**

Now enter the value to match for by entering

>   **140 < return >**
>   **< return >**

Execute the command by entering

>   **[Pg Up]**
>   **< return >**

Press any key to return to the menu. Notice that the CONTINUE command is displayed in bright video, indicating that you can now use that command. Enter

>   **< down arrow >**
>   **< return >**

The next matching record, record no. 8, is located. To return to the menu, enter

>   **< return >**

SEEK: ASSIST MODE

The ASSIST mode does not have a FIND command but uses a variation on that command called SEEK. Suppose you wanted to search for the payee SEARS. You can use the SEEK command because the PAYORDER index file, which is the current master index, is ordered by PAYTO.

SEEK is also available in the DOT PROMPT mode and works like FIND in that it searches the index file, not the data base file. Enter

>   **[Pg Up]**
>   **< return >**

dBASE III Plus requests that you enter the expression to seek in the index file.

The difference between SEEK and FIND is encountered here. The FIND command assumes you are entering the characters for which to search, while SEEK allows you to enter both literal and symbolic items as search criteria (see Memory Variables in Chapter 7). In this instance, this means you must enclose the characters in quotation marks. Enter

>   **"SEARS" < return >**

The pointer has been positioned to the record for which you were searching. Remember that SEEK, like FIND, does not display any data when a match is made. If no record can be found, it displays No find. To see the record that was found, you must use another command, such as DISPLAY, which outputs data. Enter

       <return>
       r
       <down arrow>
       <return>
       <return>

Return to the menu by entering

       <return>

COPYING: ASSIST MODE

The COPY command is accessed from the ORGANIZE menu. Enter

       o

Begin a copy command by entering

       <down arrow> (2 times)
       <return>

Enter the name of the new file you are going to create.

       testfile<return>

The command option box appears. You can now select scopes, fields, or a selection criterion. In this case, copy the entire file by entering

       <return>

Return to the menu by entering

       <return>

FILE COMMAND: ASSIST MODE

The commands to erase, rename, and list files are accessed through the TOOLS menu. Enter

       t

For example, to list files, enter

       <down arrow> (2 times)
       <return>

You can now select the disk to list. Enter

> **< return >**

dBASE III Plus lists a variety of options for listing files. For example, list index files by entering

> **< down arrow >**
> **< return >**

Return to the menu by entering

> **< return >**

Exit the ASSIST mode by entering

> **< Esc >**

SUMMARY

This chapter describes commands that are used to maintain your data base files as records are added, removed, and altered.

1. **Finding Individual Records.** One of the primary tasks in file maintenance is finding individual records. There are two methods employed by *dBASE III Plus* that do just that:
    LOCATE. The LOCATE command performs a sequential search of the data base file to find selected records, using a FOR clause. The LOCATE command can be used to search the data base for any valid *dBASE III Plus* expression. After finding the first matching record, the CONTINUE command will move the pointer to the next qualifying record, if any. The CONTINUE command can be repeated until the end of the file is reached.
    FIND. The FIND command does not search the data base file, but rather the index file. This allows the search to proceed at a high speed even in large data base files because of the binary-type of organization used in the index file. The FIND command searches only for records based on the index key.
2. **Copying.** *dBASE III Plus* allows you to copy all or part of a data base file. The source data base is always taken from the active data base file. Examples:

COPY TO (newfile)	Duplicates a data base file.
COPY STRUCTURE To (newfile)	Copies the data base file structure only.
COPY TO (newfile) FOR (expr.)	Copies selected records to a newfile.

3. **Deleting and Recalling.** *dBASE III Plus* allows you to remove records from a data base file by a two-step process. Records are marked as deleted using the DELETE command or the **[CTRL/u]** command during the full-screen editing commands of EDIT, BROWSE, CHANGE, or APPEND. Records are not removed when they are marked, but are maintained in the file until a pack is performed. Records marked for deletion can be unmarked using the RECALL command or the **[CTRL/u]** command in full-screen editing modes prior to a pack. Records cannot be recalled after a pack.

Packing a file changes the numbers of the records. Index files related to a packed data base file must be reindexed.

Deleted records can be ignored by using the SET DELETED ON command. When the DELETED function is ON, the data base functions as if the deleted records had been removed.

The DELETED() function is used to select records according to their deletion status. DELETED() equals .T. if a record is marked for deletion, and .F. if the record is not marked.

ANSWER KEY

Exercise 1

LOCATE FOR DTOC(date)="02/02/85" <return>

or

LOCATE FOR date=CTOD("02/02/85") <return>

(You should find record no. 8)

Exercise 2

LOCATE FOR "CAN"$item <return>

(You should find record no. 2)

Exercise 3

REPLACE amount WITH 5.94 FOR amount=105.94 <return>

Exercise 4

INDEX ON payto TO payto <return>
INDEX ON amount TO amount <return>

REPORTS AND

STATISTICS

IN THIS CHAPTER YOU WILL learn about *dBASE III Plus* techniques that allow you to generate sophisticated outputs such as column reports with subtotals and mailing labels. You will also learn how *dBASE III Plus* allows you to create and retain statistical information about the data in the data base file, and how that information can be integrated into *dBASE III Plus* reports.

To begin this chapter you should have *dBASE III Plus* loaded into the computer in the usual manner. If you are using *dBASE III Plus* in the ASSIST mode, exit the mode by entering <Esc>.

STATISTICAL COMMANDS AND SPECIAL FUNCTIONS

dBASE III Plus has three commands that produce statistics about the data base file: SUM, COUNT, and AVERAGE. The SUM command is used to total the values of fields in a data base file. To see how this works, place a data base file in use by entering

    USE expenses<return>

The SUM command will create totals for all the NUMERIC fields in the data base file. Enter

SUM < return >

The program displays

```
9 records summed
CAT    AMOUNT
1170   744.30
```

The command displays the number of records used to calculate the sum, as well as the names of the fields and the values.

The SUM command can also accept a list of field or numeric expressions. For example, totaling the CAT field doesn't make much sense. You could limit the command by entering

SUM amount < return >

The program displays

```
9 records summed
amount
744.30
```

The SUM command will also total selected records based on a logical criterion. This is accomplished by adding a FOR clause to the command. For example, you might want to know the total of all the expenses in category 130. Enter

SUM amount FOR cat=130 < return >

The program displays

```
2 records summed
amount
104.88
```

The SUM command can operate on numeric expressions as well as NUMERIC fields. If you enter a numeric expression, the program evaluates the expression for each record and adds the value to the total. For example, you could calculate what the total expense would be if the amounts were increased by 10, 20, or 30 percent. Enter

SUM amount,amount*1.1,amount*1.2,amount*1.3 < return >

The program displays

```
9 records summed
amount    amount*1.1    amount*1.2    amount*1.3
B.        818.730       893.160       967.590
```

The SUM command is very often used with a SET FILTER command. For example, you could set the filter for February records. Enter

SET FILTER TO MONTH(date)=2< return >
SUM amount< return >

The value you obtain is the total for the two February records only. To remove the filter, enter

SET FILTER TO< return >

Exercise 1   Enter a command that will sum all the expenses made in January. The correct command can be found at the end of the chapter.

COUNT and AVERAGE

The COUNT command is a more limited version of the SUM. COUNT simply counts the number of records in the data base file. Used by itself, it totals all the records in the data base file. However, the real value of COUNT is for counting selected records. For example, you can find out how many expenses have been entered into category 140 by entering

COUNT FOR cat=140< return >

Exercise 2   Enter a command that will count the number of expenses that are deductible. The correct command can be found at the end of the chapter.

The AVERAGE command is the same as the SUM command, with the exception that the totals are divided by the number of records summed. Enter

AVERAGE< return >

The program displays

```
    9 records averaged
CAT AMOUNT
130  82.70
```

The AVERAGE command also accepts numeric expressions. Enter

AVERAGE amount*1.3< return >

The average shown is the average increased by 30 percent. The AVERAGE command can be used with a FOR clause to average selected records. You can compare the average expenses in January and February by entering

AVERAGE amount FOR MONTH(date)=1< return >
AVERAGE amount FOR MONTH(date)=2< return >

MEMORY VARIABLES

The *dBASE III Plus* statistical commands have one great drawback. They may be capable of calculating important information concerning the records in the data base file, but the display on the screen is temporary. As soon as the screen display is cleared, the data are gone. For these statistics to be of greater use, there must be some way to store their values and integrate them into the *dBASE III Plus* system.

dBASE III Plus solves this problem by the use of memory variables. The program allows the user to store up to 256 different items of data (a total of 6000 characters) in the memory area.

The word *memory* is used in many different ways in the computer field. In *dBASE III Plus*, *memory* or *memory area* refers to a specific block of internal memory used by the programs. The term memory in this text will be used to refer to the *dBASE III Plus* memory area unless otherwise specified.

The memory can be thought of as a scratch pad on which you write down information about the data base files with which you are working. The memory is different from the data base file in several ways:

1. The memory area is not associated with any data base file. Data stored in the memory are accessible even if no data base file is open.

2. Data stored in the memory area are erased when you quit the *dBASE III Plus* program.

3. No structure is required for the memory area. You can create a memory variable at any time. You can store character, number, date, and logical values in the memory. You cannot store memo data in the memory.

There are two ways to store an item in the memory area:

1. **Indirect.** Some *dBASE III Plus* commands like SUM, COUNT, and AVERAGE can store their results in memory variables.

2. **Direct.** This method uses the STORE command to enter a value directly into the memory.

Memory variables, like fields, can be up to ten characters long and consist of letters, numbers, and the underscore characters.

When you are creating memory variables, take care not to create one that has the same name as a field in the active data base file. If this occurs, dBASE III Plus always references the field instead of the memory variable. When the data base is closed, the memory variable can be referenced. If the same names cannot be avoided, dBASE III Plus allows you to distinguish a memory variable by using M–> before the name. Example: M–>TOTEXP.

Memory variables have a tremendous number of uses in *dBASE III Plus*. To begin, you can return to the problem of how to integrate the results of statistical commands into the *dBASE III Plus* system.

Suppose you want to show each expense in your file as a percentage of the total amount of expenses in that file. Without using memory variables, you would have to proceed as follows: calculate the total amount of expenses. Enter

SUM amount< return >

The program displays the value 744.30. To remember that value, you might jot it down on a piece of paper. Enter a command that will display each amount as a percentage of the total. Enter

LIST amount/744.3*100< return >

The program displays

```
Record#   amount/744.30*100
   7               6.44
   1               9.19
   8               0.80
   3              35.56
   9              23.51
   4               7.99
   5               8.14
   6               5.95
   2               2.41
```

The only way that the total could be included in the calculation was to enter it manually into the formula as a numeric literal.

Memory variables allow you to perform the same task by an alternate method. Instead of just calculating the sum, you can create a memory variable that will represent the value calculated by the SUM command. Enter

SUM amount TO totexp< return >

What have you accomplished? You have created a new entity in the *dBASE III Plus* system, called TOTEXP. If you use the name TOTEXP in expressions or commands, *dBASE III Plus* will substitute the value of that memory variable into that expression or calculation. For example, you could use the ? command to display the value of a memory variable. Enter

? totexp< return >

The program displays the value stored in the memory variable TOTEXP. Once the value is stored in the memory, it can be referenced repeatedly. Enter

? totexp/9< return >

The command prints the average of the amounts. You can now use the memory variable as part of the command that lists the percentages. Enter

LIST amount/totexp*100< return >

You could store the totals for January and February in memory variables. Enter

> **SUM amount TO jan FOR MONTH(date)=1 <return>**
> **SUM amount TO feb FOR MONTH(date)=2 <return>**

You can now ask *dBASE III Plus* to display the values stored in the memory. Enter

> **? jan,feb,totexp<return>**

The program displays

> L.   180.94   744.30

You can use memory variables in logical expressions as well. For example, if you have entered the commands correctly, the sum of JAN plus FEB should equal TOTEXP. Enter

> **? jan+feb=totexp<return>**

dBASE III Plus displays .T., indicating that the statement is true.

Exercise 3   Enter the commands necessary to find what percent of the total expense is deductible. The correct commands can be found at the end of the chapter.

DISPLAYING THE MEMORY

dBASE III Plus has commands that allow you to list the current contents of the memory. DISPLAY MEMORY lists the memory variables that are currently active. Enter

> **DISPLAY MEMORY<return>**

The program displays

```
TOTEXP      pub   N      744.30  (      744.30000000)
JAN         pub   N      563.36  (      563.36000000)
FEB         pub   N      180.94  (      180.94000000)
     3 variables defined,      27 bytes used
   253 variables available,   5973 bytes available
```

The "pub" stands for "public variable." dBASE III Plus recognizes two types of variables, public and private. This distinction has meaning only when you are programming dBASE III Plus. Operations that create variables at the DOT PROMPT or the ASSIST mode are always public variables.

DIRECT MEMORY STORAGE

dBASE III Plus provides a means of directly defining memory variables. Suppose you wanted to list the items in the EXPENSES file as percentages of the total income for January. You can create a memory variable called INCOME by entering

income=1200 < return >

Display the memory variables by entering

DISPLAY MEMORY < return >

The program displays

```
TOTEXP      pub   N        744.30  (       744.30000000)
JAN         pub   N        563.36  (       563.36000000)
FEB         pub   N        180.94  (       180.94000000)
INCOME      pub   N        1200    (      1200.00000000)
    4 variables defined,        36 bytes used
  252 variables available,    5964 bytes available
```

You can now use the variable to create an output. Enter

LIST amount/income*100 FOR MONTH(date)=1 < return >

The program displays

```
Record#     AMOUNT/INCOME*100
      7            4.00
      1            5.70
      3           22.06
      4            4.96
      5            5.05
      6            3.69
      2            1.50
```

You can calculate the percent of income spent for expenses by entering

? jan/income*100 < return >

You can create a memory variable for text data by entering a text literal as the value for the variable. Enter

key="SEARS" < return >
DISPLAY MEMORY < return >

The program displays

```
TOTEXP      pub   N        744.30  (       744.30000000)
JAN         pub   N        563.36  (       563.36000000)
FEB         pub   N        180.94  (       180.94000000)
INCOME      pub   N        1200    (      1200.00000000)
KEY         pub   C   "SEARS"
    5 variables defined,        43 bytes used
  251 variables available,    5957 bytes available
```

Note that KEY shows a C to indicate that this is a character-type memory variable. You can create a logical memory variable by using .T. or .F. to represent a true or false value. Enter

test=.T. < return >
DISPLAY MEMORY < return >

The program displays

```
TOTEXP      pub  N       744.30  (      744.30000000)
JAN         pub  N       563.36  (      563.36000000)
FEB         pub  N       180.94  (      180.94000000)
INCOME      pub  N      1200     (     1200.00000000)
KEY         pub  C   "SEARS"
TEST        pub  L   .T.
     6 variables defined,       45 bytes used
   250 variables available,   5955 bytes available
```

The L indicates a logical value. Date variables can be created using the special date functions. Enter

today=CTOD("03/01/85") < return >
DISPLAY MEMORY < return >

The program displays

```
TOTEXP      pub  N       744.30  (      744.30000000)
JAN         pub  N       563.36  (      563.36000000)
FEB         pub  N       180.94  (      180.94000000)
INCOME      pub  N      1200     (     1200.00000000)
KEY         pub  C   "SEARS"
TEST        pub  L   .T.
TODAY       pub  D   03/01/85
     7 variables defined,       54 bytes used
   249 variables available,   5946 bytes available
```

You could use the date variable, TODAY, in a command. The following command calculates the number of days from the TODAY date of each expense. Enter

LIST today−date < return >

The program lists the days between the dates. You can use the AVERAGE command to find the average number of days. Enter

AVERAGE today−date < return >

The program tells you that each expense was an average of 39 days from the TODAY date.

SAVING VARIABLES

As mentioned previously, memory variables are not saved as part of data base files. When you quit the program, the memory variables are lost. However, it is possible to save the memory variables for later use by creating a special memory variable file. These files store the current memory variables in a file with a .MEM extension. The command to save memory variables is SAVE TO (filename). Enter

SAVE TO testvars < return >

You can see the file you have just created by entering

DIR *.mem < return >

When you save the memory variables, you are only placing a copy of the data into a file. The variables you have created are still active. Enter

DISPLAY MEMORY <return>

dBASE III Plus still lists the variables that are active in the memory.

Alternate Form

dBASE III Plus has an alternate form that can be used to create a memory variable. The STORE command can be used in the following manner:

STORE "This is a test." TO sentence <return>
DISPLAY MEMORY <return>

The program displays

```
TOTEXP      pub   N        744.30  (        744.30000000)
JAN         pub   N        563.36  (        563.36000000)
FEB         pub   N        180.94  (        180.94000000)
INCOME      pub   N          1200  (       1200.00000000)
KEY         pub   C   "SEARS"
TEST        pub   L   .T.
TODAY       pub   D   03/01/85
SENTENCE    pub   C   "This is a test."
     8 variables defined,        71 bytes used
   248 variables available,    5929 bytes available
```

The advantage of the STORE command is that you can create a series of variables with the same value in a single command. Enter

STORE 0 TO t1,t2,t3,t4,t5 <return>
DISPLAY MEMORY <return>

The program displays

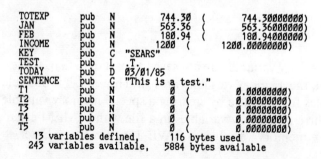

```
TOTEXP      pub   N        744.30  (        744.30000000)
JAN         pub   N        563.36  (        563.36000000)
FEB         pub   N        180.94  (        180.94000000)
INCOME      pub   N          1200  (       1200.00000000)
KEY         pub   C   "SEARS"
TEST        pub   L   .T.
TODAY       pub   D   03/01/85
SENTENCE    pub   C   "This is a test."
T1          pub   N             0  (          0.00000000)
T2          pub   N             0  (          0.00000000)
T3          pub   N             0  (          0.00000000)
T4          pub   N             0  (          0.00000000)
T5          pub   N             0  (          0.00000000)
    13 variables defined,       116 bytes used
   243 variables available,    5884 bytes available
```

This feature is handy when you are creating programs.

Memory variables are listed in the order in which they are created.

SPECIAL MEMORY VARIABLES

In addition to the 256 memory variables that *dBASE III Plus* allows you to create, the program recognizes several special memory functions. These functions are used to display information about the system's status. For example, the date and time used by DOS can be accessed in *dBASE III Plus* by using the memory functions DATE() and TIME(). Enter

? DATE(), TIME()< return >

The program displays a date and a character string representing the time according to DOS. These functions are always available regardless of the data base file in use. When a data base file is in use, *dBASE III Plus* keeps track of certain conditions as memory variables.

BOF()   True if the pointer is at the beginning of the file; false at all other times.

EOF()   True if the pointer is at the end of the file; false at all other times.

RECNO()   A numeric value equal to the current pointer position.

Enter

? RECNO(), BOF(), EOF()< return >

These functions are used primarily in programming, but they can be accessed at any time a file is open.

MODIFICATIONS OF THE MEMORY AREA

Once a variable is created, it remains in the memory until you exit *dBASE III Plus*, unless you enter one of the commands that alters the memory's contents. If you enter a new value for a variable, it replaces the old value. Enter

```
? income < return >
income=1000 < return >
? income < return >
```

If you want to remove a variable from the memory area, you can use the RELEASE command. Enter

```
RELEASE t1 <return >
DISPLAY MEMORY <return >
```

The program displays

```
TOTEXP     pub   N        744.30  (        744.30000000)
JAN        pub   N        563.36  (        563.36000000)
FEB        pub   N        180.94  (        180.94000000)
INCOME     pub   N        1200  (      1200.00000000)
KEY        pub   C   "SEARS"
TEST       pub   L   .T.
TODAY      pub   D   03/01/85
SENTENCE   pub   C   "This is a test."
T2         pub   N           0  (         0.00000000)
T3         pub   N           0  (         0.00000000)
T4         pub   N           0  (         0.00000000)
T5         pub   N           0  (         0.00000000)
     12 variables defined,     107 bytes used
    244 variables available,   5893 bytes available
```

Notice that T1 has been removed. To clear the memory of all variables, enter

> **RELEASE ALL< return >**
> **DISPLAY MEMORY <return >**

All the variables have been removed from the memory area.

> *The RELEASE command accepts a wild card character like ? or *. For example, suppose you wanted to remove T2, T3, T4, and so on. You could enter RELEASE T?. The command selects all the two-character variables that begin with T. The * is used as a wild card for a group of characters. RELEASE T* would erase TEST, TEACHER, and TIME as well as T2.*

RESTORING VARIABLES

You can load data from a MEM (Memory) file by using the RESTORE FROM command. Enter

> **RESTORE FROM testvars< return >**
> **DISPLAY MEMORY<return >**

The program displays

```
TOTEXP     pub   N        744.30  (        744.30000000)
JAN        pub   N        563.36  (        563.36000000)
FEB        pub   N        180.94  (        180.94000000)
INCOME     pub   N        1200  (      1200.00000000)
KEY        pub   C   "SEARS"
TEST       pub   L   .T.
TODAY      pub   D   03/01/85
      7 variables defined,      54 bytes used
    249 variables available,   5946 bytes available
```

Notice that only the variables that were active at the time the file was created were retrieved. The variables added after the SAVE TO command was issued are not part of the file.

> *When the RESTORE FROM command is used, any information currently in the memory is erased before the variables are restored from the file. The RESTORE command has an optional setting that protects any variables already in the memory. Us-*

ing the ADDITIVE clause adds the stored variables to the existing variables, for example: RESTORE FROM testvars ADDITIVE.

However, if the restored file contains a variable with the same name as an existing variable, the existing variable is overwritten even when the ADDITIVE clause is used.

CLEAR ALL

The CLEAR ALL command is a special form of the CLOSE command. It is not related to the CLEAR command, which affects the screen display only. The CLOSE command is used to CLOSE files such as data base or index files. CLEAR ALL closes all data base and index files and clears all memory variables. The purpose of CLEAR ALL is to return *dBASE III Plus* to the state it was in when you loaded the program.

CLEAR ALL does not affect the status of FORMAT files. FORMAT files are explained in Chapter 8.

Enter

CLEAR ALL < return >

Notice that CLEAR ALL does not affect the data displayed on the screen. You may still have the results of a previous command displayed on the screen after a CLEAR ALL has been issued. Do not get confused. All memory variables have been released and the data base and index files closed. Enter

DISPLAY MEMORY <return >
DISPLAY STATUS < return >

The commands reveal that no data base files or memory variables are active. This is the condition of the program when it is first loaded into the computer. Enter

< return >

COLUMN REPORTS

Up to this point, all the data output from the data base files has been unformatted. Unformatted output refers to the "dumping" of information produced by commands like LIST, DISPLAY, and ?. These commands display data without regard to page length, margins, page heading, page numbers, column spacing, or any of the other characteristics of a finished report.

Formatted output takes into consideration the design and printing feature not provided for in the commands that produce raw, unformatted data.

Formatted output is generally designed for printed reports, but it can be used to send data displays to the screen or even to a disk file. The next section of this chapter describes the commands used to create, print, and revise column reports.

Because reports are related to data base files, you must have such a file open before you can create a column report. Enter

USE expenses < return >

To create a column report, begin by entering

CREATE REPORT <return >

The program then asks you to enter a name for the report. Enter

expenses < return >

dBASE III Plus will display

```
Options         Groups          Columns         Locate      Exit  10:48:24 am
Page title
Page width (positions)    80
Left margin                8
Right margin               0
Lines per page            58
Double space report       No
Page eject before printing Yes
Page eject after printing  No
Plain page                 No
```

```
CURSOR   <— —>    Delete char:    Del    Insert column: ^N   Insert:    Ins
Char:     <  >    Delete word:    ^T     Report format: F1   Zoom in:  ^PgDn
Word:   Home End  Delete column:  ^U     Abandon:       Esc   Zoom out: ^PgUp
```

CREATE REPORT | <C:> | EXPENSES.FRM | Opt: 1/9 | |

All report specifications are stored in files with .FRM extensions. That is why you can have both a data base file, EXPENSES.DBF, and a report form, EXPENSES.FRM. The report file contains a description of how the report should be printed. The actual data are drawn from the data base file.

Furthermore, even though a report is created with a specific data base in use, the report can be printed with any data base file that contains the fields mentioned in the report form. For example, if you create a report for the EXPENSES file and then make a new file with the same structure, EXP1986, the report can also be used with that file.

The fields used are the key, not the name of the data base file.

The CREATE REPORT command places *dBASE III Plus* in a menu-driven mode that assists you in the creation of column reports. The command has five menus:

Options. This menu allows you to specify actions that affect the overall format of the report like margins, line spacing, and headings.

Groups. This section allows you to create reports with one or two levels of sub-total groups. Subtotal groups are the result of two related but distinct actions: creating a report with subtotal groups, and indexing or sorting the data base file to place related records into groups. You cannot produce reports with subtotals without correctly performing both actions. The actions can be performed in any order, but they must both take place before you attempt to produce the report. Attempting to print a subtotal report with an unsequenced data base file usually produces an unexpected result.

Columns. This section is the heart of the report. It contains your specification for the data, as well as the format of the individual columns. You must use this option to specify at least one column for the report.

Locate. This option does not affect the contents or format of a report. It is used as an editing aid to jump from one section of the report specification to another. It is not necessary to use this menu.

Exit. This option is used to terminate, and if desired, save the report specification.

Turn off the editing display at the bottom of the screen by entering

[F1]

The display at the bottom is the report format display box. It is used to represent the column specifications that you have entered. Its purpose is to provide a model or preview of what the column report will look like.

```
 Options         Groups        Columns        Locate       Exit  10:50:09 am
 Page title
 Page width (positions)    80
 Left margin                8
 Right margin               0
 Lines per page            58
 Double space report       No
 Page eject before printing Yes
 Page eject after printing  No
 Plain page                 No

 Report Format
 >>>>>>>>

CREATE REPORT  |<C:>|EXPENSES.FRM          |Opt: 1/9        |       |
```

The > > > > > > > stands for the eight-character left margin, which is the default value.

The OPTIONS menu has the following items:

Page title. This is a 1- to 4-line heading printed at the top of every page of the report. When you enter a heading, it will appear at the left side of the display but will be centered between the margins when printed.

Page width. This option specifies the number of characters that will print on each line including the right and left margins. When you use special print commands to compress the printing, you need to increase the value of the page width to get more characters printed across the page. The default value is 80 characters.

Left margin. The default value is 8 characters.

Right margin. The default value is zero characters.

Lines per page. This option controls the number of printed lines per page. The form is assumed to be 66 lines (i.e., 11 inches long). The default is 58 lines of printing per page.

Double space report. Controls line spacing. The default is No (i.e., single spacing).

Page eject before printing. The default, Yes, causes a form feed to occur before the report prints.

Page eject after printing. If YES, causes a form feed following the end of the report. The default value is No.

Plain page. When YES, this option prints the page heading only on the first page of the report. All subsequent pages are printed without headings or page numbers. The default is No.

In this example, enter a page heading. Enter

> < return >

dBASE III Plus displays a box with four blank lines. You can enter up to four lines of text for the page heading. If you type lines that are wider than the box, the display will scroll to allow entry of long lines. Enter

> **EXPENSE REPORT**
> **[Pg Up]**

Next, enter the columns section of the report generator by entering

c

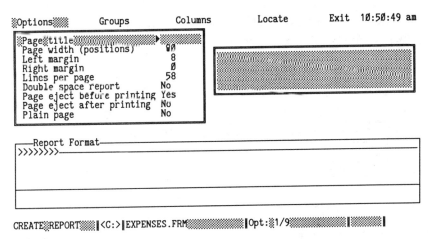

```
 Options        Groups        Columns        Locate        Exit  10:50:49 am
 Page title                        ▶
 Page width (positions)     90
 Left margin                 8
 Right margin                0
 Lines per page             58
 Double space report        No
 Page eject before printing Yes
 Page eject after printing  No
 Plain page                 No

  ┌─Report Format──────────────────────────────────────────────────┐
  >>>>>>>>─────────────────────────────────────────────────────────
  │                                                                 │
  │                                                                 │
  │                                                                 │
  └─────────────────────────────────────────────────────────────────┘

 CREATE REPORT  |<C:>|EXPENSES.FRM          |Opt: 1/9         |       |
```

Each column requires two pieces of information:

Contents. The contents of a column can be the results of any valid *dBASE III Plus* expression. The simplest column contents are fields. You can also enter numeric, character, date, or logical expressions or formulas.

Width. You are required to specify the width, in terms of number of characters, for each column. *dBASE III Plus* enters the width indicated by the entry in the contents section as a default value. You can choose to manually increase or decrease the value.

A column heading consisting of up to four lines of text can be specified, but it is not required.

If the values in the contents area are numeric, *dBASE III Plus* allows you to specify the number of decimal places. You can also request a total to be printed at the bottom of the column. To enter a column specification, enter

   < return >

```
 Options        Groups        Columns        Locate        Exit  10:53:26 am
                    ┌─────────────────────────────────────────────────────┐
                    │ Contents                                            │
                    │ Heading                                             │
                    │ Width                    0                          │
                    │ Decimal places                                     │
                    │ Total this column                                  │
                    └─────────────────────────────────────────────────────┘

  ┌─Report Format──────────────────────────────────────────────────┐
  >>>>>>>>─────────────────────────────────────────────────────────
  │                                                                 │
  │                                                                 │
  │                                                                 │
  └─────────────────────────────────────────────────────────────────┘

 CREATE REPORT  |<C:>|EXPENSES.FRM          |Column: 1         |       |
```

You can now enter the contents of the first column. In order to make entry easier, you can display a list of the fields by entering

[F10]

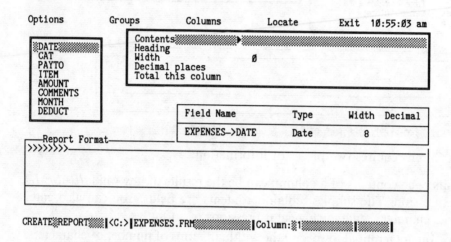

To select the DATE field, enter

< return >

dBASE III Plus automatically types the field name onto the contents line. To complete the entry, enter

< return >

The value of 8 is automatically entered into the width area. Also note that the report format display at the bottom of the screen has changed to reflect the new column. The MM/DD/YY shows you where the data will print on the final report.

You can now add a heading to be printed at the top of the column. Enter

< down arrow >
< return >
DATE OF < return >
EXPENSE < return >
[Pg Up]

The heading is added to the report format box. Note that the ; in the heading area indicates that the items will appear on separate lines. The format box also shows where the data will appear under the heading.

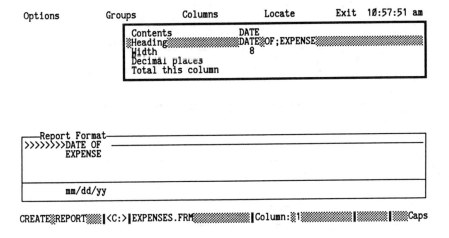

To add another column specification, enter

[Pg Dn]

The contents area can contain expressions as well as field names. For example, you can create a column that shows the day of the week that an expense was incurred by using a date function as the contents of the column. Enter

> **< return >**
> **CDOW(date) < return >**

Enter the heading as follows:

> **< down arrow >**
> **< return >**
> **DAY OF< return >**
> **WEEK< return >**
> **[Pg Up]**

Create another column by entering

> **[Pg Dn]**
> **< return >**
> **payto < return >**

Enter the heading as follows:

> **< down arrow >**
> **< return >**
> **PAYEE**
> **[Pg Up]**

The screen looks like this:

```
Options          Groups         Columns        Locate        Exit  11:00:24 am
                   ┌─────────────────────────────────────────────────────────┐
                   │ Contents            payto                                │
                   │ Heading             PAYEE                                │
                   │ Width               20                                   │
                   │ Decimal places                                          │
                   │ Total this column                                       │
                   └─────────────────────────────────────────────────────────┘




  ┌─Report Format─────────────────────────────────────────────────────────────┐
  │>>>>>>>>DATE OF   DAY OF    PAYEE           ─────────────────────────────── │
  │        EXPENSE   WEEK                                                       │
  │                                                                            │
  │                                                                            │
  │      mm/dd/yy XXXXXXXXX XXXXXXXXXXXXXXXXXXXX                               │
  └────────────────────────────────────────────────────────────────────────────┘

CREATE REPORT    |<C:>|EXPENSES.FRM            |Column: 3           |         |
```

The next column will be a numeric. Enter

> **[Pg Dn]**
> **< return >**
> **amount < return >**

Because the field is numeric, the program has inserted values in the decimal point and total areas. Enter a heading

> **< down arrow >**
> **< return >**
> **AMOUNT**
> **[Pg Up]**

dBASE III Plus *automatically assigns the field width to the width area of a numeric column. This can cause a problem with the total for that column. For example, the largest number that can appear in a numeric column that is six characters wide with two decimal places is 999.99. However, when the values in that field are totaled, it is possible that the sum will exceed 999.99. If that is the case, dBASE III Plus will round the total and eliminate the decimal places to display the larger figure. In this way, dBASE III Plus will be able to display a value up to 999,999. If the value of the total is still too large to be displayed, in this example over a million,* ****** *will appear in the total area. Should this happen, you can correct the situation by widening the column width specification to allow full display of the numbers.*

Finally, add the last column by entering

> **[Pg Dn]**
> **< return >**
> **item < return >**
> **< down arrow >**
> **< return >**
> **DESCRIPTION**
> **[Pg Up]**

The report has now been defined.

```
Options          Groups         Columns          Locate        Exit  11:01:49 am
                      ┌─────────────────────────────────────────────────────────────┐
                      │ Contents              item                                   │
                      │ Heading               DESCRIPTION                            │
                      │ Width                 20                                      │
                      │ Decimal places                                               │
                      │ Total this column                                            │
                      └─────────────────────────────────────────────────────────────┘



         ┌─Report Format──────────────────────────────────────────────────────────┐
         │ TE OF  DAY OF    PAYEE            AMOUNT DESCRIPTION              ──      │
         │ PENSE  WEEK                                                              │
         │                                                                          │
         │ /dd/yy XXXXXXXXX XXXXXXXXXXXXXXXXXXX ###.## XXXXXXXXXXXXXXXXXXXX          │
         └──────────────────────────────────────────────────────────────────────┘

CREATE REPORT  |<C:>|EXPENSES.FRM                |Column: 5             |      | Caps
```

Note the ─── at the end of the report format box. They indicate that you have used up all but 4 of the 80 characters allotted for the line width. That means that you could add one more column, but the width of the column could be no more than three characters (1 character is used for the space between columns). In this way, *dBASE III Plus* attempts to keep you from defining a report that is too wide for your paper.

Save the report form by entering

> **e**
> **< return >**

To display the report, enter

> **REPORT FORM expenses< return >**

The screen displays the report.

```
Page No.      1
01/01/80
                                    EXPENSE REPORT
DATE OF  DAY OF    PAYEE              AMOUNT DESCRIPTION
EXPENSE  WEEK

01/02/85 Wednesday CROW CANYON LUMBER  68.40 10 2 BY 4
01/10/85 Thursday  SEARS               17.95 TRASH CAN
01/15/85 Tuesday   GREEN ACRES FURN   264.68 DESKS
01/17/85 Thursday  INSTANT PRINTING    59.50 ENVELOPES
01/21/85 Monday    PG&E                60.60 TURN ON ELEC
01/25/85 Friday    PACIFIC BELL        44.28 INSTALL TELE
01/30/85 Wednesday BRITZ PRINTING      47.95 BUSINESS CARDS
02/02/85 Saturday  GIFT STORE           5.94 GROUND HOG DAY CARDS
02/05/85 Tuesday   GREEN ACRES FURN   175.00 CHAIRS
*** Total ***
                                      744.30
```

dBASE III Plus inserts the systems date at the top of each page of the report. The date is determined by the date entered into the operating system. If you want the report to show the real date, you must make sure that the proper date is entered into DOS, either manually or by the use of a battery-powered clock/calendar.

To print the report on the printer, enter the following. Make sure that your computer is properly connected to a printer before you enter this command:

REPORT FORM expenses TO PRINT <return>

The report is sent to the printer.

You can output a report for a selected group of records by adding a FOR clause. Enter the following:

REPORT FORM expenses FOR MONTH(date)=1 <return>

The program displays

```
Page No.      1
01/01/80
                          EXPENSE REPORT
DATE OF  DAY OF    PAYEE                  AMOUNT DESCRIPTION
EXPENSE  WEEK

01/02/85 Wednesday CROW CANYON LUMBER     68.40 10 2 BY 4
01/10/85 Thursday  SEARS                  17.95 TRASH CAN
01/15/85 Tuesday   GREEN ACRES FURN      264.68 DESKS
01/17/85 Thursday  INSTANT PRINTING       59.50 ENVELOPES
01/21/85 Monday    PG&E                   60.60 TURN ON ELEC
01/25/85 Friday    PACIFIC BELL           44.28 INSTALL TELE
01/30/85 Wednesday BRITZ PRINTING         47.95 BUSINESS CARDS
*** Total ***

                                         563.36
```

If an index file is open, the report will list the records in the order indicated by the index file. Enter

SET INDEX TO payorder <return>

Now display the report. Enter

REPORT FORM expenses TO PRINT <return>

The program displays

```
Page No.      1
01/01/80
                          EXPENSE REPORT
DATE OF  DAY OF    PAYEE                  AMOUNT DESCRIPTION
EXPENSE  WEEK

01/30/85 Wednesday BRITZ PRINTING         47.95 BUSINESS CARDS
01/02/85 Wednesday CROW CANYON LUMBER     68.40 10 2 BY 4
01/15/85 Tuesday   GREEN ACRES FURN      264.68 DESKS
01/17/85 Thursday  INSTANT PRINTING       59.50 ENVELOPES
01/21/85 Monday    PG&E                   60.60 TURN ON ELEC
01/25/85 Friday    PACIFIC BELL           44.28 INSTALL TELE
01/10/85 Thursday  SEARS                  17.95 TRASH CAN
*** Total ***

                                         563.36
```

LINE WRAPPING AND MEMO FIELDS

One important feature of the report generator is its ability to create a form of wraparound printing for fields with wide contents. This is particularly true of MEMO fields, but the principle applies to any text field.

dBASE III Plus usually assigns the width of the field or expression to the column width specification. However, in the case of wide text fields or MEMO fields, you can change the value of the width to a smaller value. This allows you to add more columns. When the report prints, *dBASE III Plus* will break the text in the field into a series of short lines and stack them up in a column. Wherever possible, *dBASE III Plus* breaks the lines at spaces in the text. The effect is similar to the wraparound typing effect in word processing programs.

If a single word is wider than the column width, *dBASE III Plus* simply chops off the extra characters and places them at the beginning of the next line. This is a very handy feature and makes the use of text fields in reports much simpler. To see how it works, you can modify the EXPENSES report form. Enter

        MODIFY REPORT expenses < return >

The program displays the REPORT menu with the specification you entered when you created the report.

Functionally, CREATE REPORT and MODIFY REPORT are the same command. They can be used interchangeably.

Now that you have entered column specifications, the LOCATE menu offers an easy way to move to the column specification you want to change. Enter

        I

The LOCATE menu actually consists of a listing of the column contents specification from each of the columns you have defined. To move to a specific column, simply highlight the item you want and press < return >. For example, to bring up the day of the week column, enter

        < down arrow >
        < return >

You can delete a column specification by entering

        [CTRL/u]

The report format box now shows what the report will look like without that column.

Changes made to a report form do not become permanent until you have saved the changes. Entering < Esc > or selecting ABANDON from the EXIT menu leaves the report form exactly as it was when you last saved it.

Move to the DESCRIPTION field by entering

        [Pg Dn]
        [Pg Dn]

Change the width of the column to 12 characters by entering

> **<down arrow> (2 times)**
> **<return>**
> **12<return>**

Now you can select to display the contents of the COMMENTS field. Enter

> **<Pg Dn>**
> **<return>**
> **comments<return>**

dBASE III Plus has automatically assigned to the COMMENTS field the 21 characters that are left on the form. Add the heading for this column. Enter

> **<down arrow>**
> **<return>**
> **COMMENTS<return>**
> **[Pg Up]**

Save the revised report. Enter

> **e**
> **<return>**

To print the report, enter

> **REPORT FORM expenses TO PRINT<return>**

The report will look like this:

```
Page No.      1
01/01/80
                             EXPENSE REPORT
DATE OF   PAYEE              AMOUNT DESCRIPTION  COMMENTS
EXPENSE

01/02/85  CROW CANYON LUMBER  68.40 10 2 BY 4
01/10/85  SEARS               17.95 TRASH CAN
01/15/85  GREEN ACRES FURN   264.68 DESKS
01/17/85  INSTANT PRINTING    59.50 ENVELOPES
01/21/85  PG&E                60.60 TURN ON ELEC This amount is a
                                                 deposit held by the
                                                 electric company
                                                 because of our
                                                 current lack of
                                                 credit. If all bills
                                                 are paid on time for
                                                 a period of one year,
                                                 this deposit will be
                                                 refunded.
01/25/85  PACIFIC BELL        44.28 INSTALL TELE At this time we will
                                                 use AT&T as our long
                                                 distance carrier.
                                                 However, other
                                                 possible long
                                                 distance services
                                                 should be examined
                                                 in light of their
                                                 potential savings.

01/30/85  BRITZ PRINTING      47.95 BUSINESS
                                    CARDS
02/02/85  GIFT STORE           5.94 GROUND HOG
                                    DAY CARDS
02/05/85  GREEN ACRES FURN   175.00 CHAIRS
*** Total ***

                             744.30
```

dBASE III Plus was able to print the contents of the MEMO field as a series of short lines that fit into the specified column width.

CALCULATIONS AND NUMERIC FORMATS

Reports can be used to print information not actually entered into the data base file. This can be done by entering character or numeric expressions into the column contents areas. Suppose you wanted to create a report that showed each expense as a percent of total expenses, and also as a percent of total income. You could use numeric expressions to accomplish this task.

Before you can create the report, you must take into consideration the numeric values you will be using in the report. For example, if you want to show the expenses as a percent of the total amount of all expenses, you will need to have a value to use for the total amount.

The total calculated by the report does not appear until the bottom of the report. There are two ways to get around this problem: (1) enter a numeric literal into the contents area, or (2) create a variable and use it in the contents area. The second method, creating a memory variable, is the better solution. By using a variable name, you can use the same report over and over again without alteration. To update the value for total expenses or income, you need only change the value of the memory variable. If you enter a literal numeric amount, you must modify the report each time a new expense is included in it.

To use a variable name in the contents area of a report form, the variable must already exist. If you try to enter the name of a variable that is not currently in the memory, *dBASE III Plus* will reject the contents expression as invalid.

> *In this example, the actual value of the total expense and income variables does not matter when you create the report form. All that matters is that dBASE III Plus can find some memory variable with that name in the memory area. You need to make sure of the actual value of those variables prior to the printing of the report.*

In this example you will need two variables: one for total income and one for total expenses. Enter

        totinc=1200 <return>
        SUM amount TO totexp <return>

Check the results of those commands by entering

        DISPLAY MEMORY <return>

The display shows that two variables are stored in memory.

```
     TOTINC      pub   N     1200  (      1200.00000000)
     TOTEXP      pub   N      744.30 (       744.30000000)
        2 variables defined,       18 bytes used
      254 variables available,   5982 bytes available
```

Now you can create the new report form. Enter

CREATE REPORT stats < return >

Enter the title for the report:

< return >
EXPENSE ANALYSIS
[Pg Up]

Enter the first column specification by entering

c

The first column will show the date. Instead of showing 01/02/85 you can use date and string functions to display a date in the form January 2. Enter

< return >
CMONTH(date)+STR(DAY(date),3)< return >

Before you go on you might want to examine the previous expression a bit more closely. The first part uses the CMONTH() function to display the full text name of the month. The + is used to join that text item to an expression that consists of a string of characters that contains the day of the month. This string is the result of two functions. The first, DAY(date), provides the number of the day of the month. However, the number returned by the DAY() function is a numeric value, and the name of the month provided by the CMONTH() function is a character string. The + will operate only if both items to be joined are text.

The problem is solved by converting the numeric value to a text string using the STR() function. STR() converts numeric values into text strings. The main function of STR() is to allow text strings to combine with numeric values. The STR() function requires that you specify the number or length of the converted string. In this case, choosing 3 means that each number will be preceded by a space.

Enter a heading for the column:

< down arrow >
< return >
DATE OF< return >
EXPENSE
[Pg Up]

Next, add a second column to the report. Enter

[Pg Dn]

Enter the payee in this column.

< return >
[F10]
< down arrow > (2 times)
< return > (2 times)

Add the heading for that column by entering

> **<down arrow>**
> **<return>**
> **PAYEE**
> **[Pg Up]**

Add the next column by entering

> **[Pg Dn]**

This column will be the amount of the expense. Enter

> **<return>**
> **[F10]**
> **<down arrow> (4 times)**
> **<return> (2 times)**

Add the heading for this column. Enter

> **<down arrow>**
> **<return>**
> **AMOUNT**
> **[Pg Up]**

The next column will be the one that uses the memory variable, TOTEXP, to express the expense as a percentage of the total. Enter

> **[Pg Dn]**
> **<return>**
> **amount/totexp*100<return>**

Add the heading by entering

> **<down arrow>**
> **<return>**
> **% OF<return>**
> **EXPENSES**
> **[Pg Up]**

Notice that *dBASE III Plus* has automatically assigned a width of 20 for this column. By its very nature, the calculation produces numbers that are much smaller than that. To prevent wasting space in the report, you must manually enter a smaller column width. Enter

> **<down arrow>**
> **<return>**
> **8<return>**

Why was 8 chosen? Widening the column to 5 would have been adequate for the numeric value, but 8 was used to allow the heading to print on two lines. Change the number of decimal places to one by entering

        <down arrow>
        <return>
        1<return>

Add another column; this one will show the expense as a percentage of the total income. Enter

        <return>
        amount/totinc*100<return>
        <down arrow>
        <return>
        % OF<return>
        INCOME
        [Pg Up]
        <down arrow>
        <return>
        8<return>
        <down arrow>
        <return>
        1<return>

Save the report by entering

        e<return>

Display the report on screen by entering

        REPORT FORM stats<return>

The report will look like this:

```
Page No.      1
01/01/80
                         EXPENSE ANALYSIS
DATE OF      PAYEE            AMOUNT     % OF      % OF
EXPENSE                               EXPENSES   INCOME

January   2  CROW CANYON LUMBER   68.40    9.2      5.7
January  10  SEARS               17.95    2.4      1.5
January  15  GREEN ACRES FURN   264.68   35.6     22.1
January  17  INSTANT PRINTING    59.50    8.0      5.0
January  21  PG&E                60.60    8.1      5.1
January  25  PACIFIC BELL        44.28    5.9      3.7
January  30  BRITZ PRINTING      47.95    6.4      4.0
February  2  GIFT STORE           5.94    0.8      0.5
February  5  GREEN ACRES FURN   175.00   23.5     14.6
*** Total ***
                                  1.1    100.0     62.0
```

ADDING NUMERIC FORMATS

One addition to reports with numeric values is numeric formats. A *numeric format* is a special character that you add to the numeric value to make the number more readable. Typical examples are such punctuation marks as commas, dollar signs, and percent signs. *dBASE III Plus* allows you to add these formatting capabilities to the column report by using the TRANSFORM() function.

As with most functions, transform can be used with any command that accepts a *dBASE III Plus* expression. Suppose you wanted to display the TOTINC figure with a comma inserted between the hundreds and thousands places. Enter

? totinc,TRANSFORM(totinc,"9,999.99")<return>

dBASE III Plus prints the value in two ways. The first is the normal *dBASE III Plus* display. The second adds formatting to the value. The TRANSFORM() function requires two arguments. The first is a numeric value or expression. The second is called a *picture string*. The picture string is a model of the formatting you want to apply to the numeric value. The nines in the picture string represent any number from 0 to 9. The other characters show *dBASE III Plus* where and how to add formatting. Because the picture portion of the function is a string value, it must be enclosed in quotation marks. Enter

? TRANSFORM(totinc,"$9,999.99")<return>

This time you added a dollar sign to the display. You can now modify your report STATS to include numeric formatting. In this example the formatting is used to clarify which figures stand for dollar amounts and which are percentages. Enter

MODIFY REPORT stats<return>

Display the AMOUNT field by entering

I
<down arrow> (2 times)
<return>

Clear the contents area by entering

<return>
[Home]
[CTRL/y]

Now enter

TRANSFORM(amount,"9,999.99")<return>

Move to the next column by entering

[Pg Dn]

This time, instead of entering an entirely new expression, you edit the existing expression. Enter

<return>

The cursor is positioned at the end of the expression. Enter

[Home]

Place the program in the INSERT mode by entering

[Ins]

Now add the following to the beginning of the formula:

TRANSFORM(

Move to the end of the expression by entering

[End]

Now complete the expression by entering

,"999.9%")<return>

Move to the next column.

[Pg Dn]

Exercise 4   Enter an expression to transform the value to a three-digit number with one decimal place and a percent sign. The correct expression can be found at the end of the chapter.

When the expression has been entered, save the change by entering

e<return>

Now display the results by entering

REPORT FORM stats<return>

The report will look like this:

```
Page No.      1
01/01/80
                          EXPENSE ANALYSIS
DATE OF     PAYEE              AMOUNT    % OF      % OF
EXPENSE                                 EXPENSES  INCOME
January  2  CROW CANYON LUMBER  68.40    9.1%      5.7%
January 10  SEARS               17.95    2.4%      1.5%
January 15  GREEN ACRES FURN   264.68   35.5%     22.0%
January 17  INSTANT PRINTING    59.50    7.9%      4.9%
January 21  PG&E                60.60    8.1%      5.0%
January 25  PACIFIC BELL        44.28    5.9%      3.6%
January 30  BRITZ PRINTING      47.95    6.4%      4.0%
February  2 GIFT STORE           5.94    0.8%      0.5%
February  5 GREEN ACRES FURN   175.00   23.5%     14.5%
```

What has happened to the totals? The totals no longer appear because the TRANSFORM() function changed the column contents from a numeric expression to a character expression. If you need both formats and totals, a custom report can be created. This technique is explained in Part II of this book under Custom Reports.

REPORTS WITH SUBTOTALS

Creating reports with subtotals requires two separate but related actions. You must create a report with subtotal groupings specified and you must SORT or INDEX your data base file in order to bring together all the records that belong to the same grouping.

Subtotal reports operate on the basis of a *control break*. In a control break report, a field is selected as the control field (e.g., budget category). The idea behind a control break report is that the program will process all the records as long as the value in the control field does not change. When a change in the control value is detected, the program performs a break. The break can in theory be any sort of action. However, in terms of the report form there are two possible actions *dBASE III Plus* will perform: print a subtotal and/or begin printing at the top of a new page.

Because subtotals are triggered by a change in the control field, you must SORT or INDEX the file before you print so that all the records that belong under one subtotal are grouped together.

The SORT or INDEX does not have to be performed before you create the report, only before you print it.

Suppose you wanted to print a report that displays subtotals totaled by category. The first step is to decide what the control field or expression will be. In this case the CAT field is the one that will control the subtotals. Remember that you have previously created an index file, CATORDER, that orders the file by CAT. Enter

```
SET INDEX TO catorder < return >
LIST cat < return >
```

The file is now ordered correctly for a subtotal report. Instead of creating a new report, you can modify an existing report, EXPENSES. Enter

```
MODIFY REPORT expenses < return >
```

You can modify the report's title to reflect the modifications you are making in the report.

```
< return >
[End] (2 times)
 BY CATEGORY < return >
[Pg Up]
```

The next step is to set the subtotal information, which is stored under the GROUPS menu. Enter

g

```
Options        ▓Groups▓        Columns        Locate        Exit  11:07:23 am
               ┌──────────────────────────────────────────────────────┐
               │▓Group▓on▓expression▓░░░░░░░░░░░░░░░░░░░░░░░░░░░░░░░░░░░░│
               │ Group heading                                         │
               │ Summary report only        No                        │
               │ Page eject after group                                │
               │ Sub-group on expression                               │
               │ Sub-group heading                                     │
               └──────────────────────────────────────────────────────┘
```

The GROUPS menu has six items:

Group on expression. This expression defines the subtotal group.

Group heading. This heading is printed each time a new grouping is encountered.

Summary report only. A summary report prints only the subtotal information and none of the detail (i.e., records). The default is NO summary report (i.e., print all records).

Page eject after group. This option tells *dBASE III Plus* to begin each new subtotal group at the top of a new page. This physically separates each subtotal group so that no two groups appear on the same page.

Sub-group on expression and **Sub-group heading.** These entries define a secondary subtotal group within the primary grouping.

The first item to enter is the field or expression that will be used as the control break criterion. In this case the expression will be the CAT field. Enter

    <return>
    [F10]

The program lists the names of the fields that can be used. Select the CAT field by entering

    <down arrow>
    <return>
    <return>

The next step is to add a subtotal category heading. The heading will print at the beginning of each group of related records. Keep in mind that the entire heading will be composed of the heading text and the value of the active control break expression. For example, if you define the subtotal heading as CATEGORY #, then the heading for the category 120 will read CATEGORY # 120. Enter

    <down arrow>
    CATEGORY #<return>

dBASE III Plus automatically enters No values for the summary report and page ejection options.

Before you save the report specification, delete the COMMENTS column. This deletion is not directly related to the creation of subtotals but it will make the report display simpler for the purpose of this example. Move to the COMMENTS column by entering

I
[Pg Dn]
<return>

Delete the column by entering

[CTRL/u]

Save the revised report by entering

e<return>

Display the subtotal report by entering

REPORT FORM expenses TO PRINT<return>

The report will look like this:

```
Page No.      1
01/01/80
                      EXPENSE REPORT BY CATEGORY

  DATE OF  PAYEE              AMOUNT DESCRIPTION
  EXPENSE


** CATEGORY #    110
   01/02/85 CROW CANYON LUMBER    68.40 10 2 BY 4
** Subtotal **
                                  68.40

** CATEGORY #    120
   01/15/85 GREEN ACRES FURN     264.68 DESKS
   02/05/85 GREEN ACRES FURN     175.00 CHAIRS
** Subtotal **
                                 439.68

** CATEGORY #    130
   01/21/85 PG&E                  60.60 TURN ON ELEC
   01/25/85 PACIFIC BELL          44.28 INSTALL TELE
** Subtotal **
                                 104.88

** CATEGORY #    140
   01/10/85 SEARS                 17.95 TRASH CAN
   01/17/85 INSTANT PRINTING      59.50 ENVELOPES
   01/30/85 BRITZ PRINTING        47.95 BUSINESS
                                        CARDS
   02/02/85 GIFT STORE             5.94 GROUND HOG
                                        DAY CARDS
** Subtotal **
                                 131.34
*** Total ***
                                 744.30
```

The report shows totals for each of the budget categories in the file. The important factor to keep in mind is that control break reports, like this one, are dependent on the previous indexing or sorting of the file. If the file has not been sequenced properly, the report will print showing subtotals each time a new category appears.

Subtotal reports can be used with FOR clauses to select records for the report. The following command will print the subtotal report for those records that are dated in January. Enter

REPORT FORM expenses FOR MONTH(date)=1 <return>

The same report prints but the records selected are for January only.

SPECIAL OPTION CLAUSES

dBASE III Plus has three special clauses that work only with the REPORT FORM command. The purpose of these clauses is to change temporarily some of the settings entered into the report form. The advantage of the clauses is that they do not permanently affect the report form but do change the printing of a specific report.

The SUMMARY clause causes the report to print as a summary report even though the report was created as a detailed report. A summary report prints the subtotal headings, the subtotals, and the totals specified in the report form. However, none of the individual records will be displayed. As an example, enter

REPORT FORM expenses SUMMARY <return>

The report displays as follows:

```
Page No.     1
01/01/80
                        EXPENSE REPORT BY CATEGORY

DATE OF   PAYEE              AMOUNT DESCRIPTION
EXPENSE


** CATEGORY /   110
** Subtotal **
                          68.40

** CATEGORY /   120
** Subtotal **
                         439.68

** CATEGORY /   130
** Subtotal **
                         104.88

** CATEGORY /   140
** Subtotal **
                         131.34
*** Total ***
                         744.30
```

The HEADING clause is used to specify an additional heading that will print at the top of the report form on the same line where the page number is printed. The purpose of this clause is to allow you to enter a notation that will appear on the report that reflects the options and conditions under which the report was printed. For example, if you use a FOR clause to limit the records selected for a report, the HEADING clause enables you to add text to the report explaining what you did. Keep in mind that the HEADING clause affects only the first line on each page. The remainder of the report stays the same. Enter

> **REPORT FORM expenses FOR MONTH(date)=1 HEADING "January of 1985"<return>**

The top of the report shows the additional text specified in the HEADING clause.

```
Page No.     1           January of 1985
01/01/80
                      EXPENSE REPORT BY CATEGORY

DATE OF  PAYEE           AMOUNT DESCRIPTION
EXPENSE
```

Note that the text used with the HEADING clause is a text literal that must be enclosed in quotation marks.

You can use a memory variable with the HEADING clause if you have defined a memory variable as a character variable. For example, if you entered HEAD1="Subtotal Report", you could then use the variable name with the HEADING clause (e.g., REPORT FORM expenses HEADING head1).

The NOEJECT clause suppresses the form feed issued by a report form prior to its printing. Also note that the REPORT FORM command can be used with scopes and the WHILE clause (as explained in Chapter 6).

CONDITIONAL FUNCTIONS

A conditional function is one that allows you to substitute expressions based on some logical condition. For example, when you print the DEDUCT field you will get either a .T. or .F. symbol. Enter

> **LIST deduct<return>**

dBASE III Plus will display

```
Record#  DEDUCT
      1  .T.
      3  .T.
      9  .T.
      5  .F.
      6  .F.
      2  .F.
      4  .T.
      7  .F.
      8  .F.
```

If you are familiar with *dBASE III Plus*, you may recognize that these symbols stand for true or false values. However, to someone who does not have experience with the program, the display may be confusing. The IIF() function can be used to create a substitution. For example, if the DEDUCT field is true you might display Deductible. If it were false, then you could display Not Deductible.

The IIF() function requires three pieces of information: (1) a logical expression that can be evaluated as either true or false, (2) a value that the function will assume if the expression is true, and (3) a value that the function will assume if the expression is false.

```
                  If TRUE
IIF(  expression  ,  value 1  ,  value 2  )
                  If FALSE
```

You can use the IIF() function to solve the problem posed by the LOGICAL field, DEDUCT. In the following command, the IIF() function tests the contents of the field DEDUCT. If DEDUCT is true, the word Deductible is displayed. If DEDUCT is false, the words Not Deductible are displayed. Note that the text is surrounded by quotation marks. Enter

LIST IIF(deduct,"Deductible","Not Deductible")< return >

dBASE III Plus will display

```
Record#  IIF(deduct,"Deductible","Not Deductible")
   1     Deductible
   3     Deductible
   9     Deductible
   5     Not Deductible
   6     Not Deductible
   2     Not Deductible
   4     Deductible
   7     Not Deductible
   8     Not Deductible
```

The IIF() function can also be used with the SUM command to find the difference between two types of amounts. Suppose you wanted to know the difference between the total of the deductible items and the total of the nondeductible items. One way to do this would be to take two sums and subtract the totals.

Exercise 5   Try to find the difference by the method described above. The command to this can be found at the end of the chapter.

The IIF() function can provide the answer in a much simpler manner. Enter

SUM IIF(deduct,amount,amount*–1)< return >

dBASE III Plus displays the difference, 390.86. This function was able to find the difference by going through the file and summing a positive amount when the DEDUCT field was true and a negative amount when the DEDUCT field was false. The net result was not the sum of all the amounts but the difference.

The IIF() function can be added to report forms in order to print conditional information as part of a column report. Enter

CREATE REPORT deduct< return >

Move the cursor to the column section by entering

     < right arrow >
     < right arrow >

Create a column that will print the PAYTO field. Enter

     < return >
     payto< return >
     < down arrow >
     < return >
     PAID TO
     [Pg Up]
     [Pg Dn]

    The next column will contain an IIF() function. This column will print Deductible or Not Deductible depending on the value of the DEDUCT field. The contents area will scroll to the right to allow you to enter a longer formula than can be seen on the screen. Enter

     < return >
     IIF(deduct,"Deductible","Not Deductible")< return >
     < down arrow >
     < return >
     Deductible?< return >
     [Pg Up]

The screen will look like this:

```
Options          Groups       Columns       Locate      Exit  01:44:47 am
                        Contents          IIF(deduct,"Deductible","Not Deducti
                        Heading           Deductible?
                        Width             14
                        Decimal places
                        Total this column
```

    Bring up a new column entry box by entering

     [Pg Dn]

Next, add another column with the IIF() function. This column will print nondeductible items as negative numbers and deductible amounts as positive. Enter

     < return >
     IIF(deduct,amount,amount*−1)< return >
     < down arrow >
     < return >
     Amount< return >
     [Pg Up]

The screen will show

```
Options          Groups        Columns        Locate      Exit  01:49:25 am
                 ┌────────────────────────────────────────────────────────┐
                 │ Contents            IIF(deduct,amount,amount*-1)         │
                 │ Heading             Amount                              │
                 │ Width               9                                   │
                 │ Decimal places      2                                   │
                 │ Total this column   Yes                                 │
                 └────────────────────────────────────────────────────────┘
```

Save the report form by entering

> **< right arrow >**
> **< right arrow >**
> **< return >**

To see the effect of the IIF() functions in this report, enter

> **REPORT FORM deduct** **< return >**

dBASE III Plus will display

```
Page No.      1
01/01/80


PAID TO                 Deductible?        Amount

CROW CANYON LUMBER      Deductible          68.40
GREEN ACRES FURN        Deductible         264.68
GREEN ACRES FURN        Deductible         175.00
P G & E                 Not Deductible     -60.60
PACIFIC BELL            Not Deductible     -44.28
SEARS                   Not Deductible     -17.95
INSTANT PRINTING        Deductible          59.50
BRITZ PRINTING          Not Deductible     -47.95
GIFT STORE              Not Deductible      -5.94
*** Total ***

                                           390.86
```

The report displays the values determined by the IIF() functions, not strictly the contents of the data base fields. The ability to transform the contents of fields by using a conditional function like IIF() adds a new dimension to your reports.

In this example, the cryptic display of the LOGICAL fields, .T. or .F. is replaced with a much more readable text item.

The IIF() function can be nested. This means that you can perform a second or third level of test to determine the value of the function. Look at the command below. In that command the first test is for category 110. If true, Assets is displayed.

What is unusual about this function is that the third part of the function does not contain a value but another IIF() function. This means that if the category is not 110, then the function tests to see if the category is 120. If that is true, then Fixed is displayed. If that is also false, then Other is displayed. Enter

> **LIST IIF(cat=110,'Assets',IIF(cat=120,"Fixed","Other"))** **< return >**

dBASE III Plus displays

```
Record# iif(cat=110,"Assets",IIF(cat=120,"Fixed","Other"))
      1 Assets
      3 Fixed
      9 Fixed
      5 Other
      6 Other
      2 Other
      4 Other
      7 Other
      8 Other
```

Nesting functions in this way allows you to select from more than two options. However, the commands do get difficult to read, and you should take care to enter the proper number of parentheses.

> In the programming section of this book you will learn about other methods employed in dBASE III Plus to carry out conditional operations.

SUMMARY

Statistical Commands

SUM field list FOR expression. This command is used to find the total of a group of records.

COUNT FOR expression. This counts the number of records.

AVERAGE field list FOR expression. This command is used to calculate the average of a group of records.

Memory Variables

Memory variables allow you to store information in the data base memory that does not belong in any of the individual records. This information is usually statistical information about the data base such as sums, averages, and counts of records.

The information stored in the memory stays active until you exit *dBASE III Plus* or enter a CLEAR MEMORY command. The memory is not cleared when you open or close a data base file.

Variables can be saved by creating a special file with the SAVE TO command. Variables are loaded back into memory with the RESTORE FROM command.

Report Forms

Report forms are used to generate column reports. The column reports can contain field information or any valid *dBASE III Plus* expression including functions and memory variables.

Report forms automatically account for page breaks.

ANSWER KEY

Exercise 1

SUM amount FOR MONTH(date)=1 <return>

Exercise 2

COUNT FOR deduct <return>

Exercise 3

SUM amount TO notax FOR deduct <return>
? notax/totexp*100 <return>

76.26 percent is deductible.

Exercise 4

TRANSFORM(amount/totinc*100,"999.9%")

Exercise 5

SUM amount FOR deduct TO A
SUM amount FOR .NOT.deduct TO B
? A-B

The total will be 390.86.

## 8

MAILING LISTS

AND LABELS

So FAR YOU HAVE USED THE EXPENSES file to illustrate all the data base commands and techniques you have learned. In this chapter you will learn the methods involved in handling mailing lists.

Mailing lists are not in and of themselves unusual. They are created and manipulated like any other data base file such as the EXPENSES file. The reason for creating a new data base is that data bases that consist of lists of people raise some interesting problems and tasks because of the nature of the information. In this chapter you will learn how *dBASE III Plus* handles the tasks and problems associated with this type of data base.

Begin by loading *dBASE III Plus*. If you are in the *dBASE III Plus* ASSIST mode, exit the mode by entering <Esc>.

CREATING THE DATA BASE

The first step is to create a data base for the list. Enter

    CREATE clients< return >

Enter the following structure using the method explained in Chapter 1. When you have finished, use the LIST STRUCTURE command to make sure your file has the structure shown below.

```
Field  Field Name  Type       Width  Dec
   1   TITLE       Character      3
   2   FIRST       Character     20
   3   LAST        Character     20
   4   STREET      Character     30
   5   CITY        Character     20
   6   STATE       Character      2
   7   ZIP         Character      5
   8   DOB         Date           8
```

ENTERING DATA

Next, enter data records into the file by entering

APPEND < return >

Enter the records shown below:

```
Dr Walter  LaFish    1591 Ellis Street    Concord       CA  94596  09/13/51
Ms Nancy   Farber    1703 Pine Street     Philadelphia  PA  19103  05/10/41
Ms Alice   Mullen    234 Cedar Lane       San Jose      CA  94435  06/17/48
Mr Terry   Kamrin    33 Westlake Court    Los Angles    CA  90876  04/19/53
Ms Carolyn Rigiero   18 Plainfield Avenue Shrewsbury    MA  01610  07/19/43
Mr Karl    Lafong    278 Valley Drive     Garden City   NY  10345  11/14/54
```

STRING FUNCTIONS

One of the most important skills to master in dealing with data bases like this one, which contain primarily text information, is the handling of *dBASE III Plus* functions that manipulate text. These functions, called string functions, were described briefly earlier. To review:

UPPER()—converts a text string to uppercase.

LOWER()—converts a text string to lowercase.

STR()—converts a numeric value into a text string.

ASC()—converts a letter to a numeric value equal to the ASCII code value of the letter.

dBASE III Plus provides additional functions that are helpful when dealing with CHARACTER fields. When you work with mailing lists, for instance, the TRIM() function is indispensable. In creating such a list you need to combine the contents of the TITLE, FIRST, and LAST fields by using the concatenation operator, the plus sign. Enter

LIST title+first+last < return >

The program displays

```
Record#   title+first+last
     1    Dr Walter        LaFish
     2    Ms Nancy         Farber
     3    Ms Alice         Mullen
     4    Mr Terry         Kamrin
     5    Ms Carolyn       Rigiero
     6    Mr Karl          Lafong
```

What is wrong with this listing? The answer is that *dBASE III Plus* prints out each field in its entirety, including any spaces not used. The result is that the items are listed in columns. This is fine for a column-type report but not appropriate for a mailing address. The TRIM() function is used to eliminate the trailing spaces in CHARACTER fields. Enter

LIST TRIM(first)+last < return >

The program displays

```
Record#   TRIM(first)+last
     1    WalterLaFish
     2    NancyFarber
     3    AliceMullen
     4    TerryKamrin
     5    CarolynRigiero
     6    KarlLafong
```

The TRIM() function eliminated the trailing spaces, but now there is nothing to separate the first name from the last. The solution to the problem is to add a space between the fields. Note that in the following command there is a space between the quotation marks. Enter

LIST TRIM(first)+" "+last < return >

The program displays

```
Record#   TRIM(first)+" "+last
     1    Walter LaFish
     2    Nancy Farber
     3    Alice Mullen
     4    Terry Kamrin
     5    Carolyn Rigiero
     6    Karl Lafong
```

Entering spaces between quotation marks can be confusing because it is hard to tell exactly how many spaces have been entered. *dBASE III Plus* provides a function called SPACE() that creates a blank or series of blanks based on the number used with the function. To create a single space, enter SPACE(1). Enter the following command, which takes advantage of the SPACE() function.

LIST TRIM(first)+SPACE(1)+last < return >

This has the same effect as the previous command. The advantage of the SPACE() function is that it explicitly shows the number of spaces. When you want only a single space, entering " " is shorter than SPACE(1). SPACE() has the advantage of accepting any valid *dBASE III Plus* numeric expression as an argument. In the next section of this chapter you will see that ability put to use.

You can add other constants to the text by using text literals surrounded by quotation marks. For example, you might have noticed that you did not enter the periods following the titles "Mr" and "Ms." Since every record requires a period, it is faster to omit the period from each record and add it as a text literal at the point of output.

The same logic applies to other values that will be the same for each record. For example, if your mailing list consists of people who all live in the same state, it is a waste of time to enter the state over and over again. You can fill in the state with a REPLACE ALL command, or better yet, simply add the state as a text literal when you print a report or labels.

The command below trims the TITLE field and adds a period and a space after each title. Enter

LIST TRIM(title)+". "+TRIM(first)+SPACE(1)+last < return >

The program displays

```
Record#  TRIM(title)+". "+TRIM(first)+" "+last
      1  Dr. Walter LaFish
      2  Ms. Nancy Farber
      3  Ms. Alice Mullen
      4  Mr. Terry Kamrin
      5  Ms. Carolyn Rigiero
      6  Mr. Karl Lafong
```

SUBSTRINGS

A substring is a part of a larger text item; it allows you to make use of part of the data contained in a text field. The substring function is SUBSTR(). It requires two arguments, and a third is optional. The first argument is the text string, which is the source of the substring. The text can be a literal, a field, or any valid *dBASE III Plus* string expression. The second argument is a number that indicates the character with which the substring will begin. The third item, which is optional, defines the length of the substring. If no length is specified, *dBASE III Plus* assumes that the remainder of the string should be used. For example, you could list the first letter of the first name. The SUBSTR() function below picks out a portion of the FIRST field beginning with the first character in the string for a length of one character. Enter

LIST SUBSTR(first,1,1) < return >

The program displays

```
Record#  SUBSTR(first,1,1)
      1  W
      2  N
      3  A
      4  T
      5  C
      6  K
```

You can combine substring functions with other string operations to create a desired effect. Enter

LIST TRIM(title)+". "+SUBSTR(first,1,1)+". "+SPACE(1)+last <return>

The program displays

```
Record#  TRIM(title)+". "+SUBSTR(first,1,1)+"."+SPACE(1)+last
     1   Dr. W. LaFish
     2   Ms. N. Farber
     3   Ms. A. Mullen
     4   Mr. T. Kamrin
     5   Ms. C. Rigiero
     6   Mr. K. LaFong
```

ZIP CODE ORDER

The data base you are working with is complete with zip codes. However, in everyday practice, this is not always the case. Mailing lists often lack zip codes, especially lists gathered from telephone directories. To get the zip codes for the address in your mailing list, you could use a zip code guide to look up the address and find the correct zip code.

Looking up each address in the zip code directory can be tedious. However, *dBASE III Plus* can help make this process a great deal more efficient. The trick is to sequence your data base file in exactly the same order as the zip code directory. When that is done, you will find it is a much simpler matter to move through the guide and your data base file adding the necessary zip codes.

The key is to get *dBASE III Plus* to order the file properly. First, the directory is ordered by state. Next, within each state the directory is ordered by city. Within each city, the addresses are ordered by street. Then within each street, addresses are listed by number.

The first two sequencing criteria are simple because they correspond to specific fields, STATE and CITY. However, street name and street address both fall in the same field. Furthermore, the street number precedes the street name. In order to get *dBASE III Plus* to place the file in the proper order, you must find a way to treat the street name and the street number as separate items

Look at the data entered into the STREET field. Enter

LIST street <return>

The program displays

```
Record#  street
     1   1591 Ellis Street
     2   1703 Pine Street
     3   234 Cedar Lane
     4   33 Westlake Court
     5   18 Plainfield Avenue
     6   278 Valley Drive
```

Notice that a definite pattern exists in the way that the addresses are written. The street number is separated from the street name by a space character. Depending upon the length of the street number, the space will occur at the 5th, 4th, or 3rd character position.

dBASE III Plus has a special function called AT(). The purpose of AT() is to perform a search of a string to determine the number of the position within a string of a specified letter or group of letters. The AT() function finds only the first instance of a string even if the character or characters appear more than once. The AT() function returns a value of zero if no match is found. You can use this function to determine the position of the first space in the STREET field by entering

LIST AT(SPACE(1),street)<return>

The program displays

```
Record#  AT(SPACE(1),street)
   1                5
   2                5
   3                4
   4                3
   5                3
   6                4
```

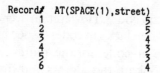

The $ is a logical operator that evaluates as either true or false. The AT() function evaluates as a numeric value. For example, "C"$"ABC" evaluates as .T. but AT("C", "ABC") evaluates as the numeric value 3, corresponding to the position of C in ABC.

The function is able to pick out the position of the space in the STREET field of each record. While this does not solve the problem, it provides the missing piece of information that will allow you to use the SUBSTR() function.

Suppose you wanted to list just the street names. You could use the SUBSTR() function with the AT() function to begin a substring at the first character after the space in each STREET field. Enter

LIST SUBSTR(street,AT(SPACE(1),street)+1)<return>

The program displays

```
Record#  SUBSTR(street,AT(SPACE(1),street)+1)
   1     Ellis Street
   2     Pine Street
   3     Cedar Lane
   4     Westlake Court
   5     Plainfield Avenue
   6     Valley Drive
```

Before you go on you might want to look more closely at the expression you have just entered. It is a good example of the concept of nesting, mentioned earlier. The AT() function is nested inside the SUBSTR() function. When *dBASE III Plus* encounters the expression, the functions most deeply nested are evaluated first.

AT(SPACE(1),street)+1 evaluates as a single number. That number is then passed to the SUBSTR() function: SUBSTR(street, nested value).

You can use the AT() and SUBSTR() functions to isolate the number portion of the address. This time the substring begins with the first character in the STREET field and ends one character before the space. Enter

LIST SUBSTR(street,1,AT(SPACE(1),street)) < return >

The program displays

```
Record#  SUBSTR(street,1,AT(SPACE(1),street))
      1  1591
      2  1703
      3  234
      4  33
      5  18
      6  278
```

You might have noticed that while the number portion of the street address has been isolated from the rest of the address, the numeric values are not aligned properly for sequencing order. For proper numeric order the numbers should be right-justified so that the ones column of each number falls underneath the ones column of the previous number. You can correct this problem by padding the front of the display with spaces. In this example, you could decide that no address would have more than four digits and use the value of 5 to determine the number of spaces with which to pad the display. Enter

LIST SPACE(5-AT(" ",street))+SUBSTR(street,1,AT(" ",street)) < return >

The program displays

```
Record#  SPACE(5-AT(" ",street))+SUBSTR(street,1,AT(SPACE(1),street))
      1  1591
      2  1703
      3   234
      4    33
      5    18
      6   278
```

You can see that a very large function can evaluate into a small list of figures. You now have figured out the steps needed to order a mailing list in the same fashion as the zip code directory. Instead of using the expression to list records, you can use it as an index key expression. The following command should be entered as a single command. Do not press < return > until the end of the command. *dBASE III Plus* will accept a command this large. Enter

INDEX ON state+city+SUBSTR(street,AT(" ",street)+1)+
SPACE(5-AT(" ",street))+SUBSTR(street,1,AT(" ",street)) to ziporder < return >

The file is now sequenced in the same order as the zip code directory. You can use the editing commands, EDIT, BROWSE, and CHANGE to add any missing zip codes.

To close the index file, enter

CLOSE INDEX < return >

DUPLICATES

Another problem that frequently occurs in mailing list data base files is duplication of entries. *dBASE III Plus* provides a special form of the INDEX command that helps eliminate duplicate records. To see how this technique operates, create a duplicate problem by using the COPY command and a special form of APPEND. First position the pointer at the top of the file. Enter

GO TOP < return >

Now copy the first three records to a new file. Enter

COPY NEXT 3 TO dups < return >

You can add those records back to the active file by using the APPEND FROM command. APPEND FROM draws records from other data base files instead of entering them manually. Note that data copied with APPEND FROM depend on common fields in both data base files. Data are copied into the receiving data base file for those fields that occur in both files. Enter

APPEND FROM dups < return >

The three records are added to the active data base file. This means that there are now three duplicates in the file. Enter

LIST first,last < return >

dBASE III Plus has a special option that helps eliminate duplicate records called SET UNIQUE ON. This command affects the operation of the INDEX command. When the UNIQUE is set ON and a file is indexed, only records with unique values for the key expression will be included in the index file. If two or more records have the same index key, only the first record will be added to the index file.

To eliminate the duplicates, enter

SET UNIQUE ON < return >

To index a file, make the key large enough to eliminate all the likely duplicates. In this example you will use FIRST, LAST, and STREET. Enter

INDEX ON first+last+street TO dups < return >

The program tells you that six records have been indexed. Enter

LIST first,last,street < return >

Only the records with a unique key appear. The other records have not been eliminated, nor do they appear, because their record numbers have not been included in the index file. If you close the index you will see the records. Enter

CLOSE INDEX < return >
LIST first,last,street < return >

The duplicate records are still part of the data base file.

DELETING THE DUPLICATES

If you want to remove the duplicate records permanently from the data base file, you can do so by following these steps:

1. With the index file closed, mark all records for deletion.
2. Open the unique index file.
3. Recall all the records that appear in the index file.
4. Pack the file.

Begin by marking all the records for deletion by entering

DELETE ALL < return >

Now open the unique index file. Enter

SET INDEX TO dups < return >

Remove the deletion marks from the unique records. Enter

RECALL ALL < return >

Only six records were recalled out of the nine in the file. Now pack the file. Enter

PACK < return >

The unique records are copied into the revised file and the duplicates are eliminated. You can now erase the index file DUPS since it is no longer needed. Enter

CLOSE INDEX < return >
ERASE dups.ndx < return >

The duplicates could have been eliminated by another method. First open the unique index file (e.g., SET INDEX TO dups). Then copy the records to a new file (e.g., COPY TO clientsI). The CLIENTSI.DBF file would contain only the unique records. While this method is simpler and quicker from a command point of view, it creates two client data base files. To avoid confusion you would want to erase the old file, CLIENTS.DBF, and rename the new file as CLIENTS. In the end both methods require about the same number of commands.

LABEL FORMS

Now that you have created and maintained your mailing list data base file, you are ready to produce labels.

dBASE III Plus allows you to create label forms that will print the contents of your data base file in mailing label format. As with the CREATE REPORT command, you must have the data base file (or one with a similar structure) open when you create a label. Enter

>**USE clients**
>**CREATE LABEL maillab < return >**

The LABEL FORM menu appears:

```
Options                      Contents                  Exit  06:57:43 am
┌──────────────────────────────────────────────────┐
│ Predefined size:          3 1/2 x 15/16 by 1       │
├──────────────────────────────────────────────────┤
│  Label width:                35                    │
│  Label height:                5                    │
│  Left margin:                 0                    │
│  Lines between labels:        1                    │
│  Spaces between labels:       0                    │
│  Labels across page:          1                    │
└──────────────────────────────────────────────────┘
```

The LABEL FORM command displays a menu bar with three choices:

1. **OPTIONS.** This menu defines the format of the label.
2. **CONTENTS.** This menu allows you to define the contents of the label in terms of the specific fields and functions to be used.
3. **EXIT.** This menu allows you to save or abandon the label definition.

The result of the CREATE LABEL command will be a label form stored in a file with an .LBL extension. In this example, the file will be MAILLAB.LBL.

The OPTIONS menu is automatically displayed. There are two ways to select the format for the label:

1. **Predefined size.** *dBASE III Plus* has five predefined label sizes built into the program. The first size, the default format, is for the most common type of label. This label is 3 1/2 inches by 15/16 inch.
2. **Manual size.** *dBASE III Plus* allows the user to customize a label size manually.

Although the predefined label's length is 15/16 inch, it is the distance between the top of one label to the top of the next that is important. If you want to measure a label to find out if it can be used with *dBASE III Plus*, this is the method used. If the distance measured is one inch, it will print properly in the default format. Note that the default format defines the label height as 5 lines with one line skipped in between; thus, each label uses 6 lines of vertical space. Most computer printers automatically print 6 lines of text per vertical inch.

The last item on the menu is Labels across page:. The setting is currently 1. Enter

<return>

The next label format appears. It is identical to the previous format with the exception that it will print two labels across. Enter

<return>

The next format appears. It also prints the same size label but three across. Enter

<return>

The next label format appears. This format is different from the others in that it uses a label that is 4 inches by 1 7/16 inch.

Once again the key is the space between the tops of the labels. The format uses 8 lines for the label and 1 line as space, a total of 9 lines or 1.5 inches of vertical printing for each label.

Display the last format by entering

<return>

This format prints three labels across in a slightly different format than the original. Enter

<return>

The original format appears. You can now move to the contents area. Enter

c

dBASE III Plus will display

```
Options                  Contents              Exit  07:01:15 am
                         ┌──────────────────────────────────────┐
                         │ Label contents 1:░░░░░░░░░░░░░░░░░░░░░ │
                         │                2:░░░░░░░░░░░░░░░░░░░░░ │
                         │                3:░░░░░░░░░░░░░░░░░░░░░ │
                         │                4:░░░░░░░░░░░░░░░░░░░░░ │
                         │                5:░░░░░░░░░░░░░░░░░░░░░ │
                         └──────────────────────────────────────┘
```

You are now ready to enter the contents on the line of the label. Enter

<return>

The first line of the label will print the name of the client. Enter

TRIM(title)+". "+TRIM(first)+SPACE(1)+last < return >

The label display scrolled to allow you to enter a long expression. Remember it is not the length of the expression that counts when you are printing but the length of the character string produced by the expression. Enter the second line of the label. If you need to see a list of the fields in the data base file, entering **[F10]** will display the fields.

< down arrow >
street < return >
< down arrow >

Now enter the city, state, and zip code.

< return >
TRIM(city)+", "+state+SPACE(1)+zip < return >

The screen will look like this:

```
Options                    Contents                    Exit  07:03:54 am
                  ┌─────────────────────────────────────────────────┐
                  │ Label contents 1:  TRIM(title)+". "+TRIM(first)  │
                  │                2:  street                        │
                  │                3:  TRIM(city)+", "+state+SPACE(  │
                  │                4:                                │
                  │                5:                                │
                  └─────────────────────────────────────────────────┘
```

Save the label form by entering

e
< return >

PRINTING LABELS

To display the label on the screen, enter

LABEL FORM maillab < return >

The labels will scroll by in the label format. To print the mailing labels you need to add the TO PRINT clause to the LABEL FORM command. However, printing labels often creates some practical problems not associated with printing on full sheets of paper. The alignment of the labels can be tricky. The best way to proceed is to print a single label, usually the first one in the file, several times to insure the correct alignment. Enter

GO TOP < return >

The command to print a single label is LABEL FORM maillab TO PRINT NEXT 1. Since you are going to have to print at least a couple of labels to check the alignment, it would be helpful not to have to type in this command each time. This is a good place to use the function keys. You can use a SET command to program one of these keys (with the exception of **[F1]**) to type out the command. Enter

SET FUNCTION 10 TO "LABEL FORM maillab TO PRINT NEXT 1;"<return>

The ; at the end of the definition stands for the < return > at the end of the command. Enter

[F10]

The label prints. Enter

[F10]

The label prints again. If the alignment is correct, you can begin printing the labels by entering

LABEL FORM maillab TO PRINT <return>

SELECTIVE LABEL PRINTING

The LABEL FORM command will accept FOR clauses, WHILE clauses, and scopes that allow you to select certain labels to print without having to print the entire file. The scopes allow you to print a specific number of records onto labels. Suppose you wanted to print out the first two people on the mailing list. Enter

GO TOP <return>

Now use the label command to print just the first two labels. Enter

LABEL FORM maillab TO PRINT NEXT 2 <return>

The first two labels print.

Suppose the next time you print you want to continue from where you left off. First, position the pointer at the next record that needs to be printed. Enter

3 <return>
LABEL FORM maillab TO PRINT NEXT 2 <return>

This process is very useful when you are sequentially processing records from a large data base file. You can print a specified number each week until you have processed the entire list.

LABELS WITH A FOR CLAUSE

You can be selective with a logical rather than a physical criterion by adding a FOR clause to the LABEL command.

Suppose you wanted to print labels only for everyone but people who reside in California. You would use a FOR clause that tests for the STATE field not being equal to CA. Enter

LABEL FORM maillab TO PRINT FOR state#"CA" <return>

SEQUENCED LABELS

If you are planning to send your mail by some bulk rate, you need to produce the labels so that they are in zip code sequence. You can accomplish this by first indexing the file before it is printed.

To index by zip code, enter

INDEX ON zip TO codes <return>

Now print the labels. Enter

LABEL FORM maillab TO PRINT <return>

SUMMARY

dBASE III Plus has a built-in program for generating labels. The program has four preset label sizes, or you can manually create a label size up to 16 lines long.

In order to place more than one field on a line in a label form, you must use the *dBASE III Plus* string operators and functions to assemble the fields in a single text string to print on that line.

The LABEL FORM command prints the labels.

dBASE III Plus has a special indexing technique used for eliminating duplicates from lists.

SET UNIQUE affects the way index files are created. When UNIQUE is ON, any index files that are created will store only one record number for each unique key expression. This means that if records have duplicate keys, only the first record will be recorded in the index file.

UNIQUE does not actually delete records; it simply creates index files that ignore the duplicates. To create a file without duplicates, INDEX a file with the UNIQUE ON. Then use the COPY command to copy the records. The UNIQUE index will cause only records with unique keys to be copied.

UNIQUE stays ON until you specifically turn it off again. It is not automatically turned off when you close an index or data base file.

CUSTOM SCREEN

DISPLAYS

Up to this point, all the output directed to the screen has been in the form of standard screen displays built directly into the *dBASE III Plus* program. This chapter concerns the methods by which the user can directly control information displayed on the *dBASE III Plus* screen by creating custom screen displays and data entry forms.

The subjects covered in this chapter are also significant because they introduce concepts that will appear again when you work with Part II of this book, the programming section. *dBASE III Plus*, as is true of most programs, requires the creation of custom screen displays for programming menus and displays. The same techniques used in this chapter will be applied to those custom programs.

This chapter assumes that you have loaded the *dBASE III Plus* program and that you are at the DOT PROMPT, ready to enter a command. If you are in the *dBASE III Plus* ASSIST mode, exit the mode by entering <Esc>.

ADDRESSING THE SCREEN

When you enter a command like LIST, DISPLAY, or ?, the information is printed following whatever data are already on the screen. The location of data displayed by these commands is not directly under your control. *dBASE III Plus* provides a special command that allows you to control the exact position at which the data are to be displayed. The basic concept views the screen as a grid of cells with each cell having the capability of displaying a single character. The IBM PC screen display has 2000 such cells. They are arranged in 25 lines and 80 columns.

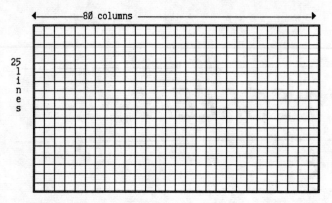

The rows and columns are numbered beginning with zero, not one. This means that rows are numbered 0 through 24 and columns are numbered 0 through 79. The @/SAY command is used to place information at a specific row and column location on the screen. For example, you could display the systems time on the screen by entering

@ 10,10 SAY TIME()< return >

TIME() is a special function built into dBASE III Plus. *It returns the systems time used by DOS.*

The first character of the time display appears in the 11th row and the 11th column of the screen display. (Remember that row 10 is the 11th row.) The rest of the information in the time display fills the cells to the right of the initial location. Enter

@ 20,40 SAY TIME()< return >

If you tell *dBASE III Plus* to display data in a portion of the screen that already contains data, the new data will overwrite the old. Enter

@ 10,10 SAY TIME()< return >

The new time replaces the old time. To clear the screen display of all data, enter

CLEAR< return >

You can use the @/SAY command to display information stored in the data base file on the screen. Open the EXPENSES data base file by entering

USE expenses< return >

You can display the data in the active record by using the field names with the @/SAY command. For example, to display the date entered in the active record, enter

@ 10,5 SAY date < return >
@ 11,5 SAY itom < roturn >

You can place another copy of the same information somewhere else on the screen. Enter

@ 5,15 SAY item < return >

@/SAY operates with any valid *dBASE III Plus* expression. For example, enter the following command to display an expression:

@ 18,0 SAY CMONTH(date)+STR(YEAR(date),5) < return >

Clear the screen by entering

CLEAR < return >

INPUT AREAS

In addition to the ability to display data on the screen, *dBASE III Plus* can create input areas on the screen through which data can be directly input into a data base record. The @/GET command functions in a similar manner to the @/SAY, with two additions. First, the display is in reverse video. Second, the area can be activated as an input area when the READ command is used.

As an example, display the contents of the fields AMOUNT and DATE. Enter

@ 10,5 GET date < return >
@ 12,5 GET amount < return >

The date and amount are displayed. To activate these display areas you need to enter a READ command. Enter

RFAD < return >

The cursor jumps to the first character in the first input area. Enter

< down arrow >

The cursor jumps to the next display area. Enter

< up arrow >

You can move the cursor up and down, or left and right, as you would move it in any *dBASE III Plus* full-screen mode like EDIT or APPEND. Any changes that you make while in an input area are entered into the record just as if you were in the EDIT mode. For example, if you changed the date, the date in the record would be changed. Enter

> **0103 < return > < return >**
> **DISPLAY < return >**

Note that the date has been changed. The @/GET command allows you to make changes from any part of the screen. You are no longer restricted to entering data in the standard *dBASE III Plus* screen format.

The @/SAY and @/GET commands can be combined in a single command that displays data and creates an input area next to the data. The command is commonly used to create a prompted input area. First clear the screen.

> **CLEAR < return >**

Next enter the @/SAY/GET command.

> **@ 10,0 SAY "Enter the date of the check" GET date < return >**

The screen shows

    Enter the date of the check 01/03/85

dBASE III Plus automatically leaves a space between the prompt and the input area. To access the input area, enter

> **READ < return >**

The cursor is now positioned in the input area. Change the date back to the original entry. Enter

> **010285 < return >**
> **DISPLAY < return >**

The record is updated. The @/SAY/GET has the ability to display descriptive prompts that explain more about the fields than can be done with the ten-character field names.

> *The contents of MEMO fields cannot be displayed using @/SAY. A GET command can display the memo, but the [**CTRL/Home**] key must still be used to display and edit the contents of the MEMO field.*

FORMAT FILES

The @/SAY/GET/READ commands place into the user's hands the necessary tools for creating the type of screen displays provided by the full-screen editing commands in *dBASE III Plus* (i.e., APPEND, EDIT, CHANGE, and INSERT). *dBASE III Plus* allows the user to specify an alternate screen format to be used with these commands.

Alternate screen formats are produced by creating a special file called a *format file*. A format file is a text file that contains a series of @/SAY, @/GET, or @/SAY/GET commands. The SET FORMAT command allows the user to specify an alternate screen format when the APPEND, EDIT, CHANGE, and INSERT commands are invoked.

To create a format file, the *dBASE III Plus* word processor can be used. The word processor is also used to create memos and program files. It is handy but limited as it is not meant to be a full-featured word processing program. To gain access to the word processor, use the MODIFY COMMAND command. Enter

MODIFY COMMAND expenses.fmt< return >

Adding the .FMT extension to the filename specifies the file as a format file. You have now entered the *dBASE III Plus* word processing mode. Your task is to enter a series of @/SAY/GET commands that will create a personalized screen format. Enter the first command.

@ 5,30 SAY "Enter the date:" GET date< return >

The command above has no immediate effect. *dBASE III Plus* simply records it. The effect takes place when this file is invoked as a format. The command will display the prompt and create an input area for the DATE field. Enter the following:

@ 6,30 SAY "Enter the payee:" GET payto
@ 8,30 SAY "Enter the amount:" GET amount
@ 11,0 SAY "Item Description:" GET item

When you have completed the entry of these four commands, save the format file by entering

[CTRL/End]

You did not have to use all the fields in the data base for the format file. You can create formats that use only some, or all, of the fields. Note further that you can display the fields in any order you choose. They do not have to be displayed in the order in which they appear in the file structure.

INVOKING A FORMAT FILE

Now that you have created a format file, you must learn how to invoke it for use with the full-screen editing commands. The first step is to put the data base file in use. Enter

USE expenses< return >

Enter the EDIT mode by entering

EDIT <return >

The screen displays the *dBASE III Plus* default screen format. The field names are listed vertically, and next to the field names is the input area. In this case, you want to substitute your screen format for the *dBASE III Plus* default.

```
DATE        01/02/85
CAT            110
PAYTO       CROW CANYON LUMBER
ITEM        10 2 BY 4
AMOUNT        68.40
COMMENTS    memo
MONTH       January
DEDUCT      Y
```

First exit the EDIT mode by entering

>   **<Esc>**

The SET FORMAT command is used to invoke a format file. Enter

>   **SET FORMAT TO expenses.fmt<return>**

The effect of the SET FORMAT command is delayed until you enter one of the commands that uses screen displays such as APPEND or EDIT. Enter

>   **EDIT<return>**

The screen now displays

```
                   Enter the date:  01/02/85
                   Enter the payee: CROW CANYON LUMBER
                   Enter the amount:  68.40

    Item Description: 10 2 BY 4
```

The EDIT command still operates as it normally does. Enter

>   **[Pg Dn]**

The next record appears in the format display. The format file acts like a template through which you can view the data stored in a data base file. Exit the EDIT mode by entering

>   **<Esc>**

Enter

>   **APPEND<return>**

The APPEND command picks up the same format as the EDIT command. The format file will stay active until you deactivate it.

To deactivate a format, first return to the DOT PROMPT by entering

>   **<Esc>**

The command to deactivate a format file is CLOSE FORMAT. Enter

>   **CLOSE FORMAT<return>**

The format file is closed. This means that the full-screen commands will use the default *dBASE III Plus* format once again. You can test to see if this is so by entering

      APPEND < return >

The screen display has returned to the default style. Exit the APPEND mode by entering

      < Esc >

CHANGING A FORMAT FILE

Format files can be changed and updated at any time, enabling you to adjust the format file to changes in the file structure, or to improve the appearance of the display.

> *You cannot edit a format file that is currently open. You must close the format file before any changes can be made. This can be easy to forget since format files stay active even when you close data base files. Even the CLEAR ALL command does not affect a format file. You must use either the CLOSE FORMAT or SET FORMAT TO command to close the format file before you attempt to make changes.*

To make additions to the format file, enter

      MODIFY COMMAND expenses.fmt < return >

The four lines of the format file appear on the screen.

ADDING SYSTEMS INFORMATION

The most common type of commands to place in a format file are ones that display a prompt and an input area. However, you can use the @/SAY command to add text or other types of information to the screen display. For example, you might want to place a heading at the top of the screen. To do so, add a line to the top of the format file by entering

      [CTRL/n]
      @ 1,20 SAY "Expenses Entry Screen" < return >

You can also use the *dBASE III Plus* special function to display information such as the systems date and the record number. Because the systems date and record number functions do not return character values, conversion functions are required. Enter

      [CTRL/n] (2 times)
      @ 3,0 SAY "Date:"+DTOC(DATE()) < return >
      @ 3,60 SAY "Record Number"+STR(RECNO(),5) < return >

The 5 used in the STR function was chosen arbitrarily. If you have a file with record numbers that exceed five digits, you should use a larger number.

Next, add another field to the display. This time it will be the DEDUCT field. Enter

> **[Pg Dn]**
> **@ 15,0 SAY "Enter Y if the item is tax deductible" GET deduct< return >**

Save the file by entering

> **[CTRL/End]**

Now display the new screen format. Enter

> **SET FORMAT TO expenses< return >**
> **APPEND< return >**

The screen will look like this:

```
                          Expenses Entry Screen
    Date: 01/01/80                                        Record Number    10
                              Enter the date:    /  /
                              Enter the payee:
                              Enter the amount:        .

    Item Description:

    Enter Y if the item is tax deductible  ?
```

Enter

> **[Pg Up]**

The previous record appears in the screen format. Exit the APPEND mode by entering

> **< Esc >**

There are some special considerations to keep in mind when you are creating a format file.

1. *dBASE III Plus* permits you to create more than one input area for the same field. The data entered in the last input area will be the data stored in the data base. Since this can be rather confusing, you should avoid displaying the same field more than once. If you display the same field by accident, *dBASE III Plus* will not consider it an error. You must take care not to make this mistake.

2. The movement of the cursor is determined by the order of the GET commands in the format file, not by their location on the screen. Below are two sets of GET commands.

Example A	Example B
@ 1,0 GET date	@ 1,0 GET date
@ 6,0 GET amount	@ 3,0 GET payto
@ 3,0 GET payto	@ 6,0 GET amount

Both sets of commands create the same screen display. However, in Example A, the cursor appears in the DATE field first, then jumps to the AMOUNT field on line 6, and then back to the PAYTO field on line 3. In example B, the cursor moves from DATE to PATYO to AMOUNT.

This is especially important to keep in mind when you are placing two or more GET commands on the same line. For example, suppose you needed to display two columns of input areas. Look at the commands below.

Example A	Example B
@ 1,0 GET date	@ 1,0 GET date
@ 1,40 GET payto	@ 2,0 GET amount
@ 2,0 GET amount	@ 1,40 GET payto
@ 2,40 GET item	@ 2,40 GET item

In Example A the cursor appears to move down the column of GETS on the left side of the screen, and then down the column of GETS on the right side. In Example B, the cursor moves horizontally from left to right on the first line, and then jumps to the beginning of the second line. Keep this in mind as you design more complicated format files.

INPUT AREA OPTIONS

The concept of format files illustrates that data input areas are really special parts of the *dBASE III Plus* system. *dBASE III Plus* has a number of commands and functions that affect the input areas and how they function.

For instance, input areas normally are blank when a new record is appended to the data base. The SET CARRY command changes this so that each new record is immediately filled with an exact copy of the previous record in the data base file. The normal setting for the SET CARRY command is OFF, meaning that new records appear as blanks. Turn the CARRY ON by entering

SET CARRY ON < return >

Now enter

APPEND < return >

The new record, 10, now contains an exact duplicate of the data entered into record no. 9. CARRY ON is designed to make data entry easier if the records contain similar information. For example, if you were entering a mailing list, you might find that the city, state, and zip tend to remain the same for groups of consecutive records. Setting the CARRY ON would allow you simply to change the name and street, and have the rest automatically entered. Exit the APPEND mode by entering

        < Esc >

The CARRY can be turned OFF by entering

        SET CARRY OFF< return >

Another aspect of the input area under the control of the user is the attributes used to indicate a display area. The *dBASE III Plus* style is to display the input area in reverse video. However, this can be changed. Enter

        SET DELIMITERS to "[ ]"< return >
        APPEND< return >

Notice that now the input area appears in the same video as the rest of the text.

    Users will note that SET INTENSITY affects the display of the status line.

Exit the APPEND mode by entering

        < Esc >

The reverse video can be redisplayed by entering

        SET INTENSITY ON< return >

The markings used to indicate the beginning and end of the input area are another aspect of the input area that is directly controllable. The default is to use no markings. Changing this requires two commands: SET DELIMITERS TO and SET DELIMITERS ON/OFF. The first command specifies what characters should be used to mark the input area; the second turns on their display. Enter

        SET DELIMITERS TO "[]"< return >
        SET DELIMITERS ON< return >
        APPEND< return >

The screen will look like this:

```
                        Expenses Entry Screen
  Date: 01/01/80                                      Record Number    10
                        Enter the date:  [  /  / ]
                        Enter the payee:  [                 ]
                        Enter the amount: [    .   ]

  Item Description: [                   ]

  Enter Y if the item is tax deductible  [?]
```

The input areas are marked by square brackets. Exit the APPEND mode by entering

> **<Esc>**

To return the delimiters to the default settings, enter

> **SET DELIMITERS OFF<return>**
> **SET DELIMITERS TO DEFAULT<return>**

BELL AND CONFIRM

There are two other characteristics of input areas that can be controlled by SET commands. When data entered into a field fills the field (e.g., entering a date), *dBASE III Plus* beeps and skips to the next field. This characteristic of the *dBASE III Plus* ENTRY mode is not permanent and can be changed. The beep is controlled by the SET BELL command, and the movement of the cursor is controlled by SET CONFIRM.

When the BELL is off, no beep is issued when the field is filled. Enter

> **SET BELL OFF<return>**
> **APPEND<return>**
> **010186**

Notice that the cursor advances in silence. Exit the ENTRY mode by entering

> **<Esc>**

The CONFIRM setting controls the movement of the cursor when a field is filled. The default setting is OFF (i.e., the cursor advances to the next field automatically). When SET is ON, the cursor advances only when a <return> has been entered. Enter

> **SET CONFIRM ON<return>**
> **APPEND<return>**
> **010186**

Notice that the cursor remains in the DATE field. To advance to the next field, enter

> **<return>**

Exit the ENTRY mode by entering

> **<Esc>**

The CONFIRM and BELL settings are independent of each other. You can turn the BELL back on and still keep the CONFIRM on. Enter

> **SET BELL ON<return>**
> **APPEND<return>**
> **010186**

Notice that the cursor remains in the DATE field but the beep is sounded. Exit the ENTRY mode by entering

<Esc>

SET STATUS

The status of the SET commands can be found by using the DISPLAY STATUS command. Enter

DISPLAY STATUS<return>
<return>

The second screen display looks like this:

```
ALTERNATE  - OFF   DELETED    - OFF   FIXED      - OFF   SAFETY      - ON
BELL       - ON    DELIMITERS - ON    HEADING    - ON    SCOREBOARD  - ON
CARRY      - OFF   DEVICE     - SCRN  HELP       - ON    STATUS      - ON
CATALOG    - OFF   DOHISTORY  - OFF   HISTORY    - ON    STEP        - OFF
CENTURY    - OFF   ECHO       - OFF   INTENSITY  - ON    TALK        - ON
CONFIRM    - ON    ESCAPE     - ON    MENU       - ON    TITLE       - ON
CONSOLE    - ON    EXACT      - OFF   PRINT      - OFF   UNIQUE      - OFF
DEBUG      - OFF   FIELDS     - OFF
Programmable function keys:
F2  - assist;
F3  - list;
F4  - dir;
F5  - display structure;
F6  - display status;
F7  - display memory;
F8  - display;
F9  - append;
F10 - edit;
```

As you can see, there are more SETS listed than have been discussed so far. Throughout this book SET commands will be discussed as they relate to the various topics.

THE SET MENU

dBASE III Plus provides an interactive menu display that lists the SET commands and also allows you to modify their status. Enter

SET<return>

The SET menu appears. The SET menu is divided into five sections.

1. **OPTIONS.** This section contains 26 SET commands including some of the commands discussed in this chapter.
2. **SCREEN.** The screen section controls the color setting of the screen display.
3. **KEYS.** This section allows you to program the function keys.

4. **DISK.** This menu allows you to set the default drive and search path.

5. **FILES.** This menu allows you to specify format files.

To change SET, position the highlight to the SET you want to change and press < return >.

To exit the menu, enter < Esc >.

PICTURING INPUT AREAS

Once you have begun to use format files to customize the appearance of entry screens, a number of additional ways are opened in which you can control the entry of data. The process involves adding PICTURE clauses to the @/SAY/GET commands in the format file.

The PICTURE clause can contain two types of specifications:

1. **Function.** A picture function is a specification that affects the entire input field. For example, the A function restricts entry into the area of alphabetical characters only.

2. **Template.** Template specifications can be entered to specify the input of individual characters. For example, AXXX would specify that you must enter an alphabetical character in the first position but that any character can be entered into the other three positions. Templates are position-specific and allow character-by-character control of input areas.

Template and function specifications are entered as string values following the PICTURE clause. Functions are always placed at the beginning of the string and are preceded by an @ sign. If a function and template are both used with the PICTURE clause, the function is entered first and separated from the template by a space.

Both functions and templates can be used with only those field types that match the function or template specification. In the following sections you will learn how these functions can be used. Enter

USE expenses< return >

ACCOUNTING FORMATS

dBASE III Plus provides three functions that help change numeric values into accounting formats. These functions operate only with NUMERIC fields or numeric expressions.

C   **Credit.** This function displays the letters CR following a positive number.

X   **Debit.** This function displays the letters DR following a negative number.

(**Parenthesis.** This function displays a negative number in parentheses.

For example, the following command displays the value stored in the AMOUNT field as a CR. Enter

> @ 10,10 SAY amount PICTURE "@C" < return >

To display a negative number as a debit, enter

> @ 10,10 SAY amount*-1 PICTURE "@X" < return >

To display a value with parentheses, enter

> @ 10,10 SAY amount*-1 PICTURE "@(" < return >

You can use the C and X functions together to print either CR or DR. Example:

> @ 10,10 SAY amount*-1 PICTURE "@CX" < return >
> @ 10,10 SAY amount PICTURE "@CX" < return >

If the (function and the X function are used in the same template, the last function in the string takes precedence. Examples:

@ 10,10 SAY amount PICTURE "@X(" will produce (68.40)
@ 10,10 SAY amount PICTURE "@(X" will produce 68.40 DB

The previous function can operate only with SAY, not with GET.

OTHER NUMERIC FUNCTIONS

B   **Left-Justified.** This function displays numeric values left-justified. The data in the field are still stored in the right-justified mode but only appear left-justified on the screen. This helps eliminate spaces between a numeric input area and a prompt. For example, enter

> CLEAR < return >
> @ 1,10 SAY "Enter amount" GET amount < return >
> @ 2,10 SAY "Enter amount" GET amount PICTURE "@B" < return >

The screen appears as below:

```
Enter amount 68.40
Enter amount  68.40
```

The B function suppresses the spaces on the left in the NUMERIC field.

Z   **Zero as Blank.** This function displays a blank when a numeric value is equal to zero.

PICTURE FUNCTIONS—DATES

dBASE III Plus allows you to display dates in two ways. The default is the American date format, MM/YY/DD. A picture format function can be used to display the date in the European format, DD/MM/YY. Enter

> **CLEAR** < return >
> **@ 10,0 GET date** < return >
> **@ 11,0 GET date PICTURE "@E"** < return >

The screen shows the change in date formats:

```
01/02/85
02/01/85
```

STRING PICTURE FUNCTIONS

The ! function can automatically capitalize the characters entered into a field. Enter

> **CLEAR** < return >
> **lastname=SPACE(10)** < return >
> **@ 10,10 GET lastname PICTURE "@!"** < return >
> **READ**

Enter

> **la fish** < return >

The letters appear as capitalized even though you entered lowercase letters.

The A function restricts entry to alphabetical characters only. Enter

> **@ 15,10 GET lastname PICTURE "@A"** < return >
> **READ**

Enter

> **1**

dBASE III Plus refuses to allow the entry of the numeric character in the field. Enter

> **< Esc >**

You can combine the A and ! functions to specify only uppercase alphabetical characters. Example: @ 15,10 GET lastname PICTURE "@A!"

SCROLLING

dBASE III Plus provides a function that allows the user to conserve screen display space for input areas. The purpose of this function is to allow entry into large text fields without displaying the entire field. This function can be used with any size field but makes sense mostly with fields that are so large that they are hard to display on the screen. Enter

```
CLEAR<return>
remarks=SPACE(150)<return>
@ 10,10 SAY "REMARKS" GET remarks PICTURE "@S40"<return>
READ
```

Enter the following:

This is an example of entering text into a field that will scroll.<return>

Note how the input area scrolled as you entered the text. Thus you can easily display fields that would normally be too large for the screen display.

TEMPLATES

Templates, like functions, help control the input and output areas. The template functions are

9   Enters 0–9, +, or −. No blank spaces.
Enters numeric digits and blank spaces.
A   Enters alphabetic characters only. No spaces.
N   Enters letters and digits. No special characters or spaces.
X   Any character.
!   Converts alpha characters to uppercase. Accepts all other characters.
L   Accepts only logical data (e.g., T, t, F, f, Y, y, N, n). In effect, this turns individual character positions into LOGICAL fields.
Y   Accepts only logical data (Y, y, N, n).
$ Displays dollar signs in place of leading zeros.
*   Displays * instead of leading zeros.
.   Specifies a decimal place. This is used with fields that do not already have decimal portions. The effect is used for display only.

The main difference between functions and templates is that the template affects only specific characters while the function controls the entire field or expression. The most common use of the template is to insert punctuation into numeric displays. Enter

```
CLEAR<return>
@ 10,10 SAY amount*100 PICTURE "9,999.99"<return>
@ 11,10 SAY amount*100 PICTURE "$$$,$$$.99"<return>
@ 12,10 SAY amount*100 PICTURE "9,999.9999"<return>
```

The screen displays

```
6,840.00
$$6,840.00
6,840.0000
```

You can combine template functions to control the format of each character. Suppose you use product numbers that begin with three letters and end with four numbers. The following command would restrict input to that format. Example: @ 10,10 SAY item PICTURE "AAA9999"

FORMATTING SPECIAL ENTRIES

Another important use of templates is to speed the entry of data into fields that use special formats. The most common example of this type of template is for entry of phone numbers. Enter

> **CLEAR** < return >
> **phone=SPACE(14)** < return >

You can automatically enter the parentheses and dashes as part of the display template. Enter

> **@ 10,10 SAY "Phone:" GET phone PICTURE "(999)9999999"** < return >
> **READ**

Enter

> **4159550202**

The characters in the template allow you to enter just the numbers. Enter

> **@ 11,10 SAY phone** < return >

The data appear with the template characters and the data entry combined. This type of template can save many keystrokes.

DISPLAY ONLY CHARACTERS

In the previous example, you may have noticed that the formatting characters entered into a field like PHONE would be the same for each record that contained such a field. Storing these characters in each field is a waste of space. While in small files with only a few fields, the issue is not significant, large data bases, with many fields that contain repetitive characters, can waste a lot of disk space and eventually slow down the processing speed of the program.

dBASE III Plus offers a special picture function that displays the characters in the input area but does not pass them on to the data area. This means that the user still gets the visual effect, but disk space is not wasted storing these characters. Enter

```
CLEAR<return>
number=SPACE(10)<return>
@ 10,10 SAY "Phone:" GET number PICTURE "@R (999)9999999"<return>
READ
```

Enter

```
4159550202
```

The template includes more characters than the variable. Enter

```
@ 11,10 SAY number<return>
```

This time only the characters that were entered were stored in the variable, saving four characters. The R function can be used to display the data so that these appear with the formatting characters. Enter

```
@ 10,10 SAY "Phone:" GET number PICTURE "@R (999)9999999"<return>
```

By using the R function you can make it appear that characters are part of the file without wasting disk space to store them.

RANGES

Another clause that can be used with the @/GET to control input areas is the RANGE clause. This clause operates on NUMERIC fields to control the entry of values. You can specify an upper and/or lower limit for the entry value. Enter

```
CLEAR<return>
age=0<return>
```

To restrict the entry to ages 18 to 65, enter

```
@ 10,10 SAY "Enter Age" GET age RANGE 18,65<return>
READ
```

Enter

```
17<return>
```

dBASE III Plus beeps and displays the message RANGE is 18 to 65 (press SPACE). This message appears at the bottom of the screen in *dBASE III Plus*. Enter

```
<space bar>
66<return>
```

Once again the entry is rejected. Enter

> **<space bar>**
> **65<return>**

This time the entry is within the range and can be entered. A single range number can be used to set an upper limit only. For example, the following command would limit the values entered to 65 or greater.

> **@ 10,10 SAY "Enter Age" GET age RANGE 65,**

The next command would limit the value entered to less than 65.

> **@ 10,10 SAY "Enter Age" GET age RANGE ,65**

Note that the placement of the comma is crucial when only a single value is specified.

> *When a single value is used, the message displayed when an invalid entry is made may be confusing. For example, in the case of the Range 65, entering a value less than 65 results in the message RANGE is 65 to None (press SPACE).*
> *dBASE III Plus simply uses the text None when no value is specified. However, it is easy to think that the None refers to a value of zero, making the message seem incorrect. The None actually indicates "no limit."*

RANGES OF DATES

Perhaps even more useful is the ability of the RANGE function to operate on dates. Date values can be used to set entry limits. For example, in updating a file you might want to limit the date entry to a date greater than the one already entered. This could eliminate many typing mistakes. In this case you can use the value stored in the DATE field of the EXPENSES file. Enter

> **CLEAR<return>**
> **@ 10,10 SAY "Enter Date" GET date RANGE date+1,<return>**
> **READ<return>**

Enter

> **010185**

The program rejects the entry and displays the message RANGE is 01/03/85 to None (press SPACE). Enter

> **<space bar>**
> **<Esc>**

You can limit the entry to a range of dates by supplying a beginning and ending date. For example, suppose you wanted to limit the dates to the remainder of the year. Enter

CLEAR< return >
@ 10,10 SAY "Enter Date" GET date RANGE date+1,CTOD("12/31/85")< return >
READ< return >

Enter

010186

dBASE III Plus rejects the entry as beyond the acceptable range of dates. Note that you were required to use the CTOD(), character to date, conversion function to enter a literal date.

ADDING PICTURE CLAUSES TO A FORMAT FILE

Picture clauses have a wide range of applications. However, the majority of them require programming. At this point you can apply the picture formats directly to a format file. Enter

MODIFY COMMAND expenses.fmt< return >

Change the format file to contain the picture clauses shown below. (The changes are indicated in bold.) Enter

```
@ 1,20 SAY "Expenses Entry Screen"
@ 3,0 SAY "Date: "+DTOC(DATE())
@ 3,60 SAY "Record Number "+STR(RECNO(),5)
@ 5,30 SAY "Enter the date: " GET date PICTURE "@E"
@ 6,30 SAY "Enter the payee:" GET payto PICTURE "@!"
@ 8,30 SAY "Enter the amount:" GET amount PICTURE "@B"
@ 11,0 SAY "Item Description:" GET item PICTURE "@S8!"
@ 15,0 SAY "Enter Y if the item is tax deductible " GET deduct PICTURE "Y"
@ 20,0 SAY "Enter Budget Category Number" GET cat PICTURE "9,999"
```

Save the file by entering

[CTRL/End]

Activate the format file by entering

SET FORMAT TO expenses< return >
APPEND< return >

The screen will look like this:

```
                           Expenses Entry Screen
     Date: 01/01/80                                          Record Number   10
                               Enter the date:    /  /
                               Enter the payee:
                               Enter the amount: .

     Item Description:

     Enter Y if the item is tax deductible   Y


     Enter Budget Category Number
```

Enter

031585

dBASE III Plus rejects the entry because the entry area has been switched to the European format with the E picture function. Enter the date in the correct format.

<space bar>
150386

Next enter

bacon east pharmacy<return>

Note that the data appear as uppercase even though you typed in lowercase letters. This is, once again, the effect of a picture function. Enter

2.56<return>

The number appears left-justified in the field. Enter the description

first aid kit<return>

In this case there were two active functions. The first enabled you to make a scrolling entry in the field. The second converted the entry to uppercase. The next field is a LOGICAL field. Note that the default value of the LOGICAL field is Y, not the usual ?. Enter

y

Finally, enter the budget category.

100

Note that a comma was automatically inserted in the field. Enter

<up arrow>

The number is justified and the comma disappears. Enter

[Pg Dn]
<Esc>

To view the data without the format file, enter

CLOSE FORMAT <return>
EDIT <return>

The screen displays the data as they are actually stored in the record.

```
DATE        03/15/86
CAT            120
PAYTO       BACON EAST PHARMACY
ITEM        FIRST AID KIT
AMOUNT        2.56
COMMENTS    memo
MONTH
DEDUCT      Y
```

Exit the EDIT mode by entering

<Esc>

PRINTING FORMS

The @/SAY commands stored in the format file can be used to create printed forms. A printed form differs from a column report in that each record prints on its own page.

The @/SAY commands allow you to specify at which row and column location the data should be printed.

When sending output to the printer, GET commands have no meaning.

You can create a form that will print out the contents of records in a formatted manner, in much the same way that you created the format file used for screen display. There are, however, some important differences:

1. When sending output to the printer, GET commands have no meaning. Therefore only @/SAY commands can be included in the file.

2. Since the printed page has more lines, and possibly more columns, than the screen display, you can use row numbers that exceed 24 and column numbers that exceed 79.

3. Formats designed for the printer should proceed logically from the top of the page toward the bottom, and from the left side of the paper to the right. Attempting to print at a point farther up or to the left of the current print-

ing position will cause *dBASE III Plus* to feed an entire page and begin at that point on a new page. Example:

Example A

@ 3,0 SAY date
@ 5,0 SAY payto
@ 2,0 SAY RECNO()

Example B

@ 2,0 SAY RECNO()
@ 3,0 SAY date
@ 5,0 SAY payto

Example A will cause an entire blank page to be printed between the PAYTO field and the RECNO() function. Example B will print properly on one page.

4. If you want to use the same format for both screen and printer, you must limit the format row and column position to those that fit on the screen. Attempting to display a format on the screen that is beyond row 24 or column 79 will cause an error and halt the display.

With these differences in mind, you can prepare a format file that will print out the data stored in the record onto a printed form. Enter

MODIFY COMMAND prtform < return >

The following format file will print out the contents of a single record on each page. Note that in the following section, a < return > is assumed at the end of every line. Enter

@ 5,40 SAY "Record Number "
@ PROW(),PCOL() SAY RECNO() PICTURE "@B"

The second line of the format file introduces two new functions, PROW() and PCOL(). The functions represent the numeric value of the cursor position on the printed page for row and column. What does it mean to talk about a "cursor" on the printed page? The answer is that the position of the printing element of the printer is similar to the position of the cursor on the screen.

dBASE III Plus keeps track of two different sets of positions. One is the screen cursor row and column; the other is the printer row and column.

ROW() and COL() display the values of the screen cursor.

For example, after the command @ 5,40 SAY "Record Number", the printer row is 5 and the printer column is 54. The reason is that the printing began at column 40 and there were 14 characters in the string. This is important because you need to know where the last print ended so that you can place the following item next to it. Because the RECNO() function is a number, it would normally need to be converted before you could print it with the same command as a text string. By using the PROW() and PCOL() functions to determine where the last item left off, you can simply issue another command to print at that spot. This avoids the need to use the STR conversion function. It also provides an opportunity to use a picture clause to print the RECNO() as a left-justified number, eliminating any unwanted space between the text and the record number.

The remainder of the format file uses this same technique to avoid type mismatches and allows you to utilize some of the picture functions you learned in this chapter. Enter

```
@ 10,10 SAY "Date of the expense: "
@ PROW(),PCOL() SAY date
@ 12,10 SAY "Payee:            "+payto
@ 14,10 SAY "Amount of Expense:     "
@ PROW(),PCOL() SAY AMOUNT PICTURE "@R $999.99"
@ 20,10 SAY "Description: "+item
@ 22,10 SAY "Is this item tax deductible (Y/N) "
@ PROW(),PCOL() SAY deduct PICTURE "@Y"
```

When the file is complete, you can save it by entering

[CTRL/End]

PRINTING A FORMAT FILE

Now that the format file has been created, you can direct the output to the printer instead of the screen by using the SET DEVICE command. There are two devices that *dBASE III Plus* recognizes, SCREEN and PRINT (printer). Enter

SET DEVICE TO PRINT <return>

Position the pointer to the record to be printed. Enter

GO TOP <return>

To print the format file, use the DO command. Enter

DO prtform.fmt <return>

The record is printed on the printer. To print another, move the pointer to the next record. Enter

SKIP <return>

Now print the file again. Enter

DO prtform.fmt <return>

You can see that the same format file can be used over and over again to print different records. You may want to select a record for printing by a criterion such as date. Enter

LOCATE FOR MONTH(date)=3 < return >
DO prtform.fmt < return >

The first record with a March date, record 11, prints.

Once the device has been set to PRINT, all @/SAY commands will send data to the printer. To return the @/SAY output to the screen, enter

SET DEVICE TO SCREEN < return >

With a little imagination you can see that this ability of *dBASE III Plus* to send formatted output to the printer as well as the screen enables you to create and print a variety of forms based on the information in your data base files.

There are several limitations to this method, but the *dBASE III Plus* programming language can automate the process you have just carried out manually. All the concepts discussed in this chapter will be employed when custom forms and reports are created in Part II of this book.

DRAWING BOXES

dBASE III Plus has a special variation on the @ command that allows boxes to be drawn on the screen. The boxes are created by using the IBM PC's extended character set. These characters do not appear on the keyboard, but they can be entered by using the [**Alt**] key and the numbers on the numeric keypad. The IBM extended character set can draw single and double lines. As an experiment, enter the following command. The commands are entered by holding down the [**Alt**] key while you type the number on the numeric keypad. You cannot use the numbers on the top row of the keyboard, only the numeric keypad. Enter

[Alt/180]
[Alt/179]

These two characters display vertical lines, both single and double. You can draw a box with single lines by entering

CLEAR < return >
@ 1,0 TO 5,79 < return >

A box is drawn at the top of the screen. You can draw a double box by entering

@ 1,0 TO 5,79 DOUBLE < return >

The boxes can be added to format files. Enter

> **CLOSE FORMAT** <return>
> **MODIFY COMMAND expenses.fmt** < return >

Enter

> **[CTRL/n]**
> **@ 4,0 TO 10,79 DOUBLE** < return >

Save the file by entering

> **[CTRL/End]**

Display the format by entering

> **GO TOP** < return >
> **SET FORMAT TO expenses.fmt** < return >
> **EDIT** <return >

The box appears as part of the format file.

> *In theory, boxes can be part of format files that are printed. The problem is that many printers do not recognize the full IBM extended character set. If your printer does not recognize the characters, the box may not print, or it may print as a series of characters other than the ones that appear on the screen.*

PAINTING SCREENS

Now that you have learned the basic concepts of formatted output to both the screen and the printer, you will find that *dBASE III Plus* provides a special means of creating screen or print formats.

The primary difficulty in creating formats is that it is hard to know the exact row and column location that will look best for your formatted output. *dBASE III Plus* provides a feature that allows you to lay out a screen or print format visually so that you can see the actual position of the fields and text as they will appear in the final format.

The command is CREATE SCREEN. This command operates in two steps:

1. You visually lay out a screen format. The format is stored in a screen file. Screen files have an .SCR extension.

2. When the screen file is complete, you can create a format file (.FMT extension) based on the layout in the screen file (.SCR extension). Both the .SCR and .FMT files will have the same name.

It is important to keep in mind that format files (.FMT extension) created with the painting command contain exactly the same type of commands as you would manually enter with the MODIFY COMMAND command. That means that you can change any format file with MODIFY COMMAND even if it was originally designed by using the CREATE SCREEN command.

The main advantage of the CREATE SCREEN command is that you get to see what the final format will look like as the layout is created.

To create a screen format, enter

CREATE SCREEN exp < return >

The SCREEN FORMAT menu has four parts:

1. **SETUP.** SETUP is used to select data base files and fields to be used in the screen display. You can use an existing data base or create a new one as you create the screen display. You can create a screen format with fields from more than one data base file. (For more information about multiple data bases, see Chapter 10.)

2. **MODIFY.** This option allows you to specify attributes of individual fields such as their picture formats and templates. This function can also be used to create new fields.

3. **OPTIONS.** This menu allows you to add single- and double-line boxes to the display.

4. **EXIT.** This menu is used to save or erase the screen format.

First, select the data base file for which the screen format will be created. Enter

< return >

A box appears with the list of data base files. Highlight EXPENSES and enter < return >.

PLACING FIELDS ON THE LAYOUT

The screen layout program is divided into two parts: the menu portion, which is currently active, and the blackboard portion, which is not active. The **[F10]** key is used to toggle back and forth between the two modes. Enter

[F10]

The menu display disappears, and you can position the cursor to any place on the screen. The status line now shows the row and column number of the cursor position.

Suppose you want to begin the screen format by placing the DATE field at row

2, column 20. Move the cursor to row 2, column 20 with the directional arrow keys. When the cursor is in the proper position, return to the menu by entering

> **[F10]**

To select a field, move to the SETUP menu by entering

> **s**

Select the LOAD DATA FIELDS option by entering

> **[Pg Dn]**
> **<return>**

Select the DATE field by entering

> **<return>**
> **<left arrow>**

The program has inserted the field name and input area for the screen at the cursor position. In the blackboard mode there are several actions you can take:

1. **Edit text.** You can enter, revise, and delete as if you were in a word processing mode. The *dBASE III Plus* editing commands are active in the blackboard mode. Deleting and inserting text will cause changes in the position of other items relative to the position of the insertion or deletion.
2. **Drag a field.** You can change the location of input areas by placing your cursor in the area, pressing <return>, and using the arrow keys to change the location of the field.
3. **Delete an input area.** You can delete an input area by placing your cursor on the area and entering **[CTRL/u]**.

For example, you might want to change the text from the field name to something more descriptive. Enter

> **Date:**

FIELDS WITHOUT LABELS

When the LOAD FIELDS option is used, the field name is always inserted into the text. If you want to insert an input area without a field name, you can do so directly from the MODIFY menu. For example, suppose you want to create a format in which the input areas are below, not next to, the text. Move the cursor to row 5, column 5. Enter

> **Payee**

Move the cursor to row 5, column 30. Enter

> **Amount**

Move the cursor to row 5, column 50. Enter

> **Description < return >**

Move the cursor to row 6, column 5. It is here that you want to place the PAYTO field, but you do not want the field name inserted. Enter

> **[F10]**

The MODIFY menu appears.
Move the highlight to the contents area by entering

> **< down arrow >**

Select the field for the input area by entering

> **< return >**

A list of fields appears in a box on the right. The first item on the list is < NewField >. Selecting < NewField > will have a similar effect on a MODIFY STRUCTURE command in that the field will be added not just to the screen format but also to the data base structure.
Move the highlight down to PAYTO and press < return >. You can now add a picture template or function. Enter

> **< down arrow > (3 times)**
> **< return >**

In this case you will want to convert entries to uppercase. Enter

> **! < return >**

Return to the blackboard by entering

> **[F10]**

The screen now shows the input area inserted at the current cursor position. Move the cursor to column 30. Enter

> **[F10]**
> **< down arrow >**
> **< return >**

Highlight the AMOUNT field. Enter

> **< return >**
> **[F10]**

The amount input area is inserted.
Next, move the cursor to column 50. Enter

[F10]
< down arrow >
< return >

Highlight the ITEM field. Enter

< return >
[F10]

The ITEM field is inserted below the text.

DRAGGING A FIELD

Once you have placed a field on the screen display, you can change the position by dragging it to another location. For example, you might want to change the location of the DATE field that appears beneath the prompt. Move the cursor to the DATE field. Enter

< return >

The blackboard enters the "drag" mode. You can now indicate the new position for the field. Move the cursor to row 3, column 20. Enter

< return >

The field has changed position. The screen should look like this:

```
Set Up              Modify           Options          Exit  01:41:38 am
                    Enter Date:
                    99/99/99
      Payee                 Amount           Description
      XXXXXXXXXXXXXXXXXXX   999.99           XXXXXXXXXXXXXXXXXXX

CREATE SCREEN    :<C:>:EXP.SCR                :Pg 01 Row 03 Col 00:Ins    :
```

Once you have created the desired screen layout, you can create the format file by entering

[F10]
e
< return >

The CREATE SCREEN command generated two files, EXP.SCR and EXP.FMT. Enter

dir exp.* < return >

The two files appear in the directory display. The SCR file contains the visual image of the screen while the .FMT file contains the @SAY/GET commands generated by that layout. Enter

TYPE exp.fmt < return >

The screen will show

```
@  2, 20  SAY  "Enter Date:"
@  3, 20  GET  EXPENSES->DATE
@  5,  5  SAY  "Payee              Amount          Description"
@  6,  5  GET  EXPENSES->PAYTO
@  6, 30  GET  EXPENSES->AMOUNT
@  6, 50  GET  EXPENSES->ITEM
```

The .FMT file contains the same type of commands that you would have manually entered to create a format file. You can now use the format file created by the CREATE SCREEN command.

> *Notice that the screen format uses the file alias name EXPENSES with each variable. This makes the format file specific to the EXPENSES data base file. For example, if you used a copy of the EXPENSES file called AMTORDER, dBASE III Plus would not be able to find EXPENSES->ITEM because the field would have the full alias name AMTORDER->ITEM. This problem can be resolved by removing the EXPENSES-> alias from the format file or using a special form of the USE command to assign the alias EXPENSES to the active file. Example: USE amtorder ALIAS expense.*
>
> *You will learn more about alias names and how they are used in Chapter 11.*

Enter

USE expenses < return >
SET FORMAT TO exp < return >
EDIT < return >

The record is displayed in the selected format. Enter

Esc
CLOSE FORMAT < return >
CLOSE DATABASE < return >

FORMATS IN ASSIST

Format files can be used and created from the ASSIST mode. Enter

ASSIST < return >

You must select a data base file before you select the format file. Attempting to select a format file with no data base file open does not cause an error message. In fact, all will appear to be correct until you enter a full-screen display mode. Then you will see that the format file is not active.

Open a data base file by entering

> **< return > (2 times)**

Move the highlight to EXPENSES and press < return >. When asked about in-dexes, enter

> **n**

Select a format file by entering

> **< down arrow >**
> **< return > (3 times)**

To activate the format file, select the APPEND mode by entering

> **u**
> **< return >**

The format is displayed. Exit the APPEND mode by entering

> **< Esc >**

There is no way to close a format file while you are in the ASSIST mode.

Screen creation and modification can also be accessed from the ASSIST menu. The CREATE menu has a selection for format. Enter

> **c**

The MODIFY menu also contains a selection for format. Enter

> **m**

CREATE FORMAT and MODIFY FORMAT are functionally the same command. They are the same as CREATE SCREEN or MODIFY SCREEN entered at the DOT PROMPT.

SUMMARY

The @ command allows you to control directly the placement of data on the screen display and the printer. The @ command views the screen or the printed page as a grid of cells, each capable of containing a single character.

The @/SAY command can place text at specific row and column locations on that grid. The command operates on both the screen display and the printer. On the screen, the rows go from 0 to 24 and the columns from 0 to 9.

The @/GET and @/SAY/GET commands operate only on the screen display, where they place data input areas. A READ command activates a GET input area to edit or enter data.

A series of @/SAY/GET commands can be placed in a format file. This file can contain only @/SAY/GET commands.

A format file can be activated by entering the SET FORMAT TO command. When a format file is active, any full-screen entry commands such as APPEND, INSERT, EDIT, and CHANGE will use the format specified in the format file to display data and fields. Format files are created manually by using the MODIFY COMMAND command or in a painting mode with the CREATE SCREEN command. Both techniques ultimately create a format file with an .FMT extension.

Format files can be deactivated by entering CLOSE FORMAT or SET FORMAT TO.

Input areas are affected by SET commands. They are

Set bell—controls beep when field is full.

Set carry—carries over data from previous record.

Set confirm—controls cursor movement when field is filled.

Set delimiter—controls the display of characters at the ends of the input areas.

Set intensity—controls the video display used for input areas.

Picture clauses can be added to @/SAY or @/GET commands to control or transform the data entry area. Picture clauses use two types of formatting codes. Picture functions affect the entire input area. Picture templates control individual characters within the input area.

The CREATE SCREEN command allows you to visualize the final format as you create the format file. Instead of entering @/SAY/GET commands, you select fields from menus and place them at various positions on the screen. *dBASE III Plus* automatically creates the format file from the screen image you lay out. The screen creation process makes creation of format files simpler, and it eliminates typing mistakes that can occur in format files.

Format files can be used to print custom-designed forms. A form is a layout that prints the contents of a single record on an entire page. Format files that are designed to be printed must contain @/SAY commands only. GET commands have no meaning when directed to the printer.

To print a format you must set the format device to the printer using the SET DEVICE command. When the device is set to PRINT, use the DO command to send the format commands to the printer. When printing a format file, you must make sure that the order of the @ commands is strictly from top to bottom, and left to right. *dBASE III Plus* cannot print backward.

MULTIPLE DATA BASE

OPERATIONS

Up to this point, you have learned to work with one active data file at a time. But *dBASE III Plus* has the ability to work with more than one file when another is open. In fact, you can work with up to ten different data base files at the same time.

Data base problems often arise that require the use of more than one file. This chapter begins with an analysis of those types of problems.

> *The subject of multiple data base files is quite extensive. In this book the subject is covered in two distinct parts. This chapter deals with problems and techniques that can be implemented manually through either the ASSIST mode or more usually through the DOT PROMPT mode. In Part II (the programming section), the topic of multiple data base files is treated from a programming perspective. The organization of this book assumes that you have worked through and understand the manual techniques before you go on to use these techniques in your programs.*

The subject of multiple file processing can be given a broad definition. This book addresses three areas concerning this topic:

1. **SUMMARY FILES.** Summary files are used to create data base files that summarize data already stored in an existing data base file. One common use of this technique is to create a file with records that reflect totals for groups of records in the original file. Summary files have a one-to-many relation-

ship to the records in the original file, meaning that each record in the summary file can be related to one or more records in the original data base file.

2. **FILE COMBINATION.** File combination allows you to take the data stored in two or more data base files and create a file that is a combination of all the data. File combination can be used to append files, update files, or create new files that contain combinations of the original files.

3. **RELATIONS.** Relations are the most advanced form of multiple file processing available in *dBASE III Plus*. In relations, data are not physically moved from one file to another. Instead, the files are connected logically. Data from the related files are joined at the point of output. Thus two files can be used to generate an output that combines the data from both files without actually creating a data base file that physically contains all the data. When the relation is terminated, the files are as they were before the relation was created.

Relations are in contrast to the other two multiple file techniques. In summary and combination files, new data records are created. Relations are usually not used to create new data records but to produce combined output. In this way relations make more efficient use of computer storage space.

This chapter assumes that you have loaded *dBASE III Plus* and are in the DOT PROMPT mode ready to enter a command. If you are in the ASSIST mode, exit by entering <Esc>.

SUMMARY FILES

In Chapter 7 you learned how to create report forms that contained summary information like subtotals showing the value of a group of related records. In a report form the subtotals are created at the point of output, either the screen or the printer, and are not stored or saved once the report has terminated.

There are many instances in which it is necessary and desirable to be able to store this type of summary information in a data base file so you can subject the data to further processing or analysis.

Summary files are really like any other data base file. The key difference is that they are produced by summarizing an existing data base file.

In Chapter 7 you encountered subtotals based on the CAT field and saw how they could be produced as part of a report. In this case, you will produce similar totals by creating a new data base file.

Place the EXPENSES file in use by entering

USE expenses

Before you can create a summary file, you must decide which field to use as the key field for creating the totals. In this example, a new data base will be created that contains the totals for each budget category. That means that you *must* index or sort the file according to the CAT field before you attempt to create the totals file.

Open the CATORDER index file by entering

SET INDEX TO catorder < return >

It would be a good idea to reindex the file at this time, because in Chapter 9 you added a new record to the EXPENSES file but did not update the CATORDER index. Thus the CATORDER index file contains only 9 of the 10 records in the file. Update the index file by entering

REINDEX < return >

You are now ready to create the new data base file that will contain the totals.

THE TOTAL COMMAND

The command that creates summary data base files is called TOTAL and does the following things:

1. It creates a new data base with the same structure as the active data base.
2. Using the key field as reference, the command creates a record in the new data base for each subtotal group in the active data base.
3. The record in the new data base will contain the total of all the records in that group if the field is numeric. If the field is not numeric, the data placed in the fields in the new data base will be the data from the first record in the subtotal group.

The TOTAL command requires two pieces of information:

1. **ON < key field >**. The key field is the one that determines the subtotal groupings. When you specify the key field, you are telling *dBASE III Plus* to create a subtotal record every time there is a change in the key field.
2. **TO < filename >**. The filename tells *dBASE III Plus* where to store the data accumulated by totaling the records in the active data base. The TOTAL command creates a data base file (.DBF extension).

To total the file on the CAT field, enter

TOTAL ON cat TO cattots < return >

The screen displays the following messages:

```
10 Record(s) totaled
 4 Records generated
```

The first item, Record(s) totaled, shows the number of records in the original file, EXPENSES, that were used to arrive at the subtotals. The second item, Records generated, tells you the number of subtotal records in the new file, CATTOTS.

The totals produced by the TOTAL command are not stored in the active data base file. To gain access to that information you must change active data base. Before you do, use the SUM command to find the total of the amounts in all the records. Later you can compare this with the total of the amounts in the new data base file to make sure the totaling was accurate. Enter

SUM amount < return >

The total in this example is 746.86. To see the totals, place the new file in use and list the records. Enter

USE cattots < return >
LIST < return >

The screen will display

```
Record#  DATE       CAT PAYTO              ITEM            AMOUNT MONTH
         DEDUCT
      1  01/02/85   110 CROW CANYON LUMBER 10 2BY 4         68.40 January
         .T.
      2  01/15/85   360 GREEN ACRES FURN   DESKS           442.24 January
         .T.
      3  01/21/85   260 PG&E               TURN ON ELEC    104.88 January
         .F.
      4  01/10/85   560 SEARS              TRASH CAN       131.34 January
         .F.
```

Check to see if the total of these four records equals the total of all the amounts in the EXPENSES file. Enter

SUM amount < return >

The total is the same, 746.86, as the total in the EXPENSES file.

The full listing is a bit confusing. All you are really concerned about is the effect of the command on the NUMERIC fields. You can display just the CAT and AMOUNT fields by entering

LIST cat,amount < return >

The screen will show

```
Record#   CAT AMOUNT
      1   110  68.40
      2   360 442.24
      3   260 104.88
      4   560 131.34
```

What has happened? The amount column shows the totals for each group of records. However, since *dBASE III Plus* subtotaled all the NUMERIC fields, the CAT numbers were also subtotaled. For example, there were three records in EX-PENSES with CAT no. 120. In the CATTOTS file the number 360 (3 times 120) appears in the CAT field. This is not the product you want. To control which NUMERIC fields will be totaled when the TOTAL command is used, you can use a FIELDS clause to select specific fields to be totaled. If you do not use the FIELDS clause, *dBASE III Plus* assumes that all NUMERIC fields should be totaled.

To correct this problem, return to the EXPENSES data base file. You can open the CATORDER index at the same time by entering

USE expenses INDEX catorder < return >

This time, use the TOTAL command with a FIELDS clause so that only the AMOUNT field will be subtotaled. Enter

TOTAL ON cat TO cattots FIELDS amount < return >

Since you have already created a data base file called CATTOTS, *dBASE III Plus* warns you that you are going to overwrite that file. Since you want to do just that, enter

y

Once again the command generates a new data base file with four records. List the contents of the new file by entering

USE cattots < return >
LIST cat,amount < return >

This time the screen displays

```
Record#   cat amount
    1     110  68.40
    2     120 442.24
    3     130 104.88
    4     140 131.34
```

The FIELDS clause prevented *dBASE III Plus* from totaling the CAT field. The result is a file that contains records that reflect the subtotals for each category in the EXPENSES file.

USING A SUMMARY FILE

A data base file created with the TOTAL command can be used just as any other data base file. However, because of the way in which it was created, the summary file has some built-in benefits. The file is automatically sorted on the key field, a result of the fact that the data base file that generated it was indexed on the CAT field.

The data base file contains the information you would usually get by creating a report form with subtotal groupings. An advantage of using the summary file is that you can create a report that prints the subtotals but does not require you to use the subtotal group feature of the REPORT command. The benefit is that you do not get the subtotal format used by the REPORT command. The following example shows a report form summary report:

```
Page No.      1
01/01/80
                          EXPENSE REPORT BY CATEGORY

  DATE OF   PAYEE              AMOUNT DESCRIPTION
  EXPENSE


** CATEGORY /   110
** Subtotal **
                        68.40

** CATEGORY /   120
** Subtotal **
                       439.68

** CATEGORY /   130
** Subtotal **
                       104.88

** CATEGORY /   140
** Subtotal **
                       131.34
*** Total ***
                       744.30
```

Now that you have created a summary file, you can use the REPORT FORM command to display the summary data. Enter

CREATE REPORT cattots < return >

Enter the title:

< return >
SAMPLE SUMMARY REPORT
[Pg Up]

Enter the column specifications by selecting the column entry mode:

c

Enter CAT as the contents of this column:

< return > cat < return >

Add the column heading by entering

< down arrow >
< return >
CATEGORY
[pg up]

Even though this column is numeric, it does not need a total. Enter

> **<down arrow>** **(3 times)**
> **<return>**

Enter the next column specification:

> **[Pg Dn]**
> **<return>**
> **amount** **<return>**
> **<down arrow>**
> **<return>**
> **AMOUNT**
> **[Pg Up]**

The screen will look like this:

```
  Options          Groups       Columns          Locate        Exit   01:35:04 am
                            ┌────────────────────────────────────┐
                            │ Contents          AMOUNT            │
                            │ Heading           AMOUNT            │
                            │ Width                  6            │
                            │ Decimal places         2            │
                            │ Total this column     Yes           │
                            └────────────────────────────────────┘




 ┌─Report Format──────────────────────────────────────────────────────────┐
 │>>>>>>>>CATEGORY AMOUNT ──────────────────────────────────────────────── │
 │                                                                          │
 │                                                                          │
 │       99999 ###.##                                                       │
 └──────────────────────────────────────────────────────────────────────── ┘
```

Conclude the report by entering

> **e** **<return>**

Display the report on the screen by entering

> **REPORT FORM cattots<return>**

The program will display the following:

```
Page No.    1
01/01/80
                           SAMPLE SUMMARY REPORT

CATEGORY AMOUNT

       110  68.40
       120 442.24
       130 104.88
       140 131.34
*** Total ***
           746.86
```

Because you did not have to use the summary feature of the REPORT FORM command, you were able to produce a more concise report.

Another advantage of using a summary file rather than a summary report is that you can index the records in a new order and not ruin the subtotals. Remember that when you produce a subtotal report, the file must be sorted or indexed on the key field. The totals in the summary file can be sequenced in any order. For example, you might want to print the report in descending order of the amounts. Enter

> **INDEX ON amount*–1 TO cattots< return >**
> **REPORT FORM cattots< return >**

The report will look like this:

```
Page No.      1
01/01/80
                         SAMPLE SUMMARY REPORT

CATEGORY AMOUNT

      120 442.24
      140 131.34
      130 104.88
      110  68.40
*** Total ***
          746.86
```

Note that amount*–1 was used to index the numeric values in descending order.

SELECTIVE SUMMARIES

The TOTAL command can be used with both FOR and WHILE clauses to select records for the totaling process. Suppose you want to create a summary file based on the CAT field for expenses that occurred in the month of January. You could use a FOR clause to select only those records that have a January date.

First, open the EXPENSES file by entering

> **USE expenses INDEX catorder< return >**

Exercise 1   Issue a TOTAL command that would summarize only the January expenses. You can use the same filename, CATTOTS, and overwrite the previous CATTOTS file. The correct command can be found at the end of the chapter.

If you entered the command correctly, you should see the following messages displayed on the screen:

```
7 Record(s) totaled
4 Records generated
```

These messages indicate that only 7 of the 10 records were included in the totaling process and that those 7 records were totaled in 4 different category totals. Display the data by entering

USE cattots < **return** >
LIST cat,amount < **return** >

The screen will display the following:

```
Record#    cat amount
     1     110  68.40
     2     120 264.68
     3     130 104.88
     4     140 125.40
```

SUMMARY BY MONTH

One problem that occurs with the TOTAL command is that the key by which the totals are accumulated must be a field. Suppose you wanted to create a summary file that totals the data based on the month of the date. Try using the DATE field as the key field.

First, place the EXPENSES data base file in use. Enter

USE expenses < **return** >

Open and update the DATEORD index file. Enter

SET INDEX TO dateord < **return** >
REINDEX < **return** >

Now enter the TOTAL command.

TOTAL ON date TO datetots < **return** >

dBASE III Plus displays the following messages:

```
10 Record(s) totaled
10 Records generated
```

What does this indicate? On the surface, the display indicates that something has gone wrong because one total was generated for each record (i.e., nothing was really summarized). The reason is that each record has a unique date. Using the DATE field as the totaling key is inadequate. However, you cannot use a function such as MONTH(date) because the TOTAL command accepts only a field as a key. MONTH(date) is a logical expression and cannot be used with TOTAL.

The solution lies in using a field that is not unique and changes only when the month changes. You might recall that this problem was anticipated when you added the MONTH field to the data base file structure.

The MONTH field contains the name of the month indicated by the date in the

DATE field. The REPLACE command can be used to update the MONTH field to make sure that each record has the correct entry in that field.

Exercise 2   Enter a command that will replace all the MONTH fields with the name of the month as indicated by the date in the DATE field. The correct command can be found at the end of the chapter.

To see the results of this command, list the MONTH field by entering

LIST month < return >

dBASE III Plus will display

```
Record# month
     1   January
     2   January
     3   January
     4   January
     5   January
     6   January
     7   January
     8   February
     9   February
    10   March
```

You now have a field that changes only when the month changes. Totaling on this field will produce the monthly totals desired. The file is still indexed on the DATE field, not the MONTH field. Since MONTH contains the text name of the month, sorting on that field would create an alphabetical order in which April and August would be the first months.

When you index a file for totaling, the key field does not have to be the one used to create the index. The purpose of the index is to place the records in order so that each change in the key field correctly produces a desired subtotal. Depending on the situation, you may find that you index on one key but select a different field as the total key.

Enter

TOTAL ON month TO montots< return >

Notice that because the totals are related to the MONTH field, it doesn't matter if the CA1 field is totaled or not. To simplify the entry of the command, the FIELDS clause is not used in this case.

Display the results of the totaling by entering

USE montots< return >
LIST month,amount

dBASE III Plus will display

```
Record# month      amount
     1   January    563.36
     2   February   180.94
     3   March        2.56
```

One problem that can occur when using the TOTAL command to create a summary file is a numeric overflow. When the TOTAL command creates the summary file, the structure of that summary file is exactly the same as the source file's structure. It is possible that the size of a NUMERIC field is too small to contain the total for that field in the summary file. For example, in the EXPENSES file the AMOUNT field is 6 characters with two decimal places. This allows for a maximum entry of 999.99. If, when creating a summary file, the total of the AMOUNT field for a given group should exceed 999.99, then a numeric overflow will occur. The data that should have been written into the record in the summary file will appear as ****.

Keep this in mind when creating summary files. You may have to enlarge the size of the NUMERIC fields in the source data base file to accommodate the totaled values as they will appear in the summary file.

If you are a dBASE II user you may recall that dBASE II allows you to create a target data base file with a different structure than the source file to use with the TOTAL command. This technique does not work with dBASE III Plus because the program will always overwrite the structure of the summary file with an exact copy of the source file's structure.

TRANSFERRING SUMMARY DATA TO *1-2-3*

One of the main reasons for creating summary files is to transfer these totals to some other application for further analysis. Most of the popular spreadsheet programs such as *1-2-3* and *SuperCalc* can create bar, line, and pie charts, a type of analysis that is not supported by *dBASE III Plus*.

Using *1-2-3* to graph the summary data from a *dBASE III Plus* file is not as complicated as you might suspect. Both applications work well together. *dBASE III Plus* is much better suited to produce summary information from raw data than is a spreadsheet program like *1-2-3*. Conversely, *1-2-3* has built-in graphics that *dBASE III Plus* does not.

The marriage of these two programs is based on the ability of *dBASE III Plus* to convert a .DBF file to a comma-separated text file, plus the ability of *1-2-3* to read data stored in a comma-separated file.

As an example, the following section explains how summary data can be transferred to *1-2-3* in order to produce a graph. The assumption is made that the user knows the basics of *1-2-3* and *1-2-3* graphing, and that a hard disk is in use with *1-2-3* stored in a directory called /LOTUS.

The first step is to convert the summary data base file into a text file. This can be done using the COPY command to copy the data to a non-*dBASE III Plus* format. Enter

```
COPY TO \lotus\month.prn FIELDS month,amount DELIMITED WITH "
<return>
```

The filename, \lotus\month.prn, contains the name of the directory, /LOTUS, and the .PRN file extension. This is done to make finding the file from *1-2-3* simpler.

1-2-3 expects text files to have a .PRN extension. *dBASE III Plus* normally creates text files with a .TXT extension. By specifying the .PRN extension in the command, the normal *dBASE III Plus* file extension is overridden.

Your work in *dBASE III Plus* is complete for now and the file is ready for *1-2-3*. Create a second data file from the CATTOTS file. Enter

> **USE cattots < return >**
> **COPY TO \lotus\cats.prn FIELDS cat,amount DELIMITED WITH " < return >**

Before you load up *1-2-3*, you can check the contents of the file by using the TYPE command. Enter

> **TYPE \lotus\cats.prn < return >**

dBASE III Plus will display

```
110,68.40
120,264.68
130,104.88
140,125.40
```

LOADING *dBASE* DATA INTO *1-2-3*

The next step is to load the *1-2-3* program and call the *dBASE III Plus* data into the worksheet. In the example shown, you will exit *dBASE III Plus* and start *1-2-3*. It is possible that if you have enough memory in your computer (640K), and you are not running any memory-resident programs such as *Sidekick,* you can use the RUN command to execute *1-2-3* from within *dBASE III Plus*.

Exit *dBASE III Plus* by entering

> **QUIT**

The next step is to load *1-2-3*. On a hard disk system, you would enter

> **cd\lotus < return >**
> **123 < return >**

When *1-2-3* loads, you are ready to import the file you want to graph by using the FILE IMPORT command. Enter

> **/fi**

1-2-3 displays the next menu.

```
A1:                                                         MENU
Text  Numbers
Enter each line of file as a single label
     A        B        C        D        E      F      G      H
```

When importing a file that was created with the DELIMITED WITH " clause, the correct file type is Numbers. Enter

> **n**

1–2–3 next displays a list of the files with a .PRN extension in that directory.

```
A1:                                                                      FILES
Enter name of file to import: C:\123\*.prn
CATS.PRN          MONTHS.PRN
        A           B         C        D        E        F        G        H
```

Highlight the CATS.PRN file and enter < return >. *1–2–3* will load the data into the worksheet.

```
A1: 110


        A        B        C
1      110      68.4
2      120    264.68
3      130    104.88
4      140     125.4
5
```

You can now use the *1–2–3* graph commands to create a graph based on the data imported from *dBASE III Plus*.

Quit *1–2–3* and return to *dBASE III Plus*. Enter

> **/qy**
> **cd\db3 < return >**
> **dbase < return >**
> **< return >**

Exit the ASSIST mode by entering

> **< Esc >**

FILE CUT AND PASTE

Another form of multiple file operation can be viewed as cutting and pasting records from file to file. The commands that allow you to perform these operations are COPY TO and APPEND FROM. The COPY command can be used to cut an existing file into a number of parts. The APPEND FROM command can be used to gather records from a number of files into a single file.

Cutting Files

The purpose of cutting files is to create smaller versions of the original file. The files can be smaller in three ways:

1. **Fewer Records.** The FOR clause can be used to select records to be copied.
2. **Fewer Fields.** The FIELDS clause can be used to copy only the data in selected fields into a new data base file.

3. **Fewer Fields and Records.** Using a command with both FIELDS and FOR clauses can select both records and fields at the same time.

The application of cutting files means more when you are programming but can also be of benefit at the command level.

Suppose you wanted to divide the EXPENSES file into separate files for each month. First place the EXPENSES file in use. Enter

USE expenses

Copy all the January records to a new file by entering

COPY TO jan FOR MONTH(date)=1 <return>

Enter the next command that will create a February file. Enter

COPY TO feb FOR MONTH(date)=2<return>

Finally, copy the March records to their own file.

COPY TO mar FOR MONTH(date)=3<return>

List the files you have just created by entering

DIR ???<return>

dBASE III Plus will display

```
Database Files    # Records    Last Update    Size
JAN.DBF                  7      10/22/86        892
FEB.DBF                  2      10/22/86        462
MAR.DBF                  1      10/22/86        376

    1730 bytes in      3 files.
```

Another use of the COPY TO command is to create a copy of a file with few fields. Enter

COPY TO simple FIELDS month,amount<return>

List the contents of the new file by entering

USE simple<return>
LIST <return>

dBASE III Plus will display

```
Record#   MONTH        AMOUNT
    1     January       68.40
    2     January       17.95
    3     January      264.68
    4     January       59.50
    5     January       60.60
    6     January       44.28
    7     January       47.95
    8     February       5.94
    9     February     175.00
   10     March          2.56
```

Combining Files

The opposite action of cutting files is pasting or combining them. To combine files you must begin with an open data base file that is either empty or already has some records.

The files that you want to combine with the open file should have at least one field in common with the active data base file. The other data base files can have fields that are not included in the structure of the open file; however, data in those fields will be ignored when the files are combined.

To illustrate how this is done, begin by opening the JAN data base file. Enter

USE jan < return >

Suppose you want to add the records in the FEB data base file to the active file JAN. Enter

APPEND FROM feb < return >

dBASE III Plus displays the message 2 Records added. *dBASE III Plus* has copied the data from the FEB data base file into the JAN data base file. The contents of FEB are not affected by the APPEND command. Only the open data base file JAN is changed.

There is nothing to stop you from adding the same file more than once. Enter

APPEND FROM feb < return >

Once more, the same two records from FEB are appended to the JAN file. When you are appending files, make sure you really mean to add the records you request or else you may wind up with a number of unwanted duplicates in the file.

The APPEND FROM command can function selectively by using a FOR clause. For example, the following command appends records from the EXPENSES data base file but only those with a March date. Enter

APPEND FROM expenses FOR MONTH(date)=3 < return >

The command selected only one of the records from EXPENSES to be added to the file.

> The APPEND FROM command can also be used to import ASCII text data into a data base file. This concept is discussed in more detail later in the book.

MULTIPLE FILES WITH DIFFERENT DATA

Up to this point in the chapter you have created variations of the original EXPENSES file. In the following section you will begin to learn how files with different but related information can be handled.

dBASE III Plus has two distinct methods of handling this type of data, representing the evolution of *dBASE* from *dBASE II* through *dBASE III Plus*. The first method is the older method originally implemented in *dBASE II*, in which related information is physically combined or updated in data base files. The second method is a newer and more advanced method by which files are logically, not physically, linked. The advantages of the newer method make it the preferred way to attack problems of this nature. However, in the interest of complete documentation of *dBASE III Plus*, the older commands will be discussed first by way of an introduction to the concepts of related data base files.

ONE-TO-MANY RELATIONSHIPS

Until this point in the book, all the information you have been working with was stored in a single data base file. However, information does not always fit into this easy-to-manage structure. In the world of information, separate groups of data are often related to each other in various ways.

As an example, consider the CAT field in the EXPENSES data base file. Its purpose is to relate each expense to a particular budget category. Although the categories in the EXPENSES data base file are listed as numbers, each number stands for an actual category name. Suppose you created a data base file called CATEGORY that had two fields: CAT and NAME. In that data base file you listed each category number and the actual name of that budget category. The file might look like this:

CATEGORY.DBF

#	Cat	Name
1	110	Office Equip
2	120	Supplies
3	130	Sales Expenses

While each of the names appears only once in the category file, the corresponding category number appears several times in the EXPENSES data base file.

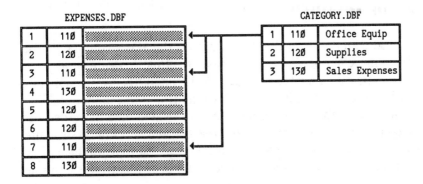

(continued)

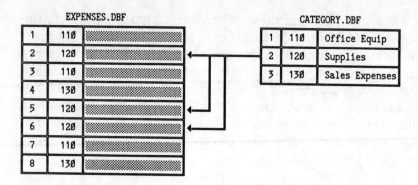

When data base files are related in this way, they are said to have a *one-to-many* relationship. This is more complex than two files that have a *one-to-one* relationship.

At some point it will be necessary to relate each item in the EXPENSES file to the matching item in the CATEGORY file in order to find the NAME of the category for each expense.

Notice that while the two files are different in most respects, one field appears in both data base files. This is called the *key field* because it is the field that relates the records in one data base file to the other. The following section will show you the various methods by which files can be related.

First, the user would create a file called CATEGORY, with the following structure:

```
1 CAT        Numeric       5
2 NAME       Character     25
```

Once the structure is created, enter the following records:

```
. LIST
Record#      CAT NAME
      1      110 OFFICE IMPROVEMENTS
      2      120 FURNITURE
      3      130 UTILITIES
      4      140 OFFICE SUPPLIES
```

The CATEGORY file now needs to be related to the EXPENSES data base file.

JOINING TWO RELATED FILES

One of the least-used commands in *dBASE III Plus* is the JOIN command. You will see as you learn more about relating data base files that there are better ways to solve the problems posed by related data base files. But JOIN gives you a place to start, and it solves the problem in a simple, straightforward manner.

The JOIN command combines the contents of two related data base files into a new file, which combines both the related data base files into a common structure.

The JOIN command requires that you supply a logical test that will be used as the basis for creating the records in the combined data base file. In this example, a new record needs to be created every time the CAT number in the EXPENSES file matches the CAT number in the CATEGORY file. The results will be a new data base file in which each record shows the EXPENSES data plus the category name.

Opening Two Files at the Same Time

In order to join two files you must have both files open together. Up to this point, you have worked with only one data base file at a time. When you open a new file, the old file is automatically closed. Look at the sequence of commands listed below:

1. USE expenses
2. LIST
3. USE category
4. LIST

When the third command is issued, it does two things. First, it closes the EXPENSES file, and then it opens the CATEGORY file. Using *dBASE III Plus* in that manner makes it impossible to have access to more than one data base file at a time.

There is another way in which files can be opened, however, allowing you to keep two or more files active at the same time. The advantage of this method is that you can simultaneously access data stored in both files.

To understand this method it is necessary to introduce the concept of *work areas*. *dBASE III Plus* allows you to operate in up to 10 different work areas. Each work area can contain one data base file. The work areas are named A, B, C, D, and so on. They can also be referred to as work areas 1, 2, 3, 4, and so forth. You can use either a number or a letter to refer to a work area. Here we refer to them as A, B, C.

The key to the use of work areas is the SELECT command. When *dBASE III Plus* is first active, the program assumes that you want to work in the first area, A. So far, you have performed all your actions in this work area.

In order to work with more than one file at a time, it is necessary to tell *dBASE III Plus* that you want to use some work area other than A. This is where the SELECT command comes in, for example: SELECT B.

The command tells *dBASE III Plus* that you want to place the next data base file you open in work area B. Look at the two following sequences of commands:

SEQUENCE A	*SEQUENCE B*
USE expenses	USE expenses
SELECT B	USE category ←close expenses
USE category	

The difference between the two sequences is the use of the SELECT command. In Sequence A, both the EXPENSES and CATEGORY files remain open at the same time. In Sequence B, the EXPENSES file is closed when the CATEGORY file is opened.

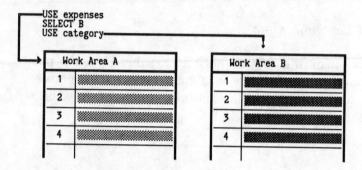

When both data base files are open, you can perform operations that use data stored in both files.

The SELECT Command

The SELECT command is really the key to working with multiple data base files. To see how this is so, begin by clearing all data base files from the memory of the program. Enter

CLEAR ALL < return >

The CLEAR ALL command does three things:

1. It clears all memory variables from the memory area.
2. It closes all data base files and index files, and turns off any data filters.
3. It selects work area A as the active work area.

In other words, this is exactly the state of your system when you first load *dBASE III Plus*.

> There is one exception to the rule. Remember that if you have a format file open, the CLEAR ALL command will not close that file. You must still enter a CLOSE FORMAT command to close the format file.

Open the EXPENSES file by entering

USE expenses < return >

Now change the active work area to B by entering

SELECT B< return >

Keep in mind that the B in the SELECT command refers to the dBASE III Plus work area that is a function of how dBASE III Plus utilizes the internal memory of the computer. The B has nothing to do with disk drive B in your computer system. The command that changes the default disk storage drive is SET DEFAULT TO B:, in which B· refers to a specific storage device.

Open the CATEGORY file by entering

USE category < return >

How can you tell that two data base files are open? One quick way to see what is going on is to use the DISPLAY STATUS command. Enter

DISPLAY STATUS < return >

dBASE III Plus will display

```
Select area:  1, Data base in Use: C:expenses.dbf   Alias: EXPENSES
          Memo file:   C:expenses.dbt
Currently Selected Database:
Select area:  2, Database in Use: C:category.dbf   Alias: CATEGORY

File search path:
Default disk drive: C:
Print destination:  PRN:
Margin =      0
Current work area =      2

Press any key to continue...
```

The display lists two active data base files, EXPENSES and CATEGORY. It also shows the work area in which each data base file is stored.

One important factor is the prompt that says Currently Selected Database:. This message is always present on the DISPLAY STATUS screen, but it is not always in the same place. In this instance it indicates that work area 2 (B) is the active work area. At the bottom of the display another line reads Current work area = 2. This also indicates which work area is currently active.

Exit the display by entering

< Esc >

What does it mean that 2 is the *active* or *selected* work area? The answer is that the data base file in the selected area is the one that will be affected by commands that change the pointer position. For example, the LIST command will list the records in the selected data base file. The unselected data base files will not be affected by the command. Enter

LIST <return >

The records in the CATEGORY data base file are displayed. To list the records in the EXPENSES data base file, you must first select the work area in which that file is located. Enter

SELECT A<return>

Now enter the command to list the data:

LIST<return>

This time, the data listed are from the EXPENSES file. Display the status report by entering

DISPLAY STATUS<return>

dBASE III Plus will display

```
Currently Selected Database:
Select area:  1, Database in Use: C:expenses.dbf    Alias: EXPENSES
        Memo file:   C:expenses.dbt

Select area:  2, Database in Use: C:category.dbf    Alias: CATEGORY

File search path:
Default disk drive: C:
Print destination:  PRN:
Margin =     Ø
Current  work  area  =        1

Press any key to continue...
```

Notice that the Currently Selected Database: message is displayed above with work area 1 (A) and that the Current work area = 1 also indicates that work area 1 is active.

DBASE III WORK AREAS

1	2	3	4	5	6	7	8	9	10
A	B	C	D	E	F	G	H	I	J
E X P E N S E S	C A T E G O R Y								

For now, you will be concerned only with two data base files and two work areas at one time. However, the principles can be applied to three, four, or more data base files being used simultaneously.

Field References and Alias Names

Up to this point in the book, whenever you wanted to refer to a field in a data base file, all you needed to do was use the field name in a command, for example: LIST cat.

When you open more than one data base file at a time, you need some method by which you can refer to a field that is used in a data base file located in another work area.

There are two reasons why this is necessary:

1. **Reference to other work areas.** Now that you can use fields from several data base files at the same time, you need a way to indicate in which file the fields are located. *dBASE III Plus* assumes that a field name refers to a field in the data base file that is open in the active work area. To combine these data with data from a file in another work area, there must be a way to refer to both work area and field.

2. **Avoid name conflicts.** Many times fields in different work areas will have the same name. You need some way of indicating which of the fields with the same name you are referring to in a command.

The problem is solved by the use of a file *alias*. The status display should still be on your screen. Look at the line that reads

```
Select area:  1, Database in Use: C:expenses.dbf   Alias: EXPENSES
```

When a data base file is opened with the USE command, *dBASE III Plus* assigns an alias name to the work area in which that file is opened. The alias name is always the name of the data base file unless specifically named something else.

> In advanced programming situations you may want to use files with different names, but assign the same alias to them. This technique is discussed in Part II.

Work area 2 is assigned the alias CATEGORY because the CATEGORY data base file was opened in that work area.

When you want to refer to a field in a specific work area, you precede the field name with the alias name. The alias name is followed by two characters, ->, and then the field name.

> Note that the -> is typed by pressing the dash key and then the > symbol, which is the uppercase character on the PERIOD key.

In this example, the CAT field in the EXPENSES data base file would be referred to as EXPENSES->CAT. On the other hand, the CAT field in the CATEGORY data base file would be referred to as CATEGORY->CAT.

	EXPENSES→CAT	
	Work Area A	

#	CAT	AMOUNT
1	▨▨▨	▨▨▨
2	▨▨▨	▨▨▨
3	▨▨▨	
4	▨▨▨	▨▨▨

	CATEGORY→CAT	
	Work Area B	

#	CAT	NAME
1	▇▇▇	▇▇▇
2	▇▇▇	▇▇▇
3	▇▇▇	▇▇▇
4	▇▇▇	▇▇▇

To see how alias names can be used, escape from the status display by entering

<Esc>

Place the pointer at the top of the EXPENSES file by entering

GO TOP <return>

Exercise 3 The next step is to place the pointer at the top of the CATEGORY file. You need to change the work area and move the pointer to the top. The correct answer is found at the end of the chapter.

You can now use the names of the fields with their alias names to display data from either data base file. Enter

? name <return>

dBASE III Plus will display

OFFICE IMPROVEMENTS

There is no need to use the alias name for this field because CATEGORY is the currently selected data base file. However, there would be nothing wrong in doing so. Enter

category-> name <return>

The result is the same. Now enter the name of a field in another work area.

? payto <return>

What happened? *dBASE III Plus* displays the message Variable not found. The reason is that *dBASE III Plus* makes the assumption that the field specified in the command is located in the active work area. In this case, that assumption is wrong. PAYTO is a field in EXPENSES that is located in work area 1. Return to the DOT PROMPT by entering

<return>

Now enter the command using the alias name

> **? expenses->payto<return>**

dBASE III Plus will display

CROW CANYON LUMBER

The program can now locate the data item you requested in the command. Enter

> **? cat<return>**

dBASE III Plus will display 110. The CAT number is drawn from the CATEGORY data base file. Enter

> **? expenses->cat<return>**

dBASE III Plus will display 110. Note that while the data happen to be the same, they are being drawn from two different sources.

Alias Letters and Names

dBASE III Plus allows you to refer to work areas in several ways. The SELECT command allows you to refer to the work area in three ways: work area number, work area letter, or work area alias name. The alias name can be used only after a data base file has been opened in that area. Enter

> **SELECT expenses<return>**

This command used the alias name EXPENSES to select work area 1. Enter

> **SELECT 2<return>**

The previous command used the work area number to select the work area. In *dBASE III Plus* the following commands would accomplish the same thing:

```
SELECT 1
SELECT A
SELECT expenses
```

When you are referring to a field in a nonactive work area, you also have a choice as to the way you can enter the alias name. *dBASE III Plus* will recognize either the full alias name of the work area or the corresponding letter. Enter

> **? expenses->amount<return>**

You can also use the letter of the work area in place of the full alias name. Enter

> **? A->amount<return>**

Both commands are interpreted by *dBASE III Plus* in the same way. The advantage of full alias names such as EXPENSES and CATEGORY is that they are easier to remember and understand. However, using alias letters is quicker when you are typing commands. The choice of which style to use is up to you.

> Because of the use of letters to indicate work areas, it is recommended that you avoid the use of files with single-letter names such as A, B, C, and so on, because they can conflict with alias names. For example, if you opened a file called B in work area A, it could cause considerable confusion.

You can combine data from more than one file in a single command. Enter

? name, A– >payto, expenses– >amount < return >

dBASE III Plus will display

```
OFFICE IMPROVEMENTS      CROW CANYON LUMBER     68.40
```

The JOIN Command

You are now ready to use the JOIN command to combine both EXPENSES and CATEGORY files into a single file in which the name of the category will be written into each record.

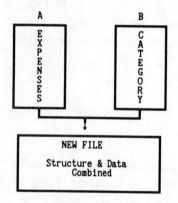

The JOIN command requires you to specify the following:

1. **WITH <alias>.** This portion of the command tells *dBASE III Plus* what unselected work area contains the file that you want to join to the one in the active work area.

2. **TO <new file>.** This portion of the command specifies the new file that will be created.

3. **FOR <condition>.** This portion of the command selects the logical link between the two files. When the condition tests true, *dBASE III Plus* creates a record in the new file that combines the data in the two data base files. When the condition is false, no joining takes place.

In order for the JOIN command to operate, it must compare all the records in the unselected file to each record in the selected file to determine if there are any matches. The process is repeated for each record in the selected file.

In addition, the JOIN command allows you to add a FIELDS clause. The FIELDS clause is used to select the fields that will be used in the structure of the new file created when the files are joined. If you do not use a FIELDS clause, *dBASE III Plus* will combine the structure of both files. The new file cannot have more than 128 fields, which is the *dBASE III Plus* limit for a single data base file.

> *If a field name appears in both source data base files, it will appear only once in the joined data base file. If the fields have the same name but are different in type or length, the structure of the field in the data base file that is in the selected area at the time of the joining will appear in the new data base file.*

In this example, you will want to join records only when the CAT number in the EXPENSES file matches the CAT number in the CATEGORY file.

To join the files, select EXPENSES as the active work area. Enter

SELECT expenses<return>

Enter the JOIN command as follows:

JOIN WITH category TO expcat FOR cat=category->cat<return>

dBASE III Plus will display the message 10 records joined. To see the resulting data base file, enter

USE expcat<return>
LIST<return>

dBASE III Plus will display

```
    DEDUCT NAME
 1  01/02/85   110 CROW CANYON LUMBER  10 2BY 4              68.40 January
    .T.    OFFICE IMPROVEMENTS
 2  01/10/85   140 SEARS               TRASH CAN             17.95 January
    .F.    OFFICE SUPPLIES
 3  01/15/85   120 GREEN ACRES FURN    DESKS                264.68 January
    .T.    FURNITURE
 4  01/17/85   140 INSTANT PRINTING    ENVOLOPES             59.50 January
    .T.    OFFICE SUPPLIES
 5  01/21/85   130 PG&E                TURN ON ELEC          60.60 January
    .F.    UTILITIES
 6  01/25/85   130 PACIFIC BELL        INSTALL TELE          44.28 January
    .F.    UTILITIES
 7  01/30/85   140 BRITZ PRINTING      BUSINESS CARDS        47.95 January
    .F.    OFFICE SUPPLIES
 8  02/02/85   140 GIFT STORE          GROUND HOG DAY CARDS   5.94 February
    .F.    OFFICE SUPPLIES
 9  02/05/85   120 GREEN ACRES FURN    CHAIRS               175.00 February
    .T.    FURNITURE
10  03/15/86   120 BACON EAST PHARMACY FIRST AID KIT          2.56 March
    .T.    FURNITURE
```

The records now show the budget category name that corresponds to the CAT number.

You might find that combining all the fields in both files creates a data base file with more information than is necessary. You can use the FIELDS clause to restrict the number of fields.

First place the EXPENSES file back into use. Enter

USE expenses < return >

Now enter another JOIN command. This time the command uses the alias letter B instead of the full alias name. This saves some typing time. Enter

JOIN WITH b TO expcat FOR cat=b– >cat
FIELDS b– >name,cat,amount < return >

dBASE III Plus will ask you if you want to overwrite the previous version of the EXPCAT file. Enter

y

Display the records in the new file by entering

USE expcat < return >
LIST <return >

dBASE III Plus will display

```
Record#  NAME                  CAT AMOUNT
     1   OFFICE IMPROVEMENTS   110  68.40
     2   OFFICE SUPPLIES       140  17.95
     3   FURNITURE             120 264.68
     4   OFFICE SUPPLIES       140  59.50
     5   UTILITIES             130  60.60
     6   UTILITIES             130  44.28
     7   OFFICE SUPPLIES       140  47.95
     8   OFFICE SUPPLIES       140   5.94
     9   FURNITURE             120 175.00
    10   FURNITURE             120   2.56
```

To close all the files in all the work areas, enter

close database < return >

The JOIN command illustrates positive and negative points about relating two data base files.

On the positive side, you can see that when files have a one-to-many relationship, the computer can automatically relate the data in one field to another. This makes it possible to avoid repetitive entry of data. For example, you may start using *dBASE III Plus* to hold a client mailing list. If the mailing list is successful, you will conduct business with the clients and store the data about the transaction in a separate file. In this way you can record several transactions with each client but have only one record of their names and addresses. The two files can be linked by a common field such as client name or client number.

On the negative side, the JOIN command implements relationships between two files in a very clumsy way. It must compare each record in one file to each record in the second file. If both files are large, the time taken to test all the permutations will increase dramatically.

Also, the JOIN command has a drawback similar to the drawback of the SORT command when it comes to updates. Since JOIN, like SORT, physically writes data to a new file, in order to update the joined file with any changes, you must perform the JOIN all over again.

The JOIN command is one of the older commands in *dBASE III Plus*. *dBASE III Plus* has another way to approach the problem of relating multiple data base files. In the next chapter you will see how these new methods make it possible to relate files logically, not phyically.

SUMMARY

The primary theme of this chapter concerned the use of more than one data base file. The first example showed how the TOTAL command can be used to create a summary file from a data base file.

The COPY TO and APPEND FROM commands can be used to cut and paste records from data base files into new files.

Two or more data base files can be placed in use at the same time by using the SELECT command to activate one of the ten *dBASE III Plus* work areas.

Each work area is assigned a number (1–10) or a letter (A–J) name. When a data base file is opened in a work area, the work area is assigned an alias name that is the same as the data base filename.

When more than one data base file is open, you can access data from a non-selected data base file by using the alias in combination with the field name, for example: B->cat.

The JOIN command combines data from two files into a new file that contains data from both files.

ANSWER KEY

Exercise 1

TOTAL ON cat TO cattots FIELDS amount FOR MONTH(date)=1

Remember to enter Y when asked if you want to overwrite the existing file.

Exercise 2

REPLACE ALL month WITH CMONTH(date)

Exercise 3

SELECT B
GO TOP

CREATING RELATIONS

In Chapter 10, you learned the basic concepts and techniques by which *dBASE III Plus* can access data from more than one file simultaneously. This ability opens up a wide variety of possibilities, many of which require programming and will be dealt with in Part II.

However, multiple data base processing can operate on the command as well as the programming level. In this chapter you will learn the concepts and techniques that allow *dBASE III Plus* to relate data logically in different files without having to join the files physically.

This chapter begins where the previous chapter ended, with *dBASE III Plus* in the command (DOT PROMPT) mode.

POINTER MOVEMENT IN WORK AREA

The concept of the pointer was introduced in the early chapters of this book. The pointer keeps track of the active record in the open data base file.

When you open more than one file at a time, each file has its own pointer. What happens to the pointer position when you issue a command? The answer is that commands that affect pointer position move only the pointer in the selected work area. The other work areas are unaffected. To illustrate the meaning of this concept, open the EXPENSES and CATEGORY data base files in work areas 1 and 2, respectively. Enter

> **USE expenses< return >**
> **SELECT 2< return >**
> **USE category < return >**
> **SELECT 1 <return >**

Suppose you wanted to get a listing of the budget CAT numbers in EXPENSES along with the corresponding names stored in the CATEGORY file. Since both files are open, you could use an alias name to refer to the NAME field in the CATEGORY file. Enter

> **LIST cat,category->name<return >**

dBASE III Plus will display

```
 1     110 OFFICE IMPROVEMENTS
 2     140 OFFICE IMPROVEMENTS
 3     120 OFFICE IMPROVEMENTS
 4     140 OFFICE IMPROVEMENTS
 5     130 OFFICE IMPROVEMENTS
 6     130 OFFICE IMPROVEMENTS
 7     140 OFFICE IMPROVEMENTS
 8     140 OFFICE IMPROVEMENTS
 9     120 OFFICE IMPROVEMENTS
10     120 OFFICE IMPROVEMENTS
```

The display is not correct because *dBASE III Plus* moves the pointer only in the active data base file. This means that the CAT field changes as each record is displayed, but the reference to the CATEGORY data base file, CATEGORY->NAME, is drawing data from the same record each time. In this case that record is the first record in the CATEGORY file.

To produce the listing you want, you need to have *dBASE III Plus* move the pointer in the unselected data base file as the pointer in the selected file area moves through the data base file.

In addition, the movement of the pointer in the unselected file cannot simply be a sequential movement through the file. Because there is a one-to-many relationship between CATEGORY and EXPENSES, the movement of the pointer in CATEGORY must be related to the CAT number that appears in the records in EXPENSES.

dBASE III Plus calls the process by which pointer movement in two data base files is logically related *setting a relation*. A *relation* is a logical instruction that links the pointer movement in two files according to the contents of a key expression.

The command that is used to relate two files in this way is SET RELATION. SET RELATION requires two pieces of information:

1. **Key expression.** The key expression is used to position the pointer in the unselected file to the desired record. When a command that moves the pointer

in the selected data base file is entered, *dBASE III Plus* evaluates the key expression for each record pointed at. The program then attempts to find a record in the unselected data base file that matches that expression.

2. **Alias name.** This is the alias name of the work area of the file that is to be linked to the selected file.

The SET RELATION command is able to find matching records much more quickly than the JOIN command for several reasons:

1. The SET RELATION command requires that the unselected data base file be indexed by the key expression before the relation is set. This means that *dBASE III Plus* does not actually search the unselected data base file, but rather it uses a high-speed search of the index file. This makes record-matching very fast.

2. SET RELATION is designed to find only the first record, if any, that matches the key expression. If there is more than one record in the unselected data base file that matches the key, SET RELATION will use only the first match.

These restrictions indicate that the unselected data base file should have one-to-many relationships with the selected data base file. This is the case with EXPENSES and CATEGORY because there is only one possible match in CATEGORY for any of the CAT numbers in EXPENSES.

SET RELATION allows a data base file to act like a look-up table for information stored in a master file.

If you are a 1–2–3 user, relations are similar in some respects to look-up tables referenced with the @VLOOPUP() function.

The first step in creating a relation is to index the data base file that will be searched. In this case the CATEGORY will be searched, so it must be indexed. Enter

SELECT category < return >

Since the link between the two files is the value in the CAT field, that should be the index key. Enter

INDEX ON cat TO category < return >

To set the relation, you must activate the EXPENSES data base file. Enter

SELECT A < return >

Work areas can be referred to by either a letter (A, B, C) or number designation (1, 2, 3). This means that the commands SELECT 1 and SELECT A accomplish the same thing. It is up to you to decide which method you prefer. In this text, the work areas are referred to by the letter designation.

You are now ready to link the files by setting a relation between them. Enter

SET RELATION TO cat INTO category<return>

dBASE III Plus does not display any visual confirmation of the fact that a relation has been set between the files in the two work areas. However, you can get information about existing relations by using the DISPLAY STATUS command. Enter

DISPLAY STATUS <return>

dBASE III Plus will display

```
Currently Selected Database:
Select area:  1, Database in Use: C:EXPENSES.DBF   Alias: EXPENSES
           Memo file:   C:EXPENSES.dbt
      Related into: CATEGORY
      Relation: cat

Select area:  2, Database in Use: C:category.dbf   Alias: CATEGORY
      Master index file:  C:category.ndx  Key: cat

File search path:
Default disk drive: C:
Print destination:  PRN:
Margin =      0
Current work area =    1

Press any key to continue...
```

dBASE III Plus shows that the file in work area 1 is related to another file by adding two lines to the status display: Related into: CATEGORY and Relation: cat. These lines show the alias name of the related work area and the field or expression that was used to link the two files.

Exit the status display by entering

<Esc>

Now you can enter the LIST command as you did before. Because the files are linked, you will get a different result. Enter

LIST cat,category->name<return>

dBASE III Plus will display

```
Record#   cat category->name
      1   110 OFFICE IMPROVEMENTS
      2   140 OFFICE SUPPLIES
      3   120 FURNITURE
      4   140 OFFICE SUPPLIES
      5   130 UTILITIES
      6   130 UTILITIES
      7   140 OFFICE SUPPLIES
      8   140 OFFICE SUPPLIES
      9   120 FURNITURE
     10   120 FURNITURE
```

Notice that each of the CAT numbers is correctly linked with the matching name in the CATEGORY file.

One of the advantages of linking files logically rather than physically is that changes are immediately recognizable and the displays are updated. For example, you might have noticed that the last record in the EXPENSES file is for a first aid kit, but the category number was entered as 120, furniture. Change the CAT to 140 by entering

```
EDIT <return>
<down arrow>
140 <return>
[CTRL/End]
```

Now list the data again by entering

```
LIST cat,payto,category->name<return>
```

dBASE III Plus will display

```
Record#   cat payto               category->name
     1    110 CROW CANYON LUMBER   OFFICE IMPROVEMENTS
     2    140 SEARS                OFFICE SUPPLIES
     3    120 GREEN ACRES FURN     FURNITURE
     4    140 INSTANT PRINTING     OFFICE SUPPLIES
     5    130 PG&E                 UTILITIES
     6    130 PACIFIC BELL         UTILITIES
     7    140 BRITZ PRINTING       OFFICE SUPPLIES
     8    140 GIFT STORE           OFFICE SUPPLIES
     9    120 GREEN ACRES FURN     FURNITURE
    10    140 BACON EAST PHARMACY  OFFICE SUPPLIES
```

Because relations are logically related, the change in the data in the EXPENSES file has an immediate effect.

RELATIONS IN REPORTS

Most of the *dBASE III Plus* output commands will work with data from more than one data base file. Take, for example, the *dBASE III Plus* REPORT FORM command.

In Chapter 7 you learned how to make columns to produce column reports. These reports can include data from files linked together by a relation. Suppose you wanted to make a report form that used the names of the budget categories instead of just their numbers.

The report form called EXPENSES created in Chapter 7 produced subtotals based on the CAT number. Now that you have learned how to relate the CAT number to a category name, you can change the report form to show the name instead of the number. To see what type of report the form currently generates, you need to have the file indexed by CAT. Enter

```
SET INDEX TO catorder<return>
```

Now display the report form by entering

REPORT FORM expenses < return >

dBASE III Plus will display

```
Page No.      1
01/01/80
                        EXPENSE REPORT BY CATEGORY

    DATE OF   PAYEE           AMOUNT DESCRIPTION
    EXPENSE

 ** CATEGORY /   110
 ** Subtotal **
                        68.40

 ** CATEGORY /   120
 ** Subtotal **
                       439.68

 ** CATEGORY /   130
 ** Subtotal **
                       104.88

 ** CATEGORY /   140
 ** Subtotal **
                       131.34
 *** Total ***
                       744.30
```

Your goal is to alter the report form so that it will display the category name instead of the category number. Enter

MODIFY REPORT expenses < return >

dBASE III Plus will display

```
Options        Groups        Columns         Locate      Exit  06:20:26 am
 ┌──────────────────────────────────┐
 │ Page title                EXPENSE │
 │ Page width (positions)    80      │
 │ Left margin               8       │
 │ Right margin              0       │
 │ Lines per page            58      │
 │ Double space report       No      │
 │ Page eject before printing Yes    │
 │ Page eject after printing  No     │
 │ Plain page                No      │
 └──────────────────────────────────┘
```

Display the subtotal group menu. Enter

g

dBASE III Plus will display

```
Options        Groups        Columns         Locate      Exit  06:20:56 am
          ┌──────────────────────────────────┐
          │ Group on expression       CAT     │
          │ Group heading             CATEGORY / │
          │ Summary report only       Yes     │
          │ Page eject after group    No      │
          │ Sub-group on expression           │
          │ Sub-group heading                 │
          └──────────────────────────────────┘
```

The Group on expression line shows the name of the CAT field. Remove CAT by entering

> **< return >**
> **[Home]**
> **[CTRL/t]**

Enter the name of the NAME field along with the alias of the file. Enter

> **category- > name < return >**

Change the HEADING field by entering

> **< down arrow >**
> **< return >**
> **[backspace]**
> **< return >**

The screen should look like this:

```
Options        Groups        Columns        Locate      Exit  Ø6:22:Ø3 am
          ┌──────────────────────────────────────────────────┐
          │ Group on expression       category->name          │
          │ Group heading             CATEGORY                 │
          │ Summary report only       Yes                      │
          │ Page eject after group    No                       │
          │ Sub-group on expression                            │
          │ Sub-group heading                                  │
          └──────────────────────────────────────────────────┘
```

Save the changes by entering

> **e**
> **< return >**

Now display the report again by entering

> **REPORT FORM expenses < return >**

dBASE III Plus will display

```
Page No.      1
Ø1/Ø1/8Ø
                           EXPENSE REPORT BY CATEGORY

DATE OF   PAYEE              AMOUNT DESCRIPTION
EXPENSE


** CATEGORY OFFICE IMPROVEMENTS
** Subtotal **
                              68.4Ø

** CATEGORY FURNITURE
** Subtotal **
                             439.68

** CATEGORY UTILITIES
** Subtotal **
                             1Ø4.88

** CATEGORY OFFICE SUPPLIES
** Subtotal **
                             131.34
*** Total ***
                             744.3Ø
```

This time the report contains the names of the categories instead of just their numbers.

You can use relations in the column specifications of a report as well. For example, in Chapter 10 you created a report form called CATTOTS. Display the current CATTOTS report by entering

REPORT FORM cattots < return >

dBASE III Plus will display

```
Page No.     1
01/01/80
                        SAMPLE SUMMARY REPORT

CATEGORY AMOUNT

     110  68.40
     120 264.68
     120 175.00
     120   0.00
     130  60.60
     130  44.28
     140  17.95
     140  59.50
     140  47.95
     140   5.94
*** Total ***
         744.30
```

Your goal is to change the column specification so that it will print the name of the category instead of the number. Enter

MODIFY REPORT cattots < return >

Move to the column specifications by entering

c

dBASE III Plus will display

```
Options          Groups        Columns         Locate       Exit  07:14:40 am
                 ┌──────────────────────────────────────────────────────┐
                 │ Contents         CAT                                  │
                 │ Heading          CATEGORY                             │
                 │ Width            8                                    │
                 │ Decimal places   0                                    │
                 │ Total this column No                                  │
                 └──────────────────────────────────────────────────────┘




┌─Report Format──────────────────────────────────────────────────────────┐
│>>>>>>>>CATEGORY AMOUNT ─────────────────────────────────────────────────│
│                                                                         │
│                                                                         │
│     99999 ###.##                                                        │
└─────────────────────────────────────────────────────────────────────────┘
```

Change the contents area by entering

> **< return >**
> **egory- > name**
> **< return >**

dBASE III Plus automatically changed the field width to accommodate the new field. Enter

> **e**
> **< return >**

Now display the report again. Enter

> **REPORT FORM cattots < return >**

dBASE III Plus will display

```
Page No.      1
Ø1/Ø1/8Ø
                       SAMPLE SUMMARY REPORT

CATEGORY               AMOUNT


OFFICE IMPROVEMENTS      68.4Ø
FURNITURE               264.68
FURNITURE               175.ØØ
FURNITURE                 Ø.ØØ
UTILITIES                6Ø.6Ø
UTILITIES                44.28
OFFICE SUPPLIES          17.95
OFFICE SUPPLIES          59.5Ø
OFFICE SUPPLIES          47.95
OFFICE SUPPLIES           5.94
*** Total ***

                        744.3Ø
```

With the relation set, the substitution is made while the report prints.

BROWSING RELATED DATA

The relation will function in the BROWSE mode as well as with a report form. Enter

> **GO TOP < return >**
> **BROWSE FIELDS category- > name,payto,amount < return >**

dBASE III Plus will display

```
NAME                  PAYTO                 AMOUNT
OFFICE IMPROVEMENTS   CROW CANYON LUMBER     68.4Ø
OFFICE SUPPLIES       SEARS                  17.95
FURNITURE             GREEN ACRES FURN      264.68
OFFICE SUPPLIES       INSTANT PRINTING       59.5Ø
UTILITIES             PG&E                   6Ø.6Ø
UTILITIES             PACIFIC BELL           44.28
OFFICE SUPPLIES       BRITZ PRINTING         47.95
OFFICE SUPPLIES       GIFT STORE              5.94
FURNITURE             GREEN ACRES FURN      175.ØØ
OFFICE SUPPLIES       BACON EAST PHARMACY     2.56
```

What makes the BROWSE mode special is that you can change, as well as display, data. What would happen if you made a change in the NAME field that is part of the data base file located in work area B? Suppose you decided to change the name OFFICE SUPPLIES to SUPPLIES FOR THE OFFICE. Enter

> **<down arrow>**
> **[CTRL/y]**
> **SUPPLIES FOR THE OFFICE <return>**

The other records with the name OFFICE SUPPLIES still show that name. Enter

> **<down arrow>**
> **<down arrow>**

When you positioned the cursor on the next entry with OFFICE SUPPLIES, *dBASE III Plus* updated the display to show the new name. Even though the name OFFICE SUPPLIES appears several times in the display, there is only *one* record in the CATEGORY data base file. If you change that record, all the records related to it will update as you move the pointer to them. Continue moving down the display by entering

> **<down arrow> (6 times)**

dBASE III Plus will display

```
NAME———————————— PAYTO———————— AMOUNT
OFFICE IMPROVEMENTS     CROW CANYON LUMBER    68.40
SUPPLIES FOR THE OFFICE SEARS                 17.95
FURNITURE               GREEN ACRES FURN     264.68
SUPPLIES FOR THE OFFICE INSTANT PRINTING      59.50
UTILITIES               PG&E                  60.60
UTILITIES               PACIFIC BELL          44.28
SUPPLIES FOR THE OFFICE BRITZ PRINTING        47.95
SUPPLIES FOR THE OFFICE GIFT STORE             5.94
FURNITURE               GREEN ACRES FURN     175.00
SUPPLIES FOR THE OFFICE BACON EAST PHARMACY    2.56
```

You can change the name back to OFFICE SUPPLIES by changing any one of the fields that are related to the same record. Enter

> **[CTRL/y]**
> **OFFICE SUPPLIES**
> **[CTRL/End]**

To see if the name was actually returned to OFFICE SUPPLIES, enter

> **LIST payto,category->name <return>**

dBASE III Plus will display

```
Record#  PAYTO                CATEGORY->NAME
     1   CROW CANYON LUMBER   OFFICE IMPROVEMENTS
     2   SEARS                OFFICE SUPPLIES
     3   GREEN ACRES FURN     FURNITURE
     4   INSTANT PRINTING     OFFICE SUPPLIES
     5   PG&E                 UTILITIES
     6   PACIFIC BELL         UTILITIES
     7   BRITZ PRINTING       OFFICE SUPPLIES
     8   GIFT STORE           OFFICE SUPPLIES
     9   GREEN ACRES FURN     FURNITURE
    10   BACON EAST PHARMACY  OFFICE SUPPLIES
```

Unlike files that are physically joined together, files that are related can be instantly updated when related records are altered.

ALIAS NAMES IN EXPRESSIONS

It should be clear that when two files are related with a SET RELATION command, the data in the corresponding records can be treated as if the files had been physically joined. For example, you can test the selected file for a condition that specifies data from the related file. Enter

LIST FOR category–>name="OFFICE" <return>

dBASE III Plus will display

```
Record#  DATE      CAT PAYTO              ITEM              AMOUNT COMMENT
S MONTH            DEDUCT
     1  01/02/85   110 CROW CANYON LUMBER  10 2BY 4          68.40 Memo
January            .T.
     2  01/10/85   140 SEARS               TRASH CAN         17.95 Memo
January            .F.
     4  01/17/85   140 INSTANT PRINTING    ENVELOPES         59.50 Memo
January            .T.
     7  01/30/85   140 BRITZ PRINTING      BUSINESS CARDS    47.95 Memo
January            .F.
     8  02/02/85   140 GIFT STORE          GROUND HOD DAY CARDS 5.94 Memo
February           .F.
    10  03/15/86   140 BACON EAST PHARMACY FIRST AID KIT      2.56 Memo
March              .T.
```

The records displayed do not contain the category name. The alias-fieldname was used to select the records; it was not part of the display. If you don't remember what command was issued to select the records, there are no data on the screen to indicate a common pattern among the records. Only the records with CAT numbers 110 and 140 appear because the corresponding name in the CATEGORY field begins with OFFICE.

FORMAT FILES

Relations can be used to create screen displays that combine data from more than one file on the same display screen. Suppose you wanted to have *dBASE III Plus* look up and display the name of the budget category when you used the EDIT or APPEND modes.

Normally the *dBASE III Plus* full-screen display mode for EDIT and APPEND shows only the fields in the currently selected data base file. However, you can get around this limitation by creating a custom screen display that includes fields from the unselected data base file.

To create a sample display, create a simple format file by using the *dBASE III Plus* screen creation mode. Enter

CREATE SCREEN twofiles <return>

First, position the cursor to the center of the screen. Access the blackboard by entering

> **[F10]**

Use the arrow keys to position the cursor at row 5 column 20. Return to the menu bar by entering

> **[F10]**

To load fields from the selected data base file, enter

> **s**
> **[Pg Dn]**
> **<return>**

The fields in the EXPENSES data base file are displayed for selection.

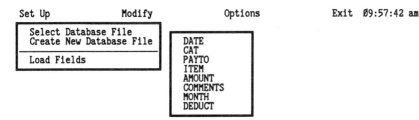

```
Set Up              Modify            Options        Exit  09:57:42 am
 ┌────────────────────────────────┐
 │ Select Database File           │  ┌─────────────┐
 │ Create New Database File       │  │ DATE        │
 ├────────────────────────────────┤  │ CAT         │
 │ Load Fields                    │  │ PAYTO       │
 └────────────────────────────────┘  │ ITEM        │
                                      │ AMOUNT      │
                                      │ COMMENTS    │
                                      │ MONTH       │
                                      │ DEDUCT      │
                                      └─────────────┘
```

Select the first five fields by entering

> **<return> <down arrow>**
> **<return> <down arrow>**
> **<return> <down arrow>**
> **<return> <down arrow>**
> **<return>**

Display the blackboard by entering

> **[F10]**

dBASE III Plus will display

```
Set Up              Modify            Options        Exit  09:58:50 am




        DATE       99/99/99
        CAT        99999
        PAYTO      XXXXXXXXXXXXXXXXXXXXX
        ITEM       XXXXXXXXXXXXXXXXXXXXX
        AMOUNT     999.99
```

Up to this point you have used the same technique as in Chapter 9. However, you are now going to add a field to the display that is part of a different data base file. Enter

> **[F10]**
> **s**

This places you at the SELECT DATABASE FILE prompt. Enter

> **< return >**

Position the highlight, using the arrow keys, on CATEGORY.DBF. Enter

> **< return >**

You can now select fields from the CATEGORY data base file. Enter

> **[Pg Dn]**
> **< return >**

dBASE III Plus will display

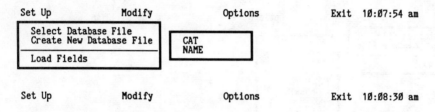

```
Set Up              Modify              Options          Exit  10:07:54 am
    ┌─────────────────────────────────┐
    │ Select Database File            │
    │ Create New Database File        │  ┌──────────┐
    │                                 │  │ CAT      │
    │ Load Fields                     │  │ NAME     │
    └─────────────────────────────────┘  └──────────┘

Set Up              Modify              Options          Exit  10:08:30 am
```

Select the NAME field by entering

> **< down arrow >**
> **< return >**

Display the blackboard by entering

> **[F10]**

dBASE III Plus will display

```
NAME      XXXXXXXXXXXXXXXXXXXXXXXXXX
CAT       99999
PAYTO     XXXXXXXXXXXXXXXXXXXX
ITEM      XXXXXXXXXXXXXXXXXXXX
AMOUNT    999.99
```

Before you conclude the screen display creation process, there is one change that still needs to be made. The NAME field should be changed from an input area (@/GET) to a display only area (@/SAY). The name of the category will be the result of the relation set between the two files and should not be directly entered.

To change the area definition, place the cursor in the NAME field area by entering

> **[CTRL/f]**

Activate the menu by entering

> **[F10]**

Toggle the field display type by entering

> < return >

Save the definition by entering

> e
> < return >

The relation that you set previously is still in effect. In case you want to check to see that this is really the case, you can display the status. Enter

DISPLAY STATUS < return >

dBASE III Plus will display

```
Currently Selected Database:
Select area:  1, Database in Use: C:expenses.dbf    Alias: EXPENSES
         Memo file:   C:expenses.dbt
         Format file: C:twofiles.fmt
    Related into: CATEGORY
    Relation: cat

Select area:  2, Database in Use: C:category.dbf    Alias: CATEGORY
    Master index file:  C:category.ndx  Key: cat

File search path:
Default disk drive: C:
Print destination:  PRN:
Margin =      0
Current work area =      1

Press any key to continue...
```

The display shows that the relation between the two data base files is still active.

Look at the line that reads Format file: C:twofiles.fmt. This indicates that the format file TWOFILES has been activated. When a format file is active, the full screen commands APPEND, EDIT, CHANGE, and INSERT are controlled by the commands in the active format file. The result will be that the screen will show data from two files for each record. Return to the COMMAND mode by entering

> < Esc >

The status display is very important because it is the one place in *dBASE III Plus* that summarizes all the file opening and relating that has taken place. Without the status display you could easily lose track of what files are active, open, selected, or related.

To get a better idea of how the format file was constructed by the CREATE SCREEN command, use the TYPE command to display its contents. Enter

TYPE twofiles.fmt < return >

dBASE III Plus will display

```
@  5, 20  SAY  "NAME"
@  5, 32  SAY   CATEGORY->NAME
@  6, 20  SAY  "CAT"
@  6, 32  GET   EXPENSES->CAT
@  7, 20  SAY  "PAYTO"
@  7, 32  GET   EXPENSES->PAYTO
@  8, 20  SAY  "ITEM"
@  8, 32  GET   EXPENSES->ITEM
@  9, 20  SAY  "AMOUNT"
@  9, 32  GET   EXPENSES->AMOUNT
```

The format file contains the alias names to indicate which fields are drawn from which files.

Activate the new screen format by entering one of the full-screen modes. Enter

> **GO TOP** < return >
> **EDIT** < return >

dBASE III Plus will display

```
NAME         OFFICE IMPROVEMENTS
CAT            110
PAYTO        CROW CANYON LUMBER
ITEM         10 2BY 4
AMOUNT       68.40
```

The relation between EXPENSES and CATEGORY makes sure that any changes in the CAT field will cause *dBASE III Plus* to change the display in the NAME field. Enter

> **120** < return >

dBASE III Plus has not changed the NAME field. You need to force the program to reread the revised record to make the update appear on the screen. Enter

> **[Pg Dn]**
> **[Pg Up]**

dBASE III Plus now shows the correct name for CAT number 120.

```
NAME         FURNITURE
CAT            120
PAYTO        CROW CANYON LUMBER
ITEM         10 2BY 4
AMOUNT       68.40
```

Return the record to CAT 110 by entering

> **110** < return >
> **[Pg Dn]**
> **[Pg Up]**

The same technique operates if you append new records to the file. Exit the EDIT mode and enter APPEND by entering

> **< Esc >**
> **APPEND** < return >

Exercise 1 Notice that *dBASE III Plus* automatically displays OFFICE SUP-
PLIES in the NAME field even though you have not entered a CAT number for
the record. Try to determine why *dBASE III Plus* would choose that record to display.
The answer can be found at the end of the chapter.

Enter the following data into the record:

> **120 < return >**
> **VIRCO EQUIPMENT <return >**
> **TABLES < return >**
> **350.45**

dBASE III Plus automatically proceeds to the next record. Return to the previous
record by entering

> **[Pg Up]**

dBASE III Plus will display

```
NAME        FURNITURE
CAT            120
PAYTO       VIRCO EQUIPMENT
ITEM        TABLES
AMOUNT      350.45
```

dBASE III Plus has correctly located the name for CAT number 120. Exit the AP-
PEND mode by entering

> **<Esc>**

REPLACING WITH RELATIONS

Relations between files can be used, as you have seen, to relate files logically. This
relation can also be used to update the data in one of the data base files with data
from another file. This updating ability is one of the most powerful uses of relations. To understand how it works and what benefit this type of updating can be,
begin with a simple example.

The EXPENSES file currently contains a field called DEDUCT. This is a
LOGICAL field that can be either true or false. The original idea of adding this
field to the data base file was to allow you to enter true for the deductible items,
and false for those that were not.

However, now that you have added categories to your data base file, you might
realize that it is not necessary to manually enter true or false into each record. It
is probably the case that all the items entered into one category have the same tax
status. For example, all CAT 140 items (office supplies) might be taxable but all
110 items (improvements) might be deductible.

The idea would be to add to the CATEGORY file a DEDUCT field for each category. *dBASE III Plus* can then be used to go through the EXPENSES file and update the DEDUCT field based on the contents of the CAT field.

This procedure would make data entry faster, since you do not need to manually enter the DEDUCT field, and more accurate, since *dBASE III Plus* would make sure that each expense was assigned the correct tax status automatically.

Begin by adding a new field to the CATEGORY data base file. First select the work area. Enter

> SELECT B< return >

Use the MODIFY STRUCTURE command to add the field DEDUCT to the CATEGORY file. After you have finished, the structure of the CATEGORY file should be

```
Field  Field Name  Type       Width
   1   CAT         Numeric        5
   2   NAME        Character     25
   3   DEDUCT      Logical        1
```

Next, enter the values for the DEDUCT field of the CATEGORY file. In this case, use the BROWSE command to make the entry.

> GO TOP < return >
> BROWSE FIELDS deduct,cat FREEZE deduct NO APPEND < return >

Enter the following:

> y
> n
> y
> n
> < Esc >

Modifying the structure of the CATEGORY file had an effect you might not have anticipated. When you modify the structure of a file, any index files associated with that file are closed. When the index file is closed, the relation that was based on that index file is also terminated. To check the status, enter

> DISPLAY STATUS < return >

dBASE III Plus will display

```
Select area:  1, Database in Use: C:expenses.dbf   Alias: EXPENSES
              Memo file:    C:expenses.dbt
              Format file: C:twofiles.fmt

Currently Selected Database:
Select area:  2, Database in Use: C:category.dbf   Alias: CATEGORY

File search path:
Default disk drive: C:
Print destination:  PRN:
Margin =      0
Current work area =     2

Press any key to continue...
```

The display shows that the relation between EXPENSES and CATEGORY is no longer active. In addition, the index file for the CATEGORY file is closed. Return to the command mode by entering

> **< Esc >**

You need to reestablish these functions to update the EXPENSES file.

Exercise 7   Set up the relation between EXPENSES and CATEGORY; first, open the CATEGORY index file; then change work areas and set the relation. The correct commands can be found at the end of the chapter.

To see if you have properly set up the relation, display the status screen.

> **DISPLAY STATUS< return >**

The top portion should look like the following display.

```
Currently Selected Database:
Select area:  1, Database in Use: C:expenses.dbf    Alias: EXPENSES
         Memo file:   C:expenses.dbt
         Format file: C:twofiles.fmt
   Related into: CATEGORY
   Relation: cat

Select area:  2, Database in Use: C:category.dbf    Alias: CATEGORY
   Master index file:  C:category.ndx  Key: cat
```

Return to the COMMAND mode by entering

> **< Esc >**

You can now update the values in the EXPENSES DEDUCT field by using the REPLACE command. In this instance, the REPLACE command changes the value in the EXPENSES DEDUCT field to match the corresponding value in the CATEGORY DEDUCT field. Because the files are related by CAT number, *dBASE III Plus* will match each record before the replacement takes place. Enter

> **REPLACE ALL deduct WITH category->deduct< return >**

dBASE III Plus displays the message 11 records replaced. Display the data by entering

> **LIST cat,deduct< return >**

dBASE III Plus will display

```
Record#   cat deduct
     1    110 .T.
     2    140 .F.
     3    120 .F.
     4    140 .F.
     5    130 .T.
     6    130 .T.
     7    140 .F.
     8    140 .F.
     9    120 .F.
    10    140 .F.
    11    120 .F.
```

The DEDUCT fields are not consistent with the DEDUCT specifications stored in the CATEGORY file.

When you are using the REPLACE command, you can replace only into the selected data base file. Refer to the line below:

REPLACE < selected > WITH < unselected >

If you attempt to place data in the unselected data base file from the selected file, *dBASE III Plus* will appear to carry out the command. When you examine the unselected data base file, you will find that no data have been changed.

Close all the files by entering

CLOSE DATABASE < return >

VIEW FILES

In this and the previous chapter, you have begun to perform tasks that require a variety of files of different types to be active at the same time. This makes working with *dBASE III Plus* more complex than when you were working with a single data base file with no relations or formats to worry about.

One way to keep track of all the files, indexes, formats, and relations is to write down which files need to be opened with which indexes. *dBASE III Plus* provides some special tools that allow you to record these facts directly into a *dBASE III Plus* file. This special file, called a *view* file, can help you manage these complex relationships more quickly and simply. The name *view* is used to indicate that when the specified data base, index, and format files are activated, your data base will reveal a certain view of the information.

View files are used to record all the files and relationships needed to carry out a particular task. The advantage of the view file is that it allows you to record all this information once and then reestablish those conditions with a single command.

Like format files, view files are controlled with three commands:

CREATE VIEW
MODIFY VIEW
SET VIEW TO

To create a view file, enter

CREATE VIEW expenses < return >

The CREATE/MODIFY view menu appears.

```
Set Up       Relate      Set Fields      Options      Exit  07:30:41 am

MAIL.DBF
EXPENSES.DBF
CLIENTS.DBF
TEST.DBF
CATTOTS.DBF
DATETOTS.DBF
MONTOTS.DBF
JAN.DBF
FEB.DBF
MAR.DBF
SIMPLE.DBF
CATEGORY.DBF
JOIN.DBF
EXPCAT.DBF
```

View files appear on the disk with a .VUE extension. For example, this file, called EXPENSES, appears on the disk as EXPENSES.VUE.

The VIEW menu has five main functions:

1. **SET UP.** This selects the data base file and index files to be opened for the view.

2. **RELATE.** This option allows you to specify a relation between two files. It performs the same function as the SET RELATION TO command.

3. **SET FIELDS.** This option allows you to specify which fields should be used. If no setting is entered, then all the fields in all the data bases are activated. The option performs the same function as the SET FIELD TO command.

4. **OPTIONS.** The OPTIONS menu allows you to activate a FORMAT file or enter a data filter. These options correspond to the SET FORMAT TO and SET FILTER TO commands.

5. **EXIT.** This option saves the view file.

Begin by selecting the data base file and index files. Move the highlight to the filename EXPENSES.DBF. Enter

< return >

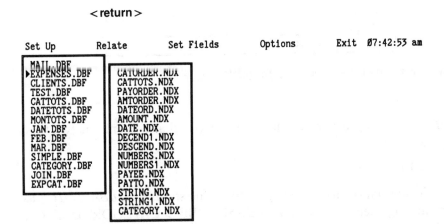

```
Set Up       Relate      Set Fields      Options      Exit  07:42:53 am

MAIL.DBF
►EXPENSES.DBF      CATORDER.NDX
CLIENTS.DBF        CATTOTS.NDX
TEST.DBF           PAYORDER.NDX
CATTOTS.DBF        AMTORDER.NDX
DATETOTS.DBF       DATEORD.NDX
MONTOTS.DBF        AMOUNT.NDX
JAN.DBF            DATE.NDX
FEB.DBF            DECEND1.NDX
MAR.DBF            DESCEND.NDX
SIMPLE.DBF         NUMBERS.NDX
CATEGORY.DBF       NUMBERS1.NDX
JOIN.DBF           PAYEE.NDX
EXPCAT.DBF         PAYTO.NDX
                   STRING.NDX
                   STRING1.NDX
                   CATEGORY.NDX
```

dBASE III Plus now lists the index files on the directory. In this case, you do not want to open an index file. Enter

> **<left arrow>**

You can now select another data base file. Move the highlight to the filename CATEGORY.DBF. Enter

> **<return>**

This time you do want to open an index file for that data base file. Move the highlight to the filename CATEGORY.NDX. Select the index file by entering

> **<return>**

The next step is to create a relation between the two files. Move to the RELATE menu by entering

> **<left arrow>**
> **r**

The RELATE menu consists of the two files that you have just selected.

```
Set Up        Relate        Set Fields      Options        Exit  07:47:43 am
                  ┌──────────────┐
                  │ EXPENSES.DBF │
                  │ CATEGORY.DBF │
                  └──────────────┘
```

You must choose the file from which the relation will be set. Since the highlight is already on EXPENSES.DBF, enter

> **<return>**

dBASE III Plus displays a list of the other active files that EXPENSES can be related to.

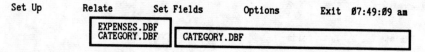

```
Set Up        Relate        Set Fields      Options        Exit  07:49:09 am
                  ┌──────────────┐┌──────────────────────────────────────┐
                  │ EXPENSES.DBF ││ CATEGORY.DBF                         │
                  │ CATEGORY.DBF ││                                      │
                  └──────────────┘└──────────────────────────────────────┘
```

The only other file selected is CATEGORY. Enter

> **<return>**

dBASE III Plus wants you to enter the key expression that will link the two files, the CAT field. Enter

> **CAT <return>**

Look at the bottom of the display, just above the status line. *dBASE III Plus* displays the message Relation Chain: EXPENSES.DBF->CATEGORY.DBF. This display indicates that you have set a relation from EXPENSES into CATEGORY.

In this example, you will not use the SET FIELDS option. The fields that are to be displayed will be controlled by the format file. Move to the OPTIONS menu by entering

> **< left arrow >**
>
> **o**

dBASE III Plus displays

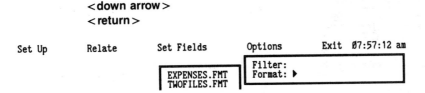

In this example, you want to specify a format file to be used. Enter

> **< down arrow >**
> **< return >**

```
Set Up        Relate        Set Fields      Options        Exit  07:57:12 am
                                                          ┌──────────────────┐
                                          ┌───────────┐   │ Filter:          │
                                          │ EXPENSES.FMT│ │ Format: ▶        │
                                          │ TWOFILES.FMT│ └──────────────────┘
                                          └───────────┘
```

dBASE III Plus displays a list of .FMT (format) files. Move the highlight to the file name TWOFILES.FMT. Enter

> **< return >**

You have created a view file that contains all the specifications you had manually entered in the previous section of this chapter. Save the view file by entering

> **e**
> **< return >**

You are now ready to use the view file that you created. First, close all the open files. Enter

> **CLOSE DATABASE < return >**

To confirm that none of the data base, index, or format files is open, enter

> **DISPLAY STATUS < return >**

dBASE III Plus will display

```
File search path:
Default disk drive: C:
Print destination:  PRN:
Margin =      0
Current work area =    1

Press any key to continue...
```

The limited display shows that no files are open at this point. Return to the COM-
MAND mode by entering

<Esc>

You can open all the files and set a relation with a single command that utilizes
the view file you created. Enter

SET VIEW TO expenses<return>

What has happened? To get the full picture, enter

DISPLAY STATUS<return>

dBASE III Plus will display

```
Currently Selected Database:
Select area:  1, Database in Use: C:EXPENSES.DBF    Alias: EXPENSES
        Memo file:     C:EXPENSES.dbt
        Format file: C:TWOFILES.FMT
    Related into: CATEGORY
    Relation: cat

Select area:  2, Database in Use: C:CATEGORY.DBF    Alias: CATEGORY
    Master index file:  C:CATEGORY.NDX  Key: cat

File search path:
Default disk drive: C:
Print destination:  PRN:
Margin =      Ø
Current work area =    1

Press any key to continue...
```

Now all the needed files have been opened with a single command. The view
file is a simple example of programming in *dBASE III Plus*. In programming, you
write down a set of commands in a file, then you execute all the commands by referring to that file. In the example of a view file, you enter the commands by selecting
from the menus of the CREATE VIEW command. Later, the SET VIEW TO command is used to activate the commands all at once.

The view file is really one big command constructed out of a number of smaller
commands. This process of building large commands from smaller ones is often
referred to as macro creation.

> The term macro *is used in many respects in the microcomputer world. Originally,
> it was used to describe command sequences used in assembly language programming.
> Programs like 1–2–3 have popularized the concept of keystroke macros. dBASE III
> Plus uses a technique called* macro substitution, *discussed in the programming sec-
> tion of the book.*

There is a great advantage to using structures like view files. Look at the chart
below. It shows that the SET VIEW command does in one entry what would otherwise take six commands to accomplish.

1. SET VIEW TO expenses	1. USE expenses
	2. SELECT B
	3. USE category INDEX category
	4. SELECT A
	5. SET FORMAT TO twofiles
	6. SET RELATION TO cat INTO category

If the relationship between these two files is one that you use often, the view file can save a great amount of time and avoid a great number of entry mistakes.

The idea of compressing sequences of *dBASE III Plus* commands into a single file is the theme behind the idea of programming in *dBASE III Plus*. View files present a preview of what programming is like and how it can improve the operation of *dBASE III Plus*.

Conclude this section by entering

CLOSE DATABASE < return >

CATALOG FILES

Another organizational tool along the lines of the view file is the catalog file. A catalog file is used to group together lists of related files.

Catalog files generally are of use to people who have a large number of data base, index, and other types of files stored in a single directory. A catalog allows you to display a list of files when you use a command that requires the entry of a filename.

Catalog provides an alternative for users who find that it is hard to keep track of the names of the files they want to use.

Catalogs are much less specific than view files. Catalog files simply store lists of files to be displayed when you are working with the *dBASE III Plus* menu.

View files do much more than list files. A view file also stores the logical relationships between files. When a view file is opened, the relationships are set as if you had just entered a sequence of *dBASE III Plus* commands.

View files are much more significant than catalog files because they are much closer to the concepts of *dBASE III Plus* programming. However, it is useful to know what the catalog files are and how they operate.

To create a catalog enter

SET CATALOG TO accounts < return >

The program displays a prompt at the bottom of the screen that asks Create new file catalog? (Y/N). Enter

y

dBASE III Plus next wants you to enter a title for the ACCOUNTS catalog. Note that CATALOG files end with a .CAT extension. Enter

accounting information< return >

What has happened is that you have turned on a recording mode. Every time you enter a command that opens a file, data base, index, format, and the like, *dBASE III Plus* records the name of that file in the catalog.

For example, place the EXPENSES file in use. Enter

USE expenses< return >

Instead of taking you back to the DOT PROMPT, *dBASE III Plus* displays a prompt. Enter a description of the data in this file. Enter

expense records< return >

Now *dBASE III Plus* displays the DOT PROMPT. Open an index file. Enter

SET INDEX TO catorder< return >

dBASE III Plus did not ask you for a description. That happens only when the file is a data base file. However, the file is recorded as part of the ACCOUNTS catalog. Now open another data base file. Enter

USE category< return >

This time the program does ask you for a description because the file is a data base file. Enter

accounts names and numbers< return >

Open an index file related to this data base file.

SET INDEX TO category< return >

So far you have entered four files into the ACCOUNTS catalog. How can you make use of the catalog? The trick is to enter a command that would normally require a filename but place a ? after the command instead of the filename. Enter

USE ?< return >

The ? signals *dBASE III Plus* to enter a full-screen menu drive mode. At the top of the display you can see the files that are part of the catalog. At the bottom of the display is the description that you entered for the highlighted item. Enter

< down arrow >

When you change the position of the highlight, the description changes. To actually place the file in use, enter

< return >

The display changes to show you the index files that are available. The box in the lower right corner displays the index key expression. If you do not want to open an index file, enter

< left arrow >

You now exit from the full-screen menu mode and return to the COMMAND mode.

Now, expand the catalog by entering the following commands that open files. Enter

USE expenses< return >
SET INDEX TO dateord < return >
SET INDEX TO amtorder< return >

dBASE III Plus *provides two special commands that can be used only when a catalog file is already in use. The commands are SET CATALOG ON and SET CATALOG OFF. These commands control which files are added to the catalog file. The default is ON, which means that any files opened become part of the catalog.*

If you set the catalog OFF, you can still use the catalog with the files already recorded, but any new files opened will not be part of the catalog.

Now enter a command that requires a filename. Enter

SET INDEX TO ?

Using the question mark in place of the filename causes the catalog to display a full-screen menu that lists all the index files in the catalog.

The box in the lower right once again shows the index key expression that was used to create the file. Move the highlight to the next file on the list by entering

< down arrow >

dBASE III Plus places the index key for that index file in the display box in the bottom right corner of the screen. To exit the menu without opening an index file, enter

< left arrow >

To close and save the active catalog, enter

SET CATALOG TO < return >

Now enter

USE ?< return >

dBASE III Plus displays the message Data Catalog has not been established. This indicates that no catalog file is open. Enter

< return >

When the catalog is not in use, the ? following commands will not be recognized by *dBASE III Plus*.

ABOUT CATALOGS

This section deals with the technical aspects of catalog files. The reason is that catalog files are really a special form of data base file. To see what that means, open the ACCOUNTS catalog. Enter

SET CATALOG TO accounts < return >

Now, display the status of the system by entering

DISPLAY STATUS < return >

dBASE III Plus will display

```
Select area:  1, Database in Use: D:expenses.dbf    Alias: EXPENSES
    Master index file:   D:amtorder.ndx  Key: amount
            Memo file:   D:expenses.dbt
Select area: 1ø, Database in Use: D:accounts.cat    Alias: CATALOG.

File search path:
Default disk drive: D:
Print destination:  PRN:
Margin =      ø
Current work area =    1

Press any key to continue...
```

What is interesting about the display is that work area 10 is currently being used. *dBASE III Plus* uses work area 10 to store the information used in the catalog.

Furthermore, you can infer that if the data are stored in a work area, that must mean catalog files are really *dBASE III Plus* data base files. The filename of the data base file is ACCOUNTS.CAT.

> The .DBF extension for data base files is a default used by dBASE III Plus when no other file extension is used. It is perfectly valid to create data base files with extensions other than .DBF. If you do create such files you must remember that these files are data base files even though they do not have the usual extension.

To test this idea, select work area 10 by entering

< Esc >
SELECT 10 < return >

List the structure of the file in this work area. Enter

LIST STRUCTURE < return >

dBASE III Plus will display

```
Structure for database: C:accounts.cat
Number of data records:         1
Date of last update    : 11/05/86
Field  Field Name  Type       Width   Dec
    1   PATH        Character     70
    2   FILE NAME   Character     12
    3   ALIAS       Character      8
    4   TYPE        Character      3
    5   TITLE       Character     80
    6   CODE        Numeric        3
    7   TAG         Character      4
** Total **                      181
```

The file ACCOUNTS.CAT records the data that is used in the catalog. The file's name and storage path are recorded along with any alias.

The type field uses the file extension .DBF, .NDX to indicate the type of file. The CODE is used to associate related files. For example, the first data base file opened is coded 1. Any index or format files used with that data base file are also coded 1.

The second data base file is coded 2, and so on. The coding system allows *dBASE III Plus* to display only index files that are related to a given data base file when you use the catalog to list index files.

Inspect one of the records by entering

EDIT <return>

dBASE III Plus will display

```
PATH        amtorder.ndx

FILE NAME   amtorder.ndx
ALIAS       AMTORDER
TYPE        ndx
TITLE       amount

CODE        1
TAG
```

This record displays the information for the index file AMTORDER. Note that AMTORDER is coded 1, which means it is related to the data base file 1 in the catalog. Enter

[Pg Up]

The next record in the catalog file is displayed.

Exit the editing mode by entering

<Esc>

Close that catalog file by entering

SET CATALOG TO <return>

VIEW AND CATALOG FILES WITH THE ASSISTANT

Catalog files can be used with the ASSIST mode as well as the DOT PROMPT mode. The main advantage of catalog files in the ASSIST mode is that they limit the number of files displayed in the option boxes to those files stored in the catalog. Enter the ASSIST mode by entering

ASSIST <return>

The screen displays the ASSISTANT menus.

```
Set Up  Create  Update  Position  Retrieve  Organize Modify Tools  06:52:50 pm
┌─────────────────────┐
│ Database file       │
├─────────────────────┤
│ Format for Screen   │
│ Query               │
├─────────────────────┤
│ Catalog             │
│ View                │
├─────────────────────┤
│ Quit dBASE III PLUS │
└─────────────────────┘
```

To activate a catalog file, enter

<down arrow> (three times)
<return> (2 times)

dBASE III Plus displays a box with the catalog files in the default disk.

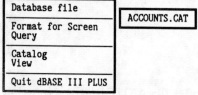

```
Set Up  Create  Update  Position  Retrieve  Organize Modify Tools  06:53:23 pm
┌─────────────────────┐
│ Database file       │   ┌──────────────┐
├─────────────────────┤   │ ACCOUNTS.CAT │
│ Format for Screen   │   └──────────────┘
│ Query               │
├─────────────────────┤
│ Catalog             │
│ View                │
├─────────────────────┤
│ Quit dBASE III PLUS │
└─────────────────────┘
```

Select the ACCOUNTS catalog file by entering

<return>

When the catalog has been opened, *dBASE III Plus* returns the highlight to the SET UP menu. You can now use the ASSIST mode to open a data base file. Enter

[Pg Up]
<return>

Instead of listing all the .DBF files, *dBASE III Plus* displays the file listed in the catalog file. In addition, a new box in the lower right-hand corner of the screen shows the description you entered into the catalog for that file.

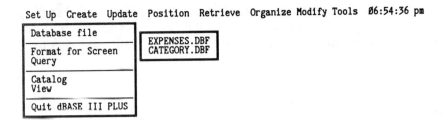

Set Up Create Update Position Retrieve Organize Modify Tools 06:54:36 pm

Database file
Format for Screen
Query
Catalog
View
Quit dBASE III PLUS

EXPENSES.DBF
CATEGORY.DBF

expenses records

Command: USE

Select the EXPENSES file by entering

< return >

dBASE III Plus asks if the file is indexed. Enter

y

The index files stored in the catalog under the same code number as the selected data base file are displayed. The catalog file aids you in making sure that the index file selected is one that matches the selected data base file. In addition, *dBASE III Plus* displays a box in the lower right-hand corner of the screen that shows the index key for the highlighted file. This further aids the user in determining which index file or files should be opened.

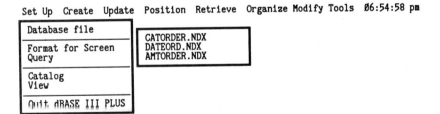

Set Up Create Update Position Retrieve Organize Modify Tools 06:54:58 pm

Database file
Format for Screen
Query
Catalog
View
Quit dBASE III PLUS

CATORDER.NDX
DATEORD.NDX
AMTORDER.NDX

cat

Command: USE EXPENSES INDEX

To select the CATORDER index file, enter

< return >
< left arrow >

Catalog files make it easier to remember which files are related to what other files. If you are working with a large number of files—data base, index, and format—catalogs can assist you by displaying smaller, selected listings when opening files.

SUMMARY

Relations

dBASE III Plus allows you to create logical links between two files by creating relations.

When a pair of files are related, one file is chosen to be the selected file while the other is unselected. The unselected file must be indexed.

The index key for the unselected file must match the key used on the SET RELATION command. Their fields do not have to match exactly but the key expressions, which may be fields or *dBASE III Plus* expressions, must contain the same information for a relation to operate correctly.

When the files are related, you can list, edit, replace, and so on. If you refer to a field in the unselected data base file, *dBASE III Plus* will find the first matching record in the unselected data base file based on the key expression and draw data from the fields in that record.

View Files

View files are used to record the files—data base, index, and format—that are needed to establish a relation. The view file can open and relate all the files with a single command.

Catalog Files

A catalog is a special data base file used for recording groups of related files. When a catalog is open, any files opened are recorded as part of the catalog.

In addition, commands that require filenames such as USE, SET INDEX TO, and the like, can use a ? in place of the filename. The ? causes *dBASE III Plus* to display a list of filenames stored in the catalog.

ANSWER KEY

Exercise 1

dBASE III Plus displays OFFICE SUPPLIES because that is the entry in the last record in the CATEGORY file. When you APPEND a new record, there is no entry in the CAT field. The relation searches the CATEGORY file but finds no matches. The pointer is positioned at the last record in the CATEGORY file, OFFICE SUPPLIES.

Exercise 2

```
SET INDEX TO category
SELECT A
SET RELATION TO cat INTO category
```

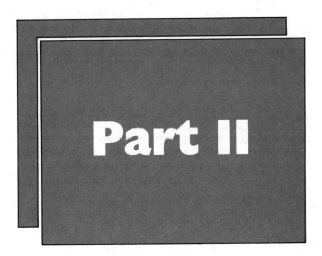

Part II

Programming with
dBASE III Plus

PROGRAMMING WITH

dBASE III PLUS

WHY PROGRAMMING?

When the word *programming* is mentioned, most people who are new to computers react by saying, "Hey, I'm not a programmer. I don't want to program."

In fact, the two ideas are not as closely related as most people think. While the majority of the people reading this book or using *dBASE III Plus* are not professional programmers, that does not mean that average users can't or won't want to use programming to make their computers work more efficiently.

The history of the microcomputer indicates very strongly that applications that permit or even encourage users to customize an application to their own specific needs are more powerful, more flexible, and in the long run, easier to use. Programming itself is not easy. But the results of programming create a customized application that can be used by people with very little experience.

As you delve deeper into the programming aspects of *dBASE III Plus*, you will find that they provide a means by which you can make *dBASE III Plus* closely reflect the environment you work in. Programming allows you to adjust *dBASE III Plus* to the user, rather than the other way around.

WHAT IS PROGRAMMING?

In the first part of this book you learned a number of procedures and techniques used in *dBASE III Plus* to handle a wide variety of data management needs. You probably noticed that the procedures varied in the number of commands required to complete a given task.

In the case of the larger, more complex operations, it would be more efficient if you could somehow create a list of commands that *dBASE III Plus* could automatically read and perform. Such a list of commands would have several advantages:

1. You would save the time and trouble of entering all the commands manually each time you wanted the job to be performed. Instead, you would simply refer to the name of the list of commands.
2. The list of commands could be changed or enlarged to perform more complicated tasks.
3. The command sequences would execute more accurately because you eliminate typing mistakes.

It is the ability to create lists of commands that makes *dBASE III Plus* more than just an ordinary data filing program. With this ability, *dBASE III Plus* can take on the personality of a computer programming language, with all the flexibility and versatility that such environments offer.

If you are not familiar with these advantages, the coming chapters will show you many of the unexpected abilities that *dBASE III Plus* has when used in the PROGRAMMING mode. If you are already familiar with programming languages such as BASIC, you will find that *dBASE III Plus* offers you the ability to construct programs in a fraction of the time that you would need for the same job performed in BASIC.

MAKING COMMAND LISTS

The simplest form of programming consists of creating lists of related commands that *dBASE III Plus* can automatically carry out. Programs can do much more than this, but the list approach is a good one to begin with.

For example, suppose you wanted to list the dates and amounts in the EXPENSES file and display the total. You would have to enter the following commands:

```
USE expenses INDEX dateord
LIST date,amount
SUM amount
```

If this was a task that you performed often, it could save you some time and effort if you were able to record the list of commands and have *dBASE III Plus* automatically play them back.

dBASE III Plus allows you to do exactly this. The method uses two commands:

1. **MODIFY COMMAND < filename >**. This command is used to create a file into which you can enter a list of *dBASE III Plus* commands. MODIFY COMMAND is really a simple word processing program in which you can edit your commands like a word processing document. You can add, delete, and revise your list of commands until you have them entered to your satisfaction.

2. **DO < filename >**. This command instructs *dBASE III Plus* to begin reading and executing the commands stored in a command file.

One important idea is that when commands are entered into a command file, they are not immediately executed as they are when you enter commands at the DOT PROMPT. Rather, *dBASE III Plus* waits until you specifically instruct the program to read that command file. Then, and only then, will the commands execute.

Suppose you wanted to create a command file that would contain the three commands listed above. You would begin by entering the MODIFY COMMAND command. Enter

MODIFY COMMAND listing < return >

You have now entered the *dBASE III Plus* EDITOR mode and can enter the commands that will make up your command file.

> *The dBASE III Plus EDITOR mode is the same mode that you enter when you are entering text into a MEMO field. dBASE III Plus uses the same editor for both tasks. This means that the features and restrictions that apply to entry of MEMO fields apply to command files.*
>
> *Thus programs written in the dBASE III Plus editor cannot exceed 4096 characters in length. You can use any word processing or editing program that creates ASCII standard files to create dBASE III Plus program files. This concept is discussed in more detail in Chapter 20.*

THE *dBASE* EDITOR

When you are using the editing program, at the very top of the screen, *dBASE III Plus* displays the name of the file that you are working on. The display will show c:listing.prg. *dBASE III Plus* adds the three-character extension .PRG (program) to any file created with MODIFY COMMAND that does not have a file extension already specified. .PRG is the default file extension for the MODIFY COMMAND command.

In Chapter 9, MODIFY COMMAND was used to create a format file with an .FMT extension. In that case the filename was entered as EXPENSES.FMT. .PRG was not added to the filename because a different extension was already specified.

As an introduction to the *dBASE* editor, begin by entering

USE

Edit your entry by using the < backspace > key to erase a character. Enter

< backspace >

The E is erased. Enter

E

The word is now complete again. As in most word processing programs, you can change the position of the cursor by using the directional arrow keys. Enter

< left arrow >

The cursor is now positioned on the E. Note that cursor movement does not erase data but merely changes the cursor's position.

If you want to move the cursor one word at a time, you can use the **[Home]** and **[End]** keys to move one word to the left and right, respectively. Enter

[Home]

The cursor is now positioned at the beginning of the word "use." Move to the end by entering

[End]

Complete the command by entering

< space bar >
expenses

The *dBASE III Plus* editor begins in the typeover mode. This means that new characters being typed automatically replace any characters that are already in the text. Enter

[Home]
category

Note that the "category" typed right over the previous name, "expenses."

You can place the editor into the insert mode by using the **[Ins]** key. Enter

[Ins]

Look at the top line of the screen. The letters "Ins" appear. This indicates that the program is now in the insert mode. Enter

> **[Home]**
> **expenses**

Note that this time "category" was not typed over when you entered "expenses." Rather, the characters were added to the line so that the characters "expensescategory" appear.

You can delete characters from the text by using the **[Del]** key. Enter

> **[Del]**

The c is removed. Enter

> **[Del]**

The next character is removed. You can remove an entire word (all the characters from the cursor position to the next space) by entering

> **[CTRL/t]**

You can remove an entire line of text by entering

> **[CTRL/y]**

The editor screen is now empty again.

> *If you are familiar with WordStar, you will recognize the editing commands as the same as those used in that word processor. Commands like [**CTRL/v**] to change the insert/overtype modes still work in* dBASE III Plus *even though the COMMAND menu shows only the [**Ins**] key.*

Begin the entry again by entering

> **USE expenses** < return >

Nothing much happens because *dBASE III Plus* ignores commands entered in the EDITOR mode. This allows you to enter as many commands as you need and correct any typing mistakes before the commands are executed.

> dBASE III Plus *displays a* < *at the right edge of the screen to indicate that a* < return > *has been entered, also similar to the display system used by* WordStar.

When entering a list of commands, you should end each line with a < return >. To simplify the text, program listings will be shown without the < return >.

Remember that when you are entering commands in a command file, a < return > must be entered at the end of each command.

Complete the entry of the program by entering the following commands:

```
LIST date,amount
SUM amount
```

SAVING A COMMAND FILE

Before a command file can be executed, it must be stored on the disk as a file. When you have completed your entry, save the file by entering

[CTRL/End]

dBASE III Plus saves the file and exits the editor. The program returns to the DOT PROMPT mode.

You can check to see if the file was actually stored on the disk by entering

DIR *.prg < return >

The screen should display the name LISTING.PRG. You can get *dBASE III Plus* to display the contents of the file by entering

TYPE listing.prg < return >

dBASE III Plus will display

```
USE expenses
LIST date,amount
SUM amount
```

Both commands confirm that *dBASE III Plus* has created a text file containing the commands entered into the editor. The program is now stored on the disk and can be recalled at any time.

Creating a program makes a permanent record of the sequence of commands required to complete a given task. This means that you do not have to remember all the details, only the name of the command file (e.g., LISTING).

> The dBASE III Plus *editor is adequate for creating simple programs. However, it has a limit of 4096 characters. This limits the size of the program you can create.*
>
> *In addition, the editing features found in many word processing programs such as block moves and copies, search and replace, and the like are not available in the dBASE III Plus editor. For that reason, users who do a lot of programming will want to use other word processing or editing programs to create and edit their dBASE III Plus programs.*
>
> *You will find a full discussion of editors and word processing in Chapter 20 under* Configuring Your dBASE III Plus System. *The programs presented in this book can be written using the dBASE III Plus editor.*

EXECUTING A COMMAND FILE

After the file has been created, you can execute the file. Execution, or running a command file, involves *dBASE III Plus* reading the text that you entered into the command file and carrying out those instructions.

dBASE III Plus always reads the command file from beginning to end unless it encounters an error while trying to execute one of the commands. When *dBASE III Plus* reaches the end of the list of commands, it returns to the DOT PROMPT mode.

The DO command is used to tell *dBASE III Plus* the name of the file in which the commands are stored. To execute the LISTING command file, enter

DO listing < return >

dBASE III Plus will display

```
Record#  date      amount
     1   01/02/85   68.40
     2   01/10/85   17.95
     3   01/15/85  264.68
     4   01/17/85   59.50
     5   01/21/85   60.60
     6   01/25/85   44.28
     7   01/30/85   47.95
     8   02/02/85    5.94
     9   02/05/85  175.00
    10   03/15/86    2.56
    11    /  /     350.45
    11  records summed
  amount
1097.31
```

> *Note that record no. II does not have a date. Number II was entered as part of the section on relations in Chapter II and no date was included. Do not be concerned about the missing date; it will be corrected later.*

The command file executes the three commands stored in the file, one after the other, after entering DO listing.

CHANGING A COMMAND FILE

One of the great advantages of program files is that they can be revised or enlarged. Suppose that after seeing the effect of LISTING, you wanted to add some additional instructions, such as clearing the screen, before the listing began. Also, you might want to close the data base file after the list has been completed.

The MODIFY COMMAND command allows you to alter the contents of an existing command file. The command is exactly the same as the one used to create the file. Enter

MODIFY COMMAND listing < return >

dBASE III Plus displays the command file exactly as you last saved it.

To add a command to the beginning of the file, use the **[CTRL/n]** command to insert a blank line at the cursor position. Enter

[CTRL/n]

Enter the command

CLEAR

Use the down arrow key to position the cursor below the last command in the file.

If you find that you cannot move the cursor past the end of the line on which you typed the SUM command, that is because you did not end that line with a <return>. Position the cursor at the end of that line and enter a <return> to correct the situation.

Enter the last command for the program.

CLOSE DATABASE

The entire program should look like this:

```
CLEAR
USE expenses
LIST date,amount
SUM amount
CLOSE DATABASE
```

Save the revised program by entering

[CTRL/End]

Execute the program by entering

DO listing <return>

The revised program executes the five commands entered into the command file. Because you cleared the screen at the beginning of your program, the list began at the top of the screen and scrolled downward. You will learn more about how screen displays can be controlled from *dBASE III Plus* programs.

VIEW FILES VS. COMMAND FILES

dBASE III Plus view files were discussed in Chapter 11. The purpose of a view file is to record all the files, data base, index, and format, that are required for a given task. In addition, view files can establish relations between data base files.

While view files are handy, their function can be duplicated or surpassed by writing a command file. Suppose you wanted to create a command file that would duplicate the function of the view file called EXPENSES that was created in Chapter 11, as well as display a list of expenses and categories.

Begin by creating the command file with the *dBASE III Plus* editor. Enter

MODIFY COMMAND cats < return >

The first task is to open the required data base, index, and format files. Enter

```
USE expenses
SET FORMAT TO twofiles
SELECT B
USE category INDEX category
SELECT A
```

The next task for the program is to create the relational link between the files. Enter

```
SET RELATION TO cat INTO category
```

Finally, enter a command that will display the records with the correct category number.

```
CLEAR
LIST payto,category->name
```

Close the files by entering

```
CLOSE DATABASE
CLOSE FORMAT
```

The entire program should look like this:

```
USE expenses
SET FORMAT TO twofiles
SELECT B
USE category INDEX category
SELECT A
SET RELATION TO cat INTO category
CLEAR
LIST payto,category->name
CLOSE DATABASE
CLOSE FORMAT
```

Save the program by entering

[CTRL/End]

Execute the program by entering

DO cats < return >

dBASE III Plus will display

```
Record#  payto               category->name
      1  CROW CANYON LUMBER  OFFICE IMPROVEMENTS
      2  SEARS               OFFICE SUPPLIES
      3  GREEN ACRES FURN    FURNITURE
      4  INSTANT PRINTING    OFFICE SUPPLIES
      5  PG&E                UTILITIES
      6  PACIFIC BELL        UTILITIES
      7  BRITZ PRINTING      OFFICE SUPPLIES
      8  GIFT STORE          OFFICE SUPPLIES
      9  GREEN ACRES FURN    FURNITURE
     10  BACON EAST PHARMACY OFFICE SUPPLIES
     11  VIRCO EQUIPMENT     FURNITURE
```

In this example the command file CATS can perform all the functions performed by the view file EXPENSES, and more. You will find that many commands that are useful in the DOT PROMPT mode can be replaced with program files of your own design. This is the advantage of learning to create program files.

When you write programs, you are using the same *dBASE III Plus* commands that you would enter in the ASSIST or DOT PROMPT modes. The line between programming and manual use of *dBASE III Plus* is more a change in mode than a radical new way of doing things.

Programming is a logical progression once you learn the basic set of *dBASE III Plus* commands and procedures.

HANDLING ERRORS

Simple programs are usually entered with few or no mistakes. However, as time goes on you will find that you may make mistakes when entering commands into a file. When *dBASE III Plus* encounters these errors, the program will stop execution.

To understand how to handle that situation when it arises, what follows purposely leads to an error. Open the CATS program file by entering

MODIFY COMMAND cats < return >

The spelling of one of the commands will be changed so that *dBASE III Plus* will not recognize it. To position the cursor, the FIND command is used. The editor uses the FIND command, **[CTRL/k]** f, to place the cursor at a specific position in the command file. Most word processing programs have an equivalent command (**[CTRL/q]**f in *WordStar*, for example). This procedure can save you time when you're looking for a specific command in a large program file.

> *The FIND command, [**CTRL/k**]f, used in the editor has no relation to the FIND command used in the DOT PROMPT mode.*

To find the SELECT command, enter

[CTRL/k]
f

Enter the command you want to locate.

SELECT <return >

The cursor is positioned at the beginning of the word "SELECT." Enter

s

to change the command to read SSELECT B. To see what *dBASE III Plus* does when it encounters this error, save the program by entering

[CTRL/End]

Execute the program by entering

DO cats <return>

dBASE III Plus will display

```
*** Unrecognized command verb.
       ?
SSELECT B
Called from - A:cats.prg
```

dBASE III Plus has stopped the execution of the program at the exact point in the command file at which the error was detected. *dBASE III Plus* displays four lines that supply the specific information as to the cause of the error to aid you in correcting the mistake.

1. **Error message.** The first line of the display is a message generated by *dBASE III Plus* specific to the type of error encountered. In this case the error message is *** Unrecognized command verb. This means that the verb, the first word in the command, is not a verb that *dBASE III Plus* recognizes.

2. **Position marker.** The second line of the display indicates where in the line *dBASE III Plus* found the item that caused the error by positioning a ? over the incorrect item. The ? is only a guide to the problem. Depending on the nature of the error, the ? may or may not actually point out what needs to be changed.

3. **Command line.** The third line of the display shows the actual line that caused the error. In this example you can clearly see the SS at the beginning of the command.

4. **Called from.** The called from display shows you what command file was being read when the error was encountered. This tells you the name of the program that needs to be modified.

In addition to that display, *dBASE III Plus* also displays a message at the bottom of the screen below the status line that shows Cancel, Ignore or Suspend? (C, I or S). *dBASE III Plus* offers you three possible actions to take at this point:

1. **CANCEL.** This command terminates the execution of the program at this point. Any files that have already been opened by the program will remain open after you cancel it. Canceling the program tells *dBASE III Plus* to stop reading the commands in the command file. It does not negate any of the effects of the commands that have executed up to this point.

    Use CANCEL when you want to stop the program so that you can correct the mistake and start the program over again.

2. **IGNORE.** This option tells *dBASE III Plus* to skip the command that it cannot understand and proceed to the next command in the program file.

This option is used when the command that causes the error is not of major significance. IGNORE allows the remainder of the program to execute beginning with the next line in the program file.

If commands later in the program depend on the result of the command you have chosen to ignore, they too may cause errors.

3. **SUSPEND.** SUSPEND allows you to halt the execution of the program temporarily. You can later restart the program from the suspended point by entering RESUME. You cannot use SUSPEND to halt the program and use MODIFY COMMAND to correct the error.

When a program is suspended, it is still held open by *dBASE III Plus* and cannot be revised. Attempting to edit the suspended command file will cause a File still open error message to appear.

Suspended programs can be canceled by entering the CANCEL command at the DOT PROMPT.

In this case you will choose to ignore the command. Enter

    i

dBASE III Plus begins to execute the next command in the program file. It encounters another error:

```
Cyclic relation.
                                ?
SET RELATION TO cat INTO category
Called from — A:cats.prg
```

The error is caused by the failure of the previous SELECT command to open a file in work area B. Because that command did not operate correctly, it is not possible to set a relation at this point.

SUSPENDING AN APPLICATION

The error now displayed on the screen poses an interesting problem. The command line is written correctly. However, the command cannot been carried out because the preconditions necessary for that command have not been correctly established. When you are not sure about those conditions, the SUSPEND option permits you to halt the execution of the program and enter commands that can display information about the current status of the system. Enter

    s

The DOT PROMPT returns. The left side of the status line displays the word "Suspended." This indicates that a program file is still open and ready to resume execution.

While the program is suspended, you can check on the system's status. Enter

DISPLAY STATUS < return >

The display shows that only one work area is being used and that any attempt to set a relation will not make any sense to *dBASE III Plus.* Enter

< Esc >

To restart the program, enter

RESUME < return >

dBASE III Plus begins reading the program file at the point where you suspended the application. Unfortunately the program produces another error. It is clear that there is no use in trying to run this application without correcting the error. Cancel the program by entering

c

When you cancel a program, the system retains any setting such as file status, print on or off, and so on, that was set by the program up to that point. It is usually a good idea to close all the open files manually before you run the program again. Enter

CLOSE DATABASE < return >
CLOSE FORMAT < return >

Now correct the mistake in the file by entering

MODIFY COMMAND cats < return >

Use the editor's FIND command to position the cursor at the line that contains the error. Enter

[CTRL/k]
f
SS < return >

Delete the extra S by entering

[Del]

Save the program by entering

[CTRL/End]

Execute the program by entering

DO cats < return >

The program runs properly this time.

344 Understanding and Using *dBASE III Plus*

VARIABLES IN COMMAND FILES

Chapter 7 showed how memory variables were used to capture and hold statistical information that is related to but not directly a part of the data base file. Memory variables play an even more important role in programming than they do in the COMMAND mode of *dBASE III Plus*.

Suppose you want to create a command file that will determine the range of dates you have entered into the EXPENSES file. The program will need to use memory variables to capture the first and last dates in the file. Before you begin the program, enter a date into record no. 11. Enter

> **USE expenses** < return >
> **GO BOTTOM** < return >
> **EDIT** <return>

Enter the date:

> **032186**

Save the record by entering

> **[CTRL/End]**

You are now ready to create a new command file that will accomplish the task you have set. Enter

> **MODIFY COMMAND range** < return >

A new command file is created by entering a new filename with the MODIFY COMMAND command. The first command in the program clears the screen display, and the USE command places the EXPENSES file in use. Enter

CLEAR
USE expenses

Next, you need to make sure that the file is ordered by date by indexing the file. Since such an index file already exists, use SET INDEX to activate that file. Then use the REINDEX command to be sure that the index is up to date. Enter

SET INDEX TO dateord
REINDEX

With the file ordered by date, you are now ready to find the first and last dates in the file. First, move the cursor to the beginning of the file. Enter

GO TOP

With the pointer positioned at the first record in the file, store that date to a variable named "first." Enter

first=date

To find the last date in the file, position the cursor at the last record. Enter

GO BOTTOM

Now store that date value to a variable named "last." Enter

last=date

You now have captured the beginning date in "first" and the ending date in "last." Use the ? (print) command to display the results. Enter

? 'The beginning date is ',first
? 'The ending date is ',last

Complete the program by closing the files you opened during the program. Enter

CLOSE DATABASE

The entire program should look like this:

```
CLEAR
USE expenses
SET INDEX TO dateord
REINDEX
GO TOP
first=date
GO BOTTOM
last=date
? 'The beginning date is ',first
? 'The ending date is    ',last
CLOSE DATABASE
```

Save the program by entering

[CTRL/End]

Execute the program by entering

DO range < return >

dBASE III Plus will display

```
Rebuilding index - A:dateord.ndx
    100% indexed          11 Records indexed
01/02/85
03/21/86
The beginning date is  01/02/85
The ending date is     03/21/86
```

The program correctly finds the range of dates in the EXPENSES file and displays them on the screen. However, the program also displays other information that is not directly related to the display of the dates.

The extra output is caused by the *dBASE III Plus* talk feature. Talk in *dBASE III Plus* is information displayed on the screen that describes and confirms the actions of certain commands. In this example, REINDEX causes the following to be displayed:

```
Rebuilding index - A:dateord.ndx
   100% indexed          11 Records indexed
```

dBASE III Plus also displays the contents of a memory variable when it is defined. This accounts for the dates that appear on the screen following the REINDEX display.

Talk is useful when you are working at the DOT PROMPT because it helps you confirm that your commands are working. However, talk is usually not desired when you are running a program because it tends to confuse the person using the program. dBASE III Plus allows you to suppress the talk by using the SET TALK OFF command. If you add the command to your program file, you can get a cleaner display. Enter

MODIFY COMMAND range <return>

The two commands shown below in bold should be added. Note that the SET TALK OFF command is added at the end of the program. Adding it there confirms that *dBASE III Plus* will return to the same display status following the program that it had when the program began.

SET TALK ON
CLEAR
USE expenses
SET INDEX TO dateord
REINDEX
GO TOP
first=date
GO BOTTOM
last=date
? 'The beginning date is ',first
? 'The ending date is ',last
CLOSE DATABASE
SET TALK OFF

Save the program by entering

[CTRL/End]

Execute the program by entering

DO range <return>

This time the program displays only the data that you specifically want displayed.

MEMORY VARIABLES AND PROGRAMS

In the previous command file, RANGE, you created two variables to help carry out the function of the program. What is the current status of those variables? Drawing on the experience you had in Chapter 7 with memory variables, you would probably assume that the variables first and last are still active in the memory area of *dBASE III Plus*. To display these values, enter

DISPLAY MEMORY <return>

The memory display shows no variables defined at all. Why?

The answer lies in the fact that *dBASE III Plus* treats memory variables defined during the execution of a program differently from memory variables defined in the DOT PROMPT mode. *dBASE III Plus* names variables defined at the DOT PROMPT public variables, while variables created during the course of a program are named private variables.

Public variables, defined by commands given at the DOT PROMPT, are available to any program. Private variables, defined during the course of a program, are erased when the program is completed.

Why make this distinction? The reason may not be obvious when you are writing simple programs. However, as programs grow into full applications, you will find it necessary to define a large number of variables. To prevent confusion when different programs use variables with the same names, *dBASE III Plus* erases the variables after each program has been completed.

If you desire to maintain a variable created during a program for some other use, you can use the PUBLIC command to tell *dBASE III Plus* not to erase the variable from the memory at the end of the program.

The PUBLIC command is a bit more sensitive than most commands in *dBASE III Plus*. In order for it to operate correctly it must be the first command in the program file. To see how PUBLIC is used, modify the RANGE program by entering

MODIFY COMMAND range <return>

Add the following command as the first line in the file. Enter

PUBLIC first,last

This command tells *dBASE III Plus* to maintain these variables after the program has completed its run. Save the program by entering

[CTRL/End]

Execute the program by entering

DO range <return>

Now display the memory. Enter

DISPLAY MEMO <return>

dBASE III Plus will display

```
FIRST        pub   D  Ø1/Ø2/85
LAST         pub   D  Ø3/21/86
      2 variables defined,      18 bytes used
    254 variables available,  5982 bytes available
```

The memory variables are retained following the conclusion of the program. The values stored in these variables can be used; for example, enter

? last–first

This tells you the number of days covered by the range of dates in the data base.

To clear the memory of public variables, use the CLEAR MEMORY command. Enter

CLEAR MEMORY <return>

The variables have been erased from the memory area. To confirm this, enter

DISPLAY MEMORY <return>

No variables are currently defined.

PROGRAMS THAT EXECUTE PROGRAMS

As you have seen, the DO command is used to execute a program. What would happen if you included a DO command as part of a program? The program would suspend its processing and read the specified command file and execute the commands stored in that file. When that was completed, the program would return to the original file and complete the execution of those commands.

The diagram below shows two programs, PROG-A and PROG-B. The process begins when you enter DO prog-a at the DOT PROMPT. This causes *dBASE III Plus* to execute the commands in PROG-A until it encounters the command DO prog-b. At this point, *dBASE III Plus* begins reading commands from PROG-B.

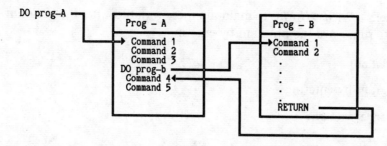

In program B a new command called RETURN is used to terminate the reading of command file PROG-B. When the RETURN is encountered *dBASE III Plus* returns to PROG-A and continues reading commands where it had left off.

The concept of calling a program from a program is called *nesting*. Programs executed from other programs are called *routines* or *subroutines*. Subroutines have many advantages. First, they allow you to break up a complex job into a series of smaller programs instead of having to create one large program. Second, you can use the same subroutine many times without having to reenter the commands.

As an example, suppose you wanted to send the output from the CATS program to the printer. You have two options:

1. You could modify the existing CATS program to send its output to the printer instead of the screen. The disadvantage of this is that if you wanted to have the program output to the screen again, you would have to remove the modifications.
2. To avoid having to add and remove the modifications, you could create a new program called PRTCATS that specifically includes outputs to the printer.

Option 2 seems to make more sense. But it does not seem very efficient to type the entire CATS program again just to add some new commands. The best solution is to use the CATS program as a subroutine of the PRTCATS program. Enter

MODIFY COMMAND prtcats < return >

The first step is to set the output for the printer. Enter

SET PRINT ON

The next step is to begin the commands stored in the CATS program. Instead of entering those commands again, use the DO command to execute the program. Enter

DO cats

When that command file has completed its work, turn off the printer and eject the paper. Enter

SET PRINT OFF
EJECT
RETURN

The RETURN command was included in this program even though you do not plan to use it as a subroutine. The reason is that it is considered good programming form in *dBASE III Plus* to end all programs with a RETURN. This is also convenient should you discover that you want to use the program as a subroutine later on.

Save the program by entering

[CTRL/End]

Before you execute the PRTCATS program, you should add a RETURN command to the end of the CATS program file.

Strictly speaking, it is not necessary to add the RETURN command at the end of the CATS subroutine. When dBASE III Plus runs out of commands to read in the CATS program, it will automatically return to the program from which it was called, even if there is no RETURN. However, the RETURN specifically ends the file and allows dBASE III Plus to close the program file and any logic associated with it.

Enter

MODIFY COMMAND cats < return >

Place the RETURN command at the end of the program, as shown in bold.

```
USE expenses
SET FORMAT TO twofiles
SELECT B
USE category INDEX category
SELECT A
SET RELATION TO cat INTO category
CLEAR
LIST payto,category->name
CLOSE DATABASE
CLOSE FORMAT
RETURN
```

Save the program by entering

[CTRL/End]

Execute the main program by entering

DO prtcats < return >

The output is sent to the printer. The advantage to the subroutine is that CATS will still perform the same as it always did. Enter

DO cats < return >

The display is sent to the screen.

Subroutines allow programs to share routines. You can develop a library of useful procedures without having to reinvent the wheel each time you create a program.

INTERACTIVE COMMANDS

Up to this point the programs that you have created have simply played back the sequence of commands you have entered into the command file. In this section you will learn how *dBASE III Plus* allows you to interact with the program as it executes. Interactive commands are ones that allow the program to pause in order to receive input from the user, which can then be captured and used by the rest of the program.

The great advantage of interactive programming is that one program can perform a variety of tasks based on the same program file. Interactive commands permit and encourage you to create more general programs. The programs are more general because the user can enter different responses each time the program is executed.

QUESTIONS AND ANSWERS

One of the basic characteristics of interactive programs is that the program initiates a dialogue with the user. This is in contrast to the previous program, which executed automatically from beginning to end with no user intervention.

In the latter program, the user is an interested but unnecessary spectator while the program executes its sequence of commands. On the other hand, interactive programs require that the user answer a question. The program halts execution and waits for user response. Following the user's entry, the program proceeds to complete its task. In this scenario the role of the user is an essential element in the design of the program. The program cannot carry out its task without some response from the user.

Because interactive programs are so important, *dBASE III Plus* provides a wide assortment of commands that implement this question-and-answer dialogue between the program and the person using the computer. The variety of ways in which the dialogue is carried out is one of the most powerful aspects of *dBASE III Plus*.

Why is this variety so important? The answer is that when you are programming an interactive application, you are indirectly communicating with a human being through the medium of a computer. If the user (who in many cases is you) cannot understand what should be entered and what effect that entry will have, the program will fail to achieve its goal. Interactive programs have to make sense to the person using the computer or the dialogue between user and program will break down

In the following chapters you will return many times to the theme of trying to find the best way to communicate with the user. In the end, interactive programming is as much art as science. The "look and feel" of a program is often as important as what it is supposed to do.

For now, a few simple interactive commands that illustrate the basic principles of this type of programming will be used. As you learn, the style of your interactive programs will improve.

First, there are some terms that occur in interactive programming that every prospective *dBASE* programmer should be familiar with:

1. **Prompt.** A prompt is a message displayed on the screen that requires users to enter a response. It is usually in the form of a question. It is also common to indicate the type of response you want the user to make. For example, the prompt Print? (Y/N) asks users if they want to print. In addition, the (Y/N) indicates that users should respond with either a Y for Yes, or an N for No.

   The goal of a prompt is to communicate as clearly as possible to users what you want them to enter. The ideal prompt asks a question that users can answer without ambiguity.

2. **User Interface.** This term refers to the overall style and approach of the dialogue between the user and the program. In working with *dBASE III Plus*, you have seen that the program employs several different user interface styles. The ASSIST mode allows you to respond with direction keys most of the time. The COMMAND mode requires you to enter whole command sentences. Variation and creativity in interface design is the mark of a good programmer.

The first interactive command that you will use is the ACCEPT command. The program that you will create will have a simple purpose: it will allow you to enter your name. The program will then use the name you entered in a line of text that will appear on the screen.

Begin by entering

MODIFY COMMAND welcome <**return**>

The first command to be entered into this program is CLEAR, to clear the screen display of any data. The importance of the CLEAR command must be understood in the context of your attempt to develop a user interface. The CLEAR command seldom has any logical function in terms of data management. However, it is one of the basic tools by which you can control what data are displayed on the screen at a given moment. Since it is those data that the user will be reading and reacting to, the decision to clear the screen is a very important one.

Wiping the screen clear before you ask the user a question is a good way to draw the user's attention to the prompt that you are going to display. Enter

CLEAR

The next command in the program will be the interactive command that pauses the program and allows the user to enter a response. The ACCEPT command has three parts:

1. **ACCEPT.** This command pauses the execution of the program. The pause will continue until the < return > key is pressed. Before the user enters < return >, up to 254 characters can be entered.
2. **Prompt.** The prompt is the portion of the command in which you specify the question that will appear on the screen when the ACCEPT command is executed. The inclusion of a prompt in the ACCEPT command is optional. Prompts are delimited with quotation marks.
3. **TO < memory variable >.** The TO clause is used to capture the text entered by the user in a memory variable. That memory variable can then be used in subsequent commands.

Enter the interactive command

ACCEPT "Please enter your name:" TO yourname

Complete the program by entering the following commands. The CLEAR command once again clears the screen. Then the next command displays a line of text that will include whatever the user entered when the program paused.

CLEAR
? "Welcome to the world of programming "+yourname

Save the program by entering

[CTRL/End]

Execute the program by entering

DO welcome < return >

When the program executes, the screen displays the prompt Please enter your name: Enter

Walter < return >

The screen clears once again and then displays

```
Welcome to the world of programming Walter
```

Execute the program again. Enter

DO welcome < return >

This time enter a different name.

Fred < **return** >

This time the message appears with the name Fred. This very simple program illustrates the basic nature of an interactive program:

1. The program asks the user a question.
2. The user enters a response.
3. The program continues. The data entered by the user are available to the remainder of the program.

The effect is to create a program that responds to the user's entries. While it is possible to create programs with no interactive command, it is unlikely that you will do so. Almost all programs require some interaction between the user and the program.

NUMERIC INPUTS

The ACCEPT command stores any data entered as character-type information. This is true even if you enter numbers. If you want to create an interactive program that takes in numeric data, the INPUT can be used. Suppose you wanted to create a program that calculated the sales tax and net cost when you enter the price of an item.

> *The INPUT command can also be used to enter character information. However, for input to accept character information, the user must remember to add delimiters to the text. This means that the user must remember to add quotation marks to the beginning and end of the text. For this reason, INPUT is used chiefly for numeric entries and ACCEPT is used for character entries.*

Begin by entering

MODIFY COMMAND tax < **return** >

The program begins by clearing the screen and displaying an entry prompt. The only difference between this program and the previous one is that the ACCEPT command is changed to INPUT because the information entered by the user should be stored as a numeric value. Enter

```
CLEAR
INPUT "Enter the price of the item: " TO price
```

Once the price has been entered, the program can then calculate and display the tax and net cost information. Enter

```
CLEAR
? "PRICE OF THE ITEM  =",price
? "AMOUNT OF SALES TAX=",price*.06
? "NET COST  =",price*1.06
```

The entire program should look like this:

```
CLEAR
INPUT "Enter the price of the item: " TO price
CLEAR
? "PRICE OF THE ITEM =",price
? "AMOUNT OF SALES TAX=",price*.06
? "NET COST =",price*1.06
```

Save the program by entering

[CTRL/End]

Execute the program by entering

DO tax < return >

The program first asks you to enter the price of the item. In this example, suppose the item costs $10.00. Enter

10

The program calculates the answers and displays them on the screen. The display will look like this:

```
PRICE OF THE ITEM =           10
AMOUNT OF SALES TAX=              0.60
NET COST =           10.60
```

Execute the program again. Enter

DO tax < return >

Enter a price that includes a decimal value:

4.49 < return >

dBASE III Plus will display

```
PRICE OF THE ITEM =         4.49
AMOUNT OF SALES TAX=              0.2694
NET COST =         4.7594
```

Note that this time the calculated values appear with four decimal places of precision. You can make the program more useful by having it round off the values to the cents place. You can do this by adding ROUND() functions to the lines that include calculations. Open the file by entering

MODIFY COMMAND tax < return >

Add the ROUND() functions as shown in bold.

```
CLEAR
INPUT "Enter the price of the item: " TO price
CLEAR
? "PRICE OF THE ITEM =",price
? "AMOUNT OF SALES TAX =",ROUND(price*.06,2)
? "NET COST =",ROUND(price*1.06,2)
```

Save the program by entering

[CTRL/End]

Execute the program by entering

DO tax < return >

Enter the amount

4.49 < return >

dBASE III Plus will display

```
PRICE OF THE ITEM =              4.49
AMOUNT OF SALES TAX=                  0.2700
NET COST =              4.7600
```

Notice that the display shows the correctly rounded values. However, you may also have noted that *dBASE III Plus* displays two zeros following the cents figure. Why? The answer can be shown in general terms about how *dBASE III Plus* decides on the number of decimal places to display as a result of a calculation. The rules are as follows:

1. **Multiplication.** If the calculation involves multiplication, the total number of decimal places displayed in the result is the total number of decimal places used in the original values. Example:

   2.00 * 1.00 = 2.0000
   3.000 * 2.00 = 6.00000

2. **Division.** When the calculation involves division, the number of decimal places in the result is determined by the SET DECIMALS command. The default value is 2 decimal places. This means that a division problem will display a minimum of two decimal places. If the numbers used in the problem contain more than two decimal places, the value will be used as a guide.

To test this concept, enter the following simple calculation using the ? command:

? 2.000*3.00 <return>

dBASE III Plus displays the answer with five decimal places: 6.00000. Now enter a division calculation.

? 2/3 <return>

dBASE III Plus displays 0.67. This is because the SET DECIMALS value is currently 2. Enter

? 2.000/3 <return>

dBASE III Plus displays 0.667 because the value 2.000 was used. You can change the SET DECIMALS value by entering

SET DECIMALS TO 4 <return>

Enter

? 2/3 <return>

dBASE III Plus displays 0.6667, which conforms to the current SET DECIMALS value. Return the SET DECIMALS value to the default by entering

SET DECIMALS TO 2 <return>

FORMATTED SCREEN DISPLAYS

In the previous program the screen interface was created by using unformatted screen display commands. *Unformatted* refers to commands that display data on consecutive rows based on the last line that was displayed. Look at the commands below:

```
CLEAR
? "Hello Joe"
```

Where on the screen will Hello Joe be displayed? The answer is that *dBASE III Plus* will place the text at the first available location. Since CLEAR places the cursor at the upper left-hand corner of the screen, the text will be displayed beginning at that position. Commands that are considered unformatted display are

```
?
INPUT
ACCEPT
LIST
DISPLAY
```

Because the appearance of the screen is so crucial to user interface design, *dBASE III Plus* allows you to handle interactive screen displays by using formatted output commands. The formatted commands are the @/SAY and @/GET commands used in Chapter 9 to create format files.

These same commands can be used in *dBASE III Plus* programs to duplicate the functions of the unformatted commands used in the tax program. Formatted commands have two main advantages:

1. **Location control.** Formatted commands allow you to display information at exact positions on the screen.
2. **Picture clauses.** Formatted commands accept picture clauses that control the display format of various items. In particular, picture clauses are useful in displaying numeric values.

To understand the differences between an unformatted and a formatted program, you can create a new program that performs exactly the same function as the tax program but uses a different style of screen programming. Enter

MODIFY COMMAND tax2 < return >

The first command in the program, the CLEAR command, remains the same. Enter

CLEAR

The next command may seem a bit odd, but it is one you must use in order to use formatted screen displays. Enter

price=0

This command is used to create a memory variable called "price." Since the actual value of price is determined by the user when the program runs, the initial value is simply set at zero. The process of creating a variable with a value of zero is often called *initialization* of a variable.

A significant question is, why is it necessary to initialize a variable? The answer is that the formatted commands in *dBASE III Plus* do not have commands that are exactly equivalent to the INPUT and ACCEPT commands.

Formatted screens handle input by the use of the @/GET-READ combination. The GET displays the current value of a field or variable at a specified screen location. When the READ command is issued, the cursor is positioned in the GET area and you can make changes or additions.

Note that you can make changes or additions only to the field or variable. The implication is that the field or variable already exists before the @/GET-READ commands are issued.

In the case of a field, it is necessary to USE the appropriate data base file before the @/GET-READ commands are issued. In the case of a memory variable, the variable must be initialized before the @/GET-READ commands.

The creation of an interactive screen display with formatted commands is a bit more complex than the unformatted method. Look at the two methods shown below:

Unformatted

INPUT "Enter Price " To price

Formatted

```
price=0
@ 10,10 SAY "Enter Price" GET "price
READ
```

The unformatted technique is the simpler of the two. The formatted technique requires more commands but provides you with a greater measure of control.

The next line in the program displays the input prompt and input area. The prompt is displayed by the SAY command, and the input area by the GET command. Enter

```
@ 10,12 SAY "Enter the Price of the item: " GET price
```

To activate the GET as an input area, use the READ command. Enter

```
READ
```

The next section of the program uses the value input into price to calculate the tax and net cost. Begin by entering the commands that display the price. Enter

```
CLEAR
@ 9,5 SAY "PRICE OF THE ITEM ="
@ 9,40 SAY price PICTURE "9,999.99"
```

Two commands were used to print a single line on the screen. The first places the text PRICE OF THE ITEM = on the screen beginning at row 9, column 5. The next command displays the value stored in the variable price at row 9, column 40. Note that the format of the price value is controlled by the PICTURE clause. Enter

```
@ 10,5 SAY "AMOUNT OF SALES TAX="
@ 10,40 SAY ROUND(price*.06,2) PICTURE "9,999.99"
```

This command places the text at column 5 and the number at column 40 of line 10. Also notice that the PICTURE clause is used to control the display format of the value that results from the calculation ROUND(price*.06,2). The PICTURE clause does not take the place of the ROUND() function but limits the display of decimal places by truncating the number. The ROUND() function is still necessary to make sure that the value is correctly rounded. Complete the program by entering

```
@ 11,5 SAY "NET COST ="
@ 11,40 SAY ROUND(price*1.06,2) PICTURE "9,999.99"
```

The entire program should look like this:

```
CLEAR
price=0
@ 10,12 SAY "Enter the Price of the item: " GET price
READ
CLEAR
@ 9,5 SAY "PRICE OF THE ITEM ="
@ 9,40 SAY price PICTURE "9,999.99"
@ 10,5 SAY "AMOUNT OF SALES TAX="
@ 10,40 SAY ROUND(price*.06,2) PICTURE "9,999.99"
@ 11,5 SAY "NET COST ="
@ 11,40 SAY ROUND(price*1.06,2) PICTURE "9,999.99"
```

Save the program by entering

[CTRL/End]

Execute the program by entering

DO tax2 < return >

The screen displays

0

```
Enter the Price of the item: ▓▓▓▓▓▓▓▓0
```

A zero appears in the upper left hand-corner. Enter

4.49

The program didn't allow for the decimal value and the screen looks like this:

```
PRICE OF THE ITEM =            4.00
AMOUNT OF SALES TAX=           0.24
NET COST =                     4.24
```

The program took the integer value 4 and calculated the net cost based on that. Obviously, some modifications are needed because

1. A zero appears at the upper left-hand corner of the screen when the program begins.
2. The input area accepts only whole numbers.

The first problem is caused by the *dBASE III Plus* talk display. When a variable is defined, *dBASE III Plus* usually places a confirming display on the screen. This display can be eliminated by using the SET TALK OFF command.

The second problem is also related to the definition of the variable price. When you enter data into a field, *dBASE III Plus* uses the file's structure as a guide to the number of decimal places allowed. When a variable is used, the initial value of the variable determines the number of decimal places allowed.

Since the current initialization command, key = 0, contains zero decimal places, *dBASE III Plus* does not allow you to enter any decimal value when the program executes. The problem can be resolved by entering a variable with the desired number of decimal places. Example:

key = 0	no decimal places
key = 0.0	one decimal place
key = 0.00	two decimal places
key = 0.000	three decimal places

Correct the problems with the program by entering

MODIFY COMMAND tax2 <return>

Make the changes as indicated below in bold print:

```
SET TALK OFF
CLEAR
price=0.00
@ 10,12 SAY "Enter the Price of the item: " GET price
READ
CLEAR
@ 9,5 SAY "PRICE OF THE ITEM ="
@ 9,40 SAY price PICTURE "9,999.00"
@ 10,5 SAY "AMOUNT OF SALEX TAX="
@ 10,40 SAY ROUND (price*.06,2) PICTURE "9,999.00"
@ 11,5 SAY "NET COST ="
@ 11,40 SAY ROUND (price*1.06,2) PICTURE "9,999.00"
SET TALK ON
```

The command SET TALK ON is added at the end of the program. It has no direct effect on the program but it is added so that *dBASE III Plus* will return to the normal display state following the execution of the program.

When SET commands like SET TALK are used in *dBASE III Plus*, they remain in effect even after the program has been completed. Thus, if you SET TALK OFF during a program, the talk will remain off after the program finishes. It is a good idea to reset the state of such commands at the end of your program. This ensures that *dBASE III Plus* will behave the same way in the COMMAND mode following the execution of your program as it did before the program was run.

Save the program by entering

[CTRL/End]

Execute the program by entering

DO tax2 <return>

dBASE III Plus will display

```
Enter the Price of the item:        0.00
```

Note that the changes you made to the program eliminate the problems you had during the previous run. The zero is not displayed at the top of the screen and the input area shows room for the entry of two decimal places. Enter

4.49

dBASE III Plus will display

```
PRICE OF THE ITEM =                   4.49
AMOUNT OF SALES TAX=                  0.27
NET COST =                            4.76
```

The program correctly calculates and displays the desired information. Using formatted output commands takes more effort but the result is a more polished program. In this book, most of the programs will use the formatted output commands to create interactive screen displays because they offer you, the programmer, more control and flexibility.

PRINTING PROGRAM LISTINGS

Now that you have created *dBASE III Plus* programs, you may want to print the command files. The method for printing command files applies to printing any ASCII text file from *dBASE III Plus*. The TYPE command displays the contents of a command or text file.

> You can use the TYPE command to display data stored in any file. However, the TYPE command in dBASE III Plus is designed to display text data. Files that contain data not stored in ASCII text format may appear scrambled when they are displayed with the TYPE command. For example, typing a .DBF file will display the data in an unformatted manner. This cannot harm the file but it seldom produces usable information. Therefore the TYPE command is used mainly with text files such as those created with MODIFY COMMAND.
>
> If you are familiar with the DOS command TYPE, you will find that the dBASE III Plus TYPE command functions in a similar manner.

To display the contents of the TAX.PRG program, enter

TYPE tax.prg < return >

The screen shows the commands. The commands are simply displayed. You cannot edit those commands. The TYPE command requires you to specify the correct file extension.

To send the output to the printer, turn the print on before you use the TYPE command. Enter

SET PRINT ON < return >
TYPE tax.prg < return >
SET PRINT OFF < return >
EJECT < return >

The TYPE command will also accept the TO PRINT clause. Using this clause can shorten the number of commands needed to print a program listing. Remember that the TO PRINT clause was used previously to send output from the LIST, LABEL, and REPORT commands to the printer. TO PRINT substitutes for both the SET PRINT ON and SET PRINT OFF commands. Enter

```
TYPE tax.prg TO PRINT <return>
EJECT <return>
```

SUMMARY

This chapter introduced the reader to the main concepts of programming in *dBASE III Plus*.

Programming consists of creating files that are lists of related commands. The lists are really word processing files that contain text written in the *dBASE III Plus* command language.

dBASE III Plus executes those commands when you enter the DO command followed by the name of the command file that you want to execute.

dBASE III Plus programs execute the same commands as you would normally enter at the DOT PROMPT. Programs allow you to create long lists of commands and execute them with a single command, saving time and eliminating mistakes.

dBASE III Plus treats commands executed from a command file the same way it does when you manually enter the commands, with one exception. If a command defines a memory variable during the execution of a *dBASE III Plus* program, *dBASE III Plus* will automatically erase the variables from the memory area following the completion of the program. This is done to avoid name conflicts between variables with the same names from different programs.

Programs can execute other programs. This allows you to build a library of small programs that can be combined to accomplish a variety of tasks without having to rewrite all the commands. When a program is executed from another program, it is called a *subroutine*. Any *dBASE III Plus* program can be a subroutine depending on how it is used.

Interactive programs are ones that carry on a dialogue with the user. The program displays a question and pauses the program to allow the user to make an entry. The entry is stored in a memory variable and can then be processed by the remainder of the commands in that program.

DECISION MAKING

CHAPTER 12 DESCRIBED TECHNIQUES OF DEVELOPING programs that consist of lists of *dBASE III Plus* commands. When the programs are run, *dBASE III Plus* reads and executes the commands in the sequence in which they are entered into the command file. The technique of pausing to allow user input was also shown. The programs described all have a linear design; that is, they proceed from beginning to end, with an occasional pause.

Despite the usefulness of these types of programs, they lack a very important element necessary for true programming—the ability to have alternate actions for different conditions. In the examples in Chapter 12, all data and input are treated the same way. What makes programming in *dBASE III Plus* even more powerful than what you have already seen is its ability to allow for *conditional structures* in programs.

THE IF COMMAND

Conditional structures allow your programs to evaluate conditions and make decisions about which commands should be carried out. The computer's ability to make decisions is very limited in nature. For instance, it can make simple judgments about the veracity of statements using the IF-THEN type statement as the basic decision-making structure. Below is a sample of an IF-THEN type statement:

If I have $10,000, *then* I will buy a new car.

The statement has two parts. One is the conditional statement, *If I have $10,000,* and the other is the action, *I will buy a new car.*

The truth or falsity of the condition determines whether the specified action will take place. If the condition evaluates as true, *if I have the money,* only then will the action be taken. If the conditional statement evaluates as false, the action is not carried out.

dBASE III Plus expresses relationships like the one discussed above as a series of command statements. Look at the sample below. *dBASE III Plus* uses an IF command to cause an evaluation of the specified condition, *money > 10000.*

```
IF money > 10000
    ? "Buy New Car"
ENDIF
```

If the condition is evaluated as true, *dBASE III Plus* reads the next command and executes it. The ENDIF has no effect if the condition is true.

```
IF money>10000 ──────────→ TRUE ──────────┐
    ? "Buy New Car"◄───────────────────────┘
ENDIF
```

If the condition is evaluated as false, *dBASE III Plus* searches for the ENDIF command. All commands between the IF and ENDIF are ignored. *dBASE III Plus* then executes the next command following the ENDIF.

```
IF money>10000 ──────────→ FALSE ──────────┐
    ? "Buy New Car"                          │
ENDIF ◄──────────────────────────────────────┘
```

Note that the command between the IF and ENDIF was indented. Although the indentation is not required, it does help make the program easier to understand. Throughout the programming section, this book uses an indented style when conditional structures are encountered.

Since indenting is a good programming habit, it is suggested that you also indent your programs. However, if you decide to save time and type all the lines at the left margin, it will make no difference in the way the program executes.

To illustrate the use of an IF/ENDIF structure, you can modify the PRTCATS program created in Chapter 12. Enter

MODIFY COMMAND prtcats < return >

The *dBASE III Plus* editor screen displays the program:

```
SET PRINT ON
DO cats
SET PRINT OFF
EJECT
RETURN
```

Suppose you want to change the program so that the user is given a choice as to whether the output should be sent to the printer. You would have to combine two techniques:

1. **Interactive.** The user is asked a question and the application records the answer.
2. **Decision making.** Once the user enters the option desired, the program must determine what command to use to carry out the selection. This is where the IF/ENDIF structure comes in.

The lines below will be added to the beginning of the program. Take care not to type over the existing commands. You can insert blank lines by using the **[CTRL/n]** command or by placing the editor into the insert mode with the **[Ins]** key.

The following section is a typical formatted input series of commands. Start by setting the talk off and clearing the screen:

```
SET TALK OFF
CLEAR
```

Next, initialize a variable to capture the user's response. The option to print or not can be expressed as a logical value (true or false).

```
printer=.N.
@ 12,0 SAY "Send to printer ? Y/N " GET printer
READ
```

There are a few points to note about the above. First, the variable Printer was defined as .N. The symbol .N. is a logical value equivalent to .F. (i.e., a false value). *dBASE III Plus* will recognize both .N. and .F. as the same false value.

You may ask why .T. or .Y., a true logical value, wasn't used instead. The answer is one of personal preference. Since a logical value must be either true or false, the one that is used to initialize the variable becomes the default that appears when the prompt is displayed for the user.

> In trying to determine the correct value to use for a default, you must take into consideration the mistakes that a user could possibly make. For example, when setting the default for a printing option, it would probably be a better solution to send the output to the screen. You can be sure that there is a screen attached to the computer, but not nearly as sure that a printer is attached and on-line. In the end, you must use your own judgment about what would be the best default value.

The next section of the program evaluates the entry of the user. The statement, IF printer, is true if the logical value printer is true. Enter

```
IF printer
```

The next line in the program, SET PRINT ON, is correct if the condition is true; leave that line as it is. You might want to indent it to show that the execution is conditional depending upon the IF statement.

The next line reads DO cats. Since a blank line is needed here, place the cursor on the DO cats line and use the [CTRL/n] command. Fill that blank line in with the ENDIF command, as below:

ENDIF

The entire program should look like this. The new commands are shown in bold.

SET TALK OFF
CLEAR
printer=.N.
@ 12,0 SAY "Send to printer ? Y/N" GET printer
READ
IF printer
    SET PRINT ON
ENDIF
DO cats
SET PRINT OFF
EJECT
RETURN

Note that the conditional logic of the IF/ENDIF commands surround the SET PRINT ON command.

```
        SET TALK OFF
        CLEAR
        printer=.N.
        @ 12,0 SAY "Send to printer ? Y/N " GET printer
        READ
    ┌──▶IF printer────────▶
    │        SET PRINT ON
    └──ENDIF◀──
        DO cats
        SET PRINT OFF
        EJECT
        RETURN
```

The SET PRINT OFF command is executed no matter what entry the user makes. Since the print is already OFF, it has no effect and won't cause an error. If the PRINT is SET ON, then it must be set off. Thus it is not necessary to make the SET PRINT OFF conditional.

Save the program by entering

      [CTRL/End]

Execute the program by entering

      DO prtcats <return>

The program displays the prompt for printing with the F displayed in the input area. Because the input area is only one character in width, no < return > following the entry is necessary. This time, enter Y for printing (assuming your printer is connected):

> y

The text is sent to the printer. Run the program again, and send the output to the screen. Enter

> **DO prtcats** < return >
> n

The output is sent to the screen, but the printer feeds a blank page. Why? The answer is that the EJECT command at the end of the program will always eject a sheet of paper even if the SET PRINT OFF command has already stopped the printing output. To complete the program, you will have to surround the EJECT command with an IF/ENDIF structure. This will avoid ejecting paper when the printer is not used for the output. Enter

> **MODIFY COMMAND prtcats** < return >

To place an IF before and an ENDIF after the EJECT command, the program is changed to read as follows (the changes are indicated by the < = = = = = = = = print):

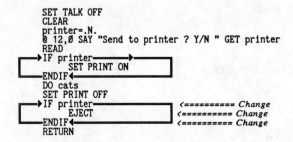

```
SET TALK OFF
CLEAR
printer=.N.
@ 12,0 SAY "Send to printer ? Y/N " GET printer
READ
IF printer
        SET PRINT ON
ENDIF
DO cats
SET PRINT OFF
IF printer                          <========== Change
    EJECT                           <========== Change
ENDIF                               <========== Change
RETURN
```

Save the program by entering

> **[CTRL/End]**

Execute the program by entering

> **DO prtcats** < return >
> n

This time the data are displayed on the screen but no paper is ejected.

One aspect of the IF/ENDIF structure is that for every IF, there must be a corresponding ENDIF in the program. Keeping the balance between the IF and ENDIF commands is aptly referred to as *balancing the structure.* Programs that contain unbalanced conditional structures can produce unpredictable results.

dBASE III Plus does not check your programs to see if the structures are balanced. *dBASE III Plus* will execute the program. However, the effect of the unbalanced structures will cause the program to operate in a different manner than you expect.

ALTERNATE ACTIONS

dBASE III Plus provides an optional command that can be used with IF/ENDIF, called ELSE. The purpose of ELSE is to allow you to specify an action that should be performed when the IF condition evaluates as false.

The ELSE command expands the ability of *dBASE III Plus* programs to make decisions.

ELSE works in the following way: imagine that you want to create a program that will evaluate whether or not a person should be allowed into an "adult" cinema. The major criterion for evaluation is the person's age. The logic works in this way:

```
IF age < 18
    @ x,y SAY 'Too young'
ELSE
    @ x,y SAY 'OK'
ENDIF
```

The series of commands will display Too young if the variable age is less than 18, or OK if the age is 18 or greater. Notice that the ENDIF follows. It should be stressed once again that every IF statement must have a matching ENDIF, even when an ELSE statement is used.

To create a new program called B:AGE, enter the following:

MODIFY COMMAND age < return >

Enter the commands below. The first portion of the program contains the usual commands to clear the screen and set the talk off:

```
CLEAR
SET TALK OFF
```

Next, enter a command at the top of the display that informs the user what kind of program is running.

```
@ 7,14 SAY 'ADULT CINEMA PROGRAM'
```

The next step, asking the user to enter his or her age, requires three commands: INITIALIZE the variable, DISPLAY the prompt, and READ the input area.

```
age=0
@ 10,10 SAY 'How old are you?' get age
READ
```

The next portion of the program evaluates the age of the user and displays the appropriate response. Enter the following:

```
CLEAR
IF age < 18
    @ 10,10 SAY 'Naughty Person !!!!'
    @ 12,8 SAY 'Come back in a few years'
ELSE
    @ 10,10 SAY [You're OK Mack !]
    @ 12,8 SAY 'Come on in !!!!!!!'
ENDIF
SET TALK ON
RETURN
```

The square bracket characters ([ ]) were used in the command @ 10,10 SAY [You're OK Mack !] because the word "you're" contains the ' character. On an IBM PC keyboard, the ' is the same character that is used to delimit a text string. If it were used to mark the string, you would get a command that looks like this:

```
@ 10,10 SAY │You│re OK Mack !'
```

dBASE III Plus would think that the string concluded at the second ' and treat the entire command as an error since there was an odd number of delimiters.

This problem is solved by using one of the alternate delimiters that *dBASE III Plus* also recognizes, such as square brackets. The entire program should read

```
CLEAR
SET TALK OFF
@ 7,14 SAY 'ADULT CINEMA PROGRAM'
age=0
@ 10,10 SAY 'How old are you? ' get age
READ
CLEAR
IF age<18
        @ 10,10 SAY 'Naughty Person !!!!'
        @ 12,8 SAY 'Come back in a few years'
    ELSE
        @ 10,10 SAY [You're OK Mack !]
        @ 12,8 SAY 'Come on in !!!!!!!!'
ENDIF
SET TALK ON
RETURN
```

Try to imagine the effect of the IF/ELSE/ENDIF structure. If the first condition, age<18, is evaluated as false, then the commands following the IF are executed until the ELSE is encountered. Then *dBASE III Plus* skips all commands until the ENDIF is found. The program then begins to execute commands following the END-IF. The effect is that all the commands from the ELSE to the ENDIF are ignored when the condition is true.

```
CLEAR
SET TALK OFF
@ 7,14 SAY 'ADULT CINEMA PROGRAM'
age=Ø
@ 1Ø,1Ø SAY 'How old are you? ' get age
READ
CLEAR
IF age<18
        @ 1Ø,1Ø SAY 'Naughty Person !!!!'
        @ 12,8 SAY 'Come back in a few years'
    ELSE
        @ 1Ø,1Ø SAY [You're OK Mack  !]
        @ 12,8 SAY 'Come on in !!!!!!!'
ENDIF
SET TALK ON
RETURN
```

On the other hand, if the condition evaluates as false, *dBASE III Plus* skips all commands until the ELSE statement is encountered and then begins to execute the commands. This option ignores all the commands between the IF and the ELSE.

```
CLEAR
SET TALK OFF
@ 7,14 SAY 'ADULT CINEMA PROGRAM'
age=Ø
@ 1Ø,1Ø SAY 'How old are you? ' get age
READ
CLEAR
IF age<18
        @ 1Ø,1Ø SAY 'Naughty Person !!!!'
        @ 12,8 SAY 'Come back in a few years'
    ELSE
        @ 1Ø,1Ø SAY [You're OK Mack  !]
        @ 12,8 SAY 'Come on in !!!!!!!'
ENDIF
SET TALK ON
RETURN
```

Save the program by entering

[CTRL/End]

Execute the program by entering

DO age <return>

dBASE III Plus will display

```
ADULT CINEMA PROGRAM

How old are you?        Ø
```

The program will ask you to enter your age. Enter

16 <return>

dBASE III Plus will display

```
Naughty Person !!!!
Come back in a few years
```

The effect is that the program responds with the statements you created for the under-18 condition. Now test the program's ability to make a decision by entering another age. Run the program again by entering

DO age < return >

The program will ask you to enter your age. Enter

45 < return >

dBASE III Plus will display

```
You're OK Mack  !
Come on in !!!!!!!
```

This time the program printed a different message. The message was the alternative setup with the ELSE command.

NESTING CONDITIONS

In situations where evaluations take place, it is often the case that the answer to one question leads to another question. For example, it may be true that when you encounter the over-18 age group, you will have to break that group into subdivisions.

Suppose you felt it was unwise to admit people over 65 years of age. You would need a way to test all the ages in the 18 or over group to find out which ones were over 65. This is accomplished by placing an IF/ELSE/ENDIF inside the ELSE/ENDIF that is already in the program. Enter

MODIFY COMMAND age < return >

dBASE III Plus displays the commands in the file. In the modifications below, you see that another IF/ELSE/ENDIF condition has been entered inside the first conditional structure. The technique of placing one function inside another is called *nesting*. It allows you to increase the complexity of the decision-making structures in your programs.

The new condition is activated when an age of 18 or over is entered. Then that age is tested again to see if it is under 65. If it is, then the first section of commands will be displayed. If not, then the group of commands following the ELSE are displayed.

Enter the commands shown in bold.

```
CLEAR
SET TALK OFF
@ 7,14 SAY 'ADULT CINEMA PROGRAM'
age=0
```

```
@ 10,10 SAY 'How old are you? ' get age
READ
CLEAR
IF age<18
    @ 10,10 SAY 'Naughty Person!!!!!'
    @ 12,8 SAY 'Come back in a few years'
ELSE age over 18
    IF age<65
        @ 10,10 SAY [You're OK Mack      !]
        @ 12,8 SAY 'Come on in !!!!!'
    ELSE age over 65
        @ 10,10 SAY 'You ought to be ashamed of yourself'
        @ 12,8 SAY 'at your age!'
    ENDIF age<65
ENDIF age<18
SET TALK ON
RETURN
```

In addition to the new commands, there is text written after the ELSE and END-IF commands. The text has no function in the program and will be ignored by *dBASE III Plus*, making it possible for you to add notations to your program to indicate which ENDIF and ELSE commands belong to which IF commands.

> As a general rule, when using comments after an ENDIF command, you should enter the condition that was used in the corresponding IF statement. For example, if you use a conditional command such as IF age<18, place the expression age<18 following the ENDIF (e.g., ENDIF IF age<18). Any text following the ENDIF will be ignored by dBASE III Plus.

Look at the diagram below. It shows how nesting should be accomplished. Notice that one conditional structure fits entirely into the high-level condition.

```
CLEAR
SET TALK OFF
@ 7,14 SAY 'ADULT CINEMA PROGRAM'
age=0
@ 10,10 SAY 'How old are you? ' get age
READ
CLEAR
IF age<18
        @ 10,10 SAY 'Naughty Person !!!!'
        @ 10,0 SAY 'Come back in a few years'
ELSE age over 18
    IF age<65
            @ 10,10 SAY [You're OK Mack  !]
            @ 12,8 SAY 'Come on in !!!!!!!'
    ELSE age over 65
            @ 10,10 SAY 'You ought to be ashamed of yourself'
            @ 12,10 SAY 'at your age!'
    ENDIF age<65
ENDIF age<18
SET TALK ON
RETURN
```

When you have completed the modifications, save the program by entering

[CTRL/End]

Execute the program by entering

DO age < return >

Test a third alternative by entering the following when the program asks for the age.

75 < return >

dBASE III Plus will display

```
You ought to be ashamed of yourself
at your age!
```

The IF/ELSE/ENDIF structure allows you to have a program that will respond in different ways depending on the input from the user. The command files can now react to the user and evaluate the entry.

In order for the IF/ELSE/ENDIF structure to work, you must anticipate the possible user responses. If you fail to take into consideration something the user might enter, you could find that your program will fail or encounter an error.

There is no absolute way to ensure that users will behave as you anticipate they will. That is why programming is as much an art as it is an exact science. The better you understand the program's user, the more you can create a program that is easy and comfortable to use.

MENUS

You have now created several simple programs. To access any one of them, you must enter the DO command followed by the name of the program file that you want to execute.

It might be useful to create a program that lists the programs you have created. Then you can simply pick the program you want from the list. A menu program does just that. It draws together a number of smaller programs, with the purpose of allowing the user to choose from alternative actions.

Usually a menu program numbers options so that users need enter only the number corresponding to the action they wish to perform.

The advantage of menus is that they make it much simpler for other people to use the programs you have created.

MENU DESIGN

While menus may have a vast variety of functions, all menus have some basic elements that remain remarkably constant no matter what type of application you are creating.

1. **Display choices.** The first task of a menu program is to display the options available to users. The menu usually uses letters or numbers to indicate options. Users enter the letter or number of the option they desire.
2. **Get choice.** Next the menu program must allow users to enter their choice. The entry is captured in a memory variable.
3. **Evaluate choice.** Finally, once the user's choice is captured as a memory variable, the program must evaluate the choice and run the program that corresponds to that choice.

The menu program you are about to create offers users four options:

1. The TAX program.
2. The PRTCATS program.
3. The AGE program
4. The RANGE program.

Begin by creating a command file that will become the menu program. In this case, the file will be called FIRSTMNU (first menu).

> It is a good idea to get in the habit of using special codes in your command filenames to indicate the type of command file. For example, since menu programs are quite common, you might want to add the letters MNU to all of your menu programs.

Enter

MODIFY COMMAND firstmnu < return >

The menu program begins with the basic housekeeping commands that usually begin a program. Clear the screen and set the talk off by entering

```
CLEAR
SET TALK OFF
```

Next, display the list of options from which the user can choose. The order in which the choices are presented is not significant. The options can be presented in any way that you see fit. Enter

```
@ 5,10 SAY 'Menu of Command Files'
@ 10,10 SAY '1) Sales Tax Program'
@ 11,10 SAY '2) Adult Cinema Program'
@ 12,10 SAY '3) Range of Dates Program'
@ 13,10 SAY '4) Budget Category Program'
```

After the choices are displayed, the user must have a way of entering an option.

ENTERING AN OPTION

The next section of the program allows users to enter their choice. Since the options are numbered, you can use a numeric value as the key for choosing an option. If you had used letters A, B, C, a character value would have to be used as a variable.

The next line is the command that initializes the variable. Enter

```
choice=0
```

Now display a prompt and read the variable. Enter

```
@ 15,10 SAY 'Enter your choice ' GET choice PICTURE "9"
READ
```

Notice that a picture clause is added to the @/SAY/GET command, for two reasons:

1. **Control of display.** When a numeric variable is defined, there is no file structure to indicate the length of the numeric variable. *dBASE III Plus* always assigns a length of 10 to the numeric variable. In this example, that would cause *dBASE III Plus* to display an entry prompt that looked like this:

   ```
   Enter your choice ▓▓▓▓▓▓▓▓▓0
   ```

   By using the PICTURE clause, the input area will be restricted to a single character. Example:

   ```
   Enter your choice ▓0
   ```

2. Since all the choices on the menu listing are single-digit numbers, it would be convenient to eliminate the need for the user to press <return> after a selection is entered. By restricting the input area to a single character with the PICTURE clause, no <return> is necessary.

You now have the number of the options that the user wants to choose. The next step is to evaluate the choice and execute the program file that corresponds to the number.

CASES

The menu as designed in this application presents you with a programming problem that can be handled with the conditional structure IF/ELSE/ENDIF. Look at the program lines below but do not enter them yet. The lines have been numbered to make reference easier.

Line 1 tests to see if the user has entered 1. If so, then the first program is executed. If the test proves false (i.e., the user has entered something other than 1), the program continues to line 4, where another IF statement tests to see if option 2 has been selected.

If option 2 is not the selection, the program skips to line 7, where another test is made. If that test is false, then the program tests again on line 10 to see if 4 is the choice.

```
[ line #1]     IF choice=1
[ line #2]         DO program1
[ line #3]     ELSE
[ line #4]         IF choice=2
[ line #5]             DO program2
[ line #6]         ELSE
[ line #7]             IF choice=3
[ line #8]                 DO program3
[ line #9]             ELSE
[ line #10]                IF choice=4
[ line #11]                    DO program4
[ line #12]                ENDIF
[ line #13]            ENDIF
[ line #14]        ENDIF
[ line #15]    ENDIF
```

While the structure shown above will do the job, *dBASE III Plus* provides another, less complex method of making the correct selection. The method structure is called a DO CASE structure.

The DO CASE structure uses three commands:

1. **DO CASE.** This command tells *dBASE III Plus* that you want the program to evaluate a series of mutually exclusive alternatives.

   The term *mutually exclusive* means that it would not be logical for two options to be valid at the same time. In the example of a menu, choosing option 2 also means that you have specifically not chosen 1, 3, or 4. Almost all menus options are mutually exclusive and can usually be evaluated by a DO CASE structure.

   DO CASE does not take an expression.

2. **CASE.** The CASE command is similar to an IF. The word CASE is followed by a *dBASE III Plus* expression that can be evaluated as true or false.

   If the CASE is true, any commands that follow it are executed. *dBASE III Plus* stops executing commands when another CASE or ENDCASE command is encountered.

   If the CASE is false, *dBASE III Plus* skips to the next CASE, if any, and evaluates its expression as true or false.

You can list as many cases as you need or desire. *dBASE III Plus* will execute the first true case. If other cases following the first true are also true, they will be ignored. That is why the DO CASE structure usually makes sense for mutually exclusive alternatives.

3. **ENDCASE.** This command marks the end of a DO CASE structure. It does not take an expression but you can enter notes or comments following the ENDCASE as you can with the ENDIF.

> There is an option command OTHERWISE that can be used with the DO CASE structure. OTHERWISE is discussed later in this chapter.

The commands listed below illustrate how the DO CASE structure can be used to accomplish the same thing as the IF/ELSE/ENDIF.

```
DO CASE
    CASE choice=1
        DO program1
    CASE choice=2
        DO program2
    CASE choice=3
        DO program3
    CASE choice=4
        DO program4
ENDCASE
```

It is quite clear that the DO CASE structure is much simpler to work with than the cascading series of IF/ELSE/ENDIF structures. Enter the following into the program file:

```
DO CASE
    CASE choice=1
        DO tax
    CASE choice=2
        DO age
    CASE choice=3
        DO range
    CASE choice=4
        DO prtcats
ENDCASE
```

> ENDCASE and DO CASE commands must be properly balanced. For every DO CASE that is included in the program, there must be a matching ENDCASE.

Complete the program by entering

```
SET TALK OFF
RETURN
```

The entire program should look like this:

```
CLEAR
SET TALK OFF
@ 5,10 SAY 'Menu of Command Files'
@ 10,10 SAY '1) Sales Tax Program'
@ 11,10 SAY '2) Adult Cinema Program'
@ 12,10 SAY '3) Range of Dates Program'
@ 13,10 SAY '4) Budget Category Program'
choice=0
@ 15,10 SAY 'Enter your choice ' GET choice PICTURE "9"
READ
DO CASE
      CASE choice=1
           DO tax
      CASE choice=2
           DO age
      CASE choice=3
           DO range
      CASE choice=4
           DO prtcats
ENDCASE
SET TALK OFF
RETURN
```

Save the program by entering

[CTRL/End]

Execute the program by entering

DO firstmnu <return>

dBASE III Plus will display

```
Menu of Command Files


1) Sales Tax Program
2) Adult Cinema Program
3) Range of Dates Program
4) Budget Category Program

Enter your choice  0
```

The menu appears. Enter

1

The TAX program executes. Enter the amount as follows:

45.67

The program calculates as it did when it was run as a single application. Run the menu program again. Enter

DO firstmnu <return>

Once again the menu is displayed. Enter

2

The AGE program is executed. Enter an age and press <return>. When the program has completed, you will return to the DOT PROMPT.

OTHERWISE

What would happen if you entered a number that was not one of the valid options, 1 through 4? Find out by entering

DO firstmnu <return>
5

The DOT PROMPT appears without any action being taken. This is logically what ought to happen. However, you might feel that some sort of message should appear that informs users that they have not paid attention to the options on the menu.

dBASE III Plus provides an optional command that can be used as part of the DO CASE structure; it is called OTHERWISE. OTHERWISE is always the last command in the DO CASE structure. It selects commands to be executed if none of the previous cases is found to be true.

The OTHERWISE command is a default option that will be carried out if none of the menu options is chosen. In this example the OTHERWISE option can be a message that indicates why no action was taken. Enter

MODIFY COMMAND firstmnu <return>

Add the lines indicated in bold.

```
CLEAR
SET TALK OFF
@ 5,10 SAY 'Menu of Command Files'
@ 10,10 SAY '1) Sales Tax Program'
@ 11,10 SAY '2) Adult Cinema Program'
@ 12,10 SAY '3) Range of Dates Program'
@ 13,10 SAY '4) Budget Category Program'
choice=0
@ 15,10 SAY 'Enter your choice ' GET choice PICTURE "9"
READ
DO CASE
    CASE choice=1
        DO tax
    CASE choice=2
        DO age
    CASE choice=3
        DO range
    CASE choice=4
        DO prtcats
```

```
   OTHERWISE
      @ 20,0 SAY "****Enter a number from 1 to 4****"
      @ 21,0 SAY "You entered "+STR(choice,1)
ENDCASE
SET TALK OFF
RETURN
```

Note the use of the STR() function on the line that reads @ 21,0 SAY "You entered "+STR(choice,1). The STR() was needed because you wanted to display text, "You entered ", along with the value of CHOICE. Keep in mind that CHOICE is a numeric variable and cannot directly be combined with a text item. The STR() function converts the numeric value into a text string. The 1 indicates that the length of the text string will be one character.

Save the program by entering

[CTRL/End]

Execute the program by entering

DO firstmnu < return >

Now enter an invalid choice.

5

dBASE III Plus will display

```
Menu of Command Files

1) Sales Tax Program
2) Adult Cinema Program
3) Range of Dates Program
4) Budget Category Program

Enter your choice  5


**** Enter a number from 1 to 4 ****
You entered 5
```

The OTHERWISE clause causes the program to display the message at the bottom of the screen. This informs users that a mistake was made while they were entering.

LOOPS

You probably are wondering about one odd characteristic of the menu program you created. It doesn't behave like menus that you have used as part of other applications. When you select an option from this menu, the action takes place but you do not return to the menu afterward. Instead the program simply stops.

If you have worked with computers at all, you expect a menu to redisplay after the action you have selected has been completed. But this one doesn't. The reason is simple. Computers don't do anything on their own. There is nothing in this program that tells *dBASE III Plus* that the menu should be redisplayed after the action has been completed.

The next logical question is "How can that be done?" The answer to that question leads to a concept called a *loop*. A loop is a structure used in a program that tells *dBASE III Plus* to go back to a previous point in the file and begin reading a specific set of commands over again.

Loops are like conditional structures in one respect: they depend upon a logical condition to activate them. Unlike conditional structures that select groups of alternative commands, a loop is used to repeat a section of a program over and over again.

Loops are controlled by logical expressions. If the expression is true, the commands controlled by the loop are repeated. When the condition is false, the loop stops repeating.

Two major commands are associated with loops in *dBASE III Plus*:

1. **DO WHILE.** This command is always followed by a logical expression that can be evaluated as true or false. If the condition is true, the commands following the loop are executed. The execution repeats until the expression associated with the DO WHILE is false.

2. **ENDDO.** This command marks the lower boundary of the loop. When an ENDDO is encountered, *dBASE III Plus* tests the expression specified in the DO WHILE command. If the condition is true, *dBASE III Plus* moves backward in the program file to the last DO WHILE command. The commands following the DO WHILE are executed again.

   If the expression is false, the program continues with the commands, if any, that follow the ENDDO.

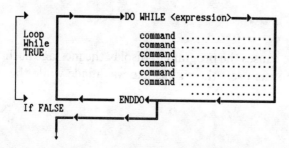

When you look at the way a DO WHILE loop is constructed, you should realize that there must be a command somewhere between the DO WHILE and the END-DO that can change the state of the logical expression controlling the loop. If you do not place such a command inside the loop, you will create an endless loop that repeats over and over, and never stops.

Before you add the loop to your menu program, it might be helpful to write some simple programs that illustrate the way loops operate.

CREATING LOOPS

As you saw in the previous section, it is necessary to have some way of making the computer repeat a sequence of commands. Most of the work that computers do is based on their ability to approach a problem from a *recursive,* rather than a *linear,* point of view.

In a *recursive* situation, the program makes references to other parts of itself, or to other programs. These references can repeat many times. When recursive programming is used you can often accomplish a lot with a small program because the commands are used over and over again.

Begin with a very simple program. These programs have very little practical use but will serve to illustrate how a loop operates.

COUNTERS

Suppose you wanted to create a program that displayed numbers from 1 to 100 on the screen. If you used a linear approach to programming, you would have to write a program that contained 100 or more commands. Example:

```
@ 10,10 SAY 1
@ 10,10 SAY 2
@ 10,10 SAY 3
@ 10,10 SAY 4
@ 10,10 SAY 5
@ 10,10 SAY 6
etc.
```

By using the recursive concept of programs that contain loops, the same task can be accomplished in a few lines.

Begin by entering

MODIFY COMMAND counter <return>

Begin with the usual setup commands. Enter

```
CLEAR
SET TALK OFF
```

Initialize a variable called counter with the first value, 1. Enter

```
counter=1
```

The next step is to begin a loop. The purpose of the loop is to repeat the commands that follow until a certain condition is met. In this case the loop will repeat until the value of counter has reached 100. To specify this to *dBASE III Plus*, you will enter a command that tells *dBASE III Plus* to DO (repeat) the loop WHILE the value of choice is less than or equal to 100. Enter

DO WHILE counter < =100

The next part of the program must answer the question, "What should happen during the loop?"

First, display the value of counter on the screen. Enter

@ 10,10 SAY counter

The first time through, the value 1 appears. Now the value of counter must be altered for two reasons:

1. First, there is no point in printing the same number over again. The idea is to print the next number, 2.
2. If you don't change the value of counter, it will never equal or exceed 100 and the loop will never stop. Remember, once you begin a loop you must include within it some command that can alter the veracity of the expression used in the DO WHILE command.

The command that you will enter is a special form of the command that stores data in memory variables. Look at the command counter = counter + 1. What does that mean? The command cannot be understood as a mathematical statement. It tells *dBASE III Plus* to take the value currently stored in the memory variable counter, add 1 to it, and store the result in the memory variable named counter.

The result of this type of command is that the value of counter increases by one each time the command is executed. It doesn't matter what the value of counter is. If counter is 1, then it becomes 2. If counter is 2, it becomes 3, and so on. The idea can be expressed in a general way:

memory variable = memory variable + number

The purpose of counter is to increase a variable by a specified increment every time the loop repeats. You will find that this simple command is used in almost every program that you write. Enter

counter=counter+1

Now you can conclude the loop by entering

ENDDO

> The ENDDO command is a single word like ENDIF and ENDCASE. As with the other structures, there must be an ENDDO for every DO WHILE used in a program.

Complete the program as usual by entering

SET TALK ON
RETURN

The entire program should look like this:

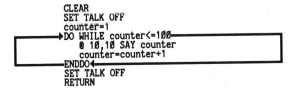

```
CLEAR
SET TALK OFF
counter=1
DO WHILE counter<=100
    @ 10,10 SAY counter
    counter=counter+1
ENDDO
SET TALK OFF
RETURN
```

The indent was added to show the effect of the DO WHILE/ENDDO commands. As in the other programs, indenting serves no function for *dBASE III Plus*, but it does make your program easier to read and understand.

Save the program by entering

[CTRL/End]

Execute the program by entering

DO counter < return >

The program displays the value of counter as it increases from 1 to 100. When the value reaches its goal, the program is terminated.

The use of the counter inside the loop allows you to control the processing by repeating the loop a specific number of times.

When you use a counter, the variable must be initialized before the loop begins. Why? You cannot test the variable if it has not already been assigned a value.

```
CLEAR
SET TALK OFF
counter=1          <--- initialize variable
DO WHILE counter<100  <--- test expression with variable
```

You must be careful not to attempt to test a data item to begin a loop before you have given it an initial value. Also, be sure the initial value given the variable will test true the first time the DO WHILE is encountered. If the variable is false the first time through, none of the commands in the loop will execute, and *dBASE III Plus* will skip to the next command following the ENDDO.

COUNTERS FOR DISPLAY COMMANDS

In the previous program, the counter structure was used in the program to control the value of a memory variable. You may have noted that the @ SAY command that displayed the value of the variable overwrote the old value each time the loop repeated. The effect was logical for the nature of that program. However, there are other times when you would want to see the results of each repetition of the loop display on the screen at the same time.

For example, suppose you want to perform the same calculation for a range of numbers and display all the results. Imagine you are considering investing money in an interest-bearing certificate, and you want to see what the compounded interest would be over the next ten years.

MODIFY COMMAND annuity < return >

Begin the program with the usual commands. Enter

```
CLEAR
SET TALK OFF
```

Now initialize two variables: one for the years of the investment, the other for the amount. Enter

```
year=1
amount=0
```

The next part of the program allows the user to enter an amount to invest. Enter

```
@ 2,0 SAY "Enter the amount you want to invest." GET amount
READ
```

Next, begin the loop. Since the goal is to project the earnings for the next 10 years, you will test the year variable for a value equal to or less than 10. Enter

```
DO WHILE year< =10
```

The commands inside the loop begin with one that calculates the value of the investment. The value 1.09 is used to represent an interest rate of 9 percent annually. The value is stored to the memory variable compound. Enter

```
compound=ROUND(amount*(1.09)^ year,2)
```

> *The formula for calculation of compound interest is principle multiplied by 1 plus the rate of interest raised to the power of the number of years.*

With the value of compound calculated, your next task is to display that value on the screen. In the previous example the value display is always on the same row. In this case, that is not adequate because you want to see the value of the annuity for each of the ten years.

An explanation lies in the nature of the @/SAY command. Remember that the @ is followed by two numeric values: one for the row and the other for the column. *dBASE III Plus* allows you to use any valid numeric value in those positions.

Thus, you could use a number, such as 10, a numeric variable, such as year, or a calculation of some kind. *dBASE III Plus* does not require that the numeric value be a literal value, only that it be a numeric value or expression of some kind. For example, if you used the variable year in an @/SAY command, the location of the display would vary depending on the current value of year.

By reading the command below you cannot tell exactly where on the screen compound will be displayed. It depends on the value of year. If year is 1, then it will appear on line 1 of the screen display. If the value is 2, then it appears on line 2, and so forth.

```
@ year,10 SAY compound
```

By adding a number to year you can make sure that the display begins lower on the screen. Look at the next example. In this case, if year is 1, the value will appear on line 5 (i.e., 1 + 4 = 5).

```
@ year+4,10 SAY compound
```

With this in mind, enter the following commands:

```
@ year+4,10 SAY "At the end of year "+STR(year,2)
@ year+4,40 SAY compound PICTURE "999,999.99"
```

Note that the STR() function is needed because year, a numeric value, cannot be combined with the text string unless it is converted to characters.

The next step is to increment the value of year by 1 and end the loop. This will do two things:

1. The next time compound is calculated, it will be for two years of the annuity.
2. When the value is displayed, it will fall one line lower on the screen display. Therefore it will not overwrite the previous value.

Enter

```
year=year+1
ENDDO
```

Complete the program with the usual commands. Enter

```
SET TALK ON
RETURN
```

The entire program should look like this:

```
        CLEAR
        SET TALK OFF
        year=1
        amount=0
        @ 2,0 SAY "Enter the amount you want to invest." GET amount
        READ
    ┌──▶DO WHILE year<=10───────────────────────────────────────────┐
    │       compound=ROUND(amount*(1.09)^year,2)                     │
    │       @ year+4,10 SAY "At the end of year "+STR(year,2)        │
    │       @ year+4,40 SAY compound PICTURE "999,999.99"            │
    │       year=year+1                                              │
    └──ENDDO◀────────────────────────────────────────────────────────┘
        SET TALK ON
        RETURN
```

Save the program by entering

[CTRL/End]

Execute the program by entering

DO annuity < return >

At the top of the screen you are prompted to enter a value. Enter

1200 < return >

dBASE III Plus will display

```
Enter the amount you want to invest.      1200

            At the end of year  1        1,308.00
            At the end of year  2        1,425.72
            At the end of year  3        1,554.03
            At the end of year  4        1,693.90
            At the end of year  5        1,846.35
            At the end of year  6        2,012.52
            At the end of year  7        2,193.65
            At the end of year  8        2,391.08
            At the end of year  9        2,606.27
            At the end of year 10        2,840.84
```

Observe that the variable year is used for three things in the ANNUITY program:

1. **Calculate annuity.** The numeric calculation depends on the value of year to determine the value of the annuity.
2. **Display year.** The variable year is also used to display the number of the year.
3. **Line of display.** The variable year is also used to determine the row portion of the @/SAY command.

The use of the loop and the variable year allows this rather short program to output a considerable amount of data. This illustrates the power of recursive programming structures.

Exercise 1   Modify the ANNUITY program to display 15 years instead of 10. The correct program listing can be found at the end of the chapter.

LOOPING THE MENU

You are now ready to apply the concept of loops to the menu program that you had created earlier in this chapter. Your goal is to create a program that repeatedly displays the menu of options so that you can choose again and again, without having to restart the program.

Load the file into the editor by entering

MODIFY COMMAND firstmnu < return >

In order to change this program to one loop, you must be able to identify the parts of the program that should be repeated as part of the loop. In the case of this program, the loop should begin (DO WHILE) with the commands that display the text of the menu. The loop should end (ENDDO) following the ENDCASE statement.

In addition, there are two commands whose position needs to be changed if the program is going to loop. First, the CLEAR command should be moved to a position in the program that includes it inside the loop. If the program is going to display the menu a number of times, you should make sure that the screen is cleared before the display each time.

On the other hand, the variable choice needs to be initialized only once no matter how many times the loop is executed. The initialization command should be moved outside the loop so that it is not repeated. The arrows below show the places in the program that must be changed to implement the menu loop.

```
CLEAR<==================================MOVE INSIDE LOOP
SET TALK OFF
@ 5,10 SAY 'Menu of Command Files'  <=======START LOOP
@ 10,10 SAY '1) Sales Tax Program'
@ 11,10 SAY '2) Adult Cinema Program'
@ 12,10 SAY '3) Range of Dates Program'
@ 13,10 SAY '4) Budget Category Program'
choice=0<============================MOVE OUTSIDE LOOP
@ 15,10 SAY 'Enter your choice ' GET choice PICTURE "9"
READ
DO CASE
      CASE choice=1
            DO tax
      CASE choice=2
            DO age
      CASE choice=3
            DO range
      CASE choice=4
            DO prtcats
ENDCASE<=================================END LOOP
SET TALK OFF
RETURN
```

When you add loops to a program, you create concerns about the position of certain commands within the program that were not as significant when the program was linear in nature.

Another factor that needs to be considered is how the loop will be maintained and ended. Answering this question is crucial to the design of a loop. You must know what condition will be used to control the loop. For example, your menu is controlled by values entered into the variable choice. When choice is equal to 1, the menu executes option 1.

If you wanted to stop the menu and exit, what number would you choose? As the program stands now, there is no option listed on the menu for exiting, because you haven't created a looping menu yet.

In this example, you will use the value 0 as the menu option that exits the program. Thus, the DO WHILE command can test whether the value of choice is equal to zero or not. If choice is not zero, the loop redisplays the menu and allows the user to enter another choice.

If the value of choice is zero, the loop will terminate, causing *dBASE III Plus* to continue reading the program file at the next command, if any, following the ENDDO. When you initialize the variable choice, you must use a value that will cause the DO WHILE command to be true when it is first encountered in the program.

```
choice=1    <================ Initialize CHOICE as 1
DO WHILE choice <> 0 <==== Test for CHOICE not equal to zero
    display menu
    enter choice
    execute option
ENDDO<==================== Test to see if CHOICE is now zero
```

Keeping in mind what you have learned about loops and variables, change your program as follows. Lines that are moved or changed are indicated by the < = = = = = =:

```
SET TALK OFF
choice=1         <=========== moved
DO WHILE choice<>0
CLEAR            <=========== moved
@ 5,10 SAY 'Menu of Command Files'
@ 10,10 SAY '1) Sales Tax Program'
@ 11,10 SAY '2) Adult Cinema Program'
@ 12,10 SAY '3) Range of Dates Program'
@ 13,10 SAY '4) Budget Category Program'
@ 15,10 SAY '0) Exit Program'
@ 17,10 SAY 'Enter your choice ' GET choice PICTURE "9"  <========changed
READ
DO CASE
        CASE choice=1
            DO tax
        CASE choice=2
            DO age
        CASE choice=3
            DO range
        CASE choice=4
            DO prtcats
        CASE choice=0
            CLEAR
            @ 10,10 SAY "Goodbye, program terminated"
        OTHERWISE
            @ 20,0 SAY "**** Enter a number from 1 to 4 ****"
            @ 21,0 SAY "You entered "+STR(choice,1)
ENDCASE
ENDDO
SET TALK OFF
RETURN
```

Save the program by entering

[CTRL/End]

Execute the program by entering

DO firstmnu < return >

Choose option 1 by entering

     1

The Sales tax program executes. Enter the amount

     12 <return>

The calculation is displayed and the program returns to the menu. What is wrong?

    You did not take into account that you need to pause after the end of the TAX program before you display the menu again. To correct this mistake, enter the following to exit the menu:

     0

The program terminates and displays the good-bye message.

THE WAIT COMMAND

One simple solution to the problem of pausing the program is the WAIT command. The WAIT command causes the program to pause execution and displays the message "Press any key to continue." on the screen. Pressing any key will cause *dBASE III Plus* to resume execution of the program with the next command in the file.

> *The WAIT command can also be used with a TO clause to capture the input to a memory variable. Example, WAIT TO choice. WAIT always stores the keystroke as a character, even if you type 0 through 9.*
>
> *In addition, you can alter the message displayed by WAIT by entering a text literal into the command. Example, WAIT "Press a key to return to the menu". You will learn more about WAIT in the systems design section of this book.*

    To pause the execution of the program after each subroutine has been executed, you can place a WAIT command following the ENDCASE. In this way, the program will pause after every case has been executed. Enter

     MODIFY COMMAND firstmnu <return>

    Below is the bottom of the FIRSTMNU program. Add the WAIT command where indicated.

```
ENDCASE
WAIT <================ add to program
ENDDO
SET TALK OFF
RETURN
```

Save the program by entering

[CTRL/End]

Execute the program by entering

DO firstmnu <return>

Now execute the TAX program by entering

1

Enter an amount:

12 <return>

This time a message, Press any key to continue, appears and the program is paused. This gives you time to inspect the results of the calculation. Now enter

<return>

The menu reappears. Now execute the CATS program by entering

4
<return>

When the program has completed its execution, a message, Press any key to continue, appears and the program is paused. Return to the menu by pressing any key (e.g., <space bar>).

The input area now shows the value 4, because the last entry made into choice was 4.

> In this program the memory variable choice is initialized only once at the beginning of the program before the loop begins. As the loop runs, choice retains the last entry until a new entry is made.

Now exit the menu by entering

0

The WAIT command pauses the program even for this option. Enter

<return>

The program is terminated and the DOT PROMPT appears.

THE EXIT COMMAND

While not a major flaw, the fact that the WAIT command pauses the program when you want to exit seems a bit out of place. *dBASE III Plus* provides you with a special command called EXIT that solves this problem. The EXIT command is used only when a DO WHILE loop is active. When an EXIT command is encountered, *dBASE III Plus* immediately jumps to the next ENDDO command and begins executing the commands following the ENDDO. This has two consequences:

1. The DO WHILE loop is immediately terminated, even if the logical condition is still true.
2. Any commands between the EXIT and the ENDDO are ignored.

Load the FIRSTMNU program into the editor by entering

MODIFY COMMAND firstmnu < return >

The object in this case is to skip the WAIT command if choice 0, exit the menu, is entered. If you place the EXIT command as the last one in the choice 0 case, the WAIT command will be skipped. This is because the WAIT command falls before the ENDDO. The EXIT command skips all commands until after the ENDDO.

```
DO WHILE choice<>0
READ (Enter zero)
DO CASE
        CASE choice=1
                commands ....
        CASE choice=2
                commands ....
        CASE choice=3
                commands ....
        CASE choice=4
                commands ....
        CASE choice=0
                commands
                EXIT
        OTHERWISE
                commands ....
ENDCASE
WAIT
ENDDO
RETURN
```

Insert the EXIT command where indicated below:

```
CASE choice=0
    CLEAR
    @ 10,10 SAY "Goodbye, program terminated"
    EXIT <=================== add command
OTHERWISE
        @ 20,0 SAY "**** Enter a number from 1 to 4 ****"
        @ 21,0 SAY "You entered "+STR(choice,1)
ENDCASE
```

The RETURN command should never be used inside a loop. If you want to terminate a program as part of a menu choice, you should use the EXIT command to jump past the ENDDO command. Then execute the RETURN at that point. If you place the RETURN command inside the loop (for example, in the same position as the

EXIT command is found in the previous program), you may cause dBASE III Plus to improperly execute the rest of the program.

The preferred programming technique is the one illustrated, in which the EXIT command is used to leave the loop, and RETURN follows the ENDDO.

Save the program by entering

[CTRL/End]

Execute the program by entering

DO firstmnu < return >

Test the EXIT command by entering

0

The program terminates without pausing for the WAIT command.

To get a better idea of how the program you created operates, run the program to test the various menu selection items.

THE GENERIC MENU PROGRAM

Many programming techniques have been described in this chapter, but there is one more structure that needs to be covered. The EXIT command provides a means by which you can create a DO WHILE loop that continues automatically until an EXIT command is encountered.

Creating this type of loop eliminates the need to use a variable to control the veracity of the DO WHILE command. This makes loops, such as those used in menus, operate until an EXIT command is used to jump out of the loop.

There is one condition you could use with the DO WHILE that will always test true, no matter what happens during the program. The current expression (choice< >0) could be replaced with a logical true value (.T.). The .T. symbol literally stands for "true."

Look at the program diagram below. It shows the use of .T. to create a never-ending loop. The EXIT command inside the loop must be placed inside an IF/ENDIF or DO CASE structure.

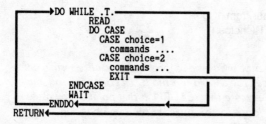

```
┌──────►DO WHILE .T.───────┐
│          READ            │
│          DO CASE         │
│            CASE choice=1  │
│              commands ....│
│            CASE choice=2  │
│              commands ... │
│              EXIT ───────┐│
│          ENDCASE         ││
│          WAIT            ││
└─────ENDDO◄───────────────┘│
RETURN◄─────────────────────┘
```

To illustrate how this type of logic is applied to a menu program, create a new program file called GENERMNU (generic menu). Enter

MODIFY COMMAND genermnu < return >

READING IN A FILE

Instead of typing in an entirely new program, you can save some time by loading a copy of the FIRSTMNU file into the editor and changing the lines that need to be altered. When you save the file, the text will be saved under the name of the file you are editing, GENERMNU. Then you will have two menus, FIRSTMNU and GENERMNU, that illustrate two variations on the basic menu design.

The *dBASE III Plus* editor allows you to combine files by using the **[CTRL/k]**r (READ A FILE) command. In this case you want to read in the contents of FIRSTMNU.PRG. The **[CTRL/k]**r command requires the entry of the full filename, including the extension .PRG.

Enter

[CTRL/k]
r
firstmnu.prg < return >

You now have the text of the FIRSTMNU program to edit, rather than starting from scratch. This is a handy technique to use when you want to create a program that is very similar to a program you have already created. Since almost all menu programs have about the same structure, you will find that you will use this technique quite often when it comes to menus.

Look at the listing below. There are two changes that need to be made:

1. Change the DO WHILE command to use the .T. (logical true value) instead of choice< >0.

2. Move the initialization command for the variable choice back into the loop. The variable is now defined as 0. The effect will be that choice will always be zero when the menu is displayed. If choice is initialized outside the loop, as is done in FIRSTMNU, then the menu will show the last value entered when it is redisplayed. Which method is the better? The choice is personal; however, setting the value of the choice to the one that exits the menu is considered standard programming style.

Make the changes as indicated.

```
SET TALK OFF
DO WHILE .T.  <=====================================changed
CLEAR
@ 5,10 SAY 'Menu of Command Files'
@ 10,10 SAY '1) Sales Tax Program'
@ 11,10 SAY '2) Adult Cinema Program'
@ 12,10 SAY '3) Range of Dates Program'
@ 13,10 SAY '4) Budget Category Program'
@ 15,10 SAY '0) Exit Program'
choice=0  <===============================changed and moved
@ 17,10 SAY 'Enter your choice ' GET choice PICTURE "9"
READ
DO CASE
      CASE choice=1
            DO tax
      CASE choice=2
            DO age
      CASE choice=3
            DO range
      CASE choice=4
            DO prtcats
      CASE choice=0
            CLEAR
            @ 10,10 SAY "Goodbye, program terminated"
            EXIT
      OTHERWISE
            @ 20,0 SAY "**** Enter a number from 1 to 4 ****"
            @ 21,0 SAY "You entered "+STR(choice,1)
ENDCASE
WAIT
ENDDO
SET TALK OFF
RETURN
```

Save the program by entering

[CTRL/End]

Execute the program by entering

DO genermnu < return >

Select option 4 by entering

4
< return >

To continue, enter

< return >

Notice that this time, the value of choice is set back to zero when the loop is redisplayed. Since zero is automatically entered as the choice, you can exit the program by entering

< return >

The program stops and you return to the *dBASE III Plus* DOT PROMPT.

Exercise 2   Create a menu program on your own that will run the programs COUNTER, ANNUITY, and LISTING. A sample program that runs these programs can be found at the end of the chapter.

SUMMARY

This chapter introduced two very important concepts required for creating nonlinear programs.

IF/ELSE/ENDIF

The IF command allows *dBASE III Plus* to process the commands in a command file selectively. The purpose of IF/ELSE/ENDIF is to tell *dBASE III Plus* what commands to read and what commands to skip in certain situations.

The simplest form is the IF/ENDIF structure. The IF command is followed by a *dBASE III Plus* expression that can be evaluated as either true or false. If the condition is false, all the commands up until the next ENDIF command will be skipped. If the expression is true, the commands execute.

The IF/ELSE/ENDIF structure contains two mutually exclusive sets of commands. If the expression is true, then all the commands between the IF and the ELSE execute. Commands entered between the ELSE and the ENDIF are skipped.

If the expression is false, all the commands following the IF until the ELSE are skipped. The commands following the ELSE until the ENDIF are executed.

dBASE III Plus allows you to nest IF/ELSE/ENDIF within IF/ELSE/ENDIF. This allows you to perform several levels of tests.

DO CASE/CASE/ENDCASE

This is a variation on the IF/ELSE/ENDIF structure. Following the DO CASE command, you can list a series of cases, each with a *dBASE III Plus* logical expression, followed by a series of commands. When the last case has been entered, the structure is completed by entering an ENDCASE command.

dBASE III Plus evaluates the CASES in the order in which they are listed in the DO CASE structure. It will execute the first set of commands for which the expression tests true. All other cases that follow are ignored, even though they might also be true.

DO CASE/ENDCASE is useful when you have a number (at least three) of mutually exclusive conditions to test for. You can nest IF/ELSE/ENDIF or other DO CASE/ENDCASE structures inside a CASE. You will see examples of this in the systems design section.

The OTHERWISE command is an optional command that can be used to create a default option within a DO CASE structure. If none of the CASEs is true, *dBASE III Plus* will execute the commands following the OTHERWISE command.

Loops

Loops are programming structures that allow you to repeat a section of a program a number of times. Loops in *dBASE III Plus* are controlled by DO WHILE/END-DO commands. The DO WHILE command is followed by a *dBASE III Plus* expression. If the expression is true, all the commands that follow are executed. When an ENDDO command is encountered, *dBASE III Plus* evaluates the expression used with the DO WHILE command once again. If the expression is still true, *dBASE III Plus* moves backward in the command file to the DO WHILE command and executes all the commands in between again.

Should the expression eventually evaluate as false, the loop is terminated and *dBASE III Plus* continues reading commands following the ENDDO command.

The EXIT command can be used to force *dBASE III Plus* to exit a loop even though the expression still evaluates as true.

You can use the logical value .T. (true) as an expression with the DO WHILE command. This creates a loop that is automatically true no matter what else takes place in the program. This is a shortcut to begin a loop. Loops that begin with .T. can be ended only by using the EXIT command to force *dBASE III Plus* to exit the loop.

ANSWER KEY

Exercise 1

The only change necessary is to the value at the end of the DO WHILE command from 10 to 15.

```
CLEAR
SET TALK OFF
year=1
amount=0
@ 2,0 SAY "Enter the amount you want to invest." GET amount
READ
DO WHILE year<=15  <---------------- change value
    compound=ROUND(amount*(1.09)^year,2)
    @ year+4,10 SAY "At the end of year "+STR(year,2)
    @ year+4,40 SAY compound PICTURE "999,999.99"
    year=year+1
ENDDO
SET TALK ON
RETURN
```

Exercise 2

```
SET TALK OFF
DO WHILE .T.
CLEAR
@ 5,10 SAY 'Menu of Command Files'
@ 10,10 SAY '1) Counter Program'
@ 11,10 SAY '2) Listing Program'
@ 12,10 SAY '3) Annuity Program'
@ 13,10 SAY '0) Exit Program'
choice=0
@ 15,10 SAY 'Enter your choice ' GET choice PICTURE "9"
READ
DO CASE
    CASE choice=1
        DO counter
    CASE choice=2
        DO listing
    CASE choice=3
        DO annuity
    CASE choice=0
        CLEAR
        @ 10,10 SAY "Goodbye, program terminated"
        EXIT
    OTHERWISE
        @ 20,0 SAY "**** Enter a number from 1 to 4 ****"
        @ 21,0 SAY "You entered "+STR(choice,1)
ENDCASE
WAIT
ENDDO
SET TALK OFF
RETURN
```

ADDITIONAL

PROGRAMMING TOOLS

THE PREVIOUS TWO CHAPTERS INTRODUCED the major commands and techniques needed to construct programs in *dBASE III Plus*. These are as follows:

1. **Creating command files.** The basis of all programming is the creation of text files that contain lists of commands, with the *dBASE III Plus* editor or some other word processing program.

    The DO command tells *dBASE III Plus* to begin reading a command file and executing the commands as if they were actually being entered from the keyboard.

2. **Interactive programming.** Interactive programming allows you to create programs that carry on a dialogue with the person using the computer. The program displays questions in the form of prompts or menus and pauses to allow the user to respond. The responses are captured in memory variables.

3. **Conditional programming.** Conditional programming allows *dBASE III Plus* to skip certain sections of the program based on logical conditions. This means that your program will execute differently depending on specific conditions.

    If you combine this ability with interactive programming, you get a program that responds to the user's input with alternative actions. The most common is a menu of choices from which the user can select different operations. Each option may in fact be an entirely different *dBASE III Plus* program.

4. **Loops.** Loops are structures that allow portions of your *dBASE III Plus* program to repeat over and over again. This repeating or recursive programming style allows small programs to process large amounts of data by repeating the crucial portion of the program.

    It also enables you to create menus that reappear after you have made an initial selection. This creates the effect of a *running* program.

The purpose of this chapter is to describe some techniques used to handle special circumstances that occur in many programming applications.

ENVIRONMENTAL INFORMATION

dBASE III Plus has a variety of functions that can be used to report information about the system you are working with. You have already encountered two of these special functions, DATE() and TIME(). DATE() returns the current systems date as a date-type variable, and TIME() returns the current time as a character string.

The other functions fall into three categories:

1. **Systems information.** These functions allow you to gather information about the overall system. They include DATE(), TIME(), and other functions that report on the status of the operating system.

2. **File information.** This is information that relates to *dBASE III Plus* files such as the number of records in the file, the size of the records, and the date of the last update to the file.

3. **Field information.** *dBASE III Plus* also has functions that display information about the fields in a data base file.

SYSTEMS INFORMATION

dBASE III Plus has a number of functions that return information about the general status of the computer and operating system. These functions are:

1. **DISKSPACE().** Calculates a numeric value equal to the total number of free bytes on the currently logged disk.

2. **OS().** Returns a character string that displays the version of DOS running in the computer.

3. **VERSION().** Displays the version of *dBASE III Plus* that is running in the computer. Version numbers are used by the manufacturer to designate revision of a program. As of the writing of this book, *dBASE III Plus* exists in two versions, *1.0* and *1.1*. Version *1.1* is not copy protected.

To see how you might use these functions, create a program called SYSSTAT (systems status) by entering

> **MODIFY COMMAND sysstat** < return >

Begin with the usual commands to clear the screen and set the talk off. Enter

```
CLEAR
SET TALK OFF
```

The next line combines a text display with the version of *dBASE III Plus*. Enter

```
@ 1,0 SAY "This computer is running "+VERSION()
```

The next line displays the version of DOS running in the computer. Enter

```
@ 2,0 SAY "Operating under "+OS()
```

Note that the functions are concatenated to the strings by using the +. The next function cannot be handled that simply. The DISKSPACE() function returns a numeric value; thus if you want to combine it with text, you must convert the numeric value to a string value.

The LTRIM() function is also used to eliminate any unneeded spaces that are created by the STR() function. In this example you have allocated a length of ten characters for the number of bytes. If the number uses only five digits, there will be five blanks preceding the number. LTRIM() will eliminate those blanks. Enter

```
@ 3,0 SAY "There are "+LTRIM(STR(DISKSPACE(),10))+" bytes free on this disk"
SET TALK ON
RETURN
```

The entire program looks like this:

```
CLEAR
SET TALK OFF
@ 1,0 SAY "This computer is running "+VERSION()
@ 2,0 SAY "Operating under "+OS()
@ 3,0 SAY "There are "+LTRIM(STR(DISKSPACE(),10))+;
" bytes free on this disk"
SET TALK ON
RETURN
```

Because of printing limitations, some of the lines of the program are divided into two parts by using a semicolon character at the end of the line. For example, in the program above, the fifth and sixth lines are really a single command. The semicolon at the end of the fifth line tells dBASE III Plus to continue reading the command on the next line.

When you are entering the commands, you can simply type them as a single command since the dBASE III Plus editor will automatically wrap the lines around. You should not type the semicolon if you combine the lines into a single entry. Keep this in mind as you work through the remainder of the book.

Save the program by entering

[CTRL/End]

Execute the program by entering

DO sysstat < return >

dBASE III Plus will display

```
This computer is running dBASE III PLUS  version 1.0
Operating under DOS 3.20
There are 17711104 bytes free on this disk
```

The screen display will vary depending on the actual version of DOS and amount of disk space used.

FILE ATTRIBUTES

dBASE III Plus allows you to report information about a data base file by using special functions that display information about the file. These commands are

1. **DBF().** Displays the name of the selected data base file.
2. **RECSIZE().** Returns the numeric value equivalent to the number of bytes in each record.
3. **RECCOUNT().** Returns a numeric value equal to the number of records in the data base file.
4. **LUPDATE().** Returns a date-type value with the date of the last update of the data base file.

You can add these functions to the SYSSTAT program. Enter

MODIFY COMMAND sysstat < return >

The first step is to open a file about which to display information. Then you can use the functions to display the information about the file. Note that DBF() returns a character string and does not have to be converted. On the other hand, RECCOUNT and RECSIZE are numeric values and must be converted to strings before they can be combined with text. The LUPDATE() function returns a date-type value, and it must be converted to a character string. Note that the LUPDATE()

was converted twice, once for the date string and once to get the day of the week (CDOW()).

Enter the commands shown in bold.

```
CLEAR
SET TALK OFF
@ 1,0 SAY "This computer is running "+VERSION()
@ 2,0 SAY "Operating under "+OS()
@ 3,0 SAY "There are "+LTRIM(STR(DISKSPACE(),10))+"bytes free on this disk"
USE expenses
@ 5,0 SAY "The current database file is "+DBF()
@ 6,0 SAY "The file contains "+LTRIM(STR(RECCOUNT(),10))+;
" records."
@ 7,0 SAY "The file was last updated on "+CDOW(LUPDATE())+;
", "+DTOC(LUPDATE())
@ 8,0 "Each Record Contains "+LTRIM (STR(RECSIZE(),10))+" characters"
```

Save the program by entering

> **[CTRL/End]**

Execute the program by entering

> **DO sysstat** <return>

dBASE III Plus will display

```
This computer is running dBASE III PLUS  version 1.0
Operating under DOS 3.20
There are 17711104 bytes free on this disk

The current database file is C:expenses.dbf
The file contains 11 records.
The file was last updated on Friday, 11/07/86
Each record contains 86 characters
```

THE FIELD FUNCTION

dBASE III Plus provides a means by which you can refer to the fields in the data base file by number rather than by name. The function is the FIELD() function. The field function requires a numeric argument from 1 to 128 corresponding to the number of each field.

For example, to display the name of the first field in the data base file, enter

> **? FIELD(1)** <return>

dBASE III Plus displays DATE. Enter

> **? FIELD(2)** <return>

dBASE III Plus displays CAT. Suppose you wanted your program to display a list of the fields in your data base file. How could this be done? One way would be to enter a series of commands, for example:

```
@ 10,0 SAY FIELD(1)
@ 11,0 SAY FIELD(2)
@ 12,0 SAY FIELD(3)
etc.
```

There are several disadvantages to this method. First, you would have to type in a command for each field that you wanted to display. Second, how would you know how many commands to enter? The number of fields might vary from data base to data base. You need to create a structure that will list the correct number of fields no matter what data base file is in use.

The answer is to create a loop that will display each field name by incrementing the number of the field by one each time it executes. The loop should terminate when you have reached a number for which there is no field name used in that data base file.

The problem is how to express this to *dBASE III Plus*. There are two concepts needed to understand the solution. First, the FIELD() function requires a numeric value to determine which field name will be displayed. However, the numeric value does not have to be a number; it could just as well be a numeric variable. For example, if you created a memory variable called "fieldnum" and assigned it a value of 1, you could then use the variable as the numeric argument for the FIELD() function. The commands below show how a variable can be used with the FIELD() functions:

A	**B**
fieldnum=1	? FIELD(1) = DATE
? FIELD(fieldnum)= DATE	? FIELD(2) = CAT
fieldnum=fieldnum+1	
? FIELD(fieldnum)= CAT	

Both column A and column B display the same results. However, in column A, by changing the value of fieldnum, the function will display the next field. This type of logic is perfect for a loop since the same command, ? FIELD(fieldnum), can be used over and over again. Changing the value of the variable will change the name printed.

Only one problem remains. How can you terminate the loop? What logical condition can you test for?

The answer lies in how *dBASE III Plus* reacts if you use a value in the FIELD() function for which there is no corresponding field. In that case, *dBASE III Plus* treats the expression as a null value. A null value can be entered as "" (i.e., two quotation marks without a space between them).

> *A null value refers to the character represented by code zero in the ASCII coding system. A null is a binary zero and can also be indicated in* dBASE III Plus *as CHR(0).*

Therefore the expression ""'FIELD(10) (i.e., a null is not equal to the field name of field 10), is true if the field has a name and false if no field 10 has been defined for that data base file.

If you use that expression as part of a DO WHILE command, the loop will continue until you have reached the last field name and then stop. Load the program into the editor by entering

MODIFY COMMAND sysstat <return>

The commands that implement that change are shown below in bold. Note that the fieldnum variable can be used for different purposes: to display the field number, as part of the FIELD() function, and to control the position on the screen where the name prints. Add those to the program.

```
CLEAR
SET TALK OFF
@ 1,0 SAY "This computer is running "+VERSION()
@ 2,0 SAY "Operating under "+OS()
@ 3,0 SAY "There are "+LTRIM(STR(DISKSPACE(),10))+"bytes free on this disk"
USE expenses
@ 5,0 SAY "The current database file is "+DBF()
@ 6,0 SAY "The file contains "+LTRIM(STR(RECCOUNT(),10))+ records."
@ 7,0 SAY "The file was last updated on "+CDOW(LUPDATE())+;
","+DTOC(LUPDATE())
@ 8,0 SAY "Each record contains "+LTRIM(STR(RECSIZE(),10))+" characters"
@ 9,0 SAY "The database contains the following fields:"
fieldnum=1
DO WHILE ""< >FIELD(fieldnum)
    @ fieldnum+9,0 SAY "Field #"+LTRIM(STR(fieldnum,3));
    +" "+FIELD(fieldnum)
    fieldnum=fieldnum+1
ENDDO
SET TALK ON
RETURN
```

Save the program by entering

[CTRL/End]

Execute the program by entering

DO sysstat <return>

The program will display the following information:

```
This computer is running dBASE III PLUS  version 1.0
Operating under DOS 3.20
There are 17711104 bytes free on this disk

The current database file is C:expenses.dbf
The file contains 11 records.
The file was last updated on Friday, 11/07/86
Each record contains 86 characters
The database contains the following fields:
Field #1 DATE
Field #2 CAT
Field #3 PAYTO
Field #4 ITEM
Field #5 AMOUNT
Field #6 COMMENTS
Field #7 MONTH
Field #8 DEDUCT
```

FIELD TYPES

dBASE III Plus provides a function that can be used to determine the type of field. The function is TYPE(), and it returns a single character corresponding to the type of the field. For example, enter

? TYPE(amount) <return>

dBASE III Plus displays N, which stands for "numeric." The other letter codes are C for "character," D for "date," L for "logical," and M for "memo." You can add this display to the SYSSTAT program. Enter

MODIFY COMMAND sysstat <return>

The trick is to nest the functions so that you can determine the type for each field beginning with the field number. The expression will look like this:

TYPE(FIELD(fieldnum))

This expression uses the inner function, FIELD(fieldnum), to provide the outer function TYPE() with the field name it requires. Nesting functions in this manner can generate some very interesting and useful results.

Below is a listing of the program that includes a line that prints the field type for each field. Enter the commands indicated in bold.

```
CLEAR
SET TALK OFF
@ 1,0 SAY "This computer is running "+VERSION()
@ 2,0 SAY "Operating under "+OS()
@ 3,0 SAY "There are "+LTRIM(STR(DISKSPACE(),10))+" bytes free on this disk"
USE expenses
@ 5,0 SAY "The current database file is "+DBF()
@ 6,0 SAY "The file contains "+LTRIM(STR(RECCOUNT(),10))+" records."
@ 7,0 SAY "The file was last updated on "+CDOW(LUPDATE())+", "+DTOC(LUPDATE())
@ 8,0 SAY "Each record contains "+LTRIM(STR(RECSIZE(),10))+" characters"
@ 9,0 SAY "The database contains the following fields:"
fieldnum=1
```

```
DO WHILE ""<>FIELD(fieldnum)
    @ fieldnum+9,0 SAY "Field #"+LTRIM(STR(fieldnum,3))+" "+FIELD(fieldnum)
    @ fieldnum+9,35 SAY TYPE(FIELD(fieldnum))
    fieldnum=fieldnum+1
ENDDO
SET TALK ON
RETURN
```

Save the program by entering

[CTRL/End]

Execute the program by entering

DO sysstat < return >

dBASE III Plus will display

```
This computer is running dBASE III PLUS  version 1.0
Operating under DOS 3.20
There are 17711104 bytes free on this disk

The current database file is C:expenses.dbf
The file contains 11 records.
The file was last updated on Friday, 11/07/86
Each record contains 86 characters
The database contains the following fields:
Field #1 DATE              D
Field #2 CAT               N
Field #3 PAYTO             C
Field #4 ITEM              C
Field #5 AMOUNT            N
Field #6 COMMENTS          M
Field #7 MONTH             C
Field #8 DEDUCT            L
```

CONVERSION STRUCTURES

It might be better if you could display the words "character," "numeric," "date," and so forth instead of just the letters. This can be done by creating a DO CASE/ENDCASE structure that will convert the letters into full words.

This is one of the most common uses of DO CASE structures, besides menus. Load the SYSSTAT file into the editor by entering

MODIFY COMMAND sysstat < return >

The concept of a lookup structure is to create a case for each of the codes that needs to be converted. In this example, the CASE commands will test for the code:

CASE TYPE(FIELD(fieldnum))="C"

The command above tests for CHARACTER fields. If the case is true, then a command is used to store the text to a memory variable. Example:

fieldtype="CHARACTER"

To make a complete conversion table, you need to repeat the process for each of the alternative codes.

Below is the revised program. Enter the commands shown in bold.

```
CLEAR
SET TALK OFF
@ 1,0 SAY "This computer is running "+VERSION()
@ 2,0 SAY "Operating under "+OS()
@ 3,0 SAY "There are "+LTRIM(STR(DISKSPACE(),10))+"bytes free on this disk"
USE expenses
@ 6,0 SAY "The file contains "+LTRIM(STR(RECCOUNT(),10))+ records."
@ 6,0 SAY "The file contains "+LTRIM(STR(RECCOUNT(),10)+" records."
@ 7,0 SAY "The file was last updated on "+CDOW(LUPDATE())+;
","+DTOC(LUPDATE())
@ 8,0 SAY "Each record contains "+LTRIM(STR(RECSIZE(),10))+" characters"
@ 9,0 SAY "The database contains the following fields:"
fieldnum=1
DO WHILE ""< >FIELD(fieldnum)
    @ fieldnum+9,0 SAY "Field #"+LTRIM(STR(fieldnum,3))
    +" "+FIELD(fieldnum)
        DO CASE
            CASE TYPE(FIELD(fieldnum))="C"
                fieldtype="CHARACTER"
            CASE TYPE(FIELD(fieldnum))="N"
                fieldtype="NUMERIC"
            CASE TYPE(FIELD(fieldnum))="D"
                fieldtype="DATE"
            CASE TYPE(FIELD(fieldnum))="L"
                fieldtype="LOGICAL"
            CASE TYPE(FIELD(fieldnum))="M"
                fieldtype="MEMO"
        ENDCASE
        @ fieldnum+9,35 SAY fieldtype <========= changed
    fieldnum=fieldnum+1
ENDDO
SET TALK ON
RETURN
```

Save the program by entering

[CTRL/End]

Execute the program by entering

DO sysstat <return>

dBASE III Plus will display

```
This computer is running dBASE III PLUS  version 1.0
Operating under DOS 3.20
There are 17711104 bytes free on this disk
```

```
The current database file is C:expenses.dbf
The file contains 11 records.
The file was last updated on Friday, 11/07/86
Each record contains 86 characters
The database contains the following fields:
Field #1 DATE          DATE
Field #2 CAT           NUMERIC
Field #3 PAYTO         CHARACTER
Field #4 ITEM          CHARACTER
Field #5 AMOUNT        NUMERIC
Field #6 COMMENTS      MEMO
Field #7 MONTH         CHARACTER
Field #8 DEDUCT        LOGICAL
```

The DO CASE structure correctly substitutes the word for the letters in the display.

CALCULATING DISK SPACE

Now that you have assembled all these data about the file, you can also perform some calculations. Suppose you wanted to display an estimate of the number of additional records that could be added to the data base file. This would require you to use two of the values that are derived from functions: DISKSPACE() and RECSIZE().

By dividing the free disk space by the record size, you can get a rough estimate of the number of records that could be added. Any additional files stored on the disk, whether they are related to *dBASE III Plus* (e.g., index files), or unrelated (e.g., DOS batch files), will take up space that could be used by *dBASE III Plus* for data storage.

Load the program into the editor by entering

MODIFY COMMAND sysstat < return >

Below is the bottom portion of the program. Add the commands shown in bold.

```
ENDDO
empty=LTRIM(STR(DISKSPACE()/RECSIZE(),9))
@ fieldnum+10,0 SAY "You have room to add approximately ";
+empty+" records."
SET TALK ON
RETURN
```

Save the program by entering

[CTRL/End]

Execute the program by entering

DO sysstat < return >

dBASE III Plus will display

```
This computer is running dBASE III PLUS  version 1.0
Operating under DOS 3.20
There are 17711104 bytes free on this disk

The current database file is C:expenses.dbf
The file contains 11 records.
The file was last updated on Friday, 11/07/86
Each record contains 86 characters
The database contains the following fields:
Field #1 DATE                DATE
Field #2 CAT                 NUMERIC
Field #3 PAYTO               CHARACTER
Field #4 ITEM                CHARACTER
Field #5 AMOUNT              NUMERIC
Field #6 COMMENTS            MEMO
Field #7 MONTH               CHARACTER
Field #8 DEDUCT              LOGICAL

You have room to add approximately 205943 records.
```

The program calculates that another 205,943 records could be added to the file. Note that the figure displayed on your computer will be different from the one shown in this illustration.

MACRO SUBSTITUTION

So far you have created a program that demonstrates the systems functions available in *dBASE III Plus*. However, there is one severe limitation. The program is specifically tied to the EXPENSES file. It would be better if the program were a general program that could be used to analyze any data base file on the disk. The key would be to replace the USE EXPENSES command with a structure that would allow the user to enter the name of the file to use interactively.

At first, the problem may not seem much different from the other interactive tasks you have learned about. But the problem is a bit more complex. To find out what that complexity consists of, create a simple program that opens a data base file interactively, and name it OPENFILE:

MODIFY COMMAND openfile < return >

Begin with the usual commands. Enter

CLEAR
SET TALK OFF

Now enter a command that allows users to enter the name of the file that they want to open. Enter

ACCEPT "Enter the file to open " TO filename

Once the filename has been entered, it can be used to open the file. Enter

USE filename

Save the program by entering

[CTRL/End]

Execute the program by entering

DO openfile <return>

Enter the name of the file you want to open:

expenses <return>

dBASE III Plus will display

```
Enter the file to open expenses
File does not exist.
           ?
USE filename
Called from — C:openfile.prg
Cancel, Ignore or Suspend (C, I or S)
```

What happened? The display indicates that the USE filename command caused the error. Naturally, the command USE filename will not execute correctly because *dBASE III Plus* cannot find a file with that name.

What is more important, the concept of the program failed. *dBASE III Plus* did not treat filename as a variable. Rather, it treated filename as a literal (i.e., the actual name of the file rather than a symbol for the filename entered by the user). Cancel the program by entering

c

Why didn't *dBASE III Plus* make the substitution and how can this problem be resolved?

The problem is caused by the nature of some *dBASE III Plus* commands that work perfectly well in the COMMAND mode but exhibit certain limitations when used in the PROGRAMMING mode. For example, *dBASE III Plus* expects that the USE command is always followed by the actual name of the file you want to open. This defeats your purpose. What you want to create is a USE command that will respond to the entry made by a user while an interactive program is running.

> The same is true of all the dBASE III Plus *commands that deal with files such as IN-DEX, SET INDEX, and the like. The technique illustrated in this section applies to all* dBASE III Plus *file-oriented commands.*

This can be done by the use of a special technique called *macro substitution*. If you have worked with programs such as *Lotus 1-2-3*, you may have encountered the term *macro.* Generally speaking, macro refers to large commands created out of small commands.

The term *macro* is applied in many ways in computer languages and applications. *dBASE III Plus* uses the term *macro substitution* to indicate a special technique for overcoming limitations in the *dBASE III Plus* language. Macro substitution is used to force *dBASE III Plus* to make a symbolic substitution into a command that normally responds only to a literal command.

To begin to understand this difficult concept, some commands will be entered at the DOT PROMPT that will illustrate what macro substitution does. The first command will store the text string EXPENSES to a memory variable called filename. Enter

filename="expenses" **<return>**

Now try to use the variable name filename with the USE command. Enter

USE filename **<return>**

dBASE III Plus takes the command literally and attempts to open the file FILENAME. As before, no file with that name exists, and the command creates an error. Enter

<return>

However, in the macro substitution technique, the & (ampersand) character is used to tell *dBASE III Plus* to treat the variable differently. Enter

USE &filename **<return>**

This time, no error message is displayed because the command was correct. The status line shows that EXPENSES has been opened. Adding the & solved the problem, but the deeper and more difficult question is why?

When *dBASE III Plus* encounters the & character in a command line, it treats the word that follows as a variable and substitutes into the command line the text stored under that variable name in the memory. The effect is that the command is read by *dBASE III Plus* as if you had typed in the command that way to begin with.

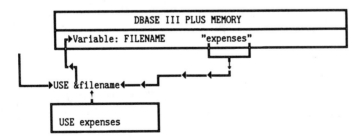

Now you can apply this technique to the PROGRAMMING mode and create a program that will open a file interactively. Create a program called SELCFILE (select file). Enter

MODIFY COMMAND selcfile **<return>**

Begin the file with the usual commands. Enter

```
SET TALK OFF
CLEAR
```

In this program you will use a formatted screen display for the interactive portion. Begin by initializing a text variable with eight spaces. Enter

```
filename=SPACE(8)
```

Next display the prompt and read the input area. Enter

```
@ 10,10 SAY "Enter file name " GET filename
READ
```

TESTING FOR A FILE

Because you are allowing users to enter the name of the file, you run the risk that they may enter a name that does not exist. *dBASE III Plus* provides a function that can test for the existence of a file and thereby avoid an error that would stop your program from running. The function is FILE(). FILE() returns a logical value, true or false, depending on the existence of the specified file. The function requires a text variable or text literal. The FILE() function tests for the entire file, including the extension name.

> A text literal refers to text enclosed in quotation marks. Example: FILE
> ("expenses.dbf").

The next command tests for the existence of the file. The literal characters .DBF are added to the filename so that the user doesn't have to enter them. Enter

```
IF FILE(filename+".dbf")
```

If the condition is true, you can use macro substitution to open the file. Once the file is open, you can run the SYSSTAT program to display data about the file. Enter

```
USE &filename
DO sysstat
```

Next enter the commands to use if the file is not found on the disk. Enter

```
ELSE
    @ 11,10 SAY "File Does Not Exist"
ENDIF
SET TALK ON
RETURN
```

The entire program should look like this:

```
CLEAR
SET TALK OFF
filename=SPACE(8)
@ 10,10 SAY "Enter file name " GET filename
READ
IF FILE(filename+".dbf")
    USE &filename
    DO sysstat
ELSE
    @ 11,10 SAY "File Does Not Exist"
ENDIF
RETURN
```

Save the program by entering

[CTRL/End]

Before you can execute this file, you need to make one change in the SYSSTAT program, which is to remove the USE EXPENSES command from that program. If it were left in the SYSSTAT, it would defeat your purpose in opening another file with macro substitution. Enter

MODIFY COMMAND sysstat <return>

Delete the line USE EXPENSES and save the revised file by entering

[CTRL/End]

Execute the program by entering

DO selcfile <return>

Enter the name of the file:

category

dBASE III Plus will display

```
This computer is running dBASE III PLUS  version 1.0
Operating under DOS 3.20
There are 17704960 bytes free on this disk

The current database file is C:category.dbf
The file contains 5 records.
The file was last updated on Friday  10/31/'06
Each record contains 30 characters
The database contains the following fields:
Field #1 CAT                    NUMERIC
Field #2 NAME                   CHARACTER
Field #3 DEDUCT                 LOGICAL

You have room to add approximately 553280 records.→
```

Run this program several times and test it by entering a nonexistent data base filename.

PROCEDURE FILES

In the last several chapters you have seen how program files can be used as subroutines of other program files. The concept can be extended several layers. For example, a menu program can call a subroutine. Then that subroutine can call another program as a subroutine.

This was the case with the FIRSTMNU program. Option 4 called the PRTCATS program. The PRTCATS program called the CATS program

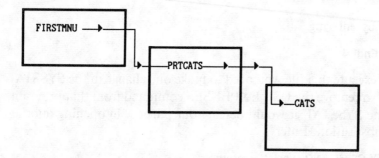

As each subroutine is called, *dBASE III Plus* tells the operating system of the computer to open another file stored on the disk so that *dBASE III Plus* can read the commands. The more levels of subroutines you call, the more files DOS is required to open. The reason this is important is that current versions of DOS have a very specific limit on the number of files that can be open at one time. The limit is 20 files.

> When you boot your computer, DOS does not automatically allow the maximum number of files. To get DOS to accept 20 open files at one time, you must set the DOS FILES command to 20. This is done by creating a text file called CONFIG. SYS and placing the file in the root directory of the disk from which the computer will be booted. The text file should contain the command FILES = 20. For more information about this type of systems operation, refer to my book entitled Getting the Most from Utilities on the IBM PC *(Bowie, MD: Brady, 1987)*.

When you count the number of open files, remember that DOS counts all files, not just data base or *dBASE III Plus* program files. For example, the *dBASE III Plus* program itself counts as several files. Each data base file, index, format, program, or other files used counts as a file.

You can see that running an application can quickly lead to a situation where too many files will be required to be open at one time.

dBASE III Plus provides a solution to the problem that has the additional benefit of increasing the speed at which the entire program will execute. The solution is called a *procedure file*. A procedure file is simply a large program file that contains the contents of several programs. Each program is marked off by a PROCEDURE command so that *dBASE III Plus* can tell one group of related commands from another.

When you want to execute the programs, before you enter the DO command, load the entire procedure file into the memory of the computer. The result is that all the commands for all the programs stored in the procedure file are available to *dBASE III Plus*, but DOS counts only one file as being open.

```
Procedure File

Procedure FIRSTMNU
      commands....


Procedure PRTCATS
      commands....

Procedure CATS
      commands.......

Procedure AGE
      commands......
```

Procedure files also help speed up the operation of the program because *dBASE III Plus* loads as many commands as possible into the memory when the procedure file is opened. Also, *dBASE III Plus* does not have to spend time opening and closing program files each time they are called during the run of the program. This saves a lot of time when you are working from menus that call other programs.

To see how a procedure file operates, create a procedure file called TESTPRO (test procedure) by entering

MODIFY COMMAND testpro

A procedure file is created in the same way as an ordinary program. Begin by entering a procedure statement to identify the first program in the procedure file. Enter

PROCEDURE firstmnu

Instead of typing the commands, use the READFILE command available in the *dBASE III Plus* editor. Enter

[CTRL/k]
r
firstmnu.prg < return >

The commands from FIRSTMNU are loaded into the active file. Move the cursor to the bottom of the file. You are now ready to load the next procedure. Enter

PROCEDURE tax

Load the commands from TAX by entering

> **[CTRL/k]**
> **r**
> **tax.prg < return >**

Repeat the process until you have created procedures for the following files:

Program name   **Procedure name**
RANGE.PRG   RANGE
AGE.PRG   AGE
PRTCATS.PRG   PRTCATS
CATS.PRG   CATS

> *It is not strictly necessary to give the procedure the same name as the program file that you copy. The name chosen for the procedure should be the name used in any DO command that calls that sequence of commands. You might decide to change the name of a routine when it is copied into the procedure file. However, make sure that any corresponding DO commands use the new name.*

When all the files have been combined, save the program by entering

> **[CTRL/End]**

> *The size of a procedure file is limited by the size of the file that the dBASE III Plus editor can handle (4096). You can construct larger procedure files by using a different editor that can handle larger files. For more information on editors and word processors that can be used to prepare program and procedure files, see Chapter 20.*

To execute the programs in the procedure file, you must first load the procedure file into the memory of the computer. This is done with a special command called SET PROCEDURE TO. Enter

> **SET PROCEDURE TO testpro < return >**

The programs have now been loaded and can be executed directly from memory without having to open any additional program files.

Execute the FIRSTMNU program by entering

> **DO firstmnu < return >**

The program runs as it usually does. The only difference is that the individual program modules are not loaded; instead, all the program files are called from the one procedure file.

> *The procedure file cuts down the number of program files opened. It does not affect other types of files such as data base files, index files, format files, and so on that may be opened during the execution of the programs stored in the procedure file. If you attempt to open too many data base files with too many index files, you can still run into a problem with DOS. The procedure file simply eliminates the need to open multiple program files when you are using subroutines in your program.*

The creation of a procedure file is usually the last step in the process of program creation. The individual programs are usually constructed and tested before they are finally combined into a finished product, the procedure file.

In addition, keep in mind that a procedure file can still call a subroutine that is stored on the disk but has not been included in the procedure file.

If a DO command in the procedure file calls a program that exists both in the procedure file and also as a separate disk file, *dBASE III Plus* will always use the procedure and ignore the disk file. If you want to correct a procedure file, you must edit the procedure file, not the original program file from which it was copied.

Test the menu by trying some of the options. When you have finished testing, exit the menu program.

To close the procedure file, enter

SET PROCEDURE TO < return >

All DO commands will now search for disk files to execute.

dBASE III Plus allows only one procedure file to open at a time.

SUMMARY

In this chapter you learned *dBASE III Plus* allows your programs to gather and analyze information concerning the program, the files, and the fields in the *dBASE III Plus* system.

Those functions are as follows:

DISKSPACE(). Returns a numeric value equal to the amount of bytes free on the default disk.

FILE(). Returns a logical value signifying whether the specified file is found on the disk.

RECCOUNT(). Returns a numeric value equal to the number of records in the selected file.

RESIZE(). Returns a numeric value equal to the number of bytes in each record of the selected file.

TYPE(). Returns a single character corresponding to the data type of a specified variable, field, or expression. If the specified argument cannot be evaluated, the character U is assigned to the function.

DBF(). Returns a character string equal to the filename and extension of the selected data base file.

FIELD(n) Returns a character string equal to the name of the field as indicated by the argument. The argument is numbered between 1 and 128 corresponding to the field's position in the file structure. If no field of that number exists in the selected data base file, the value of the function is a null, "".

OS(). Returns a character string equal to the version of the operating system running in the computer.

VERSION(). Returns a character string equal to the name of the version of *dBASE III Plus* running in the computer.

Macro Substitution

dBASE III Plus provides a means of forcing a symbolic substitution in a command where normally only a literal argument would be accepted. The ampersand (&) is used to indicate that the contents of the variable name following the & should be placed in the command as a keystroke macro. This allows you to create programs that use interactive dialog to select files to open that would not be possible without macro substitution.

Procedure Files

dBASE III Plus allows you to create large program files called *procedure files* that contain a series of subroutines. Procedure files allow you to load a program with a large number of subroutines without having DOS keep too many program files open when routines are nested. Procedure files also increase the speed at which *dBASE III Plus* reads the subroutines and executes the commands.

SYSTEMS DESIGN

The previous three chapters introduced you to the basic concepts required to produce programs that can be of use to the average business. In those chapters you learned the basic skills and tools needed to construct a system of programs that can be used to accomplish large-scale data base management tasks.

In the ensuing chapters you will learn how to put those tools to work on practical routines. The routines that you will learn to build are the basic routines needed to carry out almost any serious application.

Although some tasks may require specialized modules, almost every system will require at least one version of the following types of programs:

1. **Entry routines.** The entry routine is the most basic part of any data base system. It is used to enter information into the data base file.

   Entry routines involve the creation of formatted screen displays, verification of data, setting of default values, performance of calculations, and maintenance of necessary indexes.

2. **Retrieval/edit routines.** These routines are different from the entry routines because they raise the problem of locating data after they have been entered into the data base file.

   Retrieval is a good deal more complicated than simple entry because humans often forget how the data were entered. The key to retrieval routines is that they should offer the user as much flexibility as possible in finding information stored in the files.

3. **Reports and forms.** At some point it will be necessary to generate printed material based on the data in the files. The printing can take the form of column reports, single-page printing, or printing checks, invoices, or other business forms, some of which are preprinted and need only data filled in.

From this point on, the goal of the book is to pull together all the elements of *dBASE III Plus* that you have learned so far into routines that can be used with almost any application. In this chapter you will begin by working on the entry routines.

ENTERING DATA

The data entry routine is at the heart of any *dBASE III Plus* application. It is usually the first routine you write in any program and it is usually the first one that the user will come in contact with.

The entry routine is the simplest of the three major types of systems routines. Since you are always appending data to existing files, you can draw certain assumptions that make programming simpler than the routines that allow the user to revise existing records.

The assumption is that you have already created a format file called EXPENSES.FMT when you worked through Chapter 9. The file should contain the following commands:

```
@ 1,20 SAY "Expenses Entry Screen"
@ 3,0 SAY "Date: "+DTOC(DATE())
@ 3,60 SAY "Record Number "+STR(RECNO(),5)
@ 5,30 SAY "Enter the date: " GET date PICTURE "@E"
@ 6,30 SAY "Enter the payee:" GET payto PICTURE "@!"
@ 8,30 SAY "Enter the amount:" GET amount PICTURE "@B"
@ 11,0 SAY "Item Description:" GET item PICTURE "@S8!"
@ 15,0 SAY "Enter Y if the item is tax deductible " GET deduct PICTURE "Y"
@ 20,0 SAY "Enter Budget Category Number" GET cat PICTURE "9,999"
```

If you do not have this file, use MODIFY COMMAND to create it and enter the above commands.

The format file will be an integral part of the entry routine. Begin the creation of the routine by entering

MODIFY COMMAND expenter < return >

dBASE III Plus allows you to use any valid DOS filename for any of its files. This freedom is nice but it can be a two-edged sword. You will find that you can quickly get lost in a maze of filenames. One way to keep track of which files perform what tasks is to use a consistent coding system. For example, all the programs that specifically work with the data in the EXPENSES file might begin with EXP. In that case, EXP-ENTER (expenses entry) would be the entry routine for the EXPENSES file. EXP-EDIT (expenses edit) would be the editing routine for the EXPENSES file. One benefit of this type of coding is that you can take advantage of DOS wild card commands to call all the files that begin with EXP to another disk (e.g., COPY EXP*.* A:).

ADVANCED HOUSEKEEPING

Up to this point you have begun each program by clearing the screen and setting the talk off. That is a good start, but when you begin to construct a more complete application, you will want to take further control of the screen display.

Two additional SET commands should be used to place complete control of the screen display in the hands of the programmer:

1. **SET STATUS.** Setting the STATUS OFF will turn off the *dBASE III Plus* status line display. The status line is helpful in the COMMAND and ASSIST modes, but in a PROGRAMMING mode it may seem confusing to the user.

2. **SET SCOREBOARD.** The scoreboard is the area at the top of the screen, line 0, that *dBASE III Plus* uses to display the designations Ins and Caps when the status line is turned off. If you want to see these messages, leave the scoreboard in the default setting ON. In these examples, you will suppress the scoreboard display by turning the SET off.

Enter

```
CLEAR
SET TALK OFF
SET STATUS OFF
SET SCOREBOARD OFF
```

The next section of the program does not have any direct functional purpose in the flow of the program. Its purpose is related to the concepts discussed in Chapter 13 about interactive programs and user interface considerations.

The next two lines in the program are designed to confirm to the user that data entry has been selected. Visual confirmation has no functional purpose, but it does make the program easier for users to follow. When they enter a menu option, confirming that choice helps them feel more secure that they have actually entered the command they thought they did.

> It might be nice to allow users to escape from the option if they selected data entry by mistake. You will learn how to do this later. For now, the message will have to do.

Look at the two lines below. The first line is a variation on the @ SAY command, with which you are already familiar. The command uses the @ portion, but there is no SAY. The purpose of this command has to do with cursor location. Keep in mind that the WAIT command is an unformatted output command. That means that WAIT will display its message at the next available line on the screen. If you have just cleared the screen, that line would be line 0, at the top of the screen.

If you wanted to display the message in the middle of the screen, where it is easier for the user to follow since most people tend to focus on the center of the screen, position the cursor before you use WAIT. The @ 11,0 command places the cursor at line 11. The WAIT command uses the next available line, line 12, to display its message. Instead of using the default WAIT message (Press any key to continue), a text literal was used to make a substitute message. Enter

```
@ 11,0
WAIT "Press any Key to begin entering new records."
```

You are now ready to go on to the substantive portion of the program. The first task is to open the data base file to which you are going to add records. In addition, you should open any index files that you want updated with the new entries. Remember that if an index file is open when records are added or changed, *dBASE III Plus* automatically updates the index files. *dBASE III Plus* allows up to seven index files to be open at one time.

> Even though dBASE III Plus *allows seven index files for each data base file you have open, it is possible that you may exceed the DOS limit of 20 files open and cause a systems error.*

In this case four index files have been selected for updating. Enter

```
USE expenses INDEX catorder,amtorder,dateord,payorder
```

The next step is to store the number of records in the file to a memory variable. This is done so that at the end of the entry, you can tell the user how many records were entered in this session. Enter

```
begin=RECCOUNT()
```

The next task is to establish a loop that will allow users to enter as many records as desired. Each trip through the loop allows the entry of a single record. Users will then be asked if they wish to enter another record. Entering yes will continue the loop, while entering no will terminate it.

To accomplish this you can create a variable called expenter to control the loop. The use of the name "expenter" is again a personal preference. The idea is that if the variable that controls the main action of the program has the same name as the program, it is easier to remember what that variable is used for.

In this program the variable is initialized as a logical value, .T. Enter

```
expenter=.T.
DO WHILE expenter
```

Now that you have begun a loop, clear the screen of the previous message. Enter

```
CLEAR
```

The next command is a variation on the APPEND command. Because you want to maintain control of the program, you do not want users to enter the APPEND mode, which allows random movement within the file. The trick is to use the AP-PEND BLANK command. This command adds a new record to the end of the data base file without displaying the full screen entry mode associated with the APPEND command.

The effect is that a blank record is added to the end of the file and the pointer is positioned to that record. You can then use your format file to display the data in the record (which is entirely blank) and allow users to edit the blank fields. The effect is exactly the same as the APPEND mode except that the program maintains control of movement within the file. The user cannot flip backward to previous records but can work only with the record displayed.

At first this may seem to be a disadvantage. The idea is that you as the programmer should control the options that the user has for movement between records. When you control this process you are part of your program; thus you can make sure that any behind-the-scenes tasks such as calculation or adjustments are made correctly. When users can flip back and forth, your program may lose track of where the file pointer is located. Enter

APPEND BLANK

Now that the blank record has been added, you can display the screen format by using the EXPENSES format file and a READ command. Enter

SET FORMAT TO expenses
READ

Users now can enter data into the blank record. When the last field has been exited, the program will continue execution. The next step is to close the format file. This places the screen display back into the hands of the program.

> If a format file is left open, @ SAY commands issued from the rest of the program are not displayed on the screen. In order to add new information to the screen, you must close the format file first. Doing so does not erase the data from the screen. It merely allows you to add messages and data that are not part of the format file.

Enter

CLOSE FORMAT

The next task allows users to decide either to continue the loop (i.e., add more records) or to stop the loop (i.e., terminate the entry of records). This is done by displaying a message that confirms that the record on the screen has been recorded and another message that asks if the user wants to continue. The expenter variable is displayed and the user can enter Y or N in response to the prompt. Enter

@ 23,0 SAY "*** RECORD ENTERED ***"
@ 24,0 SAY "Enter another? (Y/N)" GET expenter
READ

The ENDDO command should follow the entry because that is the time when the loop should be reevaluated. Enter

ENDDO

If the entry is Y, the loop recycles to the top and allows the entry of another record. If the entry is N, then the program should proceed to close the files and store the entered data.

As part of the user interface, it is helpful to confirm the number of records that have been entered. This can be done by subtracting the current number of records (RECCOUNT()) from the value stored in the variable begin, which was the REC-COUNT() at the beginning of the program. The WAIT command is used to pause the display so that the user can read the message. Enter

```
CLEAR
@ 11,0 SAY "You have added "+LTRIM(STR(RECCOUNT()−begin,10));
+" records."
WAIT "Press any key to exit entry program"
```

The last part of the program is again housekeeping. This means that you should close any open files and return the sets back to their *dBASE III Plus* values. Enter

```
CLOSE DATABASE
SET TALK ON
SET STATUS ON
SET SCOREBOARD ON
RETURN
```

The entire program should look like this:

```
CLEAR
SET TALK OFF
SET STATUS OFF
SET SCOREBOARD OFF
@ 11,0
WAIT "Press any Key to begin entering new records."
USE expenses INDEX catorder,amtorder,dateord,payorder
begin=RECCOUNT()
expenter=.T.
DO WHILE expenter
    CLEAR
    APPEND BLANK
    SET FORMAT TO expenses
    READ
    CLOSE FORMAT
    @ 23,0 SAY "*** RECORD ENTERED ***"
    @ 24,0 SAY "Enter another? (Y/N)" GET expenter
    READ
ENDDO
CLEAR
@ 11,0 SAY "You have added "+LTRIM(STR(RECCOUNT()−begin,10))+" records."
WAIT "Press any key to exit entry program"
CLOSE DATABASE
SET TALK ON
SET STATUS ON
SET SCOREBOARD ON
RETURN
```

Save the program by entering

[CTRL/End]

Execute the program by entering

DO expenter < return >

The screen displays the first message.

```
Press any Key to begin entering new records.
```

Enter

< return >

The entry screen is displayed.

```
                    Expenses Entry Screen

Date: 11/08/86                                    Record Number    12

                        Enter the date:    /  /
                        Enter the payee:

                        Enter the amount: .


Item Description:


Enter Y if the item is tax deductible  Y



Enter Budget Category Number
```

Enter the following data into the screen.

```
Date: 01/01/80                                    Record Number    12

                        Enter the date:  03/14/86
                        Enter the payee: COMPUTER SUPPLY CO

                        Enter the amount: 75.50


Item Description: DISKS


Enter Y if the item is tax deductible  N



Enter Budget Category Number 140



Enter Budget Category Number    140
```

Following the last entry, the program displays a message at the bottom of the screen.

```
*** RECORD ENTERED ***
Enter Another (Y/N) T
```

In this case, you can terminate the entry by entering

    n

The program displays the following message, indicating that one record has been added to the data base file:

```
You have added 1 records.
Press any key to exit entry program
```

To complete the program, enter

    <return>

DOUBLE CHECKING

Now that you have created a basic entry program, it is time to begin looking at specific types of problems that arise during entry routines. The first problem described is called *double checking*. For example, suppose that you finish entering a screen full of data and discover that you have made a mistake. It would be helpful if the program allowed you to make corrections before the next record is entered.

To create this double check you must modify the EXPENTER program. Enter

    MODIFY COMMAND expenter <return>

The key to the double check routine is to add another loop, inside the main loop. The loop should be placed at the point in the program that follows the entry of the data.

Instead of going on to the next record, users should be prompted to confirm whether the data entered into that screen is correct. If yes, then go on to the next record. If no, the screen should be redisplayed and users allowed to make any changes they wish. Since it is possible to make several mistakes, users should be able to reedit the screen as many times as necessary.

To begin the modification of the program, move the cursor to the line following the CLOSE FORMAT command.

The first command to add creates a variable called "check." Once again, the variable is assigned a logical value of true because the question that will be displayed will be one that can be answered yes or no. Enter

check=.T.

The next step is to display a prompt at the bottom of the screen that asks users to confirm that the data entered are correct. Enter

```
@ 23,0 SAY "Is the information entered correct? (Y/N)" GET check
READ
```

This allows users to enter a true or false value into the check variable. If the value of check is false, a mistake has been found in the data entered on the screen and the information must be edited before storing the record.

To allow this sequence, a loop needs to be started. The loop will be controlled by the value in check but in a negative way. The .NOT. logical connective is used to test for a false value in check. This means that as long as check is false (the data are not correct), users can edit the screen. Enter

```
DO WHILE .NOT. check
```

Once in the loop, the commands repeat the logic used to enter the data in the first place. The format screen is opened and displayed. The READ command activates the input areas. Following the entry the format is closed. Enter

```
SET FORMAT TO expenses
READ
CLOSE FORMAT
```

You will need to ask the double check question again to allow users to repeat the double check process as many times as necessary. Enter

```
check=.T.
@ 23,0 SAY "Is the information entered correct? (Y/N)" GET check
READ
ENDDO double check routine
```

The previous ENDDO controls the double check loop. Because you are using line 23 to display the double check question, you need to clear off just that line in order to display the next message on that line. The @ 23,0 command is the same command you used at the beginning of the program to place the cursor on a certain line of the display. In addition to positioning the cursor, the @ command without a SAY will erase all the characters on the specified line to the right of the cursor position. This means that @ 23,0 will erase any data on line 23. Enter

```
@ 23,0
```

The program should now look like this:

```
CLEAR
SET TALK OFF
SET STATUS OFF
SET SCOREBOARD OFF
@ 11,0
WAIT "Press any Key to begin entering new records."
```

```
 USE expenses INDEX catorder,amtorder,dateord,payorder
 begin=RECCOUNT()
 expenter=.T.
→DO WHILE expenter─────────────────────────────────────────────────┐
    CLEAR                                                            │
    APPEND BLANK                                                     │
    SET FORMAT TO expenses                                          │
    READ                                                             │
    CLOSE FORMAT                                                     │
    check=.T.                                                        │
    @ 23,0 SAY "Is the information entered correct? (Y/N)" GET check │
    READ                                                             │
      →DO WHILE .NOT. check───────────────────────────────────────┐ │
          SET FORMAT TO expenses                                   │ │
          READ                                                     │ │
          CLOSE FORMAT                                             │ │
          check=.T.                                                │ │
          @ 23,0 SAY "Is the information entered correct? (Y/N)" GET check │ │
          READ                                                     │ │
      ─ENDDO double check routine◄──────────────────────────────┘ │
    @ 23,0                                                          │
    @ 23,0 SAY "*** RECORD ENTERED ***"                            │
    @ 24,0 SAY "Enter another? (Y/N)" GET expenter                 │
    READ                                                            │
─ENDDO expenter◄───────────────────────────────────────────────────┘
 CLEAR
 @ 11,0 SAY "You have added "+LTRIM(STR(RECCOUNT()-begin,10))+" records."
 WAIT "Press any key to exit entry program"
 CLOSE DATABASE
 SET TALK ON
 SET STATUS ON
 SET SCOREBOARD ON
 RETURN
```

This program uses two DO WHILE loops, one nested inside the other. The arrows show that the logic of the inner loop does not cross the boundaries of the outer loop. This is very important when constructing programs. The ENDDO for the inner loop must come before the ENDDO for the outer loop. If you find that the lines of your program's logic cross, you are doing something wrong.

Save the program by entering

[CTRL/End]

Execute the program by entering

DO expenter <return>

Begin the entry by entering

<return>

Fill in the record on the screen as shown below:

```
               Expenses Entry Screen
Date: 11/07/86                                    Record Number    13

                   Enter the date:   03/21/86
                   Enter the payee:  PRICE CLUB

                   Enter the amount:  45.67

Item Description: PAPER


Enter Y if the item is tax deductible  N

Enter Budget Category Number   140
```

When the record is complete, the bottom of the screen will display

```
Is the information entered correct? (Y/N) T
```

To reedit the display, enter

n

The screen will clear and the data will be redisplayed. The cursor will be positioned in the first field on the display. Move through the display and change the amount to 42.50.

Use the < return > key to move through the rest of the field until the "Is the information entered correct?" prompt is displayed again. Since the data are now correct, accept the record by entering

y

The program now asks if you want to enter more records. In this case you can exit the program by entering

n

The message tells you that one record has been entered. Complete the program by entering

< return >

TRUE OR YES

One minor point to address is that users are being prompted to enter Y or N, but the logical fields display default values of T for true, rather than Y for yes. The trick is to attach a PICTURE clause following the GET commands that display the logical variables. If the template contains a Y, then *dBASE III Plus* will show a Y instead of a T in the input area. Enter

MODIFY COMMAND expenter < return >

Add the picture clauses where indicated in bold.

```
CLEAR
SET TALK OFF
SET STATUS OFF
SET SCOREBOARD OFF
@ 11,0
WAIT "Press any Key to begin entering new records."
USE expenses INDEX catorder,amtorder,dateord,payorder
begin=RECCOUNT()
expenter=.T.
DO WHILE expenter
   CLEAR
   APPEND BLANK
```

```
       SET FORMAT TO expenses
       READ
       CLOSE FORMAT
       check=.T.
       @ 23,0 SAY "Is the information entered correct? (Y/N)" GET check PICTURE "Y"
       READ
          DO WHILE .NOT. check
             SET FORMAT TO expenses
             READ
             CLOSE FORMAT
             check=.T.
             @ 23,0 SAY "Is the information entered correct? (Y/N)" GET check PICTURE "Y"
             READ
          ENDDO double check routine
       @ 23,0
       @ 23,0 SAY "*** RECORD ENTERED ***"
       @ 24,0 SAY "Enter another? (Y/N)" GET expenter PICTURE "Y"
       READ
ENDDO expenter
CLEAR
@ 11,0 SAY "You have added "+LTRIM(STR(RECCOUNT()-begin,10))+" records."
WAIT "Press any key to exit entry program"
CLOSE DATABASE
SET TALK ON
SET STATUS ON
SET SCOREBOARD ON
RETURN
```

Save the program by entering

> **[CTRL/End]**

Execute the program by entering

> **DO expenter** < return >
> < return >

Add the following record:

DATE	03/25/86
PAYTO	**DAK PRODUCTS**
AMOUNT	**175.00**
ITEM	**ANSWERING MACHINE**
DEDUCT	**Y**
CAT	**110**

The prompt displayed a Y rather than a T as the default, making the display more consistent. It is a small point, but it illustrates the degree of control *dBASE III Plus* offers you over the screen display when programming.

Exit the program after you have entered this record.

MEMO FIELDS

At this point the EXPENSES display screen does not allow you to enter any data into the MEMO field in the EXPENSES data base file. MEMO fields present a problem for formatted screen displays. To understand what the problem is, you can simulate manually what an input area would look like for the MEMO field COMMENTS. Enter

> **USE expenses**
> **@ 10,10 GET comments** < return >

The input area appears on the screen and the word "memo" is displayed inside the area to indicate that this is a MEMO field. Activate the input area by entering

> **READ** < return >

The cursor is now in the memo area. To make an entry into a MEMO field, use the **[CTRL/Home]** command. Enter

> **[CTRL/Home]**

Instead of allowing you to enter data into the MEMO field, *dBASE III Plus* simply exited the input area and returned the cursor to the DOT PROMPT. Why? The answer is that the @/SAY/GET commands in *dBASE III Plus* do not allow you to enter data into MEMO fields. This is a limitation that is of concern only if you have memo areas in your data base files.

The question is, how can you use a MEMO field in a program when the @/SAY/GET command won't work? The solution lies in the use of the EDIT command. Remember, you don't want to use APPEND because it would allow the user to page up and down in the data base file. The program could not control that movement once the APPEND mode is entered. However, there is a way to use the EDIT mode. The *dBASE III Plus* EDIT mode will accept a scope argument that limits the editing to a single record.

To enter data into a MEMO field, you need to change both the program EXPENTER and the format file EXPENSES. First, change the format file. Enter

> **MODIFY COMMAND expenses.fmt** < return >

Change the file by adding a line for the display of the MEMO field COMMENTS. In addition, you can remove some of the picture clauses added in Chapter 9 as demonstrations. They aren't really needed now. Make the changes indicated below. The new line is shown in bold.

```
@ 1,20 SAY "Expenses Entry Screen"
@ 3,0 SAY "Date: "+DTOC(DATE())
@ 3,60 SAY "Record Number "+STR(RECNO(),5)
@ 5,30 SAY "Enter the date: "GET date < ===== remove PICTURE clause
@ 6,30 SAY "Enter the payee: " GET payto PICTURE "@!"
@ 8,30 SAY "Enter the amount: " GET amount PICTURE "@B"
@ 11,0 SAY "Item Description: " GET item < ===== remove PICTURE clause
@ 13,0 SAY "Comments: " GET comments
```

@ 15,0 SAY "Enter Y if the item is tax deductible " GET deduct PICTURE "Y"
@ 20,0 SAY "Enter Budget Category Number" GET cat < ===== **remove PICTURE**
                                                              clause

Save the program by entering

[CTRL/End]

The next step is to change the program to use the EDIT mode for data entry. Enter

MODIFY COMMAND expenter < return >

Next, using the READ command, replace the command that currently uses the EDIT command to activate the format file. In two places in the program, the READ command is used to activate the entry screen (once for the initial entry and a second time if you choose to double check your entry).

But simply changing READ to EDIT is not enough. EDIT by itself would have the same drawback as using APPEND. Once in the EDIT mode, your program would no longer control the flow of the operation. The user could leaf back and forth in the file and get confused about what is going on.

The solution is to tell *dBASE III Plus* to edit only one specific record, but which one? The record that you want to edit will always be the last record in the file because that is the one you just append as a blank.

How can that idea be expressed in a form that *dBASE III Plus* recognizes? The answer lies in the fact that the number of the last record in the file is the same as the total number of records in the file. For example, when you append record no. 14, that means there are a total of 14 records in the file. In Chapter 14 you learned that *dBASE III Plus* uses a special function, RECCOUNT(), to keep track of the number of records in the file. Look at the following command:

EDIT RECORD RECCOUNT()

The command tells *dBASE III Plus* to edit the record with a record number equal to the total number of records in the file (i.e., the last record entered in the file).

Thus the solution to the problem is to change the READ commands into EDIT RECORD RECCOUNT() commands. Make the changes where indicated in bold in the listing below.

```
CLEAR
SET TALK OFF
SET STATUS OFF
SET SCOREBOARD OFF
@ 11,0
WAIT "Press any Key to begin entering new records."
USE expenses INDEX catorder, amtorder, dateord, payorder
begin=RECCOUNT()
```

```
expenter=.T.
DO WHILE expenter
    CLEAR
    APPEND BLANK
    SET FORMAT TO expenses
        EDIT RECORD RECCOUNT() <========= change command
    CLOSE FORMAT
    check=.T.
    @ 23,0 SAY "Is the information entered correct? (Y/N)" GET check PICTURE "Y"
    READ
        DO WHILE .NOT. check
            SET FORMAT TO expenses
                EDIT RECORD RECCOUNT() <======= change command
            CLOSE FORMAT
            check=.T.
            @ 23,0 SAY "Is the information entered correct? (Y/N) GET check PICTURE "Y"
            READ
        ENDDO double check routine
    @ 23,0
    @ 23,0 SAY "***RECORD ENTERED***"
    @ 24,0 SAY "Enter another? (Y/N)" GET expenter PICTURE "Y"
    READ
ENDDO expenter
CLEAR
@ 11,0 SAY "You have added "+LTRIM(STR(RECCOUNT()-begin,10))+" records."
WAIT "Press any key to exit entry program"
CLOSE DATABASE
SET TALK ON
SET STATUS ON
SET SCOREBOARD ON
RETURN
```

The use of RECORD RECCOUNT() varies from the suggested method shown in the dBASE III Plus manual. The dBASE III Plus manual suggests using EDIT NEXT 1 to solve the problem with MEMO fields on formatted screen displays. This solution is adequate if you do not include a way to double check the data entered. The EDIT NEXT 1 command changes the position of the pointer so that it is possible, if index files are open, that the double check will display a different record than the one that was entered. RECORD RECCOUNT() always positions the pointer to the newest entry in the file.

Save the program by entering

[CTRL/End]

Execute the program by entering

DO expenter <return>

Proceed past the prompt and enter the following data:

DATE   **03/29/86**
PAYTO   **COMPUTER CURRENTS**
AMOUNT **15.00**
ITEM   **SUBSCRIPTION**

When you come to the MEMO field, enter

  [CTRL/Home]

This time, the *dBASE III Plus* editor appears, ready for you to enter a memo. Enter

  This is a biweekly publication.

Save the memo by entering

  [CTRL/End]

Enter the next two fields as follows:

DEDUCT **Y**
CAT   **140**

To test the double check routine, enter the following at the prompt.

  n

dBASE III Plus displays the same record for editing. To accept the data as is, enter

  [CTRL/End]

Enter another record.

  y
  03/29/86
  DAK PRODUCTS < return >
  2.00
  CABLE < return >
  y
  140 < return >

Exit the program by entering

  y
  n
  < return >

CANCELING THE PROGRAM

One of the features included in the EXPENTER program is a screen that confirms that the user has chosen to enter new records. That screen raises a problem, however, because if users realize they don't want to enter records, there really isn't anything that can be done about it. In order to make the message more meaningful, you need to allow users to escape from the routine.

dBASE III Plus offers an interesting command to allow you to exit the program, called ON ESCAPE. This command controls the action that *dBASE III Plus* will take if the <Esc> key is pressed. Normally, when <Esc> is pressed during the execution of a program, *dBASE III Plus* behaves in the same way as if an error had been encountered. *dBASE III Plus* pauses the execution of the program and displays the message ** INTERRUPTED **. You will be asked to CANCEL, SUSPEND, or IGNORE, as you would if an error were encountered.

The ON ESCAPE command specifies some command that should be executed instead of the usual *dBASE III Plus* pause and display. For example, if you want to stop the execution of the program, you could enter a command like this:

ON ESCAPE RETURN

This command tells *dBASE III Plus* to execute a RETURN command if the <Esc> key is pressed, causing the program to terminate smoothly. To set the <Esc> key back to its normal function, use the following command:

ON ESCAPE

Add the command to the EXPENTER program by entering

MODIFY COMMAND expenter <return>

Below is the top portion of the EXPENTER program. Add the lines shown in bold.

```
CLEAR
SET TALK OFF
SET STATUS OFF
SET SCOREBOARD OFF
ON ESCAPE RETURN
@ 11,0 "Press ESCAPE to cancel program" <========== changed
WAIT "Press any other key to begin entering new records." <========= changed
ON ESCAPE
USE expenses INDEX catorder, amtorder, dateord, payorder
begin=RECCOUNT()
expenter=.T.
```

Save the program by entering

[CTRL/End]

Execute the program by entering

DO expenter <return>

Instead of entering the usual < return >, enter

<Esc>

The program is automatically terminated and *dBASE III Plus* returns to the DOT PROMPT. Keep in mind that you exited the program before the SET ESCAPE command could reset the < Esc > key to its normal function. Enter

DISPLAY STATUS < return >

At the bottom of the display you will see On Escape: RETURN. This indicates that the escape key will still execute a RETURN command when pressed. Enter

<Esc>

< Esc > issues a RETURN command. *dBASE III Plus* reacts by telling you that RETURN is not valid unless you are executing a program. Enter

< return >

To set the escape back to it original function, enter

ON ESCAPE < return >

MULTIPLE SCREEN FORMATS

The EXPENTER program shows the use of the format file to display the actual fields used in the data base file. If you look at the program you will see that there is nothing about it that refers to any of the fields in the data base file. This makes it easy to change the screen display format for the program by changing the format file. It also is easier to adapt this program to use with almost any data base file with which you want to work.

In the case of the EXPENSES file, you have only eight fields, but *dBASE III Plus* allows you to create data base files with 128 fields. There may be times when you cannot or do not want to display all the fields to be entered at one time. Placing too many fields on the screen can often make the display harder to read and pay attention to. In situations like these, it makes sense to divide the screen display into a series of smaller panels, each displaying a limited number of fields.

The key to this type of design is to include a READ command in the format file at the place in the file that you want to end each panel. To illustrate how such a multipanel format file would operate, create a new format file called EXP-SPLIT.FMT by entering

MODIFY COMMAND expsplit.fmt < return >

Begin the file by entering a command that will draw a box on the screen display. Enter

@ 5,0 TO 15,79 DOUBLE

Next, enter a series of @/SAY/GET commands similar to the beginning portion of the EXPENSES format file. The title of the screen display indicates that there is a second part, Part B, to the entry screen. Enter

```
@ 6,20 SAY "Expenses Entry Screen Part A"
@ 7,20 SAY "Press [Pg Dn] for Part B"
@ 8,10 SAY "Date: "+DTOC(DATE())
@ 8,60 SAY "Record Number "+LTRIM(STR(RECNO(),5))
@ 10,30 SAY "Enter the date: " GET date
@ 12,30 SAY "Enter the payee:" GET payto PICTURE "@!"
@ 14,30 SAY "Enter the amount:" GET amount
```

Instead of entering the remainder of the fields for display, enter a READ command. This causes the display to be divided into two parts at this point. Enter

READ

Now continue by entering the commands to display Part B of the screen display.

```
@ 5,0 TO 18,79 DOUBLE
@ 6,20 SAY "Expenses Entry Screen Part B"
@ 7,20 SAY "Press [Pg Up] for Part A"
@ 8,10 SAY "Date: "+DTOC(DATE())
@ 8,60 SAY "Record Number "+LTRIM(STR(RECNO(),5))
@ 11,10 SAY "Item Description:" GET item
@ 13,10 SAY "Comments: " GET comments
@ 15,10 SAY "Enter Y if the item is tax deductible " GET deduct PICTURE "Y"
@ 17,10 SAY "Enter Budget Category Number" GET cat
```

The entire format file should look like this:

```
@ 5,0 TO 15,79 DOUBLE
@ 6,20 SAY "Expenses Entry Screen  Part A"
@ 7,20 SAY "  Press [Pg Dn] for Part B"
@ 8,10 SAY "Date: "+DTOC(DATE())
@ 8,60 SAY "Record Number "+LTRIM(STR(RECNO(),5))
@ 10,30 SAY "Enter the date: " GET date
@ 12,30 SAY "Enter the payee:" GET payto PICTURE "@!"
@ 14,30 SAY "Enter the amount:" GET amount
READ
@ 5,0 TO 18,79 DOUBLE
@ 6,20 SAY "Expenses Entry Screen  Part B"
@ 7,20 SAY "  Press [Pg Up] for Part A"
@ 8,10 SAY "Date: "+DTOC(DATE())
@ 8,60 SAY "Record Number "+LTRIM(STR(RECNO(),5))
@ 11,10 SAY "Item Description:" GET item
@ 13,10 SAY "Comments: " GET comments
@ 15,10 SAY "Enter Y if the item is tax deductible " GET deduct PICTURE "Y"
@ 17,10 SAY "Enter Budget Category Number" GET cat
```

Save the program by entering

[CTRL/End]

Exercise 1   Before you can use the new format file with the EXPENTER program, you must make some changes in the EXPENTER program. Try to determine what changes these are. The answer can be found at the end of the chapter.

When you have completed the changes, enter

DO expenter < return >

Move past the initial screen display by entering

< return >

dBASE III Plus will display

```
           Expenses Entry Screen  Part A
             Press [Pg Dn] for Part B
   Date: 11/07/86                            Record Number 17

             Enter the date:   ▓▓/▓▓/▓▓

             Enter the payee:  ▓▓▓▓▓▓▓▓▓▓▓▓▓▓▓▓▓

             Enter the amount: ▓▓▓.▓▓
```

Enter

033086
MICROAMERICA < return >
400.00

dBASE III Plus automatically displays the second screen.

```
           Expenses Entry Screen  Part B
             Press [Pg Up] for Part A
   Date: 11/07/86                            Record Number 17

   Item Description: ▓▓▓▓▓▓▓▓▓▓▓▓▓▓▓▓▓▓▓

   Comments:  memo

   Enter Y if the item is tax deductible  Y

   Enter Budget Category Number ▓▓▓▓▓
```

Enter

MODEM < return >

The cursor is now positioned in the MEMO field. Enter

[CTRL/Home]
[CTRL/End]

The MEMO field operates correctly. Continue the entry:

> **y**
> **120** **<return>**

The program asks if the information is correct. Test the double check routine by entering

> **n**

Part A is displayed. Enter

> **[Pg Dn]**

Part B is displayed. Enter

> **[Pg Dn]**

Once again the program asks if you want to accept the entry. Enter

> **y**

Exit the program by entering

> **n**
> **<return>**

DEFAULT VALUES

Default values refer to values that are entered automatically into the field of new records before entry begins. These default values are of three types:

1. **Constants.** If the default value is a constant, that means that the same value is always inserted in the field each time a new record is entered. For example, you might want to insert the system's date automatically into the DATE field. This assumes that you are entering records that should be dated with the real time that you entered them. For example, the DATE() function would place that date into the field each time a new record was added.

   Constants can even be simple numbers or text strings. What they all have in common is that the same data are placed in each new record. For example, your mailing list file might always default to the same state if you don't do out-of-state business.

   In this example, you will make the date of the expense default to the systems date.

2. **Sequential defaults.** A sequential default refers to the use of a default value to automatically number records in sequence like check or invoice numbers.

You can let the user edit the default value or prohibit the user from changing the sequence number, depending on your needs. Sequential defaults save time and prevent mistakes by automatically numbering the records for you.

In this example, you will create a field for check number and have the program automatically number the checks.

3.   **Ditto defaults.** A ditto default is a variation on the idea of a sequential default. A ditto default carries over the entry made in the same field from the previous record. This type of default makes sense when you are likely to enter a series of records that tend to share some common attribute. For example, you might be entering expenses that all have the same date or budget code.

In this example, you will have the program carry over the last budget code used into each new record.

The key to creating defaults is to use the REPLACE command to place data in the record after it has been appended but before the record is displayed. The following section illustrates the basic techniques required for each of the three kinds of defaults.

Exercise 2   To illustrate the use of sequential defaults, you will need to add a field to the EXPENSES file. The field is used for the check number and should be called "check." The field should be a numeric-type field with a length of four characters and no decimal places. When you have added the field, place the starting check number. For this example, 1125 is the check field of record no. 17. Hints are provided at the end of the chapter.

Exercise 3   Now that you have created a new field, the EXPSPLIT.FMT file needs to be modified to display that field. Add a line to the first part of the display that will show the check number field. Place the input area on line 9. Hints are provided at the end of the chapter if you need them.

Now that you have prepared the way, you are ready to change your program to create the default values. Load the program into the editor by entering

MODIFY COMMAND expenter < return >

Below is the beginning section of the program. What sort of changes need to be made? The answer lies in the fact that the default values for the ditto and sequential type of defaults have to come from the last record in the file. The idea is to find the last record in the EXPENSES data base file. Use the values for check and cat to determine the default values for the new record that will be added. For example, the new check number should be one more than the last check number entered.

The first change takes place following the ON ESCAPE command. It is at this point that you need to locate the last record entered into the EXPENSES file to determine what category and what check numbers were entered into that record.

The first change is that the USE command has had the INDEX clause removed. The reason is that if the index files were active, the last record in the file would be the last record according to the index order. The combination of USE expenses and GO BOTTOM locate the last record.

Then two variables, lastcheck and lastcat are defined. They will carry the value of the cat and check over into the new record. Note the use of program notes indicated by the * and && commands. A program note has no functional purpose and is ignored when *dBASE III Plus* reads the program file. The purpose of program notes is to document what the program is doing and what the commands are used for. This is very important when it comes to revising a program written by someone else, because your only guide to what he or she was doing is the program notes included in the file.

The * allows you to enter a full line note. Anything on a line that begins with an * is ignored by *dBASE III Plus*. You can also add program notes to the end of a command by entering &&. Any text following the && is ignored by *dBASE III Plus* when it reads the command file.

> Most of the programs in this book contain very few program notes. Though this seems to contradict the previous statement about the importance of adding notes to your programs, it does not. First, all the programs are annotated as you enter them by the text that explains each section of code as you enter it. Second, because of space limitations and the large number of program listings in this book, I have decided to include only a minimal number of program notes. But you should feel free to add notations of your own that explain in your own words what the various sections of code are designed to do.
>
> Also keep in mind that although dBASE III Plus does not execute comments or notes, they do take up space in the program file and dBASE III Plus must still read the notes to find the next valid command. This means that there may be some slight slowing of your program if you add a large number of notes. However, the slight degradation in speed is usually more than made up for in the readability of your program.

After all the default values have been gathered, SET INDEX TO opens the index files that will need to be updated. Enter the lines shown in bold.

```
CLEAR
SET TALK OFF
SET STATUS OFF
SET SCOREBOARD OFF
ON ESCAPE RETURN
@ 11,0
WAIT "Press any Key to begin entering new records."
ON ESCAPE
USE expenses
GO BOTTOM
* get default values
lastcheck=lastcheck+1      && starting check number
lastcat=cat      && last category used
SET INDEX TO catorder,amtorder,dateord,payorder
```

The next section of the program contains only one new command, but it is very important. The REPLACE command places the data gathered for the default. Note that the REPLACE command follows the APPEND BLANK. You must first create the record before you can place any data in it.

The DATE field is replaced with the systems date as calculated by the DATE() function. The check number is replaced with the value of the lastcheck variable plus 1, and the CAT field is replaced with the same value as was entered into the last record in the data base file.

One other change must be made. Keep in mind that you have added a new field to the file structure called "check," which is exactly the same name that you used for the variable that controlled the double check routine. Therefore, you will have to make a change to avoid a conflict between the names. This can be done by changing the name of the variable, or by using the M-> alias to indicate the places where check refers to the memory variable.

Enter the lines shown in bold.

```
begin=RECCOUNT()
expenter=.T.
DO WHILE expenter
    CLEAR
    APPEND BLANK
        REPLACE date WITH DATE(),cat WITH lastcat;
        ,check WITH lastcheck+1
    SET FORMAT TO expsplit
    EDIT RECORD RECCOUNT()
    CLOSE FORMAT
    check=.T.
        @ 23,0 SAY "Is the information entered correct? (Y/N)";
        GET M->check PICTURE "Y"
    READ
        DO WHILE .NOT. M->check
        SET FORMAT TO expsplit
        EDIT RECORD RECCOUNT()
        CLOSE FORMAT
        check=.T.
            @ 23,0 SAY "Is the information entered correct? (Y/N)";
            GET M->check PICTURE "Y"
        READ
    ENDDO double check routine
    @ 23,0
    @ 23,0 SAY "*** RECORD ENTERED ***"
    @ 24,0 SAY "Enter another? (Y/N)" GET expenter PICTURE "Y"
READ
```

The final section of the program is concerned with preparing the variables for the next record, if any. The GO RECCOUNT() command is very important, and its use is required by the effect of the EDIT command. Unlike READ, EDIT affects the position of the pointer. After EDIT is used, the pointer is moved to the next record. In the program you want to make sure that the default values are initialized from the data in the last record entered. The GO RECCOUNT() makes sure that the pointer is repositioned to that record before the default values are reinitialized.

Note that the GO (also GOTO) command can accept a numeric value in the form of a number, a variable, or a numeric function like RECCOUNT() or RECNO().

The value of the check is incremented by 1. Note that it is the value in the CHECK field that is incremented, giving you the opportunity to change the check numbering sequence if necessary. The value in the current record's CAT field is placed into lastcat. Enter the commands shown in bold.

```
* prepare defaults
GO RECCOUNT()
lastcheck=check+1
lastcat=cat
ENDDO expenter
CLEAR
@ 11,0 SAY "You have added "+LTRIM(STR(RECCOUNT()-begin,10))+" records."
WAIT "Press any key to exit entry program"
CLOSE DATABASE
SET TALK ON
SET STATUS ON
SET SCOREBOARD ON
RETURN
```

The entire program should look like this:

```
CLEAR
SET TALK OFF
SET STATUS OFF
SET SCOREBOARD OFF
ON ESCAPE RETURN
@ 11,0
WAIT "Press any Key to begin entering new records."
ON ESCAPE
USE expenses
* get default values
GO BOTTOM
lastcheck=check   && starting check number
lastcat=cat       && last category used
SET INDEX TO catorder,amtorder,dateord,payorder
begin=RECCOUNT()
expenter=.T.
DO WHILE expenter
   CLEAR
   APPEND BLANK
   REPLACE date WITH DATE(),cat WITH lastcat,check WITH lastcheck
   SET FORMAT TO expsplit
   EDIT RECORD RECCOUNT()
   CLOSE FORMAT
   check=.T.
   @ 23,0 SAY "Is the information entered correct? (Y/N)" GET M->check PICTURE "Y"
   READ
      DO WHILE .NOT. M->check
         SET FORMAT TO expsplit
         EDIT RECORD RECCOUNT()
         CLOSE FORMAT
         check=.T.
         @ 23,0 SAY "Is the information entered correct? (Y/N)" GET M->check PICTURE "Y"
```

```
      READ
    ENDDO double check routine
  @ 23,Ø
  @ 23,Ø SAY "*** RECORD ENTERED ***"
  @ 24,Ø SAY "Enter another? (Y/N)" GET expenter PICTURE "Y"
  READ
  * prepare defaults
    GO RECCOUNT()
    lastcheck=lastcheck+1
    lastcat=cat
ENDDO expenter
CLEAR
@ 11,Ø SAY "You have added "+LTRIM(STR(RECCOUNT()-begin,1Ø))+" records."
WAIT "Press any key to exit entry program"
CLOSE DATABASE
SET TALK ON
SET STATUS ON
SET SCOREBOARD ON
RETURN
```

Save the program by entering

[CTRL/End]

Execute the program by entering

DO expenter < return >
< return >

The main display screen appears like this:

```
                 Expenses Entry Screen  Part A
                     Press [Pg Dn] for Part B
         Date: 11/Ø7/86                              Record Number 18
                          Enter check #:  1126
                          Enter the date:  11/Ø7/86

                          Enter the payee: ████████████████

                          Enter the amount: ████.██
```

Note that the new check number is automatically entered for you. Also note that the systems date is automatically entered into the DATE field. To accept the check number, enter

< return >

Next, enter the following data:

033086
QUILL < return >
79.95

The screen flips to Part B.

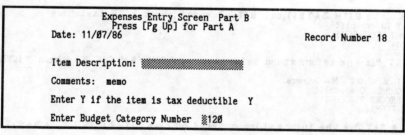

```
                 Expenses Entry Screen  Part B
                     Press [Pg Up] for Part A
         Date: 11/Ø7/86                              Record Number 18

         Item Description: ████████████████████████

         Comments:  memo

         Enter Y if the item is tax deductible  Y

         Enter Budget Category Number  █12Ø
```

The budget category number has automatically been entered, based on the previous record. Enter

> **DISPLAY RACK** < return >
> < return >
> < return >
> **140** < return >

Since these data are correct, continue to the next record by accepting the defaults. This can be done by entering

> < return >
> < return >

The next screen appears.

```
                     Expenses Entry Screen  Part A
                        Press [Pg Dn] for Part B
        Date: 11/07/86                                  Record Number  19
                         Enter check #  :   1127
                         Enter the date:   11/07/86

                         Enter the payee:  ▒▒▒▒▒▒▒▒▒▒▒▒▒▒▒

                         Enter the amount:  ▒▒▒.▒
```

The check number has automatically been incremented to 1127. Enter

> < return >
> **03/30/86**
> **MICROAMERICA** < return >
> **45** < return >

Screen B appears. The category number on that screen is automatically entered as 140. This is the same value used in the previous record, an example of the ditto-type default. Complete the screen by entering

> **PRINTER CABLE** < return >
> < return > **(3 times)**

Exit the program by entering

> **y**
> **n**

The screen confirms that you have entered 2 records. Exit by entering

> < return >

BATCHING/AUDIT TRAILS

Another common variation on the theme of entry program is called *batch entry*. Instead of making entries directly into the master file, you enter all the new records into a separate file with the same structure, called a *batch* file.

The advantage of this type of entry is that the new records can be entered and analyzed or double checked before they are actually combined with the main file. This type of entry is usually found in financial accounting systems. For example, in a double entry bookkeeping system all the new records entered should balance before they are added to the main file. Also, it is a good idea to print a copy of the transaction or records that were entered so that there is a paper record of each computer session. This paper record is called an *audit trail*.

There are also some computer-oriented considerations that make batch entry desirable. One is the problem of blank records. Note that the system you have designed for entry of data appends a blank record before each entry screen is displayed. If the user starts to enter a new record and then decides to quit the program, the blank record on the screen is added to the file. In real life situations, this happens very often. The result is that the file accumulates a number of blank records.

The solution is to delete blank records as they are entered. However, if your data base is large, packing out the deleted records may delay processing considerably each time you need to remove a single blank record.

However, if entry is made into a batch, the blanks can be eliminated when the batch is combined with the main file, eliminating the need to pack the main file.

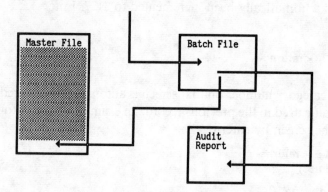

The next section of this chapter shows how batch entry is achieved, how audit trails can be produced, and how blank records can be eliminated.

Because this program is somewhat different from the previous version of the entry program, you will want to give it a different name. Enter

MODIFY COMMAND expbatch <return>

To save time, copy the contents of EXPENTER into this file. Then you will need to make changes only in the code, instead of typing the entire program. Enter

[CTRL/k]
r
expenter.prg <return>

Nothing much will be changed in the new program until after the default values have been stored as memory variables. At that point, no actual data will have been entered into the master file, EXPENSES. You will have only copied the default value from the file.

You will need to duplicate a file that has the same structure as EXPENSES but no records. The COPY STRUCTURE command will do just that. The COPY STRUCTURE command is preceded by a SET SAFETY OFF. Safety refers to the *dBASE III Plus* routine that prompts you every time a file is overwritten. In this program, each new batch will wipe out any old batches on the disk. To keep the safety message off the screen, the SAFETY is set OFF.

After the new file, EXPADD, has been created, it is placed in use. Because its structure is an exact duplicate of EXPENSES, the section of the program that is concerned with actual data entry will be left unchanged.

Also note that the command SET INDEX TO catorder, amtorder, dateord, payorder should be deleted from the program. In batch entry programs, index files can be updated when the batch file is combined with the master. Enter the commands in bold and eliminate the SET INDEX command.

```
CLEAR
SET TALK OFF
SET STATUS OFF
SET SCOREBOARD OFF
ON ESCAPE RETURN
@ 11,0
WAIT "Press any Key to begin entering new records."
ON ESCAPE
USE expenses
* get default values
GO BOTTOM
lastcheck=check        && starting check number
lastcat=cat      && last category used
SET SAFETY OFF
COPY STRUCTURE TO EXPADD
USE expadd
SET INDEX TO catorder,amtorder,dateord,payorder < =====delete
```

The next change in the program comes after all the records have been entered. Below is the section of the program that follows the ENDDO for the main entry loop. The first group of changes creates the audit trail report. First, the SUM command is used to find the total of all the amounts entered. In a double entry program, credits and debits may be balanced at this point. A line is added to the screen display to show the total to the user. After the WAIT (the message has been altered), a report form is used to print out data about the transactions. You will need to design that report form before you can run this program. Enter the new commands and changes shown in bold.

```
ENDDO expenter
CLEAR
SUM amount TO entertot
@ 11,0 SAY "You have added "+LTRIM(STR(RECCOUNT()-begin,10))+" records."
@ 12,0 SAY "The records add up to "+LTRIM(STR(entertot,10,2))
WAIT "Press any key to print audit report"<=============changed
* print audit report
REPORT FORM expaudit TO PRINT NOEJECT
EJECT
```

After the printing, you are ready to combine the file. The idea of the following group of commands is to allow the user to accept or reject the batch of entries. To do this a variable called "ok" is defined as a logical value true. The user is then asked to enter Y or N to determine if the batch should be accepted. An IF command is used to evaluate the entry. If the entry is Y, then the files are combined.

The technique used in this example begins by opening the master data base file and any index files that should be updated. The APPEND FROM command is used to copy the files from the EXPADD file into the EXPENSES file. A FOR clause is added to the APPEND FROM command to eliminate any blank records. The specific test is for an amount greater than zero. The assumption is made that any valid record would contain some amount and that blank records would have an amount of zero.

On the other hand, if the batch is not OK, the program skips the APPEND FROM and the master file is unchanged.

> *It makes sense to allow users to correct any mistakes that caused them to reject the batch. This routine and others like it are discussed in Chapter 16.*

Enter the commands shown in bold. Note that the SET SAFETY ON command is added near the end of the file.

```
CLEAR
OK=.T.
@ 14,0 SAY "Add this batch to file?" GET ok PICTURE "Y"
READ
IF ok
     USE expenses INDEX catorder,amtorder,dateord,payorder
     APPEND FROM expadd FOR amount>0
ENDIF
CLOSE DATABASE
SET SAFETY ON
SET TALK ON
SET STATUS ON
SET SCOREBOARD ON
RETURN
```

The entire program should look like this:

```
CLEAR
SET TALK OFF
SET STATUS OFF
SET SCOREBOARD OFF
ON ESCAPE RETURN
@ 11,0
WAIT "Press any Key to begin entering new records."
ON ESCAPE
USE expenses
* get default values
GO BOTTOM
lastcheck=check  && starting check number
lastcat=cat      && last category used
SET SAFETY OFF
COPY STRUCTURE TO EXPADD
USE expadd
begin=RECCOUNT()
expenter=.T.
DO WHILE expenter
    CLEAR
    APPEND BLANK
    REPLACE date WITH DATE(),cat WITH lastcat,check WITH lastcheck+1
    SET FORMAT TO expsplit
    EDIT RECORD RECCOUNT()
    CLOSE FORMAT
    check=.T.
    @ 23,0 SAY "Is the information entered correct? (Y/N)" GET M->check PICTURE "Y"
    READ
        DO WHILE .NOT. M->check
           SET FORMAT TO expsplit
           EDIT RECORD RECCOUNT()
           CLOSE FORMAT
           check=.T.
           @ 23,0 SAY "Is the information entered correct? (Y/N)" GET M->check PICTURE "Y"
           READ
        ENDDO double check routine
    @ 23,0
    @ 23,0 SAY "*** RECORD ENTERED ***"
    @ 24,0 SAY "Enter another? (Y/N)" GET expenter PICTURE "Y"
    READ
    * prepare defaults
    GO RECCOUNT()
    lastcheck=lastcheck+1
    lastcat=cat
ENDDO expenter
CLEAR
SUM amount TO entertot
@ 11,0 SAY "You have added "+LTRIM(STR(RECCOUNT()-begin,10))+" records."
@ 12,0 SAY "The records add up to "+LTRIM(STR(entertot,10,2))
WAIT "Press any key to print audit report"
* print audit report
REPORT FORM expaudit TO PRINT NOEJECT
EJECT
CLEAR
OK=.T.
@ 14,0 SAY "Add this batch to file?" GET ok PICTURE "Y"
READ
IF ok
    USE expenses INDEX catorder,amtorder,dateord,payorder
    APPEND FROM expadd FOR amount>0
ENDIF
CLOSE DATABASE
SET SAFETY ON
SET TALK ON
SET STATUS ON
SET SCOREBOARD ON
RETURN
```

Save the program by entering

[CTRL/End]

Exercise 4   Before you can begin using the revised program, you must create a report form called EXPAUDIT to print when the REPORT FORM command is executed. Use the CREATE REPORT command to design a report that will print the DATE, CAT, PAYTO, ITEM, and AMOUNT fields and show a total for the AMOUNT column. If you need help, see Chapter 7 for more information about report forms. Below is a sample of such a report.

```
Page No.      1
11/07/86
                              BATCH ENTRY REPORT

DATE        CAT PAYTO          DESCRIPTION          AMOUNT

03/31/86    140 RV PAPER       BINDING MATERIAL      33.92
*** Total ***
            140                                      33.92
```

After you have created the report form, execute the new program by entering

DO expbatch < return >

Enter the following record

> < return >
> **033186**
> **RV PAPER** < return >
> **33.92BINDING MATERIAL** < return >
> < return > **(3 times)**

Exit the program by entering

> **y**
> **n**

The program displays

```
You have added 1 records.
The records add up to 33.92
Press any key to print audit report
```

Enter the following to start the printing

> < return >

The report form prints out the audit trail for the program. Accept the batch by entering

> **y**

The records in the batch have been added to the main file.

Batch processing does not really alter the logic of the program substantially. It reflects a minor change, but one that is needed in certain circumstances.

SUMMARY

The subject of this chapter is the types of programs that can be used to aid entry of data into files.

The entry routines have a basic concept common to all data base entry programs.

1. A screen format is used as the entry form. That format can be a single screen or a series of screens that can be paged using the **[Pg Up]** and **[Pg Dn]** keys.
2. A loop is created that appends a blank record to the file, displays the screen format, and allows the user to make entries into fields.
3. If the entry screen does not contain memo files, you can use the READ command to display the entry screen. READ does not allow MEMO field entry. If that is required, the EDIT command must replace READ. In this chapter, EDIT RECORD RECCOUNT() was used to edit the last record in the file.
4. A double check routine can be added to allow users to make corrections to the entry screen before they enter the next record.
5. The ON ESCAPE command allows you to assign a specific command to execute when <Esc> is pressed.
6. Default values can be stored in the records before they are displayed. This allows the program to automatically enter data that would otherwise have to be manually entered.

    Defaults have three forms. Constant defaults replace the fields with the same data for each new record. Sequential defaults are used for numbering fields consecutively such as invoice or check numbers. Ditto defaults carry over the entry made in the same field in the previous record.
7. Batch files are used in special situations where each group of records being entered needs to be checked before it is added to the main file. This type of processing checks for such things as amounts in balance and also helps eliminate unwanted records like blanks before they are added to the master file.

ANSWER KEY

Exercise 1

In order to use the format file that you just created, you must change the name of the format file used in the SET FORMAT TO command in the EXPENTER.PRG file. The listing below shows the changes you should make.

```
CLEAR
SET TALK OFF
```

```
SET STATUS OFF
SET SCOREBOARD OFF
@ 11,0
WAIT "Press any Key to begin entering new records."
USE expenses INDEX catorder,amtorder,dateord,payorder
begin=RECCOUNT()
expenter=.T.
DO WHILE expenter
   CLEAR
   APPEND BLANK
   SET FORMAT TO expsplit <============= change file name
   EDIT RECORD RECCOUNT()
   CLOSE FORMAT
   check=.T.
   @ 23,0 SAY "Is the information entered correct? (Y/N)" GET check PICTURE "Y"
   READ
       DO WHILE .NOT. check
           SET FORMAT TO expsplit <================ change file name
           EDIT RECORD RECCOUNT()
           CLOSE FORMAT
           check=.T.
           @23,0 SAY "Is the information entered correct? (Y/N)" GET check PICTURE "Y"
           READ
       ENDDO double check routine
   @ 23,0
   @ 23,0 SAY "***RECORD ENTERED***"
   @ 24,0 SAY "Enter another? (Y/N)" GET expenter PICTURE "Y"
   READ
ENDDO expenter
CLEAR
@ 11,0 SAY "You have added "+LTRIM(STR(RECCOUNT()-begin,10))+" records."
WAIT "Press any key to exit entry program"
CLOSE DATABASE
SET TALK ON
SET STATUS ON
SET SCOREBOARD ON
RETURN
```

Exercise 2

Place the EXPENSES file in use: USE expenses. Change the structure by entering:
MODIFY STRUCTURE. The structure should look like this when you are done.

```
Structure for database: C:EXPENSES.dbf
Number of data records:          17
Date of last update       : 11/07/86
Field    Field Name    Type        Width    Dec
   1     DATE          Date           8
   2     CAT           Numeric        5
   3     PAYTO         Character     20
```

4	ITEM	Character	20	
5	AMOUNT	Numeric	6	2
6	COMMENTS	Memo	10	
7	MONTH	Character	15	
8	DEDUCT	Logical	1	
9	CHECK	Numeric	4	
Total			90	

You can place the value in the record in a variety of ways. The following command will do the trick:

```
REPLACE check WITH 1125 RECORD 17
```

Exercise 3

Load the format file into the editor with MODIFY COMMAND EXPSPLIT.FMT. Below is the file with a line added to display the CHECK field.

```
@ 5,0 TO 15,79 DOUBLE
@ 6,20 SAY "Expenses Entry Screen Part A"
@ 7,20 SAY " Press [Pg Dn] for Part B"
@ 8,10 SAY "Date:"+DTOC(Date())
@ 8,60 SAY "Record Number "+LTRIM(STR(RECNO(),5))
@ 9,30 SAY "Enter check #: "GET check <=========added
@ 10,30 SAY "Enter the date: " GET date
@ 12,30 SAY "Enter the payee: " GET payto PICTURE "@!"
@ 14,30 SAY "Enter the amount: " GET amount
READ
@ 5,0 TO 18,79 DOUBLE
@ 6,20 SAY "Expenses Entry Screen Part B"
@ 7,20 SAY " Press [Pg Up] for Part A"
@ 8,10 SAY "Date: "+DTOC(DATE())
@ 8,60 SAY "Record Number "+LTRIM(STR(RECNO(),5))
@ 11,10 SAY "Item Description:" GET item
@ 13,10 SAY "Comments: " GET comments
@ 15,10 SAY "Enter Y if the item is tax deductible " GET deduct PICTURE "Y"
@ 17,10 SAY "Enter Budget Category Number " GET cat
```

PROGRAMS THAT EDIT

DATA FILES

IN THE PREVIOUS CHAPTER YOU LEARNED how to use *dBASE III Plus* programming to create custom-designed entry routines. Once data have been entered, you will need programs that allow users to retrieve the records that have been entered in order to inspect and revise them.

dBASE III Plus provides you with a number of tools for finding, displaying, and editing records. This chapter explores ways in which these tools can be combined with the techniques of interactive programming to create routines that guide users through the tasks required to retrieve and revise records in an existing data base file.

THE BASIC SEARCH ROUTINE

Adding editing or retrieval programs consists of two basic parts:

1. **Search.** The search portion of the program lets users specify a criterion by which the data base file can be searched for specific records.
2. **Display and edit.** Once the desired record has been located, the program should display the data and allow users to make any changes they want.

The second part of the program is very similar to the technique used in the previous chapter to enter new records. The main difference is that you will not be appending blank records, but editing existing records. The first part, the search routine, is the part that really distinguishes editing from entering programs.

You will create as simple an editing program as possible. From there, you will look at the weaknesses of that program and examine a variety of ways to improve and expand the editing concept. Begin by creating a new program file, EXPEDIT (expenses edit). Enter

MODIFY COMMAND expedit < return >

Enter the usual housekeeping-type commands to begin the edit program.

```
CLEAR
SET TALK OFF
SET STATUS OFF
```

The next step is to open the data base file that you want to work with (i.e., EXPENSES). The index files are also opened at this point. Why are they opened? If you are not sure, see Question 1 at the end of the chapter.

Enter

```
USE expenses INDEX catorder,amtorder,dateord,payorder
```

You are now ready to search for a record interactively. The first step is to create a loop. The loop is designed to repeat the search routine as many times as the user desires. To do this, a logical variable called "expedit" is created with a true value. Then a DO WHILE command begins the loop. Enter

```
expedit=.t.
DO WHILE expedit
```

Now that the loop has been initialized, the first step is to ask the user what record has to be edited. To find that record, you need to pick a key item of data that identifies the record. Suppose you wanted to locate the record by virtue of the name in the PAYTO field. The program needs to do the following:

1. Create a variable that will contain the data to search for.
2. Allow the user to fill in the variable with the search key.
3. Search the PAYTO field for a name that matches the one the user entered.
4. Display the matching record and allow the user to edit the data.

The first step is to create the variable that will serve as the search key. The next series of commands clears the screen and places a heading, RETRIEVE A RECORD BY PAYEE, at the top of the screen. Then a variable named "key" is defined as

20 spaces. Why was KEY defined as 20 spaces? The explanation can be found at the end of the chapter under Question 2.

Enter

```
CLEAR
@ 5,20 SAY "RETRIEVE A RECORD BY PAYEE"
key=SPACE(20)
```

The next step is to allow the user to enter a specific name into the key variable. This can be done interactively by using @/SAY/GET to display the variable and READ to allow entry. Note the use of the @! function in the picture clause. The @! is used to automatically convert all entries to uppercase characters. Enter

```
@ 10,10 SAY "Enter payee " GET key PICTURE "@!"
READ
```

After the user has entered the name, the program should go on to locate the record that matches the entry. However, before you proceed to that section of the program, you need to consider how the loop that you started might eventually be ended.

In this example, you may decide that if the user didn't enter a name but left the key variable blank, you should exit the editing program. In order to implement that logic, it is necessary to test the contents of key to see if it is all blanks, or if a name was entered. The following IF command structure tests for a blank key. If key is blank, the loop is exited, which leads to the termination of the program.

> You should never use a RETURN to terminate a program inside a DO WHILE loop. Use EXIT to jump to the RETURN outside the loop.

Enter

```
IF key=SPACE(20)
    EXIT
ENDIF
```

If key is not blank, the next task is to locate the record in the data base file that contains a PAYTO that matches the key. To do this you can use the LOCATE command. Notice that a TRIM() function is used for the search instead of just key. The reason is that you want to allow the user to enter a partial name into key and still find a match. For example, enter MICRO and find MICROAMERICA, enter CROW and find CROW CANYON LUMBER. Enter

```
LOCATE FOR payto=TRIM(key)
```

> If you wanted to allow for a substring match, you could use the $ operator. For example, if you wanted to search for ACRES but weren't sure if you entered GREEN ACRES FURN or ACRES FURN, you would need to change the LOCATE command to read LOCATE FOR TRIM(key)$payto. The command tells dBASE III Plus to locate the first record for which the key data are some part of the PAYTO field.

The LOCATE command affects the position of the pointer. At this stage in the program the pointer has been positioned at the correct record. You can now display the data in the record by using a format file. If you want the record to appear exactly as the user entered it, you can use the same format file. If you want to show the user a different look, you can use a different format file from the one used in the entry program. In this example, you will use the EXPENSES format file. The READ command activates the input areas and allows the user to perform revisions. Enter

```
SEI FORMAT TO expenses
READ
```

After the record has been changed, you are ready to conclude the routine by closing the format and sending the loop back for another search. The SET commands and RETURN take care of the necessary housekeeping. Enter

```
    CLOSE FORMAT
ENDDO
SET TALK ON
SET STATUS ON
CLOSE DATABASE
RETURN
```

The entire program looks like this:

```
CLEAR
SET TALK OFF
SET STATUS OFF
USE expenses INDEX catorder,amtorder,dateord,payorder
expedit=.t.
DO WHILE expedit
    CLEAR
    @ 5,20 SAY "RETRIEVE A RECORD BY PAYEE"
    key=SPACE(20)
    @ 10,10  SAY "Enter payee " GET key PICTURE "@!"
    READ
    IF key=SPACE(20)
        EXIT
    ENDIF
    LOCATE FOR payto=TRIM(key)
    SET FORMAT TO expenses
    READ
    CLOSE FORMAT
ENDDO
SET TALK ON
SET STATUS ON
```

Save the program by entering

[CTRL/End]

Execute the program by entering

DO expedit < return >

The program displays the key entry screen.

```
              RETRIEVE A RECORD BY PAYEE

Enter payee  ▓▓▓▓▓▓▓▓▓▓▓▓▓▓▓▓▓
```

Enter the name of a payee that you want to search for:

   crow <return>

The program finds and displays the record as shown below:

```
                    Expenses Entry Screen
Date: 01/01/80                                      Record Number    1
                    Enter the date:  11/07/86
                    Enter the payee: CROW CANYON LUMBER

                    Enter the amount: 68.40

Item Description: 10 2BY 4

Comments:  memo

Enter Y if the item is tax deductible  Y



Enter Budget Category Number    120
```

You are now free to edit the record or proceed to another search. In this case, exit the record by entering

   [Pg Dn]

The search screen appears again. Enter

   micro <return>

The program displays the record for MICROAMERICA, record no. 17. Change the date to March 29 by entering

   032986

Continue to the next search by entering

   [Pg Dn]

Check to see if the change was actually recorded by searching for the same record. Enter

   micro <return>

The date appears as you revised it, 03/29/86.

What would happen if the program failed to find a matching payee? Enter

xxxx <return>

What has happened? The program displays a blank record. Which record is it? The display indicates the record is 21. Remember that the file contains only 20 records. The screen display is attempting to display a record that is really the end of the EXPENSES file. Any data that you would enter now would not be recorded.

Since this screen display is very confusing, you can make the edit program more coherent by adding commands that handle an unsuccessful search more clearly. Return to the SEARCH menu by entering

[Pg Dn]

To exit the program, enter a blank search key:

<return>

The program terminates and you return to the *dBASE III Plus* DOT PROMPT mode.

THE NOT FOUND ROUTINE

Any program that searches needs to account for the possibility that the search will not locate a record that matches the search key. The way the EXPEDIT program is now designed, an unsuccessful search will show a blank record and meaningless screen display. To make the program more logical, you need a series of commands that test for a successful search.

Load the program into the editor by entering

MODIFY COMMAND expedit.prg <return>

The key to this modification is to use the FOUND() function. After a search is executed, the FOUND() is true if the pointer is at any position in the file other than the end of the file. If the pointer is at the end of the file, FOUND() will evaluate as false. For example, the command IF FOUND() can be used to determine whether or not the search is successful.

Below is the center section of the program. To account for an unsuccessful search, an IF command with the FOUND() function is placed immediately after the LOCATE command. This makes sense because you should test for the pointer location before you decide what to display on the screen.

If the condition is true, then the commands to display and edit the record appear. If the condition is false (i.e., the end of file has been reached), a message is displayed at the bottom of the screen indicating that what you were looking for was not found. The WAIT command displays the message and pauses the program until the user is ready to continue. Add the lines indicated in bold.

```
      IF key=SPACE(20)
            EXIT
      ENDIF
      LOCATE FOR payto=TRIM(key)
        IF FOUND()
            SET FORMAT TO expenses
            READ
            CLOSE FORMAT
        ELSE
            WAIT " *** NOT FOUND *** Any Key to Continue"'
        ENDIF
ENDDO
```

The entire program should look like this:

```
      CLEAR
      SET TALK OFF
      SET STATUS OFF
      USE expenses INDEX catorder,amtorder,dateord,payorder
      expedit=.t.
   ┌─▶DO WHILE expedit──────────────────────────────────────────┐
   │      CLEAR                                                   │
   │      @ 5,20 SAY "RETRIEVE A RECORD BY PAYEE"                 │
   │      key=SPACE(20)                                          │
   │      @ 10,10  SAY "Enter payee " GET key PICTURE "@!"        │
   │      READ                                                    │
   │  ┌─▶IF key=SPACE(20)────────────────────────────────┐       │
   │  │      EXIT                                         │       │
   │  └──ENDIF◀────────────────────────────────────────── │      │
   │      LOCATE FOR payto=TRIM(key)                             │
   │  ┌─▶IF FOUND()──────────────────────────────────────────┐   │
   │  │      SET FORMAT TO expenses                          │   │
   │  │      READ                                            │   │
   │  │      CLOSE FORMAT                                    │   │
   │  │  ELSE                                                │   │
   │  │      WAIT " *** NOT FOUND ***  Any Key to Continue"  │   │
   │  └──ENDIF◀─────────────────────────────────────────────┘   │
   └──ENDDO◀──────────────────────────────────────────────────── ┘
      SET TALK ON
      SET STATUS ON
      CLOSE DATABASE
RETURN
```

Save the program by entering

[CTRL/End]

Execute the program by entering

DO expedit < return >

Enter

xxx < return >

This time the program does not display an empty record but shows the message that indicates that no payee xxx has been entered into the file. Enter

< return >

The program is ready to search again. Enter

SEARS < return >

The correct record is displayed. Enter

[Pg Dn]

Exit the program by entering

< return >

FAST SEARCHES

The previous version of the EXPEDIT program has a major defect. The defect is not apparent when you run the program because it is related to the time that it takes to find various records in the data base file. Since EXPENSES is a very small file, it doesn't seem to make much difference if the record you are searching for is at the beginning or the end of the file.

However, this will not be the case when the data base file is larger. The LOCATE command performs a sequential search of the data base file. This means that *dBASE III Plus* tests each record in sequence to see if it matches the search key. The larger the data base file, the longer this search will take.

But *dBASE III Plus* has another method of searching that takes advantage of files that have indexes. Searching an indexed file cuts the amount of time needed to find records in large data base files to a small fraction of the time required for sequential searches.

The EXPEDIT works well as an example, but for practical editing the program ought to be modified to use the *dBASE III Plus* fast search method.

For more details about searching and index files, see Chapter 6.

The fast search method requires two basic changes:

1. The data base file must be indexed on the field that is going to be searched.
2. The LOCATE command is replaced by the SEEK command.

To implement these changes, load the EXPEDIT program into the editor.

MODIFY COMMAND expedit < return >

Interestingly, the change to a fast search requires very little modification of the program. Only two lines are actually changed. The USE command is changed very slightly. Since the search will be conducted on the PAYTO field, the master index file should be the PAYORDER index. Remember that the master index file is the first one in the list if you are opening more than one index file. The other index files can be listed in any order.

The other change is that the LOCATE command is replaced with a SEEK command. SEEK uses a much simpler syntax than LOCATE. To find the key value, all you need to enter is SEEK TRIM(key). The reason that SEEK appears to be a simpler command is that it automatically searches the master index file for matching data. You do not need to tell the SEEK command which field to search because that is already decided when you select the master index. This also tells you that it is very important to make sure that the master index file logically matches the search key. In this case the PAYORDER index contains the PAYTO field information. Enter the additions and changes indicated in bold.

```
CLEAR
SET TALK OFF
SET STATUS OFF
USE expenses INDEX payorder,catorder, amtorder,dateord
expedit=.t.
DO WHILE expedit
    CLEAR
    @ 5,20 SAY "RETRIEVE A RECORD BY PAYEE"
    key=SPACE(20)
    @ 10,10 SAY "Enter payee " GET key PICTURE "@!"
    READ
    IF key=SPACE(20)
        EXIT
    ENDIF
    SEEK TRIM(key)
    IF FOUND()
        SET FORMAT TO expenses
        READ
        CLOSE FORMAT
    ELSE
        WAIT "***NOT FOUND*** Any Key to Continue"
    ENDIF
ENDDO
SET TALK ON
SET STATUS ON
CLOSE DATABASE
RETURN
```

Save the program by entering

> **[CTRL/End]**

Execute the program by entering

> **DO expedit < return >**

Enter

> **RV < return >**

The matching record is displayed. In a small file like this one, you will be hard pressed to notice the difference made by the fast search. However, the difference will be crucial when the file contains even a few hundred records.

The INDEX/SEEK method of locating records should be used on all but the smallest data base files.

Exit the program by entering

[Pg Dn]
<return>

The FXPEDIT program did not include a double check routine like the one used in the EXPENTER program. The reasoning is that since you can go back and edit any of the records, double checking after each entry would be a redundant feature. If you desire to add a double check, you can carry over the code added to EXPENTER into the EXPEDIT file.

SEARCHING BY DIFFERENT CRITERIA

The program you have designed works well but it has a major limitation. The search is always carried out on the same field, PAYTO. If you think about retrieving data from a data base file, you might want the ability to perform the same type of search using criteria other than PAYTO to locate the records.

Your next task in programming search routines is to create a program that allows the user to select from several different fields as the basis for the search.

In addition, you may have noticed that PAYTO is a CHARACTER field. Is it possible to search for other field types such as NUMERIC or DATE? If so, what types of changes need be made to perform those types of searches?

To answer those questions you will create a program called MULIFIND (multiple finds) that will provide the user with several ways to locate records. The example will also illustrate search on NUMERIC and DATE fields, as well as CHARACTER fields. The program allows users to search three fields for records, PAYTO, DATE, and AMOUNT.

Begin by initializing a new file in the editor.

MODIFY COMMAND mulifind <return>

The beginning of the program is almost identical to the beginning of the EXPEDIT program. The only difference is that in this program the index files are not opened at the same time as the EXPENSES file. The reason is that you cannot decide which index should be the master index file until the user has decided which field in the data base file will be searched. Enter

CLEAR
SET TALK OFF

```
SET STATUS OFF
USE expenses
expedit=.t.
DO WHILE expedit
  CLEAR
```

The first change in the logic of the program takes place at this point in the program. In the EXPEDIT program you displayed the search key input screen at this point. But because this program allows the use of one of several key fields, you must first display a menu from which the user will pick the desired search field.

The menu created in this program uses a shortcut method for creating screen displays, like menus that consist of consecutive lines of text. The commands used are the TEXT/ENDTEXT commands. When *dBASE III Plus* encounters the TEXT command, any lines that follow are treated as if they were ? commands with text entered in quotation marks. Look at the commands below.

```
? "Hello Joe"
? "How are you today?"
? "Who cares?"
```

The same text can be displayed using a TEXT/ENDTEXT command sequence. Contrast the commands below with the previous method.

```
TEXT
Hello Joe
How are you today?
Who cares
ENDTEXT
```

Both sets of commands will have exactly the same effect. The TEXT/ENDTEXT is simpler when you are using several lines of text in a row, as you do in a menu display. Enter

```
TEXT

              Edit Existing Records

              1. Search by Payee
              2. Search by Date
              3. Search by Amount
              0. Quit

ENDTEXT
```

Next, allow users to enter their choice of search field by displaying an interactive prompt and storing the answer in the variable choice. Enter

```
choice=0
@ 10,15 SAY "Enter search option" GET choice PICTURE "9"
READ
```

The next section of the program actually carries out the procedures for searching different fields.

Four changes occur, depending on which field is selected:

1. **Heading.** The heading at the top of the screen should reflect the field selected.
2. **Prompt.** The entry prompt should also reflect the selected field.
3. **Key.** The previous changes are of a cosmetic nature. However, if you intend to search different fields that are not all the same type, you must initialize the key variables to the same data type as the field you will be searching.
4. **Master index.** In addition to selecting the data type for the key variable, you must select a master index file that contains index data from the selected field.

To implement these changes, a DO CASE structure can be used. Three cases, corresponding to the three search fields, will select a heading, a prompt, a value for key, and a master index file.

Begin by entering the first CASE. Enter

```
DO CASE
CASE choice=1
     heading="RETRIEVE A RECORD BY PAYEE"
     prompt="Enter Payee"
     key=SPACE(20)
     SET INDEX TO payorder,catorder,amtorder,dateord
```

The variables heading and prompt are used to confirm the selection of option 1. The key variable is initialized as a character variable of 20 blanks. Finally, the PAYORDER file is selected as the master index. The order of the other index files is not important.

Next enter the commands needed to prepare for a search on a DATE-type field:

```
CASE choice=2
     heading="RETRIEVE A RECORD BY DATE"
     prompt="Enter Date"
```

How can you initialize a variable as a date-type variable? One way is to use the CTOD()—character to date—function to convert a group of characters into *dBASE III Plus* date-type variables. Enter

```
key=CTOD("  /  /  ")
```

Finally, open the DATEORD file as the master index file:

```
SET INDEX TO dateord,payorder,catorder,amtorder
```

The next section prepares for each by AMOUNT. Enter

```
CASE choice=3
     heading="RETRIEVE A RECORD BY AMOUNT"
     prompt="Enter Amount"
     key=0.00
     SET INDEX TO amtorder,dateord,payorder,catorder
```

Note that 0.00 was used as the initial value for key. The decimal places were necessary if you wanted to be able to enter decimal numbers for the search.

The next part of the DO CASE structure is the OTHERWISE clause. In this case the OTHERWISE can be used to exit the loop and the program. In other words, entering a number that is not 1, 2, or 3 automatically terminates the program. Enter

```
OTHERWISE
    EXIT
ENDCASE
```

Now that you have selected the field and the other values necessary to define the search parameters, you can allow users to enter the search criterion. Note that the @ SAY commands use the variable names "heading" and "prompt" instead of literal text as they did in the EXPEDIT program. Enter

```
CLEAR
@ 5,20 SAY heading
@ 10,10 SAY prompt GET key PICTURE "@!"
READ
```

The next section of code might come as a surprise. The section is needed in order to TRIM() the entry if choice 1, PAYTO field, is selected. Using TRIM() will cause an error if key is not a character-type variable. TRIM(key) when key is a number or a date will cause *dBASE III Plus* to treat the command as an error, which will halt the execution of the program.

The problem can be solved by using the TYPE() function to test the data type of key. If key is character, type C, then the TRIM(key) expression is used with SEEK. If the data type is numeric or date, the command SEEK key will be used. Using the IF command at this point avoids the type mismatch error. Enter

```
IF TYPE("key")="C"
    SEEK TRIM(key)
ELSE
    SEEK key
ENDIF
```

From this point on, the program is identical to the EXPEDIT program. First the test is performed to determine if there is a matching item in the file. Then the record is displayed on the screen for editing. The program then loops back to the SEARCH menu. Enter

```
    IF FOUND()
        SET FORMAT TO expenses
        READ
        CLOSE FORMAT
    ELSE
        WAIT " *** NOT FOUND *** Any Key to Continue"
```

```
    ENDIF
ENDDO
SET TALK ON
SET STATUS ON
CLOSE DATABASE
RETURN
```

The entire program should look like this:

```
CLEAR
SET TALK OFF
SET STATUS OFF
USE expenses
expedit=.t.
DO WHILE expedit
    CLEAR
    TEXT
                    Edit Existing Records

                    1. Search by Payee
                    2. Search by Date
                    3. Search by Amount
                    0. Quit
    ENDTEXT
    choice=0
    @ 10,15 SAY "Enter search option" GET choice PICTURE "9"
    READ
    DO CASE
        CASE choice=1
            heading="RETRIEVE A RECORD BY PAYEE"
            prompt="Enter Payee"
            key=SPACE(20)
            SET INDEX TO payorder,catorder,amtorder,dateord
        CASE choice=2
            heading="RETRIEVE A RECORD BY DATE"
            prompt="Enter Date"
            key=CTOD("  /  /  ")
            SET INDEX TO dateord,payorder,catorder,amtorder
        CASE choice=3
            heading="RETRIEVE A RECORD BY AMOUNT"
            prompt="Enter Amount"
            key=0.00
            SET INDEX TO amtorder,dateord,payorder,catorder
        OTHERWISE
            EXIT
    ENDCASE
    CLEAR
    @ 5,20 SAY heading
    @ 10,10  SAY prompt GET key PICTURE "@!"
    READ
    IF TYPE("key")="C"
        SEEK TRIM(key)
    ELSE
        SEEK key
    ENDIF
    IF FOUND()
        SET FORMAT TO expenses
        READ
        CLOSE FORMAT
    ELSE
        WAIT " *** NOT FOUND ***  Any Key to Continue"
    ENDIF
ENDDO
SET TALK ON
SET STATUS ON
CLOSE DATABASE
RETURN
```

Notice the number of command structures used in the program. The arrows and lines show how each structure controls a section of the program for selection or repetition. Also note the proper nesting of each layout within the containing structure. Save the program by entering

[CTRL/End]

Execute the program by entering

DO mulifind < return >

The menu of search options is displayed.

```
Edit Existing Records

1. Search by Payee
2. Search by Date
3. Search by Amount
0. Quit


Enter search option 0
```

Enter the option to search by date:

2

The screen displays

```
_____
             RETRIEVE A RECORD BY DATE

      Enter Date ▓/▓/▓
_____
```

Enter a date to search for:

032986

The program finds the first record with that date.

```
_____
               Expenses Entry Screen
Date: 11/07/86                        Record Number    15

                    Enter the date:  03/29/86
                    Enter the payee: COMPUTER CURRENTS

                    Enter the amount: 15.00

Item Description: SUBSCRIPTION

Comments:  memo

Enter Y if the item is tax deductible  N

Enter Budget Category Number    140
_____
```

You are now free to revise this record if you wish. Exit the record by entering

[Pg Dn]

The program returns to the menu display. This time, try an amount. Enter

3

The program displays

RETRIEVE A RECORD BY AMOUNT

Enter Amount   *0.00*

Enter

42.50

The program displays the record:

Expenses Entry Screen

Date: 11/07/86   Record Number   13

                        Enter the date: 03/21/86
                        Enter the payee: PRICE CLUB

                        Enter the amount: 42.50

Item Description: PAPER

Comments: memo

Enter Y if the item is tax deductible N

Enter Budget Category Number   140

Return to the menu by entering

[Pg Dn]

You can test the program by trying the other option and searching for nonexistent records.

When you have finished, exit the program by entering the following at the main menu:

<return>

MULTIPLE MATCHES

It may have occurred to you that the editing programs you have been creating are not finding all the records that match the criteria, only the first matching record in the file. For example, there are several records that have the same date or the same payee, but the editing programs have all displayed only one of those records.

The program needs to be able to display all the records that match for the same criterion if it is to be of practical use. Load the program into the editor so that you can make the necessary changes.

MODIFY COMMAND mulifind <return>

Before you begin to make changes to the program, you need to think about how you can get the program to display the desired series of records, not just the first record that matches. The key to the problem is the index file that arranges the record in order, according to the key field. Suppose you have several records with the same date. If the program correctly finds the first record in the file with that date, what would you have to do to position the pointer?

The answer is that all the records with the same key data (e.g., date) would be grouped together. In order to get to those records you need only move the pointer to the next record using the SKIP command.

You can repeat SKIP until you reach a record that does not match the key criterion.

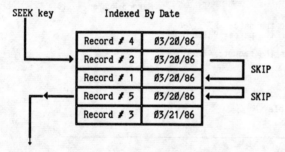

The logic of this type of program is very important in programming. The idea is that the fast search can find the first record. You then create a loop in which you skip to the next record, test to see if it still matches the key criterion, and if so, process the record. In this example that means to display the record for editing. This process continues until a record that does not match is found. The search then terminates.

To implement this type of program, you need to change the program in several different places. The first modifications occur in the DO CASE structure. Each case now needs to store the actual name of the field being searched to a variable called "fieldname." The reason this is necessary is that later you will have to test data in each successive record for a match in the key field. Since SEEK works only for the first record in the file that matches, you will use the fieldname to perform that test. Enter the new commands shown in bold.

```
DO CASE
    CASE choice=1
        heading="RETRIEVE A RECORD BY PAYEE"
        prompt="Enter Payee"
```

```
            key=SPACE(20)
            SET INDEX TO payorder,catorder,amtorder,dateord
                fieldname="PAYTO"
        CASE choice=2
            heading="RETRIEVE A RECORD BY DATE"
            prompt="Enter Date"
            key=CTOD("  /  /  ")
            SET INDEX TO dateord,payorder,catorder,amtorder
                fieldname="DATE"
        CASE choice=3
            heading="RETRIEVE A RECORD BY AMOUNT"
            prompt="Enter Amount"
            key=0.00
            SET INDEX TO amtorder,dateord,payorder,catorder
              fieldname="AMOUNT"
        OTHERWISE
            EXIT
ENDCASE
```

The next change occurs following the user's input after the SEARCH CHOICE choice menu. The change is to the IF structure that chooses the type of SEEK command to use. The program currently looks like this:

```
IF TYPE("key")="C"
    SEEK TRIM(key)
ELSE
    SEEK key
ENDIF
```

This section of the program is fine when you intend to test only one record each time you search. However, if you intend to test a series of records as potential matches, you would like to make sure that the key variable can be used without having to change the command to adjust for a different data type. This section can be rewritten as shown below in bold. Make the changes indicated.

```
CLEAR
@ 5,20 SAY heading
@ 10,10 SAY prompt GET key PICTURE "@!"
READ
    IF TYPE("key")="C"
        key=TRIM(key)
    ENDIF
    SEEK key
```

The advantage of the change is that the variable key can be used without any special functions to make the test for matching. The change points out a principle of programming. Depending on how the program evolves, you may find that commands that work perfectly well in a simpler program need to be revised when you add what may appear to be an unrelated feature to the program.

The next section of the program contains the changes that actually accomplish the multiple records display that you desire. The first match is treated the same way as it was previously. Now look at the commands below in bold. The difference occurs after the first record has been edited. Instead of sending the program back to the SEARCH menu, the SKIP command is used to position the pointer at the next record in the file.

You need to test the contents of the key field to determine whether or not this record should also be displayed. A DO WHILE loop is started by testing if the contents of the key field (filled in by the variable fieldname using macro substitution) matches the value in the variable key.

If that test is true, a variable "more" is initialized as true. A message is displayed: Display next match?. If the user enters Y or <return>, the next matching record is displayed. If the user enters N, the loop terminates and the program goes back to the SEARCH menu.

If the user selects to display the record, the record is placed into the editing display. The process repeats until all matching records have been displayed or the user selects to terminate the loop. Enter the commands shown in bold.

```
    IF FOUND()
       SET FORMAT TO expenses
       READ
       CLOSE FORMAT
          SKIP
          DO WHILE &fieldname=key
              more=.T.
              @ 23,0 SAY "Display next match?" GET more PICTURE "Y"
              READ
              IF .NOT. more
                  EXIT
              ENDIF more records
              SET FORMAT TO expenses
              READ
              CLOSE FORMAT
              SKIP
          ENDDO more matching records
       ELSE
          WAIT " *** NOT FOUND *** Any Key to Continue"
       ENDIF
    ENDDO
    SET TALK ON
    SET STATUS ON
    CLOSE DATABASE
    RETURN
```

The entire program should look like this:

```
CLEAR
SET TALK OFF
SET STATUS OFF
USE expenses
expedit=.t.
DO WHILE expedit
    CLEAR
    TEXT

                        Edit Existing Records

                        1. Search by Payee
                        2. Search by Date
                        3. Search by Amount
                        0. Quit

    ENDTEXT
    choice=0
    @ 10,15 SAY "Enter search option" GET choice PICTURE "9"
    READ
    DO CASE
        CASE choice=1
            heading="RETRIEVE A RECORD BY PAYEE"
            prompt="Enter Payee"
            key=SPACE(20)
            SET INDEX TO payorder,catorder,amtorder,dateord
            fieldname="PAYTO"
        CASE choice=2
            heading="RETRIEVE A RECORD BY DATE"
            prompt="Enter Date"
            key=CTOD("  /  /  ")
            SET INDEX TO dateord,payorder,catorder,amtorder
            fieldname="DATE"
        CASE choice=3
            heading="RETRIEVE A RECORD BY AMOUNT"
            prompt="Enter Amount"
            key=0.00
            SET INDEX TO amtorder,dateord,payorder,catorder
            fieldname="AMOUNT"
        OTHERWISE
            EXIT
    ENDCASE
    CLEAR
    @ 5,20 SAY heading
    @ 10,10  SAY prompt GET key PICTURE "@!"
    READ
    IF TYPE("key")="C"
        key=TRIM(key)
    ENDIF
    SEEK key
    IF FOUND()
        SET FORMAT TO expenses
        READ
        CLOSE FORMAT
        SKIP
        DO WHILE &fieldname=key
            more=.T.
            @ 23,0 SAY "Display next match?" GET more PICTURE "Y"
            READ
            IF .NOT. more
                EXIT
            ENDIF more records
            SET FORMAT TO expenses
            READ
            CLOSE FORMAT
            SKIP
        ENDDO more matching records
    ELSE
        WAIT " *** NOT FOUND ***  Any Key to Continue"
    ENDIF
ENDDO
SET TALK ON
SET STATUS ON
CLOSE DATABASE
RETURN
```

Save the program by entering

[CTRL/End]

Execute the program by entering

DO mulifind <return>

Enter

2

Search for the following date by entering

032986

The program finds the first record with that date, record no. 15. Exit this record by entering

[Pg Dn]

At the bottom of the screen a message appears that asks if you want to see the next match. Note that in this program, if the search key was unique, the message would not appear and the program would have returned to the SEARCH menu. Enter

<return>

Record no. 16 appears. Enter

[Pg Dn]

The message indicates that there is another match. Enter

<return>

This time it is record no. 17. Enter

[Pg Dn]

The program returns to the menu display because that was the last record that matched.

Now use the program to display all the records with a payee named DAK.

You can feel free to test the program as much as you like. When you have finished, exit the program and return to the DOT PROMPT.

MEMO FIELDS

One small aspect of the program has been neglected. The READ command does not allow you to edit MEMO fields. In order to allow editing of MEMO fields, you must change the READ commands used for full-screen editing to EDIT NEXT 1 commands. Note that not all READ commands need be changed, only those that are used to activate the format file for full-screen editing of the records in EXPENSES.

Exercise 1 Modify the program to allow editing of MEMO fields. The correct program listing is shown at the end of the chapter.

MORE FIELDS

Exercise 2 The program MULIFIND is a prototype that can be reworked to fit a wide variety of applications. To test your understanding of the logic of the program, modify MULIFIND to search also for budget categories by searching the CAT field. If you are worried about ruining your MULIFIND program, create a new file and read in the commands from MULIFIND using the [**CTRL/K**]r command.

 The correct listing can be found at the end of the chapter.

BROWSING

The design of the MULIFIND program has one small drawback. It assumes that the user has a good acquaintance with the data that have been entered. The design is very good when the user has a source document with a name, invoice number, and so on that needs to be tracked down.

 At other times, however, you might find the most effective way to look at the records in a data base file is by displaying the important parts of each file in a list. When you see a record that you might want to edit, you can pick from the list. This type of interface is very handy and easy to use when examining records without having a specific one in mind.

 From a technical point of view, the program you are going to create shows how you can display a number of records on the screen at one time and allow users to choose records as they would choose options from a menu.

 Begin by creating a program called EXPBROW (expenses browse) by entering

MODIFY COMMAND expbrow < return >

Start the program with the usual housekeeping set of commands. Enter

```
CLEAR
SET TALK OFF
SET STATUS OFF
SET SCOREBOARD OFF
```

Open the data base and index files. Note that the DATEORD index file is the master index. The records in this program will be listed in date order.

```
USE expenses INDEX dateord,catorder,payorder,amtorder
```

The next two commands are used to program the function keys to enter specific characters. In this program, the user will be instructed to use the function keys instead of entering letter commands. (It doesn't make any real difference, but people seem to like programs that use function keys.) Enter

```
SET FUNCTION 9 TO "N"
SET FUNCTION 10 to "Q"
```

The next step is to begin a loop. The purpose of this loop is to display all the records in the file so that the user can select the records for editing. A loop that processes all the records in the file usually begins with the condition .NOT.EOF(). This expression reads "not end of file." Thus the command is DO WHILE .NOT.EOF() (do while not end of file). Enter

```
DO WHILE .NOT. EOF()
```

Now you are ready to begin processing. The concept of this browse program is to pick out a few key fields in that data base file and display a list of records. In this example, the DATE, PAYTO, AMOUNT, and CAT fields will be displayed.

The first step is to display at the top of the screen a few lines of text that will serve as a screen heading. Note that the last command in the sequence below draws a single line box around the heading lines. Enter

```
* DISPLAY SCREEN HEADING
CLEAR
@ 3,10 SAY "EXPENSES FILE RECORDS"
@ 4,40 SAY "Date:"+dtoc(date())+" Time:"+time()
@ 4,0 SAY "#"
@ 4,5 SAY "DATE"
@ 4,15 SAY "PAYEE"
@ 4,40 say "AMOUNT"
@ 4,65 say "CATEGORY"
@ 2,0 TO 5,79
```

Because the screen is limited to 25 lines of text, the program will need to pause after a certain number of records to let the user edit one of the records before the rest are displayed. The number can vary. If you really want, you can probably squeeze 22 records onto the screen. Although 20 is a better number, in this example you will display only 7 records at a time. This is because you need to see how multiple pages are handled and you have only 20 records in EXPENSES at this point. The logic of the program does not change when you change the number of lines displayed on the screen.

If you keep the number of records on the screen to ten or fewer, you can use single-digit entry. If you use more than ten records at a time in browse, you would have to widen the input area to accept a two-digit number. Another alternative to two-digit numbers is to use letters instead.

The first task is to initialize two variables: line, which will be used to determine the screen vertical position, and begindisp (begin display), which will hold the number of the record that is the first record displayed on a given screen.

The first record displayed on each screen is an important reference point to record. If you know the first record, you can then redisplay the entire screen. Later in the program you will see how this variable is used. Enter

```
*INITIALIZE VARIABLES
line=1
begindisp=RECNO()
* begin display of records
```

The actual display of the records begins by drawing a box around the area on the screen in which the records will appear. The box is not a functional part of the program, but a cosmetic aspect that helps users concentrate on the area of the screen in which you are displaying data.

```
@ 6,0 TO 14,79
```

Since the display of records needs to be limited, you have to create a DO WHILE loop that displays the maximum number of records on each screen. The loop will use the variable "line" to keep track of the number of records displayed. If line exceeds a certain value, the display is paused. Take into consideration that you might encounter the end of the file at some point during this loop. This means that you must test for two conditions, both of which must be true, or the display look is paused:

1. The value of line is less than the specified number.
2. The expression .NOT.EOF() is true.

The .AND. connective can be used to join the two conditions into a compound condition. Enter

```
DO WHILE line<8.AND..NOT.EOF()
```

Once you have entered this loop, you will display each of the four fields. The horizontal positions will be the same for each record. However, the tricky part is the value used for the vertical address. In these commands the value line+6 is used to calculate the number of the row. Since line begins as 1, the first record will appear at row 6+1 (i.e., row 7). At the bottom of the loop, the value of line is incremented so that the next time through the loop the data will be printed one line lower. Note also the use of the line to automatically number the records as they are displayed. The numbering does not correspond to their actual record numbers. The user will simply choose a record, 1 through 7, as if they were menu items. Enter

```
@ line+6,1 SAY str(line,2)+":"
@ line+6,5 SAY date
@ line+6,15 SAY payto
@ line+6,40 SAY amount PICTURE "999.99"
@ line+6,65 say cat PICTURE "9999"
```

The next step is to prepare the program for the display of the next record by moving the pointer to the next record in the file (SKIP) and incrementing the value of line by 1. Enter

```
SKIP
line=line+1
```

Now end the screen display loop. The loop will repeat until 7 records have been displayed, or the end of the file is encountered. Enter

```
ENDDO display one screen
```

The next section of the program handles the actions that should take place once a full screen of records has been displayed. The first section is a special prompt that will be displayed if the end of the file is reached. This is helpful to the user to know that all the records in the file have been displayed. Enter

```
IF EOF()
    @ line+6,10 SAY "**Last Record in File**"
ENDIF end of file marker
```

Next, display the three options for the user to take:

1. **Enter number.** This option allows the user to enter the number of the record to be edited. The record selected will then appear in a full-screen display format.

2. **[F9].** This key causes the program to display the next group of records in the file.

3. **[F10].** This key causes the program to terminate. The key allows the user to escape from the browse at any time.

The next group of commands creates a variable called "action." Action is defined as a single blank character. A prompt is displayed and the action variable accessed for input by a READ command. Enter

```
action=SPACE(1)
@ 24,0 SAY "Enter Number or F9 next screen or F10 to Quit" GET action
READ
```

Following the READ, the value of action should be evaluated with a DO CASE. Enter

DO CASE

The first case to be evaluated is the result of the **[F9]** key. Remember that **[F9]** was assigned a value of N by the SET FUNCTION command at the beginning of the program. **[F9]** displays the next screen. This is a very simple option. A special form of the @ command is used to clear the screen from column zero, row down. The value of line is then set back to 1. This causes the next record to be displayed at row 7 once again. Enter

CASE action="N"
    @ 4,0 CLEAR
    line=1

The next case is **[F10]** the QUIT command. **[F10]** will simply exit the loop. Enter

CASE action="Q"
    EXIT

The final and most complex option allows users to edit the selected record. Since this section is more complicated than the others, it might help to study in some detail what has to be done.

The key is to position the pointer at the record indicated by the user. Once that is done, the format file EXPENSES can be used to place the file into a full-screen EDIT mode. After the editing takes place, you will want to display the same menu of files from which the user has just selected.

Begin with the first task, positioning the pointer at the selected record. This is not a straightforward matter because the user is entering a number, chosen from 1 through 7, that corresponds to the position of the record on the screen, not the actual record number.

The value of action tells you in a relative way which record users want to edit. For example, if users enter 3, they are selecting the third record from the top of the list. However, in terms of pointer position it is more important to think of the selected record's distance from the bottom of the list because that is where the pointer is currently positioned.

After each screen display, the value of line is 8. If users want to edit record no. 3, the pointer must be moved backward 5 records in the file.

In the commands below, the variable move is calculated to indicate the number of steps needed to position the pointer. First action, which is a character variable, is converted to a numeric value with the VAL() function. Then that number is subtracted from the value of line. The result is multiplied by negative one because the movement will be backward in the file. Enter

CASE action>"0"
move=(line−VAL(action))*−1

The SKIP command positions the pointer backwards. Enter

```
SKIP move
```

Now you can display the EXPENSES format and allow users to edit. Enter

```
SET FORMAT TO expenses
READ
CLOSE FORMAT
```

The last trick is to use the value stored in begindisp. Remember that at the beginning of the loop you stored the record number of the first record on the display to this variable. You can now reestablish the screen display for the user. Enter

```
     ** redisplay browse **
       GOTO begindisp
   ENDCASE
ENDDO end of file reached
```

The program concludes with the usual housekeeping commands.

```
SET STATUS ON
SET SCOREBOARD ON
SET TALK ON
CLOSE DATABASE
RETURN
```

The entire program should look like this:

```
CLEAR
SET TALK OFF
SET STATUS OFF
SET SCOREBOARD OFF
USE expenses INDEX dateord,catorder,payorder,amtorder
SET FUNCTION 9 TO "N"
SET FUNCTION 10 to "Q"
DO WHILE .NOT. EOF()
   * DISPLAY SCREEN HEADING
   CLEAR
   @ 3,10  SAY "EXPENSES FILE RECORDS"
   @ 3,40 SAY "Date:"+dtoc(date())+"  Time:"+time()
   @ 4,1  SAY "/"
   @ 4,5  SAY "DATE"
   @ 4,15 SAY "PAYEE"
   @ 4,40 say "AMOUNT"
   @ 4,65 say "CATEGORY"
   @ 2,0 TO 5,79
   *INITIALIZE VARIABLES
   line=1
   begindisp=RECNO()
   * begin display of records
   @ 6,0 TO 14,79
   DO WHILE line<8.AND..NOT.EOF()
      @ line+6,1  SAY str(line,2)+"."
      @ line+6,5  SAY date
      @ line+6,15 SAY payto
      @ line+6,40 SAY amount PICTURE "999.99"
      @ line+6,65 say cat PICTURE "9999"
      SKIP
      line=line+1
   ENDDO display one screen
```

```
  ┌──►IF EOF()─────
  │   │    @ line+6,1Ø SAY "**Last Record in File**"
  │   └──ENDIF end of file marker◄──
  │     ACTION=SPACE(1)
  │     @ 24,Ø SAY "Enter Number or F9 next screen or F1Ø to Quit" GET act
  │     READ
  │   ┌─►DO CASE─────
  │   │      CASE action="N"
  │   │            @ 4,Ø CLEAR
  │   │            line=1
  │   │      CASE action="Q"
  │   │            EXIT
  │   │      CASE action>"Ø"
  │   │            move=(line-VAL(action))*-1
  │   │            suspend
  │   │            SKIP move
  │   │            SET FORMAT TO expenses
  │   │            READ
  │   │            CLOSE FORMAT
  │   │            ** redisplay browse **
  │   │            GOTO begindisp
  │   └──ENDCASE◄──
  └──ENDDO end of file reached◄──
      SET STATUS ON
      SET SCOREBOARD ON
      SET TALK ON
      CLOSE DATABASE
      RETURN
```

Save the program by entering

[CTRL/End]

Execute the program by entering

DO expbrow <return>

The program will display

#	DATE	EXPENSES FILE RECORDS PAYEE	Date:11/Ø7/86 Time:Ø2:34:29 AMOUNT	CATEGORY
1.	Ø1/Ø2/85	CROW CANYON LUMBER	68.4Ø	11Ø
2.	Ø1/1Ø/85	SEARS	17.95	14Ø
3.	Ø1/15/85	GREEN ACRES FURN	264.68	12Ø
4.	Ø1/17/85	INSTANT PRINTING	59.5Ø	14Ø
5.	Ø1/21/85	PG&E	6Ø.6Ø	13Ø
6.	Ø1/3Ø/85	PACIFIC BELL	44.28	13Ø
7.	Ø2/Ø2/85	BRITZ PRINTING	47.95	14Ø

Display the next group of records by entering

[F9]

The screen will display

#	DATE	EXPENSES FILE RECORDS PAYEE	Date:11/Ø7/86 Time:Ø2:35:49 AMOUNT	CATEGORY
1.	Ø2/Ø2/85	GIFT STORE	5.94	14Ø
2.	Ø2/Ø5/85	GREEN ACRES FURN	175.ØØ	12Ø
3.	Ø3/14/86	COMPUTER SUPPLY CO	75.5Ø	14Ø
4.	Ø3/15/86	BACON EAST PHARMACY	2.56	1ØØ
5.	Ø3/15/86	VIRCO EQUIPMENT	35Ø.45	12Ø
6.	Ø3/21/86	PRICE CLUB	45.67	14Ø
7.	Ø3/25/86	DAK PRODUCTS	175.ØØ	11Ø

Edit a record by entering

3

The screen format displays the record in full-screen layout. You can make any editing changes desired.

If you want to allow editing of the MEMO field, change the READ command following the SET FORMAT TO expenses command to EDIT NEXT 1.

To continue, enter

[Pg Dn]

The program returns to the browse display of the same records. Exit the program by entering

[F10]

Run the program again to get a feel for the interface. The browse is an alternative design for the basic editing program. It provides the user with more information to help in choosing the records to edit. In addition, the user does not have to manually enter a name or an amount that can easily be typed incorrectly. Instead, the user simply picks from a menu of information already displayed on the screen.

The browse program takes the concept developed in the menus designed in Chapter 13 and extends the design. In Chapter 13, literal choices were written into the menu. In the EXPBROW program you can see that the menu options are filled in with data from the data base file. The options change as each group of records is displayed.

MORE BROWSE OPTIONS

The browse/menu-type interface has a great potential in *dBASE III Plus* programming. For example, it will not take very much to add some interesting features to the previous program.

The first feature will be a menu that allows you to select different index orders for the browse. In that way, the records can be presented in date, payee, amount, or category order. In addition, you may want to allow the user to mark records as deleted. You will be surprised how little the basic structure of the program has to be revised to allow this increased flexibility.

Load the program into the editor by entering

MODIFY COMMAND expbrow <return>

The first part of the program remains unchanged except for the order of the index files in the USE statement. This may seem like an odd thing to be concerned about, considering that it has been stressed that the order of the index files, with the exception of the master file, is irrelevant.

In this case, the order does matter because of a shortcut that will be taken later in the program. The main idea is that the order of the index files should match the order of the menu options shown below. For example, if the third menu option is Indexed by Amount, then the third index file opened should be amtorder. Enter

```
CLEAR
SET TALK OFF
SET STATUS OFF
SET SCOREBOARD OFF
USE expenses INDEX dateord,payorder,amtorder,catorder
```

The first modification is to insert a menu display at the beginning of the program. The menu is implemented by using the TEXT/ENDTEXT method. Insert the commands shown in bold below into the program:

```
TEXT

        BROWSING EXPENSE RECORDS
        Choose an Index Order

        1. By Date
        2. By Payee
        3. By Amount
        4. By Category

ENDTEXT
```

Following the menu, it is necessary to allow the user to input one of the menu options and then set the index order accordingly. A variable is created called ordernum (index order number). The default is 1. Users can enter a different number value if they desire. Enter

```
ordernum=1
@ 20,0 SAY "Enter number " GET ordernum PICTURE "9"
READ
```

Here comes the interesting part. The user has entered a numeric value into ordernum that corresponds to the number of one of the index files. *dBASE III Plus* assigns a number to each of the index files opened beginning with 1. The SET ORDER command switches one of the open index files for the index file. For example, SET ORDER TO 3 makes the third index file (in this example AMTORDER) the master index.

The shortcut comes when you place the numeric variable, ordernum, into the SET ORDER command. Thus whatever number is entered by the user becomes the master index number. The shortcut eliminates the need to use an IF or DO CASE structure to select the proper index file. Enter

```
SET ORDER TO ordernum
GO TOP
SET FUNCTION 2 TO "D"
```

It is necessary to follow the SET ORDER command with a GO TOP command. Unlike SET INDEX, SET ORDER does not affect the position of the pointer. To make sure that the browse begins at the first index record, you need to use the GO TOP to position the pointer at the logical beginning of the file. The SET FUNC-TION command will be used later to delete records. It is not related to the index commands but it needs to be set at this point in the program.

Once the correct index has been selected, the browse portion of the program pro-ceeds unchanged. The next modification comes after the display loop. However, there is one addition that ought to be made, now that you are working with deleting records: the insertion of an IF condition that tests records for the deletion mark.

If the records are deleted, a message is displayed beside the record. Otherwise nothing is displayed. Insert the lines shown in bold. Enter

```
DO WHILE line8.AND..NOT.EOF()
     @ line+6,1 SAY str(line,2)+":"
     @ line+6,5 SAY date
     @ line+6,15 SAY payto
     @ line+6,40 SAY amount PICTURE "999.99"
     @ line+6,65 say cat PICTURE "9999"
          IF DELETED()
               @ line+6,70 SAY "*Deleted*"
          ENDIF
     SKIP
     line=line+1
ENDDO display one screen
```

The next change to the program allows the user to select deletion in addition to the other options. In order to make the prompts easier to read, they have been divided into two commands, one printing on line 23, the other on line 24.

Following that, a CASE is added to the DO CASE structure that deletes the specified record. When [**F2**] is pressed, the user is asked to enter the menu number of the record to delete. This case uses the same logic as the editing option to posi-tion the pointer to the selected record. The record is marked for deletion and the menu redisplayed. Insert the commands shown in bold below:

```
IF EOF()
     @ line+6,10 SAY "**Last Record in File**"
ENDIF end of file marker
ACTION=SPACE(1)
```

```
    @ 23,0 SAY "Enter Number to Edit Record"
    @ 24,0 SAY "F2 to Delete | F9 next screen | F10 to Quit" GET action
READ
DO CASE
      CASE action="D"
          @ 23,0 CLEAR
          @ 23,0 SAY "Enter number to DELETE " GET action
          READ
          move=(line-VAL(action))*-1
          SKIP move
          DELETE
          GOTO begindisp
      CASE action="N"
        @ 4,0 CLEAR
        line=1
      CASE action="Q"
        EXIT
      CASE action>"0"
        move=(line-VAL(action))*-1
        SKIP move
        SET FORMAT TO expenses
        READ
        CLOSE FORMAT
        ** redisplay browse **
        GOTO begindisp
      ENDCASE
ENDDO end of file reached
```

The entire program should look like this. The shading is used to dramatize how one loop is nested inside of a larger loop. In this book, shading, in addition to the lines and arrows, will be added to help you visualize the logic of the program. The shading has no functional purpose but simply serves to emphasize the structure of the program.

```
CLEAR
SET TALK OFF
SET STATUS OFF
SET SCOREBOARD OFF
USE expenses INDEX dateord,payorder,amtorder,catorder
TEXT

                BROWSING EXPENSE RECORDS
                Choose an Index Order

                1. By Date
                2. By Payee
                3. By Amount
                4. By Category

ENDTEXT
ordernum=1
@ 20,0 SAY "Enter number " GET ordernum PICTURE "9"
READ
SET ORDER TO ordernum
GO TOP
SET FUNCTION 2 TO "D"
```

```
                    SET FUNCTION 9 TO "N"
                    SET FUNCTION 10 to "Q"
                  ►DO WHILE .NOT. EOF()
                    * DISPLAY SCREEN HEADING
                    CLEAR
                    @ 3,10  SAY "EXPENSES FILE RECORDS"
                    @ 3,40  SAY "Date:"+dtoc(date())+"  Time:"+time()
                    @ 4,1   SAY "/"
                    @ 4,5   SAY "DATE"
                    @ 4,15  SAY "PAYEE"
                    @ 4,40  say "AMOUNT"
                    @ 4,65  say "CATEGORY"
                    @ 2,0 TO 5,79
                    *INITIALIZE VARIABLES
                    line=1
                    begindisp=RECNO()
                    * begin display of records
                    @ 6,0 TO 14,79
                  ►DO WHILE line<8.AND..NOT.EOF()
                        @ line+6,1   SAY str(line,2)+"."
                        @ line+6,5   SAY date
                        @ line+6,15  SAY payto
                        @ line+6,40  SAY amount PICTURE "999.99"
                        @ line+6,65  say cat PICTURE "9999"
                      ►IF DELETED()
                        @ line+6,70 SAY "*Deleted*"
                        ENDIF
                        SKIP◄
                        line=line+1
                    ENDDO display one screen◄
                    IF EOF()
                        @ line+6,10 SAY "**Last Record in File**"
                    ENDIF end of file marker
                    ACTION=SPACE(1)
                    @ 23,0 SAY "Enter Number to Edit Record"
                    @ 24,0 SAY "F2 to Delete | F9 next screen | F10 to Quit" GET action
                    READ
                  ►DO CASE
                      CASE action="D"
                          @ 23,0 CLEAR
                          @ 23,0 SAY "Enter number to DELETE " GET action
                          READ
                          move=(line-VAL(action))*-1
                          SKIP move
                          DELETE
                          GOTO begindisp
                      CASE action="N"
                          @ 4,0 CLEAR
                          line=1
                      CASE action="Q"
                          EXIT
                      CASE action>"0"
                          move=(line-VAL(action))*-1
                          SKIP move
                          SET FORMAT TO expenses
                          READ
                          CLOSE FORMAT
                          ** redisplay browse **
                          GOTO begindisp
                      ENDCASE◄
                  ENDDO end of file reached◄
                    SET STATUS ON
                    SET SCOREBOARD ON
                    SET TALK ON
                    CLOSE DATABASE
                    RETURN
```

Save the program by entering

[CTRL/End]

Execute the program by entering

DO expbrow <return>

The program displays the INDEX ORDER menu.

```
BROWSING EXPENSE RECORDS
Choose an Index Order

1. By Date
2. By Payee
3. By Amount
4. By Category



Enter number  1
```

Choose payee order by entering

> **2**

The program displays the records like this:

```
          EXPENSES FILE RECORDS      Date:11/07/86  Time:02:41:27
#    DATE        PAYEE              AMOUNT                    CATEGORY

1. 03/15/86  BACON EAST PHARMACY       2.56                    100
2. 02/02/85  BRITZ PRINTING           47.95                    140
3. 03/29/86  COMPUTER CURRENTS        15.00                    140
4. 03/14/86  COMPUTER SUPPLY CO       75.50                    140
5. 01/02/85  CROW CANYON LUMBER       68.40                    110
6. 03/25/86  DAK PRODUCTS            175.00                    110
7. 03/29/86  DAK PRODUCTS              2.00                    140
```

Delete the third record by entering

> **[F2]**
> **3**

The screen is redisplayed and the *Deleted* mark appears next to the third record on the display.

```
          EXPENSES FILE RECORDS      Date:11/07/86  Time:02:42:50
#    DATE        PAYEE              AMOUNT                    CATEGORY

1. 03/15/86  BACON EAST PHARMACY       2.56                    100
2. 02/02/85  BRITZ PRINTING           47.95                    140
3. 03/29/86  COMPUTER CURRENTS        15.00                    140 *Deleted*
4. 03/14/86  COMPUTER SUPPLY CO       75.50                    140
5. 01/02/85  CROW CANYON LUMBER       68.40                    110
6. 03/25/86  DAK PRODUCTS            175.00                    110
7. 03/29/86  DAK PRODUCTS              2.00                    140
```

Exit the program by entering

> **[F10]**

Run the program several times and test the various index orders.

Recall deleted records by entering

```
USE expenses <return>
RECALL ALL  <return>
CLOSE DATABASE <return>
```

Exercise 3   You may have noted that the EXPBROW program did not pack the deleted records at the end of the program. You want to make sure that there are some deleted records before you pack. In order to do that you must search the data base file to find at least one deleted record. If you find one, ask if the user wants to pack the file. If you do not find any deleted records, it is not necessary to ask about packing. A version of EXPBROW modified as described is shown at the end of the chapter.

SUMMARY

In this chapter you learned how to create routines that would allow the user to locate, display, and revise data.

The edit programs consist of two parts:

1. **SEARCH.** Locate the desired record.
2. **EDIT.** Display the data for editing.

The searching can be done by either the sequential or the random access method. The sequential method uses the LOCATE command to search the actual data base for matching data. This method can become quite slow if the data base file contains a large number of records.

The random method allows you to take advantage of the high-speed search *dBASE III Plus* can perform in indexed data base files. To use the high-speed search you must make sure that the index files are up to date and accurate. This type of searching uses the SEEK command to position the pointer at the correct record.

An alternative to the standard search routine is a browse-type routine in which the parts of the records are displayed on a menu from which the user can simply select. This type of interface makes it easier to find records when one is not exactly sure how they were entered.

ANSWER KEY

Question 1

The index files are not opened to index the data base file in a special order. They are opened because the editing program allows the user to change data. If the data changed is part of the key information for one of the index files, the index files must be open in order to be updated for any changes.

Question 2

The PAYTO field was defined as 20 characters. By making key 20 blanks, you allow for the entry of a search key that is as large as the entire field.

Exercise 1

Note that when EDIT NEXT 1 is added to this program, the pointer is automatically moved to the next record. Therefore, in addition to changing READ to EDIT NEXT 1 you must remove the SKIP commands as indicated.

```
CLEAR
SET TALK OFF
SET STATUS OFF
USE expenses
expedit=.t.
DO WHILE expedit
    CLEAR
    TEXT

              Edit Existing Records

          1. Search by Payee
          2. Search by Date
          3. Search by Amount
          0. Quit
    ENDTEXT
    choice=0
    @ 10,15 SAY "Enter search option" GET choice PICTURE "9"
    READ
    DO CASE
        CASE choice=1
            heading="RETRIEVE A RECORD BY PAYEE"
            prompt="Enter Payee"
            key=SPACE(20)
            SET INDEX TO payorder,catorder,amtorder,dateord
            fieldname="PAYTO"
        CASE choice=2
            heading="RETRIEVE A RECORD BY DATE"
            prompt="Enter Date"
            key=CTOD("  /  /  ")
            SET INDEX TO dateord,payorder,catorder,amtorder
            fieldname="DATE"
        CASE choice=3
            heading="RETRIEVE A RECORD BY AMOUNT"
            prompt="Enter Amount"
            key=0.00
```

```
            SET INDEX TO amtorder,dateord,payorder,catorder
            fieldname="AMOUNT"
     OTHERWISE
            EXIT
     ENDCASE
     CLEAR
     @ 5,20 SAY heading
     @ 10,10 SAY prompt GET key PICTURE "@!"
     READ
     IF TYPE("key")5"C"
            key=TRIM(key)
     ENDIF
     SEEK key
     IF FOUND()
       SET FORMAT TO expenses
       EDIT NEXT 1 <=========change
       CLOSE FORMAT
       *SKIP <===========delete
       DO WHILE &fieldname=key
         more=.T.
         @ 23,0 SAY "Display next match?" GET more PICTURE "Y"
         READ
         IF .NOT. more
              EXIT
         ENDIF more records
         SET FORMAT TO expenses
         EDIT NEXT 1 <=======change
         CLOSE FORMAT
         *SKIP <========delete
       ENDDO more matching records
     ELSE
            WAIT "***NOT FOUND***Any Key to Continue"
     ENDIF
  ENDDO
  SET TALK ON
  SET STATUS ON
  CLOSE DATABASE
  RETURN
```

Exercise 2

Changes are shown in bold.

```
CLEAR
SET TALK OFF
SET STATUS OFF
USE expenses
expedit=.t.
DO WHILE expedit
    CLEAR
```

```
TEXT

    Edit Existing Records

    1. Search by Payee
    2. Search by Date
    3. Search by Amount
            4. Search By Category
    0. Quit
ENDTEXT
choice=0
@ 10,15 SAY "Enter search option" GET choice PICTURE "9"
READ
DO CASE
    CASE choice=1
        heading="RETRIEVE A RECORD BY PAYEE"
        prompt="Enter Payee"
        key=SPACE(20)
        SET INDEX TO payorder,catorder,amtorder,dateord
        fieldname="PAYTO"
    CASE choice=2
        heading="RETRIEVE A RECORD BY DATE"
        prompt="Enter Date"
        key=CTOD("  /  /  ")
        SET INDEX TO dateord,payorder,catorder,amtorder
        fieldname="DATE"
    CASE choice=3
        heading="RETRIEVE A RECORD BY AMOUNT"
        prompt="Enter Amount"
        key=0.00
        SET INDEX TO amtorder,dateord,payorder,catorder
        fieldname="AMOUNT"
    CASE choice=4
        heading="RETRIEVE A RECORD BY CATEGORY"
        prompt="Enter Amount"
        key=0
        SET INDEX TO catorder, dateord,payorder,amtorder
        fieldname="CAT"
    OTHERWISE
        EXIT
    ENDCASE
    CLEAR
    @ 5,20 SAY heading
    @ 10,10 SAY prompt GET key PICTURE "@!"
    READ
    IF TYPE("key")5"C"
        key=TRIM(key)
    ENDIF
    SEEK key
```

```
            IF FOUND()
               SET FORMAT TO expenses
               EDIT NEXT 1
               CLOSE FORMAT
               DO WHILE &fieldname=key
                  more=.T.
                  @ 23,0 SAY "Display next match?" GET more PICTURE "Y"
                  READ
                  IF .NOT. more
                     EXIT
                  ENDIF more records
                  SET FORMAT TO expenses
                  EDIT NEXT 1
                  CLOSE FORMAT
               ENDDO more matching records
            ELSE
                WAIT "***NOT FOUND***Any Key to Continue"
            ENDIF
ENDDO
SET TALK ON
SET STATUS ON
CLOSE DATABASE
RETURN
```

Exercise 3

Additions are marked in bold:

```
CLEAR
SET TALK OFF
SET STATUS OFF
SET SCOREBOARD OFF
USE expenses INDEX dateord,payorder,amtorder,catorder
TEXT

            BROWSING EXPENSE RECORDS
            Choose an Index Order

            1. By Date
            2. By Payee
            3. By Amount
            4. By Category
ENDTEXT
ordernum=1
@ 20,0 SAY "Enter number " GET ordernum PICTURE "9"
READ
SET ORDER TO ordernum
GO TOP
SET FUNCTION 2 TO "D"
SET FUNCTION 9 TO "N"
```

```
SET FUNCTION 10 TO "Q"
DO WHILE .NOT. EOF()
    *DISPLAY SCREEN HEADING
    CLEAR
    @ 3,10 SAY "EXPENSES FILE RECORDS"
    @ 3,40 SAY "Date: "+dtoc(date())+" Time:"+time()
    @ 4,1 SAY "#"
    @ 4,5 SAY "DATE"
    @ 4,15 SAY "PAYEE"
    @ 4,40 say "AMOUNT"
    @ 4,65 say "CATEGORY"
    @ 2,0 to 5,79
    *INITIALIZE VARIABLES
    line=1
    begindisp=RECNO()
    *begin display of records
    @ 6,0 TO 14,79
    DO WHILE line<8 .AND. .NOT. EOF()
        @ line+6,1 SAY str(line,2)+"."
        @ line+6,5 SAY date
        @ line+6,15 SAY payto
        @ line+6,40 SAY amount PICTURE "999.99"
        @ line+6,65 say cat PICTURE "9999"
        IF DELETED()
            @ line+6,70 SAY "*Deleted*"
        ENDIF
        SKIP
        line=line+1
    ENDDO display one screen
    IF EOF()
        @ line+6,10 SAY "**Last Record in File**"
    ENDIF end of file marker
    ACTION=SPACE(1)
    @ 23,0 SAY "Enter Number to Edit Record"
    @ 24,0 SAY "F2 to Delete | F9 next screen | F10 to Quit" GET action
    READ
    DO CASE
        CASE action="D"
            @ 23,0 CLEAR
            @ 20,0 SAY " Enter number to DELETE " GET action
            READ
            move=(line-VAL(action))*-1
            SKIP move
            DELETE
            GOTO begindisp
        CASE action="N"
            @ 4,0 CLEAR
            line=1
        CASE action="Q"
            EXIT
```

```
            CASE action>"0"
                 move=(line-VAL(action))*-1
                 SKIP move
                 SET FORMAT TO expenses
                 READ
                 CLOSE FORMAT
                 **redisplay browse**
                 GOTO begindisp
            ENDCASE
ENDDO end of file reached
*check for deleted records
LOCATE FOR DELETED()
IF FOUND()
        packit=.F.
        CLEAR
        @ 10,10 SAY "Pack Deleted Records? (Y/N) " GET packit PICTURE "Y"
        READ
        IF packit
            PACK
        ENDIF packit true
ENDIF deleted record found
SET STATUS ON
SET SCOREBOARD ON
SET TALK ON
CLOSE DATABASE
RETURN
```

CUSTOM PRINTED

REPORTS

IN CHAPTER 15 YOU LEARNED how to create entry programs; Chapter 16 taught you to create programs that allowed you to display and revise the data that had been entered. Chapter 17 is the last basic systems design chapter in the book.

This chapter concentrates on the basic programming techniques used to create printed outputs based on the data in the data base file. Printer outputs can take many forms (e.g., column reports, printed forms, or special printed forms like checks or W2-Forms). Many report tasks are simple column reports that can be handled with the *dBASE III Plus* report generator (e.g., CREATE REPORT, REPORT FORM commands).

Custom reports are needed to handle a wide variety of printing tasks that the REPORT command cannot. They allow you almost total control over what prints at each position on each page.

Even though custom report outputs may vary greatly, all reports have certain things in common. The programs in this chapter illustrate the basic techniques used to create and print reports of all types.

FORMATTED AND UNFORMATTED OUTPUTS

dBASE III Plus allows you to use two types of commands to output data to the printer: formatted and unformatted. Formatted commands are the @/SAY commands, which send data to specific addresses on the output grid. Unformatted commands are those like LIST and ?, which print data on the next available line. Both commands can be used to produce printed outputs. In general, it is better to use the formatted output commands to send data to the printer. However, since unformatted outputs also can be used, and because they are easier to work with, a simple example that contrasts both methods will be used.

Before you begin to create reports, a larger data base file than the EXPENSES file should be made. The reason is that reports are printed on pages and page printing creates special problems that your program needs to account for. The EXPENSES file contains only 19 records. It will be easier to test the program if you have a data base file of about 80 records. A data base of this size assures you that the program is able to correctly print a second page. Usually, if the program works correctly for two pages, you can safely assume that the rest of the report will format correctly.

To create this file you can simply use the COPY and APPEND commands to create a file that contains four duplicates of every record in EXPENSES. First place EXPENSES in use. Enter

USE expenses < return >

Next, copy the data to a new file. Enter

COPY TO prtdata < return >

Now use print data. Enter

USE prtdata < return >

Append another copy of the EXPENSES data. Enter

APPEND FROM expenses < return >

Repeat this command two more times. Count the number of records by entering

? RECCOUNT()

You now have 76 records with which to test your printing programs.

UNFORMATTED OUTPUT

The first step is to design a program that will output the data from a file. This program is not very complicated but needs a lot of modification. Preparing it will serve to illustrate all the components that go into a printing program.

Create a program file called UNFORM (unformatted) by entering

MODIFY COMMAND unform <**return**>

The program begins with the usual housekeeping commands and the USE command, which opens that data base file. In this report you start out using the smaller data file, EXPENSES. Enter

```
CLEAR
SET TALK OFF
SET STATUS OFF
USE expenses
```

Once the file has been opened, you can begin to print the data. The first step is to turn on the printing of unformatted outputs with the SET PRINT ON command. When the print is on, any data sent to the screen is also sent to the printer. Enter

```
SET PRINT ON
```

> *This is true even of information like talk that is created by* dBASE III Plus. *If you do not set the talk off when you print, any talk that appears on the screen will also appear on the printer.*

The next section of the program is a loop. In this case the program will process all the records stored in the data base file, so you will use the condition NOT. EOF() as the logical condition in the DO WHILE. Enter

```
DO WHILE .NOT. EOF()
```

The loop executes two commands:

1. **PRINT A LINE.** The data from each record are printed out.
2. **SKIP.** The pointer is positioned at the the next record in the file.

Enter

```
    ? date,payto,amount,cat,deduct
    SKIP
ENDDO
```

The loop will print out the four fields specified for each of the records in the file. When the loop has finished, all the records will have been printed.

> dBASE III Plus *will hold the last line output in its buffer. If you were to stop the printing at this point, you would find that all but the last record had printed. You must always remember to force the last line out of the buffer area by printing an extra blank line, or using the EJECT command to send a form feed instruction to the printer.*

The next section of the program will print some summary information about the file. To mark off the summary data from the previous list, you can draw a line of = characters. *dBASE III Plus* allows you to take shortcuts when repeating the

same character. Instead of having to print a line of = signs, the REPLICATE()
function will automatically repeat the character a specified number of times. In
this case, 60 repetitions will be sufficient. Enter

```
? REPLICATE("=",60)
```

The SUM command is used to find the total of the AMOUNT field. Then that
total and the number of records is printed. Enter

```
SUM amount TO total
? "The sum of the amounts is",total
? "Total number of records is",RECCOUNT()
```

When the program has printed all the data, you are ready to complete the printing cycle by turning the print off and ejecting the paper. The *dBASE III Plus* EJECT
command sends a form feed character (ASCII 12) to the printer. Most printers will
then eject the paper to the top of the next form.

> How does the printer know where the top of the form is? The answer is that all printers
> are provided with default values for the length of a page, as well as other important
> printing characteristics. These default settings are usually controlled by DIP switches
> inside the printer. Some newer printers allow you to control these defaults with but-
> tons on the front of the printer. The usual default value for page length is 66 lines.
> As you print, the printer keeps track of the number of lines printed. When a form
> feed is sent, the printer subtracts the number of lines printed from 66 and sends that
> number of blank lines.

Enter

```
SET PRINT OFF
EJECT
CLOSE DATABASE
SET TALK ON
SET STATUS ON
RETURN
```

The entire program should look like this:

```
CLEAR
SET TALK OFF
SET STATUS OFF
USE expenses
SET PRINT ON
DO WHILE .NOT. EOF()
        ? date,payto,amount,cat,deduct
        SKIP
ENDDO
? REPLICATE("=",60)
SUM amount TO total
? "The sum of the amounts is",total
? "Total number of records is",RECCOUNT()
SET PRINT OFF
EJECT
CLOSE DATABASE
SET TALK ON
SET STATUS ON
```

Save the program by entering

[CTRL/End]

Execute the program by entering

DO unform <return>

The program will print out the following:

```
Ø1/Ø2/85 CROW CANYON LUMBER    68.4Ø   11Ø .T.
Ø1/1Ø/85 SEARS                 17.95   14Ø .F.
Ø1/15/85 GREEN ACRES FURN     264.68   12Ø .F.
Ø1/17/85 INSTANT PRINTING      59.5Ø   14Ø .F.
Ø1/21/85 PG&E                  6Ø.6Ø   13Ø .T.
Ø1/3Ø/85 PACIFIC BELL          44.28   13Ø .T.
Ø2/Ø2/85 BRITZ PRINTING        47.95   14Ø .F.
Ø2/Ø2/85 GIFT STORE             5.94   14Ø .F.
Ø2/Ø5/85 GREEN ACRES FURN     175.ØØ   12Ø .F.
Ø3/15/86 BACON EAST PHARMACY    2.56   1ØØ .F.
Ø3/15/86 VIRCO EQUIPMENT      35Ø.45   12Ø .F.
Ø3/14/86 COMPUTER SUPPLY CO    75.5Ø   14Ø .F.
Ø3/21/86 PRICE CLUB            45.67   14Ø .F.
Ø3/25/86 DAK PRODUCTS         175.ØØ   11Ø .T.
Ø3/29/86 COMPUTER CURRENTS     15.ØØ   14Ø .T.
Ø3/29/86 DAK PRODUCTS           2.ØØ   14Ø .T.
Ø3/29/86 MICROAMERICA         4ØØ.ØØ   12Ø .F.
Ø3/3Ø/86 QUILL                 79.95   14Ø .F.
Ø3/31/86 RV PAPER              33.92   14Ø .F.
=========================================================
The sum of the amounts is      1924.35
Total number of records is        19
```

SUPPRESSING THE SCREEN DISPLAY

The simple program that you just executed can be improved in a number of ways. Load the program into the editor by entering

MODIFY COMMAND unform <return>

Unformatted outputs always send their output to the screen, even when they are printing. It might make the program look cleaner if you found a way to suppress the screen display portion of it while the printing is taking place. The SET CONSOLE command controls output sent to the screen. The *dBASE III Plus* default is to set the console on (i.e., the screen displays data). Setting the console off keeps data from being displayed on the screen. The result in this program is that the data being printed are not echoed on the screen. Add the lines shown below in bold.

```
CLEAR
SET TALK OFF
SET STATUS OFF
USE expenses
? "PRINTING............."
SET CONSOLE OFF
SET PRINT ON
DO WHILE .NOT. EOF()
```

```
    ? date,payto,amount,cat,deduct
    SKIP
ENDDO
? REPLICATE("=",60)
SUM amount TO total
? "The sum of the amounts is",total
? "Total number of records is",RECCOUNT()
SET PRINT OFF
EJECT
SET CONSOLE ON
CLEAR
? "PRINTING COMPLETE"
CLOSE DATABASE
SET TALK ON
SET STATUS ON
```

Note that the messages meant to print on the screen are issued while the PRINT is off and the CONSOLE is on.

Save the program by entering

[CTRL/End]

Execute the program by entering

DO unform <return>

This time the program prints but no data are displayed on the screen.

SUBSTITUTIONS

One reason for using a program to make a listing like this program's is that you can perform logical operations while printing that are much more difficult to do when you are printing with report forms. For example, you might want to print the word "deductible" for each record that contains a true value in DEDUCT instead of just the T.

What makes this possible is a special form of the ? command, ??. The double question mark command works exactly like the ? with one important exception. The ? command precedes each line that it prints with a line-feed/carriage return. The commands below print the name on two different lines.

? "Joe" (line feed/carriage return, then JOE)
? "Smith" (line feed/carriage return, then SMITH)

The ?? does not precede the text with a line feed. Rather, it prints the data on the same line as the preceding text at the next available column. The two commands below print the first and last names on the same line.

? "JOE" (line feed/carriage return, then JOE)
?? " SMITH" (print SMITH)

This distinction is important because it is no longer necessary to have all the data that need to be printed on the same line, entered in a single ? command. It is possible to separate the items that will be printed with other commands. Those commands can be conditional commands that select text to print based on some logical condition. The commands below show that the word "deductible" will be printed only if the DEDUCT value is true.

```
IF deduct
     ?? "Deductible"
ENDIF
```

To illustrate how such changes can be used to print conditional text, load the program into the editor by entering

MODIFY COMMAND unform < return >

In the program below, two sections have been added as conditional text (i.e., text that prints on only some of the lines, depending on logical conditions). In the listing, the first section is used to determine which dates fell on Saturdays or Sundays. Such a distinction is very helpful when you are trying to make employer-related determinations, such as overtime. The DOW() function is used to determine the day of the week of each date. The second section is used to determine the deductible records.

Note the use of the ? and ?? commands. The first item on each line uses a ?. All the other items that might potentially be printed on that line are printed with a ??.

Also note that it is necessary to print either the word "weekend" or nine spaces to make sure all the columns line up. If you print "weekend" on some lines but not on others, the total number of characters on each line would be different, causing the columns not to line up.

Printing spaces ensures that the other items will always line up properly. The deductible condition does not need spaces because it falls at the end of the line.

Enter the commands shown in bold.

```
CLEAR
SET TALK OFF
SET STATUS OFF
USE expenses
? "PRINTING    ...."
SET CONSOLE OFF
SET PRINT ON
DO WHILE .NOT. EOF()
    IF DOW(date)=1.OR.DOW(date)=7
        ? "Weekend"+SPACE(2)
    ELSE
        ? SPACE(9)
    ENDIF
    ?? date,payto,amount,cat  <============ changed
    IF deduct
```

```
        ?? SPACE(2)+"Deductible"
    ENDIF
  SKIP
ENDDO
? REPLICATE("=",60)
SUM amount TO total
? "The sum of the amounts is",total
? "Total number of records is",RECCOUNT()
SET PRINT OFF
EJECT
SET CONSOLE ON
CLEAR
? "PRINTING COMPLETE"
CLOSE DATABASE
SET TALK ON
SET STATUS ON
RETURN
```

Save the program by entering

[Ctrl/End]

The effect of the IF/ENDIF structure could be achieved by using the IIF() function discussed in Chapter 7. For example, the print line could be written like this:

? ?? date,payto,amount,cat,IIF(deduct,SPACE(2)+"Deductible",SPACE(1))

The IIF() function would print when DEDUCT was true and would not print when deduct was false. The IF/ENDIF structure is a more standard programming approach. The IIF() function will execute slightly faster since it requires only one command line to execute. The overall effect of the two methods will be identical.

Execute the program by entering

DO unform <return>

The output will look like this:

```
          01/02/85  CROW CANYON LUMBER    68.40   110  Deductible
          01/10/85  SEARS                 17.95   140
          01/15/85  GREEN ACRES FURN     264.68   120
          01/17/85  INSTANT PRINTING      59.50   140
          01/21/85  PG&E                  60.60   130  Deductible
          01/30/85  PACIFIC BELL          44.28   130  Deductible
Weekend   02/02/85  BRITZ PRINTING        47.95   140
Weekend   02/02/85  GIFT STORE             5.94   140
          02/05/85  GREEN ACRES FURN     175.00   120
Weekend   03/15/86  BACON EAST PHARMACY    2.56   100
Weekend   03/15/86  VIRCO EQUIPMENT      350.45   120
          03/14/86  COMPUTER SUPPLY CO    75.50   140
          03/21/86  PRICE CLUB            45.67   140
          03/25/86  DAK PRODUCTS         175.00   110  Deductible
Weekend   03/29/86  COMPUTER CURRENTS     15.00   140  Deductible
Weekend   03/29/86  DAK PRODUCTS           2.00   140  Deductible
Weekend   03/29/86  MICROAMERICA         400.00   120
Weekend   03/30/86  QUILL                 79.95   140
          03/31/86  RV PAPER              33.92   140
==============================================================
The sum of the amounts is     1924.35
Total number of records is         19
```

ACCUMULATORS

In the previous example the SUM command was used to find the total of the amounts in the file that was printed. Although the method works, it works in a very inefficient way. The program requires *dBASE III Plus* to process the entire file twice. The first time through the data base file, each record is printed. Then to get the total, the program must go back to the beginning of the file and add together all the AMOUNT fields to find the total. When the data base file is small, the time wasted is not considerable. But in large data base files the time used up by making a second pass through the data base file is very important.

The problem gets worse when you want to gather several different types of totals. For example, suppose you wanted to get a total of all the deductible items, a total of all the nondeductible items, plus totals by each budget category. If you used the SUM command, you would have to make one full pass through the entire data base file for each type of total. This would make the program take much longer to complete the processing.

However, there is a way to avoid processing the data base file more than once. The trick is to create a series of memory variables that function as accumulators for the various totals. The amounts are added to the accumulators as each record is being printed. When the file has been printed, the values for the totals are already stored in the memory. All you need to do is print them; you don't have to go back through the data base file again.

As an illustration of the use of accumulators, you will modify the UNFORM program to calculate several different totals:

1. Totals for deductible and nondeductible items.
2. Totals for each of the four budget categories.
3. A total for all records.

Load the program into the editor by entering

MODIFY COMMAND unform < return >

The first change that needs to be made is to create a series of variables that will be used to hold the various totals. Note that the STORE command allows you to assign the same value to a list of variables with one command. Enter the commands shown below in bold.

```
CLEAR
SET TALK OFF
SET STATUS OFF
* initialize accumulators
STORE 0 TO ded,nonded,cat1,cat2,cat3,cat4,all
USE expenses
```

The next change in the program comes inside the processing loop. Position your cursor following the section of the program that reads

```
IF deduct
    ?? SPACE(2)+"Deductible"
ENDIF
```

The first line to insert at that point is a command that will accumulate the total for all the records. Enter

```
* calculate totals
all=all+amount
```

The next section will calculate the deductible and nondeductible items. In this case, an IF structure can be used to add the deductible items to the DED accumulator and the nondeductible items to the NONDED accumulator. Enter

```
IF deduct
    ded=ded+amount
ELSE
    nonded=nonded+amount
ENDIF deductible totals
```

The next addition to the program is a DO CASE structure. Because there are more than two accumulators to choose from when calculating budget categories, the DO CASE is more practical than using several IF structures. Enter

```
DO CASE
    CASE cat=110
        cat1=cat1+amount
    CASE cat=120
        cat2=cat2+amount
    CASE cat=130
        cat3=cat3+amount
    CASE cat=140
        cat4=cat4+amount
ENDCASE
```

The next change comes at the end of the program. This is where you want to display the information gathered during the processing of the file. The commands are simply instructions for printing each of the accumulators. Add the commands shown in bold.

The SUM command should be removed from the program because it is not needed any longer. Note also that one of the lines, ? "The sum of the amounts is", has been changed to use the ALL variable.

```
? REPLICATE("=",60)
? "The sum of the amounts is",all  <=========changed
? "Total number of records is",RECCOUNT()
? "Deductible ",ded
```

```
? "Non Deductible ",nonded
? "Category 110 ",cat1
? "Category 120 ",cat2
? "Category 130 ",cat3
? "Category 140 ",cat4
SET PRINT OFF
EJECT
SET CONSOLE ON
```

The entire program should look like this:

```
CLEAR
SET TALK OFF
SET STATUS OFF
* initialize accumulators
STORE 0 TO ded,nonded,cat1,cat2,cat3,cat4,all
USE expenses
? "PRINTING..........."
SET CONSOLE OFF
SET PRINT ON
DO WHILE .NOT. EOF()
    IF DOW(date)=1.OR.DOW(date)=7
        ? "Weekend"+SPACE(2)
    ELSE
        ? SPACE(9)
    ENDIF
    ?? date,payto,amount,cat
    IF deduct
        ?? SPACE(2)+"Deductible"
    ENDIF
    * calculate totals
    all=all+amount
    IF deduct
        ded=ded+amount
    ELSE
        nonded=nonded+amount
    ENDIF deductible totals
    DO CASE
        CASE cat=110
            cat1=cat1+amount
        CASE cat=120
            cat2=cat2+amount
        CASE cat=130
            cat3=cat3+amount
        CASE cat=140
            cat4=cat4+amount
    ENDCASE
    SKIP
ENDDO
? REPLICATE("=",60)
? "The sum of the amounts is",all
? "Total number of records is",RECCOUNT()
? "Deductible      ",ded
? "Non Deductible ",nonded
? "Category 110    ",cat1
? "Category 120    ",cat2
? "Category 130    ",cat3
? "Category 140    ",cat4
SET PRINT OFF
EJECT
SET CONSOLE ON
CLEAR
? "PRINTING COMPLETE"
CLOSE DATABASE
SET TALK ON
SET STATUS ON
RETURN
```

Save the program by entering

[Ctrl/End]

Execute the program by entering

DO unform < return >

The program will create an output like this:

```
         01/02/85 CROW CANYON LUMBER    68.40   110  Deductible
         01/10/85 SEARS                 17.95   140
         01/15/85 GREEN ACRES FURN     264.68   120
         01/17/85 INSTANT PRINTING      59.50   140
         01/21/85 PG&E                  60.60   130  Deductible
         01/30/85 PACIFIC BELL          44.28   130  Deductible
Weekend  02/02/85 BRITZ PRINTING        47.95   140
Weekend  02/02/85 GIFT STORE             5.94   140
         02/05/85 GREEN ACRES FURN     175.00   120
Weekend  03/15/86 BACON EAST PHARMACY    2.56   100
Weekend  03/15/86 VIRCO EQUIPMENT      350.45   120
         03/14/86 COMPUTER SUPPLY CO    75.50   140
         03/21/86 PRICE CLUB            45.67   140
         03/25/86 DAK PRODUCTS         175.00   110  Deductible
Weekend  03/29/86 COMPUTER CURRENTS     15.00   140  Deductible
Weekend  03/29/86 DAK PRODUCTS           2.00   140  Deductible
Weekend  03/29/86 MICROAMERICA         400.00   120
Weekend  03/30/86 QUILL                 79.95   140
         03/31/86 RV PAPER              33.92   140
=============================================================
The sum of the amounts is       1924.35
Total number of records is           19
Deductible              365.28
Non Deductible         1559.07
Category 110            243.40
Category 120           1190.13
Category 130            104.88
Category 140            383.38
```

This program provides a variety of accumulated totals without having to pass through the data base file more than once. As the data base files in your system increase in size, you will want to take care in writing programs to avoid commands that cause the program to sequentially process the data base file more than is absolutely necessary.

Exercise 1   Although programming is a complex business, you will find that you can borrow techniques used in one program to solve similar problems in another. So far the UNFORM program has printed the data base file in the order that was entered. Suppose you wanted to print the file in some indexed order; how would you modify the program?

The answer is that you would use the same sort of routine that you added to the EXPBROW editing program, which allows users to select an index order before the main part of the program prints the data. Referring to the changes made in EXPBROW, try to modify UNFORM to work with the four index files used in the EXPBROW file. A listing of a program that does this can be found at the end of the chapter.

To do this exercise, make a copy of the UNFORM program called UNFORM1 and make your changes. The next section of this chapter works with the UNFORM program without these changes.

PAGE BREAKS

You can probably guess what would happen if you changed the data base file from EXPENSES to PRTDATA. Because PRTDATA contains four times as many records as EXPENSES, the program will print four times as many records. The problem is that there are more records than can fit onto a single page. At this point, the UNFORM program has no way of knowing when the end of the page is approaching or what to do when that end is reached.

The key modification is to place a conditional structure in the program that tests to see if the text is too far down the page to print. The test will then eject the page and continue the printing at the top of the next page.

dBASE III Plus supplies a function that makes this test quite simple, called PROW(), printer row. The PROW() function keeps track of the last row printed on the page. For example, you could enter a command like this into a program:

```
IF PROW() > 54
```

When the printing begins at the top of the page, PROW() is assigned a value of zero. As each row prints, the value of PROW() is incremented. When the row counter reaches 56 lines, PROW() > 54 becomes true. You can then use that true condition to perform an EJECT. This feeds the paper form to the top of the next page and resets the value of PROW() to zero again.

Because the first line on the page is zero, not one, PROW() > 54 tests for 56 (55 + 1) lines printed on a page. Note that the standard 11-inch sheet of paper is 66 lines long (PROW() equals 65).

To modify the program to print correctly on more than one page, load the program into the editor by entering

MODIFY COMMAND unform < return >

There are two small changes to make. First, change the USE expenses command to USE prtdata. Then add the following commands shown in bold following the SKIP command. The command tests for the printing row and ejects to the next page when it gets too low.

```
DO CASE
   CASE cat=110
        cat1=cat1+amount
   CASE cat=120
        cat2=cat2+amount
   CASE cat=130
        cat3=cat3+amount
   CASE cat=140
        cat4=cat4+amount
ENDCASE
SKIP
   IF PROW()>54        <========== add command
      EJECT            <========== add command
   ENDIF               <========== add command
ENDDO
? REPLICATE("=",60)
? "The sum of the amounts is",all
```

Save the program by entering

[CTRL/End]

Execute the program by entering

DO unform < return >

The program correctly prints out the first page and then advances to a second page to complete the printing.

Exercise 2 So far, the assumption has been made that you are using continuous-feed paper. What would you need to do to this program to allow you to print on single sheets?

The answer is that you would need to pause the program after each page was ejected. Try to modify UNFORM to stop after every page and wait for the user to continue. Note that if you want to display an unformatted message on the screen, such as with the WAIT command, you must turn the print off and the console on. A sample program with this modification can be found at the end of the chapter.

FORMATTED OUTPUT

There are still a number of improvements that can be made in this report. However, they will not be made but added to a new report that will use formatted output commands to create a column-type report.

The formatted commands are the @/SAY commands. Note that when you send output to the printer, @/GET commands have no meaning. The @ SAY commands can be used to address locations on the printed page in the same way that they can be used to address locations on the screen display.

dBASE III Plus uses the command SET DEVICE to control which device, the screen or the printer, will receive the output of the @ SAY commands. The default setting is to send @ SAY output to the screen.

1. **SET DEVICE TO PRINT.** This command directs all subsequent @ SAY commands to the printer. @ GET commands are always sent to the screen.

    If you take a screen display that contains @/SAY, @/GET, and @/SAY/GET commands, and redirect the output to the printer, the @ SAY commands will be sent to the printer but the GETS will still be displayed on the screen. It is usually necessary to modify screen layouts such as format files before they can be used for printing forms.

2. **SET DEVICE TO SCREEN.** This command sends all subsequent @ SAY output to the screen display.

In using @ SAY commands directed toward the printer, some restrictions need to be considered. The most important is that the formatted output commands sent to the printer must proceed in a strict top to bottom, left to right fashion. Notice in the commands below that the row portion of the commands specifies printing at row 1, then row 3, then row 2. The commands would present no problem if they were sent to the screen for display; but when sent to the printer, *dBASE III Plus* cannot print backwards. The result is that the first two lines will be printed on one page, while the third will cause *dBASE III Plus* to skip to the second line of the next page.

```
@ 1,0 SAY "First line"  <----- Prints on line 1
@ 3,0 SAY "Third line"  <----- Prints on line 3
@ 2,0 SAY "Second line" <----- Prints on line 2, next page
```

The same type of problem can occur when you are printing from left to right. Look at the commands below.

```
@ 1,0 SAY "My Name is Sam"
@ 1,10 SAY "Hello Sam"
```

At first it might seem that these two commands shouldn't cause a problem. But, if you look carefully, you will see that the text printed at column 0 extends past column 10. The second command will begin to print "Hello" over "Sam." *dBASE III Plus* does not care if you overprint text, but it is a consideration you must keep in mind. What makes this more of a problem than it might seem at first is the use of variables. Look at the commands below:

```
@ 1,0 SAY TRIM(payto)
@ 1,10 SAY amount
```

Will these commands overprint? The answer depends on the actual length of the two fields. If PAYTO is more than 10 characters, then the fields will over print.

dBASE III Plus provides a means of avoiding this type of problem by using a special function, PCOL(), printer column. The PCOL() function is a numeric value equal to the current printing column position on the page. You can make sure that one field follows directly after the other by changing the column specification from an absolute location (e.g., column 10) to a PCOL() function. Look at the commands below:

```
@ 1,0 SAY TRIM(payto)
@ 1,PCOL()+1 SAY amount
```

The PCOL()+1 tells *dBASE III Plus* to print the amount one column to the left of the last character printed. You can increase the amount of space between the fields by adding a larger number to the PCOL() function.

The PCOL() function is reset to zero when a carriage return/line feed is sent to the printer or the page is ejected.

By using PCOL() and PROW(), you can create a printing program that uses relative addressing with formatted @ SAY commands to create column-type reports.

HEADERS, FOOTERS, AND PAGE NUMBERS

In this report you will also learn the techniques used to create page headings and footings, including automatic page numbering. As an illustration, create a report program called FORMTRP (formatted report) by entering

MODIFY COMMAND formrpt < return >

The program begins the same way as the unformatted program:

```
CLEAR
SET TALK OFF
SET STATUS OFF
* initialize accumulators
STORE 0 TO ded,nonded,cat1,cat2,cat3,cat4,all
```

Next, two variables are defined. RECNUM will be used to number automatically each of the lines that prints. Note that you will not use the RECNO() function to number the records. If the file were to be indexed while printing, the actual record numbers would not be consecutive. The PAGENUM variable would be used to keep track of the pages that are printed and print the actual page number at the bottom of the page. Enter

```
recnum=1
pagenum=1
```

The next section of the program prepares you to begin the processing of the records. First, the data base file is opened. In this case the records will be printed without an index file open. A message is displayed on the screen to tell the user that printing is taking place.

The SET DEVICE TO PRINT command redirects the output of the @ SAY commands to the printer. The DO WHILE command creates a loop that will continue until all the records in the file have been processed. Enter

```
USE prtdata
@ 10,10 SAY "PRINTING. Please Wait ........"
SET DEVICE TO PRINT
DO WHILE .NOT. EOF()
```

PAGE BEGINNINGS AND ENDINGS

In the UNFORM program you tested the amount of text printed on each page to determine whether or not a page break was necessary. The concept of page endings can also be extended to the beginning of each page.

When printing column-type reports, you are often required to print special information at the top and bottom of each page. This information occurs only once on each page. The remainder of the page is filled in with repetition of commands that print individual records.

The most common piece of information printed at the bottom of the page is the page number.

The type of information printed at the beginning of each page may be a heading or title for the report, as well as headings for each of the columns. In addition, the insertion of the date on which the report was printed is a common feature.

The trick to adding page headings and footings is to test for the proper conditions at the beginning of the loop. What sort of tests can be used? To determine if you need to print a page ending, you can test for a certain value in PROW() (e.g., PROW() > 54). A page heading can be determined by testing to see if the PROW() is at the beginning of a page (e.g., PROW() < 1).

Which test should come first? The answer is that you should test first for the end of the page, then the beginning. The reason is that following a page ending, you should automatically print a page beginning on the new page. This is accomplished when the page ending sequence resets the PROW() to 0, at the time that the completed page is ejected from the printer.

Begin the loop by entering the page ending routine. In this case, row 54, line 55 on the page is used as the last printed line. Enter

```
* Page end routine
IF PROW()>54
```

In this program you want to print the page number at the bottom of every page. As part of the page ending routine, you will need to print the page number before you eject the page. Enter

```
@ 60,35 SAY "Page :"+LTRIM(STR(pagenum,3))+" - "
```

Next, you can eject the page, resetting the PROW() to zero. Also note that you must increment the value of PAGENUM to make sure that the next page is numbered in sequence. Enter

```
    EJECT
    pagenum=pagenum+1
ENDIF end of page routine
```

Next, enter the page heading routine. This routine will print if the PROW() has just been reset. This is true when the program first begins and after each subsequent page ending. Thus the page beginning routine will print on all the pages of the report. Enter

```
* page heading routine
IF PROW()<1
```

The heading routine consists of a series of @ SAY commands that creates three lines of text. The first line begins at row 4. A title is printed, EXPENSES REPORT. A PCOL() function is used to print the date of the report on the same line but 10 spaces further to the right. The PCOL() is used here as a convenience to avoid having to count the number of letters in EXPENSES REPORT. Enter

```
@ 4,10 SAY "EXPENSES REPORT"
@ 4,PCOL()+10 SAY "Date of Report:"
@ 4,PCOL()+2 SAY DATE()
```

The next group of commands prints the headings for each of the columns that will be printed. Enter

```
@ 5,0 SAY "#"
@ 5,10 SAY "DATE"
@ 5,20 SAY "PAYEE"
@ 5,45 SAY "AMOUNT"
@ 5,60 SAY "CATEGORY"
```

The final part of the heading is a REPLICATE() function that prints a line of dashes. Enter

```
    @ 6,0 SAY REPLICATE(" - ",65)
ENDIF
```

With the header and footer routines resolved, go to the section of the loop that prints the lines for each record in the file. The first command prints a number for each record. The number is simply a consecutive numbering of the lines, not the actual record number. Enter

```
*print a line
@ PROW()+1,0 SAY LTRIM(STR(recnum,3))+":"
```

Note the use of the expression PROW()+1. This function tells *dBASE III Plus* to print these data one line lower than the last line printed. This command accomplishes two things. First, it places the data on the next available line for printing. Second, by printing, it establishes the current line as the new value for PROW(). For example, when the last line of the page heading routine prints on line 6, the

PROW() value is 6. The command to print at PROW()+1 places the text on line 7 (6 + 1). That also means that the next time a PROW() function is used, *dBASE III Plus* will assign the value of 7 to that function.

In practical terms, any data that you want to print on the same row as the last piece of data should use the row address of PROW().

Use PROW()+1 again only when you want to move onto the next line for printing. In this case, all the rest of the data is meant for the same line on the page, so enter

```
@ PROW(),10 SAY date
@ PROW(),20 SAY payto
@ PROW(),45 SAY amount PICTURE "9,999.99"
@ PROW(),60 SAY cat PICTURE "9999"
IF deduct
     @ PROW(), PCOL()+2 SAY "*Deductible*"
ENDIF
```

Note that formatted output commands allow you to use PICTURE functions to control formatting, in particular, formatting of numbers.

The next section of the loop is used to calculate the accumulators for the totals desired. This section is unaffected by the change from unformatted to formatted output commands. Enter

```
* calculate totals
recnum=recnum+1
all=all+amount
IF deduct
     ded=ded+amount
ELSE
     nonded=nonded+amount
ENDIF deductible totals
DO CASE
     CASE cat=110
          cat1=cat1+amount
     CASE cat=120
          cat2=cat2+amount
     CASE cat=130
          cat3=cat3+amount
     CASE cat=140
          cat4=cat4+amount
ENDCASE
SKIP
ENDDO
```

The final section of the program executes only after all the records have been processed. The printing consists of the totals at the end of the program. Before you print the totals you might want to test the PROW() to see if there is enough room left at the bottom of the page to print the total summary, or determine if that should be held over for the next page. Enter

```
IF PROW()>45
    @ 55,30 SAY "Totals on next page...."
    @ 60,35 SAY "Page - "+LTRIM(STR(pagenum,3))+" - "
    EJECT
    pagenum=pagenum+1
    @ 6,0 SAY "Total Information:"
ENDIF
```

Once you have determined the page that the totals should print on, you can actually print the data. Enter

```
*print totals
@ PROW()+1, 0 SAY REPLICATE("=",65)
@ PROW()+1,20 SAY "The sum of the amounts is"
@ PROW() ,44 SAY all PICTURE "99,999.99"
@ PROW()+1,20 SAY "Total number of records is"
@ PROW() ,44 SAY RECCOUNT() PICTURE "99,999"
@ PROW()+2,20 SAY "Deductible"
@ PROW() ,44 SAY all PICTURE "99,999.99"
@ PROW()+1,20 SAY "Not Deductible"
@ PROW() ,44 SAY all PICTURE "99,999.99"
@ PROW()+2,20 SAY "Category 110"
@ PROW() ,44 SAY cat1 PICTURE "99,999.99"
@ PROW()+1,20 SAY "Category 120"
@ PROW() ,44 SAY cat2 PICTURE "99,999.99"
@ PROW()+1,20 SAY "Category 130"
@ PROW() ,44 SAY cat3 PICTURE "99,999.99"
@ PROW()+1,20 SAY "Category 140"
@ PROW() ,44 SAY cat4 PICTURE "99,999.99"
@ 60,35 SAY "Page - "+LTRIM(STR(pagenum,3))+" - "
```

You may wonder why column 44 was used for printing the value of the total accumulators. The reason is that the totals are meant to line up with the values in the amount column.

The amount column was printed at column 45; why choose 44 for the totals? The reason has to do with the PICTURE clause. In the main loop, each AMOUNT field is printed at column 45 with a picture clause template that looks like this: "9,999.99." That template has five characters to the left of the decimal point. However, it is possible that some of the totals may require numbers with more places to the left of the decimal. The total uses a template that has six characters to the left of the decimal point: "99,999.99." To make sure that the decimal points line up on the same column, you need to begin the @ SAY one column to the left: $45 - 1 = 44$.

Complete the program by entering

```
EJECT
SET DEVICE TO SCREEN
```

```
@ 10,10
@ 10,10 SAY "Printing Complete."
CLOSE DATABASE
SET TALK ON
SET STATUS ON
RETURN
```

The entire program should look like this. The shading indicates the main loop of the program

```
CLEAR
SET TALK OFF
SET STATUS OFF
* initialize accumulators
STORE Ø TO ded,nonded,cat1,cat2,cat3,cat4,all
recnum=1
pagenum=1
USE prtdata
@ 1Ø,1Ø SAY "PRINTING.  Please Wait ........"
SET DEVICE TO PRINT
DO WHILE .NOT. EOF()
    * Page end routine
    IF PROW()>54
        @ 6Ø,35 SAY "Page -"+LTRIM(STR(pagenum,3))+"-"
        EJECT
        pagenum=pagenum+1
    ENDIF end of page routine
    * page heading routine
    IF PROW()<1
        @ 4,1Ø SAY "EXPENSES REPORT"
        @ 4,PCOL()+1Ø SAY "Date of Report:"
        @ 4,PCOL()+2 SAY DATE()
        @ 5,Ø  SAY "#"
        @ 5,1Ø SAY "DATE"
        @ 5,2Ø SAY "PAYEE"
        @ 5,45 SAY "AMOUNT"
        @ 5,6Ø SAY "CATEGORY"
        @ 6,Ø SAY REPLICATE("-",65)
    ENDIF
    *print a line
    @ PROW()+1,Ø SAY LTRIM(STR(recnum,3))+"."
    @ PROW(),1Ø SAY date
    @ PROW(),2Ø SAY payto
    @ PROW(),45 SAY amount PICTURE "9,999.99"
    @ PROW(),6Ø SAY cat PICTURE "9999"
    IF deduct
        @ PROW(), PCOL()+2 SAY "*Deductible*"
    ENDIF
    * calculate totals
    recnum=recnum+1
    all=all+amount
    IF deduct
        ded=ded+amount
    ELSE
        nonded=nonded+amount
    ENDIF deductible totals
    DO CASE
        CASE cat=11Ø
            cat1=cat1+amount
        CASE cat=12Ø
            cat2=cat2+amount
        CASE cat=13Ø
            cat3=cat3+amount
        CASE cat=14Ø
            cat4=cat4+amount
    ENDCASE
    SKIP
ENDDO
```

```
→IF PROW()>45
       @ 55,30 SAY "Totals on next page...."
       @ 60,35 SAY "Page -"+LTRIM(STR(pagenum,3))+"-"
       EJECT
       pagenum=pagenum+1
       @ 6,0 SAY "Total Information:"
  ENDIF
  *print totals
  @ PROW()+1, 0 SAY REPLICATE("=",65)
  @ PROW()+1,20 SAY "The sum of the amounts is  "
  @ PROW(),44 SAY all PICTURE "99,999.99"
  @ PROW()+1,20 SAY "Total number of records is "
  @ PROW(),44 SAY RECCOUNT() PICTURE "99,999"
  @ PROW()+2,20 SAY "Deductible                "
  @ PROW(),44 SAY all PICTURE "99,999.99"
  @ PROW()+1,20 SAY "Not Deductible            "
  @ PROW(),44 SAY all PICTURE "99,999.99"
  @ PROW()+2,20 SAY "Category 110              "
  @ PROW(),44 SAY cat1 PICTURE "99,999.99"
  @ PROW()+1,20 SAY "Category 120              "
  @ PROW(),44 SAY cat2 PICTURE "99,999.99"
  @ PROW()+1,20 SAY "Category 130              "
  @ PROW(),44 SAY cat3 PICTURE "99,999.99"
  @ PROW()+1,20 SAY "Category 140              "
  @ PROW(),44 SAY cat4 PICTURE "99,999.99"
  @ 60,35 SAY "Page -"+LTRIM(STR(pagenum,3))+"-"
  EJECT
  SET DEVICE TO SCREEN
  @ 10,10
  @ 10,10 SAY "Printing Complete."
  CLOSE DATABASE
  SET TALK ON
  SET STATUS ON
  RETURN
```

Note that most of the program is contained within the DO WHILE .NOT. EOF() loop. Most of the commands inside the loop are controlled by conditional structures, IF and DO CASE. Only a few commands execute absolutely every time the loop is processed. These commands print the main print line and the grand total accumulator. The other command that executes every time is the SKIP. The SKIP is crucial to the program because it moves the pointer through the data base file.

Save the program by entering

[CTRL/End]

Execute the program by entering

DO formrpt < return >

The program will generate a column report.

BASIC PARTS

Before you go on to the next topic, control break reports, it might be useful to review the basic parts of a column-type report.

*The term "control break" refers to a particular type of programming strategy. It should not be confused with the [**Ctrl**] or [**Break**] keys on the keyboard.*

The figure below shows the basic parts of a printed report.

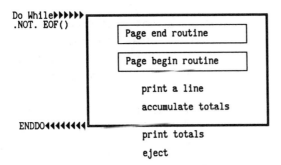

The parts of the program are:

1. **DO WHILE/ENDDO.** Create a loop that processes all the records in the file.
2. Test for end of page.
3. Test for beginning of page.
4. Print line.
5. Store values to accumulators.
6. After loop, print totals and eject.

You can add sequencing and selection to the program by adding commands that index and/or filter the data base file before the main line of processing takes place:

1. **SELECTION.** Add a SET FILTER command to the beginning of the program to restrict the records printed on the report by some logical condition.
2. **SEQUENCING.** Open an index file to control the sequence of the records.

Below is an example of how you would print the FORMRPT selecting only the January records, printed in payee order:

```
CLEAR
SET TALK OFF
SET STATUS OFF
* initialize accumulators
STORE 0 TO ded,nonded,cat1,cat2,cat3,cat4,all
recnum=1
pagenum=1
   USE prtdata INDEX payorder
   SET FILTER TO MONTH(date)=1
@ 10,10 SAY "PRINTING. Please Wait ........"
SET DEVICE TO PRINT
```

CONTROL BREAKS

A control break is a report that performs special actions based on a change in a key value or field. The most common use of control breaks is to print subtotals, but the break can be used for other tasks as well. The group report feature used by the CREATE REPORT command, discussed in Chapter 7, makes use of the control break concept.

Suppose you wanted to create a report that printed subtotals for each month. In this program, you can make the total section for each month as specialized as you desire. Because the report is custom-designed, you do not have to be limited to the subtotal format used in commands such as REPORT FORM.

To change FORMRPT to a control break report, it is necessary to understand how control breaks are achieved. The first step is to decide on a criterion that will be used to determine when a break should occur. For example, if you wanted to break the report after each month, the criterion would be any change in the value MONTH(date). Control breaks are achieved by creating a loop within the main loop, which is usually a DO WHILE .NOT. EOF() loop.

The subloop begins by assuming the first month (e.g., January, month 1) is the control value. The loop processes each record until a new value is encountered in the control field—in this example, a date with a month value of 2, February. When this value is encountered, the break routine is executed. The routine would print whatever subtotal information has been accumulated. Then the new value, 2 for February, would become the new control value, and the loop would continue until the next month was encountered.

In this way, you can process a file and create subtotals along the way, as well as summary totals that print at the end of the report. You can include page breaks in the control breaks and begin each new section on a new page.

For a control break program to operate, the data base file *must* be indexed on the field or expression that will be used to determine the control break. For example, if you wanted to break based on change of date, you would need to sort or index the data base file on the DATE field.

To see how control breaks are accomplished, load the FORMRPT program into the *dBASE III Plus* editor. Enter

MODIFY COMMAND formrpt < return >

The first change to make in the program is to add an index file to the USE prtdata command.

Then following the DO WHILE .NOT. EOF() command, you need to insert the lines indicated in bold. The first command establishes the value of a variable called "control." The variable control will be used to determine when the control break should occur. Then the STORE command is used to create three variables that will be used to accumulate subtotal information that will be printed when the control break occurs. The initialization of the subtotal variables takes place within the main loop. This is because you will want to have the subtotal accumulators set back to zero each time a subtotal is printed.

The last command added is a DO WHILE command, which loops the record printing part of the program until the value in the record no longer matches the control value, or you have reached the end of the file:

```
CLEAR
SET TALK OFF
SET STATUS OFF
* initialize accumulators
STORE 0 TO ded,nonded,cat1,cat2,cat3,cat4,all
recnum=1
pagenum=1
USE prtdata INDEX prtdata < ==============changed
@ 10,10 SAY "PRINTING. Please Wait ........"
SET DEVICE TO PRINT
DO WHILE .NOT. EOF()
    control=CMONTH(date)
    STORE 0 TO dedsub,nonsub,allsub
    DO WHILE control=CMONTH(date).AND..NOT.EOF()
    * Page end routine
```

The program remains unchanged until you encounter the section that accumulates the totals. Here you need to add programming statements that accumulate the subtotals. Add the commands shown in bold.

```
* calculate totals
recnum=recnum+1
all=all+amount
    allsub=allsub+amount
IF deduct
    ded=ded+amount
        dedsub=dedsub+amount
ELSE
    nonded=nonded+amount
        nonsub=nonsub+amount
ENDIF deductible totals
```

The final alteration is the entry of the commands that execute whenever the control break occurs. The key is to enter an ENDDO command for the inner control break loop, following the SKIP command. At that point, you force the program to determine if the month value of the current record still matches the control value. If not, the inner loop terminates and the control break occurs. The subtotals are printed and the next ENDDO returns the program to the top of the main loop unless the end of the file has been reached. Enter the commands shown in bold.

```
        SKIP
ENDDO control break
@ PROW()+1,0 SAY REPLICATE(" - ",65)
@ PROW()+1,20 SAY "Total for"
@ PROW(),PCOL()+1 SAY control
@ PROW(),44 SAY allsub PICTURE "99,999.99"
@ PROW()+1,20 SAY "Deductible"
@ PROW(),44 SAY dedsub PICTURE "99,999.99"
@ PROW()+1,20 SAY "Non Deductible"
@ PROW(),44 SAY nonsub PICTURE "99,999.99"
@ PROW()+2,0 SAY SPACE(1)
ENDDO all records process all records
```

The entire program should look like this:

```
CLEAR
SET TALK OFF
SET STATUS OFF
* initialize accumulators
STORE Ø TO ded,nonded,cat1,cat2,cat3,cat4,all
recnum=1
pagenum=1
USE prtdata INDEX prtdata
@ 1Ø,1Ø SAY "PRINTING.  Please Wait ........"
SET DEVICE TO PRINT
DO WHILE .NOT. EOF()
   control=CMONTH(date)
   STORE Ø TO dedsub,nonsub,allsub
   DO WHILE control=CMONTH(date).AND..NOT.EOF()
      * Page end routine
      IF PROW()>54
         @ 6Ø,35 SAY "Page -"+LTRIM(STR(pagenum,3))+"-"
         EJECT
         pagenum=pagenum+1
      ENDIF end of page routine
      * page heading routine
      IF PROW()<1
         @ 4,1Ø SAY "EXPENSES REPORT"
         @ 4,PCOL()+1Ø SAY "Date of Report:"
         @ 4,PCOL()+2 SAY DATE()
         @ 5,Ø  SAY "#"
         @ 5,1Ø SAY "DATE"
         @ 5,2Ø SAY "PAYEE"
         @ 5,45 SAY "AMOUNT"
         @ 5,6Ø SAY "CATEGORY"
         @ 6,Ø SAY REPLICATE("-",65)
      ENDIF
      *print a line
      @ PROW()+1,Ø SAY LTRIM(STR(recnum,3))+"."
      @ PROW(),1Ø SAY date
      @ PROW(),2Ø SAY payto
      @ PROW(),45 SAY amount PICTURE "9,999.99"
      @ PROW(),6Ø SAY cat PICTURE "9999"
      IF deduct
         @ PROW(), PCOL()+2 SAY "*Deductible*"
      ENDIF
      * calculate totals
      recnum=recnum+1
      all=all+amount
      allsub=allsub+amount
      IF deduct
         ded=ded+amount
         dedsub=dedsub+amount
      ELSE
         nonded=nonded+amount
         nonsub=nonsub+amount
      ENDIF deductible totals
```

```
        ►DO CASE
           CASE cat=110
                cat1=cat1+amount
           CASE cat=120
                cat2=cat2+amount
           CASE cat=130
                cat3=cat3+amount
           CASE cat=140
                cat4=cat4+amount
          ENDCASE◄
     SKIP
    ENDDO control break ◄
    @ PROW()+1,0 SAY REPLICATE("-",65)
    @ PROW()+1,20 SAY "Total for"
    @ PROW(),PCOL()+1 SAY control
    @ PROW(),44 SAY allsub PICTURE "99,999.99"
    @ PROW()+1,20 SAY "Deductible"
    @ PROW(),44 SAY dedsub PICTURE "99,999.99"
    @ PROW()+1,20 SAY "Non Deductible"
    @ PROW(),44 SAY nonsub PICTURE "99,999.99"
    @ PROW()+2,0 SAY SPACE(1)
   ENDDO all records processed◄
►IF PROW()>45
    @ 55,30 SAY "Totals on next page...."
    @ 60,35 SAY "Page -"+LTRIM(STR(pagenum,3))+"-"
    EJECT
    pagenum=pagenum+1
    @ 6,0 SAY "Total Information:"
  ENDIF◄
*print totals
@ PROW()+1, 0 SAY REPLICATE("=",65)
@ PROW()+1,20 SAY "The sum of the amounts is  "
@ PROW(),44 SAY all PICTURE "99,999.99"
@ PROW()+1,20 SAY "Total number of records is "
@ PROW(),44 SAY RECCOUNT() PICTURE "99,999"
@ PROW()+2,20 SAY "Deductible             "
@ PROW(),44 SAY all PICTURE "99,999.99"
@ PROW()+1,20 SAY "Not Deductible         "
@ PROW(),44 SAY all PICTURE "99,999.99"
@ PROW()+2,20 SAY "Category 110           "
@ PROW(),44 SAY cat1 PICTURE "99,999.99"
@ PROW()+1,20 SAY "Category 120           "
@ PROW(),44 SAY cat2 PICTURE "99,999.99"
@ PROW()+1,20 SAY "Category 130           "
@ PROW(),44 SAY cat3 PICTURE "99,999.99"
@ PROW()+1,20 SAY "Category 140           "
@ PROW(),44 SAY cat4 PICTURE "99,999.99"
@ 60,35 SAY "Page -"+LTRIM(STR(pagenum,3))+"-"
EJECT
SET DEVICE TO SCREEN
@ 10,10
@ 10,10 SAY "Printing Complete."
CLOSE DATABASE
SET TALK ON
SET STATUS ON
RETURN
```

Note that the control break program is characterized by a loop within a loop. The outer loop controls the processing so that all the records in the data base file are eventually printed. The inner loop is more specific. It prints until a control break is required.

> To create a report with sub subtotals, you would create a third loop inside the second loop that would perform a control break on a secondary criterion. The index file for the data base would have to sequence the records correctly to match up with both control breaks.

Save the program by entering

[CTRL/End]

Note that before you can execute this program, you must create the PRTDATA.NDX index file that is required. Enter

> **USE prtdata** < return >
> **INDEX ON date TO prtdata** < return >
> **CLOSE DATABASE** < return >

Execute the program by entering

> **DO formrpt** < return >

The program prints the report with subtotal breaks for each month. The subtotal breaks will print the sum of the expenses and the totals for deductible and nondeductible items as well.

ADDING SUBHEADINGS

Now that you have created subtotal breaks in the report, you might want to enhance the report by adding subtotal headings. Subtotal breaks are printed after the records for that group. A subtotal heading needs to print *before* the records for that group. To accomplish this, you will change the program in a few simple lines. Load the program into the editor by entering

> **MODIFY COMMAND formrpt** < return >

The main change is to enter two commands between the inner and outer loops that print a subtotal heading. However, this causes a slight problem with the major page heading on the first page. The first time through, the section heading would print before the page heading. To remedy this situation, you simply add commands to print the heading at the top of the first page. From then on, the loops and conditionals will correctly print the page headings and footings. Enter the commands shown in bold.

```
SET DEVICE TO PRINT
* initial page heading
@ 4,10 SAY "EXPENSES REPORT"
@ 4,PCOL()+10 SAY "Date of Report:"
@ 4,PCOL()+2 SAY DATE()
@ 5,0 SAY "#"
@ 5,10 SAY "DATE"
@ 5,20 SAY "PAYEE"
@ 5,45 SAY "AMOUNT"
@ 5,60 SAY "CATEGORY"
@ 6,0 SAY REPLICATE(" - ",65)
DO WHILE .NOT. EOF()
```

```
control=CMONTH(date)
STORE 0 TO dedsub,nonsub,allsub
  * print section heading
  @ PROW()+1,0 SAY "Expenses for"
  @ PROW(),PCOL()+1 SAY CMONTH(date)+STR(YEAR(date),5)
DO WHILE control=CMONTH(date).AND..NOT.EOF()
  * Page end routine
```

Save the program by entering

[CTRL/End]

Execute the program by entering

DO formrpt < return >

The program prints with headings preceding each section, and totals following each section.

SPECIAL PRINTER CONTROLS

For the most part the printed output from *dBASE III Plus* uses the default setting in your printer as far as character style and pitch are concerned. However, you might know that your printer is capable of creating a number of specialized effects that can be used to enhance the reports that you print. If you are not aware of the capabilities of your printer, take a look at the manual that was provided with it. It usually contains samples of the type of print you printer can produce.

The effects that can be performed vary from printer to printer. Here are some of the most common characteristics:

1. **Pitch.** Printers can vary the number of characters per horizontal inch that are printed. The usual default is 10-pitch (i.e., printing 10 characters per inch).
2. **Underline.** Many printers can underline text as it is printed.
3. **Bold/enhanced.** Most printers provide the ability to print some characters darker than usual. This can be done in one of two ways. The double-strike method prints each character twice, making the print darker. The other method is to print twice but offset the second strike by some small fraction, usually 1/120 of an inch. This makes the character not only darker, but thicker.
4. **Special Fonts.** Some printers provide special character sets such as italic and double-width letters.

dBASE III Plus can access all the features provided by your printer by sending special codes to the printer that vary the way text is printed. These codes vary among printers. In this section the assumption is that you are working with an Epson or Epson-compatible printer such as an Okidata 193. While not every printer uses the exact same codes as the Epson, the method applies to all printers. You simply need to look up the specific codes in your printer manual.

WHAT YOU FIND IN THE PRINTER MANUAL

Using special printer effects is really quite simple. The hardest part may be reading your printer manual to find the codes that you need to enter. Many manuals have several listings of codes, some in numeric order, others in order by type of feature. For example, you might see something like this in your printer manual:

DEC	Hex	Symbol	Function
15	0F	SI	Shift In. Empties the buffer and turns Compressed Mode (17.16 cpi) ON. Cannot work with Emphasized, Elite or Pica Mode. Stays on until canceled by CHR$(18).

In another section of the same manual you might see the same information listed in this way.

Print Width
Codes

CHR$(15)	Turns Compressed Mode ON
CHR$(18)	Turns Compressed Mode OFF

BASIC, like dBASE III Plus, *uses the decimal number version of the code, not the hex(adecimal) number.*

Both sections are saying the same thing; that is, they are describing how to place your printer in the compressed printing mode. The code that performs this action is shown in four different representations.

15	decimal value
0F	hexadecimal value
SI	ASCII symbol name
CHR$(15)	BASIC language function

All of the above are different names for the same thing, the ASCII code, which *dBASE III Plus* represents by the special function CHR(15).

Note that the BASIC language representation, CHR$(15), is the closest to the dBASE III Plus *function. The only difference is that BASIC requires a $ while dBASE III Plus does not.*

ASCII character 15 cannot be typed from the keyboard. It must be entered by way of the CHR() function. Suppose you were working with an Epson or compatible printer. You could print out the FORMRPT in the compressed mode by entering

```
SET PRINT ON <return>
?? CHR(15) <return>
SET PRINT OFF <return>
EJECT <return>
```

The ?? command is used to send the character to the printer instead of the ? command. The ?? is used to avoid sending a carriage return/line feed character that causes the printer to feed a line that the ? would normally send.

Now execute the report by entering

```
DO formrpt <return>
```

The entire report is compressed. To return the printer to normal, you have two options:

1. **Turn off the printer.** When you turn off the printer and then turn it back on, the printer resets itself to the default values for pitch and style.
2. **Issue another code.** You can issue another code to the printer that will turn the printing pitch back to 10-pitch, the default.

In this case you can try the harder method. The code that turns the printer back to 10-pitch printing is CHR(18). Enter

```
SET PRINT ON <return>
?? CHR(18) <return>
SET PRINT OFF <return>
EJECT <return>
```

Now execute the report by entering

```
DO formrpt <return>
```

This time, the report prints at normal pitch.

Another common character used to set printer effects is the <Esc> code. In *dBASE III Plus* that code is issued by using CHR(27). For example, the Epson code for printing a continuous underline is <Esc> − 1. In *dBASE III Plus* you would create that code string by entering a command like this:

```
? CHR(27)+"−1"
```

Note that the <Esc> symbol stands for ASCII character 27. The − and the 1 are treated as normal text characters (i.e., delimited with quotation marks). The code that turns off underlining is

```
? CHR(27)+"−0"
```

One handy way to deal with codes like these is to store them to memory variables. For example, you could define the codes for underlining by entering

```
begin=CHR(27)+"−1" <return>
end=CHR(27)+"−0" <return>
```

Now that you have a set of variables, add them to the text that you want to print. Enter

```
SET PRINT ON <return>
? begin+"This text is underlined"+end <return>
? "This text is not underlined" <return>
EJECT <return>
```

The codes added to the first line create a continuous underline.

You can add print attributes to a report by defining your codes at the beginning of the program and using them whenever you want to highlight data. Once you turn a printer effect on, you must remember to turn it off again. Also, some modes or effects are not compatible with other modes. For example, in an Epson scheme, compressed cannot be combined with emphasized printing. Other modes can be combined. Your printer manual is the best source for the different types of effects produced by code combinations.

Load the program into the editor by entering

```
MODIFY COMMAND formrpt <return>
```

In the section of program shown below, a series of special printer effects has been listed. Each code sequence is assigned to a variable. There are two advantages to this technique:

1. You can use the words rather than the code sequences in the remainder of the program.
2. If you want to use the same program on a different printer, you simply need to change the code definitions to match the coding sequence for that particular printer. It is not necessary to go through the entire program and change all the codes.

Enter the lines shown in bold:

```
CLEAR
SET TALK OFF
SET STATUS OFF
* define special print codes
compress=CHR(15)
enlarge=CHR(18)
double=CHR(14)
emph=CHR(27)+"E"
normal=CHR(27)+"F"
```

```
underon=CHR(27)+"-1"
underoff=CHR(27)+"-0"
elite=CHR(27)+"M"
pica=CHR(27)+"P"
* initialize accumulators
```

Now that you have defined printing variables, you can add them to the report. Below, you see lines that have been changed to include the print variables. Note that when print variables are added to a DATE-type field, it is necessary to convert the date to characters. The reason is that the printer variables are character-type data. If these data are combined with other data types such as date or numeric, you must convert the data to characters to avoid a type mismatch error. Enter the changes shown below in bold. The changes are used to set off the various headings from the main text of the report.

```
SET DEVICE TO PRINT
* initial page heading
@ 3,0 SAY emph+underon+double+"EXPENSES REPORT"+underoff+normal
@ 4,0 SAY underoff+emph+"Date of Report:"
@ 4,PCOL()+2 SAY DTOC(DATE())+normal
@ 5,0 SAY "#"
@ 5,10 SAY "DATE"
@ 5,20 SAY "PAYEE"
@ 5,45 SAY "AMOUNT"
@ 5,60 SAY "CATEGORY"
@ 6,0 SAY REPLICATE(" - ",65)
DO WHILE .NOT. EOF()
    control=CMONTH(date)
    STORE 0 TO dedsub,nonsub,allsub
    @ PROW()+1,0 SAY elite+"Expenses for"+pica
        @ PROW(),PCOL()+1 SAY emph+underon+CMONTH(date);
        +STR(YEAR(date),5)+normal+underoff
ENDIF print section heading
```

Another change is to use the compressed print mode to print the deductible flag in compressed text while the remainder of the line is printed normally. When you change pitch on a line, it can cause problems with column alignment. Keep in mind that ten columns at 10-pitch use up more physical space than do ten columns at 17.6 pitch.

In this case, since the item that has the change in pitch is the last one on the line, you will not disturb the column alignment by changing to compressed mode. Enter the change shown in bold.

```
IF deduct
    @ PROW(), PCOL()+2 SAY compress+"*Deductible*"+enlarge
ENDIF
```

Save the program by entering

[CTRL/End]

Execute the program by entering

DO formrpt < return >

The report prints and includes the various printer effects that you specified.

PRINTED FORMS AND CONVERSION

The *dBASE III Plus* formatted printing commands allow you to fill out all types of preprinted forms. This is done by using the @ SAY commands to place the text at specific locations on the form. Most business forms like checks and invoices are available in continuous-form, pin-feed format so that you can use these preprinted forms in your computer printer.

In this next section you will learn how you can create a program that will write checks based on the data in a data base file. The programs will illustrate how data can be placed on forms and also how *dBASE III Plus* can convert data to meet the format used on the form. In this example the conversion takes the numeric amount in the AMOUNT field and changes it to the text required for writing checks.

Before you begin creating the actual text of the program, it is important to consider how you can calculate the positions on a printed form. There are three numbers to keep in mind:

1. **Line height.** The height of the printed line is not the same as the height of the characters on the line. When measuring line height, it is the distance from the bottom of one line to the bottom of the next that counts. There are two common line heights used by most computer forms: 1/6th inch and 1/8th inch. By far, 1/6th inch is the more common. Printers can set the height of the line using a special code. Line height refers to the amount of space between printed lines. Changing the line height does not change the vertical size of the printed characters. Changing line height has the effect of squeezing the lines closer together. For example, the Epson-type printer would use the following codes:

    ? CHR(27)+ "0"   sets line height to 1/8"
    ? CHR(27)+ "2"   sets line height to 1/6"

    On the Epson, 1/6 inch is the factory default setting.
2. **Form length.** This value sets the length of the form. The default is 11 inches. This means that whenever a form feed is sent to the printer, it moves to the top of the next form, assuming that each form is 11 inches long.

However, many preprinted forms such as checks, invoices, and billing statements are not 11 inches long; the typical length is 7 inches. In order to have the form feeds move between 7-inch rather than 11-inch forms, you will need to issue a code that controls the form length. In the Epson printer the following command sets the form length.

```
? CHR(27)+"C"+CHR(0)+CHR(7)      7-inch form
? CHR(27)+"C"+CHR(0)+CHR(11)     11-inch form
```

The last character is the number of inches on the form. If the form should not be an even number (e.g., 6.5 inches), you can set the form in terms of the number of lines on a page. For example, a 6.5-inch form printing at 1/6-inch line height will total 39 lines. The following codes set the form length in terms of lines:

```
? CHR(27)+"C"+CHR(39)      6.5-inch form
? CHR(27)+"C"+CHR(66)      11-inch form
```

3. **Pitch.** The pitch tells you the number of characters or columns for horizontal measurement. If the printing is taking place at 10 pitch, the usual size for most printers, every 10 columns covers one inch.

Knowing how spacing is allocated by the printer, you can then measure the form you have and find the location for each data item. For example, if the name of the payee should be printed 5 inches from the top of the form and 1.5 inches from the left edge of the form, you would use a command like this:

```
@ 30,15 SAY payto
```

Laying out a complex form is tedious but the results can save you a great deal of time. Create the sample check printing program by entering

MODIFY COMMAND prtcheck <return>

The program begins by opening two data base files. The first is the EXPENSES. The second, which is opened in word area B, is called NUMBTEXT and is assigned the alias words. Note that NUMBTEXT does not yet exist. You will create it later. Its purpose is to provide the words that go with numeric value (e.g., 12 = TWELVE).

The program then asks users to enter the date to be used on the checks and the first check in the file to print. Enter

```
CLEAR
SET TALK OFF
USE expenses
SELECT B
USE numbtext INDEX numbtext ALIAS words
SELECT expenses
```

```
beginprt=0
prtdate=CTOD(" / / ")
@ 10,10 SAY "Enter date of Checks " GET prtdate
@ 12,10 SAY "Enter first check to print " GET beginprt
READ
```

A LOCATE command is used to find the first check number. The assumption is made that you will print all the checks in consecutive order from this point on.

```
LOCATE FOR check=beginprt
CLEAR
```

The next section of the program sets the form length to 7 inches. The assumption is made that you are printing on a 7-inch form. The top part is a check stub and the bottom part is the actual check. Enter

```
* set form length
SET PRINT ON
? CHR(27)+"C"+CHR(0)+CHR(7)
SET PRINT OFF
```

The rest of the program is a loop that prints the check data on the stub and the check. Note that inside the loop is a command, DO CONV, that calls a subroutine, CONV. That CONV program will use the numeric value stored in the variable value to create a text string called FULLTEXT that is the word version of the amount. Enter

```
* main processing
DO WHILE .NOT. EOF()
    @ 10,10 SAY "Printing check #"+LTRIM(STR(check,5))
    SET DEVICE TO PRINT
    @ 10,10 SAY prtdate
    @ 10,20 SAY payto
    @ 10,40 SAY amount PICTURE "99,999.99"
    @ 10,60 SAY item
    @ 26,65 SAY CMONTH(prtdate)
    @ PROW(),PCOL()+1 SAY DAY(prtdate)
    @ PROW(),PCOL()+4 SAY STR(YEAR(prtdate)-1900,2)
    @ 30,5 SAY payto
    value=amount
    DO conv
    @ 32,0 SAY fulltext
    @ 32,70 SAY amount PICTURE "99,999.99"
    @ 35,0 SAY item
    SET DEVICE TO SCREEN
    EJECT
    SKIP
ENDDO
CLOSE DATABASE
SET TALK ON
RETURN
```

Save the program by entering

[CTRL/End]

The next step is to create a file called NUMBTEXT. The file has the following structure.

Field	Field Name	Type	Width	Dec
1	NUMBER	Character	2	
2	WORD	Character	20	
** Total **			23	

Fill in the file with the following data:

```
Record#  NUMBER  WORD
      1       1  ONE
      2       2  TWO
      3       3  THREE
      4       4  FOUR
      5       5  FIVE
      6       6  SIX
      7       7  SEVEN
      8       8  EIGHT
      9       9  NINE
     10      10  TEN
     11      11  ELEVEN
     12      12  TWELVE
     13      13  THIRTEEN
     14      14  FOURTEEN
     15      15  FIFTEEN
     16      16  SIXTEEN
     17      17  SEVENTEEN
     18      18  EIGHTEEN
     19      19  NINETEEN
     20      20  TWENTY
     21      30  THIRTY
     22      40  FORTY
     23      50  FIFTY
     24      60  SIXTY
     25      70  SEVENTY
     26      80  EIGHTY
     27      90  NINETY
```

Create an index for this file by entering

INDEX ON number TO numbtext < return >

Now you are ready to create the conversion program. Enter

MODIFY COMMAND conv <return>

The purpose of this program is to convert numeric values as high as 99,999.99 from numbers to words.

The program begins with a PUBLIC command. This is because the variable "fulltext" needs to be preserved when you return to the main program. Without the PUBLIC command, the fulltext variable would be erased from the memory when the CONV program completes. Enter

PUBLIC fulltext

The next step is to select the WORDS data base file. This file contains the words that relate to the numbers. A variable called "dollar" is also created that will eventually contain the text version of the numeric value. Enter

```
SELECT words
dollar=""
```

The next section of the program creates a text string for the cents portion of the value. If there are no cents, 00 is assigned to the cents variable. The INT() function is used to truncate any decimal portion of the value. For example, the expression INT(value)=value tests to see if value has a decimal portion. Note that the structure also needs to test if the cents value has one or two digits, since a leading zero needs to be added to single-digit numbers. Enter

```
* calculate cents
IF INT(value)=value
    centtext="00"
ELSE
    cents=(value-INT(value))*100
    IF cents>10
        centtext=STR(cents,2)
    ELSE
        centtext="0"+STR(cents,1)
    ENDIF singe or double digit
ENDIF convert cents
```

The next section finds the words for any values in the thousands. First the value is tested to see if it is over 999. If so, the value is divided between those greater than 19,000 and those equal to or below 19,000. Values below 20 can be expressed in a single word. Higher values require two words, one for the tens value and one for the ones value. The words are found by using the SEEK command to find the number in the NUMBER field and storing the matching word to the dollar string.

Note that the command value=value-thousands*1000 reduces the value of value so that only the hundreds are left. This program reduces the value until all the parts have been translated into text. Enter

```
value=INT(value)
* check for thousands
IF value>999
    thousands=INT(value/1000)
    value=value-thousands*1000
    IF thousands>19
    tens=SUBSTR(STR(thousands,2),1,1)+"0"
    ones=SUBSTR(STR(thousands,2),2,1)
    SEEK tens
```

```
          dollar=TRIM(word)
          SEEK ones
          dollar=dollar+" "+TRIM(word)+"THOUSAND "
      ELSE
        IF thousands>9
            SEEK STR(thousands,2)
            dollar=TRIM(word)+" THOUSAND "
        ELSE
            SEEK STR(thousands,1)
            dollar=TRIM(word)+" THOUSAND "
        ENDIF
      ENDIF
ENDIF
```

Next, you need to look up the hundreds value. Since hundred can be only 1 to 9, the structure is simpler than the thousands structure. Enter

```
* hundreds
IF value>99
    hundreds=INT(value/100)
    value=value-hundreds*100
    SEEK STR(hundreds,1)
    dollar=dollar+TRIM(word)+" HUNDRED"
ENDIF
```

The final conversion section takes the dollar value left, from 1 to 99, and converts it to words. The structure used is an exact duplicate of the structure used for converting thousands, but the word "dollar" has replaced "thousand." Enter

```
IF value>0
    IF value>19
      tens=SUBSTR(STR(value,2),1,1)+"0"
      ones=SUBSTR(STR(value,2),2,1)
      SEEK tens
      dollar=dollar+" "+TRIM(word)
      SEEK ones
      dollar=dollar+" "+TRIM(word)+" DOLLARS "
    ELSE
      IF value>9
          SEEK STR(value,2)
          dollar=dollar+TRIM(word)+" DOLLARS"
      ELSE
          SEEK STR(value,1)
          dollar=dollar+TRIM(word)+" DOLLARS "
      ENDIF
    ENDIF
ENDIF
```

Finally the dollars and cents are combined into a single string. In addition, a series of ***** are added to the front of the words so that each check will print a full 69-character text, so that no one can type in extra words. Enter

```
fulltext=dollar+" AND "+centtext+"/100 CENTS"
pad=REPLICATE("*",69-LEN(fulltext))
fulltext=pad+fulltext
SELECT expenses
RETURN
```

The entire program should look like this:

```
PUBLIC fulltext
SELECT words
dollar=""
* calculate cents
IF INT(value)=value
    centtext="00"
ELSE
    cents=(value-INT(value))*100
    IF cents>10
        centtext=STR(cents,2)
    ELSE
        centtext="0"+STR(cents,1)
    ENDIF singe or double digit
ENDIF convert cents
value=INT(value)
* check for thousands
IF value>999
    thousands=INT(value/1000)
    value=value-thousands*1000
    IF thousands>19
        tens=SUBSTR(STR(thousands,2),1,1)+"0"
        ones=SUBSTR(STR(thousands,2),2,1)
        SEEK tens
        dollar=TRIM(word)
        SEEK ones
        dollar=dollar+" "+TRIM(word)+" THOUSAND "
    ELSE
        IF thousands>9
            SEEK STR(thousands,2)
            dollar=TRIM(word)+" THOUSAND "
        ELSE
            SEEK STR(thousands,1)
            dollar=TRIM(word)+" THOUSAND "
        ENDIF
    ENDIF
ENDIF
* hundreds
IF value>99
    hundreds=INT(value/100)
    value=value-hundreds*100
    SEEK STR(hundreds,1)
    dollar=dollar+TRIM(word)+" HUNDRED"
ENDIF
IF value>0
    IF value>19
        tens=SUBSTR(STR(value,2),1,1)+"0"
        ones=SUBSTR(STR(value,2),2,1)
        SEEK tens
        dollar=dollar+" "+TRIM(word)
        SEEK ones
        dollar=dollar+" "+TRIM(word)+" DOLLARS "
    ELSE
        IF value>9
            SEEK STR(value,2)
            dollar=dollar+TRIM(word)+" DOLLARS"
        ELSE
            SEEK STR(value,1)
            dollar=dollar+TRIM(word)+" DOLLARS "
        ENDIF
    ENDIF
ENDIF
```

```
fulltext=dollar+" AND "+centtext+"/100 CENTS"
pad=REPLICATE("*",69-LEN(fulltext))
fulltext=pad+fulltext
SELECT expenses
RETURN
```

Save the program by entering

[CTRL/End]

Execute the program by entering

DO prtcheck < return >

Enter the date and starting check number. Enter

033086
1125 < return >

The program prints out the data from the records in the check format. Note how the conversion program translates the values into words and pads the words with *****.

Exercise 3   Now that you have entry, edit, and printing programs, you can unite the three programs in a single unit. Your task is to create a menu program that allows users to select among the three programs, EXPENTER, EXPEDIT, and UNFORM. A sample menu program can be found at the end of the chapter.

SUMMARY

dBASE III Plus can print data and text using two types of commands:

1. **Unformatted.** Unformatted commands place text on the next available row or column. The commands usually used to print data are ?, ??, or TEXT/ENDTEXT for large blocks of text without variables.

    The ? sends a carriage return/line feed character before it prints; the ?? does not. Commands printed with the ?? are placed on the same print row. ? begins on a new print row.

    Unformatted output is sent to the printer using the SET PRINT ON/OFF commands.

2. **Formatted.** Formatted commands address specific parts of the printed page. @/SAY commands are used. The output is directed to the printer by the SET DEVICE command. SET DEVICE TO PRINT directs the output of @/SAY commands to the printer. @/GET commands are not affected by SET DEVICE.

dBASE III Plus uses two special functions to hold the current printing position:

1. **PROW().** This function is the numeric value of the current print row. Addressing an output command such as @ PROW()+1,0 places the text on the next line on the page.
2. **PCOL().** This function is the numeric value of the current column position of the printer.

Programs that print column reports have the following parts:

1. **Main loop.** This loop processes all the selected records by printing a line for each record. The SKIP command is used to move the pointer through the data base file.
2. **Page break.** A conditional structure is needed to determine when the printing has reached the end of a page. The PROW() function can be tested to determine the need to add a page break. The EJECT command issues a form feed to the printer and resets the PROW() to zero.
3. **Page heading and footing.** These routines print headings at the top of each page. Footings are used for printing page numbers.

You can also add control breaks to print subtotals when a specified value changes.

ANSWER KEY

Exercise 1

The new lines needed to create an index listing are shown in bold.

```
CLEAR
SET TALK OFF
SET STATUS OFF
*initialize accumulators
STORE 0 TO ded,nonded,cat1,cat2,cat3,cat4, all
USE expenses INDEX dateord,payorder,amtorder,catorder
TEXT

          BROWSING EXPENSE RECORDS
          Choose an Index Order

          1. By Date
          2. By Payee
          3. By Amount
          4. By Category
```

```
ENDTEXT
ordernum=1
@ 20,0 SAY "Enter number " GET ordernum PICTURE "9"
READ
SET ORDER TO ordernum
GO TOP
? "PRINTING . . . . . . . ."
SET CONSOLE OFF
SET PRINT ON
DO WHILE .NOT. EOF()
    IF DOW(date)=1 .OR. DOW(date)=7
        ? "Weekend"+SPACE(2)
    ELSE
        ? SPACE(9)
    ENDIF
    ?? date,payto,amount,cat
    IF deduct
        ?? SPACE(2)+"Deductible"
    ENDIF
    *calculate totals
    all=all+amount
    IF deduct
        ded=ded+amount
    ELSE
        nonded=nonded+amount
    ENDIF deductible totals
    DO CASE
        CASE cat=110
            cat1=cat1+amount
        CASE cat=120
            cat2=cat2+amount
        CASE cat=130
            cat3=cat3+amount
        CASE cat=140
            cat4=cat4+amount
    ENDCASE
    SKIP
ENDDO
? REPLICATE("=",60)
? "The sum of the amounts is",all
? "Total number of records is",RECCOUNT()
? "Deductible      ",ded
? "Non Deductible ",nonded
? "Category 110 ",cat1
? "Category 120 ",cat2
? "Category 130 ",cat3
? "Category 140 ",cat4
SET PRINT OFF
EJECT
```

```
SET CONSOLE ON
CLEAR
?"PRINTING COMPLETE"
CLOSE DATABASE
SET TALK ON
SET STATUS ON
RETURN
```

Exercise 2

The new lines needed to create a program that pauses after each page is printed, to allow single-sheet feeding, are shown in bold.

```
CLEAR
SET TALK OFF
SET STATUS OFF
*initialize accumulators
STORE 0 TO ded,nonded,cat1,cat2,cat3,cat4, all
USE prtdata
? "PRINTING . . . . . . . ."
SET CONSOLE OFF
SET PRINT ON
DO WHILE .NOT. EOF()
    IF DOW(date)=1 .OR. DOW(date)=7
        ? "Weekend"+SPACE(2)
    ELSE
        ? SPACE(9)
    ENDIF
    ?? date,payto,amount,cat
    IF deduct
        ?? SPACE(2)+"Deductible"
    ENDIF
    *calculate totals
    all=all+amount
    IF deduct
        ded=ded+amount
    ELSE
        nonded=nonded+amount
    ENDIF deductible totals
    DO CASE
        CASE cat=110
            cat1=cat1+amount
        CASE cat=120
            cat2=cat2+amount
        CASE cat=130
            cat3=cat3+amount
        CASE cat=140
            cat4=cat4+amount
    ENDCASE
    SKIP
```

```
        IF PROW()>54
            EJECT
            SET PRINT OFF
            SET CONSOLE ON
            WAIT "Put paper into printer. Any key to continue."
            SET CONSOLE OFF
            SET PRINT ON
        ENDIF pause and display message
ENDDO
? REPLICATE("=",60)
? "The sum of the amounts is",all
? "Total number of records is",RECCOUNT()
? "Deductible     ",ded
? "Non Deductible ",nonded
? "Category 110 ",cat1
? "Category 120 ",cat2
? "Category 130 ",cat3
? "Category 140 ",cat4
SET PRINT OFF
EJECT
SET CONSOLE ON
CLEAR
?"PRINTING COMPLETE"
CLOSE DATABASE
SET TALK ON
SET STATUS ON
RETURN
```

Exercise 3

```
SET TALK OFF
SET STATUS OFF
expmenu=.T.
DO WHILE expmenu
    *SET TALK and SET STATUS added to loop
    *because the program called by the menu
    *turn on TALK and STATUS when they finish
    *adding these commands is simpler than removing
    *the others from each program
    SET TALK OFF
    SET STATUS OFF
    CLEAR
    TEXT

            EXPENSES PROGRAM MENU

        1. Enter New Expenses
        2. Display/Edit Existing Records
        3. Print Expense Report
        0. Exit Program
```

```
            ENDTEXT
            program=0
            @ 18,20 SAY "Enter Option" GET program PICTURE "9"
            READ
            DO CASE
                 CASE program=1
                      DO expenter
                 CASE program=2
                      DO expedit
                 CASE program=3
                      DO unform
                 OTHERWISE
                      EXIT
            ENDCASE
      ENDDO expmenu loop
      SET TALK ON
      SET STATUS ON
      RETURN
```

18

ADVANCED

PROGRAMMING

TECHNIQUES

THE PREVIOUS THREE CHAPTERS HAVE GIVEN YOU the basic types of routines that are needed in every system. In this chapter you will learn more sophisticated routines that apply in more specialized situations. The goal of this chapter and the ensuing ones is to introduce you to *dBASE III Plus* techniques that are somewhat beyond the basic programming structure discussed in the previous chapters.

HIGHLIGHTED MENUS

The history of microcomputer software has shown that menus are an effective way of communicating with the person using your program. In this book you have learned how to create the basic type of menu most commonly used. In this concept, text is displayed showing users what options they can choose from. The options can be a way of selecting programs (e.g., FIRSTMNU), or selecting records to edit (e.g., EXPBROW).

In all these menus the user's response can be in the form of a keystroke, number, letter, or function key. However, another popular method of menu selection is similar to the one *dBASE III Plus* uses in the ASSIST mode. By using the cursor key, users can position a highlight to an option and press < return > to select that option. You can create that type of menu using *dBASE III Plus*. The key is to use a command that controls the video attributes of the screen display, as well as a special function that allows you to use the cursor arrow keys as user input.

1. **SET COLOR TO.** This command allows you to select the video attributes of the next text items displayed on the screen. The meaning of "video attribute" changes depending on the type of screen display and adapter you are using. The IBM PC and compatible world recognizes a variety of screen types. The two most common are MONO (monochrome) and CGA(color/graphics adapter). What sometimes makes the distinction confusing is that the IBM marketplace has hybrid display options also.

   For example, a color/graphics adapter may be hooked up to a monitor that displays only one color (green or amber). This is the type of display used by most Compaq computers in the graphics mode. From a programming point of view, those displays behave like color screens in which the color appears as shades of green, most of which look pretty much alike.

   On the other hand, the Hercules adapter adds graphics ability to Monochrome screen displays like the Amdek 310A. However, from a *dBASE III Plus* point of view, a Hercules adapter is a monochrome adapter.

   If you are not sure which type you have, enter

   ```
   SET COLOR TO U <return>
   <return>
   <return>
   ```

   If you have a monochrome-type display, the screen shows an underline every time you enter < return >. If your computer is using a color/graphics display, the screen produces blank lines; not even the DOT PROMPT is displayed. To return the display to normal, type the following command. The command will not appear on the screen even though the cursor will move:

   ```
   SET COLOR TO <return>
   ```

   SET COLOR TO returns the screen to normal display.

2. **INKEY().** This function allows you to capture the keystroke entered by the user as a numeric value matching the ASCII value of the key pressed. This allows you to determine if special keys like cursor arrows, Home, or End were pressed. The INKEY() function allows you to extend your interactive pro-

gramming to allow user input from the entire keyboard, not just the alphanumeric portion of the keyboard.

How do these two functions work together to create a highlight menu?

1. The SET COLOR command is used to create a highlight by displaying one of the menu options in a different color from the rest.
2. The INKEY() function allows the user to change the highlighted option by entering a function key.

HOW SET COLOR WORKS

The SET COLOR command changes the display attribute of text. Below is a simple program that demonstrates how color can be changed in response to a user entry.

The key to screen display attributes is the SET COLOR TO command, which sets three different types of color:

SET COLOR TO normal, enhanced, border

1. **NORMAL.** The normal color is the color used for normal text display. The default colors are white letters on a black background.
2. **ENHANCED.** The enhanced color is used by *dBASE III Plus* to highlight special areas of the screen. For example, data input areas are displayed in the enhanced color. The default colors are black letters on a white background.
3. **BORDER.** The border area is the portion of the screen that is above, below, to the left, and to the right of the text area. You cannot place characters in this area, so only the background color is relevant. The default color is black.

Colors are set by using letter codes. The NORMAL and ENHANCED colors are set by entering a pair of letters, one for the foreground color and one for the background color. The BORDER area requires only a background color. The colors available in *dBASE III Plus* are:

```
             MONOCHROME  VIDEO  ATTRIBUTES
             Used with SET COLOR TO command

   Letter        Video
   Code          Display

     U            Underlined Text

     I            Inverse Text
                  (Dark letters, light Background)
```

```
                    COLORS CODES
                 For SET COLOR TO command

        Letter           Color
        Code             Displayed

          N              Black (No Color)

          B              Blue

          G              Green

          R              Red

          W              White

         BG              Cyan (Blue Green)

         RB              Magenta (Red Blue)

         GR              Brown (Green Red)

          +              Bright Color

          *              Blinking Color
```

For example, to change the NORMAL text to white on blue and the ENHANCED text to red on blue with a blue border, enter

SET COLOR w/b,r/b,b

The programs in this section assume you are working with monochrome display. If you are not, change the I (inverse color) attribute to a color combination that you like. For example, B/W creates a blue letter on a white background. Enter

MODIFY COMMAND colors < return >

The program below changes colors whenever a < return > is pressed. Enter

```
CLEAR
SET TALK OFF
SET STATUS OFF
ON ESCAPE EXIT
@ 1,0 SAY "Press RETURN to change color or ESC to exit"
sample="THIS IS A SAMPLE MENU ITEM"
DO WHILE .T.
    @ 10,10 SAY sample
    WAIT ""
    SET COLOR TO I
    @ 10,10 SAY sample
    WAIT ""
    SET COLOR TO
ENDDO
ON ESCAPE
SET COLOR TO
CLEAR
SET TALK ON
SET STATUS ON
```

Save the program by entering

[CTRL/End]

Execute the program by entering

DO colors < return >

Press < return >. The color changes. Enter < return > again. The color changes back to normal. Exit the program by entering

< Esc >

The idea is that by printing text in a different color, you create the illusion of a moving cursor.

KEY PRESS RESPONSE

The second part of the concept is to find a way to use such special keys as the cursor arrows as user inputs. Unlike color, this solution is not a command but a function. The INKEY() function is a numeric value that *dBASE III Plus* records, based on the last keystroke entered. *dBASE III Plus* assigns a numeric value to each key on the keyboard. When no keys are being pressed, INKEY has a value of zero. IN-KEY() is hard to demonstrate without creating a program. Enter

MODIFY COMMAND keys < return >

The program listed below shows the way INKEY() can be used. First, a variable is defined to hold the numeric value of the key. In this case it is called "key." The loop, shown in bold, is used to test for a key being pressed. Because INKEY() equals zero when no key is pressed, the expression KEY=0 creates a loop that continues until the user enters a keystroke. Then the keystroke's value is placed into KEY, and the number and character symbol for that key are displayed. Enter

```
SET TALK OFF
SET STATUS OFF
CLEAR
DO WHILE .T.
    key=0
      DO WHILE key=0
        key=INKEY()
      ENDDO
    IF key=6
      EXIT
    ENDIF
    @ 10,10 SAY "Key pressed was "+CHR(key)
    @ 11,10 SAY "ASCII value:"+STR(key,3)
```

```
ENDDO
SET TALK ON
SET STATUS ON
```

Save the program by entering

[CTRL/End]

Execute the program by entering

DO keys < return >

The screen begins as a blank. Enter

< down arrow >

The program displays the character symbol and the value of the keystroke.

```
Key pressed was ↑
ASCII value: 24
```

Pressing the down arrow key in dBASE III Plus *produces ASCII code character 24, which in the IBM PC character set is shown as an arrow pointing up.*

This tells you that pressing the down arrow key sets the value of INKEY() to 24. Enter

[F1]

The screen displays

```
Key pressed was ∟
ASCII value: 28
```

The **[F1]** key is assigned a value of 28. Continue exploring the keyboard. When you have finished, enter

[End]

The program was designed to stop when you pressed **[End]** because that key has a value of 6 and the DO WHILE loop was controlled by the conditional structure that tested for that keystroke:

```
IF key=6
    EXIT
ENDIF
```

The chart below shows the values returned by the INKEY() function for some special keys on the IBM PC keyboard.

SPECIAL KEYS CODES FOR INKEY() FUNCTION	
Key	Value Returned by INKEY()
<left arrow>	19
<right arrow>	4
<up arrow>	5
<down arrow>	24
[Home]	1
[End]	6
[Pg Up]	18
[Pg Dn]	3
[Ins]	22
[Del]	7
[Tab]	9
<return>	13
<backspace>	127
[–] gray key	45
[+] gray key	43
[F1]	28
[F2]	–1
[F3]	–2
[F4]	–3
[F5]	–4
[F6]	–5
[F7]	–6
[F8]	–7
[F9]	–8
[F1Ø]	–9

Using the [SHIFT], [CTRL], and [ALT] in combination with the special keys produces different values. For example, using [SHIFT] with the [F1] to [F10] keys produces values from 84 through 93, respectively. [CTRL] [F1] through [F10] yields 94 through 103, and [ALT] yields 104 through 113.

However, the keys listed in the chart are the most significant since they can be used by themselves without requiring another key in combination.

A HIGHLIGHT MENU

These two elements can be combined in a program that allows you to select menu options with a highlight. The menu covers the same programs used in Exercise 3 at the end of Chapter 17: EXPENTER, EXPEDIT, UNFORM. Enter

MODIFY COMMAND highmnu < return >

The first section of the program begins by starting a menu loop. The first action in the loop is to display a menu for the four items from which the user can choose. Note that the menu display is different from the usual menu for two reasons:

1. The menu does not include numbers or letters for each choice. The items are simply listed.
2. The SET COLOR command is used to display the first menu item in a different type of video (Inverse) than the other items. This item is the highlighted item on the menu.

Enter

```
SET TALK OFF
SET STATUS OFF
highmnu=.T.
DO WHILE highmnu
    SET TALK OFF
    SET STATUS OFF
    * display options
    @ 20,0 SAY "Use "+CHR(24)+" to move highlight."
    @ 21,0 SAY "Or use RETURN to select highlighted item."
    @ 10,10 TO 15,40 DOUBLE
    SET COLOR TO I
    @ 11,11 SAY "Enter Expenses"+SPACE(15)
    SET COLOR TO
    @ 12,11 SAY "Edit Expenses"+SPACE(16)
    @ 13,11 SAY "Print Report"+SPACE(17)
    @ 14,11 SAY "Exit"+SPACE(25)
```

The next part of the program has a simple but interesting purpose: to give users the feeling that they can change the position of the highlight by pressing the down arrow key. This is done by using the INKEY() function to capture the incoming keystroke. If that keystroke is 24 (i.e., down arrow), then you need to move the highlight down to the next item. Of course, moving the highlight is simply an illusion created by making two displays:

1. Display the item that is currently in inverse video, in normal video.
2. Display the next item below in inverse video.

If you make this swap each time the arrow is pressed, the user gets the feeling that pressing the down arrow key moves the highlight.

To simplify the program, move the highlight to the top of the list after the user has moved to the last item on the list. The variable "position" is used to determine what the current position of the highlight is.

Each case prints two lines, one in normal, the other in highlighted video. The position variable is also changed to reflect the newly highlighted option. Enter

```
key=0
position=1
DO WHILE key#13
  key=0
  DO WHILE key=0
      key=INKEY()
  ENDDO
  IF key=24
     DO CASE
       CASE position=1
         SET COLOR TO
         @ 11,11 SAY "Enter Expenses"+SPACE(15)
         SET COLOR TO I
         @ 12,11 SAY "Edit Expenses"+SPACE(16)
         position=2
       CASE position=2
         SET COLOR TO
         @ 12,11 SAY "Edit Expenses"+SPACE(16)
         SET COLOR TO I
         @ 13,11 SAY "Print Report"+SPACE(17)
         position=3
       CASE position=3
         SET COLOR TO
         @ 13,11 SAY "Print Report"+SPACE(17)
         SET COLOR TO I
         @ 14,11 SAY "Exit"+SPACE(25)
         position=4
       CASE position=4
         SET COLOR TO
         @ 14,11 SAY "Exit"+SPACE(25)
         SET COLOR TO I
         @ 11,11 SAY "Enter Expenses"+SPACE(15)
         position=1
     ENDCASE
  ENDIF down arrow pressed
ENDDO return pressed
```

The loop above continues until a <return> is pressed. Then the program skips to the next section. This section consists of a fairly standard menu execution DO

CASE structure. The variable position is now used to determine which program should be executed. Enter

```
SET COLOR TO
DO CASE
    CASE position=1
        DO expenter
    CASE position=2
        DO expedit
    CASE position=3
        DO unform
    CASE position=4
        EXIT
ENDCASE
ENDDO menu loop
SET TALK ON
SET STATUS ON
RETURN
```

The entire program should look like this. The shading is used to show the two major loops in the program nested within each other.

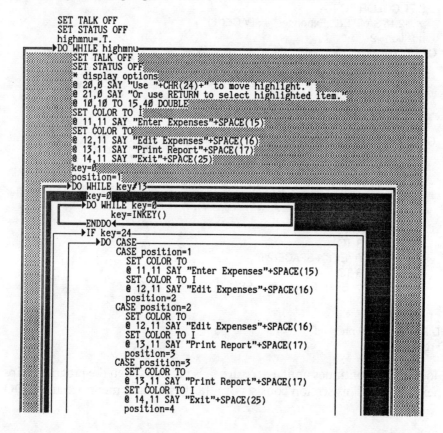

```
SET TALK OFF
SET STATUS OFF
highmnu=.T.
DO WHILE highmnu
    SET TALK OFF
    SET STATUS OFF
    * display options
    @ 20,0 SAY "Use "+CHR(24)+" to move highlight."
    @ 21,0 SAY "Or use RETURN to select highlighted item."
    @ 10,10 TO 15,40 DOUBLE
    SET COLOR TO I
    @ 11,11 SAY "Enter Expenses"+SPACE(15)
    SET COLOR TO
    @ 12,11 SAY "Edit Expenses"+SPACE(16)
    @ 13,11 SAY "Print Report"+SPACE(17)
    @ 14,11 SAY "Exit"+SPACE(25)
    key=0
    position=1
    DO WHILE key#13
        key=0
        DO WHILE key=0
            key=INKEY()
        ENDDO
        IF key=24
            DO CASE
                CASE position=1
                    SET COLOR TO
                    @ 11,11 SAY "Enter Expenses"+SPACE(15)
                    SET COLOR TO I
                    @ 12,11 SAY "Edit Expenses"+SPACE(16)
                    position=2
                CASE position=2
                    SET COLOR TO
                    @ 12,11 SAY "Edit Expenses"+SPACE(16)
                    SET COLOR TO I
                    @ 13,11 SAY "Print Report"+SPACE(17)
                    position=3
                CASE position=3
                    SET COLOR TO
                    @ 13,11 SAY "Print Report"+SPACE(17)
                    SET COLOR TO I
                    @ 14,11 SAY "Exit"+SPACE(25)
                    position=4
```

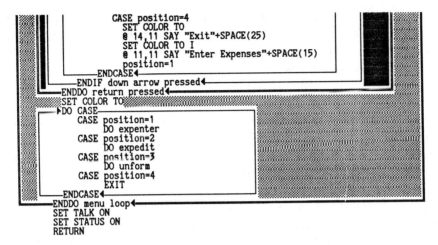

```
                    CASE position=4
                         SET COLOR TO
                         @ 14,11 SAY "Exit"+SPACE(25)
                         SET COLOR TO I
                         @ 11,11 SAY "Enter Expenses"+SPACE(15)
                         position=1
                    ENDCASE
               ENDIF down arrow pressed
          ENDDO return pressed
          SET COLOR TO
          DO CASE
                    CASE position=1
                         DO expenter
                    CASE position=2
                         DO expedit
                    CASE position=3
                         DO unform
                    CASE position=4
                         EXIT
          ENDCASE
     ENDDO menu loop
     SET TALK ON
     SET STATUS ON
     RETURN
```

Save the program by entering

[CTRL/End]

Execute the program by entering

DO highmnu < return >

The menu appears like this on the screen:

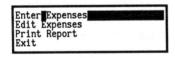

```
Enter Expenses
Edit Expenses
Print Report
Exit
```

```
Use ↑ to move highlight.
Or use RETURN to select highlighted item.
```

Test the menu by moving the highlight to the program you want to execute and pressing < return >.

The SET COLOR command and INKEY() function can be combined to create a user interface that allows the user to feel that cursor movements are selecting items from a menu. This interface mimics the one used in the ASSIST mode; it adds another method of communicating with the person using your programs.

SYSTEMS USING MULTIPLE FILES

The previous chapters on systems design assumed that you were working with a single data base file. Part of the power of *dBASE III Plus* is its ability to operate with several files at the same time. The need to create systems with multiple data base files is dictated by the nature of the data you are trying to store.

Many business tasks require data base systems that use more than a single data base file. For example, suppose you wanted to create a data base system that would allow you to create invoices for orders that you receive. Why would invoicing be different from recording expenses?

The reasons become apparent when you ask the following question: How many fields should you create for items on each invoice? If you say one, then you can place only one item on each invoice record. If you say ten, that means you must create a file with ten duplicate sets of fields for the items, prices, and descriptions. Even if you were to do that, you would still face the possibility that some invoices require more than ten items. On the other hand, smaller invoices would waste all those fields.

The best solution to this type of problem is to create two related data base files. The master file would contain all the information about the invoice that needs to be recorded only once, such as the invoice number, date, and customer information. The second file is called the *transaction file*. In this file you can place all the details about each invoice item, such as part number, description, amount, and quantity. The two files are linked at a common piece of data (e.g., invoice number).

Each invoice item would be recorded as a separate record in the transaction file linked to a unique invoice number in the master file. The advantage of this system is that you can enter as many or as few items as you like for each invoice. In addition, you can use other files to provide lists of customers and products. These files can provide automatic look up of addresses, product information, and pricing.

The relationship between master and transaction file is common to many applications. In the ensuing chapters you will learn how a system that uses several data base files to contain all the information is constructed. The specific subject is an invoicing system, but the principle can be applied to a wide variety of problems that exhibit the one-to-many relations that the invoice problem does.

CREATING THE FILES

To carry out this program, you will need to create four new data base files and some index files as well. The files will be

CUST	customer names and addresses
PRODUCT	Sproduct information and pricing
DETAILS	this file holds the individual invoice items
INVOICE	this file holds the master record for each invoice

Begin by creating the file INVOICE with the following structure:

Structure for database: C:invoice.dbf

Field	Field Name	Type	Width	Dec
1	CONUM	Numeric	5	
2	INVDATE	Date	8	
3	INUM	Numeric	8	
4	ITEMS	Numeric	3	
5	TOTAL	Numeric	8	2
6	TAXRATE	Numeric	5	1
7	TAX	Numeric	8	2
8	NET	Numeric	8	2
9	PAID	Logical	1	
10	DATEPAID	Date	8	
** Total **			63	

Create an index for this file by entering

INDEX ON inum TO invoice < return >

Create the file that will hold the detailed information called DETAIL with the following structure:

Structure for database: C:details.dbf

Field	Field Name	Type	Width	Dec
1	CONUM	Numeric	5	
2	INVDATE	Date	8	
3	INUM	Numeric	8	
4	PNUM	Character	10	
5	ITEM	Character	30	
6	PRICE	Numeric	6	2
7	QUANTITY	Numeric	4	
8	TOTAL	Numeric	8	2
** Total **			80	

Create an index for this file by entering

INDEX ON inum TO details < return >

The next file will hold the customer information. It will be called CUST and should have the following structure:

Structure for database: C:cust.dbf

Field	Field Name	Type	Width	Dec
1	CONUM	Numeric	5	
2	COMPANY	Character	25	
3	STREET	Character	25	
4	CITY	Character	25	
5	STATE	Character	2	
6	ZIP	Character	5	

7	AREACODE	Character	3
8	PHONE	Character	8
9	CONTACT	Character	30
** Total **			129

Enter the following records into the CUST file:

```
Record#  CONUM COMPANY                STREET                 CITY          STATE ZIP
AREACODE PHONE     CONTACT
      1  1000 Northwood Enterprises   150 Gates Ave          San Deigo     CA    94102
415      322-9999 Dave Smith
      2  1001 Winter Productions      890 Tennessee Street   Eureka        CA    94107
345      355-0399 Walter La Fish
      3  1002 Bay Cities Enterprises  1250 Main Street       Walnut Creek  CA    94546
415      515-9292 Carolyn Regiero
      4  1003 Taylor Made Copy Systems 1053 Shary Circle     Concord       CA    94518
415      535-0303 Herb
```

This file will not need an index.

Create the fourth file, the product inventory file called PRODUCTS, with the following structure:

Structure for database: C:**products.dbf**

Field	Field Name	Type	Width	Dec
1	PNUM	Character	10	
2	NAME	Character	25	
3	INSTOCK	Numeric	4	
4	COST	Numeric	8	2
5	MARKUP	Numeric	2	
** Total **			50	

Enter the following records into this file:

```
Record# PNUM    NAME                    INSTOCK    COST MARKUP
     1  PC-400  IBM COMPATIBLE  2 FLOPPY       5  950.00     23
     2  PC-400H IBM COMPATIBLE 20 MEGA HD      4 1350.00     21
     3  MONO-1  MONOCHROME MONITOR            6  125.00     27
     4  T321    TOSHIBA 321 PRINTER           8  450.00     23
     5  PARA-6  PARALLEL PRINTER CABLE       15   12.00     35
     6  HERC-1  HERCULES PRINTER ADAPTER      6  210.00     25
```

Create an index for this file by entering

INDEX ON pnum TO products < return >

You now have the files necessary to create the invoice entry system. Close any open files by entering

CLOSE DATABASE < return >

ENTERING THE DATA

The program that will create the invoices will actually be a series of related programs. Four programs will be needed to complete the sample system.

The main program, INVOICE, creates a new batch of invoices. INVOICE will function to open the correct files and allow the user to select a customer. The rest of the operation will be carried on by three subroutines.

1. **MAKEINV.** This routine allows you to fill out the details of each invoice. After each invoice is complete, the program returns to INVOICE for the next customer.
2. **INVPRT.** This program is used to print the invoices entered in MAKEINV. It will execute after the entire batch of invoices has been filled out. This is a more efficient way than printing after each invoice is filled out.
3. **UPDATEINV.** This program is used to update the inventory and detail files with the data contained in the batch file.

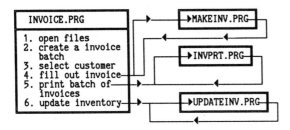

THE MAIN PROGRAM

The overall goal of this program system is to create an easy way of filling out invoice information on the screen. While the programming techniques become more complex, the result ought to be a simpler way for users to do their work.

dBASE III Plus allows you to create programs, like the ones in this chapter, that switch back and forth between several data base files without making the user aware that these complex operations are taking place.

The main advantage to users of these multiple-file operations is that they can avoid entering the same data over and over again. By storing the customer and product data in separate files, the information can be added to the invoice by selection from lists, rather than manual entry. As always, the idea is to cut down on time and errors by selection rather than manual entry.

Although the subject of these programs is INVOICE, the techniques can be applied to almost any data management task.

Begin the creation of the main program by entering

MODIFY COMMAND invoice <return>

Enter the usual housekeeping commands:

```
CLEAR
SET TALK OFF
SET STATUS OFF
SET SAFETY OFF
CLEAR
```

The next section of the program is used to obtain the correct starting invoice number and date for the batch you are about to enter. The assumption is that you want to number the invoices consecutively and use the same date for all the invoices entered into the same batch.

The starting invoice number is found by searching the INVOICE file for the last invoice number used. The user is allowed to override this number by entering a value manually. Enter

```
@ 10,10 SAY "CREATING INVOICE BATCH ........."
* initialize invoice number and date
USE invoice INDEX invoice
GO BOTTOM
startinv=inum+1
batchdate=CTOD("  /  /  ")
@ 11,10 SAY "The First Invoice will be:"
@ 11,COL()+1 GET startinv
@ 12,10 SAY "Press RETURN to accept or enter new number"
READ
@ 14,10 SAY "Enter date for this batch " GET batchdate
READ
```

Now that the date and invoice number are entered, you are ready to open the files needed for invoice processing. Four files will be used.

	Work Area A	Work Area B	Work Area C	Work Area D
Database File	INVBATCH	CUST	PRODUCTS	INVOICE
Index File	none	none	PRODUCTS	INVOICE
Alias	DETAILS	CUSTOMER	PRODUCTS	MASTER

The DETAILS file is not used directly; a copy of its structure is used to simplify keeping track of which details need to be printed. All the details in the INVBATCH file will be printed and then appended to the DETAILS file. Enter

```
* create new batch
USE details
COPY STRUCTURE TO invbatch
USE invbatch ALIAS details
SELECT B
```

```
USE cust ALIAS customer
SELECT C
USE products INDEX products
SELECT D
USE invoice ALIAS master
SELECT details
```

The next section of the program contains a loop that allows the user to select a customer from the CUST file, and then create an invoice for that customer. The procedure is similar to that used in EXPEDIT in Chapter 16. The main difference is that the search is conducted in the CUST data base file, opened in work area C. The goal is simply to position the pointer in the CUST data base file to the proper record. That record can be used to display data about the customer when needed. Enter

```
batch=.T.
DO WHILE batch
        * selected customer from file
        CLEAR
        @ 1,0 SAY "Invoice date  =  "
        @ 1,COL()+1 SAY batchdate
        @ 2,0 SAY "Invoice numb.=  "
        @ 2,COL()+1 SAY startinv
        findcust=.F.
        SELECT CUSTOMER <========= selects CUST database
        DO WHILE .NOT.findcust
            @ 10,0 CLEAR
            customer=SPACE(30)
            @ 10,10 SAY "Enter name of customer" get customer PICTURE "@!"
            READ
            * verify customer
            LOCATE FOR UPPER(company)=TRIM(customer)
            IF FOUND()
                @ 11,9 TO 16,40
                @ 12,10 SAY company
                @ 13,10 SAY street
                @ 14,10 SAY TRIM(city)+", "+state+" "+zip
                @ 15,10 SAY "("+areacode+")"+phone
                @ 17,10 SAY "Correct ? (Y/N)" GET findcust PICTURE "Y"
                READ
            ELSE
                @ 15,10 SAY "**** NOT FOUND *****"
                WAIT "Press any key to search again"
            ENDIF
        ENDDO find customer
```

Once the customer has been selected, the program calls the MAKEINV subroutine to fill out the actual details of the invoice. When the MAKEINV routine is complete, the program asks the user if there is another invoice to enter. The loop continues until all the invoices have been created. Enter

```
    DO makeinv
    CLEAR
    @ 20,10 SAY "Add another Invoice? (Y/N)" GET batch PICTURE "Y"
    READ
    IF .NOT. batch
        EXIT
    ENDIF
    startinv=startinv+1
ENDDO batch
* batch complete
```

The next section of the program executes when the batch entry is complete. Note that the INVPRT and UPDATEINV programs are entered as notes. This allows you to test the entry portion of the program before you create the other two routines. The entry of the commands as notes is to show you where in this program those routines will be called. Enter

```
*DO invprt
*DO updateinv
SET SAFETY ON
SET TALK ON
SET STATUS ON
CLOSE DATABASE
RETURN
```

The entire program should look like this:

```
CLEAR
SET TALK OFF
SET STATUS OFF
SET SAFETY OFF
CLEAR
@ 10,10 SAY "CREATING INVOICE BATCH ........."
* initialize invoice number and date
USE invoice INDEX invoice
GO BOTTOM
startinv=inum+1
batchdate=CTOD("  /  /  ")
@ 11,10 SAY "The First Invoice will be:"
@ 11,COL()+1 GET startinv
@ 12,10 SAY "Press RETURN to accept or enter new number"
READ
@ 14,10 SAY "Enter date for this batch " GET batchdate
READ
* create new batch
USE details
COPY STRUCTURE TO invbatch
USE invbatch ALIAS details
SELECT B
USE cust ALIAS customer
SELECT C
USE products INDEX products
SELECT D
USE invoice ALIAS master
SELECT details
batch=.T.
```

```
┌─▶DO WHILE batch
│          * selected customer from file
│          CLEAR
│          @ 1,0 SAY "Invoice date = "
│          @ 1,COL()+1 SAY batchdate
│          @ 2,0 SAY "Invoice numb.= "
│          @ 2,COL()+1 SAY startinv
│          findcust=.F.
│          SELECT CUSTOMER
│        ┌─▶DO WHILE .NOT.findcust
│        │        @ 10,0 CLEAR
│        │        customer=SPACE(30)
│        │        @ 10,10 SAY "Enter name of customer" get customer PICTURE "@!"
│        │        READ
│        │        * verify customer
│        │        LOCATE FOR UPPER(company)=TRIM(customer)
│        │      ┌─▶IF FOUND()
│        │      │        @ 11,9 TO 16,40
│        │      │        @ 12,10 SAY company
│        │      │        @ 13,10 SAY street
│        │      │        @ 14,10 SAY TRIM(city)+", "+state+" "+zip
│        │      │        @ 15,10 SAY "("+areacode+")-"+phone
│        │      │        @ 17,10 SAY "Correct ? (Y/N)" GET findcust PICTURE "Y"
│        │      │        READ
│        │      ELSE
│        │      │        @ 15,10 SAY "**** NOT FOUND *****"
│        │      │        WAIT "Press any key to search again"
│        │      └─ENDIF◀
│        └─ENDDO find customer◀
│          DO makeinv
│          CLEAR
│          @ 20,10 SAY "Add another Invoice? (Y/N)" GET batch PICTURE "Y"
│          READ
│        ┌─▶IF .NOT. batch
│        │       EXIT
│        └─ENDIF◀
│          startinv=startinv+1   && increment invoice number
└─ENDDO batch entry◀
          * batch complete
          *DO invprt
          *DO updateinv
          SET SAFETY ON
          SET TALK ON
          SET STATUS ON
          CLOSE DATABASE
          RETURN
```

Save the program by entering

[CTRL/End]

INVOICE DETAIL

The next portion of the program, MAKEINV, is the entry of the details of the invoice. Enter

MODIFY COMMAND makeinv < return >

This program is designed in a similar manner to the EXPBROW program in Chapter 16. The entry screen is designed to show a screen header and footer.

The header is a box at the top of the screen that shows the invoice date and number, and the name and address of the customer. The footer is a box that displays the number of items entered and the total amount of the invoice. The footer display keeps a running total as you enter items. The center of the screen allows you to enter the actual details of items, prices, and quantities.

The first portion of the program displays the screen heading, footing, and column headings. This display remains throughout the entry of the details. Enter

```
* make invoice program
SELECT details <======== selects DETAILS database file
STORE 0 TO items,itemtotal
* display customer information
CLEAR
@ 0,0 TO 4,78 DOUBLE
@ 1, 3 SAY "Date of Invoice:"
@ 1, 20 SAY batchdate
@ 2, 3 SAY "Invoice Number:"
@ 2, 20 SAY startinv
@ 1, 39 SAY "Customer:"
@ 1, 50 SAY CUSTOMER->COMPANY
@ 2, 50 SAY CUSTOMER->STREET
@ 3, 50 SAY TRIM(city)+", "state+" "+zip
* display bottom totals
@ 22, 5 SAY "Number of Items:"
@ 22, 23 SAY items PICTURE "999"
@ 22, 45 SAY "Total for Invoice:"
@ 22, 64 SAY itemtotal PICTURE "99,999.99"
@ 21,0 TO 23,78 DOUBLE
* display headings
@ 5, 0 SAY "Item #       Description"+;
"              Cost     Price    Quantity      Total"
```

The next section of the program is a loop that adds detail records to the DETAILS data base file. The line variable is used to place each item on a different line. The append blank adds records to the DETAILS data base file because that is the file currently selected. Enter

```
line=6
more=.T.
DO WHILE more
     APPEND BLANK
```

What should happen next? You must place into the new detail record the information that will link this detail with the invoice being created. The REPLACE command is used to store the CONUM (customer's company number), the INVDATE (invoice date), and the STARTINV (invoice number), in the record automatically.

```
REPLACE conum WITH customer->conum,invdate with batchdate,inum WITH startinv
```

The next step is to allow the user to enter the product number for the first item. Enter

```
@ line,0 GET pnum PICTURE "@!"
READ
```

After the number has been entered, the program can search the PRODUCT file to find the name, cost, and markup of selected items. Note that the alias is used to search the PRODUCTS data base file with a value stored in the DETAILS data base file. Enter

```
* find product
SELECT products
SEEK details->pnum
```

If the product is located in the PRODUCTS data base file, the data stored about the product can be transferred to the record in the DETAILS file. The selling price can be calculated by using the cost and markup values. The data are displayed on the screen and the user is allowed to enter the quantity sold. Enter

```
IF FOUND()
    SELECT details
    REPLACE item WITH products->name,;
    price WITH products->cost*(1+products->markup*.01)
    @ line,11 SAY item
    @ line,38 SAY products->cost PICTURE "9999.99"
    @ line,47 SAY price PICTURE "9999.99"
    @ line,58 GET quantity PICTURE "999"
```

Allowance is made for items not currently in the PRODUCT file. If the PNUM is not found, a message is placed in the ITEM field. The user can then manually enter the description, price, and quantity. Enter

```
ELSE
    SELECT details
    REPLACE item WITH "*Not in Inventory",price WITH 0
    @ line,11 GET item
    @ line,38 SAY "N/A"
    @ line,47 GET price PICTURE "9999.99"
    @ line,58 GET quantity PICTURE "999"
ENDIF
READ
```

The next step is to calculate the total for the item (quantity times price), and add the item to the values displayed in the screen footer. The screen footer shows the running total for the invoice. Enter

```
REPLACE total WITH quantity*price
@ line, 66 SAY total PICTURE "9,999.99"
items=items+1
itemtotal=itemtotal+total
@ 22, 23 SAY items PICTURE "999"
@ 22, 64 SAY itemtotal PICTURE "99,999.99"
```

Next, the user is asked if she wants to enter another item. Enter

```
@ line+1,0 SAY "Enter Another Item? (Y/N)" GET more PICTURE "Y"
READ
```

If YES, the line is incremented and the loop executes again. Enter

```
    IF more
        @ line+1,0
        line=line+1
    ENDIF
ENDDO more items
```

If no, that invoice is complete. The program then transfers the summary data to the master invoice file. There is now one master invoice record for each series of related details. Enter

```
SELECT master
APPEND blank
REPLACE conum WITH details->conum,invdate WITH batchdate;
,items WITH M->items,total WITH itemtotal,paid WITH .F.;
,inum WITH startinv
```

The next section allows the user to add sales tax to the invoice. Enter

```
@ 6,0 CLEAR
@ 6,10 SAY "Items:"
@ 7,10 SAY "Total:"
@ 8,10 SAY "Tax rate:"
@ 9,10 SAY "Tax:"
@ 10,10 SAY "Net Due:"
@ 6,30 SAY items PICTURE "99,999"
@ 7,30 SAY total PICTURE "99,999.99"
@ 8,30 GET taxrate
READ
REPLACE tax with ROUND(taxrate*total*.01,2)
REPLACE net WITH tax+total
@ 9,30 SAY tax PICTURE "99,999.99"
@ 10,30 SAY net PICTURE "99,999.99"
```

The program has now filled out both the detail and master records for the invoice, and returns to INVOICE. Enter

```
WAIT
RETURN
```

The entire program should look like this:

```
* make invoice program
SELECT details sales
STORE 0 TO items,itemtotal
* display customer information
CLEAR
@ 0,0 TO 4,78 DOUBLE
```

```
@ 1,  3  SAY "Date of Invoice:"
@ 1, 20  SAY  batchdate
@ 2,  3  SAY "Invoice Number:"
@ 2, 20  SAY  startinv
@ 1, 39  SAY "Customer:"
@ 1, 50  SAY  CUSTOMER->COMPANY
@ 2, 50  SAY  CUSTOMER->STREET
@ 3, 50  SAY  TRIM(city)+", "+state+" "+zip
* display bottom totals
@ 22,  5  SAY "Number of Items:"
@ 22, 23  SAY  items PICTURE "999"
@ 22, 45  SAY "Total for Invoice:"
@ 22, 64  SAY  itemtotal PICTURE "99,999.99"
@ 21,Ø TO 23,78 DOUBLE
* display headings
@ 5,  Ø  SAY "Item #       Description                      "+;
"Cost    Price   Quantity  Total"
line=6
more=.T.
DO WHILE more
        APPEND BLANK
        REPLACE conum WITH customer->conum,invdate with batchdate,;
        inum WITH startinv
        @ line,Ø GET pnum PICTURE "@!"
        READ
        * find product
        SELECT products
        SEEK details->pnum
        IF FOUND()
            SELECT details
            REPLACE item WITH products->name,;
            price WITH products->cost*(1+products->markup*.Ø1)
            @  line,11  SAY  item
            @  line,38  SAY  products->cost PICTURE "9999.99"
            @  line,47  SAY  price  PICTURE "9999.99"
            @  line,58  GET  quantity PICTURE "999"
        ELSE
            SELECT details
            REPLACE item WITH "*Not in Inventory",price WITH Ø
            @  line,11  GET  item
            @  line,38  SAY  " N/A"
            @  line,47  GET  price   PICTURE "9999.99"
            @  line,58  GET  quantity PICTURE "999"
        ENDIF
        READ
        REPLACE total WITH quantity*price
        @ line, 66  SAY  total PICTURE "9,999.99"
        items=items+1
        itemtotal=itemtotal+total
        @ 22, 23  SAY  items PICTURE "999"
        @ 22, 64  SAY  itemtotal PICTURE "99,999.99"
        @ line+1,Ø SAY "Enter Another Item? (Y/N)" GET more PICTURE "Y"
        READ
        IF more
            @ line+1,Ø
            line=line+1
        ENDIF
ENDDO more items
SELECT master
APPEND blank
REPLACE conum WITH details->conum,invdate WITH batchdate;
,items WITH M->items,total WITH itemtotal,paid WITH .F.;
,inum WITH startinv
@ 6,Ø CLEAR
@ 6,10 SAY "Items:"
@ 7,10 SAY "Total:"
@ 8,10 SAY "Tax rate:"
@ 9,10 SAY "Tax:"
@ 10,10 SAY "Net Due:"
@ 6,30 SAY items PICTURE "99,999"
@ 7,30 SAY total PICTURE "99,999.99"
@ 8,30 GET taxrate
READ
REPLACE tax with ROUND(taxrate*total*.Ø1,2)
REPLACE net WITH tax+total
@ 9,30 SAY tax PICTURE "99,999.99"
@ 10,30 SAY net PICTURE "99,999.99"
WAIT
RETURN
```

Save the program by entering

[CTRL/End]

You are now ready to try the program. Enter

DO invoice < return >

The screen will display

```
CREATING INVOICE BATCH ........
The First Invoice will be:        1
Press RETURN to accept or enter new number
```

Since the files are empty, the program uses 1 as the starting invoice number. Enter

145 < return >

The screen now shows

```
CREATING INVOICE BATCH ........
The First Invoice will be:        145
Press RETURN to accept or enter new number

Enter date for this batch  ■/■/■
```

Enter the date for this batch.

111786

The next screen allows you to select the company for the invoice.

```
Invoice date = 11/17/86
Invoice numb.=        145

Enter name of customer ▉▉▉▉▉▉▉▉▉▉▉
```

Enter

BAY < return >

The screen will show

```
Invoice date = 11/17/86
Invoice numb.=        145



        Enter name of customer BAY
        ┌─────────────────────────────┐
        │ Bay Cities Enterprises       │
        │ 1250 Main Street             │
        │ Walnut Creek, CA 94546       │
        │ (415)-515-9292               │
        └─────────────────────────────┘
        Correct ? (Y/N) N
```

The name and address of the company are shown. Suppose this is not the correct company. Enter

```
<return>
nor <return>
```

The program finds a new company:

```
Invoice date = 11/17/86
Invoice numb.=         145
```

```
Enter name of customer NOR
┌─────────────────────────────┐
│ Northwood Enterprises        │
│ 150 Gates Ave                │
│ San Diego, CA 94102          │
│ (415)-322-9999               │
└─────────────────────────────┘
Correct ? (Y/N) N
```

Accept this company by entering

```
<return>
```

The next screen is the item entry screen.

```
┌──────────────────────────────────────────────────────────────────┐
│ Date of Invoice: 11/17/86        Customer:  Northwood Enterprises  │
│ Invoice Number:         145                 150 Gates Ave          │
│                                             San Diego              │
└──────────────────────────────────────────────────────────────────┘
Item #       Description           Cost    Price   Quantity   Total
███████


┌──────────────────────────────────────────────────────────────────┐
│    Number of Items:   0          Total for Invoice:      0.00      │
└──────────────────────────────────────────────────────────────────┘
```

Enter a product number:

```
PC-400 <return>
```

The program finds the product in the PRODUCT file and displays the data for that item.

```
┌──────────────────────────────────────────────────────────────────┐
│ Date of Invoice: 11/17/86        Customer:  Northwood Enterprises  │
│ Invoice Number:         145                 150 Gates Ave          │
│                                             San Diego              │
└──────────────────────────────────────────────────────────────────┘
Item #       Description           Cost     Price   Quantity   Total
PC-400       IBM COMPATIBLE 2 FLOPPY 950.00 1168.50 ███


┌──────────────────────────────────────────────────────────────────┐
│    Number of Items:   0          Total for Invoice:      0.00      │
└──────────────────────────────────────────────────────────────────┘
```

Enter the quantity:

```
1 <return>
```

The program calculates the total for that item. Note that the bottom of the screen now shows the running total of items and their value. The program also is prompting you for the entry of another item.

```
┌─────────────────────────────────────────────────────────────────────┐
│ Date of Invoice: 11/17/86        Customer:  Northwood Enterprises     │
│ Invoice Number:        145                  150 Gates Ave             │
│                                             San Diego                 │
└─────────────────────────────────────────────────────────────────────┘
Item #        Description            Cost     Price    Quantity  Total
PC-400    IBM COMPATIBLE  2 FLOPPY  950.00   1168.50      1      1,168.50
Enter Another Item? (Y/N) Y




┌─────────────────────────────────────────────────────────────────────┐
│  Number of Items:    1              Total for Invoice:  1,168.50      │
└─────────────────────────────────────────────────────────────────────┘
```

Enter the next item:

T321 <return>
1 <return>

The new item is added to the invoice display and the running totals.

```
┌─────────────────────────────────────────────────────────────────────┐
│ Date of Invoice: 11/17/86        Customer:  Northwood Enterprises     │
│ Invoice Number:        145                  150 Gates Ave             │
│                                             San Diego                 │
└─────────────────────────────────────────────────────────────────────┘
Item #        Description            Cost     Price    Quantity  Total
PC-400    IBM COMPATIBLE  2 FLOPPY  950.00   1168.50      1      1,168.50
T321      TOSHIBA 321 PRINTER       450.00    553.50      1        553.50
Enter Another Item? (Y/N) Y




┌─────────────────────────────────────────────────────────────────────┐
│  Number of Items:    2              Total for Invoice:  1,722.00      │
└─────────────────────────────────────────────────────────────────────┘
```

Enter another item for this invoice:

PARA-6 <return>
1 <return>

The screen now shows

```
┌─────────────────────────────────────────────────────────────────────┐
│ Date of Invoice: 11/17/86        Customer:  Northwood Enterprises     │
│ Invoice Number:        145                  150 Gates Ave             │
│                                             San Diego                 │
└─────────────────────────────────────────────────────────────────────┘
Item #        Description            Cost     Price    Quantity  Total
PC-400    IBM COMPATIBLE  2 FLOPPY  950.00   1168.50      1      1,168.50
T321      TOSHIBA 321 PRINTER       450.00    553.50      1        553.50
PARA-6    PARALLEL PRINTER CABLE     12.00     16.20      1         16.20
Enter Another Item? (Y/N) Y




┌─────────────────────────────────────────────────────────────────────┐
│  Number of Items:    3              Total for Invoice:  1,738.20      │
└─────────────────────────────────────────────────────────────────────┘
```

Complete the invoice by entering

>   n

The summary screen appears:

```
┌─────────────────────────────────────────────────────────────────────┐
│  Date of Invoice: 11/17/86        Customer:  Northwood Enterprises    │
│  Invoice Number:          145                150 Gates Ave            │
│                                              San Diego                │
└─────────────────────────────────────────────────────────────────────┘
  Item /     Description                  Cost   Price   Quantity  Total
             Items:                   3
             Total:            1,738.20
             Tax rate:
             Tax:
             Net Due:
```

Enter the sales tax rate:

>   **6.5 < return >**

The program calculates the tax and displays

```
┌─────────────────────────────────────────────────────────────────────┐
│  Date of Invoice: 11/17/86        Customer:  Northwood Enterprises    │
│  Invoice Number:          145                150 Gates Ave            │
│                                              San Diego                │
└─────────────────────────────────────────────────────────────────────┘
  Item /     Description                  Cost   Price   Quantity  Total
             Items:                   3
             Total:            1,738.20
             Tax rate:        6.5
             Tax:               112.98
             Net Due:         1,851.18
  Press any key to continue...
```

Enter

>   **< return >**

The program has now completed the MAKEINV routine and returns to the main program, INVOICE. A prompt asks you if you want to enter another invoice:

```
  Add another Invoice? (Y/N) Y
```

Enter

>   y

The screen displays the company search screen.

```
  Invoice date =  11/17/86
  Invoice numb.=         146
```

```
        Enter name of customer
```

Note that the invoice number has automatically been incremented to 146. Select a customer by entering

>   **bay < return >**
>   y

Fill out the invoice as shown below:

```
Date of Invoice: 11/17/86      Customer:  Bay Cities Enterprises
Invoice Number:        146                1250 Main Street
                                          Walnut Creek

Item #     Description           Cost    Price   Quantity  Total
MONO-1     MONOCHROME MONITOR    125.00  158.75     3      476.25
HERC-1     HERCULES PRINTER ADAPTER 210.00 262.50   3      787.50
Enter Another Item? (Y/N) Y
```

```
Number of Items:    2              Total for Invoice:  1,263.75
```

When you have completed the invoice, enter 6.5% sales tax. When asked if you want to enter another, enter N. The program terminates and returns you to the DOT PROMPT.

What should have happened is that you added two records to the master file, INVOICE, and five records to the DETAILS file (three for the first invoice and two for the second). To check the success of the program, enter

>   **USE invoice** < return >
>   **LIST** <return >

dBASE III Plus will display

```
Record#  CONUM INVDATE   INUM ITEMS   TOTAL TAXRATE      TAX     NET PAID DATEPAID
      1   1000 11/17/86    145     3 1738.20     6.5   112.98 1851.18 .F.    /  /
      2   1002 11/17/86    146     2 1263.75     6.5    82.14 1345.89 .F.    /  /
```

The two master entries are in the file. They show the invoice number, the customer number, the number of items, the total, the tax rate, and the tax amount. Enter

>   **USE invbatch** < return >
>   **LIST** <return >

dBASE III Plus displays

```
        Record#  CONUM INVDATE     INUM PNUM     ITEM                              PRICE QUANTITY
TOTAL
      1   1000 11/17/86     145 PC-400   IBM COMPATIBLE  2 FLOPPY    1168.5    1   1168.50
      2   1000 11/17/86     145 T321     TOSHIBA 321 PRINTER         553.50    1    553.50
      3   1000 11/17/86     145 PARA-6   PARALLEL PRINTER CABLE       16.20    1     16.20
      4   1002 11/17/86     146 MONO-1   MONOCHROME MONITOR          158.75    3    476.25
      5   1002 11/17/86     146 HERC-1   HERCULES PRINTER ADAPTER    262.50    3    787.50
```

This file shows the details of each item entered. The records also contain the invoice and customer number for each item. This enables you to analyze the items sold according to customer or invoice number and link the records with either.

Close the data file by entering

CLOSE DATABASE <return>

This completes the first part of the invoice program. In the next chapter you will complete the program by adding the modules that print the invoices and update the PRODUCT file by subtracting the items sold from the inventory.

SUMMARY

This chapter illustrated two advanced programming techniques available in *dBASE III Plus*:

1. **Highlight menus.** The highlight menu gives the user the ability to select items from a menu by using the arrow keys to change the position of the highlight.

    The highlight effect is created by using two *dBASE III Plus* commands that may at first seem to be totally unrelated.

    a. **SET COLOR TO.** The SET COLOR command is used to create the contrasting video displays that create the highlight. By changing the position of the highlight on the screen display, you can create the illusion of a moving cursor.

    b. **INKEY().** The INKEY() function allows you to capture input from the user in the form of nonalphanumeric keys. The INKEY() function returns a numeric value corresponding to the ASCII value of the key. A zero value indicates no keystroke entered by the user.

2. **Multiple data base processing.** The INVOICE program showed how data that compose a single sheet of paper, such as an invoice, are really stored in a series of related data base files. The primary data are stored in a master and detail files. In addition, supporting information is stored in customer and product inventory files.

    The SELECT command is used to move back and forth between these files, while the user simply enters the proper codes into the screen display. The use of multiple files is transparent to the user.

    > *The term "transparent" refers to commands that do not affect the screen display directly. For example, when a program executes a SELECT command, there is no change visible on the screen. The user is unaware that anything has changed.*

Appendix to Chapter 18

The INKEY() function discussed in this chapter is not the only function of its type in *dBASE III Plus*. The READKEY() function also exists. Its use is a variation on the INKEY() function. READKEY() is directly related to the full-screen editing commands provided by *dBASE III Plus* and discussed in the first part of this book.

The primary purpose of the READKEY() function is to help you determine if changes have been made while you were editing a full-screen display. The READKEY() applies to displays created by the EDIT, APPEND, CHANGE, BROWSE, and INSERT commands. In addition, formatted screen displays created with @/SAY/GET and using READ to access the input area also change the READKEY() value. Since the interactive commands are not recommended for programming, the use of READKEY() with @/SAY/GET and READ is the one most helpful to programmers.

The value of READKEY() is determined by two things:

1.   The key that was used to exit the full-screen editing.
2.   Whether or not changes were made during the editing.

For example, if you enter a command to EDIT a single record, EDIT NEXT 1, and exit the display by pressing **[CTRL/End]**, the value of READKEY() will be

15   if no changes were made
271   if changes were made in the record

dBASE III Plus adds a value of 256 to the key value if changes were made.

Below is a sample program that utilizes READKEY() to determine if a key has been pressed during editing of the record. The record is displayed by using the @/SAY/GET commands shown in lines 7 through 11.

Following the READ command, READKEY() is tested. If the value is greater than 256, the program can take actions based on a change in data. In this program the new data is displayed beside the old data and the user is asked to confirm the changes. If the user enters N, the old values are replaced in the record.

If the READKEY() is below 256, then the program tells the user that no data has been changed.

```
[line #1]    SET TALK OFF
[line #2]    CLEAR
[line #3]    USE EXPENSES
[line #4]    oldamt = amount
[line #5]    olddate = date
```

```
[line #6]   oldpayto = payto
[line #7]   @ 5,0 SAY "Date" GET date
[line #8]   @ 6,0 SAY "Payee" GET payto
[line #9]   @ 7,0 SAY "Amount" GET amount
[line #11] READ
[line #12] IF READKEY() > 256
[line #13]       @ 10,10 SAY "Data Has been Changed"
[line #14]       @ 11,10 SAY "Old"
[line #15]       @ 11,30 SAY "New"
[line #16]       @ 12,10 SAY olddate
[line #17]       @ 12,30 SAY date
[line #18]       @ 13,10 SAY oldpayto
[line #19]       @ 13,30 SAY payto
[line #20]       @ 14,10 SAY oldamt
[line #21]       @ 14,30 SAY amount
[line #22]       alter = .t.
[line #23]       @ 16,10 SAY "Save Changes? (Y/N)" GET alter PICTURE "Y"
[line #24]       READ
[line #25]       IF .NOT. alter
[line #26]            REPLACE date WITH olddate,payto WITH oldpayto,amount WITH oldamt
[line #27]       ENDIF
[line #28] ELSE
[line #29]       @ 10,10 SAY "Data Displayed but No Changes Made"
[line #30] ENDIF
[line #31] CLOSE DATABASE
[line #32] SET TALK ON
[line #33] RETURN
```

COMPLETING THE

INVOICE PROGRAM

IN THE PREVIOUS CHAPTER YOU LEARNED how to create a program that used multiple data base files to store data about invoices. The program illustrates a very important principle about computer-based information systems. The point is that the forms of organization used by computers often require you to look at the information from a different perspective.

For example, when a manual system is used for invoices, all the information placed on a single piece of paper (i.e., the invoice), appears to be a single unit. When computerizing, the usual reaction is to place all this information in a single computer-based unit (i.e., a single record in a data base file). But this is not correct. The invoice is really composed of information from a variety of different files, as listed below:

1. **Heading.** The heading consists of customer data, name, and address, that does not change with each invoice.

2. **Details.** The individual items ordered reflect movement of inventory information to a particular customer. The records in the data base file that record this transfer are a different type from the records that record customer information.

    There are really two records—one that shows the inventory item and one that shows where that item was transferred.

3. **Summary.** Because more than one item can be transferred during a transaction, there is a need to keep track of the summary information, such as the total of all the items, sales tax, and freight charges. These figures are related to the detail information but cannot logically be stored in the same file.

The most difficult part of creating a data base system is understanding what types of information are really implied by a manual task. The analysis should attempt to break the task down into the smallest possible unit (i.e., the lowest common denominator). From those small parts you can always reassemble the larger structures.

For example, printing an invoice requires you to retrieve information stored in three files: customer data, master invoices, and item details. When the data is printed on the invoice, it will appear to readers as a single unit. Readers do not see that the data were drawn from multiple sources.

That is exactly the problem you face as a designer of data base structures. You are usually presented with the final product and asked to create a computer program that will duplicate the product, only with less effort and more accuracy. The key is to be able to break up that final product into its parts and establish a method by which all the parts can be related to one another.

There is an advantage to this apparent fragmentation of the data. You can assemble the data to create reports that look at the data in a variety of ways. For example, you might produce a list of all products sold, or all transactions with one customer.

You may have noticed that the master invoice file contains the PAID and DATEPAID fields. By filling in this information you can now produce an accounts receivable file by listing all the unpaid invoices for each customer.

With that plan in mind you can create a *pseudocode* (i.e., a listing of ideas and tasks rather than actual *dBASE III Plus* commands). Pseudocode can take many forms. Some programmers write out the command sequence by using English phrases instead of *dBASE III Plus* commands. Other forms of pseudocode are flowcharts, that is, diagrams that show the parts of a program and what the logical flow is from one part to another.

In this case a diagram will be used. The diagram will show only the major parts of the program: the menu options presented to the user and the .PRG files that carry out each option.

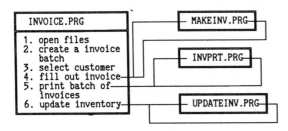

Pseudocode's purpose is to help you develop a framework from which you can actually write the program. The amount of detail included in your pseudocode depends on how much help you need in actually programming the code. As you become more familiar with various programming structures, the pseudocode can be reduced to a simple diagram, like the one above.

According to the diagram there are still two routines needed to complete the INVOICE program.

PRINTING FROM MULTIPLE DATA BASES

The key problem that you are faced with now is how to gather the data stored in the various files and print a single page for each invoice. Note that the invoice is really more of an idea than an actual data item. The invoice is in effect something that you assemble, when needed, from the components stored in a variety of related files.

Create a file INVPRT.PRG by entering

MODIFY COMMAND invprt <return>

The hard part has already been done (i.e., the data base files that are required for this program are still open). All you need to do is select the data bases and print the data that belong on each invoice.

Begin by selecting the INVBATCH file in the details work area. Enter

```
CLEAR
SELECT details
```

Why you begin with the details has to do with why you created a batch file in the first place. Unlike the other files open, the batch has data that are specific to this session. Since that is true, all you need to do is proceed through the INVBATCH file and print the details in that file. When you have finished, all the invoices for this entry session will have been printed.

In order to process them, place the pointer back at the top of the details file. Enter

```
GO TOP
```

Next, begin a loop that will process all the records in that file. Enter

```
DO WHILE .NOT. EOF()
```

Now that you have begun this loop, the first task is to fill out the top of the invoice form. The top consists of your company's name and address and the customer data. In addition, the date and number of the invoice usually appear at the top of the form.

To get this information you need to make sure that the records active in the MASTER and CUSTOMER files match the invoice number and customer number of the first record in the DETAIL file.

First, select the MASTER file and move the pointer to the record with the same invoice number as the active record in the DETAILS file. Note that the MASTER file is indexed and a SEEK command can be used to search the index key, INUM. Enter

```
SELECT master
SEEK details->inum
```

Next, select the CUSTOMER file and find the record that matches the customer number in the DETAILS file. Note that CUSTOMER is not indexed, so a SEEK command cannot be used. Instead, a LOCATE command is used.

```
SELECT customer
LOCATE FOR conum=details->conum
```

> *The CUSTOMER file is not indexed because the number of customers is probably small compared to the size of the other file. The LOCATE command is slower than the SEEK but can be used when the search will not take very long. If you find that the CUSTOMER file is so large that the delay is too long, you can create an index file for CUSTOMER and perform a SEEK.*

Now the pointers in all three files are pointing at the records that match the invoice that needs to be printed.

You can now return to the DETAILS data base work area and begin printing. As an aid to the user, a message indicating which invoice is being printed appears on the screen. Enter

```
SELECT details
SET DEVICE TO SCREEN
@ 10,10 SAY "Printing Invoice #"+STR(master->inum,5)
SET DEVICE TO PRINT
```

The first part of the invoice to print is the name of your company, in this example Krummy Computer. In addition, the invoice number and the date, drawn from the MASTER file, are also printed. Enter

```
@ 5, 0 SAY "KRUMMY COMPUTER"
@ 6, 0 SAY "3725 OLD YORK ROAD"
@ 6, 50 SAY "DATE:"
@ 6, PCOL()+1 SAY master->invdate
@ 7, 0 SAY "PACHECO, CA 94549"
@ 8, 0 SAY "(415)-343-9303"
@ 8, 50 SAY "Invoice # "
@ 8, PCOL()+1 SAY master->inum
@ 10, 0 SAY REPLICATE("=",75)
```

Next, the address of the customer is printed. Enter

```
@ 11, 0 SAY "CUSTOMER:"
@ 11, 27 SAY customer->company
@ 12, 27 SAY customer->street
@ 13, 27 SAY TRIM(customer->city)+", "+customer->state+" "+;
customer->zip
@ 17, 0 SAY "Attention: "+customer->contact
@ 18, 0 SAY REPLICATE("=",75)
```

Finally, the headings for the columns are printed. Enter

```
* print headings
@ 19,0 SAY "Item #"
@ 19,10 SAY "Description"
@ 19,44 SAY "Price"
@ 19,50 SAY "Quantity"
@ 19,64 SAY "Total"
@ 20,0 SAY REPLICATE("=",75)
```

The next section of the program entails another loop. Its purpose is to print all the records in the DETAILS file that contain the same invoice number as the active record in the MASTER file. In this way all the related records are printed on the same invoice.

The testing condition is, therefore, inum=master->inum (i.e., DO WHILE the invoice number equals the invoice number in the master file). In addition, you need to test for the end of the file in case the invoice you are printing is the last one in the file. The line variable is set to the vertical location of the first detail line, 21. Enter

```
line=21
DO WHILE inum=master->inum.AND..NOT.EOF()
```

The next section of the program simply prints the invoice information for each record on the same invoice number. Enter

```
@ line,0 SAY pnum
@ line,10 SAY item
@ line,40 SAY price PICTURE "99,999.99"
@ line,50 SAY quantity PICTURE "9,999"
@ line,60 SAY total PICTURE "99,999.99"
SKIP
line=line+1
ENDDO
```

Once the loop has processed all the details for one invoice number, you need to print the summary data at the bottom of the invoice. The alias name is used to draw the necessary data from the MASTER file. Enter

```
* print summary
@ 50,0 SAY "Total number of items:"
@ 50,PCOL()+1 SAY master->items
```

```
@ 51,0 SAY "Total of items"
@ 51,60 SAY master->total PICTURE "99,999.99"
@ 52,0 SAY "Sales Tax (rate "+STR(master->taxrate,3,1)+"%)"
@ 52,60 SAY master->tax PICTURE "99,999.99"
@ 53,0 SAY "Net Due"
@ 53,60 SAY master->tax+master->total PICTURE "99,999.99"
ENDDO
```

The ENDDO tests for the End Of the File. If not EOF, the invoice number of the active record becomes the key for printing the next invoice. This process repeats until all the records in DETAILS have been printed on an invoice.

Conclude the program by entering

```
SET DEVICE TO SCREEN
EJECT
EJECT
RETURN
```

The entire program should look like this:

```
CLEAR
SELECT details
GO TOP
DO WHILE .NOT. EOF()
    SELECT master
    SEEK details->inum
    SELECT customer
    LOCATE FOR conum=details->conum
    SELECT details
    SET DEVICE TO SCREEN
    @ 10,10 SAY "Printing Invoice #"+STR(master->inum,5)
    SET DEVICE TO PRINT
    @ 5, 0  SAY "KRUMMY COMPUTER"
    @ 6, 0  SAY "3725 OLD YORK ROAD"
    @ 6, 50 SAY "DATE:"
    @ 6, PCOL()+1 SAY master->invdate
    @ 7, 0  SAY "PACHECO, CA 94549"
    @ 8, 0  SAY "(415)-343-9303"
    @ 8, 50 SAY "Invoice # "
    @ 8, PCOL()+1 SAY master->inum
    @ 10, 0  SAY REPLICATE("=",75)
    @ 11, 0  SAY "CUSTOMER:"
    @ 11, 27 SAY  customer->company
    @ 12, 27 SAY  customer->street
    @ 13, 27 SAY  TRIM(customer->city)+", "+customer->state+" "+;
customer->zip
    @ 17, 0 SAY "Attention: "+customer->contact
    @ 18, 0  SAY REPLICATE("=",75)
    * print headings
    @ 19,0 SAY "Item #"
    @ 19,10 SAY "Description"
    @ 19,44 SAY "Price"
    @ 19,50 SAY "Quantity"
    @ 19,64 SAY "Total"
    @ 20,0 SAY REPLICATE("=",75)
    line=21
    DO WHILE inum=master->inum.AND..NOT.EOF()
        @ line,0 SAY pnum
        @ line,10 SAY item
        @ line,40 SAY price PICTURE "99,999.99"
        @ line,50 SAY quantity PICTURE "9,999"
        @ line,60 SAY total PICTURE "99,999.99"
        SKIP
        line=line+1
    ENDDO
```

```
* print summary
@ 50,0 SAY "Total number of items:"
@ 50,PCOL()+1 SAY master->items
@ 51,0 SAY "Total of items"
@ 51,60 SAY master->total PICTURE "99,999.99"
@ 52,0 SAY "Sales Tax (rate "+STR(master->taxrate,3,1)+"%)"
@ 52,60 SAY master->tax PICTURE "99,999.99"
@ 53,0 SAY "Net Due"
@ 53,60 SAY master->tax+master->total PICTURE "99,999.99"
ENDDO
SET DEVICE TO SCREEN
EJECT
EJECT
RETURN
```

Save the program by entering

[CTRL/End]

UPDATING FILES WITH FILES

The final portion of this program is a procedure that will change the amount of the items in stock to reflect the items listed in the details file. This means that as the items are entered into invoices, they will automatically be deducted from the inventory file. The programming concept is the idea of updating files not with direct manual entry but with data entered into another file.

The technique is similar to the one employed in printing an invoice. One file is used to locate the match record in another file. The difference is that the action taken is not an output, printing, but an input. The REPLACE command is used to change the value in the INSTOCK field in the PRODUCTS data base file. Begin by creating a new command file called UPDATEIN by entering

MODIFY COMMAND updatein < return >

Once again, the program begins by selecting the DETAILS data base file. This file is used because it contains records that list which products have been sold and their quantity. Note that the pointer needs to be positioned at the top of the file to begin the processing. Enter

```
SELECT details
GO TOP
```

The next section is a loop that processes all the records in DETAILS.

```
DO WHILE .NOT. EOF()
```

The next step is to search the PRODUCTS data base file to locate the record with the part number, pnum, that matches the part number in the invoice detail record. Note that PRODUCTS is an indexed file and a SEEK command can be used. Enter

```
SELECT products
SEEK details->pnum
```

When the matching product is found, a REPLACE command subtracts the quantity in the DETAILS file from the INSTOCK field in the PRODUCTS file. If no match is found, the program skips to the next records.

```
IF FOUND()
      REPLACE instock WITH instock-details->quantity
ENDIF
SELECT details
  SKIP
FNDDO
```

The process continues until all the records in the file have been processed.

The next section of the program completes the invoice cycle by adding the data in the INVBATCH file to the DETAILS file. Enter

```
USE details INDEX details
APPEND FROM invbatch
RETURN
```

The entire program should look like this:

```
        SELECT details
        GO TOP
   ┌──▶DO WHILE .NOT. EOF()──────────────────────────────────┐
   │         SELECT products                                  │
   │         SEEK details->pnum                               │
   │    ┌──▶IF FOUND()──────────────────────────────────────┐│
   │    │         REPLACE instock WITH instock-details->quantity│
   │    └───ENDIF◀──                                          │
   │         SELECT details                                   │
   │         SKIP                                             │
   └───ENDDO◀────────────────────────────────────────────────┘
        USE details INDEX details
        APPEND FROM invbatch
        RETURN
```

Save the program by entering

[CTRL/End]

You need to make one more change. Load the INVOICE program and remove the * from in front of the DO invprt and DO updatein commands. Then execute the system by entering

DO invoice < return >

The screen displays

```
CREATING INVOICE BATCH .........
The First Invoice will be:      147
Press RETURN to accept or enter new number
```

The invoice number has automatically been incremented to 147. Enter

< return >
111886

Select the customer by entering

nor <return>
y

Fill out an invoice like the one below:

```
Date of Invoice: 11/18/86        Customer:  Northwood Enterprises
Invoice Number:       147                   150 Gates Ave
                                            San Diego

Item #      Description          Cost    Price    Quantity  Total
PC-400      IBM COMPATIBLE  2 FLOPPY  950.00  1168.50     1    1,168.50
T321        TOSHIBA 321 PRINTER  450.00   553.50     1      553.50
HERC-1      HERCULES PRINTER ADAPTER  210.00  262.50     1      262.50
MONO-1      MONOCHROME MONITOR   125.00   158.75     1      158.75
PARA-6      PARALLEL PRINTER CABLE   12.00    16.20     1       16.20
Enter Another Item? (Y/N) Y
```

```
Number of Items:    5              Total for Invoice:  2,159.45
```

Enter a 6.5% sales tax.

```
Date of Invoice: 11/18/86        Customer:  Northwood Enterprises
Invoice Number:       147                   150 Gates Ave
                                            San Diego

Item #      Description          Cost    Price    Quantity  Total
            Items:              5
            Total:          2,159.45
            Tax rate:           6.0
            Tax:              129.57
            Net Due:        2,289.02
```

Create another invoice for Taylor that looks like this:

```
Date of Invoice: 11/18/86        Customer:  Taylor Made Copy Systems
Invoice Number:       148                   1053 Shary Circle
                                            Concord

Item #      Description          Cost    Price    Quantity  Total
PC-400H     IBM COMPATIBLE 20 MEGA HD  1350.00  1633.50    2    3,267.00
PARA-6      PARALLEL PRINTER CABLE   12.00    16.20     2       32.40
Enter Another Item? (Y/N) Y
```

```
Number of Items:    2              Total for Invoice:  3,299.40
```

Use a 6% sales tax.

```
┌─────────────────────────────────────────────────────────────────┐
│  Date of Invoice: 11/18/86        Customer:  Taylor Made Copy Systems │
│  Invoice Number:       148                   1053 Shary Circle       │
│                                              Concord                 │
└─────────────────────────────────────────────────────────────────┘
   Item #      Description              Cost    Price   Quantity  Total
               Items:            2
               Total:        3,299.40
               Tax rate:         6.5
               Tax:            214.46
               Net Due:      3,513.86
```

When asked if you want any more invoices, enter N. The invoices will print and the inventory updated. To check on the inventory, enter

USE products < return >
LIST < return >

```
Record#  PNUM      NAME                         INSTOCK    COST MARKUP
      1  PC-400    IBM COMPATIBLE  2 FLOPPY         4     950.00    23
      2  PC-400H   IBM COMPATIBLE 20 MEGA HD        2    1350.00    21
      3  MONO-1    MONOCHROME MONITOR              5     125.00    27
      4  T321      TOSHIBA 321 PRINTER             7     450.00    23
      5  PARA-6    PARALLEL PRINTER CABLE         12      12.00    35
      6  HERC-1    HERCULES PRINTER ADAPTER        5     210.00    25
```

Compare the results with your original entries.

```
Record#  PNUM      NAME                         INSTOCK    COST MARKUP
      1  PC-400    IBM COMPATIBLE  2 FLOPPY         5     950.00    23
      2  PC-400H   IBM COMPATIBLE 20 MEGA HD        4    1350.00    21
      3  MONO-1    MONOCHROME MONITOR              6     125.00    27
      4  T321      TOSHIBA 321 PRINTER             8     450.00    23
      5  PARA-6    PARALLEL PRINTER CABLE         15      12.00    35
      6  HERC-1    HERCULES PRINTER ADAPTER        6     210.00    25
```

You can see that the invoice program has updated the inventory listing.

SUMMARY

This chapter details two additional multiple-file techniques.

1. **Printing.** You can use the data from several files to create a single document by opening the data base files and selecting records and fields to print from any of the files.

2. **Updates.** You can use the same idea of opening multiple data base files to update one file from data entered into another file. Instead of using the OUTPUT commands, the update is accomplished using a REPLACE command to change the data in the fields of one of the data base files.

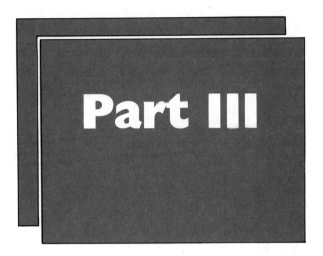

Part III

The *dBASE III Plus* System

SYSTEMS

CONFIGURATION

CONFIGURING *dBASE III Plus*

The most basic alteration you can make to the *dBASE III Plus* system takes place when you first load the program into the memory of the computer. When you do so, the program automatically searches the current directory for a file with the name CONFIG.DB (configure data base). The file is a standard DOS ASCII text file used to alter the default setting in *dBASE III Plus*.

The file consists of one or more commands. Each command contains a keyword and a value. The keyword identifies the part of the system you want to modify, while the value specifies the exact change you want to implement.

Keywords fall into two categories. The first class are keywords that provide initial values for the *dBASE III Plus* environmental SET commands. For example, if you are operating a color system, you might want to set the screen color automatically whenever the program is loaded. The command below could be placed in the CONFIG.DB file:

color=w/b,b/w,b

The command above sets the screen colors to white on blue. To perform the same operation in *dBASE III Plus*, you would use the SET form of the command. For example:

SET COLOR TO w/b,b/w,b

The second class of keywords used in the CONFIG.DB file affects the use of memory by *dBASE III Plus*. Because these commands affect memory usage and therefore the entire computer system, they can be issued only while *dBASE III Plus* is loading. Once *dBASE III Plus* has loaded, there is no way to change the amount of memory allocated to the program by quitting the program and reloading it.

Another common use of the CONFIG.DB file is to set the default data drive when the system is loaded. This is most often necessary when you are working with a floppy disk system. For example, the following keyword entered into the CONFIG.DB file sets the default disk drive to B:

DEFAULT=b:

There are eight keywords in the *dBASE III Plus* system that can be implemented only from the CONFIG.DB file.

There are two keywords that affect the user interface of the program:

1. **COMMAND** = <dbase command>. This keyword specifies a *dBASE III Plus* command that will be automatically executed when the program has loaded. Whether you realize it or not, you probably already have experience with this keyword. *dBASE III Plus* is supplied with a CONFIG.DB file that contains the command COMMAND=assist. This means that when the program is loaded, the ASSIST command is automatically issued. That is why the program automatically displays the ASSIST menus. If you change or remove this keyword from the file, *dBASE III Plus* will start in the DOT PROMPT mode.

2. **PROMPT** = <text>. This keyword allows you to specify an alternative to the DOT PROMPT that *dBASE III Plus* normally displays.

    For example, PROMPT=Enter a command: would tell *dBASE III Plus* to display Enter a command: instead of the DOT PROMPT. Note that no quotation marks were used to indicate that Enter a command: is text. There is no SET command that alters the prompt once it has been changed by a configuration keyword. To get the program back to the normal prompt, you must change the CONFIG.DB file, quit, and reload the program.

The group of keywords below affects the amount of memory allocated to special features of *dBASE III Plus*. They are primarily of interest to programmers who find they need more memory for variables or screen displays than is normally provided by *dBASE III Plus*. In most cases, you would use only these keywords if your program failed because of memory limits. If you don't run into a problem, you don't have to worry about these keywords.

1. **BUCKET** = <value between 1 and 31>. This value sets the total amount of memory used for @ GET commands. The default is 2 (2048 bytes).
2. **GETS** – <value between 35 and 1023>. This sets the total number of screen input areas created with @ GET at one time. The default is 128.
3. **MAXMEM** = <value between 256 and 720>. This keyword sets the amount of memory *dBASE III Plus* reserves for its own use. Additional memory can be used by the RUN command to execute another program while *dBASE III Plus* remains resident in the memory of the computer. The default is 256K. If you want to run additional programs, keeping *dBASE III Plus* at the minimum memory size allows more memory for additional programs.
4. **MVARSIZ** = <value between 1 and 31>. This keyword sets the amount of memory, in kilobytes, available for use by memory variables. You still are limited to 256 memory variables. This keyword changes the total amount of memory usable by the 256 variables.

The final class of keywords is used to select the method of editing text. This means that you can select some other program, usually a word processing program, to perform the text editing function usually performed by the *dBASE III Plus* word processor.

1. **TEDIT** = <program>. The program specified by this keyword is used when you issue a MODIFY COMMAND command.
2. **WP** = <program>. This keyword selects the program to be used when you edit a MEMO field.

These keywords require additional memory to run the external word processing program. To use an external word processor, you must have enough memory to load both programs. For example, if you wanted to use *WordStar* as your text editor, you would need 256K for *dBASE III Plus* and 128K for *WordStar*, a total of 384K of internal memory.

If you do not have enough memory to operate both the word processing program and *dBASE III Plus*, you will not become aware of it until you attempt to use the text editor. *dBASE III Plus* allows you to specify the program in the CONFIG.DB file and it does not check to see if you have sufficient memory to run both programs. Until you enter a MODIFY COMMAND command, you will not know if this is a problem.

CHANGING THE CONFIGURATION

Because the CONFIG.DB file is a text file, it can be changed by any program that edits ASCII text files. This includes the DOS program EDLIN, word processing programs like *Word* and *WordStar*, and the *dBASE III Plus* editor. The *dBASE III Plus* editor is invoked by entering MODIFY COMMAND. While MODIFY COMMAND is usually thought of as a way to create program files, it can be used to edit any ASCII text file.

> *The* dBASE III Plus *editor is limited to editing files that are 4K (4096 bytes) in size.*

The *dBASE III Plus* editor assumes that the file you are working with has a .PRG extension. You can edit any file with the editor as long as you specify the extension if it is not .PRG.

To change the CONFIG.DB file, enter

> **MODIFY COMMAND config.db < return >**

The *dBASE III Plus* editor displays the contents of the file, or creates a new one if no file exists. If you have the original configuration file supplied with *dBASE III Plus*, you will set a command, COMMAND=ASSIST, as the first and only command in the file.

Remove this command by entering

> **[CTRL/y]**

As an example, you can change the DOT PROMPT to something a bit more meaningful. Enter

> **PROMPT=Ready, enter a command: < return >**

You can also turn the status line display off by entering

> **STATUS=off < return >**

Save the file by entering

> **[CTRL/End]**

Note that the changes made in the CONFIG.DB file have no effect on the current display. Exit the program by entering

> **QUIT < return >**

Now reload the program by entering

> **dbase < return >**

Notice that the prompt has been changed, and the status line does not appear in the screen. Enter

> **CLEAR** < return >

The status line can be redisplayed but the prompt cannot be changed unless you alter the configuration file, exit, and reload the program. First, erase the CONFIG.DB file by entering

> **ERASE** config.db < return >

Exit and reload the program. Enter

> **QUIT** <return>
> **dbase** < return >

The DOT PROMPT and the status line appear. It is not necessary to have a CONFIG.DB file at all. If none is present on your disk, *dBASE III Plus* loads and uses the default values. The ASSIST mode is not a default. If you want to continue loading the program into the ASSIST mode, create a new CONFIG.DB with the keyword command COMMAND = assist entered into the file.

CHANGING THE EDITOR

There are a number of reasons why you would want to replace the *dBASE III Plus* editor with a word processing program. Some of the most important reasons are listed below:

1. **File size.** The *dBASE III Plus* editor is limited to a file of 4096 characters. Most word processing programs allow files whose size is limited only by the disk space available. Even those that have internal memory limits usually allow for editing documents much larger than 4096 characters.
2. **Editing features.** The *dBASE III Plus* editor has a limited number of text editing features. It can insert, delete, search, replace, and read and write files. However, it does not have the ability to copy or move text. In programming, copying and moving can save a tremendous amount of time.
    Many programs allow editing of files at one time through the use of windows. All these features can be very handy to have when writing programs.
3. **Familiar command.** If you already know how to use a word processing program, replacing the *dBASE III Plus* editor with that program will avoid the necessity of learning a new system of text editing.

For these reasons it is desirable to use a word processing program in place of the *dBASE III Plus* editor. In order to use a word processing program as part of the *dBASE III Plus* system, the following must be considered:

1. The program must be able to edit and save ASCII files. For example, *Word-Star, WordStar 2000, Word, WordPerfect* and *XyWrite* meet this qualification. *MultiMate* requires a special conversion program to change files to and from ASCII format to *MultiMate* format. Otherwise, it will not operate correctly.

2. The program must be loadable with an argument. This means that you should be able to load the word processing program and specify a file that you want to edit at the same time. The following command is used to load *WordStar*.

ws menu.prg <return>

That command will load *WordStar* and immediately place it into the editing mode, editing a file called MENU.PRG. MENU.PRG is the argument for the command to load *WordStar*. This ability is important because *dBASE III Plus* must pass the name of the file you are editing to the word processing program.

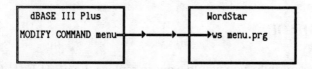

3. The system contains enough memory to run both *dBASE III Plus* and the word processing program.

4. The program files have been placed in the correct directories so that DOS can find them. This aspect of integration of programs causes the most problems. For example, *WordStar 3.31* can be run only from a directory that contains the *WordStar* OVR (overlays) files. Other programs require that a DOS Path be open to the directory in which the word processing program is stored. *WordPerfect* and *WordStar 2000* require a path.

While in theory it is possible to perform this operation on a floppy disk computer, it is seldom practical. *dBASE III Plus* files do not leave much space on the A disk for additional word processing files. For example, the DBASE.OVL file, which is stored on the #2 system disk, takes up 272,385 bytes of disk space. On a 360K diskette (362,496 bytes for file storage) that leaves only about 90,000 bytes. *WordStar* version *3.31* requires three files (WS.COM, WSMSGS.OVR, and WSOVLY1,OVR) to operate. They total 116,736 bytes of disk space. You could store the files on drive B, leaving about 245,760 bytes for *dBASE III Plus* data and programs.

In most cases it is a practical necessity to have a hard disk drive in order to implement an external word processing program. However, hard disks have problems that must also be considered. The following sections of this chapter detail the implementing of specific word processing programs with *dBASE III Plus*.

DOS CONCEPTS

One important issue is the role of DOS in interfacing external programs with *dBASE III Plus*. While a detailed discussion of DOS does not fit in this book, it is necessary to cover some DOS concepts that directly affect the task you are attempting to perform.

The first issue is the COMMAND.COM file. This file is part of the basic operation of DOS and is referred to as the *command interpreter*. As its name implies, this file contains the instructions that allow the computer to translate DOS commands into actions.

What is not obvious about DOS is the way it works with this file. To allow maximum memory for programs, DOS allows a program to erase the COMMAND.COM data from its memory. This frees up more space for programs and data. When the program is terminated, DOS remembers the drive and directory from which the COMMAND.COM file was originally loaded. DOS calls this filename the COMSPEC (command processor specification). When you turn on the computer, DOS automatically assumes that the COMSPEC is the root directory of the drive from which the computer was booted. Whenever you exit a program, DOS attempts to load the COMMAND.COM file from that drive and directory.

Most of the time you would never notice the process. However, when programs use two disks to load on a floppy system, as does *dBASE III Plus*, you may find that when you exit the program, DOS displays the message Place disk with COMMAND.COM in drive. This is caused by the fact that you do *not* have a copy of the COMMAND.COM file on the #2 system disk. Copying the COMMAND.COM file onto the disk eliminates the problem since the system can then reload the command interpreter.

If you are working with a hard disk and have correctly configured the disk so that the computer can boot directly from it, the COMSPEC is set at C:\COMMAND.COM. You can test this by using the *dBASE III Plus* function GETENV(). The name GETENV stands for *get environmental data*. To determine the current COMSPEC, enter

? GETENV("comspec") <return>

dBASE III Plus displays C:\COMMAND.COM.

Another more significant item to be considered in interfacing external programs with *dBASE III Plus* is the DOS system of directories. The purpose of directories is to store programs and data in distinct areas of the hard disk to avoid unwieldy file directories. But this poses a technical problem. To get access to a program, for example, a word processing program in another directory, you need to open a search path so that DOS will know where the program you want to operate is located.

A path is the name of a directory or list of directories that DOS should search to find a program. If no path is set, then DOS will search only the active directory for the program.

Suppose you have a hard disk with *dBASE III Plus* and *WordPerfect. dBASE III Plus* is stored in a directory called \DBASE and *WordPerfect* is stored in a directory called \WP. In order for *dBASE III Plus* to operate with the word processing program, DOS must be provided with the correct path to find the word processing program.

The best way to implement the path is to execute a PATH command before you load *dBASE III Plus*. This can be done as part of a batch file or be manually entered before you run the program. The batch file makes more sense since you might forget about the necessary path command. Below is an example of a file that opens a path to both the \DOS and the \WP directories. This will enable you to operate DOS commands and *WordPerfect* from within *dBASE III Plus*. The file can be created using the *dBASE III Plus* MODIFY COMMAND. Enter

```
PATH \DOS;\WP
CD\DB3
DBASE
```

PROBLEMS WITH *WORDSTAR 3.31*

WordStar is an exception to the discussion about paths. *WordStar* was developed before the use of subdirectories in MS DOS was common. Even copies of *WordStar* sold recently have never been updated to operate with the subdirectories. The result is that opening a path to the *WordStar* subdirectory will not allow you to run the program from within *dBASE III Plus*. In the case of *WordStar,* the simplest solution is to copy the three main files (WS.COM, WSMSGS.OVR, and WSOVLY1.OVR) into the same directory as *dBASE III Plus*.

The same problem will occur with other word processing programs that do not understand directories.

The new release of *WordStar 4.0* will correct this limitation.

RUNNING WORD PROCESSORS

The previous discussion covered the basic concepts required to operate word processing programs from within *dBASE III Plus* by setting the TEDIT and WP keywords in the CONFIG.DB file. Now you can look at the steps needed to integrate a word processing program with *dBASE III Plus*.

1. **Set the correct paths.** Before you run *dBASE III Plus*, open a path to the directories in which the programs you want to interface with *dBASE III Plus* are located. Example: PATH\WP

   In addition, it is probably a good idea always to open an additional path to the directory that contains the MS DOS utility programs, such as FOR-MAT, BACKUP, and DISKCOPY. Additional paths can be added to a PATH command by using semicolons to separate the path names. Example: PATH\DOS; \WP

2. **Edit the CONFIG.DB file.** This is done to access directly the word processing program of your choice when you enter MODIFY COMMAND or edit a MEMO field. For example, if you wanted to use *WordPerfect* as your editor, you would enter the following commands. Note that WP refers to the *Word-Perfect* program file, WP.EXE.

   > **MODIFY COMMAND config.db < return >**
   > **TEDIT=wp < return >**
   > **WP=wp < return >**
   > **[CTRL/End]**
   > **QUIT < return >**
   > **dbase < return >**

3. **Invoke the editor.** Once these steps have been taken, *dBASE III Plus* will call the word processing program specified in the CONFIG.DB file whenever text editing is required. For example, if you have carried out steps 1 and 2, you can now edit a file by entering

   > **MODIFY COMMAND config.db < return >**

   dBASE III Plus will display the CONFIG.DB file as a document in the specified program.

4. **Editing MEMO fields.** There is one slight difference between the way a word processing program is invoked for MEMO field editing and for the MODIFY COMMAND editing.

   When MODIFY COMMAND is used, the filename passed to the word processing program is the one specified by you in the *dBASE III Plus* command. If no extension is specified, *dBASE III Plus* adds the .PRG extension automatically.

   However, when you use the word processing program to edit the contents of a MEMO field, *dBASE III Plus* must perform some additional manipulations. Remember that memos are stored in a large text file that has a .DBT extension. When you edit a memo, *dBASE III Plus* copies the contents of the field, if any, to a file called DBASEDIT.TMP. It is the DBASEDIT.TMP that your word processing program will edit. If you are using a program that displays the name of the file you are editing, you will see DBASEDIT.TMP displayed.

One advantage of using an external word processing program is to create memos larger than the 4096-character limit imposed by the *dBASE III Plus* editor. Should you attempt to use a file containing large memos with a copy of *dBASE III Plus* that uses the *dBASE III Plus* editor, any text beyond the 4096 limit will be truncated. Large memo files can be maintained only in a system that always uses an external word processing program.

5. **Exiting the word processing program.** Entering the word processing mode, even when the word processor is external to *dBASE III Plus*, remains the same. However, that is not the case with exiting the word processing mode. Once *dBASE III Plus* has turned over execution to the external program, you must follow the conventions and command structure of that program until you have exited that program completely.

    Remember that *exiting* refers to the command that would normally take you to DOS when working in the word processing program alone. *dBASE III Plus* commands such as <Esc> will not function while you are word processing.

6. **Performance.** Every time you edit a file or a MEMO field, *dBASE III Plus* must load the entire program. You may find that the time required to load a large word processing program degrades the performance of the program considerably. One compromise is to use the external word processing program for editing command files, but use the *dBASE III Plus* editor for MEMO fields. This can be done by specifying only the TEDIT keyword and not using the WS keyword in the CONFIG.DB file.

WORDSTAR

Using *WordStar* may seem like a cliché in the computer business, but despite many features that it lacks, it is one of the best programs to use as an editor for *dBASE III Plus*. There are several reasons for this. First, the *dBASE III Plus* editing commands are modeled after *WordStar*. This means that you will have a smooth transition when you go from the *dBASE III Plus* editor to *WordStar*.

Another reason is *WordStar*'s nondocument mode. As you will learn if you look at the other word processing programs discussed in this section, *WordStar* has an advantage when it comes to entering a text editing mode. *WordStar* has two editing modes, D for document and N for nondocument. You select the mode manually by entering the letter. But remember, when a program is used as an external word processor for *dBASE III Plus*, you do not have the opportunity to select the document or nondocument mode. How is the mode selected?

In *WordStar* the answer is simple and straightforward. *WordStar* allows you to select the mode that should be used when the program is started with an argument (e.g., WS MENU.PRG). If you select nondocument as the default mode, the program will always start up in the nondocument mode.

If you are a *WordStar* user, you may never have noticed this setting because you always select the mode manually from the opening menu. The default setting, installed when you buy *WordStar,* is to use the document mode. To turn *WordStar* into an editor for *dBASE III Plus*, you must use the *WordStar* install program to change the setting of the DEFAULT DOCUMENT type. Once this is done, *WordStar* will function properly in any editing situation.

Note that *WordStar* displays only standard ASCII characters. For example, the lines and boxes used by *dBASE III Plus* consist of the characters produced by the IBM extended character set. If you include these characters in your file, they will not be displayed in *WordStar.*

SIDEKICK

The *Sidekick* notepad can be used to edit and revise ASCII text files, making it usable as an editor for *dBASE III Plus*. However, unlike the other programs discussed in Chapter 3 that can be used as an external word processing program, the *Sidekick* notepad is part of the memory-resident *Sidekick* program. This has several implications:

1. **Speed.** Since the notepad is already in memory, it takes less time to use the notepad because the program does not have to load each time you want to edit. Using the *Sidekick* activate command, CTRL–Alt or Left Shift–Right Shift, you can pop up the editor at any time, including while *dBASE III Plus* is running the application.

    Note that once *Sidekick* loads a file, the file remains in memory. This means that revision can be made and then saved with a single keystroke.

2. **Windows.** *Sidekick*'s notepad does not take the place of the *dBASE III Plus* word processor; it operates in addition to it. Therefore you can edit two files at once—one in the *dBASE III Plus* editor and the other in *Sidekick*. *Sidekick* also makes it possible to copy text from one program to another.

Sidekick is probably the best way to edit *dBASE III Plus* programs. It is fast and contains all the important commands found in *WordStar.* If you have not used

Sidekick to edit, you don't know what you are missing. Even if you don't have the program, it is worth the investment for this use alone.

WORDSTAR 2000

WordStar 2000 is a more sophisticated program than *WordStar* when it comes to working with directories. With the proper path open, you can run *WordStar 2000* from any directory on the hard disk.

Although not mentioned in the documentation, *WordStar 2000* can also be started with an argument; example: WS2 MENU.PRG. But there is one small problem. *WordStar 2000* does not make the same distinction between document and non-document modes. *WordStar 2000* uses a system of format files that controls various document qualities. ASCII files are created by selecting a special format, UN-FORM.FRM. However, the process of selecting a format cannot be specified when you start the program as an external word processor for *dBASE III Plus*.

When *WordStar 2000* is used to create a new file from *dBASE III Plus*, you will need to select the UNFORM.FRM format manually .

This additional step is required only when you are creating a *new* file. If you are editing a file that already exists in ASCII format, *WordStar 2000* will sense that and automatically enter its ASCII editing mode. Note that when you edit a MEMO field, you are creating a new file (DBASEDIT.TMP) each time.

WORDPERFECT

WordPerfect can be used as an external word processor for *dBASE III Plus*. You must make sure that a path has been opened to the *WordPerfect* directory before you run *dBASE III Plus*.

If you are creating a new file, *WordPerfect* will display an error message as it loads. The message reads ERROR: File not found. The message will appear for a moment and then *WordPerfect* will display the editing screen. What caused the error message?

The answer is that when *WordPerfect* is started with an argument (e.g., WP MENU.PRG), it assumes the file specified (MENU.PRG) already exists. In case this file is new, *WordPerfect* displays the error message. Interestingly, *WordPerfect* will then proceed to create the file anyway. In other words, the error message has no effect; it is strictly intended as an informational message. Note that when you edit a MEMO field, you are creating a new file (DBASEDIT.TMP) each time.

In order to save a standard ASCII text file from *WordPerfect,* use the [**CTRL/F5**] command to display the TEXT SAVE menu. Option 1 from this menu saves the text as an ASCII file.

When you exit *WordPerfect,* you do not need to save the document because it was already saved as an ASCII text file using the **[CTRL/F5]** 1 command. Exit by entering

       [F7]
       n
       y

WORD

Word has the qualities required by a word processing program to function successfully as the *dBASE III Plus* editor. Once the proper DOS path is set, *Word* can edit a file anywhere on the hard disk. In addition, *Word* will load a file specified as an argument when *Word* is loaded (e.g., WORD MENU.PRG).

One small problem does occur when editing a new file. *Word* automatically assumes certain document formatting attributes that are assigned to the new file. To save this file as an ASCII standard file, you need to change the FORMAT setting on the TRANSFER menu. When you save the document, you would enter the TRANSFER SAVE command

       <Esc>
       ts

Word displays the TRANSFER SAVE menu. On the right side of the menu, the formatted option is displayed with two options: Yes and No. The No option selects saving the file as an ASCII standard file. If the document you are working on is a new one, the Yes option will be selected. Note that when you edit a MEMO field, you are creating a new file (DBASEDIT.TMP) each time.

Enter

       <Tab>
       n
       <return>

If the document you are editing was already an ASCII file, *Word* automatically sets the format setting to No.

XyWRITE

While *XyWrite* has the two main attributes that are required to interface with *dBASE III Plus*, it has a quirk that prevents the program from working smoothly with *dBASE III Plus*. *XyWrite* will run from any directory (if the proper path is opened) and it will accept an argument when it is started. The limitation is that the argument is restricted to a file that has already been created. This means that when attempting to create a new file or to edit a MEMO field, *XyWrite* will consider the command an error and refuse to enter the editing mode. This makes *XyWrite* a poor choice as an external word processing program for *dBASE III Plus*.

If you really like *XyWrite,* it will operate from *dBASE III Plus*, but you will have to manually enter the name of the file you want to edit.

THE RUN COMMAND

Another one of the basic tools of program integration is the RUN command. RUN allows you to issue DOS commands from within *dBASE III Plus*, giving you access to DOS utilities like DISKCOPY and FORMAT, as well as a wide variety of applications such as spreadsheet and graphics programs.

The RUN command provides a means by which the power of DOS and other programs can be tapped by *dBASE III Plus*. Furthermore, you can use the *dBASE III Plus* programming language to create programs that carry out DOS functions using menus and prompts of your own design.

The basic structure of the RUN command is quite simple:

RUN <valid MS DOS command>

As a simple example you can execute the DOS command VER. The VER command displays the version of DOS current in the memory of the computer. Enter

RUN ver <return>

The version name is displayed and *dBASE III Plus* brings back the DOT PROMPT. The RUN command can also be abbreviated by using an !. Enter

!ver <return>

It is important to keep in mind that there are two types of commands supplied with DOS. One class of commands is called *internal*. These commands are stored in the COMMAND.COM file and loaded automatically when the system is booted. (When the RUN command is used, *dBASE III Plus* must first load the COMMAND.COM file before it can carry out the DOS command.)

The other class of commands is called *external* commands. External commands are really complete programs that perform special actions such as disk formatting and disk copying. They are called DOS commands because they are usually supplied with MS DOS. From a functional point of view, they are external programs like the word processing programs discussed in the previous sections.

Thus in order to run the *external* commands, you must satisfy the same preconditions required by the word processing programs. The key is that a PATH be specified to the directory that contains the DOS external command programs or they cannot be accessed by *dBASE III Plus* or a *dBASE III Plus* program.

> *The PATH command cannot be issued with the RUN command in* dBASE III Plus. *Using PATH with the RUN command will not change the PATH set in DOS before you ran* dBASE III Plus.
>
> *The SET PATH TO command found in* dBASE III Plus *does not change the DOS path, but alters the path used by* dBASE III Plus *commands. Using the SET PATH TO command does not affect commands issued with the RUN command. The PATH cannot be changed by running a DOS batch file with the RUN command that contains a PATH command. This means that you must open the paths you need before you run* dBASE III Plus.

In the following sections you will learn how the RUN command, combined with other *dBASE III Plus* commands, can create *dBASE III Plus* programs that carry out functions normally accomplished with DOS.

USING RUN IN PROGRAMS

The RUN command (!) provides *dBASE III Plus* with the ability to call and execute external programs while *dBASE III Plus* is running. If sufficient memory is present in the computer, you can run DOS programs like FORMAT, CHKDSK, or full applications like *Lotus 1-2-3*.

dBASE III Plus allows you to create programs that use the RUN command to execute external programs from a running *dBASE III Plus* command file. The potential is that *dBASE III Plus* can be used as an application integrator.

The program listed below is a simple example of how DOS commands such as FORMAT, DISKCOPY, and BACKUP can be controlled through a *dBASE III Plus* program.

Create a command file called DOSFUNC (DOS functions) by entering

MODIFY COMMAND dosfunc < return >

Enter the following program:

```
SET TALK OFF
SET STATUS OFF
dosfunc=.I.
DO WHILE dosfunc
    CLEAR
    TEXT
        DOS COMMANDS

        F = Format a disk in drive A.
        D = Duplicate a floppy disk.
        B = Backup all data files.
        Q = Quit DOS menu.
```

```
        ENDTEXT
option=SPACE(1)
        @ 12,10 SAY "Enter letter for DOS action: " GET option PICTURE "!"
        READ
        DO CASE
            CASE option="F"
                TEXT
                This procedure will wipe out
                all data on the disk in drive A:
                ENDTEXT
                WAIT
                RUN format a:
            CASE option="D"
                RUN diskcopy a: a:
            CASE option="B"
                RUN backup c:\db3\*.dbf a:
        ENDCASE
ENDDO
SET TALK ON
SET STATUS ON
RETURN
```

Save the program by entering

[CTRL/End]

Before you execute this program make sure you have some disks to use for copying, formatting, and backing up. Execute the program by entering

DO dosfunc <return>

You can experiment with the functions listed from the menu.

TURN KEY APPLICATIONS

dBASE III Plus allows you to execute a command file directly when the program loads. There are two methods by which this can be done.

1. **DOS argument.** A DOS argument is an item that follows the command you use to start a program. In the case of *dBASE III Plus*, this argument is taken to be the name of a command file that you want to execute when the program starts. For example, the normal way to start *dBASE III Plus* is to enter

    dbase <return>

    Suppose you wanted to run the DOSFUNC program immediately upon loading *dBASE III Plus*. You would enter the following command at DOS.

dbase dosfunc <return>

>*dBASE III Plus* would still display the *dBASE III Plus* logo screen. If you do not enter <return>, *dBASE III Plus* will wait for a few seconds and execute the specified program.

2. **Command keyword.** The CONFIG.DB file can also be used to execute an application whenever *dBASE III Plus* loads. To execute the DOSFUNC program each time the *dBASE III Plus* program loads, change the COMMAND keyword in the CONFIG.DB file to read COMMAND=DO dosfunc.

The advantage of the keyword technique is that you do not have to remember the argument each time *dBASE III Plus* is loaded. On the other hand, the argument technique allows *dBASE III Plus* to load normally if you don't specify an argument. Any command file specified as an argument will take precedence over the COMMAND keyword.

Also note that the *dBASE III Plus* QUIT command can be included in applications so that your program will automatically terminate *dBASE III Plus* when the program is complete.

SUMMARY

dBASE III Plus allows you to customize its operation in three ways:

1. **CONFIG.DB.** *dBASE III Plus* will search for a file called CONFIG.DB when it loads. Keywords used in the file can set a number of attributes for the *dBASE III Plus* system. Some keywords alter the way memory is used. The function of these keywords cannot be duplicated by *dBASE III Plus* SET commands.

2. **TEXT EDITING.** Since there are limits to the *dBASE III Plus* editor, *dBASE III Plus* allows you to substitute a word processing or text editing program that you prefer. The WP and TEDIT keywords are used to specify the alternative editor.

3. **TURN KEY.** *dBASE III Plus* allows you to specify a command file to execute whenever *dBASE III Plus* is loaded.

dBASE III PLUS *AND*

OTHER APPLICATIONS

THIS CHAPTER REVIEWS THE BASIC CONCEPTS required to transfer data between applications. Specifically the chapter explains how *dBASE III Plus* can send data to word processing and spreadsheet applications. Note that integrated software like *Symphony* and *Framework* are classified as spreadsheets.

WORD PROCESSING

While *dBASE III Plus* has a great deal of power to handle data base information on its own, it is also capable of working with word processing programs to create form letters using data stored in data base files.

Using *dBASE III Plus* with a word processing program allows you to take advantage of the best features of both programs in order to produce the mailings that you need to make. *dBASE III Plus* offers the power of its selection and indexing abilities in creating, entering, revising, and selecting data for form letters. On the other hand, the word processing programs have the ability to handle text formats such as wrapping lines, setting margins, and adding special printing effects, like proportional spacing and special fonts (e.g., italic) to the text.

Although the idea of combining data and features of two different types of programs may seem very difficult, it is much simpler than many procedures normally carried out with a word processor or data base alone. What makes the process seem difficult is that you need to plan very carefully, ahead of time, exactly how the two programs will work together.

Once you have learned the basic concepts, you will find that interfacing word processing programs with *dBASE III Plus* is one of the most productive computing times you have ever spent.

Most word processing programs cannot understand a *dBASE III Plus* data base file. What is required to integrate *dBASE III Plus* files with word processing programs is to convert the *dBASE III Plus* file into a standard data format that the word processing program can understand.

The COPY TO [TYPE] method uses the COPY command to copy fields and records to a specified type of non-*dBASE III Plus* file. Since the file types are built into *dBASE III Plus*, no additional programming is required.

When creating an ASCII format file from a data base file, there are two primary questions to be concerned with:

1. How are fields marked in the ASCII file?
2. How are records marked in the ASCII file?

It is the answer to those questions that characterizes the file format. The simplest format used by *dBASE III Plus* is the SDF (Standard Data Format). An SDF file does not mark the fields in any way. The fields, including trailing blanks, are strung together. Each record is ended with a carriage return/line feed code. The result is that each record takes up one line of text. The file will contain one line for each record in the data base file.

USE clients < return >

To create an SDF format file from a data base file, enter

COPY TO standard SDF < return >

dBASE III Plus automatically adds a .TXT extension to all non-*dBASE III Plus* files. The file you just created will appear in the disk directory as STANDARD.TXT. To see the effect, enter

TYPE standard.txt < return >

The file displays on the screen. Because each record is wider than the 80-column screen display, the lines are broken by the screen display. This may give you the impression that the file is more fragmented than it really is. To view the file more accurately, enter

MODIFY COMMAND standard.txt < return >

The screen displays the file as it would be used by the word processor. The + signs on the right side of the display indicate that the lines are wider than the screen can display.

The SDF format is not widely used with word processing programs because it does not provide a simple means of identifying fields. You will learn later in this book what the SDF file format allows you to do. Enter

< Esc >

In the case of creating lists for word processing programs, the most commonly used format is one in which the fields are marked by a particular character. The format is called DELIMITED because each field is marked. To create a DELIMITED ASCII file, enter

COPY TO maillist DELIMITED < return >

You have just created a file called MAILLIST.TXT that contains the data in the DELIMITED ASCII format. To inspect the format, enter

TYPE maillist.txt < return >

The screen displays the text file with the delimited format.

```
"Dr","Walter","LaFish","1591","Ellis","St","Conco",CA
"Ms","Nancy","Farber","1703","Pine","St","Phila",PA
"Ms","Alice","Mullen","234","Cedar","La","San",Jose
"Ter","Kamrin","33","Westlake","Court","Lo","Angle",CA
"Ms","Carolyn","Riglero","18","Plainfield","Av","Shrew",MA
"Mr","Karl","Lafong","278","Valley","Dr","Garde",City
```

The DELIMITED format is different from the SDF format in three respects:

1. In the DELIMITED format, all fields are separated by a comma.
2. Fields have been trimmed of their trailing spaces. The DELIMITED format creates a smaller file because it does not transfer the unnecessary blanks. This is important for word processing because the user needn't insert all those blanks into form letters.
3. All the CHARACTER fields are surrounded by quotation marks.

The DELIMITED format is not very easy to read. Its value lies in the fact that it can be used to fill in form letters created with various word processing programs, specifically, *WordStar, WordStar 2000,* and *Microsoft Word. WordPerfect* is not able to use this file format.

One of the main reasons for storing mailing list information in *dBASE III Plus* instead of in a word processing program file has to do with the features that *dBASE III Plus* offers. If a file is sorted or indexed before it is copied to a non-*dBASE III Plus* format, the records in the ASCII file will appear in index order. For example, to create an ASCII file ordered by zip code, you would enter the following commands:

```
USE clients < return >
INDEX ON zip TO ziporder < return >
COPY TO maillist DELIMITED < return >
```

The process of selection is typically of more importance than sequencing when form letters are involved. The ability to select a group of records logically for a specific mailing allows you to target your mailings more effectively. The more data you store about the individuals in your mailing list, the more precise you can be in selecting people to mail to.

FOR clauses and data filters depend on the use of a logical expression. A logical expression is one that *dBASE III Plus* can judge to be either true or false. For example, you might want to limit the mailing to people in the state of California. Below are two command sequences that accomplish this task:

```
USE clients < return >
COPY TO maillist FOR UPPER(state)="CA" < return >
```

and

```
USE clients < return >
SET FILTER TO UPPER(state)="CA"  < return >
COPY TO maillist DELIMITED  < return >
SET FILTER TO  < return >
```

Up to this point, the assumption has been that the data in the *dBASE III Plus* fields are exactly as you want to use them in your form letter. However, problems can arise with special field types, specifically DATES, and entries like NAME.

DATES are stored in a special numeric format and are converted when they are copied into a non-*dBASE III Plus* file. For example, the date 03/15/86 entered into a *dBASE III Plus* DATE field will appear as 19860315 in the delimited file. This date form is useless for form letters.

Once you have created the delimited mail list file, you can combine the data with a form letter created with *WordStar, WordStar 2000, Microsoft Word,* or any other word processing program that operates with delimited ASCII files.

WORDSTAR, WORDSTAR 2000 AND WORD FORM LETTERS

WordStar is the oldest software program discussed in this section, but its method of form letter production (called MAILMERGE) is the basic model used by most programs. *WordPerfect,* though different, follows a similar pattern.

The first step in creating a form letter is to know the number of fields, and the order in which they appear in the DELIMITED file. In this example, the DELIMITED file was created with these commands.

```
USE clients <return>
COPY TO maillist FIELDS company,name,address,city,state,zip,salutation
DELIMITED <return>
```

WORDSTAR

Create a *WordStar* document by choosing the D command from the *WordStar* Opening Menu.

The key to creating form letters is to use two special DOT commands.

.DF (data file). This command tells *WordStar* what file contains data to be used with the form letter. Without *dBASE III Plus*, you would have to enter the data manually in a *WordStar* nondocument file. A *WordStar* nondocument file is an ASCII standard file.

.RV (read variable). This command allows *WordStar* to assign names to the fields stored in the delimited file. *dBASE III Plus* does not place any information in the delimited file that indicates what the names of the fields are, or should be. That information is stored in the *dBASE III Plus* file header, and is not copied into the delimited file. The names assigned to the fields in *WordStar* are independent of the field names in *dBASE III Plus*. In *WordStar,* the terms *variable* and *field* are used interchangeably.

Below is a typical form letter written in *WordStar* that will merge with the delimited data prepared by *dBASE III Plus*. Note that the file is MAILLIST.TXT (the .TXT extension is added by *dBASE III Plus*).

```
.df maillist.txt
.rv company,name,street,city,state,zip,salutation

&company&
&name&
&street&
&city&, &state& &zip&
```

Dear *&salutation&*

Thank you for your interest in our company.

Regards,

Walter La Fish
President
.pa

In *WordStar,* & (ampersand) is used to mark a word as a field or variable. A variable can be used as many times as you like in the body of a document.

WORDSTAR 2000 FORM LETTERS

WordStar 2000 operates under the same concepts as *WordStar,* but the DOT commands have been changed to menu-oriented commands. To create a form letter with *WordStar 2000,* use the EDIT command from the opening menu. Select a format that is appropriate for this document.

When you reach the EDITING mode, you must enter commands that will designate this document as a form letter. The first command in the document will be the one that tells *WordStar 2000* what file contains the data. The .DF command in *WordStar* is replaced with the CTRL-OMS command in *WordStar 2000.* The OMS stands for Option Mailmerge Select data file. Enter

> **[CTRL/o]**
> **ms**
> **maillist.txt < return >**

If you are working in the normal *WordStar 2000* display mode, you see nothing new on your screen. Display the command tags by entering

> **[CTRL/o]**
> **d**

You now see the command tag that looks like this:

    [SELECT DATA FILE MAILLIST.TXT]

The next entry is the REPEAT command. The REPEAT command establishes a loop. The other end of the loop is marked by a NEXT command. The concept is similar to a DO WHILE and ENDDO pairing in *dBASE III Plus*. Enter

> **[CTRL/o]**
> **mr < return >**

Next is the LOAD DATA statement. It performs the same function as the .RV in *WordStar.* Enter

    [CTRL/o]
    ml
    company,name,street,city,state,zip,sal <return>

The document looks like this:

```
[SELECT DATA FILE MAILLIST.TXT]
[LOAD DATA company,name,street,city,state,zip,sal]
[REPEAT UNTIL END OF DATA]
```

Now enter the body of the letter. The &, the variable marker, is used exactly the same as it is in *WordStar.* Enter

&company&
&name&
&street&
&city&, &state& &zip&

Dear &salutation&

Thank you for your interest in our company.

Regards,

Walter La Fish
President

At the end of the document there are two other commands that must be entered. First is the command that creates a new page. Enter

    [CTRL/o]
    p

The final command completes the form letter loop. Enter

    [CTRL/o]
    mn

The letter looks like this:

```
[SELECT DATA FILE MAILLIST.TXT]
[REPEAT UNTIL END OF DATA]
[LOAD DATA company,name,street,city,state,zip,sal]
&company&
&name&
&street&
&city&, &state& &zip&

Dear &salutation&
```

```
Thank you for your interest in our company.

Regards,

Walter La Fish
President
[PAGE]————————————————————————————
[NEXT COPY]
```

Save the letter and print by entering

[CTRL/q]

p

MICROSOFT *WORD*

Word's merge abilities are similar to *WordStar* and *WordStar 2000*. The main difference is that *Word* does not place its field definition statement in the form letter. Instead, *Word* places it in the data file, or in a special file called a *header* file.

In the *Word* scheme, field names are assigned to the variables by virtue of the first line in the data file. Unlike *WordStar* products, *Word* assumes that the first entry in the data file is *not* a record, but a header line that contains the names of the fields.

dBASE III Plus took care to strip out all the field names from the delimited file. *Word* was designed to anticipate this problem. In *Word*, you can merge data from consecutive data files, allowing you to create a data file that has only one line, the field name header, and merge it before you call the MAILLIST.TXT file.

Word will treat the two consecutive files as if they were one large file. The result is that the first line read can be used as the field headings, and the data in the MAILLIST.TXT fills in the variables.

Instead of &, *Word* uses special characters produced by the CTRL-[and the CTRL-] to mark fields in the text. *Word* also uses the control bracket characters to indicate merge commands in the text.

When you enter CTRL-[, *Word* places a < < (ASCII character 174) in the text. Entering CTRL-] produces > > (ASCII character 175).

To create a form letter in *Word*, begin with a clear window. The first command in the letter defines the data file. In this case, there will be two names in the data file command. The first is the header file, and the second is the delimited dBASE III Plus file. Enter

To maintain consistency with the Word *manual, a hyphen has been placed between the CTRL and the bracket character, in the keystroke below. But the hyphen should not be typed. The keystroke requires that you press and hold down the CTRL key, then press the bracket character.*

```
CTRL-[
data header.txt,maillist.txt
CTRL-]
```

You can now create the document that you want to use as the form letter. Variables are marked using the CTRL-[and the CTRL-] commands. Enter

<<company>>
<<name>>
<<street>>
<<city>>, <<state>> <<zip>>
Dear *<<salutation>>*

Thank you for your interest in our company.

Regards,

Walter La Fish
President

The next step is to create a header file. The header file will serve as the link between the data in MAILLIST.TXT and the fields in the form letter. Because *Word* allows you to work with multiple windows, you can create the header file without having to save the form letter. Enter

```
<Esc>
wsh
10 <return>
```

This creates a window at the bottom of the screen. Clear the window of text so that you can make a new document. Enter

```
<Esc>
tcw
```

You can now enter a new document into the window. Note that the following text is simply a list of field names, in the order in which the fields appear in the file, MAILLIST.TXT. No special commands or keystrokes are needed. Enter

company,name,street,city,state,zip,salutation <return>

Now save the document as HEADER.TXT. Enter

```
<Esc>
ts
header.txt <return>
```

Close the window by entering

```
<Esc>
wc2 <return>
```

You are now ready to produce the form letters. The PRINT MERGE command produces the form letters. Keep in mind that unless you use the PRINT MERGE command, the < < and the > > characters will be printed as ordinary text. Enter the keystrokes below to produce the form letters.

> **<Esc>**
> **pm**

WORDPERFECT

WordPerfect adds a layer of complexity to the process of integrating *dBASE III Plus* files into form letters. *WordPerfect* requires special characters to be inserted into the file to mark the fields and records in the data file.

When you manually enter data into a *WordPerfect* list document, you are required to enter a [**CTRL/r**] character at the end of every field, and a [**CTRL/e**] at the end of every record.

To use a comma-separated file with *WordPerfect,* you must use the file conversion utility supplied with the program to convert the *dBASE III Plus* delimited file into a *WordPerfect* secondary merge file.

This utility is available in WordPerfect *Version 4.2 only.*

WordPerfect uses special codes to mark the placement of the fields in its form letters. The concept is much the same as that of the other word processing programs mentioned, in that the data are assigned to the field sequentially. The main difference is that *WordPerfect* does not use descriptive names for the fields but simply assigns them consecutive numbers.

The advantage of this system is that *WordPerfect* does not need a defined variables command or a file header. The fields are always assigned the same names, F1, F2, F3, and so on. The disadvantage is that the name F1 does not remind you of what the field contains.

A field is entered into the *WordPerfect* text by using the [**Alt/F9**] command. (The [**Alt/F9**] command allows you to enter special merge codes.) The F code is used to enter a field specification. Which field is specified by entering the number of the field that you want. If you were to start a new document, to enter the COMPANY field, you would enter

> **[Alt/F9]**
> **f1 <return>**

WordPerfect inserts a symbol into the text that looks like this:

^F1^

Enter the next field by entering

> <return>
> [Alt/F9]
> f2 <return>

Continue this process until you have created a form letter with all seven fields, that looks like this:

```
^F1^
^F2^
^F3^
^F4^, ^F5^ ^F6^

Dear ^F7^,

Thank you for your interest in our company.

Regards,

Walter La Fish
President
```

When the document is complete, save the file by entering

> [F7]
> y
> form <return>
> <return>

SPREADSHEET PROGRAMS

By far the two most popular types of applications run on microcomputers are word processors and spreadsheets. Among the many reasons why this is so is that both applications are visually oriented.

In the previous section you saw how *dBASE III Plus* relates and interacts with word processing programs. In this section you will see how *dBASE III Plus* can exchange data with a variety of spreadsheet programs.

The *dBASE III Plus* COPY and APPEND commands both accept the TYPE clause. This clause allows *dBASE III Plus* to write and read data into the following non-*dBASE III Plus* formats.

1. **Delimited.** This format operates with comma-separated ASCII standard text files. In these files each data item is separated by commas. Each record is marked with a carriage return/line feed character.

    Delimited files do not include trailing blank spaces. They generally take up less disk space than an equivalent *dBASE III Plus* file that contains space characters for characters in the file not filled with actual information.

2. **SDF.** SDF stands for Standard Data Format. This type of file stores data as a series of items separated by spaces. Each record is ended with a carriage return/line feed character.

    SDF files do not specifically mark one data item (i.e., field) from another. Fields can be calculated by counting characters including all spaces.

    The SDF format most closely resembles the way *dBASE III Plus* stores data. An SDF file is about the same size as an equivalent *dBASE III Plus* file.

3. **DIF.** DIF stands for Data Interchange Format. The format was first used with *VisiCalc* on Apple II computers. DIF is similar to the other file types in that it contains only ASCII text data. However, the DIF format is much more complicated than either the delimited or SDF formats. The format adds a variety of numeric indicators that numerically place each data item in a matrix. Since DIF is primarily used by spreadsheet programs, this matrix orientation is understandable.

    Spreadsheets treat rows and columns equally. *dBASE III Plus* treats rows in a DIF file as records; columns are treated as fields.

4. **SYLK.** This stands for Symbolic Link format. Like DIF, SYLK is a spreadsheet oriented text format. The format was designed by Microsoft to be used as a replacement for the less complex DIF format. However, SYLK is far less popular than DIF in the spreadsheet world. The best known program using SYLK is Microsoft's *Multiplan*.

    SYLK contains only text data, but it is a complex format like DIF that is designed to place data in a spreadsheet maxtrix. *dBASE III Plus* treats rows as records and columns as fields in the SYLK.

5. **WKS.** This format creates files that are compatible with *Lotus 1–2–3*. The WKS format is different from the other formats in that it contains information in binary rather than ASCII text format. *dBASE III Plus* treats rows as records and columns as fields.

All these formats can copy on data. Formulas or special functions used in spreadsheets are not copied into dBASE III Plus. *Only the last calculated value of those formulas can be appended to* dBASE III Plus.

By adding the TYPE clause to a COPY command, you can create a copy of your selected data base file in one of the above formats.

The following command will create a *Lotus*-compatible file.

COPY TO lotus.wks WKS

To create a DIF format file, enter

COPY TO lotus.wks DIF

To add records to a *dBASE III Plus* data base file from a non-*dBASE III Plus* file, you would attach the TYPE clause to an APPEND FROM command.

To read in data from a DIF file, enter

APPEND FROM sample.dif DIF

To copy data from a *Lotus 1–2–3* file, enter

APPEND FROM sample.wks WKS

TRANSLATION OF FILES

The following section is a listing of the leading spreadsheet programs and the types of files they can read or translate. For each spreadsheet there are several points to consider. First, what types of alien files will the program read directly, if any? Second, what types of files can be translated through a utility provided with the program? In addition, you might want to know if the translation utilities are integrated into the main program menu or operate outside the program.

In the descriptions of each program, the term ASCII file will mean a standard DOS text file such as a *Lotus* PRN file. The term SDF (Standard Data Format) will stand for a text file that contains lines of text padded with space characters that end with a carriage return character. A delimited file is one in which the data items are separated by commas and/or quotation marks.

The term DIF stands for Data Interchange Format. This was formerly used by *VisiCalc* to interchange data with other applications. While *VisiCalc* is pretty much a memory in today's PC market, the format remains one of the most widespread file formats.

This listing can also give you a clue as to how to translate files that do not directly have a *dBASE III Plus* type equivalent.

1–2–3 VERSION 1A

This release of *1–2–3* reads ASCII text files directly from the program menu using the File Import command. The files can be SDF (text option) or delimited (numbers option). To write an SDF format text file, you can use the PRINT FILE command.

From the *Lotus* ACCESS menu you can run a file translation utility. The utility can translate:

VisiCalc to *1–2–3* (formulas and data)
DIF to *1–2–3* (data only)
dBASE II to *1–2–3* (data only)

1-2-3 to DIF (data only)

1-2-3 to *dBASE II* (data only)

As you can see, *1-2-3* keeps up the tradition that manufacturers allow you to translate a full *VisiCalc* worksheet (others) to *1-2-3* (theirs), but not the other way around.

1-2-3 RELEASE *2*

From the main program menu, you can read and write the same style text file. Release *2* reads version *1A* spreadsheets but only writes Release *2* format worksheets. From the ACCESS menu you can perform the following translations.

1-2-3 1A to *1-2-3 2* (formulas and data), *dBASE II* or *III* (data only), *Symphony* (formulas and data)

1-2-3 2 to *1-2-3 1A* (formulas and data), *dBASE II* or *III* (data only), *Symphony* (formulas and data)

dBASE II or *III* to *1-2-3 1A, 1-2-3 2,* or *Symphony* (data only)

Jazz (if you have them in IBM disk format) to *1-2-3 1A, 1-2-3 2,* or *Symphony* (I assume formulas and data, but I don't have any way of proving it)

Symphony to *1-2-3 1A* or *2* (spreadsheet data and formulas only), *dBASE II* and *III* (data only)

VisiCalc to *1-2-3 1A, 1-2-3 2, Symphony* (formulas and data)

DIF to *1-2-3 1A, 1-2-3 2, Symphony* (data only)

SYMPHONY

Symphony is structured just about the same way as *1-2-3* version *1A*. From the application's menu you can retrieve *1-2-3* worksheets, data, and formulas. *Symphony* also has menu options to read in SDF and delimited text files. The command FILE IMPORT, is found on the *Symphony* SERVICES menu. *Symphony* can also write an SDF printer file using the PRINT SETTINGS command to specify the print destination as a file.

The *Symphony* ACCESS menu runs a translate utility that performs the following conversion:

VisiCalc to *Symphony* (formulas and data)

DIF to *Symphony* (data only)

dBASE II to *Symphony* (data only)
Symphony to DIF (data only)
Symphony to *dBASE II* (data only)

MULTIPLAN 1.0, 1.2

Multiplan does not directly read an ASCII file from its menu. It can write an SDF file using the PRINT FILE command. *Multiplan* also saves files in a symbolic format. The term SYLK (symbolic link) is used for files in this format. This is a Microsoft-designed ASCII format that is limited to a few Microsoft products. *RBASE 5000* and *dBASE III Plus* read these files as data, however.

Multiplan 2.0

Multiplan 2.0 has greatly improved its file translation ability. Unlike the *Lotus* products, *Multiplan* integrates its file translation ability directly into the program. In *Multiplan 2.0,* the TRANSFER OPTIONS menu contains a new option called OTHER. When OTHER is selected, *Multiplan* directly reads into a *Multiplan* worksheet, *VisiCalc, 1-2-3,* and *Symphony* (spreadsheet only) file formulas and data. When a file is saved in the OTHER mode, it is stored in a *1-2-3 1A* format. *Multiplan* reads in macros, but they will not function since *Multiplan* macros have a very different structure.

Multiplan 2.0 is supplied with a utility program that performs translations not fully supported from the program menu. The program, called CONVERTD, does the following:

Read in: SDF text files, delimited text files, SYLK *Multiplan* files, or *Lotus 1-2-3 1A* worksheets.
Write out: SDF text files, delimited files, SYLK *Multiplan* files.

The CONVERTD program also shows an option for a *dBASE II* text file. However, this option produces a delimited text file, not a *dBASE II* DBF file.

SUPERCALC 2 AND 3

Both programs write SDF files from the main program menu. *SuperCalc 2* and *3* use the OUTPUT DISPLAY DISK command to create a text file.

SuperCalc 2 and*3* do not have a command to read in text data in the SDF or delimited formats. Note that *SuperCalc* does command a command /X, EXECUTE, that reads SDF format text files, but its purpose is to execute those characters as keystrokes much in the same way that *1–2–3* executes macros.

In addition, both programs have a utility modestly named SUPER DATA IN-TERCHANGE. The SUPER DATA INTERCHANGE program converts the following:

SuperCalc 2 or *3* to delimited text files (data only)

SuperCalc 2 or *3* to DIF (called SDF in *SuperCalc* for some reason) (data only)

Delimited to *SuperCalc 2* or *3* (data only)

DIF to *SuperCalc 2* or *3* (data only)

SUPERCALC 4

SuperCalc 4 is a good deal more sophisticated than versions *2* and *3* when it comes to data integration. Like *Multiplan*, the program is designed to integrate smoothly with the industry leader. *SuperCalc 4* contains two menu options, //Import and //Export, that contain commands that perform the following conversions:

SuperCalc 4 to *1–2–3* version *1A* (formulas and data)

SuperCalc 4 to *SuperCalc 3* (formula and data)

SuperCalc 4 to DIF (data only)

SuperCalc 4 to SUPER DATA INTERCHANGE (data only)

SuperCalc 4 to delimited text file (data only)

1–2–3 version *1A* or *2* to *SuperCalc 4* (formulas and data)

DIF to *SuperCalc 4* (data only)

SUPER DATA INTERCHANGE to *SuperCalc 4* (data only)

Delimited text file to *SuperCalc 4* (data only)

SDF text files to *SuperCalc 4* (data only)

VisiCalc to *SuperCalc 4* (formulas and data)

FRAMEWORK II

Framework II has an IMPORT and EXPORT command located on the DISK AC-TION menu. Since *Framework* is an integrated program, some of the conversion options are directed toward word processing applications. *Framework* can make the following conversions:

dBASE II or *III* to *Framework II* (data only)

IBM DCA text format to *Framework II* (word processing)

WordStar to *Framework II* (word processing)

MultiMate to *Framework II* (word processing)

Lotus 1–2–3 to *Framework II* (formula and data)

DIF to *Framework II* (formula and data)

Framework II to *dBASE II* or *III* (data only)

Framework II to IBM DCA format (word processing)

Framework II to *WordStar* (word processing)

Framework II to *MultiMate* (word processing)

Framework II to *Lotus 1–2–3* (formula and data)

Framework II to DIF (data only)

VP PLANNER

Planner is a combination of spreadsheet and data base. *VP Planner* uses a menu structure that is almost identical to *1–2–3* in the spreadsheet portion of the program. *VP*, in its spreadsheet mode, reads and writes files that are in the *Lotus 1–2–3* format. This also means that programs that read *1–2–3* files can read *VP Planner* files. This makes *VP Planner* as easy to integrate with other spreadsheets as *Lotus 1–2–3* is.

In addition to the *Lotus* format spreadsheet files, *VP Planner* expands the FILE IMPORT menu to include the ability to read DIF format files, SDF text files, and delimited text files. The FILE XTRACT menu is expanded to include SDF and DIF text files. This means that you can create these files without having to run a conversion program.

PFS PROFESSIONAL PLAN

Plan integrates the conversion process into its FILE SAVE and FILE GET menus. *Plan* will read and write the following file types:

Plan to *1–2–3 1A* (formulas and data)

Plan to *1–2–3 2* (formulas and data)

Plan to delimited text file (data only)

Delimited to *Plan* (data only)

1-2-3 1A to *Plan* (formulas and data)

1-2-3 2 to *Plan* (formulas and data)

Plan can also output an SDF file from its PRINT menu by selecting the disk as the destination device.

JAVELIN

Javelin is quite different in structure from the standard spreadsheet. But in the worksheet mode it is capable of importing data from two types of non-*Javelin* files: delimited text files, and *1-2-3* worksheet files. Because *Javelin* does not use the same formula setup as *1-2-3*, only the data will be transferred from a *1-2-3* spreadsheet.

SUMMARY

dBASE III Plus can exchange data with a variety of word processing and spreadsheet applications.

COPY and APPEND commands use a TYPE clause that allows you to read and write five different types of non-*dBASE III Plus* files.

1. **Delimited**. This type operates with a comma-separated ASCII standard text files. In these files each data item is separated by commas. Each record is marked with a carriage return/line feed character.

    Delimited files do not include trailing blank spaces. They generally take up less disk space than an equivalent *dBASE III Plus* file, which contains space characters for all the characters in the file not filled with actual information.

2. **SDF.** SDF stands for Standard Data Format. This type of file stores data as a series of items separated by spaces. Each record is ended with a carriage return/line feed character.

3. **DIF.** DIF stands for Data Interchange Format. The format was first used with *VisiCalc* on Apple II computers. DIF is similar to the other file types in that it contains only ASCII text data. Spreadsheets treat rows and columns equally. *dBASE III Plus* treats rows in a DIF file as records; columns are treated as fields.

4. **SYLK.** This stands for Symbolic Link format. Like DIF, SYLK is a spreadsheet-oriented text format. SYLK contains only text data, but it is a complex format like DIF that is designed to place data in a spreadsheet matrix.

5. **WKS.** This format creates files that are compatible with *Lotus 1-2-3*. The WKS format is different from the other formats in that it contains information in binary rather than ASCII text format. *dBASE III Plus* treats rows as records and columns as fields.

RUNTIME+

AND COMPILERS

THIS CHAPTER DEVIATES FROM THE CONVENTIONS of the others in this book by being less of a hands-on tutorial. Its purpose is to discuss compilers and explain how they work with *dBASE III Plus* programs, files, indexes, and reports.

The chapter covers two different techniques. The first is the RUNTIME+ module supplied with *dBASE III Plus*. RUNTIME+ creates a coded version of a *dBASE III Plus* program, whose main purpose is to prevent users from making changes in a program. However, you must still run the program using a version of *dBASE III Plus*.

The second part of the chapter discusses true compilers. A true compiler creates a version of your *dBASE III Plus* program that can operate without *dBASE III Plus*.

RUNTIME+ is not nearly as significant as a true compiler, but since it is included in *dBASE III Plus*, the first section of this chapter will deal with it.

RUNTIME+

The RUNTIME+ system can be a bit confusing because the *dBASE III Plus* manual refers to "compiling" with the RUNTIME+ module. In fact, the program does not really create a compiled program. What RUNTIME+ does do is change the

ASCII standard text files that use CREATE when using the MODIFY COMMAND into encrypted files. An encrypted file is one that is encoded in a nonstandard format. The file can still be understood by *dBASE III Plus*, but it cannot be edited or displayed as you would a normal command file.

The main reason for using the RUNTIME+ system is to prevent tampering with or modification of a customized program. This is a concern of professional programmers who don't want other people reading or changing their programs.

While the beginning programmer is usually not concerned with this aspect, there is another benefit from encrypting a series of program files. The RUNTIME+ program compresses the amount of disk space used by the programs. This is done by removing program notes, spaces used for indenting, and unneeded text such as letters in a command following the fourth letter.

> Remember that dBASE III Plus *needs only the first four letters of each command. Example: REPLACE = REPL. However, if you enter a command and make a spelling mistake after the fourth character,* dBASE III Plus *will consider it an error. Example: REPLICE will cause an error while REPL will not.*

There are two programs that make up the RUNTIME+ system.

1. **DBC. dBASE Code.** This program converts *dBASE III Plus* programs in command files to encrypted files.
2. **DBL. dBASE Linker.** This program links together a series of encrypted files to make a single large file from the component programs.

Suppose you wanted to create a RUNTIME+ version of the invoice program. The first step is to create a text file that contains a listing of all the files that are used in the invoice application. Enter

   MODIFY COMMAND runtest < return >

Now enter the names of the file:

invoice.prg
makeinv.prg
invprt.prg
updatein.prg

Save the program by entering

   [CTRL/End]

When the DBC program creates the encrypted version of these files, they will be assigned the same name as the original files. For that reason you must place the files in another directory of the hard drive. You can use the RUN command to create a new DOS directory. Enter

   RUN MD\runtest < return >

Now run the DBC program. Like most compilers, the RUNTIME+ program requires a series of arguments. These arguments tell the program where to find and store files. The command below uses -r to tell DBC that the file list is found in the file RUNTEST.PRG; -o tells DBC that the encrypted files should be placed in the \RUNTEST directory. The RUN command enables you to execute DBC without exiting *dBASE III Plus*. Enter

RUN dbc -rruntest.prg -o\runtest\ <return>

The program will create four new files.

The four original files took up about 6800 bytes. The RUNTIME+ versions takes up about 4500 bytes, a savings of about 30 percent.

The next step is to create a single command file from the compiled files. The DBL program links the smaller files into one large file. The command uses -r to specify the file that contains the list of source files, -s to tell DBL where to find the code files, and -f for the name of the new program. Enter

RUN dbl -rruntest -s\runtest -fnew.prg <return>

The result is a file called NEW.PRG, which is a coded version of the original four programs.

You can now execute the program by entering

DO new <return>

The program will execute as if it were still in the original text format. Note that coded files cannot be uncoded. Therefore you must remember to save the original text files if you want to make changes in the program. These files are called the *source code* because they are the original text version of the program.

COMPILERS

Some of the most powerful and interesting additions to the family of programs related to *dBASE III Plus* are the compiler programs that have recently appeared on the market. If you are a serious *dBASE III Plus* user, you need to understand what compilers are, what they can do for you, and why their power and advantages are crucial in particular situations.

Compilers are not supplied with *dBASE III Plus* and must be purchased separately. They generally cost in the area of $500 to $600.

In previous chapters the assumption was made that the reader had access to programs besides *dBASE III Plus*, such as word processing programs. In the case of a compiler, that assumption is not made. Therefore the structure of this chapter is such that there will be more explanation and discussion, and less direct hands-on examples. To illustrate clearly what procedures and techniques are involved in the use of compilers, and the advantages they provide, this section includes sample programs that can be used with them.

HOW THE *dBASE III PLUS* LANGUAGE WORKS

The best place to begin an explanation of compilers is to look first at how the *dBASE III Plus* language, or any computer language for that matter, operates. When you enter a command into a program, you type in a series of characters. For example, the line shown below contains the word USE, which is recognized by *dBASE III Plus* as an instruction to open a file. In this case, the file is called EXPENSES.DBF.

USE expenses

When *dBASE III Plus* is operating, that command achieves the results you desire, that is, to open a file called EXPENSES. However, the command USE expenses is not something the computer really understands. For example, if you quit *dBASE III Plus* and return to DOS, what would happen if you entered USE expenses? DOS would display a message that says Bad Command or file name. Why?

DOS does not recognize the command USE expenses, because that command is not part of the DOS command language; USE is exclusive to *dBASE III Plus*. DOS has its own set of commands. For example, DOS would be able to carry out this command:

TYPE expenses.dbf

Note that the DOS command TYPE, and the *dBASE III Plus* command USE, do not perform the exact same function. Each system, DOS or *dBASE III Plus*, recognizes a set of instructions specific to the program that you are working with at that moment. Commands that work in *dBASE III Plus* will not necessarily work with *1-2-3*, or *WordStar*, or DOS. This is the common experience of every computer user. It is also a cause of much frustration, since almost every program adopts its own command structure, making each program a unique learning task.

Several important points can be inferred from this common experience:

1. The first conclusion is that the commands you enter into a program are specific to that program and do not apply across the board to the computer as a whole. Another way to look at it is that each program translates your commands into specific actions or sequences of actions.

2. Since all the programs operate on the same computer but use different commands, there must be some common command structure that all programs use to communicate directly with the hardware. In other words, the programs translate their various commands into a basic, low-level language that the computer can understand directly.

This low-level language is the basic instruction set built into the computer's microprocessor. The basic instruction set is small, usually about 100 to 200 instructions. These instructions were built into the microprocessor at the factory and are always understood by the computer.

The commands the microprocessor understands are not in the form of text, such as USE expenses. Instead, the instructions must be used in the form of a number, specifically binary. For example, the binary number 11000011 is the instruction that tells the microprocessor to return from a subroutine. The binary number 11000011 is very roughly equivalent to the RETURN command used in *dBASE III Plus* to terminate a program. Binary numbers are called *machine language* because the instructions are coded directly into a form that the computer can understand.

This means that whenever you enter a command in the form of a word, a sentence, or a special keystroke, the program you are working with must translate that command into one or more binary numbers corresponding to the low-level machine language commands that actually carry out the task.

Thus all programs that change your high level command (e.g., USE expenses) into a sequence of low-level commands (e.g., 11000011) act as translators.

3. The speed of operation of a program is, in part at least, determined by the speed at which the translation takes places. The faster the commands can be translated into binary commands, the faster the tasks are carried out.

In *dBASE III Plus*, programs are constructed by creating text files that contain lists of commands. When you execute a *dBASE III Plus* program, the commands in the file are translated into binary commands and the actions specified take place.

METHODS OF TRANSLATION

In a sense, all programs are translation devices that change your instructions into instructions that the microprocessor can understand. When you are programming *dBASE III Plus*, the program acts as a translator that interprets the text of your commands in terms of the low-level instructions that the computer understands. When you change to another program (e.g., *Lotus 1-2-3*), the command structure changes. Now *1-2-3* translates your commands into microprocessor instructions. What these two programs have in common is that they both ultimately boil down the instructions to a series of binary commands.

The translation process takes two very distinct forms.

1. **Interpreters.** As in any translating situation, one method used is to translate each instruction as it is entered.

When translating a program, an interpreter reads the instruction from the command file. The instruction is then translated into machine language. Once this has been done, the machine language instructions are executed.

Following the execution of the previous instruction, the program then reads the next instruction in the *dBASE III Plus* command file and repeats the process.

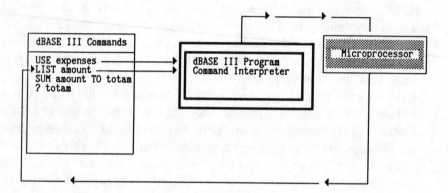

2. **Compilers.** The other method of translating a program is to take the entire program and translate all the commands at one time. When a compiler works with a command file, it fetches the first instruction and translates it into machine language. Instead of executing the machine language instruction at that point, it then reads the next instruction in the command file and translates that into machine language.

    The compiler continues this process until the entire program has been translated. Then all the translated commands are stored in a new file. The new file contains a complete translated version of the original *dBASE III Plus* program. You can now execute the compiled file instead of the original program.

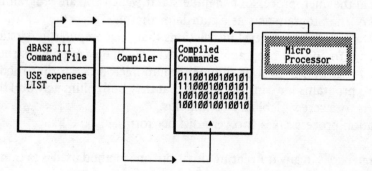

When compilers are used, there are really two programs in place. The first is the original program that contains the commands entered in *dBASE III Plus* command files. This file is called the *source code*. The translated file produced by the compiler is called the *object code*. The source code is the version that can be read and edited. The object code is strictly for the computer to read.

Both compilers and interpreters have positive and negative aspects. The main advantage of the compiler is speed. An interpreter must fetch an instruction, translate, and execute. With a compiler, all the translation is done before any of the execution is done. This means that the translation stage and the execution stage operate more quickly.

Another advantage to the compilation process concerns the processing of repetitive portions of a program. For example, suppose a program uses a loop to repeat a procedure several times. An interpreter must translate the looping instructions each time as if it has never seen them before. A compiler will translate the loop once and then execute the translated version as many times as necessary.

Compiling provides the program with a way to analyze the entire program before it is executed. For example, if a program contains an unbalanced IF/ENDIF structure, the interpreter will not be able to diagnose the problem because it only looks at one command at a time. The interpreter will execute the flawed program and produce some bizarre results. A compiler is able to detect such unbalanced structures before the program is executed because it looked at all the lines of the program prior to execution.

If you execute a program several times, an interpreter will translate the program each time it is run. The compiler will translate the program once, and from that point on, execute the translated version.

Although compilers have a variety of advantages, one should not overlook the value of an interpreter. The interpreter is much simpler to work with and to learn to use. The interpreter allows you to create a command file and immediately begin executing the program, whereas compilers require a series of steps to take place before the program will execute.

With an interpreter, syntax and command errors halt the program at exactly the point where the error occurs. This makes learning how to program much simpler and faster. Interpreters can execute a program immediately even though the program itself will run a bit slower. A compiler will not execute a program unless the entire program is free from syntax errors. While this is a good work habit to enforce, it can make program development and testing a bit more tedious.

dBASE III Plus is an interpreter. It is designed to allow users to create programs quickly and execute them immediately. In all the programming discussed in this book, *dBASE III Plus* has been used to translate the command files into actions. This translation takes place line by line as the program executes.

Until 1986 this was the only way to work with *dBASE III Plus* programs. Recently, compilers have been developed that translate *dBASE III Plus* command files into compiled programs.

WHY COMPILE?

There are four essential reasons for using a compiler for *dBASE III Plus* programs:

1. **Performance.** Because the compiler translates the entire program before it executes it, you will find that the program executes more quickly. The degree of improvement in performance is related to what type of actions the program performs. As a general rule, operations that involve calculation, screen display, or evaluation of complex conditional logic show the most improvement. Operations that require reading and writing of data from the disk show the least improvement. No matter what type of program you are working with, you will find some degree of improvement in performance when the compiled program is executed.

2. *dBASE* **not needed.** When a program has been compiled, it is directly executable by DOS; thus the program will operate directly from the C> or A> prompts. Furthermore, this means that *dBASE III Plus* does not need to be present for the program to execute.

   Another advantage is that a user with a computer, but not a *dBASE III Plus* program, can operate the program. This means that the programmer can duplicate her program, and give or sell it to other people, who can operate the program without having to buy *dBASE III Plus*.

   > It is possible to create an application without using dBASE III Plus at all. The WordTech compiler discussed in this chapter has a special utility that creates database files. All the other operations of dBASE III Plus can be carried out from within the application.

3. **Portability.** *dBASE III Plus* operates only on IBM PC or compatible computers. The compiler makes it possible to convert an existing compiled program to operate on MS DOS computers that are not 100 percent compatible with the IBM PC, but are merely MS DOS compatible.

4. **Debugging.** The nature of a compiler makes it possible, in fact necessary, to analyze the command files before they are actually executed. Compilers are very good at catching syntax errors and logical errors such as unbalanced structures.

Generally speaking, the first two reasons are the most common ones for using a compiler. In addition, some compilers may offer special commands not found in *dBASE III Plus* itself. These commands usually take the form of advanced programming functions that allow you to access some of the special attributes of the IBM PC.

Another side benefit of a compiled program is that it cannot be altered. Since all that is necessary to operate a compiled program is the object code, users cannot modify the program, but can use it only as it was compiled. The object code does not reveal how the source code created the program; thus programming techniques are kept secret. Of course, this may be seen as a disadvantage, depending on your point of view.

The advantages of compiled programs will appeal to a variety of users. One type is the person who is concerned with the speed of execution of the program. This is especially true of someone who creates an application that performs a great deal of calculations, or logical processing. The advantages of the compiler, in terms of performance, will be greatest with the latter types of applications. If your application is slow due to the time it takes to print, the compiler cannot speed up the printer. However, if you are using a laser printer, you may find that the printer is waiting for the program to compose the page. In that case, a compiled program will increase the print performance because it will increase the speed at which the page is composed.

Another type of user interested in the compiler is someone who is going to distribute a program to a number of users. For example, you might be developing a program that will be used by branch offices to keep track of client billing. If the program is compiled, you do not have to buy *dBASE III Plus* programs for all the offices.

Whatever your motivation, compiling has become a tool that can be used by *dBASE III Plus* users to broaden the uses of *dBASE III Plus* programs.

ABOUT RUNTIME+

A source of some confusion about compilers for *dBASE III Plus* is the RUNTIME+ system supplied by Ashton-Tate with the *dBASE III Plus* package. RUNTIME+ is not a compiler, although the *dBASE III Plus* documentation refers to *compiling* *dBASE III Plus* programs into RUNTIME+ programs.

RUNTIME+ is an encryption program. A true compiler will change the source code into an object code that can be run independently of the source code and its interpreter. RUNTIME+ changes the source code into an encrypted source code. The encrypted source code is a scrambled code that cannot be read or altered. However, this encrypted file is not capable of being executed directly from DOS as a compiled program would be. The RUNTIME+ version of the program still needs to be interpreted by *dBASE III Plus* in order to execute. This means that a program compiled with RUNTIME+ is not a genuine object code file, but simply a different form of source code.

The primary purpose of RUNTIME+ is to appeal to programmers who want to sell or distribute *dBASE III Plus* programs but are afraid that other people will read the source code files and find out how the programs were constructed. If the programmer wishes that information to remain a secret, the RUNTIME+ program will prevent users from examining the code of the application.

Ashton-Tate also offers a special version of *dBASE III Plus* called BRUN. BRUN is sold to programmers at a lower cost than the full *dBASE III Plus* program. Programmers are also permitted by Ashton-Tate to resell the BRUN programs along with the RUNTIME+ versions of the program code.

The BRUN programs, like *dBASE III Plus*, are copy-protected. The programmer who distributes a program on BRUN disks has the same copy protection scheme used by *dBASE III Plus* to prevent the creation of unauthorized copies of the program. Note that BRUN does not prevent the copying of the RUNTIME+ program. However, since the RUNTIME+ program is really source code, it won't function without *dBASE III Plus* or BRUN.

Ashton-Tate claims that RUNTIME+ will improve the performance of your applications. This is true to a certain degree, because RUNTIME+ eliminates many of the characters added to the source code file to make it more readable. For example, the RUNTIME+ program eliminates comments and notes and line indents and tokenizes the command words. Depending on how the original program was written, you may get a RUNTIME file that is considerably smaller than the source code.

The key thing to remember about the RUNTIME+ system is that it does not eliminate the need for a copy of *dBASE III Plus*, or the RUNTIME+ version of the program BRUN, for each copy of the program you intend to use.

WHICH CAME FIRST?

If you are a newcomer to computers, you may find the concept of compiling programs a new and engaging idea. However, compilers are really an old idea. In fact, it is the interactive, interpreter-type programs like *dBASE III Plus* or BASIC that are new.

Most computer languages are compiler-based. This is true of COBOL, FORTRAN, and PASCAL. In those programming environments you must use the compiler before you ever see your program operate. One of the most popular of the compiled languages on the IBM PC is Turbo Pascal by Borland. Turbo Pascal is not an application like *dBASE III Plus*, but a programming language.

Unlike *dBASE III Plus*, Turbo Pascal has no means of executing the source code directly. The advantage of *dBASE III Plus* and its compiler is that you can work with the *dBASE III Plus* program to design, test, and debug a program. Then when you are certain that the application is correctly written, you can compile the source code into an object code program.

> The compilers discussed in this book are not products produced by Ashton-Tate. Ashton-Tate does not sell a compiler for dBASE III Plus or any of its other products.

The combination of interpreter and compiler is one that can be used by a programmer on any level. You can directly transfer whatever skill you have as a *dBASE III Plus* programmer to the compiler. The *dBASE III Plus* compilers, along with the original *dBASE III Plus* program, offer a blend of power and ease of use that can produce sophisticated applications much more quickly than would otherwise have been possible.

THE *QUICKSILVER* COMPILER

Today, there are several programs on the market that will compile *dBASE III Plus* programs into directly executable object code files. The program that will be used as an example of how compilers work is called *Quicksilver* by WordTech Systems Inc., of Orinda, California.

One of the reasons this program was selected is that it maintains a large degree of compatibility with the main *dBASE III Plus* program. This means that data base and index files created with *dBASE III Plus* can be used by programs running under *Quicksilver.*

Conversely, data base and index files created or maintained by programs running under *Quicksilver* can in turn be used by *dBASE III Plus*. Thus data corrections can be made with *dBASE III Plus* to files normally used by a *Quicksilver* program.

Quicksilver is also compatible with files that support built-in *dBASE III Plus* functions such as the report generator (REPORT FORM command using .FRM files) and the label processor (LABEL FORM using .LBL files).

The features discussed in the following sections are specific to the *Quicksilver* compiler but also are fairly representative of the world of compilers in general, and the *dBASE III Plus* compilers in particular.

The following discussion is meant to supply you with an understanding of how a compiler system works, what it is actually like to use a compiler and a compiled program, and what type of programming strategies should be used in designing systems to run as compiled programs.

EDIT, COMPILE, LINK, AND GO

The process of creating a directly executable program consists of four parts:

1. **Edit.** The first and most important step in creating a program is the editing stage. Editing is the process by which the source code is entered into a file. In *dBASE III Plus*, the MODIFY COMMAND command is used to place the program in a text editing mode. As discussed in Chapter 3, it is possible, and in many cases desirable, to use word processing programs to create and revise the source code files.

   In creating a large application, the source code is written in small sections called *routines*. The routine is designed to carry out one specific task in the scheme of the program.

   The general design of a program usually begins with a PROGRAM menu of some type that lists the main actions that can be taken in the program. This file is referred to as the *root file*. All other program files can be traced back to this root program.

   When the application is compiled, the process begins with the root. The name of the root file becomes the name of the compiled application.

2. **Compile.** After the source code files have been created and testing and debugging completed, the source code files are compiled into object code files. In this stage there is a one-to-one correspondence between each of the source code files and the object files produced. This means that if you have ten program files, the compiler will produce ten object code files. These ten object code files will eventually become the compiled application. However, at this point they are not ready to execute.

3. **Link.** The third step in the process may come as a surprise if you have never worked with compilers before. The compiling stage does not create an executable program. In order to transform the object code files into an executable program, they must be linked.

   Linking the object files accomplishes two things. First, all the object files are combined into a single program. Second, the programs are linked with a library of special routines that specify the exact code to be used to carry out many fundamental operations.

   The linker library is another idea that at first seems quite strange if you have never worked with a compiler language before. The purpose of the library is discussed more fully later in this chapter.

   Linking with the WordTech compiler produces three files: .EXE, .OVL, and .DBC. These three files function as the final program.

4. **Go.** Once the applications have been linked, they are ready to execute directly from DOS.

The compiling procedure always moves in the same direction, (i.e., from source code to object code, and then linked program). This means that if you want to change the program, you would make your changes in the source code, compile that code, and link it again to create new program files. The larger your application, the more time it will take to compile, link, and go. The time it takes to make changes is one of the primary drawbacks in using compilers.

The general rule is that you should fully test your application in the source code form by running it under *dBASE III Plus*. When you are satisfied that the program is what you want, use the compiler.

COMMAND CHANGES

Generally speaking, *Quicksilver* will support the commands used by *dBASE III Plus*. However, the nature of a compiled program requires that some commands cannot be supported, while others are altered in their form or syntax. On the other hand, the compiler may allow the use of new commands that *dBASE III Plus* does not recognize.

The exact change will vary with different compilers. In this section you will see the types of commands supported, changed, and added by WordTech *Quicksilver.*

Quicksilver *also supports* dBASE III Plus *networking commands.*

COMMANDS NOT SUPPORTED

The majority of the differences in commands between *Quicksilver* and *dBASE III Plus* involves commands that are interactive or affect the display environment. For example, commands like BROWSE, APPEND, EDIT, CHANGE, and INSERT all use a special interactive full-screen mode for data entry and revision.

Quicksilver takes the attitude that if you are creating a program, you would create programs that would take the place of these interactive commands. In fact, commands like EDIT or APPEND are really simple programs that are already part of the *dBASE III Plus* program which was written in C language, and compiled into a DOS application.

Another class of commands that *Quicksilver* does not support are the SET commands that alter the normal output conventions. For example, the SET MENU ON/OFF command is used in *dBASE III Plus* to turn on or off the display of menus with certain interactive commands. *Quicksilver* always assumes that the MENU is set OFF. This makes sense when you consider that *Quicksilver* does not support the interactive commands that display help menus.

Another group of commands not supported by *Quicksilver* are the CREATE/MODIFY commands used to create data base files, report forms, label forms, view files, screen formats, and query files.

The compiler uses data base files, report, and label formats, created with *dBASE III Plus* during the running of the application. The reason is the same as the interactive data entry commands. The assumption is that programmers who want to allow users to create data base files and reports will create programs that perform the functions of the one built into *dBASE III Plus*.

From a practical point of view, most applications created with *dBASE III Plus* and *Quicksilver* are designed to perform specific tasks. They are not designed to function as generalized data base programs such as *dBASE III Plus*. The applications are aimed at vertical markets in which the user works with the application as it is designed. The user is not usually given the responsibility for designing labels and reports, or even data base files.

In addition, version *2.0* of *Quicksilver,* which was used in writing this book, did not support some of the new commands and functions added to *dBASE III Plus*. The @ r,c TO r,c command, which draws boxes, is not supported in *Quicksilver*. WordTech intends to support these commands in future versions. However, it is still possible to create the boxes and other designs by using the programming commands available in *Quicksilver*.

The WordTech *Quicksilver* will not support the following *dBASE III Plus* commands.

APPEND
ASSIST
BROWSE
CHANGE
CREATE, CREATE LABEL, CREATE REPORT
DIR
DISPLAY STATUS
EDIT
HELP
INSERT
LIST STATUS
MODIFY COMMAND
MODIFY REPORT, MODIFY LABEL, MODIFY STRUCTURE
SET CARRY
SET DEBUG
SET ECHO
SET HEADING

SET HELP

SET MENU

SET PATH

SET SAFETY

SET STEP

SET TALK

The interactive commands that are not supported can be replaced by creating programming structures that duplicate the function. For example, the APPEND command can be duplicated by creating a screen format using @ SAY/GET commands and using the APPEND BLANK command. First, the blank record is added to the data base file. Then the data are filled in by using the screen format display. The hardest command to duplicate is the BROWSE command because it is the most complex of the built-in *dBASE III Plus* interactive commands.

> One way to create a browse-type environment is to use the INKEY() command to allow your program to evaluate the direction of the arrow keys used by the users to exit a field. This technique is discussed in Chapter 18. The INKEY() function is supported by Quicksilver.

Another limitation is that *Quicksilver* does not support MEMO fields. Take care not to use data base files with MEMO fields in compiled applications.

CREATE FROM

In creating data base applications, the user can work around the fact that *Quicksilver* does not support commands such as CREATE, MODIFY REPORT, or LABEL. These output tasks can be duplicated by a variety of programming methods. However, the lack of a CREATE command for data base files is not quite as simple to work around. If your application is designed to include the ability to create new data base files with the structure determined by the user, you cannot solve this problem by using the usual interactive methods.

Although *Quicksilver* does not support the *dBASE III Plus* CREATE command, it does support a special form of the CREATE command called CREATE FROM. The CREATE FROM command creates a data base file from the data stored in another data base file.

The key to this technique is that the data base file that is used as the source for the creation contains the following structure:

```
Field  Field Name  Type       Width   Dec
    1   FIELD_NAME  Character     10
    2   FIELD_TYPE  Character      1
    3   FIELD_LEN   Numeric        3
    4   FIELD_DEC   Numeric        3
** Total **                      18
```

The user can be prompted by the use of @ SAY/GET commands to enter data into the special data base file. The CREATE FROM command can then employ these data to construct a new data base file with the file specifications drawn from the source file. The source file can be used again to construct a new file. Example:

CREATE userfile FROM source

The previous command uses the data stored in SOURCE (assumed to be a data base file with the special structure) to create a new file called USERFILE.

Performing a file modification is a bit tricky. You would first have the user modify the data in the SOURCE file, then create a new file from SOURCE. Then use the new file and append any old records from the old data base file. The techniques used to create and modify files are illustrated in the sample application included in this chapter.

COMMANDS ALTERED

In addition to those commands not supported by *Quicksilver,* there are changes in the way some of the *dBASE III Plus* commands operate in this compiler. For example, the statistical commands in *dBASE III Plus*—COUNT, AVERAGE, and SUM—can be used in *Quicksilver* only to store value to memory variables. *Quicksilver* does not allow these commands to place data directly on screen since it does not support the talk feature of *dBASE III Plus*. This change should not cause much of a problem, however.

COMMAND ENHANCEMENTS

Quicksilver offers some additional commands that enhance the features of *dBASE III Plus*. Some of these changes or enhancements are quite interesting and, in and of themselves, are a motivating factor in deciding to use the compiler.

@ SAY

The @ SAY command is one of the most powerful commands in *dBASE III Plus*. It gives you complete control of data output on the screen and the printer. However, there are two limitations to the @ SAY command that are fixed by *Quicksilver*.

The first limitation is typical of the limits of an interpreter. When you are using the @ SAY command to display data on the screen, it does not matter in what order you enter the commands. This is because the screen display is a reusable area, and text can overwrite previous displays.

When you are creating printed output with @ SAY commands, the situation is different. Because the interpreter processes each command as it encounters it, if you enter a sequence of @ SAY commands that are out of order, *dBASE III Plus* skips an entire page between the commands. Below are two sample displays. Example A prints correctly, but Example B prints the first two lines on one page and the third line on a new page.

Example A

@ 5,0 SAY "Hello"
@ 6,0 SAY "My Name is Walter."
@ 7,0 SAY "Can you say Walter?"

Example B

@ 5,0 SAY "Hello"
@ 7,0 SAY "Can you say Walter?"
@ 6,0 SAY "My Name is Walter."

One reason that this happens is because the interpreter cannot look ahead to the next line and see that the printing is out of order. When you are formatting complicated reports with looks and variables, it is quite easy to get unwanted form feeds because of this problem.

Quicksilver can solve this problem because it looks at all the commands used in a report before they execute. The SET FEED command recognized by *Quicksilver* eliminates these unwanted form feeds when the FEED is set OFF. Setting FEED ON returns the formatting to the same logic used in *dBASE III Plus*.

Another limitation of *dBASE III Plus* that involves the use of @ SAY is the SET DEVICE command. *dBASE III Plus* allows you to specify either the screen or the printer as output devices for the @ SAY command. When the DEVICE is set to screen, the output of the @ SAY commands is sent to the screen. When SET to PRINT, the @ SAY output is directed to the printer. However, *dBASE III Plus* does not allow you to create an ASCII text file by using @ SAY commands.

In this book, the ability to create ASCII files is shown to be one of the most powerful tools in the *dBASE III Plus* arsenal. The SET ALTERNATE command can create an ASCII text file, but only the output of unformatted commands like LIST or ? can be sent to that file. The output of the @ SAY commands is ignored by the SET ALTERNATE.

The compiler allows you to use @ SAY commands to store data in an ASCII file. This allows you to harness the greater control and power of the @ SAY command (e.g., PICTURE templates and functions) to format data for text file output.

Quicksilver accepts ALTERNATE as the name of a device in the SET DEVICE command. For example, one of the more powerful functions available with the @ SAY command is the @R template function. The @R template allows you to add characters to the input or output display without having to store them as part of your data base. This feature is commonly used to add standard characters to phone numbers. For example, if the characters 4159431200 were stored in a field called NUMBER, the following command would display the number as (415)–943–1200.

@ 10,10 SAY phone PICTURE "@R (999)-999-9999"

The data could be sent to either the screen, or the printer with *dBASE III Plus*, but not to a text file. The following program shows how a list of phone numbers would be sent to a text file in *Quicksilver.*

```
USE phonedir
SET DEVICE TO ALTERNATE
SET ALTERNATE TO plist
DO WHILE .NOT. EOF()
   @ RECNO(),10 SAY phone PICTURE "@R (999)-999-999"
   SKIP
ENDDO
CLOSE ALTERNATE
RETURN
```

Another problem associated with the use of the @ SAY and @ GET commands is the speed at which displays are placed on the screen. Because the interpreter translates each line as it is encountered, the items on the screen are displayed one at a time. When you display a complicated screen format, the items appear in the order in which they are entered into the program.

Windows

One of the most interesting features of *Quicksilver* is a complete set of windowing commands that can be implemented as part of your compiled *dBASE III Plus* program.

A window is a display that pops up in a specified area of the screen. When the window is closed, any data that had been displayed underneath the window are restored. Windows provide a means of displaying information, questions, or other programming structures without destroying the data on the screen.

Many popular programs use windows. Adding window displays to your programs can greatly enhance the appearance and visual flow of your program. Below is a picture of a typical screen display.

```
┌──────────────────────────────────────────────────────────────────┐
│ Record 169          Record Management File COMM    ▓▓▓▓▓▓▓▓▓▓▓▓    │
└──────────────────────────────────────────────────────────────────┘

  Customer
  Envelope #
  Date        11/30/85
  Print Char.     0.00
  Out Lab         0.00
  Inventory       0.00
  Processing      0.00
  Taxable         0.00
  Discount        0.00
```

```
┌──────────────────────────────────────────────────────────────────┐
│ [F1] = Help           [F2] = Edit Displayed Record   [F3]= Delete Record │
│ [Pg Dn]=Next Record   [Pg Up] = Previous Record      [End]= Exit File    │
│ [F4]= Quick Search    [F5]= Add a New Record                             │
└──────────────────────────────────────────────────────────────────┘
```

The program is designed to display a help window when the user presses **[F1]**. The next display shows the help window displayed over the data entry screen.

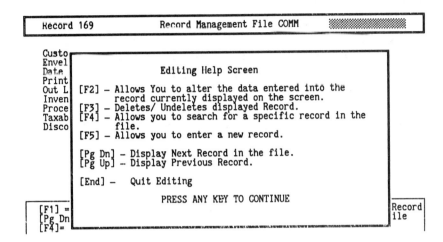

When the user presses the next key, the window is closed and the display returns to its previous appearance.

The *Quicksilver* window command approximates the standard *dBASE III Plus* command structure. All window commands begin with a W. prefix. To display a window, there are four basic window commands:

1. **W.SET WINDOW.** This command is used to create a definition in the memory of the computer of the position and size of the window. The command does not display a window but creates a definition and a descriptive name for the window. To define a window you must provide four numeric values corresponding to the coordinates of the upper left- and lower right-hand corners of the window. Example:

   W.SET WINDOW helpscrn 5,5,10,75

   The command above defines a window called helpscrn that begins at row 5, column 5 and extends to row 10, column 75. Defining a window display does not place it on the screen. You need other window commands to do that.

   The W.SET WINDOW command provides options for the type of border, single or double lines, and the color of the window and border.

2. **W.SELECT.** This command selects a window work area in a similar manner to the way the *dBASE III Plus* SELECT command activates a data file work area. *Quicksilver* allows up to 99 different windows to be displayed at the same time. Each window is stacked on top of the previous window. The command requires a numeric value from 1 to 99.

3. **W.USE.** This command actually displays the selected window on the screen. The command is roughly equivalent to a *dBASE III Plus* USE command that opens a data base file.

4. **W.CLOSE.** This command removes a window from the screen display and restores the display that was hidden by the window. If you have several windows displayed on the screen, you can specify which one to close by following the command with a numeric value corresponding to the W.SELECT number used to display the window.

The code below creates the help window shown in the previous illustrations.

```
w.set window hlp to 5,10,22,70 double
w.select 1
w.use hlp
@ 1,0 say "          Editing Help Screen"
@ 3,0 say " [F2] - Allows You to alter the data entered into the"
@ 4,0 say "       record currently displayed on the screen.       "
@ 5,0 say " [F3] - Deletes/ Undeletes displayed Record.          "
@ 6,0 say " [F4] - Allows you to search for a specific record in the"
@ 7,0 say "       file.                          "
@ 8,0 say " [F5] - Allows you to enter a new record.             "
@ 9,0 say "                          "
@ 10,0 say " [Pg Dn] - Display Next Record in the file. "
@ 11,0 say " [Pg Up] - Display Previous Record.       "
@ 12,0 say "                          "
@ 13,0 say " [End] -   Quit Editing "
words="PRESS ANY KEY TO CONTINUE"
@ 15,(60−len(words))/2 say words
    K=0
    DO WHILE K=0
        K=INKEY()
    ENDDO
w.close 1
return
```

Note that the @/SAY commands issued while the window was open refer to display locations relative to the top of the window, not the entire screen display. For example, a command that says @ 1,0 say "X" printed within a window that begins at row 5, column 10 is placed on the screen at row 1 of the window, row 6 of the screen display. The same is true of the column specification. This type of "relative" addressing makes it simpler to plan window screen displays. Commands that scroll will scroll within the window's borders.

Quicksilver contains window commands to move windows, copy windows, save windows, restore windows, add titles to window displays, change the size of windows, and more.

Note that when writing a *dBASE III Plus* program that contains window commands, you can use the *\ command so that the application can be run in *dBASE III Plus* before it is compiled.

The *\ command is a variation on the * (program note) command in *dBASE III Plus*. The *\ functions like a program note. However, the *Quicksilver* compiler will compile those commands into the finished application.

Direct Memory Commands

Another area in which *Quicksilver* adds capabilities to the *dBASE III Plus* programming language is the commands that directly modify the memory of the computer. Direct modification refers to programming instructions meant to affect specific memory locations in order to implement machine-level programs and operations. Such operations are usually beyond the scheme of most *dBASE III Plus* users. They are primarily of interest and use to advanced or professional programmers. If the information in the following section seems confusing to you, do not be concerned. Only a small percentage of people writing *dBASE III Plus* and *Quicksilver* programs will need to use these commands.

Also keep in mind that because *dBASE III Plus* does not support these commands, programs that use them can be operated and tested only as compiled applications.

MACHINE-LEVEL COMMANDS

Both *dBASE III Plus* and *Quicksilver* support the LOAD and CALL commands. The LOAD command is used to place the contents of a machine-language program into the memory of the computer. Such a program is stored in binary form and is assumed to have a .BIN extension. To create such a program you usually need to have a special programming tool called a *macro assembler*.

> *A macro assembler is a special program, a type of compiler, that allows you to create binary, machine-language programs. If macro assemblers are unfamiliar to you, you probably won't need to use the LOAD or CALL commands.*

The CALL command is used to execute the binary program placed in the memory by the LOAD command. Since use of the CALL and LOAD commands assumes you have a macro assembler or equivalent tool available, *Quicksilver* implements some machine-level commands directly.

Like the CALL and LOAD commands, these direct machine-level commands require an extensive knowledge of the IBM PC and DOS. The commands added by *Quicksilver* are

1. DOSINT
2. IN()
3. OUT()

DOSINT

Some specialized programming applications require the programmer to work very closely with the hardware in a way not accommodated by high-level languages like *dBASE III Plus*. DOS provides a variety of file- and system-related services that can be invoked by programmers to accomplish very specific tasks.

Most of the tasks required to run a program can be handled by the commands in the *dBASE III Plus* language. However, should you find a need to work closer to the machine level, the DOSINT command allows you to access DOS services directly. The majority of commonly used DOS services are provided by interrupt 33 (21 hex). This interrupt allows you to access some 46 special services. For example, function 42 of interrupt 33 is used to get the date from the operating system; function 43 is used to set the date. Function 44 will get the systems time, and function 45 will set the systems time.

Suppose you wanted to gather information about the time in the systems clock. There are several reasons why you might want to do this. First, your application may require specific timing; thus you might want to delay execution of some part of the program until a specific time. Another common use of the systems time is to generate pseudo-random numbers. Whatever your motivation, you may decide to use the DOSINT command to perform the task. Suppose you wanted to fetch the systems time. To do so you would have to execute interrupt 33 function 44.

But this is not as simple as it seems. For example, the command to execute a DOS interrupt function requires the use of decimal numbers. The computer represents values stored in its registers in hexadecimal form. First, you know that the decimal value of the interrupt is 33; that is pretty straightforward. However, the next concept is more complex. When interrupt 33 is issued, DOS uses the value stored in the A register to determine which DOS function should be executed by the interrupt.

In this case, the value should be 44 to indicate the get systems time function. However, there are two complications. First, the value placed in the A register must be in hexadecimal form. The hex value of 44 is 2C. Second, the A register (and the B, C, and D registers as well) can hold two bytes. The first byte is referred to as AL (A register, Lower order byte). The second is called the AH (A register, High order byte). The value that determines that DOS function to be carried out is the AH value. Thus you must place in the A register a decimal value equal to the hex number 2C00. 2C00 is arrived at by placing the AH first, and assuming that the AL should be zero.

You must now convert 2C00 to decimal value. This is not a simple task unless you have on hand a hex-to-decimal calculator. The result is that 2C00 in hex equals 11264 in decimal notation. Thus it is the value 11264 that selects DOS function 44. If you were programming, you could accomplish that in the following lines:

```
STORE 0 TO ar,ar,cr,dr
STORE 11264 TO ar
DOSINT 33,ar,br,cr,dr
```

Note that variables were created for all four registers. The reason is that function 44 places the systems time value into the C and D registers. It is therefore necessary to define variables for all the registers in order to capture the desired data. Note that the variables are assigned to the registers sequentially.

When the interrupt and function call are completed, the data in the C and D registers break down like this:

C register, High order byte = hour value 0–24

C register, Low order byte = minute value 0–59

D register, High order byte = seconds value 0–59

D register, Low order byte = hundredths of seconds value 0–99

It is not possible to count individual hundredths of a second because of the clock speed of the computer. The finest measurement of time is about 1/20 of a second. This means that the hundredth value can act as a pseudo-random number generator.

For example, you might print out the contents of the CR and DR registers to evaluate the systems time. The command below would be the next one on your program:

```
? cr,dr
wait
```

When the application is compiled, you may get results like this: 2079 14150. What do these numbers mean? First, you must realize that these values are decimal equivalents of hex numbers. The value in the C register, 2079, is 81F hex. This means that the hour is 8 (8 hex and 8 decimal are the same value) and the minute value is 1F hex, or 31 decimal. The time indicated by the value 2079 is 8:31 A.M.

DOS uses a 24-hour clock system, so that 8:31 P.M. would be 20:31.

The next value is 14150. Converted to hex, the value reads 3746. This means 37.46 seconds. Thus the time returned by the DOSINT command was 8:30:37.46 A.M.

The process can be reversed to set the systems date. First you would store the value of function 45 to the A register. Then place the value of the time you want to set in the C and D registers. Suppose you wanted to set the time to 9:00 A.M.

For simplicity's sake, the seconds will be assumed to be zero.

First calculate the function number. The hex value of 45 is 2D. Thus the value of the function would be 2D00 hex, or 11520 decimal. 9:00 A.M. would be 900 hex. 900 hex changes to 2304 decimal. The following program would set that date to 9:00 A.M.

```
STORE 0 TO ar,br,cr,dr
STORE 11520 TO ar
STORE 2304 TO cr
DOSINT 33,ar,br,cr,dr
? time()
wait
```

The TIME() function would display 9:00:00.

> TIME() is a dBASE III Plus *function that returns the current value of the systems time as a character string.*
>
> *If you are working on an AT-compatible computer, you may find that the time displayed is 8:59:59 instead of 9:00:00. This is caused by the elimination of wait states to speed up the processing. You can compensate for such errors by placing the value 0059 in the D register that will advance the time enough to get the correct time.*

As you can see, using the DOS interrupt requires a great deal of planning and understanding of the DOS machine-level functions, and the ability to convert hex and decimal numbers. Most of the common tasks that can be accomplished with DOS interrupts like the one shown in the example can be done using *dBASE III Plus* commands and functions, or supplemental functions added by *Quicksilver.*

> Quicksilver *adds the commands SET DATE TO and SET TIME TO, which perform the DOS interrupts necessary to set the date and the time.*

The purpose of the DOSINT command is to allow the programmer the ability to perform unusual actions based on DOS services, such as generating pseudo-random numbers.

The concept of pseudo-random numbers has been mentioned several times in this chapter. What are they and why are they needed? To answer the second part of the question first, testing a program requires data. When you want to try out a program, you usually have to create records in order to test whether or not the program will function properly when used by other people. In *dBASE III Plus* this means typing in the data manually.

Quicksilver offers you a special utility called DBCREATE, which allows you to create a *dBASE III Plus* data file and generate some sample data as records in that file. This makes testing simpler because you don't have to take the time to type in the records yourself.

In addition to this utility program, you can generate random numbers by using the DOS interrupt function to capture the value in the D register. The value is called a pseudo-random number because of the actual definition of random numbers. For example, suppose you were asked to pick a number between 1 and 100. Would the number you picked be a random number? It is not possible to say that the chosen number was random or arbitrary. The only way to know for certain that a random number has been picked is to have you continue picking numbers. The sequence would then be analyzed mathematically to see if the numbers you had chosen really fell into a pattern or were random.

When numbers are created based on the ticking of the systems clock, the numbers are not really random. However, because of the time it takes to execute a command on a computer, the effect is very close to a true random distribution of numbers. Hence, we have the term pseudo-random numbers.

Below is a sample program that will generate numbers based on the systems time.

```
STORE 0 to ar,br,cr,dr
STORE 1 TO nums
STORE 11264 TO ar
DOSINT 33,ar,br,cr,dr
seed=dr
DO WHILE nums<21
    DOSINT 33,ar,br,cr,dr
    ? dr-INT(dr/seed)*seed
    nums=nums+1
ENDDO
WAIT
```

IN AND OUT

The IN() and OUT() commands are used to access directly the input and output ports of the computer. They achieve direct control over the data sent or received by the input and output ports. These commands allow the programmer to control such operations as sounds generated by the speaker, or data sent to the serial interface. This allows programs to play music or send and receive telecommunications.

As with DOSINT, the user is required to have a full understanding of the memory organization of the PC before these functions will be of use.

The IN() function uses the decimal value of the port that is to be polled. The use of these ports is more complicated than the use of DOSINT, and a discussion of the programming techniques involved is, unfortunately, beyond the scope of this book. However, advanced versions of BASIC, like GWBASIC 3.1, commonly supplied with most computers, contain commands INP and OUT, which operate like the *Quicksilver* commands, IN and OUT. You can convert BASIC programs that use INP and OUT to run under *Quicksilver*.

A SAMPLE SESSION

In order to get the feel of what compiling an application is like, the following section will show the process by which a simple *dBASE III Plus* program is converted into a directly executable program. The program will also illustrate how *dBASE III Plus* commands can be used to create a substitute for the interactive CREATE command, which is not supported by *Quicksilver*.

The first step is to create the program just like any other *dBASE III Plus* application. This sample application consists of five files. Three of the files are programs: MENU.PRG, ROUTA.PRG, and ROUTB.PRG. The other two are format files: MENU.FMT and SCRN1.FMT.

The first program, shown below, is MENU.PRG. This is the root program, since all the other programs function as subroutines and formats. The program is designed to allow two options and an EXIT command. The first step is to create the file MENU.FMT. The file should consist of the following lines. Like all format files, the only command contained in this file are @ SAY and @ GET commands.

```
@ 8,10 SAY "Menu of Options"
@ 10,10 SAY "A. Create a database"
@ 12,10 SAY "B. Add Records"
@ 14,10 SAY "Q. Quit Program"
@ 16,10 SAY "Enter Letter" GET menuloop PICTURE "!"
```

The next file needed is the MENU.PRG file. The following shows the commands contained in that file. The first command in the file is the SET FLASH ON. Note that the first command uses the *\ symbol so that it will be ignored by the *dBASE III Plus* interpreter, but added to the compiled version of the program by *Quicksilver*.

```
*\SET FLASH ON
menuloop=SPACE(1)
DO WHILE menuloop< >"Q"
    CLEAR
    SET FORMAT TO menu
    READ
    CLOSE FORMAT
    DO CASE
        CASE menuloop="A"
                DO routa
        CASE menuloop="B"
                DO routb
    ENDCASE
ENDDO
RETURN
```

The next file to create is ROUTA.PRG. This routine will be used to create a new data base structure. The first section of the program stores the name of the new data base file to the variable name.

```
CLEAR
STORE SPACE(8) TO name
@ 10,10 SAY "Enter name of New File" GET name
READ
```

The program continues by using an existing data base file called MODEL to create a data base file called FIELDS. FIELDS has the special structure used to generate files. The MODEL data base file does not have to have any special structure. It can be any data base file with any structure whatsoever.

```
USE model
COPY TO fields STRUCTURE EXTENDED
USE fields
ZAP
```

The result is a data base file, FIELDS, that can be used to enter the data about the fields you want to create. The next section of the program uses a format file (which you have not yet created) called SCRN1 (screen #1) to allow you to enter the field specifiction data.

Note the use of the format file. First a blank record is appended, then the format file displayed. Because the SET FLASH was set on in the root program file, the format used in this program will also flash. Then after the data have been entered, the format file is closed.

```
DO WHILE .T.
    APPEND BLANK
    SET FORMAT TO scrn1
    READ
    CLOSE FORMAT
    more=SPACE(1)
    @ 20,0 SAY "Enter another? (Y/N)" GET more PICTURE "Y"
    READ
    IF more="N"
      EXIT
    ENDIF
ENDDO
```

The next section of the program is designed to generate a data base file automatically, based on the field information entered into the FIELDS data base file. This step is necessary because you will reuse the FIELDS data base each time a field file is created.

The object of this section of code is to create a data base file with the same structure as fields, with a name associated with the data base file that actually has that structure. For example, if the data base file you are defining is called CLIENTS, then the data base file with the structural specifications would be called FCLIENTS.DBF. Note that in the earlier section of the program, the filename blank was only seven characters wide. This was in anticipation of the F-------.FLD version of that file. Restricting the user entry to seven characters reserved the extra character for this use.

```
CLOSE DATABASE
CREATE &name FROM fields
CLOSE DATABASE
USE fields
screenfile="f"+TRIM(name)+".FLD"
COPY TO &screenfile
RETURN
```

The entire ROUTA.PRG program looks like this:

```
CLEAR
STORE SPACE(8) TO name
@ 10,10 SAY "Enter name of New File" GET name
READ
USE model
COPY TO fields STRUCTURE EXTENDED
USE fields
ZAP
DO WHILE .T.
   APPEND BLANK
   SET FORMAT TO scrn1
   READ
   CLOSE FORMAT
   more=SPACE(1)
   @ 20,0 SAY "Enter another? (Y/N)" GET more PICTURE "@"
   READ
   IF more="N"
      EXIT
   ENDIF
ENDDO
* make display screen
CLOSE DATABASE
CREATE &name FROM fields
CLOSE DATABASE
USE fields
screenfile="f"+TRIM(name)+".FLD"
COPY TO &screenfile
RETURN
```

Next create the SCRN1.FMT file. Enter

```
@ 3,0 SAY "Field #"
@ ROW(),COL() SAY RECNO() PICTURE "99"
@ 5,0 SAY "Field name" GET field_name PICTURE "@!"
@ 6,0 SAY "Field type" GET field_type PICTURE "@!"
@ 7,0 SAY "Field length " GET field_len
@ 8,0 SAY "Decimals" GET field_dec
```

The final program in the system is the ROUTB.PRG file. This program uses the data base files created with ROUTA, and allows data entry. ROUTB works with two data base files at the same time. In work area A, the data base file itself is used. Work area B holds the data base file used to store the specifications about the other file's structure.

The first part of the program opens both files based on the user's entry of a filename.

```
CLEAR
STORE SPACE(7) TO name
@ 10,10 SAY "Enter name of New File" GET name
READ
USE &name
SELECT B
screenfile="f"+TRIM(name)+".fld"
USE &screenfile ALIAS fields
SELECT A
```

The next section of the program uses the data in the FIELDS data base file to create a screen display based on the structure of the file. The entry is actually made into a series of memory variables called vname1, vname2, vname3, and so on. The loop displays one variable for each field in the data base file. The COUNT command stored the total number of fields in the data base file to a variable named totfields. This variable is used in the next section of the program. The READ command allows the user to enter data into the display.

```
DO WHILE .T.
    APPEND BLANK
    SELECT FIELDS
    COUNT TO totfields
    GO TOP
    CLEAR
    DO WHILE .NOT. EOF()
        fname="fname"+STR(RECNO(),1)
        vname="vname"+STR(RECNO(),1)
        STORE SPACE(field_len) TO &vname
        STORE TRIM(field_name) TO &fname
        @ RECNO(),0 SAY field_name GET &vname
        SKIP
    ENDDO
    READ
```

Following that section, the program switches work areas to begin the process of placing the data entered by the user into the actual data base file. The totfields variable is used to select the variables that correspond to the fields. For example, fname1 corresponds to the name of the first field, and vname1 contains the data to be stored in that field. The macro substitution allows the loop to replace the fields with the corresponding variables. The totfields variable makes sure that the loop stops at the correct number of replacements.

```
SELECT A
fieldnum=1
DO WHILE fieldnum<=totfields
    fieldname="fname"+STR(fieldnum,1)
    fname=&fieldname
    varname="vname"+STR(fieldnum,1)
    vname=&varname
    REPLACE &fname WITH vname
    fieldnum=fieldnum+1
ENDDO
```

Finally the user is asked to enter more data or terminate the routine.

```
more=SPACE(1)
@ 20,0 SAY "Enter another? (Y/N)" GET more PICTURE "!"
READ
```

```
            IF more="N"
                 EXIT
            ENDIF
      ENDDO
      CLOSE DATABASE
      RETURN
```

The entire ROUTB program looks like this:

```
CLEAR
STORE SPACE(7) TO name
@ 10,10 SAY "Enter name of New File" GET name
READ
USE &name
SELECT B
screenfile="f"+TRIM(name)+".fld"
USE &screenfile ALIAS fields
SELECT A
DO WHILE .T.
   APPEND BLANK
   SELECT FIELDS
   COUNT TO totfields
   GO TOP
   CLEAR
   DO WHILE .NOT. EOF()
      fname="fname"+STR(RECNO(),1)
      vname="vname"+STR(RECNO(),1)
      STORE SPACE(field_len) TO &vname
      STORE TRIM(field_name) TO &fname
      @ RECNO(),0 SAY field_name GET &vname
      SKIP
   ENDDO
   READ
   SELECT A
   fieldnum=1
   DO WHILE fieldnum<=totfields
      fieldname="fname"+STR(fieldnum,1)
      fname=&fieldname
      varname="vname"+STR(fieldnum,1)
      vname=&varname
      REPLACE &fname WITH vname
      fieldnum=fieldnum+1
   ENDDO
   more=SPACE(1)
   @ 20,0 SAY "Enter another? (Y/N)" GET more PICTURE "!"
   READ
   IF more="N"
      EXIT
   ENDIF
ENDDO
CLOSE DATABASE
RETURN
```

When you have created the program files, you are ready to compile the application. If you want to make sure that the program operates correctly, you can use the *dBASE III Plus* interpreter to run the program and test your program files. Note that the program was written to operate in full, in both the *dBASE III Plus* interpreter and *Quicksilver*. The only command that will not operate is SET FLASH, which will not affect the logic of the program. Also remember that if you wish to follow this example, you must create a *dBASE III Plus* file called MODEL.DBF. The structure and contents of MODEL are irrelevant; it can be any *dBASE III Plus* data file.

COMPILE

The next step is to compile the application. Since there are five programs in the system, you need to create an object code file for each one. However, since each file is called by a command from either the root program or one of its branches, *Quicksilver* can automatically find all the files based on their relationship to the root.

> *The call used to activate a file must be explicit for the compiler to follow the logic and compile the called program. This means that if you use macro substitution to select a subroutine, the compiler will not be able to automatically find the module. For example, DO &filename does not explicitly state the program to be performed and cannot be used by the compiler as a guide by which programs should be compiled.*

Quicksilver uses a special command called -A to automatically seek and compile routines logically called from the program. To compile the application, enter the following command at DOS.

> *In a 640K computer you can use the dBASE III Plus RUN command to execute the compiler. Example: RUN DB3C -A MENU.*

DB3C -A MENU < return >

The screen will display the creation of the object code files based on the source code files you created.

A word about the naming conventions used by *Quicksilver* is in order. As a rule, the compiler uses the name of the PRG or FMT file, and adds an @ to the beginning of the name to indicate that the file is an object code file. For example, the file MENU.PRG becomes @MENU.PRG. The file SCRN1.FMT would have an object code file @SCRN1.FMT.

Because *Quicksilver* uses one of the eight characters available for the filename as part of its identification of object files, it is best to limit your program and format files to seven character names.

Below is what the screen display shows while compiling is taking place. Note that on your screen the line numbers will print over one another and show only the final line count.

```
Serial Number : A999999 AAAA
Licensed To   : Un-registered
Quicksilver   Version 2.0B    February, 1986
Copyright (C) 1985,1986 WordTech Systems, Inc.  All Rights Reserved


Compiling MENU.PRG
LINE 1   LINE 2   LINE 3   LINE 4   LINE 5   LINE 6
LINE 7   LINE 8   LINE 9   LINE 10  LINE 11  LINE 12
LINE 13  LINE 14  LINE 15  LINE 16  LINE 17
     Constructing object file .... MENU.PRG compilation complete

Compiling ROUTB.PRG
LINE 1   LINE 2   LINE 3   LINE 4   LINE 5   LINE 6   LINE 7   LINE 8
LINE 9   LINE 10  LINE 11  LINE 12  LINE 13  LINE 14  LINE 15  LINE 16
LINE 17  LINE 18  LINE 19  LINE 20  LINE 21  LINE 22  LINE 23  LINE 24
LINE 25  LINE 26  LINE 27  LINE 28  LINE 29  LINE 30  LINE 31  LINE 32
LINE 33  LINE 34  LINE 35  LINE 36  LINE 37  LINE 38  LINE 39  LINE 40
LINE 41  LINE 42  LINE 43  LINE 44  LINE 45  LINE 46
     Constructing object file .... ROUTB.PRG compilation complete
```

```
Compiling ROUTA.PRG
    Constructing object file .... ROUTA.PRG compilation complete
LINE 1   LINE 2   LINE 3   LINE 4   LINE 5   LINE 6   LINE 7   LINE 8
LINE 9   LINE 10  LINE 11  LINE 12  LINE 13  LINE 14  LINE 15  LINE 16
LINE 17  LINE 18  LINE 19  LINE 20  LINE 21  LINE 22  LINE 23  LINE 24
    Constructing object file .... ROUTA.PRG compilation complete

Compiling SCRN1.FMT
    LINE 1   LINE 2   LINE 3   LINE 4   LINE 5   LINE 6   LINE 7
    Constructing object file .... SCRN1.FMT compilation complete

Compiling MENU.FMT
    LINE 1   LINE 2   LINE 3   LINE 4   LINE 5   LINE 6
    Constructing object file .... MENU.FMT compilation complete

Modules compiled : 5
```

LINKING

The next step after the object files have been created is linking. Linking is a step that may seem strange if you have not worked with compilers before. The concept of linking is that each computer has a special way of performing standard tasks required in any program. These tasks are closely associated with the hardware structure of the computer. For example, the size, shape, and movement of the cursor is the result of very specific routines on the IBM PC. Other MS DOS machines that are not 100 percent compatible with IBM hardware may require routines that are adjusted for those differences.

Quicksilver uses the concept of a library of standard routines that link up with your object code program. Without the link to the library, your object code files lack the machine-level specific routines that actually make the program work on the computer.

Linking object files to a library of routines has several advantages. The concept is that one set of object files can be linked to different libraries at different times, to produce programs that can execute on a variety of computers. WordTech's *Quicksilver* can be linked to work on 100 percent IBM-compatible machines. On the other hand, the library used could link the same program to an MS DOS computer that is not 100 percent compatible with IBM hardware.

By linking your source code to various libraries, you can write a program that will run on IBM-compatible computers or on computers that use MS DOS but are not 100 percent IBM-compatible. These are all things that cannot be done with *dBASE III Plus* alone. For example, *dBASE III Plus* operates only on 100 percent IBM-compatible computers. Your compiled program can operate on a more varied selection of computers.

The linking phase has two parts. First the object files are consolidated into a single program. Any redundancy is eliminated during this phase. Then the object code is linked with the selected library. The resulting linking produces three files:

one with an .EXE extension, one with a .DBC extension, and one with an .OVL extension.

To link an application, you would enter a command like this:

DB3L menu <return>

The screen display will show the following:

```
dBIII/C Linker Version 2.0  March, 1986
Copyright (C) 1985,1986 WordTech Systems, Inc.  All Rights Reserved
Serial Number : A999999-AAAA
Licensed To   : Un-registered

Phase I
Linking @MENU.PRG
Linking @MENU.FMT
Linking @ROUTA.PRG
Linking @ROUTB.PRG
Linking @SCRN1.FMT
Phase II
Linking Library : DB3PCL.LIB

    MENU.EXE        48768
    MENU.OVL        60566
    MENU.DBC         2714
```

Notice that the MENU program produced the three files with the name MENU. The root program gives its name to the entire application when it is finally linked.

Now that the application has been linked it can be operated from DOS without the presence of either *dBASE III Plus* or *Quicksilver.*

You must make sure that any supporting files, such as data base files that are required by the application, are present when the program is operated. With that exception, the program is completely independent from the original source codes files.

The compiled program will generally require more memory than running *dBASE III Plus* alone. *dBASE III Plus* requires a minimum of 256K of internal memory to operate. The compiled program will require 256K TPA. TPA, Transient Program Area, refers to the amount of memory left free after the computer loads DOS and any other memory-resident programs (e.g., ram disks or utility programs like *Sidekick*). Measuring TPA is different from measuring the amount of memory in your computer. One way to determine the TPA is to use the DOS program CHKDSK. Below are the results of a CHKDSK performed on a computer with 384K of memory installed. The display reveals that the TPA is 327K.

```
5259264 bytes total disk space
  61440 bytes in 4 hidden files
  24576 bytes in 5 directories
4063232 bytes in 330 user files
1110016 bytes available on disk

 393216 bytes total memory      <===== Total Install Memory
 335152 bytes free              <===== TPA (transient program area)
```

The CHKDSK command displays data in terms of total bytes of kilobytes. Since a kilobyte is 1024 bytes, the 335,152-byte figure calculates to 327K for the TPA.

Since the TPA in the computer is over 256K, the compiled *Quicksilver* program will operate in this computer. Keep in mind that a computer with 256K installed uses some of that memory for DOS. The exact amount changes according to the version of DOS used. In the example, 57K was used. This means that a 256K computer will have a TPA of about 199K and the compiled *Quicksilver* program will not operate.

Performance Optimizer

The linker program supplied with *Quicksilver* creates an application that is about halfway between a fully compiled application coded in 8088/8086 machine code and a *dBASE III Plus* program file coded in ASCII text commands.

The linker produces three files:

PROGRAM.**EXE**
PROGRAM.**OVL**
PROGRAM.**DBC**

When this program is executed, the .EXE and .OVL files are loaded into the memory of the computer. They then read the .DBC file for the actual commands that make up your program. The .DBC file contains a pseudo-code that is the compilation of all the .PRG files used in the *dBASE III Plus* version of your program.

The files produced by the *Quicksilver* linker achieve the main goal of compiling independently from the *dBASE III Plus* interpreter. However, the type of code produced by this linker is still a step removed from the naive machine-language of the computer.

Quicksilver allows you to take the pseudo-code stored in the .DBC file and create machine-language object files. These object files can then be linked with 8088/8086 libraries to create a machine-language version of your program. This final step will increase the speed of your application a great deal.

As a rule, you would want to fully test and debug your program before you compile it down to machine-language.

The program that complies the .DBC file is called QS.EXE. Example:

QS -f menu < return >

The command shown above creates a series of machine-language object files that transform the pseudo-code in the .DBC file into standard 8088/8086 machine-language code. Since these object files are closer to actual machine-language than the pseudo-code in the .DBC file, the program will operate at a high rate of speed.

Note the -f option used in the QS command. This option tells *Quicksilver* to create object code files that will maximize the performance of the program. When a program is run through the *Quicksilver* performance optimizer, a series of files are created. For example, the menu program would create the following files:

MENU.OBJ
MENU00.OBJ
MENU01.OBJ
MENU02.OBJ
MENU03.OBJ
MENU04.OBJ
MENU05.OBJ
MENU06.OBJ
MENU.LNK

The files with the .OBJ extension are a series of machine-language files that contain the 8088/8086 machine code equivalent of your *dBASE III Plus* .PRG files. These files are not an executable program. To organize these files into a program, it is necessary to link them using a standard 8088/8086 linker program. This program is not provided with *Quicksilver*. However, it is provided with most copies of the MS DOS system. The program is the file LINK.EXE. *Quicksilver* object files need to be linked with *Quicksilver* libraries to form an executable program. The *Quicksilver* object files and libraries are compatible with most versions of LINK.EXE supplied with MS DOS.

> *If you have a Microsoft Language compiler such as* Quicksilver, *you have another version of LINK.EXE provided with that program. This version is usually 3.00 or higher. If you want to use this linker with* Quicksilver, *you should compile the object files with the -3 option.*

In order to help run the linking process, *Quicksilver* produces a file with an .LNK extension. This file is a batch file that contains the correct instructions and specifications to link the *Quicksilver* object files to the *Quicksilver* libraries and produce the final code. For example, the file MENU.LNK contains the following:

MENU.OBJ +
MENU00.OBJ +
MENU01.OBJ +
MENU02.OBJ +
MENU03.OBJ +
MENU04.OBJ +

```
MENU05.OBJ +
MENU06.OBJ/SE:574
MENU.EXE
QSPC1.LIB + QSPC2.LIB + QS.LIB->
```

The file tells the linker what object files to link and in what order, the name of the program file to produce, MENU.EXE, and the library files to link the object files to. The /SE option sets the number of segments to be used by the LINK.EXE program. This number is automatically set by *Quicksilver*.

To complete the process and create the MENU.EXE file, you enter a command like this:

LINK @MENU.LNK < return >

When the program completes linking a file, in this example, MENU.EXE is created. This single file is a directly executable version of the original .PRG files.

Note that when a program is transformed into an executable machine-language program, the amount of disk space it takes up and the size of the TPA is requires increases. If you intend to run the program in a computer with a small memory, (e.g., 384K), you might find that the machine-language version will not run.

The -f option creates a fast version of the program but also produces a larger program that requires a larger TPA than if you used *Quicksilver* without the -f option.

You should consider the type of system you will be running the application on when deciding the type of compilation to use.

Debugging

Quicksilver also features a full, interactive debugging program. The Debugger allows you to run a compiled application in a way that makes it easy to test for and isolate errors. The Debugger will execute all *dBASE III Plus* and *Quicksilver* commands so you can see the effect of window displays.

The advantage of the Debugger is that you can see the source code commands, as well as the effect they have on the application. You can run a program from a specified point and halt execution as it runs. This program can be quite helpful in smoothing out large applications.

SUMMARY

dBASE III Plus includes two programs, DBC and BDL, that create a compressed, coded version of *dBASE III Plus* programs. These programs are not really compiled but are coded. This means that you still need *dBASE III Plus* to run the program and that they execute at about the same speed as noncoded programs.

The chief advantage of RUNTIME+ is that it prevents unauthorized changes in a program and it compresses the file size.

A main subject of this chapter is *Quicksilver*. The compiler allows you to change *dBASE III Plus* programs into independent, directly executable applications. The major advantages of a compiler are as follows:

Performance. Most programs will perform faster, several times faster in many cases, than the original *dBASE III Plus* version. Compilers are especially fast at handling internal calculations. *Quicksilver* has two levels of compiling:

1. **Pseudo-code.** This is the simplest way to compile a program. Programs compiled into *Quicksilver* pseudo-code operate in a 256K TPA.

2. **Machine code.** *Quicksilver* provides a means by which the pseudo-code can be compiled into 8088/8086 machine-language code. This increases the speed of execution dramatically. However, programs compiled in this way require more memory to operate than the pseudo-code version.

Independence. Programs compiled with *Quicksilver* do not need either *dBASE III Plus* or *Quicksilver* to operate. They are independent applications and can operate in full without copies of either program being present. This means that you can sell or distribute copies of your program to users who do not own *dBASE III Plus* or *Quicksilver.*

Portability. Programs can be linked to libraries that allow the same program to operate on computers that are not 100 percent IBM-compatible. They can also operate on both *dBASE III* and *dBASE II* files.

In addition, the compiler is capable of implementing commands that do not appear in *dBASE III Plus,* such as DOSINT (DOS interrupt).

> The version of the WordTech compiler used for this book, 2.0, also supports the networking commands implemented in dBASE III Plus. However, the compiler does not have the copy-protected restrictions that dBASE III Plus has.

If you are a serious programmer, compiling applications is a necessary part of your work that carries with it many advantages. The primary advantage is that by using *dBASE III Plus* and *Quicksilver* you can write, test, debug, and install a variety of applications in a fraction of the time it would otherwise take to do so.

INDEX

About the Author

Rob Krumm's writing career began in 1982 when he opened his own private school in Walnut Creek, California, called microCOMPUTER SCHOOLS, Inc. He found that students learned faster, and retained more, when they worked at the microcomputer with a detailed step-by-step learning guide in the application they were studying. This first "learning guide" was popularized in the best-selling Brady Book, *Understanding and Using dBASE II.*

Since that time, Rob's writing career has blossomed. One of the industry's most prolific authors, Rob has used his detailed "hands-on" style in several successful computer books covering such subjects as spreadsheets, word processors, utilities, and the *dBASE II, III,* and *III Plus* products. His columns and commentaries have appeared in the *San Francisco Examiner* and in several popular computer magazines and journals. In addition, his semi-monthly column, "The Bottom Line," can be read in the Berkeley-based *Computer Currents.*

Order Form

Indicate the titles and quantities desired below.
Enclose Check or Money order or use your credit card for payment:

☐ Enclosed is a check for $_____

☐ Charge my   ☐ MasterCard   Account # _____

                 ☐ VISA   Exp. Date _____

              Signature _____

Name _____

Address _____

City _____ State _____ Zip _____

(New Jersey residents please add applicable sales tax.)
Dept. 3

Return to: PH Mail Order Billing
                  Route 59 at Brook Hill Drive
                  West Nyack, NY 10994

Title	Code	Quantity	Price	Total
Utilities				
Hard Disk Manager	38377		$39.95	
dBASE III Plus To Go	19621		$39.95	
1-2-3 Ready-to-Run	93988		$39.95	
1-2-3 Power Pack	63540		$39.95	
Instant Ventura Publisher	46779		$39.95	
Also by Peter Norton				
Inside the IBM PC	03583		$21.95	
Inside the IBM PC book/disk	46732		$39.95	
Peter Norton's Assembly Language Book for the IBM PC				
Book	66190		$21.95	
Book/Disk	66214		$39.95	
Peter Norton's DOS Guide	66207		$19.95	
Also by Robert Jourdain				
Programmer's Problem Solver	03787		$22.95	
Turbo Pascal Express	53533		$39.95	
Inside the Norton Utilities	46788		$19.95	